Visual Basic® 2012

HOW TO PROGRAM

SIXTH EDITION

Deitel Series Page

How To Program Series

Android How to Program
C How to Program, 7/E
C++ How to Program, 9/E
C++ How to Program, Late Objects Version, 7/E
Java™ How to Program, 9/E
Java™ How to Program, Late Objects Version, 8/E
Internet & World Wide Web How to Program, 5/E
Visual Basic® 2012 How to Program
Visual C#® 2012 How to Program, 5/E
Visual C++® 2008 How to Program, 2/E
Small Java™ How to Program, 6/E
Small C++ How to Program, 5/E

Simply Series

Simply C++: An App-Driven Tutorial Approach
Simply Java™ Programming: An App-Driven Tutorial Approach
Simply Visual Basic® 2010, 4/E: An App-Driven Tutorial Approach

CourseSmart Web Books

www.deitel.com/books/CourseSmart/

C++ How to Program, 7/E, 8/E & 9/E
Simply C++: An App-Driven Tutorial Approach
Java™ How to Program, 7/E, 8/E & 9/E

Simply Visual Basic 2010: An App-Driven Approach, 4/E
Visual Basic® 2012 How to Program
Visual Basic® 2010 How to Program
Visual C#® 2012 How to Program, 5/E
Visual C#® 2010 How to Program, 4/E

Deitel Developer Series

C++ for Programmers, 2/E
Android for Programmers: An App-Driven Approach
C# 2010 for Programmers, 3/E
Dive Into iOS 6: An App-Driven Approach
iOS 6 for Programmers: An App-Driven Approach
Java™ for Programmers, 2/E
JavaScript for Programmers

LiveLessons Video Learning Products

www.deitel.com/books/LiveLessons/

Android® App Development Fundamentals
C++ Fundamentals
C# Fundamentals
iOS 6 App Development Fundamentals
Java™ Fundamentals
JavaScript Fundamentals
Visual Basic® Fundamentals

To receive updates on Deitel publications, Resource Centers, training courses, partner offers and more, please register for the free *Deitel Buzz Online* e-mail newsletter at:

www.deitel.com/newsletter/subscribe.html

and join the Deitel communities on Twitter®

@deitel

Facebook®

facebook.com/DeitelFan

and Google+

gplus.to/deitel

To communicate with the authors, send e-mail to:

deitel@deitel.com

For information on government and corporate *Dive-Into Series* on-site seminars offered by Deitel & Associates, Inc. worldwide, visit:

www.deitel.com/training/

or write to

deitel@deitel.com

For continuing updates on Prentice Hall/Deitel publications visit:

www.deitel.com
www.pearsoninternationaleditions.com/deitel

Visit the Deitel Resource Centers that will help you master programming languages, software development, Android and iPhone/iPad app development, and Internet- and web-related topics:

www.deitel.com/ResourceCenters.html

Visual Basic® 2012

HOW TO PROGRAM

SIXTH EDITION **Paul Deitel**
Deitel & Associates, Inc.

Abbey Deitel
Deitel & Associates, Inc.

Harvey Deitel
Deitel & Associates, Inc.

International Edition contributions by

B. R. Chandavarkar

National Institute of Technology Karnataka, Surathkal

DEITEL

PEARSON

Boston   Columbus   Indianapolis   New York   San Francisco   Upper Saddle River
Amsterdam   Cape Town   Dubai   London   Madrid   Milan   Munich   Paris   Montréal   Toronto
Delhi   Mexico City   São Paulo   Sydney   Hong Kong   Seoul   Singapore   Taipei   Tokyo

Vice President and Editorial Director: **Marcia J. Horton**
Executive Editor: **Tracy Johnson**
Associate Editor: **Carole Snyder**
Director of Marketing: **Christy Lesko**
Marketing Manager: **Yezan Alayan**
Marketing Assistant: **Jon Bryant**
Director of Production: **Erin Gregg**
Managing Editor: **Scott Disanno**
Associate Managing Editor: **Robert Engelhardt**
Publisher, International Edition: **Angshuman Chakraborty**
Publishing Administrator and Business Analyst, International Edition: **Shokhi Shah Khandelwal**
Associate Print & Media Editor, International Edition: **Anuprova Dey Chowdhuri**
Acquisitions Editor, International Edition: **Sandhya Ghoshal**
Publishing Administrator, International Edition: **Hema Mehta**
Project Editor, International Edition: **Karthik Subramanian**
Senior Manufacturing Controller, Production, International Edition: **Trudy Kimber**
Operations Specialist: **Lisa McDowell**
Art Director: **Anthony Gemmellaro**
Cover Design: **Jodi Notowitz**
Cover Photo: **majeczka/Shutterstock**
Media Project Manager: **Renata Butera**

Pearson Education Limited
Edinburgh Gate
Harlow
Essex CM20 2JE
England

and Associated Companies throughout the world

Visit us on the World Wide Web at:
www.pearsoninternationaleditions.com

© Pearson Education Limited 2014

ISBN 10: 0-273-79328-4
ISBN 13: 978-0-273-79328-1

British Library Cataloguing-in-Publication Data

A catalogue record for this book is available from the British Library

10 9 8 7 6 5 4 3 2 1

14 13 12 11 10

Typeset in AGaramond Regular by GEX Publishing Services

Printed and bound by Courier Westford in The United States of America

The publisher's policy is to use paper manufactured from sustainable forests.

To the Microsoft Visual Basic Language Team
Paul, Abbey and Harvey Deitel

Trademarks

Brief Contents

Chapters 16–31 are PDF documents posted online at the book's Companion Website (located at www.pearsoninternationaleditions.com/deitel).

Companion Website Online Content

Chapters 16–31 and Appendix F are PDF documents posted online at the book's Companion Website (located at www.pearsoninternationaleditions.com/deitel).

Contents

Chapters 16–31 are PDF documents posted online at the book's Companion Website (located at www.pearsoninternationaleditions.com/deitel).

10   Contents

3 Introduction to Visual Basic Programming 93

4 Introduction to Problem Solving and Control Statements 135

8 Files   320

9 Object-Oriented Programming: Classes and Objects   346

13 Web App Development with ASP.NET   480

14 Windows Forms GUI: A Deeper Look   532

15 Graphics and Multimedia   **588**

Online Chapters   **631**

A Operator Precedence Chart   **632**

B Primitive Types   **634**

C Number Systems   **635**

D ASCII Character Set   **647**

E Unicode®   **648**

Companion Website Online Content

Chapters 16–31 and Appendix F are PDF documents posted online at the book's Companion Website (located at www.pearsoninternationaleditions.com/deitel).

Preface

Welcome to the Visual Basic® 2012 computer programming language and the world of Microsoft® Windows® and Internet and web programming with Microsoft's .NET platform. Please read the book's back cover and inside back cover—these concisely capture the book's essence. In this Preface we provide more details.

This book is appropriate for information technology and business students in novice-level and intermediate-level Visual Basic courses. The book is also used by professional programmers.

At the heart of the book is the Deitel signature *live-code approach*—rather than using code snippets, we present concepts in the context of complete working programs followed by sample executions. Read the Before You Begin section after this Preface for instructions on setting up your computer to run the code examples. The source code is available at www.deitel.com/books/vb2012htp and www.pearsoninternationaleditions.com/deitel. Use the source code we provide to *compile and run each program* as you study it—this will help you master Visual Basic and related Microsoft technologies faster and at a deeper level.

We believe that this book and its supplements for students and instructors will give you an informative, engaging, challenging and entertaining introduction to Visual Basic. If you have questions, we're easy to reach at deitel@deitel.com—we'll respond promptly. For book updates, visit www.deitel.com/books/vb2012htp, join our social media communities on Facebook (www.deitel.com/DeitelFan), Twitter (@deitel), Google+ (gplus.to/deitel) and LinkedIn (bit.ly/DeitelLinkedIn), and subscribe to the *Deitel Buzz Online* newsletter (www.deitel.com/newsletter/subscribe.html).

Visual Basic® 2012, the Visual Studio® 2012 IDE, .NET 4.5, Windows® 7 and Windows® 8

The new Visual Basic 2012 and its associated technologies motivated us to write *Visual Basic 2012 How to Program*. These are some of the key features of this new edition:

- *Use with Windows 7, Windows 8 or both.* The book is designed so that you can continue to use Windows 7 now and begin to evolve to Windows 8, if you like, or you can move right to Windows 8. All of the code examples in Chapters 1–19 and 23–31 were tested on *both* Windows 7 and Windows 8. The code examples for the Windows-8-specific chapters—Chapter 20 (Windows 8 UI and XAML), Chapter 21 (Windows 8 Graphics and Multimedia) and Chapter 22 (Building a Windows Phone 8 App)—were tested *only* on Windows 8.

- *Modular multi-GUI treatment with Windows Forms, Windows 8 UI and WPF.* The printed book features Windows Forms GUI; optional online chapters contain treatments of WPF GUI and the new Windows 8 UI. Windows 8 UI apps are called *Windows Store apps*. In Chapter 20, you'll learn how to create and test Windows Store apps and upload them to Microsoft's Windows Store.

- *Modular treatment of graphics and multimedia with Windows 8 and WPF.* The book features optional online chapters on both Windows 8 Graphics and Multimedia (Chapter 21) and WPF Graphics and Multimedia (Chapter 28).

- *Database with LINQ to Entities.* In the previous edition of this book, we discussed LINQ (Language Integrated Query) to SQL (Microsoft's SQL Server database system). Microsoft stopped further development on LINQ to SQL in 2008 in favor of the newer and more robust LINQ to Entities and the ADO.NET Entity Framework, which we've switched to in this edition, keeping the discussion friendly for novices.

- *SQL Server database.* We use Microsoft's free SQL Server Express 2012 (which installs with the free Visual Studio Express 2012 for Windows Desktop) to present the fundamentals of database programming. Chapters 12–13 and online Chapters 24–25 use database and LINQ capabilities to build an address-book desktop app, a web-based guestbook app, a bookstore app and an airline reservation system app.

- *ASP.NET 4.5.* Microsoft's .NET server-side technology, ASP.NET, enables you to create robust, scalable web-based apps. In Chapter 13, you'll build several apps, including a web-based guestbook that uses ASP.NET and the ADO.NET Entity Framework to store data in a database and display data in a web page. The chapter also discusses the IIS Express web server for testing your web apps on your local computer.

- *Building a Windows Phone 8 App.* Windows Phone 8 is Microsoft's latest operating system for smartphones. It features multi-touch support for touchpads and touchscreen devices, enhanced security features and more. In online Chapter 22, you'll build a complete working Windows Phone 8 app and test it on the Windows Phone simulator; we'll discuss how to upload apps to the Windows Phone Store.

- *Building a Windows Azure™ Cloud Computing App.* Windows Azure is a cloud computing platform that allows you to develop, manage and distribute your apps in the cloud. Online Chapter 26 shows you how to build a Windows Azure app that can store data in the cloud.

- *Asynchronous programming with* `async` *and* `await`. Asynchronous programming is simplified in Visual Basic 2012 with the new `Async` and `Await` capabilities. We introduce asynchronous programming with `Async` and `Await` in online Chapter 23.

Object-Oriented Programming

- *Late objects approach.* We defer the discussion of creating custom classes until Chapter 9, but in the early chapters, we still use lots of existing objects. Chapter 10 discusses how to create powerful new classes quickly by using inheritance to "absorb" the capabilities of existing classes, and presents the crucial concepts of polymorphism, abstract classes and interfaces.

- *Rich coverage of programming fundamentals.* Chapters 4 and 5 present a friendly treatment of control statements and problem solving.

- *A clear, example-driven presentation of classes, objects, inheritance, polymorphism and interfaces.*

- *Optional case study: Using the UML to develop an object-oriented design and Visual Basic implementation of an Automated Teller Machine (ATM).* The UML™ (Unified Modeling Language™) is the industry-standard graphical language for modeling object-oriented systems. We introduce the UML in the early chapters. Optional online Chapters 30 and 31 include an *optional* case study on object-oriented design using the UML. We design and implement the software for a simple automated teller machine. We analyze a typical *requirements document* that specifies the system to be built. We determine the *classes* needed to implement that system, the *attributes* the classes need to have, the *behaviors* the classes need to exhibit and we specify how the classes must *interact* with one another to meet the system requirements. From the design we produce a complete working Visual Basic implementation. Students often report a "light bulb moment"—the case study helps them "tie it all together" and truly understand object orientation.

- *Three programming paradigms.* We discuss *structured programming*, *object-oriented programming* and *generic programming*.

Interesting, Entertaining and Challenging Exercises

- Extensive self-review exercises *and* answers are included for self-study.

- Many chapters include a multiple-choice Quick Quiz.

- Each chapter concludes with a substantial set of exercises, which generally includes simple recall of important terminology and concepts, identifying the errors in code samples, writing individual program statements, writing small portions of Visual Basic classes, writing complete programs and implementing major projects. Figure 1 lists a small sampling of the book's hundreds of exercises, including selections from our *Making a Difference* exercises set, which encourage you to use computers and the Internet to research and solve significant social problems—we hope you'll approach these exercises with *your own* values, politics and beliefs.

Exercises		
Abstract Methods	Cafeteria Survey App	`DateInformation` Class
Account Information App	Calculator GUI	Diameter, Circumference and
Account Inheritance Hierarchy	Carbon Footprint Calculator	Area
Airline Reservations system	Car-Pool Savings Calculator	Digit Extraction
Alarm Clock GUI	Coin Tossing	Displaying Tabular Data
Arithmetic Calculator App	Computer-Assisted Instruction:	`Concantenating Strings`
Array Sorting App	Reducing Student Fatigue	Duplicate Elimination
Average Calculator App	Computerization of Health	Duplicate Word Removal
Baseball Database App	Records	`Employee` Class
Blackjack Modification	Concentric Circles	Enforcing Privacy with Cryp-
Body Mass Index Calculator	Credit Checker App	tography

Fig. 1 | A sampling of the book's exercises. (Part 1 of 2.)

Exercises		
Enhanced Drawing App	Polling	Table of Decimal, Octal,
Enhanced Exam Analysis App	Polymorphism and Extensibility	Hexadecimal and Binary
Evaluating Poker Hands	Present Value Calculator App	Equivalents
Find the Smallest and Largest	Protected vs. Private Access	Table of Powers App
Values	Pyramid	Target-Heart-Rate Calculator
Gas Pump	Querying an Array of Invoice	Tax Plan Alternatives; The
Guess the Number App	Objects	"Fair Tax"
Image Flasher	Quiz Average App	Telephone-Number Word
Image Reflector App	Radio GUI	Generator
Inheritance Advantages	Random Lines	Temperature Converter App
Invoice Class	Reading Grades into a Two-	Triangles of Asterisks
Large-Type Displays for Peo-	Dimensional Array	Using the Debugger: Discount
ple with Low Vision	Retail Sales Calculator App	Calculator App
Lottery Number Generator	Road Sign Test App	Using the Debugger: Factorial
MDI Text Editor	Sales Commissions	App
Miles Per Gallon App	Savings Account Class	Using the Debugger: Savings
Modifying the Internal Data	Screen Saver App	Calculator App
Representation of a Class	Shape Hierarchy	Using the Debugger: Sibling
Multiples	Simple Calculator App	Survey App
Notepad GUI	Simple Drawing App	Vending Machine App
Nutrition Information XML	Snake PolyLine App	Wage Calculator with Tax
Document	Sorting and Ascending and	Calculations
Package Inheritance Hierarchy	Descending Order	Web-Based Address Book
Page Hit Counter	Speech-Controlled Drawing	World Population Growth
Parking Charges	App	Writing a Grade Report to a
Phone-Book Web Service	Square Class	File
Pig Latin	Student Inheritance Hierarchy	

Fig. 1 | A sampling of the book's exercises. (Part 2 of 2.)

Other Features

- *Illustrations and figures.* Abundant tables, line drawings, UML diagrams, programs and program outputs are included.

- *Focus on business and personal utility examples.*

- *Windows Forms GUI is integrated throughout the core chapters.* The core content focuses on Windows Forms GUI apps.

- *We use LINQ to query files, databases, XML and collections.* The introductory LINQ to Objects chapter (Chapter 11), is intentionally simple and brief to encourage instructors to begin covering LINQ technology early. We take a deeper look, using LINQ to Entities (Chapters 12–13 and online Chapters 24–25) and LINQ to XML (online Chapters 19, 25 and 26).

- *Integrated Using the Debugger sections and exercises* in the core printed book. Students use the debugger to locate and fix logic errors.

- *Strings, files and databases are covered early.*

- *Introduction to Web app development with ASP.NET is in the core print book.*

- *Local type inference.* When you initialize a local variable in its declaration, you can omit the variable's type—the compiler *infers* it from the initializer value.

- *Object initializers.* For new objects, you can use object initializer syntax (similar to array initializer syntax) to assign values to the new object's `public` properties and `public` instance variables.

- *We emphasize the IDE's* **IntelliSense** *feature* that helps you write code faster and with fewer errors.

- *Optional parameters.* You can specify method parameters with default values—if a corresponding method argument is not provided in the method call, the compiler inserts the optional parameter's default value in the call.

- *"Quick Fix" window.* We show how to use the IDE's **Error Correction Options** window to quickly fix certain common programming errors simply by clicking the suggested fix, which is displayed in a window in the code editor.

- *We show how to use* **DataTips** *and visualizers* to view object contents in the code window during debugging.

- *Integrated exception handling.* We introduce exception handling early (Chapter 7, Arrays) to ensure that we do not access an array element outside the array's bounds. Chapter 9, Object-Oriented Programming: Classes and Objects, shows how to indicate an exception when a member function receives an invalid argument. We cover the complete details of exception handling in online Chapter 16, Exception Handling: A Deeper Look.

- *Visual Basic XML capabilities.* Extensible Markup Language (XML) is pervasive in the software-development industry, e-business and throughout the .NET platform. In optional online Chapter 19, we introduce XML syntax and programmatically manipulate the elements of an XML document using LINQ to XML. XAML is an XML vocabulary that's used to describe graphical user interfaces, graphics and multimedia. We discuss XAML in optional online Chapters 20–21 and 27–28.

- *Web app development with ASP.NET 4.5 and ASP.NET AJAX.* Optional online Chapter 24 extends Chapter 13's ASP.NET discussion with a case study on building a password-protected, web-based bookstore app. We also introduce in Chapter 24 ASP.NET AJAX controls and use them to add AJAX functionality to web apps to give them a look and feel similar to that of desktop apps.

Companion Website

The printed book contains the core content (Chapters 1–15) for introductory course sequences. Several optional online chapters are available for advanced courses and professionals. Figure 2 lists the chapters that are available in searchable PDF format on the book's password-protected Companion Website at:

    www.pearsoninternationaleditions.com/deitel

See the inside front cover of the book for an access code.

Online chapters

Chapter 16, Exception Handling: A Deeper Look

Chapter 17, Strings and Characters: A Deeper Look

Chapter 18, Files and Streams: A Deeper Look

Chapter 19, XML and LINQ to XML

Chapter 20, Windows 8 UI

Chapter 21, Windows 8 Graphics and Multimedia

Chapter 22, Windows Phone 8 Case Study

Chapter 23, Introduction to Concurrency: Async and Await

Chapter 24, Web App Development with ASP.NET: A Deeper Look

Chapter 25, Web Services

Chapter 26, Building a Windows Azure Cloud Computing App

Chapter 27, Windows Presentation Foundation (WPF) GUI

Chapter 28, WPF Graphics and Multimedia

Chapter 29, Data Structures and Generic Collections

Chapter 30, ATM Case Study, Part 1: Object-Oriented Design with the UML

Chapter 31, ATM Case Study, Part 2: Implementing an Object-Oriented Design

Index (The online index includes the content from the printed book and the online content. The printed book index covers only the printed material.)

Fig. 2 | Optional online chapters in *Visual Basic 2012 How to Program.*

VideoNotes

The Companion Website also includes extensive *VideoNotes*—watch and listen as co-author Paul Deitel discusses key code examples in the core chapters of the book. VideoNotes allow for self-paced instruction with easy navigation, including the ability to select, play, rewind, fast-forward and stop within each video.

We've created a jump table that maps each VideoNote to the corresponding figures in the book (www.deitel.com/books/vb2012htp/jump_table.pdf). VideoNotes are free with the purchase of a *new* textbook.

1. Go to www.pearsonhighered.com/deitel/.

2. Scroll to *Visual Basic 2012 How to Program* and click **Companion Website**.

3. Click the **Register** button.

4. On the registration page, enter your student access code found beneath the scratch-off panel on the inside front cover of this book. Do not type the dashes. You can use lower- or uppercase. The access code can be used *only once*. This subscription is valid for twelve months upon activation and is *not transferable*. If this access code on your book has already been revealed, it may no longer be valid.

5. Once your personal Login Name and Password are confirmed, you can begin using the *Visual Basic 2012 How to Program* Companion Website.

Book Overview and Chapter Dependencies

This section discusses the book's modular organization to help instructors plan their syllabi.

Introduction to Visual Basic and Visual Studio 2012 Express

Chapter 1, Introduction to Computers, the Internet and Visual Basic, introduces computing fundamentals and Microsoft's .NET platform. If you do not need to cover these fundamentals, you should still cover the **Painter** app test-drive. The vast majority of the book's examples will run on Windows 7 and Windows 8 using *Visual Studio Express 2012 for Windows Desktop*, which we test-drive in Section 1.14. Online Chapters 20–21 can be run *only* on Windows 8 using *Visual Studio Express 2012 for Windows 8*. There are other versions of *Visual Studio Express 2012* for web development and Windows Phone development—we cover these in the corresponding chapters.

Chapter 2, Dive Into Visual Studio Express 2012 for Windows Desktop, shows how to develop a simple GUI app that displays text and an image. We'll look at Visual Studio Express 2012 for Windows 8 in more depth in online Chapter 20.

Introduction to Visual Basic Fundamentals

The chapters in this module of the book:

- Chapter 3, Introduction to Visual Basic Programming
- Chapter 4, Introduction to Problem Solving and Control Statements
- Chapter 5, Problem Solving and Control Statements: Part 2
- Chapter 6, Methods
- Chapter 7, Arrays
- Chapter 8, Files

present Visual Basic programming fundamentals (data types, operators, control statements, methods, arrays and files). These chapters should be covered in order. Chapter 7 introduces exception handling with an example that demonstrates accessing an element outside an array's bounds.

Object-Oriented Programming

The chapters in this module of the book:

- Chapter 9, Object-Oriented Programming: Classes and Objects
- Chapter 10, Object-Oriented Programming: Inheritance and Polymorphism
- Chapter 11, Introduction to LINQ
- Chapter 16, Exception Handling: A Deeper Look
- Chapter 30, ATM Case Study, Part 1: Object-Oriented Design with the UML
- Chapter 31, ATM Case Study, Part 2: Implementing an Object-Oriented Design

discuss object-oriented programming, including classes, objects, inheritance, polymorphism, interfaces and exception handling. Chapter 11, Introduction to LINQ, introduces Microsoft's Language Integrated Query (LINQ) technology, which provides a uniform syntax for manipulating data from various data sources, such as arrays and, as you'll see in later chapters, collections, XML and databases. This chapter can be deferred, but it's required for many of the later chapters starting with Chapter 12, Databases and LINQ. Online Chapters 30–31 present an *optional* object-oriented design and implementation case study that requires the Visual Basic and object-oriented programming concepts presented in Chapters 3–7 and 9–10.

Windows Forms Graphical User Interfaces (GUIs), Graphics and Multimedia

There are now three GUI technologies in Windows—Windows Forms (which is a legacy technology), Windows 8 UI (available *only* on Windows 8) and Windows Presentation Foundation (WPF). We surveyed instructors teaching Visual Basic and they still prefer Windows Forms for their classes, so Windows Forms GUI is integrated throughout most of the book. Chapter 14, Windows Forms GUI: A Deeper Look, covers additional Windows Forms GUI controls and Chapter 15, Graphics and Multimedia, introduces graphics and multimedia. For those who wish to present or study Microsoft's more recent GUI, graphics and multimedia technologies, we provide online introductions to Windows 8 UI, graphics and multimedia (online Chapters 20–21) and WPF GUI, graphics and multimedia (online Chapters 27–28).

Strings and Files

We introduce Strings beginning in Chapter 3 and use them throughout the book. We introduce files beginning in Chapter 8. Online Chapter 17, Strings and Characters: A Deeper Look, investigates Strings in more depth, and online Chapter 18, Files and Streams: A Deeper Look, discusses files in more depth.

Databases and an Introduction to Web App Development

Chapter 12, Databases and LINQ, introduces database app development using the ADO.NET Entity Framework and LINQ to Entities. The chapter's examples require Visual Basic, object-oriented programming and Windows Forms concepts presented in Chapters 3–11. The final example in Chapter 13, Web App Development with ASP.NET requires the LINQ and database techniques presented in Chapter 12.

Extensible Markup Language (XML)

Online Chapter 19, XML and LINQ to XML, introduces XML, which is used in several later chapters. The first few sections of this chapter are required to understand the XAML markup that's used to build Windows 8 GUI, graphics and multimedia apps (Chapters 20–21), Windows Phone 8 apps (Chapter 22) and WPF GUI, graphics and multimedia apps (Chapters 27–28). The remainder of the chapter discusses LINQ to XML, which allows you to manipulate XML using LINQ syntax. These capabilities are used in Chapters 25 and 26.

Windows 8 UI, Graphics and Multimedia; Windows Phone

The online chapters in this module of the book:

- Chapter 20, Windows 8 UI
- Chapter 21, Windows 8 Graphics and Multimedia
- Chapter 22, Windows Phone 8 Case Study

present Windows 8 UI, graphics and multimedia, and Windows Phone 8 app development. These chapters can be used *only* on computers running Windows 8—they depend on event-handling concepts that are presented throughout the early chapters and the introduction to XML at the beginning of online Chapter 19 (see Section 19.1 for details). Developing a Windows Phone 8 app is similar to developing a Windows 8 UI app.

Asynchronous Programming

Online Chapter 23, Introduction to Concurrency: `Async` and `Await`, demonstrates .NET's and Visual Basic's new simplified asynchronous programming capabilities. These are commonly used in Web app and Web service development among many other uses.

Web App Development and Web Smervices

The chapters in this module of the book:

- Chapter 24, Web App Development with ASP.NET: A Deeper Look
- Chapter 25, Web Services
- Chapter 26, Building a Windows Azure™ Cloud Computing App

continue our discussion of Web app development from Chapter 13 and introduce web services, including a case study on cloud computing with Windows Azure. Online Chapters 25 and 26 depend on the LINQ to XML discussion in Chapter 19.

Windows Presentation Foundation (WPF) GUI, Graphics and Multimedia

The chapters in this module of the book

- Chapter 27, Windows Presentation Foundation (WPF) GUI
- Chapter 28, WPF Graphics and Multimedia

discuss Windows Presentation Foundation GUI, graphics and multimedia. These chapters can be used on computers running Windows 7 or Windows 8 and depend on event-handling concepts that are presented throughout the early chapters and the introduction to XML at the beginning of online Chapter 19.

Teaching Approach

Visual Basic 2012 How to Program contains a rich collection of examples. We concentrate on building good software and stress program clarity.

Live-Code Approach. The book is loaded with "live-code" examples. Most new concepts are presented in the context of complete working Visual Basic apps, followed by one or more executions showing program inputs and outputs. In the few cases where we show a code snippet, to ensure correctness we first tested it in a complete working program then copied the code from the program and pasted it into the book.

Syntax Shading. For readability, we syntax shade the code, similar to the way most integrated-development environments and code editors syntax color code. Our syntax-shading conventions are:

```
comments appear like this
keywords appear like this
constants and literal values appear like this
all other code appears in black
```

Code Highlighting. We place light blue rectangles around each program's key code.

Using Fonts for Emphasis. We place the key terms and the index's page reference for each defining occurrence in **bold blue** text for easy reference. We emphasize on-screen components in the **bold Helvetica** font (for example, the **File** menu) and Visual Basic program text in the Lucida font (for example, Dim count As Integer = 5).

Objectives. The opening quotes are followed by a list of chapter objectives.

Illustrations/Figures. Abundant tables, line drawings, UML diagrams, programs and program outputs are included.

Programming Tips. We include programming tips to help you focus on important aspects of program development. These tips and practices represent the best we've gleaned from a combined seven decades of programming and teaching experience.

Good Programming Practice
The Good Programming Practices *call attention to techniques that will help you produce programs that are clearer, more understandable and more maintainable.*

Common Programming Error
Pointing out these Common Programming Errors *reduces the likelihood that you'll make them.*

Error-Prevention Tip
These tips contain suggestions for exposing and removing bugs from your programs; many describe aspects of Visual Basic that prevent bugs from getting into programs.

Performance Tip
These tips highlight opportunities for making your programs run faster or minimizing the amount of memory that they occupy.

Portability Tip
The Portability Tips *help you write code that will run on a variety of platforms.*

Software Engineering Observation
The Software Engineering Observations *highlight architectural and design issues that affect the construction of software systems, especially large-scale systems.*

Look-and-Feel Observation
These observations help you design attractive, user-friendly graphical user interfaces that conform to industry norms.

Summary Bullets. We present a section-by-section, bullet-list summary of each chapter.

Terminology. We include an alphabetized list of the important terms defined in each chapter with the page number of each term's defining occurrence for easy reference.

Self-Review Exercises and Answers. Extensive self-review exercises *and* answers are included for self-study.

Exercises. Each chapter concludes with additional exercises including:

- simple recall of important terminology and concepts
- What's wrong with this code?

- What does this code do?
- Using the Debugger
- writing individual statements and small portions of methods and classes
- writing complete methods, classes and programs
- major projects.

Check out our Programming Projects Resource Center for lots of additional exercise and project possibilities (www.deitel.com/ProgrammingProjects/).

Index. We've included an extensive index for reference. Defining occurrences of key terms in the index are highlighted with a **bold blue** page number.

Instructor Supplements

The following supplements are available to *qualified instructors only* through Pearson Education's Instructor Resource Center (www.pearsoninternationaleditions.com/deitel):

- *Solutions Manual* contains solutions to *most* of the end-of-chapter exercises. **Please do not write to us requesting access to the Pearson Instructor's Resource Center. Access is restricted to college instructors teaching from the book. Instructors may obtain access only through their Pearson representatives.** If you're not a registered faculty member, contact your Pearson representative or visit. Exercise Solutions are *not* provided for "project" exercises. Check out our Programming Projects Resource Center for lots of additional exercise and project possibilities:

  www.deitel.com/ProgrammingProjects

- *Test Item File* of multiple-choice questions (approximately two per book section)
- *Customizable PowerPoint® slides* containing all the code and figures in the text, plus bulleted items that summarize the key points in the text.

Microsoft DreamSpark™

Professional Developer and Designer Tools for Students
Microsoft provides many of its professional developer tools to students for free via a program called DreamSpark (www.dreamspark.com). See the website for details on verifying your student status so you take advantage of this program.

Acknowledgments

We'd like to thank Barbara Deitel of Deitel & Associates, Inc. for long hours devoted to this project. She painstakingly researched the new capabilities of Visual Basic 2012, .NET 4.5, Windows 8, Windows Phone 8, Windows Azure and other key topics.

We're fortunate to have worked with the dedicated team of publishing professionals at Pearson Higher Education. We appreciate the guidance, wisdom and energy of Tracy Johnson, Executive Editor, Computer Science. Carole Snyder did an extraordinary job recruiting the book's reviewers and managing the review process. Bob Engelhardt did a wonderful job bringing the book to publication.

Reviewers

We wish to acknowledge the efforts of our reviewers. The book was scrutinized by academics teaching Visual Basic courses and industry experts. They provided countless suggestions for improving the presentation. Any remaining flaws in the book are our own.

Sixth edition reviewers: Wu He (Old Dominion University), Ken Tucker (Microsoft MVP and Software Developer, Sea World), José Antonio González Seco (Parliament of Andalusia) and Jim Wooley (Slalom Consulting, Microsoft Visual Basic MVP, Author of LINQ in Action).

Other recent edition reviewers: Douglas B. Bock (MCSD.NET, Southern Illinois University Edwardsville), Dan Crevier (Microsoft), Amit K. Ghosh (University of Texas at El Paso), Marcelo Guerra Hahn (Microsoft), Kim Hamilton (Software Design Engineer at Microsoft and co-author of *Learning UML 2.0*), Huanhui Hu (Microsoft Corporation), Vitek Karas (Microsoft), Narges Kasiri (Oklahoma State University), James Edward Keysor (Florida Institute of Technology), Helena Kotas (Microsoft), Charles Liu (University of Texas at San Antonio), Chris Lovett (Software Architect at Microsoft), Bashar Lulu (INETA Country Leader, Arabian Gulf), John McIlhinney (Spatial Intelligence; Microsoft MVP 2008 Visual Developer, Visual Basic), Ged Mead (Microsoft Visual Basic MVP, DevCity.net), Anand Mukundan (Architect, Polaris Software Lab Ltd.), Dr. Hamid R. Nemati (The University of North Carolina at Greensboro), Timothy Ng (Microsoft), Akira Onishi (Microsoft), Jeffrey P. Scott (Blackhawk Technical College), Joe Stagner (Senior Program Manager, Developer Tools & Platforms), Erick Thompson (Microsoft) and Jesús Ubaldo Quevedo-Torrero (University of Wisconsin–Parkside, Department of Computer Science)

As you read the book, we'd sincerely appreciate your comments, criticisms and suggestions for improving the text. Please address all correspondence to:

```
deitel@deitel.com
```

We'll respond promptly. We really enjoyed writing this book—we hope you enjoy reading it!

Paul Deitel
Harvey Deitel

The publishers wish to thank Somitra Kr Sanadhya of Indraprastha Institute of Information Technology, Delhi for reviewing the content of the International Edition.

About the Authors

Paul Deitel, CEO and Chief Technical Officer of Deitel & Associates, Inc., is a graduate of MIT, where he studied Information Technology. Through Deitel & Associates, Inc., he has delivered hundreds of programming courses to industry clients, including Cisco, IBM, Siemens, Sun Microsystems, Dell, Fidelity, NASA at the Kennedy Space Center, the National Severe Storm Laboratory, White Sands Missile Range, Rogue Wave Software, Boeing, SunGard Higher Education, Nortel Networks, Puma, iRobot, Invensys and many more. He and his co-author, Dr. Harvey M. Deitel, are the world's best-selling programming-language textbook/professional book/video authors.

Paul was named as a Microsoft® Most Valuable Professional (MVP) for C# in 2012. According to Microsoft, "the Microsoft MVP Award is an annual award that recognizes exceptional technology community leaders worldwide who actively share their high quality, real world expertise with users and Microsoft."

2012 C# MVP

Dr. Harvey Deitel, Chairman and Chief Strategy Officer of Deitel & Associates, Inc., has over 50 years of experience in computing. Dr. Deitel earned B.S. and M.S. degrees in Electrical Engineering from MIT and a Ph.D. in Mathematics from Boston University. He has extensive college teaching experience, including earning tenure and serving as the Chairman of the Computer Science Department at Boston College before founding Deitel & Associates, Inc., in 1991 with his son, Paul Deitel. The Deitels' publications have earned international recognition, with translations published in Chinese, Korean, Japanese, German, Russian, Spanish, French, Polish, Italian, Portuguese, Greek, Urdu and Turkish. Dr. Deitel has delivered hundreds of programming courses to corporate, academic, government and military clients.

Deitel Dive-Into Series Programming Languages Training

Deitel & Associates, Inc., founded by Paul Deitel and Harvey Deitel, is an internationally recognized authoring and corporate training organization, specializing in computer programming languages, object technology, mobile app development and Internet and web software technology. The company's training clients include many of the world's largest companies, government agencies, branches of the military, and academic institutions. The company offers instructor-led training courses delivered at client sites worldwide on major programming languages and platforms, including Visual Basic®, Visual C#®, Visual C++®, C++, C, Java™, XML®, Python®, object technology, Internet and web programming, Android app development, Objective-C and iPhone app development and a growing list of additional programming and software development courses.

Through its 37-year publishing partnership with Prentice Hall/Pearson, Deitel & Associates, Inc., publishes leading-edge programming college textbooks, professional books and *LiveLessons* video courses. Deitel & Associates, Inc. and the authors can be reached at:

    deitel@deitel.com

To learn more about Deitel's *Dive-Into*® *Series* Corporate Training curriculum, visit:

    www.deitel.com/training

To request a proposal for worldwide on-site, instructor-led training at your organization, e-mail deitel@deitel.com.

Individuals wishing to purchase Deitel books and *LiveLessons* video training can do so through www.deitel.com. Bulk orders by corporations, the government, the military and academic institutions should be placed directly with Pearson. For more information, visit

    www.informit.com/store/sales.aspx

Before You Begin

This section contains information you should review before using this book and instructions to ensure that your computer is set up properly for use with this book.

Font and Naming Conventions

We use fonts to distinguish between features, such as menu names, menu items, and other elements that appear in the program-development environment. Our convention is to emphasize IDE features in a sans-serif bold Helvetica font (for example, **Properties** window) and to emphasize program text in a sans-serif Lucida font (for example, bool x = true).

Software

This textbook uses the following software:

- Microsoft Visual Studio Express 2012 for Windows Desktop
- Microsoft Visual Studio Express 2012 for Web (Chapters 13 and 24–26)
- Microsoft Visual Studio Express 2012 for Windows 8 (Chapters 20–21)
- Microsoft Visual Studio Express 2012 for Windows Phone (Chapter 22)

Each is available free for download at www.microsoft.com/express. The Express Editions are fully functional, and there's no time limit for using the software.

Hardware and Software Requirements for the Visual Studio 2012 Express Editions

To install and run the Visual Studio 2012 Express Editions, ensure that your system meets the minimum requirements specified at:

www.microsoft.com/visualstudio/eng/products/compatibility

Microsoft Visual Studio Express 2012 for Windows 8 works *only* on Windows 8.

Viewing File Extensions

Several screenshots in *Visual Basic 2012 How to Program* display file names with file-name extensions (e.g., .txt, .cs or .png). Your system's settings may need to be adjusted to display file-name extensions. Follow these steps to configure your Windows 7 computer:

1. In the **Start** menu, select **All Programs**, then **Accessories**, then **Windows Explorer**.
2. Press *Alt* to display the menu bar, then select **Folder Options...** from **Windows Explorer**'s **Tools** menu.
3. In the dialog that appears, select the **View** tab.
4. In the **Advanced settings:** pane, uncheck the box to the left of the text **Hide extensions for known file types**. [*Note:* If this item is already unchecked, no action needs to be taken.]
5. Click OK to apply the setting and close the dialog.

Follow these steps to configure your Windows 8 computer:

1. On the **Start** screen, click the **Desktop** tile to switch to the desktop.
2. On the task bar, click the **File Explorer** icon to open the **File Explorer.**
3. Click the **View** tab, then ensure that the **File name extensions** checkbox is checked.

Obtaining the Code Examples

The examples for *Visual Basic 2012 How to Program* are available for download at

```
www.deitel.com/books/vb2012htp/
```

If you're not already registered at our website, go to www.deitel.com and click the **Register** link below our logo in the upper-left corner of the page. Fill in your information. There's no charge to register, and we do not share your information with anyone. We send you only account-management e-mails unless you register separately for our free e-mail newsletter at www.deitel.com/newsletter/subscribe.html. *You must enter a valid e-mail address.* After registering, you'll receive a confirmation e-mail with your verification code. Click the link in the confirmation email to go to www.deitel.com and sign in.

Next, go to www.deitel.com/books/vb2012htp/. Click the **Examples** link to download the ZIP archive file to your computer. Write down the location where you save the file—most browsers will save the file into your Downloads folder.

Throughout the book, steps that require you to access our example code on your computer assume that you've extracted the examples from the ZIP file and placed them at C:\Examples. You can extract them anywhere you like, but if you choose a different location, you'll need to update our steps accordingly. You can extract the ZIP archive file's contents using tools such as WinZip (www.winzip.com), 7-zip (www.7-zip.org) or the built-in capabilities of **Windows Explorer** on Window 7 or **File Explorer** on Windows 8.

Visual Studio Theme

Visual Studio 2012 has a **Dark** theme (the default) and a **Light** theme. The screen captures shown in this book use the **Light** theme, which is more readable in print. If you'd like to switch to the **Light** theme, in the **TOOLS** menu, select **Options...** to display the **Options** dialog. In the left column, select **Environment**, then select **Light** under **Color theme**. Keep the **Options** dialog open for the next step.

Displaying Line Numbers and Configuring Tabs

Next, you'll change the settings so that your code matches that of this book. To have the IDE display line numbers, expand the **Text Editor** node in the left pane then select **All Languages**. On the right, check the **Line numbers** checkbox. Next, expand the Visual Basic node in the left pane and select **Tabs**. Make sure that the option **Insert spaces** is selected. Enter **3** for both the **Tab size** and **Indent size** fields. Any new code you add will now use three spaces for each level of indentation. Click **OK** to save your settings.

Miscellaneous Notes

- Some people like to change the workspace layout in the development tools. You can return the tools to their default layouts by selecting **Window > Reset Window Layout**.

- Many of the menu items we use in the book have corresponding icons shown with each menu item in the menus. Many of the icons also appear on one of the toolbars at the top of the development environment. As you become familiar with these icons, you can use the toolbars to help speed up your development time. Similarly, many of the menu items have keyboard shortcuts (also shown with each menu item in the menus) for accessing commands quickly.

You are now ready to begin your Visual Basic studies with *Visual Basic 2012 How to Program*. We hope you enjoy the book!

Introduction to Computers, the Internet and Visual Basic

The chief merit of language is clearness.
——Galen

Our life is frittered away with detail. . . . Simplify, simplify.
—Henry David Thoreau

Man is still the most extraordinary computer of all.
—John F. Kennedy

Objectives

In this chapter you'll learn:

- Basic hardware, software and data concepts.

- The different types of programming languages.

- The history of the Visual Basic programming language and the Windows operating system.

- What cloud computing with Windows Azure™ is.

- Basics of object technology.

- The history of the Internet and the World Wide Web.

- The parts that Windows, .NET, Visual Studio 2012 and Visual Basic 2012 play in the Visual Basic ecosystem.

- To test-drive a Visual Basic 2012 drawing app.

1.1 Introduction

Welcome to Visual Basic 2012 which, from this point forward, we'll refer to simply as Visual Basic. Visual Basic is a powerful computer programming language that's appropriate for building substantial information systems. This book explains how to develop software with Visual Basic.

You're already familiar with the powerful tasks computers perform. Using this textbook, you'll write instructions commanding computers to perform those kinds of tasks and you'll prepare yourself to address new challenges.

Computers process *data* under the control of sequences of instructions called **computer programs.** These programs guide the computer through *actions* specified by people called **computer programmers.** The programs that run on a computer are referred to as **software.** In this book, you'll learn *object-oriented programming*—today's key programming methodology that's enhancing programmer productivity and reducing software development costs. You'll create many *software objects* that model both abstract and real-world *things.* And you'll build Visual Basic apps (applications) for a variety of environments including the *desktop* and *tablets*—and new to this edition of the book—"the *cloud*" and even *mobile devices* like *smartphones.*

1.2 Hardware and Moore's Law

A computer consists of various devices referred to as **hardware,** such as the keyboard, screen, mouse, hard disks, memory, DVD drives, printer and processing units. Every year or two, the capacities of computer hardware have approximately *doubled* inexpensively. This remarkable trend often is called **Moore's Law,** named for the person who identified it, Gordon Moore, co-founder of Intel—the leading manufacturer of the processors in today's computers and **embedded systems**, such as smartphones, appliances, game controllers, cable set-top boxes and automobiles.

Moore's Law and *related* observations apply especially to

- the amount of *memory* that computers have for running programs and processing data
- the amount of *secondary storage* (such as hard disk storage) they have to hold programs and data over longer periods of time
- their *processor speeds*—the speeds at which computers execute their programs (i.e., do their work).

Similar growth has occurred in the communications field, in which costs have plummeted as enormous demand for communications *bandwidth* (i.e., information-carrying capacity) has attracted intense competition. We know of no other fields in which technology improves so quickly and costs fall so rapidly. Such phenomenal improvement is truly fostering the *Information Revolution* and creating significant career opportunities.

1.3 Data Hierarchy

Data items processed by computers form a **data hierarchy** that becomes larger and more complex in structure as we progress from the simplest data items (called "bits") to richer data items, such as characters, fields, and so on. Figure 1.1 illustrates a portion of the data hierarchy.

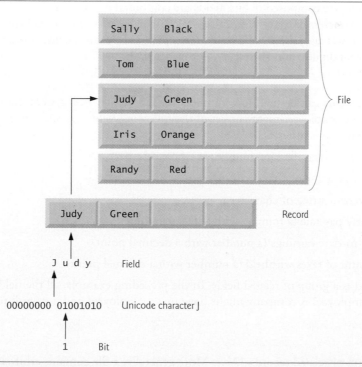

Fig. 1.1 | Data hierarchy.

Bits

The smallest data item in a computer can assume the value 0 or the value 1. Such a data item is called a **bit** (short for "binary digit"—a digit that can assume either of *two* values). It's remarkable that the impressive functions performed by computers involve only the simplest manipulations of 0s and 1s—*examining a bit's value*, *setting a bit's value* and *reversing a bit's value* (from 1 to 0 or from 0 to 1). We discuss binary numbers in more detail in Appendix C, Number Systems.

Characters

It's tedious for people to work with data in the low-level form of bits. Instead, we prefer to work with *decimal digits* (0–9), *uppercase letters* (A–Z), *lowercase letters* (a–z), and *special symbols* (e.g., $, @, %, &, *, (,), –, +, ", :, ? and /). Digits, letters and special symbols are known as **characters**. The computer's **character set** is the set of all the characters used to write programs and represent data items on that device. Computers process only 1s and 0s, so every character is represented as a pattern of 1s and 0s. The **Unicode** character set contains characters for many of the world's languages. Visual Basic supports several character sets, including 16-bit Unicode® characters that are composed of two **bytes**—each byte is composed of eight bits. See Appendix D for more information on the **ASCII** (**American Standard Code for Information Interchange**) character set—the popular *subset* of Unicode that represents uppercase and lowercase letters in the English alphabet, digits and some common *special characters*.

Fields

Just as characters are composed of bits, **fields** are composed of characters or bytes. A field is a group of characters or bytes that conveys meaning. For example, a field consisting of uppercase and lowercase letters could be used to represent a person's name, and a field consisting of decimal digits could represent a person's age.

Records

Several related fields can be used to compose a **record**. In a payroll system, for example, the record for an employee might consist of the following fields (possible types for these fields are shown in parentheses):

- Employee identification number (a whole number)
- Name (a string of characters)
- Address (a string of characters)
- Hourly pay rate (a number with a decimal point)
- Year-to-date earnings (a number with a decimal point)
- Amount of taxes withheld (a number with a decimal point)

Thus, a record is a group of related fields. In the preceding example, all the fields belong to the *same* employee. A company might have many employees and a payroll record for each one.

Files

A **file** is a group of related records. [*Note:* More generally, a file contains arbitrary data in arbitrary formats. In some operating systems, a file is viewed simply as a *sequence of bytes*—

any organization of the bytes in a file, such as organizing the data into records, is a view created by the programmer.] It's not unusual for an organization to have thousands or even millions of files, some containing billions or even trillions of characters of information. You'll work with files in Chapter 8.

Database

A database is a collection of data that's organized for easy access and manipulation. The most popular database model is the *relational database* in which data is stored in simple *tables*. A table includes *records* composed of *fields*. For example, a table of students might include first name, last name, major, year, student ID number and grade point average fields. The data for each student is a record, and the individual pieces of information in each record are the fields. You can *search*, *sort* and otherwise manipulate the data based on its relationship to multiple tables or databases. For example, a university might use data from the student database in combination with data from databases of courses, on-campus housing, meal plans, etc. We discuss databases in Chapters 12–13.

Big Data

The amount of data being produced worldwide is enormous and growing explosively. Figure 1.2 shows various common byte measurements. According to IBM, approximately 2.5 quintillion bytes (2.5 *exabytes*) of data are created daily and 90% of the world's data was created in just the past two years![1] According to an IDC study, approximately 1.8 *zettabytes* (equal to 1.8 trillion gigabytes) of data was used worldwide in 2011.[2]

Unit	Consists of	Which is approximately
1 kilobyte (KB)	1024 bytes	10^3 (1024 bytes, exactly)
1 megabyte (MB)	1024 kilobytes	10^6 (1,000,000 bytes)
1 gigabyte (GB)	1024 megabytes	10^9 (1,000,000,000 bytes)
1 terabyte (TB)	1024 gigabytes	10^{12} (1,000,000,000,000 bytes)
1 petabyte (PB)	1024 terabytes	10^{15} (1,000,000,000,000,000 bytes)
1 exabyte (EB)	1024 petabytes	10^{18} (1,000,000,000,000,000,000 bytes)
1 zettabyte (ZB)	1024 exabytes	10^{21} (1,000,000,000,000,000,000,000 bytes)

Fig. 1.2 | Byte measurements.

1.4 Computer Organization

Regardless of differences in *physical* appearance, computers can be envisioned as divided into various logical units or sections.

Input Unit

This "receiving" section obtains information (data and computer programs) from input devices and places it at the disposal of the other units for processing. Most information is

1. www-01.ibm.com/software/data/bigdata/.
2. www.emc.com/collateral/about/news/idc-emc-digital-universe-2011-infographic.pdf.

entered into computers through keyboards, touch screens and mouse devices. Other forms of input include receiving voice commands, scanning images and barcodes, reading from secondary storage devices (such as hard drives, DVD drives, Blu-ray Disc™ drives and USB flash drives—also called "thumb drives" or "memory sticks"), receiving video from a webcam or smartphone and having your computer receive information from the Internet (such as when you download videos from YouTube or e-books from Amazon). Newer forms of input include position data from GPS devices, and motion and orientation information from accelerometers in smartphones or game controllers (such as Microsoft® Kinect™, Nintendo's Wii™ Remote and Sony's PlayStation® Move).

Output Unit

This "shipping" section takes information that the computer has processed and places it on various **output devices** to make it available for use outside the computer. Most information that's output from computers today is displayed on screens; printed on paper ("going green" discourages this); played as audio or video on PCs and media players (such as Apple's iPods) and giant screens in sports stadiums; transmitted over the Internet or used to control other devices, such as robots, 3D printers and "intelligent" appliances.

Memory Unit

This rapid-access, relatively low-capacity "warehouse" section retains information that's entered through the input unit, making it immediately available for processing when needed. The memory unit also retains processed information until it can be placed on output devices by the output unit. Information in the memory unit is *volatile*—it's typically *lost* when the computer's power is turned off. The memory unit is often called either **memory** or **primary memory**—on desktop and notebook computers it commonly contains as much as 16 GB (gigabytes).

Arithmetic and Logic Unit (ALU)

This "manufacturing" section performs *calculations*, such as addition, subtraction, multiplication and division. It also contains the *decision* mechanisms that allow the computer, for example, to *compare* two items from the memory unit to determine whether they're equal. In today's systems, the ALU is usually implemented as part of the next logical unit, the CPU.

Central Processing Unit (CPU)

This "administrative" section *supervises* the operation of the other sections. The CPU tells the input unit when information should be read into the memory unit, tells the ALU when information from the memory unit should be used in calculations and tells the output unit when to send information from the memory unit to certain output devices. Many of today's computers have multiple CPUs and, hence, can perform many operations simultaneously. A **multi-core processor** implements multiple CPUs on a single "microchip"—a *dual-core processor* has *two* CPUs and a *quad-core processor* has *four* CPUs. Many of today's desktop computers have quad-core processors that can execute billions of instructions per second. In this book you'll use Microsoft's new Async technology to write programs that can keep CPUs running in parallel to get your computing tasks done faster.

Secondary Storage Unit

This is the long-term, high-capacity "warehousing" section. Programs or data not actively being used by the other units normally are placed on secondary storage devices (such as your *hard drive*) until they're again needed, possibly hours, days, months or even years later. Information on secondary storage devices is *persistent*—it's *preserved* even when the computer's power is turned off. Secondary storage data takes much longer to access than information in primary memory, but the cost per unit of secondary storage is much less than that of primary memory. Examples of secondary storage devices include CD drives, DVD drives and flash drives, some of which can hold up to 768 GB. Typical hard drives on desktop and notebook computers can hold up to 2 TB. New to this edition, you'll see that storage in the cloud can be viewed as additional secondary storage accessible by your Visual Basic apps.

1.5 Machine Languages, Assembly Languages and High-Level Languages

Programmers write instructions in various programming languages (such as Visual Basic), some directly understandable by computers and others requiring intermediate *translation* steps.

Machine Languages

Any computer can *directly* understand *only* its own **machine language**, defined by its hardware architecture. Machine languages generally consist of numbers, ultimately reduced to 1s and 0s. Such languages are cumbersome for humans, who prefer meaningful words like "add" and "subtract" to indicate the operations to be performed, so the machine language numeric versions of these instructions are referred to as **code**. The term "code" has become more broadly used and now refers to the program instructions in *all* levels of programming languages.

Assembly Languages and Assemblers

Machine language was simply too slow and tedious for programmers to work with. Instead, they began using English-like *abbreviations* to represent elementary operations. These abbreviations form the basis of **assembly languages**. *Translator programs* called **assemblers** convert assembly-language code to machine language code quickly. Although assembly-language code is clearer to humans, it's incomprehensible to computers until translated to machine language code.

High-Level Languages, Compilers and Interpreters

To speed the programming process even further, **high-level languages** were developed in which single statements could be written to accomplish substantial tasks. High-level languages, such as Visual Basic, C#, C++, C, Objective-C and Java, allow you to write instructions that look almost like everyday English and contain commonly used mathematical expressions. Translator programs called **compilers** convert high-level language code into machine language code.

The process of compiling a large high-level language program into machine language can take a considerable amount of computer time. **Interpreter** programs were developed to execute high-level language programs directly (without the need for compilation), although more slowly than compiled programs.

1.6 Object Technology

Visual Basic is an object-oriented programming language. In this section we'll introduce the basics of object technology.

Building software quickly, correctly and economically remains an elusive goal at a time when demands for new and more powerful software are soaring. **Objects,** or more precisely the *classes* objects come from, are essentially *reusable* software components. There are date objects, time objects, audio objects, video objects, automobile objects, people objects, etc. Almost any *noun* can be reasonably represented as a software object in terms of *attributes* (such as name, color and size) and *behaviors* (such as calculating, moving and communicating). Software developers have discovered that using a modular, object-oriented design and implementation approach can make software-development groups much more productive than was possible with earlier techniques—object-oriented programs are often easier to understand, correct and modify.

The Automobile as an Object

Let's begin with a simple analogy. Suppose you want to *drive a car and make it go faster by pressing its accelerator pedal*. What must happen before you can do this? Well, before you can drive a car, someone has to *design* it. A car typically begins as engineering drawings, similar to the *blueprints* that describe the design of a house. These drawings include the design for an accelerator pedal. The pedal *hides* from the driver the complex mechanisms that actually make the car go faster, just as the brake pedal hides the mechanisms that slow the car, and the steering wheel hides the mechanisms that turn the car. This enables people with little or no knowledge of how engines, braking and steering mechanisms work to drive a car easily.

Before you can drive a car, it must be *built* from the engineering drawings that describe it. A completed car has an *actual* accelerator pedal to make the car go faster, but even that's not enough—the car won't accelerate on its own (we hope), so the driver must *press* the pedal to accelerate the car.

Methods and Classes

Let's use our car example to introduce some key object-oriented programming concepts. Performing a task in a program requires a **method.** The method houses the program statements that actually perform the task. It *hides* these statements from its user, just as a car's accelerator pedal hides from the driver the mechanisms of making the car go faster. In object-oriented programming languages, we create a program unit called a class to house the set of methods that perform the class's tasks. For example, a class that represents a bank account might contain one method to *deposit* money to an account, another to *withdraw* money from an account and a third to *inquire* what the account's current balance is. A class that represents a car might contain methods for accelerating, breaking and turning. A class is similar in concept to a car's engineering drawings, which house the design of an accelerator pedal, steering wheel, and so on.

Making Objects from Classes

Just as someone has to *build a car* from its engineering drawings before you can actually drive a car, you must *build an object* from a class before a program can perform the tasks that the class's methods define. The process of doing this is called *instantiation*. An object is then referred to as an **instance** of its class.

Reuse

Just as a car's engineering drawings can be *reused* many times to build many cars, you can *reuse* a class many times to build many objects. Reuse of existing classes when building new classes and programs saves time and effort. Reuse also helps you build more reliable and effective systems, because existing classes and components often have gone through extensive *testing* (to locate problems), *debugging* (to correct those problems) and *performance tuning*. Just as the notion of *interchangeable parts* was crucial to the Industrial Revolution, *reusable classes* are crucial to the software revolution that's been spurred by object technology.

Software Engineering Observation 1.1

Use a building-block approach to creating your programs. Avoid reinventing the wheel—use existing pieces wherever possible. This software reuse is a key benefit of object-oriented programming.

Messages and Method Calls

When you drive a car, pressing its gas pedal sends a *message* to the car to perform a task—that is, to go faster. Similarly, you *send messages to an object*. Each message is implemented as a **method call** that tells a method of the object to perform its task. For example, a program might call a particular bank-account object's *deposit* method to increase the account's balance.

Attributes and Instance Variables

A car, besides having capabilities to accomplish tasks, also has *attributes*, such as its color, its number of doors, the amount of gas in its tank, its current speed and its record of total miles driven (i.e., its odometer reading). Like its capabilities, the car's attributes are represented as part of its design in its engineering diagrams (which, for example, include an odometer and a fuel gauge). As you drive an actual car, these attributes are carried along with the car. Every car maintains its *own* attributes. For example, each car knows how much gas is in its own gas tank, but *not* how much is in the tanks of *other* cars.

An object, similarly, has attributes that it carries along as it's used in a program. These attributes are specified as part of the object's class. For example, a bank-account object has a *balance attribute* that represents the amount of money in the account. Each bank-account object knows the balance in the account it represents, but *not* the balances of the *other* accounts in the bank. Attributes are specified by the class's **instance variables**.

Encapsulation

Classes **encapsulate** (i.e., wrap) attributes and methods into objects—an object's attributes and operations are intimately related. Objects may communicate with one another, but they're normally not allowed to know how other objects are implemented—implementation details are *hidden* within the objects themselves. This **information hiding**, as we'll see, is crucial to good software engineering.

Inheritance

A new class of objects can be created quickly and conveniently by **inheritance**—the new class absorbs the characteristics of an existing class, possibly customizing them and adding unique characteristics of its own. In our car analogy, an object of class "convertible" certainly *is an* object of the more *general* class "automobile," but more *specifically*, the roof can be raised or lowered.

Object-Oriented Analysis and Design (OOAD)

Soon you'll be writing programs in Visual Basic. Perhaps, like many programmers, you'll simply turn on your computer and start typing. This approach may work for small programs (like the ones we present in the early chapters of this book), but what if you were asked to create a software system to control thousands of automated teller machines for a major bank? Or suppose you were asked to work on a team of thousands of software developers building the next U.S. air traffic control system? For projects so large and complex, you should not simply sit down and start writing programs.

To create the best solutions, you should follow a detailed **analysis** process for determining your project's **requirements** (i.e., defining *what* the system is supposed to do) and developing a **design** that satisfies them (i.e., deciding *how* the system should do it). Ideally, you'd go through this process and carefully review the design (and have your design reviewed by other software professionals) before writing any code. If this process involves analyzing and designing your system from an object-oriented point of view, it's called an **object-oriented analysis and design (OOAD) process**. Languages like Visual Basic are object oriented. Programming in such a language, called **object-oriented programming (OOP)**, allows you to implement an object-oriented design as a working system.

The UML (Unified Modeling Language)

Although many different OOAD processes exist, a single graphical language for communicating the results of *any* OOAD process has come into wide use. This language, known as the *Unified Modeling Language (UML)*, is now the most widely used graphical scheme for modeling object-oriented systems. We present our first simple UML diagrams in Chapters 4 and 5, then use them in our deeper treatment of object-oriented programming. In our optional ATM Software Engineering Case Study in Chapters 30–31 we present a subset of the UML's features as we guide you through a simple object-oriented design experience.

1.7 Internet and World Wide Web

In the late 1960s, ARPA—the Advanced Research Projects Agency of the United States Department of Defense—rolled out plans to network the main computer systems of approximately a dozen ARPA-funded universities and research institutions. The computers were to be connected with communications lines operating at a then-stunning 56 Kbps (1 Kbps is equal to 1,024 bits per second), at a time when most people (of the few who even had networking access) were connecting over telephone lines to computers at a rate of 110 bits per second. Academic research was about to take a giant leap forward. ARPA proceeded to implement what quickly became known as the ARPAnet, the precursor of today's **Internet**.

Things worked out differently from the original plan. Although the ARPAnet enabled researchers to network their computers, its main benefit proved to be the capability for quick and easy communication via what came to be known as electronic mail (e-mail). This is true even on today's Internet, with e-mail, instant messaging, file transfer and social media such as Facebook and Twitter, enabling billions of people worldwide to communicate quickly and easily.

The protocol (set of rules) for communicating over the ARPAnet became known as the **Transmission Control Protocol (TCP)**. TCP ensured that messages, consisting of sequentially numbered pieces called *packets*, were properly routed from sender to receiver, arrived intact and were assembled in the correct order.

The Internet: A Network of Networks

In parallel with the early evolution of the Internet, organizations worldwide were implementing their own networks for both intraorganization (that is, within an organization) and interorganization (that is, between organizations) communication. A huge variety of networking hardware and software appeared. One challenge was to enable these different networks to communicate with each other. ARPA accomplished this by developing the Internet Protocol (IP), which created a true "network of networks," the current architecture of the Internet. The combined set of protocols is now called **TCP/IP**.

Businesses rapidly realized that by using the Internet, they could improve their operations and offer new and better services to their clients. Companies started spending large amounts of money to develop and enhance their Internet presence. This generated fierce competition among communications carriers and hardware and software suppliers to meet the increased infrastructure demand. As a result, **bandwidth**—the information-carrying capacity of communications lines—on the Internet has increased tremendously, while hardware costs have plummeted.

The World Wide Web: Making the Internet User-Friendly

The **World Wide Web** (simply called "the web") is a collection of hardware and software associated with the Internet that allows computer users to locate and view multimedia-based documents (documents with various combinations of text, graphics, animations, audios and videos) on almost any subject. The introduction of the web was a relatively recent event. In 1989, Tim Berners-Lee of CERN (the European Organization for Nuclear Research) began to develop a technology for sharing information via "hyperlinked" text documents. Berners-Lee called his invention the **HyperText Markup Language** (HTML). He also wrote communication protocols such as **HyperText Transfer Protocol** (HTTP) to form the backbone of his new hypertext information system, which he referred to as the World Wide Web.

In 1994, Berners-Lee founded an organization, called the **World Wide Web Consortium** (W3C, www.w3.org), devoted to developing web technologies. One of the W3C's primary goals is to make the web universally accessible to everyone regardless of disabilities, language or culture.

In this book, you'll use Visual Basic and other Microsoft technologies to build web-based apps.

1.8 Visual Basic

The Visual Basic programming language evolved from BASIC, developed in the 1960s at Dartmouth College for introducing novices to fundamental programming techniques. When Bill Gates founded Microsoft in the 1970s, he implemented BASIC on several early personal computers. In the late 1980s and the early 1990s, Microsoft developed the Microsoft Windows **graphical user interface (GUI)**—the visual part of the operating system with which users interact. With the creation of the Windows GUI, the natural evolution of BASIC was to Visual Basic, introduced by Microsoft in 1991 to make programming Windows apps easier.

Visual Basic 6 was introduced in 1998. It was designed to make programming fast and easy, however it was not intended for building industrial strength apps. In 2002, Microsoft released Visual Basic .NET—a more robust language that's appropriate for the most demanding app development tasks, especially for building today's large-scale enterprise apps, and web-based, mobile and cloud apps.

Visual Basic 2012 is one of the most *productive* programming languages, requiring less development time than other popular high-level programming languages such as Java, C, C++ and C#—the sister language to Visual Basic.[3]

1.8.1 Object-Oriented Programming

Visual Basic is *object oriented*—we've discussed the basics of object technology and will present a rich treatment of object-oriented programming throughout the book. Visual Basic has access to the powerful .NET Framework Class Library—a vast collection of pre-built components that enable you to develop apps quickly (Fig. 1.3). We'll say more about .NET in Section 1.9.

Some key capabilities in the .NET Framework Class Library	
Database	Computer networking
Building web apps	Debugging
Graphics	Multithreading
Input/output	File processing
Networking	Security
Permissions	Web communication
Mobile	Graphical user interface
String processing	Data structures

Fig. 1.3 | Some key capabilities in the .NET Framework Class Library.

1.8.2 Event-Driven Programming

Visual Basic is event driven. You'll write programs that respond to user-initiated events such as mouse clicks, keystrokes, timer expirations and—new in Visual Basic 2012—*touches* and *finger swipes*—geatures that are so widely used on smartphones and tablets.

1.8.3 Visual Programming

Visual Basic is a *visual programming language*—in addition to writing program statements to build portions of your apps, you'll also use Visual Studio's graphical user interface (GUI) to conveniently drag and drop predefined objects like *buttons* and *textboxes* into place on your screen, and label and resize them. Visual Studio will write much of the GUI code for you.

---

3. www.drdobbs.com/jvm/the-comparative-productivity-of-programm/240005881.

1.8.4 Internet and Web Programming

Today's apps can be written with the aim of communicating among the world's computers. As you'll see, this is the focus of Microsoft's .NET strategy. In Chapters 13 and 24, you'll build web-based apps with Visual Basic and Microsoft's ASP.NET technology.

1.8.5 Other Key Contemporary Programming Languages

Figure 1.4 summarizes some other important programming languages. The last four are object-oriented languages that have capabilities comparable to those of Visual Basic. C, which is not object oriented, is an ancestor of the other four languages in the figure.

Programming language	Description
C	C was implemented in 1972 by Dennis Ritchie at Bell Laboratories. It initially became widely known as the UNIX operating system's development language. Today, most of the code for general-purpose operating systems is written in C or C++.
C++	C++, an extension of C, was developed by Bjarne Stroustrup in the early 1980s at Bell Laboratories. C++ provides several features that "spruce up" the C language, but more important, it provides capabilities for *object-oriented programming*. It's often used in applications with stringent performance requirements such as operating systems, real-time systems, embedded systems and communications systems. Visual C++ is Microsoft's version of the language.
Java	In the 1990s, Sun Microsystems (now part of Oracle) developed the C++-based object-oriented programming language called Java. A key goal of Java is to be able to write programs that will run on a great variety of computer systems and computer-control devices—this is sometimes called *write once, run anywhere*. Java is used to develop large-scale enterprise applications, to enhance the functionality of web servers (the computers that provide the content we see in our web browsers), to provide applications for consumer devices (e.g., smartphones, tablets, television set-top boxes, appliances, automobiles and more) and for many other purposes.
C#	In 2000, Microsoft announced the C# programming language. C# has roots in the C, C++ and Java programming languages. It has similar capabilities to Java and is appropriate for the most demanding application development tasks, especially for building today's large-scale enterprise applications, and web-based, mobile and cloud-based apps. The latest versions of Visual Basic have capabilities comparable to those of C#.
Objective-C	Objective-C is another object-oriented language based on C. It was developed at Stepstone in the early 1980s and later acquired by Next, which in turn was acquired by Apple. It has become the key programming language for the Mac OS X desktop operating system and all iOS-based devices, such as iPods, iPhones and iPads.

Fig. 1.4 | Other programming languages.

1.9 Microsoft's .NET

In 2000, Microsoft announced its **.NET initiative** (www.microsoft.com/net), a broad vision for using the Internet and the web in the development, engineering, distribution and use of software. Rather than forcing you to use a single programming language, .NET permits you to create apps in *any* .NET-compatible language (such as Visual Basic, C#, Visual C++ and many others). Part of the initiative includes Microsoft's ASP.NET technology, which is used to build web applications that users interact with via their web browsers.

1.9.1 .NET Framework

The **.NET Framework** contains the .NET Framework **Class Library**, which provides many capabilities that you'll use to build substantial Visual Basic apps quickly and easily. The .NET Framework Class Library has *thousands* of valuable *prebuilt* classes that have been tested and tuned to maximize performance. You'll learn how to create your own classes, but you should *re-use* the .NET Framework classes when possible to speed up the software development process, while enhancing the quality and performance of the software you develop.

1.9.2 Common Language Runtime

The **Common Language Runtime (CLR)**, another key part of the .NET Framework, executes .NET programs and provides functionality to make them easier to develop and debug. The CLR is a **virtual machine (VM)**—software that manages the execution of programs and hides from them the underlying operating system and hardware. The source code for programs that are executed and managed by the CLR is called *managed code*. The CLR provides various services to managed code, such as integrating software components written in different .NET languages, error handling between such components, enhanced security, automatic memory management and more. Unmanaged-code programs do not have access to the CLR's services, which makes unmanaged code more difficult to write.[4]

1.10 Microsoft's Windows® Operating System

Microsoft's Windows is the most widely used desktop operating system worldwide. **Operating systems** are software systems that make using computers more convenient for users, app developers and system administrators. They provide *services* that allow each app to execute safely, efficiently and *concurrently* (i.e., in parallel) with other apps. Other popular desktop operating systems include Linux and Mac OS X. Popular *mobile operating systems* used in smartphones and tablets include Microsoft's Windows Phone, Google's Android, Apple's iOS (for iPhone, iPad and iPod Touch devices) and BlackBerry OS. Figure 1.5 presents the evolution of the Windows operating system.

---

4. msdn.microsoft.com/en-us/library/8bs2ecf4.aspx.

Version	Description
Windows in the 1990s	In the mid-1980s, Microsoft developed the Windows **operating system** based on a graphical user interface with buttons, textboxes, menus and other graphical elements. The various versions released throughout the 1990s were intended for personal computing. Microsoft entered the corporate operating systems market with the 1993 release of *Windows NT.*
Windows XP and Windows Vista	*Windows XP* was released in 2001 and combined Microsoft's corporate and consumer operating system lines. It remains popular today—according to a 2012 Netmarketshare study, it's used on more than 40% of Windows computers (netmarketshare.com/operating-system-market-share.aspx?qprid=10&qpcustomd=0). *Windows Vista*, released in 2007, offered the attractive new Aero user interface, many powerful enhancements and new apps and enhanced security. But Vista never caught on— today, it has "only" six percent of the total desktop operating systems market share (that's still a pretty significant number; netmarketshare.com/operating-system-market-share.aspx?qprid=10&qpcustomd=0).
Windows 7	*Windows 7*, now the most widely used version of Windows, includes enhancements to the Aero user interface, faster startup times, further refinement of Vista's security features, touch-screen with multi-touch support, and more. Windows 7 had a 43% market share, and overall, Windows (including Windows 7, Windows XP and Windows Vista) had over 90% of the desktop operating system market share worldwide (netmarketshare.com/operating-system-market-share.aspx?qprid=10&qpcustomd=0). The core chapters of this book use Windows 7, Visual Studio 2012 and Visual Basic 2012.
Windows 8 for Desktops and Tablets	Windows 8, released in 2012 provides a similar **platform** (the underlying system on which apps run) and *user experience* across a wide range of devices including personal computers, tablets and the Xbox Live online game service. The new look-and-feel features a Start screen with *tiles* that represent each app, similar to that of *Windows Phone*—Microsoft's operating system for smartphones. Windows 8 features *multi-touch* support for *touchpads* and *touchscreen* devices, enhanced security features and more.
Windows 8 UI (User Interface)	Visual Basic 2012 supports the new Windows 8 UI (previously called "Metro") which has a clean look-and-feel with minimal distractions to the user. Windows 8 apps feature a *chromeless window*—there's no longer a border around the window with the typical interface elements such as title bars and menus. These elements are *hidden*, allowing apps to fill the *entire* screen, which is particularly helpful on smaller screens such as tablets and smartphones. The interface elements are displayed in the *app bar* when the user *swipes* the top or bottom of the screen by holding down the mouse button, moving the mouse in the swipe direction and releasing the mouse button; this can be done with a *finger swipe* on a touchscreen device. We discuss Windows 8 and the Windows 8 UI in Chapter 20 and Windows Phone 8 in Chapter 22.

Fig. 1.5 | The evolution of the Windows operating system.

Windows Store

You can sell Windows 8 UI desktop and tablet apps or offer them for free in the Windows Store. The fee to become a registered Windows Store developer is $49 for individuals and $99 for companies. However the fee is waived for Microsoft DreamSpark program students (see the Preface). For Windows 8 UI apps, Microsoft retains 30% of the purchase price and distributes 70% to you, up to $25,000. If revenues for your app that exceed that amount, Microsoft will retain 20% of the purchase price and distribute 80% to you.

The Windows Store offers several business models for monetizing your app. You can charge the full price for your app before download, with prices starting at $1.49. You can also offer a time-limited trial or feature-limited trial that allows users to try the app before purchasing the full version, sell virtual goods (such as additional app features) using in-app purchases and more. To learn more about the Windows Store and monetizing your apps, visit msdn.microsoft.com/en-us/library/windows/apps/br229519.aspx.

1.11 Windows Phone 8 for Smartphones

Windows Phone 8 is a pared down version of Windows 8 designed for *smartphones*. These are *resource-constrained devices*—they have less memory and processor power than desktop computers, and limited battery life. Windows Phone 8 has the *same* core operating systems services as Windows 8, including a common file system, security, networking, media and Internet Explorer 10 (IE10) web browser technology. However, Windows Phone 8 has *only* the features necessary for smartphones, allowing them to run efficiently, minimizing the burden on the device's resources.

New to this edition of the book, you'll use Visual Basic 2012 to develop your own Windows Phone 8 apps. Just as the Objective-C programming language has increased in popularity due to iOS app development for iPhone, iPad and iPod touch, Visual Basic is sure to become even more popular as the demand for Windows Phones increases. International Data Corporation (IDC) predicts that Windows Phone will have over 19% of the smartphone market share by 2016, second only to Android and ahead of Apple's iPhone.[5] You'll learn how to develop Windows Phone apps in Chapter 22.

1.11.1 Selling Your Apps in the Windows Phone Marketplace

You can sell your own Windows Phone apps in the **Windows Phone Marketplace** (www.windowsphone.com/marketplace), similar to other app commerce platforms such as Apple's App Store, Google Play (formerly Android Market), Facebook's App Center and the Windows Store. You can also earn money by making your apps free for download and selling *virtual goods* (e.g., additional content, game levels, e-gifts and add-on features) using *in-app purchase*.

1.11.2 Free vs. Paid Apps

A recent study by Gartner found that 89% of all mobile apps are free, and that number is likely to increase to 93% by 2016, at which point in-app purchases will account for over 40% of mobile app revenues.[6] Paid Windows Phone 8 apps range in price from $1.49

---

5.   www.idc.com/getdoc.jsp?containerId=prUS23523812.
6.   techcrunch.com/2012/09/11/free-apps/.

(which is higher than the $0.99 starting price for apps in Google Play and Apple's App Store) to $999.99. The average price for mobile apps is approximately $1.50 to $3, depending on the platform. For Windows Phone apps, Microsoft retains 30% of the purchase price and distributes 70% to you. At the time of this writing, there were over 100,000 apps in the Windows Phone Marketplace.[7]

1.11.3 Testing Your Windows Phone Apps

You can test your phone apps on the Windows Phone Emulator that Microsoft provides with the Windows Phone 8 SDK (software development kit). To test your apps on a Windows phone and to sell your apps or distribute your free apps through the Windows Phone Marketplace, you'll need to join the *Windows Phone Dev Center*. There's an annual fee of $99; the program is *free* to DreamSpark students (for more information about Dream-Spark, see the Preface). The website includes development tools, sample code, tips for selling your apps, design guidelines and more. To join the Windows Phone Dev Center and submit apps, visit `dev.windowsphone.com/en-us/downloadsdk`.

1.12 Windows Azure™ and Cloud Computing

Cloud computing allows you to use software and data stored in the cloud—i.e., accessed on remote computers (or servers) via the Internet and available on demand—rather than having it stored on your desktop, notebook computer or mobile device. Cloud computing gives you the flexibility to increase or decrease computing resources to meet your resource needs at any given time, making it more cost effective than purchasing expensive hardware to ensure that you have enough storage and processing power at their occasional peak levels. Using cloud computing services also saves money by shifting the burden of *managing* these apps to the service provider. New to this edition of the book, in Chapter 26 you'll use Microsoft's **Windows Azure**—a cloud computing platform that allows you to develop, manage and distribute your apps in the cloud. With Windows Azure, your apps can store their data in the cloud so that the data is available at all times from any of your desktop computer and mobile devices. Verified DreamSpark students can download Visual Studio 2012 Professional which includes built-in support for Windows 8 and Windows Azure.[8] You can sign up for a free 90-day trial of Windows Azure at `www.windowsazure.com/en-us/pricing/free-trial/`.

1.13 Visual Studio Integrated Development Environment

Visual Basic programs are created using Microsoft's Visual Studio—a collection of software tools called an **Integrated Development Environment** (IDE). The **Visual Studio 2012** IDE enables you to *write, run, test* and *debug* Visual Basic programs quickly and conveniently. It also supports Microsoft's Visual C#, Visual C++ and F# programming languages. You'll use Visual Studio to develop Visual Basic apps featuring the new Windows 8 UI.

---

7. `windowsteamblog.com/windows_phone/b/windowsphone/archive/2012/06/20/announcing-windows-phone-8.aspx`.

8. `www.dreamspark.com/Product/Product.aspx?productid=44`.

1.14 Test-Driving the Visual Basic Advanced Painter App in Visual Studio 2012

In this section, you'll "test-drive" an existing app that enables you to draw on the screen using the mouse. In Chapter 2, you'll write your first simple Visual Basic programs.

The **Advanced Painter** app allows you to draw with different brush sizes and colors. The elements and functionality in this app are typical of what you'll learn to program in this text. The following steps show you how to test-drive the app. You'll run and interact with the working app.

1. *Checking your setup.* Confirm that you've set up your computer properly by reading the Before You Begin section located after the Preface.

2. *Locating the app directory.* Open a Windows Explorer (File Explorer on Windows 8) window and navigate to the C:\Examples\ch01 directory (Fig. 1.6)—we assume you placed the examples in the C:\Examples folder.

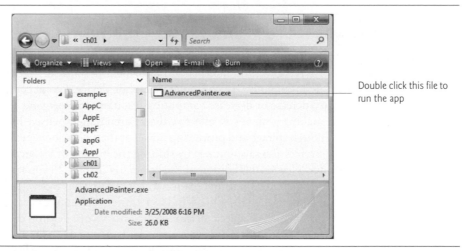

Double click this file to run the app

Fig. 1.6 | Contents of C:\Examples\ch01.

3. *Running the Advanced Painter app.* Now that you're in the proper directory, double click the file name AdvancedPainter.exe (Fig. 1.6) to run the app (Fig. 1.7). [*Note:* Depending on your system configuration, Windows Explorer or File Explorer might not display file name extensions. To display file name extensions (like .exe in Fig. 1.6) on Windows 7, type *Alt + T* in Windows Explorer to open the **Tools** menu, then select **Folder options....** In the **Folder Options** window, select the **View** tab, uncheck **Hide extensions for known file types** and click **OK**. On Windows 8, click the **View** tab in the **File Explorer** window, then ensure that **File name extensions** is selected.]

Figure 1.7 labels several graphical elements—called **controls**. These include GroupBoxes, RadioButtons, a Panel and Buttons (these controls and many others are discussed in depth throughout the text). The app allows you to draw with a red, blue, green or black brush of small, medium or large size. You can also undo your previous operation or clear the drawing to start from scratch.

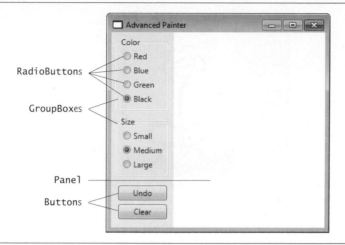

RadioButtons

GroupBoxes

Panel

Buttons

Fig. 1.7 | Visual Basic **Advanced Painter** app.

By using existing controls—which are objects—you can create powerful apps much faster than if you had to write all the code yourself.

The brush's properties, selected in the `RadioButtons` labeled **Black** and **Medium**, are *default settings*—the initial settings you see when you first run the app. You'll program default settings in your apps to provide visual cues for users to choose their own settings. Now you'll choose your own settings as a user of this app.

4. *Changing the brush color and size.* Click the `RadioButtons` labeled **Red** to change the color of the brush and **Small** to change the size of the brush. Position the mouse over the white `Panel`, then press and hold down the left mouse button to draw with the brush. Draw flower petals, as shown in Fig. 1.8.

Fig. 1.8 | Drawing with a new brush color.

5. *Changing the brush size.* Click the `RadioButton` labeled **Green** to change the color of the brush again. Click the `RadioButton` labeled **Large** to change the size of the brush. Draw grass and a flower stem, as shown in Fig. 1.9.

Fig. 1.9 | Drawing with a new brush size.

6. **Finishing the drawing.** Click the **Blue** and **Medium** RadioButtons. Draw rain-drops, as shown in Fig. 1.10, to complete the drawing.

Close box

Fig. 1.10 | Finishing the drawing.

7. **Closing the app.** Close your running app by clicking its **close box**, 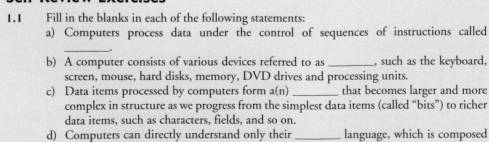 (Fig. 1.10).

Self-Review Exercises

1.1   Fill in the blanks in each of the following statements:
   a) Computers process data under the control of sequences of instructions called _____.
   b) A computer consists of various devices referred to as _____, such as the keyboard, screen, mouse, hard disks, memory, DVD drives and processing units.
   c) Data items processed by computers form a(n) _____ that becomes larger and more complex in structure as we progress from the simplest data items (called "bits") to richer data items, such as characters, fields, and so on.
   d) Computers can directly understand only their _____ language, which is composed only of 1s and 0s.

    e) The three types of computer programming languages discussed in the chapter are machine languages, _____ and _____.

    f) Programs that translate high-level-language programs into machine language are called _____.

    g) A(n) _____ processor implements several CPUs on a single "microchip"—a dual-core processor has two CPUs and a quad-core processor has four CPUs.

1.2 Fill in the blanks in each of the following statements:

    a) Objects, or more precisely the _____ that objects come from, are essentially reusable software components.

    b) You send messages to an object. Each message is implemented as a method _____ that tells a method of the object to perform its task.

    c) A new class of objects can be created quickly and conveniently by _____; the new class absorbs the characteristics of an existing class, possibly customizing them and adding unique characteristics of its own.

    d) To create the best solutions, you should follow a detailed analysis process for determining your project's _____ (i.e., defining what the system is supposed to do) and developing a design that satisfies them (i.e., deciding how the system should do it).

    e) Visual Basic is _____ driven. You'll write programs that respond to mouse clicks, keystrokes, timer expirations and—new in Visual Basic 2012—touches and finger swipes.

    f) Microsoft's Visual Basic is a(n) _____ programming language—in addition to writing program statements to build portions of your apps, you'll also use Visual Studio's graphical user interface (GUI) to conveniently drag and drop predefined objects like buttons and textboxes into place on your screen, and label and resize them.

    g) C++ provides several features that "spruce up" the C language, but more important, it provides capabilities for _____-oriented programming.

    h) A key goal of Java is to be able to write programs that will run on a great variety of computer systems and computer-controlled devices. This is sometimes called _____.

1.3 Fill in the blanks in each of the following statements:

    a) The _____ executes .NET programs.

    b) The CLR provides various services to _____ code, such as integrating software components written in different .NET languages, error handling between such components, enhanced security and more.

    c) The ability of a program to run without modification across multiple platforms is known as platform _____.

    d) Visual Studio is a(n) _____ in which Visual Basic programs are developed.

    e) The new Windows 8 look-and-feel features a Start screen with _____ that represent each app, is similar to that of *Windows Phone 8*—a Microsoft operating system for smartphones.

    f) Windows 8 apps feature a(n) _____ window; there's no longer a border around the window with the typical interface elements such as title bars and menus.

    g) You can sell your own Windows Phone apps in the _____.

    h) You can test your phone apps on the Windows Phone _____ app that Microsoft provides with the Windows Phone SDK (software development kit).

1.4 State whether each of the following is *true* or *false*. If *false*, explain why.

    a) Software objects model both abstract and real-world things.

    b) The most popular database model is the *relational database* in which data is stored in simple *tables*. A table includes *records* and *fields*.

    c) A database is a collection of data that's organized for easy access and manipulation.

d) Secondary storage data takes much longer to access than data in primary memory, but the cost per unit of secondary storage is much higher than that of primary memory.

e) High-level languages, such as Visual Basic, C#, C++, C, Objective-C and Java, allow you to write instructions that look almost like everyday English and contain commonly used mathematical expressions.

f) An object has attributes that it carries along as it's used in a program.

g) The Transmission Control Protocol (TCP) ensures that messages, consisting of sequentially numbered pieces called bytes, are properly routed from sender to receiver, arrive intact and are assembled in the correct order

h) The information-carrying capacity of communications lines on the Internet has increased tremendously, while hardware costs have increased.

i) You can build web-based apps with Visual Basic and Microsoft's ASP.NET technology.

j) Java has become the key programming language for the Mac OS X desktop operating system and all iOS-based devices, such as iPods, iPhones and iPads.

k) Microsoft's ASP.WEB technology is used to create web apps.

l) Microsoft's Windows operating system is the most widely used desktop operating system worldwide.

m) Windows 8 is designed for resource-constrained devices that have less memory and processor power than desktop computers, and limited battery life.

n) Visual Basic 2012 also can be used to develop Windows Phone 8 apps.

1.5 Arrange these byte measurements in order from smallest to largest: terabyte, megabyte, petabyte, gigabyte and kilobyte.

Answers to Self-Review Exercises

1.1 a) computer programs. b) hardware. c) data hierarchy. d) machine. e) assembly languages, high-level languages. f) compilers. g) multi-core.

1.2 a) classes. b) call. c) inheritance. d) requirements. e) event. f) visual. g) object. h) write once, run anywhere.

1.3 a) Common Language Runtime (CLR) of the .NET Framework. b) managed. c) independence. d) IDE. e) tiles. f) chromeless. g) Windows Phone Marketplace. h) Emulator.

1.4 a) True. b) True. c) True. d) False: The cost per unit of secondary storage is much lower than that of primary memory. e) True. f) True. g) False. Packets—not bytes. h) False. Hardware costs have decreased. i) True. j) False. The language is Objective-C, not Java. k) False. It's ASP.NET technology. l) True. m) False. Windows Phone 8 is designed for resource-constrained devices. n) True.

1.5 kilobyte, megabyte, gigabyte, terabyte, petabyte.

Exercises

1.6 Fill in the blanks in each of the following statements:

a) The programs that run on a computer are referred to as _____.

b) Systems such as smartphones, appliances, game controllers, cable set-top boxes and automobiles that contain small computers are called _____.

c) Just as characters are composed of bits, _____ are composed of characters or bytes.

d) Information on secondary storage devices is _____; it's preserved even when the computer's power is turned off.

e) Translator programs called _____ convert high-level language code into machine language code.

    f) In object-oriented programming languages, we create a program unit called a(n) _____ _____ to house the set of methods that perform its tasks.

    g) Use a building-block approach to creating your programs. Avoid reinventing the wheel—use existing pieces wherever possible. Such software _____ is a key benefit of object-oriented programming.

1.7   Fill in the blanks in each of the following statements:

    a) Although many different OOAD processes exist, a single graphical language for communicating the results of *any* OOAD process has come into wide use. This language, known as the _____, is now the most widely used graphical scheme for modeling object-oriented systems.

    b) Tim Berners-Lee developed the _____ for sharing information via hyperlinked text documents on the web.

    c) The CLR is a(n) _____ machine. It is software that manages the execution of programs and hides from them the underlying operating system and hardware.

    d) Microsoft's Windows _____ is a cloud computing platform that allows you to develop, manage and distribute your apps in the cloud.

    e) By using existing controls—which are objects—you can create powerful apps much faster than if you had to write all the code yourself. This is a key benefit of software _____.

1.8   State whether each of the following is *true* or *false*. If *false*, explain why.

    a) The smallest data item in a computer can assume the value 1 or the value 2. Such a data item is called a bit (short for "binary digit"—a digit that can assume either of *two* values).

    b) The Unicode character set is a popular subset of ASCII that represents uppercase and lowercase letters, digits and some common special characters.

    c) Each of the following is a form of computer output: data displayed on screens, printed on paper, played as audio or video on PCs and media players, used to control other devices, such as robots, 3D printers and "intelligent" appliances.

    d) Reuse helps you build more reliable and effective systems, because existing classes and components often have gone through extensive testing, debugging and performance tuning.

    e) One of the W3C's primary goals is to make the web universally accessible to everyone regardless of disabilities, language or culture.

    f) The .NET Framework Class Library has millions of valuable prebuilt classes that have been tested and tuned to maximize performance.

    g) .NET programs can run on any platform.

    h) Windows 8, released in 2012, is designed to provide a similar platform (the underlying system on which apps run) and user experience across all of your devices including personal computers, smartphones, tablets and Xbox Live.

    i) Most mobile apps are sold for a small fee.

1.9   What is meant by the data hierarchy of data items processed by a computer?

1.10   Explain the various logical units of a computer.

1.11   In programming, what is the need for intermediate translation? Name the various translation programs.

1.12   Categorize each of the following items as either hardware or software:

    a) Secondary Memory unit

    b) Assembler

    c) Interpreter

    d) Server

    e) TCP/IP

1.13 Translator programs such as assemblers and compilers convert programs from one language to another. Determine which of the following statements are *true* and which are *false*:

    a) Compilers convert high-level language code into machine language code.

    b) Assembly Language code is comprehensible to computers.

    c) The process of compiling a large high-level language program into machine language can take a considerable amount of computer time.

1.14 Expand each of the following acronyms:

    a) TCP

    b) HTTP

    c) CPU

    d) OOAD

    e) GUI

1.15 What is an object? Explain the attributes and behaviors of an object, taking an automobile (car) as an example.

1.16 What is an OOAD? What is an OOP?

1.17 What is a unified modeling language (UML)? How are UML and OOAD processes related?

1.18 What is a protocol? Name a protocol used for communicating over the ARPAnet. What are the advantages of this protocol?

1.19 What is the difference between HTML and HTTP?

1.20 What is the .NET Framework Class Library? List its capabilities.

1.21 "Visual Basic is an event-driven and visual programming language". Justify.

1.22 What is CLR? What are the different services provided by the CLR to manage code?

1.23 Write a short note on the evolution of the Windows operating system.

1.24 What is cloud computing? What are its advantages? How is it related to Windows Azure?

Making a Difference Exercises

1.25 *(Test Drive: Carbon Footprint Calculator)* Some scientists believe that carbon emissions, especially from the burning of fossil fuels, contribute significantly to global warming and that this can be combatted if individuals take steps to limit their use of carbon-based fuels. Organizations and individuals are increasingly concerned about their "carbon footprints." Websites such as TerraPass

    www.terrapass.com/carbon-footprint-calculator/

and Carbon Footprint

    www.carbonfootprint.com/calculator.aspx

provide carbon footprint calculators. Test drive these calculators to determine your carbon footprint. Exercises in later chapters will ask you to program your own carbon footprint calculator. To prepare for this, use the web to research the formulas for calculating carbon footprints.

1.26 *(Test Drive: Body Mass Index Calculator)* Obesity can cause significant increases in illnesses such as diabetes and heart disease. To determine whether a person is overweight or obese, you can use a measure called the body mass index (BMI). The United States Department of Health and Human Services provides a BMI calculator at www.nhlbisupport.com/bmi/. Use it to calculate your own BMI. A forthcoming exercise will ask you to program your own BMI calculator. To prepare for this, use the web to research the formulas for calculating BMI.

1.27 *(Attributes of Hybrid Vehicles)* In this chapter you learned some basics of classes. Now you'll "flesh out" aspects of a class called "Hybrid Vehicle." Hybrid vehicles are becoming increasingly popular, because they often get much better mileage than purely gasoline-powered vehicles. Browse the web and study the features of four or five of today's popular hybrid cars, then list as many of their hybrid-related attributes as you can. Some common attributes include city-miles-per-gallon and highway-miles-per-gallon. Also list the attributes of the batteries (type, weight, etc.).

1.28 *(Moore's Law Predictor)* A computer consists of various devices referred to as hardware, such as the keyboard, screen, mouse, hard disks, memory, DVD drives and processing units. Every year or two, the capacities of computer hardware have approximately doubled inexpensively. This remarkable trend is often called Moore's Law, named for the person who identified it, Gordon Moore, co-founder of Intel. Moore's Law and related observations apply especially to the amount of memory, the amount of secondary storage, and the processor speeds. Develop an application to predict the above three parameters based on Moore's Law for the next 10 years. Compare the predicted results with the real situation assuming you would have run this application 10 years ago.

2

Dive Into® Visual Studio Express 2012 for Windows Desktop

Seeing is believing.
—Proverb

Form ever follows function.
—Louis Henri Sullivan

Intelligence ... is the faculty of making artificial objects, especially tools to make tools.
—Henri-Louis Bergson

Objectives

In this chapter you'll learn:

- The basics of the Visual Studio Express 2012 for Windows Desktop Integrated Development Environment (IDE) for writing, running and debugging your apps.

- Visual Studio's help features.

- Key commands contained in the IDE's menus and toolbars.

- The purpose of the various kinds of windows in the Visual Studio Express 2012 for Windows Desktop IDE.

- What visual app development is and how it simplifies and speeds app development.

- Use visual app development to create, compile and execute a simple Visual Basic app that displays text and an image.

2.1 Introduction

Visual Studio 2012 is Microsoft's Integrated Development Environment (IDE) for creating, running and debugging apps (also called applications) written in various .NET programming languages. This chapter provides an overview of the Visual Studio 2012 IDE and shows how to create a simple Visual Basic app by dragging and dropping predefined building blocks into place—a technique known as **visual app development**.

2.2 Overview of the Visual Studio 2012 IDE

There are several versions of Visual Studio available. This book's examples are based on the **Visual Studio Express 2012 for Windows Desktop**. See the Before You Begin section that follows the Preface for information on installing the software. Our screen captures and discussions focus on Visual Studio Express 2012 for Windows Desktop. The examples will work on full versions of Visual Studio as well—though some options, menus and instructions might differ. From this point forward, we'll refer to the Visual Studio Express 2012 for Windows Desktop IDE simply as "Visual Studio" or "the IDE." We assume that you have some familiarity with Windows.

Introduction to Microsoft Visual Basic Express 2012 for Windows Desktop
We use the > character to indicate the selection of a *menu item* from a *menu*. For example, we use the notation **FILE > Open File...** to indicate that you should select the **Open File...** menu item from the **File** menu.

To start Visual Studio Express 2012 for Windows Desktop, select **Start > All Programs > Microsoft Visual Studio 2012 Express > VS Express for Desktop** (on Windows 8, click the **VS for Desktop** tile on the **Start** screen). Once the Express Edition begins execution, the **Start Page** displays (Fig. 2.1) Depending on your version of Visual Studio, your **Start Page** may look different. The **Start Page** contains a list of links to Visual Studio resources and web-based resources. At any time, you can return to the **Start Page** by selecting **VIEW > Start Page**.

Links on the Start Page
The **Start Page** links are organized into two columns. The left column's **Start** section contains options that enable you to start building new apps or to continue working on existing ones. The **Recent** section contains links to projects you've recently created or modified. You can also create new projects or open existing ones by clicking the links in the **Start** section.

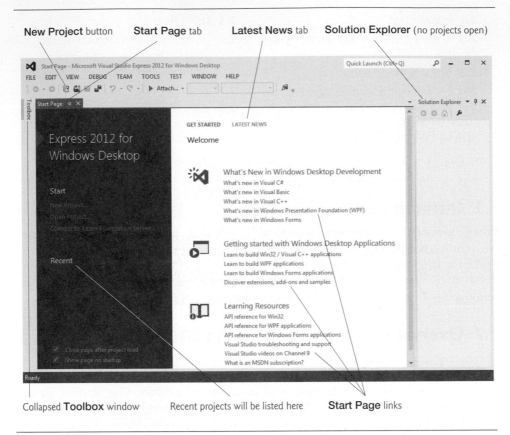

New Project button Start Page tab Latest News tab Solution Explorer (no projects open)

Collapsed **Toolbox** window Recent projects will be listed here **Start Page** links

Fig. 2.1 | **Start Page** in Visual Basic Express 2012 for Windows Desktop.

The right column contains two tabs—**GET STARTED** (selected by default) and **LATEST NEWS**. The links in the **GET STARTED** tab provide information about the programming languages supported by Visual Studio and various learning resources. An Internet connection is required for the IDE to access most of this information.

The **LATEST NEWS** tab includes an **Enable RSS Feed** button. Once you click this button, the IDE will display links to the latest Visual Studio developments (such as updates and bug fixes) and to information on advanced app-development topics. To access more extensive information on Visual Studio, you can browse the MSDN (**Microsoft Developer Network**) library at

```
msdn.microsoft.com/library
```

The MSDN site contains articles, downloads and tutorials on technologies of interest to Visual Studio developers. You can also browse the web from the IDE by selecting **VIEW > Other Windows > Web Browser**. To request a web page, type its URL into the location bar (Fig. 2.2) and press the *Enter* key—your computer, of course, must be connected to the Internet. The web page that you wish to view appears as another tab in the IDE (Fig. 2.2).

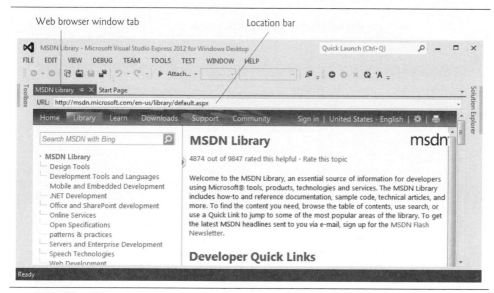

Fig. 2.2 | **MSDN Library** web page in Visual Studio.

Creating a New Project

To begin app development in Visual Basic, you must create a new project or open an existing one. You select **FILE > New Project...** to create a new project or **FILE > Open Project...** to open an existing one. From the **Start Page**'s **Start** section, you can also click the links **New Project...** or **Open Project...**. A **project** is a group of related files, such as the Visual Basic code and any images that might make up an app. Visual Studio organizes apps into projects and **solutions**, which contain one or more projects. Multiple-project solutions are used to create large-scale apps. Most apps we create in this book consist of a solution containing a single project.

New Project Dialog and Project Templates

When you select **FILE > New Project...** or click the **New Project...** link on the **Start Page**, the **New Project dialog** (Fig. 2.3) displays. **Dialogs** are windows that facilitate user–computer communication.

Visual Studio provides several **templates** (Fig. 2.3)—the *project types* users can create in Visual Basic and other languages. The templates include Windows Forms apps, WPF apps and others—full versions of Visual Studio provide many additional templates. In this chapter, you'll build a **Windows Forms Application**. A **Windows Forms app** is an app that executes within a Windows operating system (such as Windows 7 or Windows 8) and typically has a **graphical user interface** (**GUI**)—users interact with this *visual* part of the app. Windows apps include Microsoft software products like Microsoft Word, Internet Explorer and Visual Studio, software products created by other vendors, and customized software that you and other app developers create. You'll create many Windows apps in this text.

By default, Visual Studio assigns the name **WindowsApplication1** to a new **Windows Forms Application** project and solution (Fig. 2.3). Select **Windows Forms Application**, then click **OK** to display the IDE in **Design** view (Fig. 2.4), which contains the features that enable you to create an app's GUI.

Visual Basic **Windows Forms Application** (selected)

Default project name (provided by Visual Studio)

Description of selected project (provided by Visual Studio)

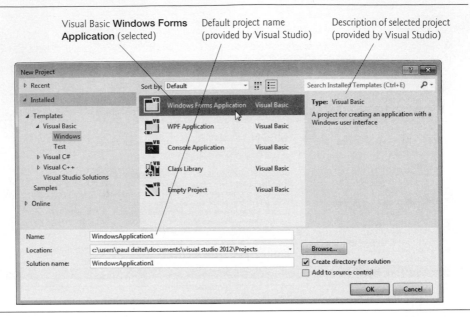

Fig. 2.3 | New Project dialog.

Menu in the menu bar

Active tab (highlighted in blue)

Solution Explorer window

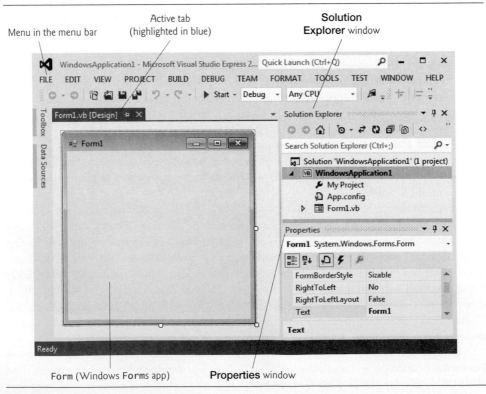

Form (Windows Forms app)

Properties window

Fig. 2.4 | **Design** view of the IDE.

Forms and Controls

The rectangle in the **Design** area titled **Form1** (called a **Form**) represents the main window of the Windows Forms app that you're creating. Visual Basic apps can have multiple Forms (windows)—however, most apps you'll create in this text will use only one Form. You'll learn how to customize the Form by adding GUI controls—in this example, you'll add a Label and a PictureBox (as you'll see in Fig. 2.20). A **Label** typically contains descriptive text (for example, "Welcome to Visual Basic!"), and a **PictureBox** displays an image. Visual Basic Express has many preexisting controls and other components you can use to build and customize your apps. Many of these controls are discussed and used throughout the book. Other controls are available from third parties.

In this chapter, you'll work with preexisting controls from the .NET Framework Class Library. As you place controls on the Form, you'll be able to modify their properties (discussed in Section 2.4). For example, Fig. 2.5 shows where the Form's title can be modified and Fig. 2.6 shows a dialog in which a control's font properties can be modified.

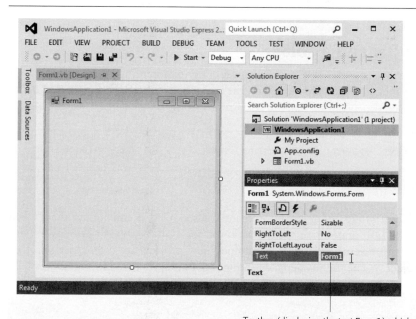

Textbox (displaying the text **Form1**) which can be modified

Fig. 2.5 | Textbox control for modifying a property in the Visual Studio IDE.

Collectively, the Form and controls make up the app's GUI. Users enter data into the app by typing at the keyboard, by clicking the mouse buttons and in a variety of other ways. Apps use the GUI to display instructions and other information for users to view. For example, the **New Project** dialog in Fig. 2.3 presents a GUI where the user clicks the mouse button to select a template type, then inputs a project name from the keyboard (the figure is still showing the default project name **WindowsApplication1** supplied by Visual Studio).

Each open document's name is listed on a tab. To view a document when multiple documents are open, click its tab. The active tab (the tab of the currently displayed document) is highlighted in blue (for example, **Form1.vb [Design]** in Fig. 2.4).

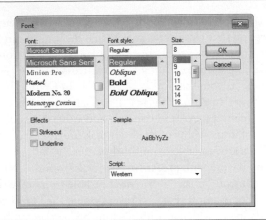

Fig. 2.6 | Dialog for modifying a control's font properties.

2.3 Menu Bar and Toolbar

Commands for managing the IDE and for developing, maintaining and executing apps are contained in menus, which are located on the menu bar of the IDE (Fig. 2.7). The set of menus displayed depends on what you're currently doing in the IDE.

| FILE | EDIT | VIEW | PROJECT | BUILD | DEBUG | TEAM | TOOLS | TEST | WINDOW | HELP |

Fig. 2.7 | Visual Studio menu bar.

Menus contain groups of related commands (also called menu items) that, when selected, cause the IDE to perform specific actions—for example, open a window, save a file, print a file and execute an app. For example, new projects are created by selecting **FILE > New Project...**. The menus depicted in Fig. 2.7 are summarized in Fig. 2.8.

Menu	Description
FILE	Contains commands for opening, closing, adding and saving projects, as well as printing project data and exiting Visual Studio.
EDIT	Contains commands for editing apps, such as cut, copy, paste, undo, redo, delete, find and select.
VIEW	Contains commands for displaying IDE windows (for example, **Solution Explorer**, **Toolbox**, **Properties** window) and for adding toolbars to the IDE.
PROJECT	Contains commands for managing projects and their files.
BUILD	Contains options for turning your app into an executable program.

Fig. 2.8 | Summary of Visual Studio menus that are displayed when a Form is in **Design** view. (Part 1 of 2.)

Menu	Description
DEBUG	Contains commands for compiling, debugging (that is, identifying and correcting problems in apps) and running apps.
TEAM	Allows you to connect to a Team Foundation Server—used by development teams that typically have multiple people working on the same app.
FORMAT	Contains commands for arranging and modifying a Form's controls. The **Format** menu appears only when a GUI component is selected in **Design** view.
TOOLS	Contains commands for accessing additional IDE tools and options for customizing the IDE.
TEST	Contains options for performing various types of automated testing on your app.
WINDOW	Contains commands for hiding, opening, closing and displaying IDE windows.
HELP	Contains commands for accessing the IDE's help features.

Fig. 2.8 | Summary of Visual Studio menus that are displayed when a Form is in **Design** view. (Part 2 of 2.)

You can access many common menu commands from the toolbar (Fig. 2.9), which contains icons that graphically represent commands. By default, the standard toolbar is displayed when you run Visual Studio for the first time—it contains icons for the most commonly used commands, such as opening a file, adding an item to a project, saving files and running apps (Fig. 2.9). The icons that appear on the standard toolbar may vary, depending on the version of Visual Studio you're using. Some commands are initially disabled (grayed out or unavailable to use). These commands are enabled by Visual Studio only when they're necessary. For example, Visual Studio enables the command for *saving* a file once you begin *editing* a file.

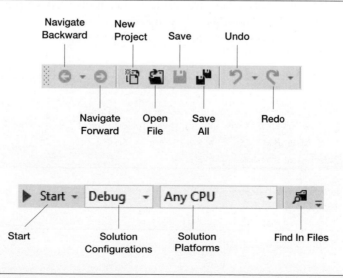

Fig. 2.9 | Standard Visual Studio toolbar.

You can customize which toolbars are displayed by selecting **VIEW > Toolbars** then selecting a toolbar from the list in Fig. 2.10. Each toolbar you select is displayed with the other toolbars at the top of the Visual Studio window. You move a toolbar by dragging its handle (⁞) at the left side of the toolbar. To execute a command via the toolbar, click its icon.

Fig. 2.10 | List of toolbars that can be added to the top of the IDE.

It can be difficult to remember what each toolbar icon represents. *Hovering* the mouse pointer over an icon highlights it and, after a brief pause, displays a description of the icon called a tool tip (Fig. 2.11). **Tool tips** help you become familiar with the IDE's features and serve as useful reminders for each toolbar icon's functionality.

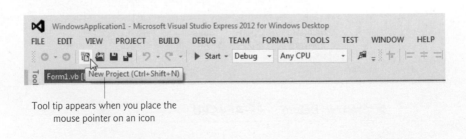

Tool tip appears when you place the
mouse pointer on an icon

Fig. 2.11 | Tool tip demonstration.

2.4 Navigating the Visual Studio IDE

The IDE provides windows for accessing project files and customizing controls. This section introduces several windows that you'll use frequently when developing Visual Basic apps. Each of the IDE's windows can be accessed by selecting its name in the **View** menu.

Auto-Hide

Visual Studio provides a space-saving feature called **auto-hide**. When auto-hide is enabled for a window, a tab containing the window's name appears along either the left, right or bottom edge of the IDE window (Fig. 2.12). Clicking the name of an auto-hidden window displays that window (Fig. 2.13). Clicking the name again hides the window. To "pin down" a window (that is, to disable auto-hide and keep the window open), click the pin icon. When auto-hide is enabled, the pin icon is horizontal (, Fig. 2.13)—when a window is "pinned down," the pin icon is vertical (, Fig. 2.14).

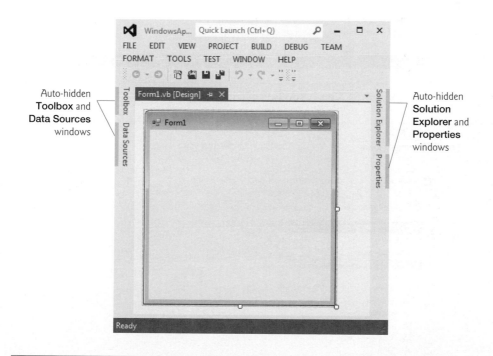

Fig. 2.12 | Auto-hide feature demonstration.

The next few sections cover three of Visual Studio's main windows—the **Solution Explorer**, the **Properties** window and the **Toolbox**. These windows display project information and include tools that help you build your apps.

Expanded **Toolbox** window   Horizontal orientation for pin icon when auto-hide is enabled

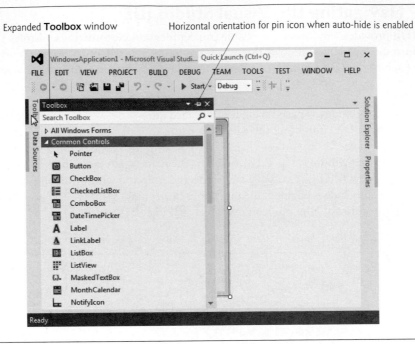

Fig. 2.13 | Displaying the hidden **Toolbox** window when auto-hide is enabled.

Toolbox "pinned down"   Vertical orientation for pin icon when window is "pinned down"

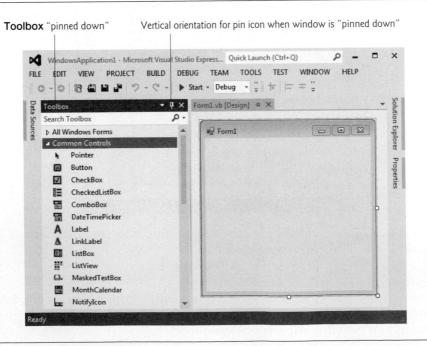

Fig. 2.14 | Disabling auto-hide—"pinning down" a window.

2.4.1 Solution Explorer

The **Solution Explorer** window (Fig. 2.15) provides access to all of a solution's files. If it's not shown in the IDE, select **VIEW > Solution Explorer**. When you open a new or existing solution, the **Solution Explorer** displays the solution's contents.

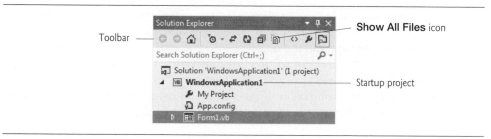

Fig. 2.15 | Solution Explorer window with an open project.

The solution's **startup project** is the one that runs when you select **DEBUG > Start Debugging** (or press the *F5* key). For a single-project solution like the examples in this book, the startup project is the only project (in this case, **WindowsApplication1**). The startup project's name appears in bold text in the **Solution Explorer** window. When you create an app for the first time, the **Solution Explorer** window lists only the project's My Project, App.config and Form1.vb files (Fig. 2.15). The Visual Basic file that corresponds to the Form shown in Fig. 2.4 is named Form1.vb (selected in Fig. 2.15). Visual Basic files use the .vb file-name extension, which is short for "Visual Basic."

By default, the IDE displays only files that you may need to edit—other files that the IDE generates are hidden. The **Solution Explorer** window includes a toolbar that contains several icons. Clicking the **Show All Files** icon (Fig. 2.15) displays all the solution's files, including those generated by the IDE (Fig. 2.16). Clicking the arrows to the left of a file

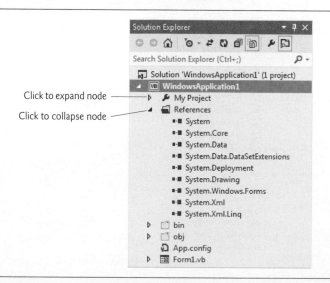

Fig. 2.16 | Solution Explorer with the **References** node expanded.

or folder *expands* or *collapses* the project tree's nodes. Try clicking the arrow to the left of **References** to display items grouped under that heading (Fig. 2.16). Click the arrow again to collapse the tree. Other Visual Studio windows also use this convention.

2.4.2 Toolbox

To display the **Toolbox** window, select **VIEW > Toolbox**. The **Toolbox** contains the controls used to customize Forms (Fig. 2.17). With visual app development, you can "drag and drop" controls onto the Form and the IDE will write the code that creates the controls for you. This is faster and simpler than writing this code yourself. Just as you do not need to know how to build an engine to drive a car, you do not need to know how to build controls to use them. *Reusing* preexisting controls saves time and money when you develop apps. You'll use the **Toolbox** when you create your first app later in the chapter.

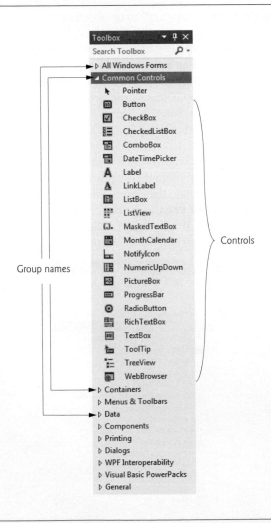

Fig. 2.17 | **Toolbox** window displaying controls for the **Common Controls** group.

The **Toolbox** groups the prebuilt controls into categories—**All Windows Forms, Common Controls, Containers, Menus & Toolbars, Data, Components, Printing, Dialogs, WPF Interoperability, Visual Basic PowerPacks** and **General** are listed in Fig. 2.17. Again, note the use of arrows, which can expand or collapse a group of controls. We discuss many of the **Toolbox**'s controls and their functionality throughout the book.

2.4.3 Properties Window

To display the **Properties** window, select **VIEW > Properties Window**. The **Properties** window displays the properties for the currently selected Form (Fig. 2.18), control or file in **Design** view. Properties specify information about the Form or control, such as its size, color and position. Each Form or control has its own set of properties—a property's description is displayed at the bottom of the **Properties** window whenever that property is selected.

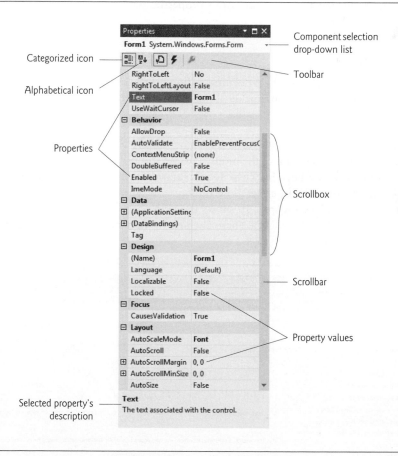

Fig. 2.18 | Properties window.

Figure 2.18 shows Form1's **Properties** window. The left column lists the Form's properties—the right column displays the current value of each property. You can sort the properties either *alphabetically* (by clicking the **Alphabetical** icon) or *categorically* (by clicking the

Categorized icon). Depending on the size of the **Properties** window, some of the properties may be hidden from view on the screen. You can scroll through the list of properties by **dragging** the **scrollbox** up or down inside the **scrollbar**, or by clicking the arrows at the top and bottom of the scrollbar. We show how to set individual properties later in this chapter.

The **Properties** window is crucial to visual app development—it allows you to modify a control's properties visually, without writing code. You can see which properties are available for modification and, in many cases, can learn the range of acceptable values for a given property. The **Properties** window displays a brief description of the selected property, helping you understand its purpose. A property can be set quickly using this window, and no code needs to be written.

At the top of the **Properties** window is the **component selection drop-down list**, which allows you to select the Form or control whose properties you wish to display in the **Properties** window (Fig. 2.18). Using the component selection drop-down list is an alternative way to display a Form's or control's properties without clicking the actual Form or control in the GUI.

2.5 Using Help

Microsoft provides extensive help documentation via the **Help** menu. Using **Help** is an excellent way to get information quickly about Visual Studio, Visual Basic and more.

Context-Sensitive Help
Visual Studio provides **context-sensitive help** pertaining to the "current content" (that is, the items around the location of the mouse cursor). To use context-sensitive help, click an item, then press the *F1* key. The help documentation is displayed in a web browser window. To return to the IDE, either close the browser window or select the IDE's icon in your Windows task bar. Figure 2.19 shows the help page for a Form's **Text** property. You can view this help by selecting the Form, clicking its **Text** property in the **Properties** window and pressing the *F1* key.

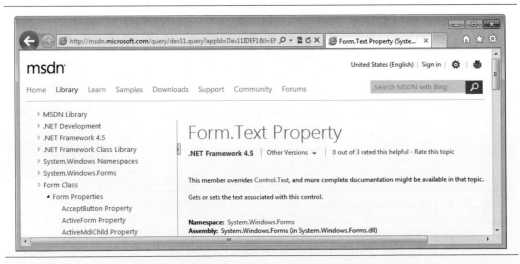

Fig. 2.19 | Using context-sensitive help.

2.6 Using Visual App Development to Create a Simple App that Displays Text and an Image

Next, we create an app that displays the text "Welcome to Visual Basic!" and an image of the Deitel & Associates bug mascot. The app consists of a single Form that uses a Label and a PictureBox. Figure 2.20 shows the final app executing. The app and the bug image are available with this chapter's examples. See the Before You Begin section following the Preface for download instructions. We assume the examples are located at C:\examples on your computer.

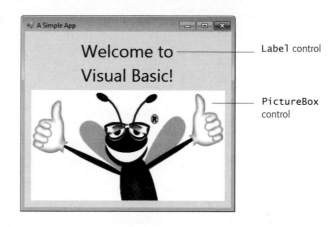

Fig. 2.20 | Simple app executing.

You won't write a single line of code. Instead, you'll use visual app development techniques. Visual Studio processes your actions (such as mouse clicking, dragging and dropping) to generate app code. Chapter 3 begins our discussion of writing app code. Throughout the book, you produce increasingly substantial and powerful apps that usually include a combination of code written by you and code generated by Visual Studio. The generated code can be difficult for novices to understand—but you'll rarely need to look at it.

Visual app development is useful for building GUI-intensive apps that require a significant amount of user interaction. To create, save, run and terminate this first app, perform the following steps:

1. *Closing the open project.* If the project you were working with earlier in this chapter is still open, close it by selecting **FILE > Close Solution**.

2. *Creating the new project.* To create a new Windows Forms app, select **FILE > New Project...** to display the **New Project** dialog (Fig. 2.21). Select **Windows Forms Application**. Name the project **ASimpleApp**, specify the **Location** where you want to save it (we used the default location) and click **OK**. As you saw earlier in this chapter, when you first create a new Windows Forms app, the IDE opens in **Design** view (that is, the app is being designed and is not executing).

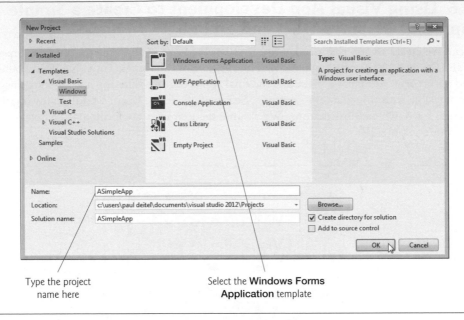

Type the project name here

Select the **Windows Forms Application** template

Fig. 2.21 | New Project dialog.

3. *Setting the text in the Form's title bar.* The text in the Form's title bar is determined by the Form's **Text** property (Fig. 2.22). If the **Properties** window is not open, select **VIEW > Properties Window**. Click anywhere in the Form to display the Form's properties in the **Properties** window. In the textbox to the right of the Text property, type "A Simple App", as in Fig. 2.21. Press the *Enter* key—the Form's title bar is updated immediately (Fig. 2.23).

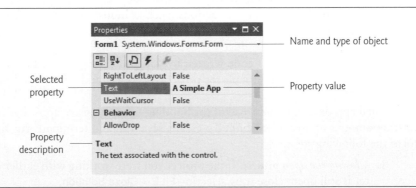

Name and type of object

Selected property

Property value

Property description

Fig. 2.22 | Setting the Form's Text property in the **Properties** window.

4. *Resizing the Form.* Click and drag one of the Form's enabled **sizing handles** (the small white squares that appear around the Form, as shown in Fig. 2.23). Using the mouse, select the bottom-right sizing handle and drag it down and to the right to make the Form larger (Fig. 2.24).

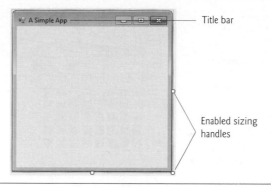

Fig. 2.23 | Form with enabled sizing handles.

Fig. 2.24 | Resized Form.

5. *Changing the Form's background color.* The **BackColor** property specifies a Form's or control's background color. Clicking BackColor in the **Properties** window causes a down-arrow button to appear next to the value of the property (Fig. 2.25). When clicked, the down-arrow button displays other options, which vary depending on the property. In this case, the arrow displays tabs for **Custom, Web** and **System** (the default). Click the **Custom tab** to display the **palette** (a grid of colors). Select the box that represents light blue. Once you select the color, the palette closes and the Form's background color changes to light blue (Fig. 2.26).

6. *Adding a Label control to the Form.* If the **Toolbox** is *not* already open, select **VIEW > Toolbox** to display the set of controls you'll use for creating your apps. For the type of app we're creating in this chapter, the typical controls we use are located in either the **All Windows Forms** group of the **Toolbox** or the **Common Controls** group. If either group name is collapsed, expand it by clicking the arrow to the left of the group name (the **All Windows Forms** and **Common Controls** groups are shown in Fig. 2.17). Next, double click the Label control in the **Toolbox**. This action causes a Label to appear in the upper-left corner of the Form

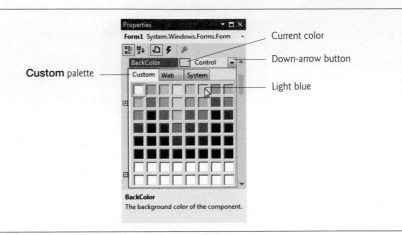

Fig. 2.25 | Changing the Form's BackColor property.

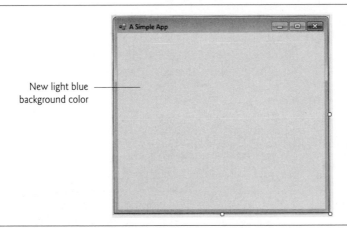

Fig. 2.26 | Form with new BackColor property applied.

(Fig. 2.27). [*Note:* If the Form is behind the **Toolbox**, you may need to hide the **Toolbox** to see the Label.] Although double clicking any **Toolbox** control places the control on the Form, you also can "drag" controls from the **Toolbox** to the Form—you may prefer dragging the control because you can position it wherever you want. The Label displays the text **Label1** by default. When you add a Label to the Form, the IDE sets the Label's BackColor property to the Form's BackColor. You can change the Label's background color by changing its BackColor property.

7. *Customizing the Label's appearance.* Select the Label by clicking it. Its properties now appear in the **Properties** window. The Label's Text property determines the text (if any) that the Label displays. The Form and Label each have their own Text property—Forms and controls can have the *same* property names (such as BackColor, Text, etc.) without conflict. Set the Label's Text property to Welcome to Visual Basic!. The Label resizes to fit all the typed text on one line. By default, the

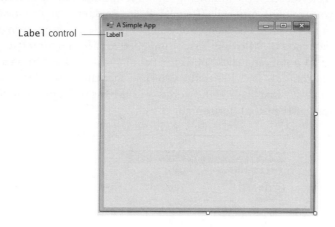

Label control ── Label1

Fig. 2.27 | Adding a Label to the Form.

AutoSize property of the Label is set to True, which allows the Label to update its size to fit all of the text if necessary. Set the AutoSize property to False so that you can resize the Label on your own. Resize the Label (using the sizing handles) so that the text fits. Move the Label to the top center of the Form by dragging it or by using the keyboard's left and right arrow keys to adjust its position (Fig. 2.28). Alternatively, when the Label is selected, you can center the Label control horizontally by selecting **FORMAT > Center In Form > Horizontally**.

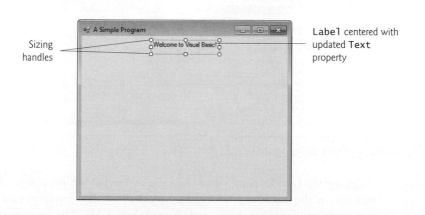

Sizing handles

Label centered with updated **Text** property

Fig. 2.28 | GUI after the Form and Label have been customized.

8. *Setting the Label's font size.* To change the font type and appearance of the Label's text, select the value of the **Font property**, which causes an **ellipsis button** to appear next to the value (Fig. 2.29). When the ellipsis button is clicked, a dialog that provides additional values—in this case, the **Font dialog** (Fig. 2.30)—

is displayed. You can select the font name (the font options may be different, depending on your system), font style (**Regular**, **Italic**, **Bold**, etc.) and font size (**16**, **18**, **20**, etc.) in this dialog. The **Sample** text shows the selected font settings. Under **Font**, select **Segoe UI**, Microsoft's recommended font for user interfaces. Under **Size**, select **24** points and click **OK**. If the `Label`'s text does not fit on a single line, it *wraps* to the next line. Resize the `Label` so that the words "`Welcome to`" appear on the `Label`'s first line and the words "`Visual Basic!`" appear on the second line. Re-center the `Label` horizontally.

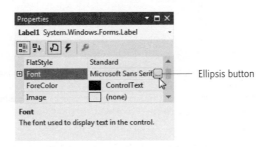

Fig. 2.29 | **Properties** window displaying the `Label`'s **Font** property.

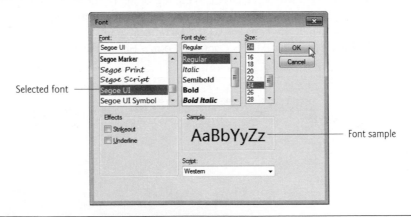

Fig. 2.30 | **Font** dialog for selecting fonts, styles and sizes.

9. *Aligning the `Label`'s text.* Select the `Label`'s **TextAlign** property, which determines how the text is aligned within the `Label`. A three-by-three grid of buttons representing alignment choices is displayed (Fig. 2.31). The position of each button corresponds to where the text appears in the `Label`. For this app, set the `TextAlign` property to `MiddleCenter` in the three-by-three grid—this selection centers the text horizontally and vertically within the `Label`. The other `TextAlign` values, such as `TopLeft`, `TopRight`, and `BottomCenter`, can be used to position the text anywhere within a `Label`. Certain alignment values may require that you resize the `Label` to fit the text better.

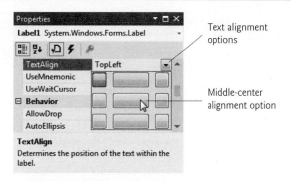

Fig. 2.31 | Centering the Label's text.

10. *Adding a PictureBox to the Form.* The PictureBox control displays images. The process involved in this step is similar to that of *Step 6*, in which we added a Label to the Form. Locate the PictureBox in the **Toolbox** (Fig. 2.17) and double click it to add it to the Form. When the PictureBox appears, move it underneath the Label, either by dragging it or by using the arrow keys (Fig. 2.32).

11. *Inserting an image.* Click the PictureBox to display its properties in the **Properties** window (Fig. 2.33). Locate and select the **Image property**, which displays a preview of the selected image or **(none)** if no image is selected. Click the ellipsis button to display the **Select Resource** dialog (Fig. 2.34), which is used to import files, such as images, for use in an app. Click the **Import...** button to browse for an image to insert, select the image file and click **OK**. We used bug.png from this chapter's examples folder. The image is previewed in the **Select Resource** dialog (Fig. 2.35). Click **OK** to use the image. Supported image formats include PNG (Portable Network Graphics), GIF (Graphic Interchange Format), JPEG (Joint Photographic Experts Group) and BMP (Windows bitmap). To scale the image to the PictureBox's size, change the **SizeMode** property to **StretchImage** (Fig. 2.36). Resize the PictureBox, making it larger (Fig. 2.37).

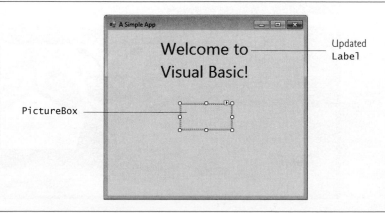

Fig. 2.32 | Inserting and aligning a PictureBox.

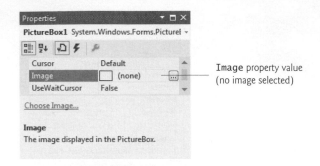

Fig. 2.33 | Image property of the PictureBox.

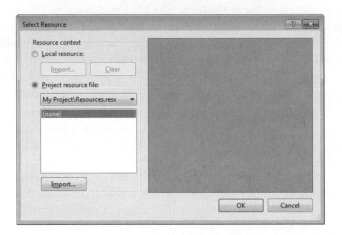

Fig. 2.34 | **Select Resource** dialog to select an image for the PictureBox.

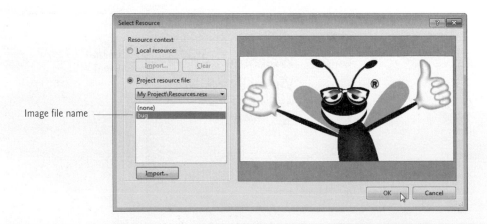

Fig. 2.35 | **Select Resource** dialog displaying a preview of selected image.

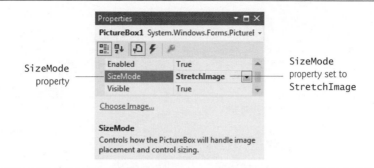

Fig. 2.36 | Scaling an image to the size of the `PictureBox`.

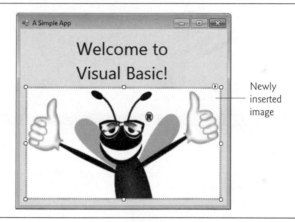

Fig. 2.37 | `PictureBox` displaying an image.

12. *Saving the project.* Select **FILE > Save All** to save the entire solution. The solution file (which has the filename extension .sln) contains the name and location of its project, and the project file (which has the filename extension .vbproj) contains the names and locations of all the files in the project. If you want to reopen your project at a later time, simply open its .sln file.

13. *Running the project.* Recall that up to this point we have been working in the IDE design mode (that is, the app being created is not executing). In **run mode**, the app is executing, and you can interact with only a few IDE features—features that are not available are disabled (grayed out). The text **Form1.vb [Design]** in the project tab (Fig. 2.38) means that we're designing the Form *visually* rather than *programmatically*. If we had been writing code, the tab would have contained only the text **Form1.vb**. If there is an asterisk (*) at the end of the text in the tab, the file has been changed and should be saved. Select **DEBUG > Start Debugging** to execute the app (or you can press the *F5* key). Figure 2.39 shows the IDE in run mode (indicated by the title-bar text **ASimpleApp (Running)**. Many toolbar icons and menus are disabled, since they cannot be used while the app is running. The running app appears in a separate window outside the IDE as shown in the lower-right portion of Fig. 2.39.

Debug menu

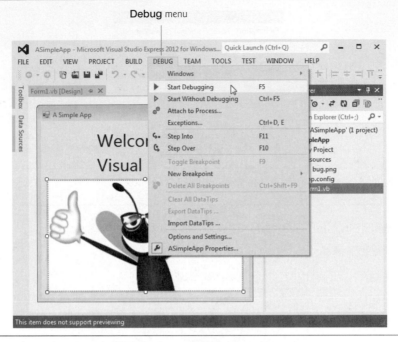

Fig. 2.38 | Debugging a solution.

IDE displays text **Running**, which signifies that the app is executing

Close box

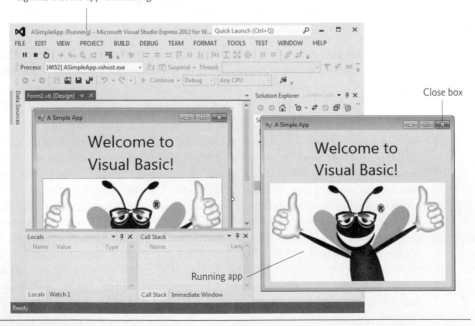

Running app

Fig. 2.39 | IDE in run mode, with the running app in the foreground.

14. *Terminating execution.* Click the running app's close box (the ▣ in the top-right corner of the running app's window). This action stops the app's execution and returns the IDE to design mode. You can also select **DEBUG > Stop Debugging** to terminate the app.

2.7 Wrap-Up

In this chapter, we introduced key features of the Visual Studio IDE. You visually designed a working Visual Basic app without writing a single line of code. Visual Basic app development is a mixture of the two styles: Visual app development allows you to develop GUIs easily and avoid tedious GUI programming. "Conventional" programming (which we introduce in Chapter 3) allows you to specify the behavior of your apps.

You created a Visual Basic Windows Forms app with one Form. You worked with the IDE's **Solution Explorer**, **Toolbox** and **Properties** windows, which are essential to developing Visual Basic apps. We also demonstrated context-sensitive help, which displays help topics related to selected controls or text.

You used visual app development to design an app's GUI quickly and easily, by dragging and dropping controls (a Label and a PictureBox) onto a Form or by double clicking controls in the **Toolbox**.

You used the **Properties** window to set a Form's Text and BackColor properties. You learned that Label controls display text and that PictureBoxes display images. You displayed text in a Label and added an image to a PictureBox. You also worked with the Label's AutoSize, TextAlign and Font properties and the PictureBox's Image and Size-Mode properties.

In the next chapter, we discuss "nonvisual," or "conventional," programming—you'll create your first apps with Visual Basic code that you write, instead of having Visual Studio write the code. You'll also learn memory concepts, arithmetic, decision making and how to use a dialog to display a message.

2.8 Web Resources

Please take a moment to visit each of these sites briefly.

www.deitel.com/VisualBasic2012/
This site lists many of the key web resources we used as we were preparing to write this book. There's lots of great stuff here to help you become familiar with the world of Visual Basic 2012.

msdn.microsoft.com/vstudio
This site is the home page for Microsoft Visual Studio. The site includes news, documentation, downloads and other resources.

msdn.microsoft.com/en-us/vstudio/hh388573.aspx
This site provides information on the newest release of Visual Basic, including downloads, community information and resources.

social.msdn.microsoft.com/forums/en-US/category/visualbasic/
This site provides access to the Microsoft Visual Basic forums, which you can use to get your Visual Basic language and IDE questions answered.

msdn.microsoft.com/en-us/magazine/default.aspx
This is the Microsoft Developer Network Magazine site. This site provides articles and code on many Visual Basic and .NET app development topics. There is also an archive of past issues.

Summary

Section 2.1 Introduction
- Visual Studio is Microsoft's Integrated Development Environment (IDE) for creating, running and debugging apps written in a variety of .NET programming languages.
- Creating simple apps by dragging and dropping predefined building blocks into place is called visual app development.

Section 2.2 Overview of the Visual Studio 2012 IDE
- The **Start Page** contains links to Visual Studio 2012 IDE resources and web-based resources.
- A project is a group of related files that compose a app.
- Visual Studio organizes apps into projects and solutions—a solutison may contain one or more projects.
- Dialogs are windows that facilitate user–computer communication.
- Visual Studio provides templates for the project types you can create, including Windows Forms apps.
- A Form represents the main window of the Windows Forms app that you're creating.
- Collectively, the Form and controls constitute the app's graphical user interface (GUI), which is the visual part of the app with which the user interacts.

Section 2.3 Menu Bar and Toolbar
- Commands for managing the IDE and for developing, maintaining and executing apps are contained in the menus, which are located on the menu bar, and as buttons on the toolbar below the menu bar.
- Menus contain groups of commands (menu items) that, when selected, cause the IDE to perform actions (for example, open a window, save a file, print a file and execute an app).
- Tool tips help you become familiar with the IDE's features.

Section 2.4 Navigating the Visual Studio IDE
- The **Solution Explorer** window lists all the files in the solution.
- The **Toolbox** contains controls for customizing Forms.
- By using visual app development, you can place predefined controls onto the Form instead of writing the code yourself.
- Clicking an auto-hidden window's name opens that window. Clicking the name again hides it. To "pin down" a window (that is, to disable auto-hide), click its pin icon.
- The **Properties** window displays the properties for a Form, control or file (in **Design** view). Properties are information about a Form or control, such as size, color and position. The **Properties** window allows you to modify Forms and controls visually, without writing code.
- Each control has its own set of properties. The left column of the **Properties** window shows the property names and the right column displays the property values. This window's toolbar contains options for organizing properties alphabetically when the **Alphabetical** icon is selected or categorically (for example, **Appearance**, **Behavior**, **Design**) when the **Categorized** icon is selected.

Section 2.5 Using Help
- Extensive help documentation is available via **Help** menu.
- Context-sensitive help brings up a list of relevant help articles. To use context-sensitive help, select an item and press the *F1* key.

Section 2.6 Using Visual App Development to Create a Simple App that Displays Text and an Image

- Visual Basic app development usually involves a combination of writing a portion of the app code and having Visual Studio generate the remaining code.

- The text that appears at the top of the Form (the title bar) is specified in the Form's Text property.

- To resize the Form, click and drag one of the Form's enabled sizing handles (the small squares around the Form). Enabled sizing handles appear as white boxes.

- The BackColor property specifies the background color of a Form. The Form's background color is the default background color for any controls added to the Form.

- Double clicking any **Toolbox** control icon places a control of that type on the Form. Alternatively, you can drag and drop controls from the **Toolbox** to the Form.

- The Label's Text property determines the text (if any) that the Label displays. The Form and Label each have their own Text property.

- A property's ellipsis button, when clicked, displays a dialog containing additional options.

- In the **Font** dialog, you can select the font for a control.

- The TextAlign property determines how the text is aligned within a Label's boundaries.

- The PictureBox control displays images. The Image property specifies the image to displayed.

- An app that is in design mode is not executing.

- In run mode, the app is executing—you can interact with only a few IDE features.

- When designing an app visually, the name of the Visual Basic file appears in the project tab, followed by [Design].

- Terminate execution by clicking the close box.

Terminology

Self-Review Exercises

2.1 Fill in the blanks in each of the following statements:

a) The technique of _____ allows you to create GUIs without writing any code.

b) A(n) _____ is a group of one or more projects that collectively form a Visual Basic app.

c) A(n) _____ appears when the mouse pointer hovers over an icon.

d) The _____ window allows you to browse solution files.

e) The properties in the **Properties** window can be sorted _____ or _____.

f) A Form's _____ property specifies the text displayed in the Form's title bar.

g) The _____ contains the controls that you can add to a Form.

h) _____ displays relevant help articles, based on the current context.

i) The _____ property specifies how text is aligned within a Label's boundaries.

2.2 State whether each of the following is *true* or *false*. If *false*, explain why.

a) ▆✕▆ toggles auto-hide for a window.

b) The toolbar icons represent various menu commands.

c) The toolbar contains icons that represent controls you can drag onto a Form.

d) Both Forms and Labels have a title bar.

e) Control properties can be modified only by writing code.

f) PictureBoxes typically display images.

g) Visual Basic files use the file extension .bas.

h) A Form's background color is set using the BackColor property.

Answers to Self-Review Exercises

2.1 a) visual app development. b) solution. c) tool tip. d) **Solution Explorer**. e) alphabetically, categorically. f) Text. g) **Toolbox**. h) context-sensitive help. i) TextAlign.

2.2 a) False. The pin icon (▆⊟▆) toggles auto-hide. ▆✕▆ closes a window. b) True. c) False. The **Toolbox** contains icons that represent such controls. d) False. Forms have a title bar but Labels do not (although they do have Label text). e) False. Control properties can be modified using the **Properties** window. f) True. g) False. Visual Basic files use the file extension .vb. i) True.

Exercises

2.3 Fill in the blanks in each of the following statements:

a) Creating simple apps by dragging and dropping predefined building blocks into place is called _____.

b) _____ is a group of related files that compose an app.

c) _____ are windows that facilitate user-computer communication.

d) Collectively, the _____ and _____ constitute the app's graphical user interface (GUI).

e) _____ tips help to become familiar with the IDE's features.

2.4 State whether each of the following is *true* or *false*. If *false*, explain why.

a) The **Solution Explorer** window lists all the files in the solution.

b) The Toolbox contains controls for customizing projects.

c) By using visual app development, you can place predefined controls onto the Form instead of writing the code yourself.

d) Clicking an auto-hidden window's name opens that window. Clicking the name again hides it.

e) The TextAlign property determines how the text is aligned within a form's boundaries.

2.5 Some features that appear throughout Visual Studio perform similar actions in different contexts. Explain and give examples of how the ellipsis buttons, down-arrow buttons and tool tips act in this manner. Why do you think the Visual Studio IDE was designed this way?

2.6 Briefly describe each of the following terms:
   a) Templates
   b) Windows Forms app
   c) Startup project
   d) Label
   e) Active tab
   f) Icons

Note Regarding Exercises 2.7–2.11

In the following exercises, you're asked to create GUIs using controls that we have not yet discussed in this book. These exercises give you practice with visual app development only—the apps do not perform any actions. You place controls from the **Toolbox** on a Form to familiarize yourself with what each control looks like. We have provided step-by-step instructions for you. If you follow these, you should be able to replicate the screen images we provide.

2.7 *(Notepad GUI)* Create the GUI for the notepad as shown in Fig. 2.40.

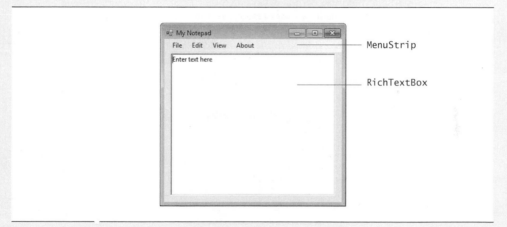

Fig. 2.40 | Notepad GUI.

   a) *Manipulating the Form's properties.* Change the Text property of the Form to My Notepad. Change the Font property to 9pt Segoe UI.
   b) *Adding a MenuStrip control to the Form.* Add a MenuStrip to the Form. After inserting the MenuStrip, add items by clicking the **Type Here** section, typing a menu name (for example, **File**, **Edit**, **View** and **About**) and then pressing *Enter*.
   c) *Adding a RichTextBox to the Form.* Drag this control onto the Form. Use the sizing handles to resize and position the RichTextBox as shown in Fig. 2.40. Change the Text property to Enter text here.

2.8 *(Calendar and Appointments GUI)* Create the GUI for the calendar as shown in Fig. 2.41.
   a) *Manipulating the Form's properties.* Change the Text property of the Form to My Scheduler. Change the Font property to 9pt Segoe UI. Set the Form's Size property to 275, 400.
   b) *Adding Labels to the Form.* Add two Labels to the Form. Both should be of equal size (231, 23; remember to set the AutoSize property to False) and should be centered in

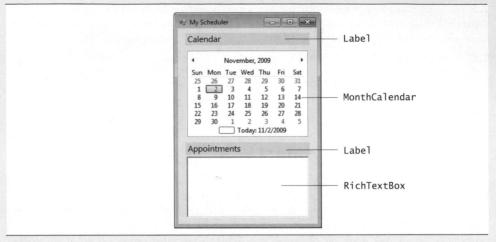

Fig. 2.41 | Calendar and appointments GUI.

the Form horizontally, as shown. Set the Label's Text properties to match Fig. 2.41. Use 12-point font size. Also, set the BackColor property to Yellow.

c) *Adding a MonthCalendar control to the Form.* Add this control to the Form and center it horizontally in the appropriate place between the two Labels.

d) *Adding a RichTextBox control to the Form.* Add a RichTextBox control to the Form and center it below the second Label. Resize the RichTextBox accordingly.

2.9   *(Calculator GUI)* Create the GUI for the calculator as shown in Fig. 2.42.

Fig. 2.42 | Calculator GUI.

a) *Manipulating the Form's properties.* Change the Text property of the Form to Calculator. Change the Font property to 9pt Segoe UI. Change the Size property of the Form to 258, 210.

b) *Adding a TextBox to the Form.* Set the TextBox's Text property in the **Properties** window to 0. Stretch the TextBox and position it as shown in Fig. 2.42. Set the TextAlign property to Right—this right aligns text displayed in the TextBox.

c) *Adding the first Panel to the Form.* Panel controls are used to group other controls. Add a Panel to the Form. Change the Panel's BorderStyle property to Fixed3D to make the inside of the Panel appear recessed. Change the Size property to 90, 120. This Panel will contain the calculator's numeric keys.

d) *Adding the second Panel to the Form.* Change the Panel's BorderStyle property to Fixed3D. Change the Size property to 62, 120. This Panel will contain the calculator's operator keys.

e) *Adding the third (and last)* Panel *to the Form.* Change the Panel's BorderStyle property to Fixed3D. Change the Size property to 54, 62. This Panel contains the calculator's **C** (clear) and **C/A** (clear all) keys.

f) *Adding* Buttons *to the Form.* There are 20 Buttons on the calculator. Add a Button to the Panel by dragging and dropping it on the Panel. Change the Text property of each Button to the calculator key it represents. The value you enter in the Text property will appear on the face of the Button. Finally, resize the Buttons, using their Size properties. Each Button labeled 0-9, *, /, -, = and . should have a size of 23, 23. The **00** Button has size 52, 23. The **OFF** Button has size 54, 23. The **+** Button is sized 23, 81. The **C** (clear) and **C/A** (clear all) Buttons are sized 44, 23.

2.10 *(Alarm Clock GUI)* Create the GUI for the alarm clock as shown in Fig. 2.43.

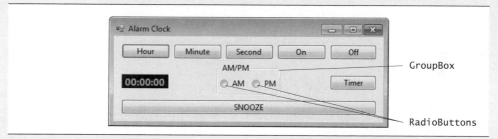

Fig. 2.43 | Alarm clock GUI.

a) *Manipulating the* Form's *properties.* Change the Text property of the Form to Alarm Clock. Change the Font property to 9pt Segoe UI. Change the Size property of the Form to 438, 170.

b) *Adding* Buttons *to the Form.* Add seven Buttons to the Form. Change the Text property of each Button to the appropriate text. Align the Buttons as shown.

c) *Adding a* GroupBox *to the Form.* GroupBoxes are like Panels, except that GroupBoxes display a title. Change the Text property to AM/PM, and set the Size property to 100, 50. Center the GroupBox horizontally on the Form.

d) *Adding* **AM/PM** RadioButtons *to the* GroupBox. Place two RadioButtons in the GroupBox. Change the Text property of one RadioButton to AM and the other to PM. Align the RadioButtons as shown.

e) *Adding the time* Label *to the Form.* Add a Label to the Form and change its Text property to 00:00:00. Change the BorderStyle property to Fixed3D and the BackColor to Black. Use the Font property to make the time bold and 12pt. Change the ForeColor to Silver (located in the **Web** tab) to make the time stand out against the black background. Position the Label as shown.

2.11 *(Radio GUI)* Create the GUI for the radio as shown in Fig. 2.44. [*Note:* The image used in this exercise is located in the examples folder for Chapter 2.]

a) *Manipulating the* Form's *properties.* Change the Font property to 9pt Segoe UI. Change the Form's Text property to Radio and the Size to 427, 194.

b) *Adding the* **Pre-set Stations** GroupBox *and* Buttons. Set the GroupBox's Size to 180, 55 and its Text to Pre-set Stations. Add six Buttons to the GroupBox. Set each one's Size to 23, 23. Change the Buttons' Text properties to 1, 2, 3, 4, 5, 6, respectively.

c) *Adding the* **Speakers** GroupBox *and* CheckBoxes. Set the GroupBox's Size to 120, 55 and its Text to Speakers. Add two CheckBoxes to the GroupBox. Set the Text properties for the CheckBoxes to Rear and Front.

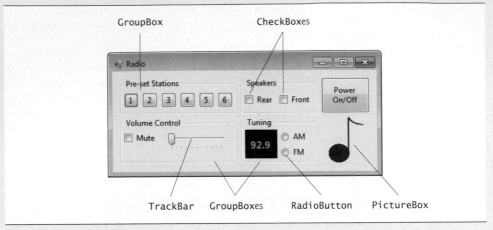

Fig. 2.44 | Radio GUI.

d) *Adding the **Power On/Off** Button.* Add a Button to the Form. Set its Text to Power On/Off and its Size to 75, 55.

e) *Adding the **Volume Control** GroupBox, the **Mute** CheckBox and the **Volume** TrackBar.* Add a GroupBox to the Form. Set its Text to Volume Control and its Size to 180, 70. Add a CheckBox to the GroupBox. Set its Text to Mute. Add a TrackBar to the GroupBox.

f) *Adding the **Tuning** GroupBox, the radio station Label and the **AM/FM** RadioButtons.* Add a GroupBox to the Form. Set its Text to Tuning and its Size to 120, 70. Add a Label to the GroupBox. Set its AutoSize to False, its Size to 50, 44, its BackColor to Black, its ForeColor to Silver, its font to 12pt bold and its TextAlign to MiddleCenter. Set its Text to 92.9. Place the Label as shown in the figure. Add two RadioButtons to the GroupBox. Set the Text of one to AM and of the other to FM.

g) *Adding the image.* Add a PictureBox to the Form. Set its SizeMode to StretchImage and its Size to 55, 70. Set the Image property to MusicNote.gif (located in the examples folder for Chapter 2).

Introduction to Visual Basic Programming

3

Comment is free, but facts are sacred.
—C. P. Scott

The creditor hath a better memory than the debtor.
—James Howell

When faced with a decision, I always ask, "What would be the most fun?"
—Peggy Walker

Objectives

In this chapter you'll learn:

- To write simple Visual Basic programs.
- To use the Windows Forms designer to position, size and align controls.
- To write statements that input data from the user and display results to the user.
- To declare and use data of various types.
- To use variables to store data for later use in a program.
- To use arithmetic operators to perform calculations.
- How precedence determines the order in which arithmetic operators are applied.
- To write decision-making statements.
- To use equality and relational operators to compare values.

3.1 Introduction

In this chapter, we introduce Visual Basic programming with program code. We demonstrate how to display information on the screen and obtain information from the user at the keyboard. You'll use graphical user interface (GUI) controls to allow users to interact visually with your programs. GUIs (pronounced "goo-ees") give your app a distinctive *look-and-feel*.

Sample GUI
GUIs are built from GUI controls (which are sometimes called **components** or **widgets**—short for "window gadgets"). GUI controls are objects that can display information on the screen or enable users to interact with an app via the mouse, keyboard or other forms of input (such as voice commands). Figure 3.1 shows a Visual Studio Express 2012 window that contains various GUI controls.

Near the top of the window is a *menu bar* containing the menus **FILE**, **EDIT**, **VIEW**, **DEBUG**, **TEAM**, **TOOLS**, **TEST**, **WINDOW** and **HELP**. Below the menu bar is a *tool bar* of

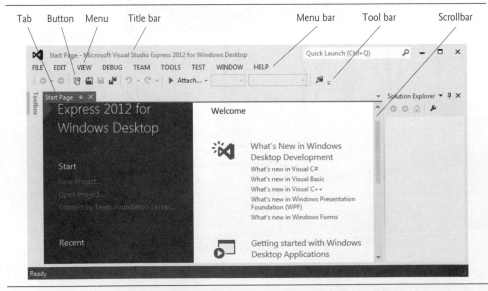

Fig. 3.1 | GUI controls in the Visual Studio Express 2012 window.

buttons, each with a defined task, such as creating a new project or opening an existing one. A *scrollbar* is located at the right side of the **Start Page**'s **Welcome** section. Usually, scrollbars appear when there's more information than can be displayed in certain types of controls.

The **Start Page** is shown on a *tab*—if multiple documents are open, the user can click a document's tab to view it. These controls form a user-friendly interface through which you've been interacting with the Visual Studio Express 2012. As you'll see, the .NET framework provides many predefined controls.

3.2 Programmatically Displaying Text in a Label

In Chapter 2, we showed how to create a simple GUI app using *visual* programming. We defined the app's appearance by *dragging and dropping* GUI controls onto a Form and setting properties in *design mode*—without writing *any* program code. The app you created in Section 2.6 displayed text and an image but did not perform any other actions.

You'll generally build your apps with a combination of visual programming and conventional programming techniques. In this section, you'll modify the Label's text programmatically, causing the text displayed on the Form to change when you execute the program. You'll also learn how to write code that performs an action when the Form *loads*—that is, when the app executes and displays the Form.

We begin by considering the app's code and sample execution (Fig. 3.2). In Section 3.2.2, we'll guide you step-by-step through the process of creating this app by modifying the one you created in Section 2.6.

```vb
1  ' Fig. 3.2: ASimpleApp.vb
2  ' Programmatically changing a Label's text.
3  Public Class ASimpleApp
4     ' called when the program loads the Form
5     Private Sub ASimpleApp_Load(sender As Object,
6        e As EventArgs) Handles MyBase.Load
7
8        Label1.Text = "Visual Basic is fun!"
9     End Sub ' ASimpleApp_Load
10 End Class ' ASimpleApp
```

Fig. 3.2 | Programmatically changing a Label's text.

3.2.1 Analyzing the Program

Line Numbers and Sample Outputs

All of our program listings include *line numbers*—these are not part of Visual Basic. The line numbers help us refer to specific parts of a program. In Section 3.2.2, you'll learn how to display line numbers in program files. Each program in the book is followed by one or more sample outputs that demonstrate the program's execution.

Comments

Line 1 of Fig. 3.2 begins with a single-quote character ('), which indicates that the remainder of the line is a comment. Comments improve the code's readability—you can write anything you want in a comment. Comments can be placed either on their own lines (we call these "full-line comments"; as in lines 1–2) or at the end of a line of Visual Basic code (we call these "end-of-line comments"; as in lines 9 and 10). The compiler ignores comments—they do not cause the computer to perform any actions when a program runs. The comment in line 1 simply indicates the figure number (Fig. 3.2) and the file name (`ASimpleApp.vb`) in which we stored this program. The comment in line 2 provides a brief description of the program. By convention, we begin each program this way.

Classes

Windows Forms apps consist of pieces called classes, which are logical groupings of methods and data that simplify program organization. **Methods** perform tasks and can return information when the tasks are completed. Lines 3–10 define a class that represents our `Form`. These lines collectively are called a **class declaration**. We discuss the method in lines 5–9 shortly. Every Windows Forms app consists of at least one class that typically contains one or more methods that perform tasks.

Keywords

The words **Public** and **Class** (line 3) are examples of keywords. **Keywords** are words reserved for use by Visual Basic. The complete list of keywords can be found at:

```
msdn.microsoft.com/library/dd409611.aspx
```

Class Names and Identifiers

The name of the `Class`—`ASimpleApp` in line 3—is an **identifier**, which is a series of characters consisting of letters, digits and underscores (_). Identifiers cannot begin with a digit and cannot contain spaces. Examples of valid identifiers are `value1`, `Welcome1`, `xy_coordinate`, `_total` and `grossPay`. The name `7Welcome` is not a valid identifier because it begins with a digit; `input field` is not valid because it contains a space.

Good Programming Practice 3.1

By convention, every word in a class name should begin with an uppercase letter—this is known as "Pascal case."

Common Programming Error 3.1

You cannot use a keyword as an identifier, so it's an error, for example, to use the keyword Double *as a class name. The Visual Basic compiler helps you locate such errors in your programs. Though keywords cannot be used as identifiers, they* can *be used in comments.*

Visual Basic Is Not Case Sensitive

Visual Basic keywords and identifiers are *not* **case sensitive**. Uppercase and lowercase letters are considered to be identical, so `ASimpleApp` and `asimpleapp` are interpreted as the same identifier. Although keywords appear to be case sensitive, they're not. Visual Basic applies its "preferred" case (that is, the casing used in Fig. 3.2) to each letter of a keyword, so when you type `class`, for example, the IDE changes the lowercase `c` to uppercase, as in `Class`, even though `class` would be correct.

Blank Lines and Whitespace

Line 7 (Fig. 3.2) is a blank line. Blank lines, space characters and tab characters are used throughout a program to make it easier to read. These are called **whitespace**. Blank lines are ignored by the compiler.

The Form's **Load** Event and Method `ASimpleApp_Load`

GUIs are **event driven**. When the user interacts with a GUI component, the interaction—known as an **event**—causes the program to perform a task by "calling" a method. Common events (user interactions) include clicking a `Button`, selecting an item from a menu, closing a window and moving the mouse. All GUI controls, including `Form`s, have events associated with them. A method that performs a task in response to an event is called an **event handler**, and the process of responding to events is known as **event handling**. Most of a GUI app's functionality executes based on events. Event handling methods are called automatically. You'll learn how to call existing methods yourself later in this chapter. You'll learn how to create and call your own methods in Chapter 6.

A common event for a `Form` is its **Load event**, which occurs just before a `Form` is displayed on the screen—typically as a result of executing the program. This is where you perform tasks that should occur before the user sees the `Form`. Lines 5–9 define the method `ASimpleApp_Load` as the `Form`'s Load event handler. When this event is **raised** (that is, the event occurs), method `ASimpleApp_Load` executes to perform its task—changing the text in the `Label`. At the end of line 6, the clause

```
Handles MyBase.Load
```

indicates that method `ASimpleApp_Load` is the one that will be called to handle the `Form`'s Load event. The IDE automatically inserts this clause for you when you create the event handler. We'll discuss the contents inside the parentheses in lines 5–6 in later chapters.

Defining a Method

The keyword **Sub** (line 5) begins the **method declaration** (the code that will be executed by this method). The keywords **End Sub** (line 9) close the method declaration. The **body of the method declaration** appears between the lines of code containing the keywords `Sub` and `End Sub`. `Sub` is short for "subroutine"—an early term for method. Methods are also sometimes called **procedures**. The end-of-line comments in lines 9 and 10 improve readability by indicating which method or class ends at those lines.

Good Programming Practice 3.2

Follow a method's `End Sub` *with an end-of-line comment containing the name of the method that the* `End Sub` *terminates.*

Indentation

Lines 4–9 are indented three spaces relative to lines 3 and 10. Indentation improves program readability—in this case making it clear that method ASimpleApp_Load is part of the class ASimpleApp. We show how to set the IDE's indent size in Section 3.2.2.

Line 8 in the method body is indented three additional spaces to the right relative to lines 5 and 9. This emphasizes that line 8 is part of method ASimpleApp_Load's body. The indentation is whitespace and is ignored by the compiler. In Visual Basic, the IDE indents the statements in a method's body for you.

*Modifying a **Label**'s Text with Code*

Line 8 in Fig. 3.2 does the "real work" of the program, displaying the phrase Visual Basic is fun!. Line 8 instructs the computer to perform an **action**—namely, to change the text on the Label to the characters contained between the double quotation marks. These characters and the surrounding double quotes are called **string literals** or simply **strings**.

The entire line is called a **statement**. When this line executes, it changes the Label's Text property to the message Visual Basic is fun!. This updates the text on the Form (Fig. 3.2). The statement uses the **assignment operator** (=) to give the Text property a new value. The statement is read as, "Label1.Text *gets* the value "Visual Basic is fun!"."

The expression Label1.Text contains two identifiers (that is, Label1 and Text) separated by the **dot separator** (.). The identifier to the right of the dot separator is the **property name**, and the identifier to the left of the dot separator is the name of the Label control. When you add a Label to a Form, the IDE gives it the name Label1 by default for the first Label you add—you'll learn how to change the IDE-assigned names in Section 3.4. After the statement in line 8 executes, the program reaches the keywords End Sub, which indicate that this method has completed performing its task. The keywords **End Class** (line 10), indicate the end of the Class.

*Note About **Public** and **Private***

We did not discuss the keywords Public (line 3) and Private (line 5). Most classes you'll define begin with keyword Public and most event-handling methods begin with the keyword Private. We'll discuss each of these keywords in detail when we formally present classes in Chapter 9, Object-Oriented Programming: Classes and Objects.

3.2.2 Modifying ASimpleApp to Programmatically Change the Label's Text Property

Now that we've presented the program (Fig. 3.2), we provide a step-by-step explanation of how to modify the version of ASimpleApp you created in Section 2.6.

Loading the Project

Open the project ASimpleApp from the ASimpleApp folder in the Chapter 3 examples folder. To do this, select **FILE > Open Project…** in the IDE and locate the project's .sln file or double-click the .sln file in Windows Explorer. This is the same program you created in Chapter 2.

*Naming the **Form** Class*

In larger programs, you might have several Forms—giving each one a name helps programmers understand the purpose of each Form and improves program clarity. Change the name of the file from `Form1.vb` to `ASimpleApp.vb` by right clicking the file in the **Solution Explorer**, selecting **Rename** and typing the new file name. A dialog will appear asking if you want to rename all references to `Form1` in the project—click **Yes**. Next, double click this file to open it in design mode. Select the `Form` by clicking it. Notice in the **Properties** window that the IDE changed the `Form`'s name from `Form1` to `ASimpleApp` when you changed the file name. You can also rename a file by selecting it in the **Solution Explorer**, then changing the **File Name** property in the **Properties** window.

Viewing the Form's Code
There are several ways to view the code for `ASimpleApp`:

1. Right click the `Form` and select **View Code**.
2. Right click the `ASimpleForm.vb` file in the **Solution Explorer** and select **View Code**.
3. Select **Code** from the **View** menu.

Figure 3.3 shows `ASimpleApp.vb`'s initial contents. The editor window contains some Visual Basic code generated by the IDE.

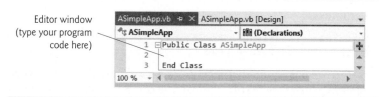

Fig. 3.3 | `ASimpleApp.vb`'s initial contents.

Syntax Shading
The code coloring scheme used by the IDE—called **syntax-color highlighting**—helps you visually differentiate program elements. Keywords appear in dark blue. Comments are colored green. Other program elements use different colors. We simulate the IDE's syntax coloring with syntax shading—bold dark blue for keywords, gray for comments, bold light blue for literals and constants, and black for all other text. One example of a literal is the string assigned to `Label1.Text` in line 8 of Fig. 3.2. You can customize the colors shown in the code editor by selecting **TOOLS > Options...**, then in the **Options** dialog select **Fonts and Colors** to display the options for changing the fonts and colors of various code elements.

Configuring the Editor Window
Visual Studio provides many ways to personalize your coding experience. In the Before You Begin section that follows the Preface, we show how to configure the IDE to display line numbers at the left side of the editor window and how to specify indent sizes that match our code examples.

Creating the Event Handler Method ASimpleApp_Load
Click the **ASimpleApp.vb [Design]** tab in the IDE to view the Windows Forms designer. Double clicking any control creates that control's default event handler (if it does not already exist) and switches to *code view*. For a `Form`, the default is the `Load` event handler. Double click the blue background of the `Form` to create the event handler now. The IDE

automatically names an event handler with the name of the control (ASimpleForm), an underscore (_) and the name of the event that the method handles (Load). Figure 3.4 shows the code editor with the new event handler method.

```
ASimpleApp.vb* ⊹ ×   ASimpleApp.vb [Design]*
  ⚡ (ASimpleApp Events)                              ⚡ Load
  1  ⊟Public Class ASimpleApp
  2
  3  ⊟    Private Sub ASimpleApp_Load(sender As Object, e As EventArgs) Handles MyBase.Load
  4
  5      End Sub
  6  End Class
  7
100 %  ⚡ ◄
```

Fig. 3.4 | ASimpleApp.vb's Load event handler.

Line 3 is too long to fit on a single line in our book, so we split the line into two lines as shown in lines 5–6 of Fig. 3.2. To improve readability, long statements may be split over several lines. In earlier versions of Visual Basic, you had to use the **line-continuation character** (_) to do this as follows:

```
Private Sub ASimpleApp_Load(sender As Object, _
    e As EventArgs) Handles MyBase.Load
```

Line-continuation characters are not required in most cases, so we'll use them only when necessary. For the few cases in which they're still required, the compiler will tell you if you do not include them.

Common Programming Error 3.2

Splitting a statement over several lines without including the line-continuation character is sometimes a syntax error—a violation of Visual Basic's rules for creating correct programs (that is, one or more statements are not written correctly). Syntax errors occur for various reasons, such as missing parentheses and misspelled keywords. If you get error messages after splitting a long line of code, insert a line-continuation character.

Common Programming Error 3.3

Failure to precede the line-continuation character (_) with at least one whitespace character is a syntax error.

Writing Code and Using IntelliSense

In the editor window, add the comments from lines 1, 2, 4, 9 and 10 of Fig. 3.2. Also, split the first line of method ASimpleApp_Load's first line as shown in Fig. 3.2. Then click the line before End Sub, press *Enter* and type the code contained in line 8 of Fig. 3.2. As you begin typing, a small window appears (Fig. 3.5). This IDE feature, called *IntelliSense*, lists keywords, class names, **members** of a class (which include property and method names) and other features that start with the same characters you've typed so far. Tabs (**Common** and **All**) are provided in the *IntelliSense* window so that you can view either the most commonly used matches or all available matches.

As you type characters, *IntelliSense* highlights the first item that matches the characters typed so far, then displays a tool tip containing information about that item. You can type

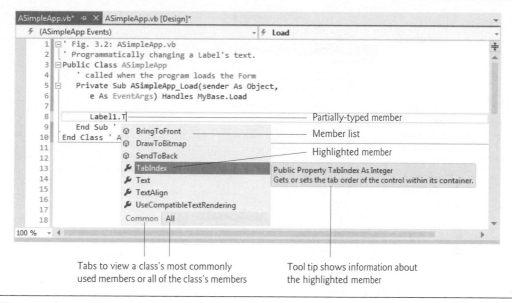

Fig. 3.5 | *IntelliSense* feature of Visual Studio.

the complete item name (for example, Label1 or Text), or you can let the IDE insert the complete name for you by double clicking the item's name in the list, or by pressing the *Space* or *Tab* keys. When the complete name is provided, the *IntelliSense* window closes. Notice that once you type the dot (.) after Label1, the *IntelliSense* window shows *only* the members of class Label that can be used on the right side of the dot. This also helps you learn about the control or class you're using.

While the *IntelliSense* window is displayed, pressing the *Ctrl* key makes the window transparent so you can see the code behind the window. Also, if you accidentally close *IntelliSense* (normally by pressing the *Esc* key), you can display it at any time by pressing *Ctrl* and the *Spacebar*.

Compiling and Running the Program
You're now ready to compile and run the program. To do so, select **DEBUG > Start Debugging** (or press *F5* or the toolbar button ▶). The statement in line 8 displays Visual Basic is fun! on the Label. When you run a program, the IDE first compiles it. You can also compile the program without running it by selecting **BUILD > Rebuild Solution** (this menu option's name changes based on your project's name). This creates a new file with the project's name and the .exe file-name extension (ASimpleApp.exe). This file executes on the .NET Framework. The **.exe file extension** indicates that the file is **executable**.

Compilation Errors, Error Messages and the Error List Window
Go back to the app in the IDE. When you type a line of code and press the *Enter* key, the IDE responds either by applying syntax-color highlighting or by generating an error. When an error occurs, the IDE places a *blue squiggle* below the error and provides a description of the error in the **Error List** window. If the **Error List** window is not visible in the IDE, select **VIEW > Error List** to display it. In Fig. 3.6, we intentionally omitted the

Omitted parenthesis character (syntax error)

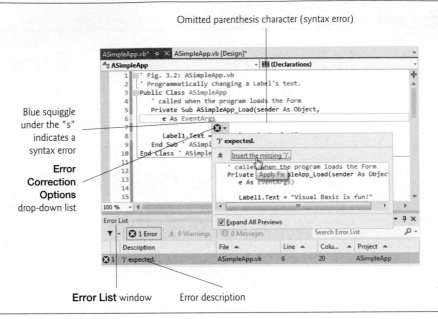

Blue squiggle under the "s" indicates a syntax error

Error Correction Options drop-down list

Error List window   Error description

Fig. 3.6 | Syntax error indicated by the IDE.

parenthesis and `Handles MyBase.Load` at the end of line 6. The error contains the text "')' **expected.**" and specifies that the error is in column 20 of line 6. This informs you that a right parenthesis is missing in line 6. You can double click an error message in the **Error List** to jump to the line of code that caused the error. For some errors (such as this one), the IDE shows the **Error Correction Options** drop-down list and allows you to simply click a link to fix the error.

 Error-Prevention Tip 3.1

*One syntax error can lead to multiple entries in the **Error List** window. Fix the errors in the order they appear—fixing one error might make the others disappear.*

3.3 Addition Program

We'll now build an `Addition` app (Fig. 3.7) that allows the user to enter two integers (whole numbers) then click an **Add Button** to calculate their sum and display the result. First, we'll discuss the GUI and the app's code. Then, we'll show how to lay out the GUI and create the `addButton_Click` event handler (lines 5–16) that's called when the user clicks the button. The sample output that follows the code shows the GUI after the user has entered two integers and clicked the **Add** button to display the result.

```
1    ' Fig. 3.7: Addition.vb
2    ' Addition program that adds two integers entered by the user.
3    Public Class Addition
```

Fig. 3.7 | Addition program that adds two integers entered by the user. (Part 1 of 2.)

```
 4        ' adds two integers and displays the result
 5        Private Sub addButton_Click(sender As Object,
 6           e As EventArgs) Handles addButton.Click
 7
 8           Dim number1 As Integer ' first number entered by the user
 9           Dim number2 As Integer ' second number entered by the user
10           Dim total As Integer ' sum of the two integers
11
12           number1 = number1TextBox.Text ' get the first number entered
13           number2 = number2TextBox.Text ' get the second number entered
14           total = number1 + number2 ' add the two numbers
15           resultLabel.Text = "The sum is " & total ' display the total
16        End Sub ' addButton_Click
17    End Class ' Addition
```

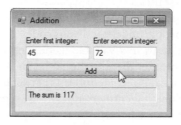

Fig. 3.7 | Addition program that adds two integers entered by the user. (Part 2 of 2.)

The Addition Program's GUI

The GUI for this program consists of three Labels, two TextBoxes and a Button. As you've seen, Labels display text information. The app user cannot directly modify the text on a Label, but as you saw in Fig. 3.2, a Label's text can be changed programmatically by modifying the Label's Text property. The Labels **Enter first integer:** and **Enter second integer:** are called **prompts**, because they direct the user to take a specific action.

A **TextBox** is an area in which a program can display text or the user can type text via the keyboard. TextBoxes are typically used to obtain information from the app's user. Like a Label, a TextBox's **Text** property can be used to change the text that's displayed in a TextBox. As you'll see in this program, the Text property can also be used to get information the user types in a TextBox.

A **Button** is a control the user clicks to trigger a specific action in the program. When the user clicks the **Add** Button, this app reads the values typed by the user in the two Text-Boxes, adds the values and displays the result. The text displayed on a Button is specified using its Text property.

Variable Declarations and Naming

Lines 8–10 are declarations, which begin with keyword **Dim**. The words number1, number2 and total are identifiers for variables—locations in the computer's memory where values can be stored for use by a program. *All variables must be declared before they can be used.* The declarations in lines 8–10 specify that the variables number1, number2 and total are data of type **Integer**; that is, these variables store **integer** values (that is, whole numbers such as 919, –11, 0 and 138624). Types defined as part of the Visual Basic language, such as `Integer`, are known as **primitive types** and their type names are keywords. The primitive types are listed in Fig. 3.8.

Primitive types				
Boolean	Byte	Char	Date	Decimal
Double	Integer	Long	SByte	Short
Single	String	UInteger	ULong	UShort

Fig. 3.8 | Primitive types.

A variable name can be any valid identifier. Variables of the same type can be declared in separate statements or in one statement with each variable in the declaration separated by a comma. The latter format uses a **comma-separated list** of variable names.

You should choose meaningful variable names to make your programs "self-documenting." This helps other people understand your code.

By convention, the first word in a variable-name identifier begins with a lowercase letter. Every word in the name after the first should begin with an uppercase letter—this is known as "camel case." For example, identifier `firstNumber` has a capital `N` beginning its second word, `Number`. Although identifiers are not case sensitive, using this convention helps make your programs more readable.

Using Variables to Store the Values Entered by the User
Line 12 uses an assignment operator (=) to give a value to variable `number1`. The statement is read as, "`number1` *gets* the value returned by `number1TextBox.Text`." We call the entire statement an **assignment statement** because it assigns a value to a variable. The expression `number1TextBox.Text` gets the value that the user typed in the `TextBox`. Line 13 assigns `number2` the value that the user entered in the `number2TextBox`.

What if the User Doesn't Enter an Integer?
Technically, the user can type any character into a `TextBox` as input. For this program, if the user types a noninteger value, such as `"hello,"` a **runtime error** (an error that has its effect at execution time) occurs. The message displayed in Fig. 3.9 appears when you run

Error message ——

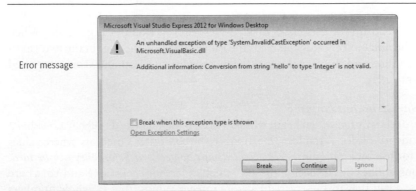

Fig. 3.9 | Dialog displaying a runtime error.

the app using **DEBUG > Start Debugging** (or press *F5*). You can terminate the program by selecting **DEBUG > Stop Debugging** or by clicking **Break** in the dialog. In Chapter 7, we'll introduce how to handle such errors to make programs more robust—that is, able to handle runtime errors and continue executing.

Using Variables in a Calculation

The assignment statement in line 14 (Fig. 3.7) calculates the sum of the `Integer` variables `number1` and `number2` and assigns the result to variable `total`. The statement is read as, "`total` *gets* the value of `number1 + number2`." The expression to the right of the = is always evaluated first before the assignment occurs. The addition (+) operator is called a **binary operator**, because it has two **operands**—`number1` and `number2`.

> **Good Programming Practice 3.3**
>
> *The Visual Basic IDE places a space on either side of a binary operator, such as the addition operator, to make the operator stand out and improve the statement's readability.*

Displaying the Result in `resultLabel`

Line 15 displays the total of the two values by assigning a new value to the `resultLabel`'s `Text` property. The expression

```
"The sum is " & total
```

uses the **string concatenation operator**, **&**, to combine the string literal `"The sum is "` and the value of the variable `total` (the `Integer` variable containing the sum calculated in line 14). The string concatenation operator is a binary operator that joins two strings together, resulting in a new, longer string. If one of the operands is a number, the program automatically creates a string representation of the number.

3.4 Building the Addition Program

Follow the steps in Section 2.6 to create a new Windows Forms app named `Addition`. In the **Solution Explorer**, right click `Form1.vb`, select **Rename**, then rename the file `Addition.vb`.

Setting the Form's Font

In the **Solution Explorer**, double click `Addition.vb` to view the `Form` designer. Select the `Form` and use the **Properties** window to change the `Font` property to `Segoe UI 9pt`. By default, controls added to the `Form` will use the `Form`'s font.

Changing the Names of Controls

Figure 3.10 shows the `Addition` program's GUI with the names we used for each control. When you build a GUI, you'll typically want to rename each control. The name of a control is actually a variable that can be used to interact with that control. For example, in Fig. 3.2 we used `Label1.Text` to access and change the `Label`'s `Text` property. In that expression, `Label1` is the variable name that you can use to interact with the control programmatically. You can change a control's variable name by selecting the control and modifying its **Name property** (listed in the **Properties** window as **(Name)**). We'll use this technique to change the names of all the controls in this GUI, which will enable us to easily identify the Form's controls in the program code.

number1Label

number1TextBox

addButton

resultLabel

number2Label

number2TextBox

Fig. 3.10 | Addition program's GUI with the variable names of the controls.

Setting the Form's Text Property

In the Windows Forms designer, click the Form to select it. Then use the **Properties** window to change the Form's Text property to Addition. This is displayed in the Form's title bar.

Creating the number1Label

Next, you'll create the number1Label. Visual Studio provides design tools that help you lay out a GUI. When you drag a control across a Form, **snap lines** appear to help you position the control with respect to the Form's edges and other controls. As you move a control close to another control or close to the edge of the Form, the IDE moves it a bit for you—and quickly—hence the term "snap into place." Drag a Label from the **Toolbox** onto the Form and position it near the Form's upper-left corner. Figure 3.11 shows the two snap lines that appear when you drag the Label near the upper-left corner. These snap

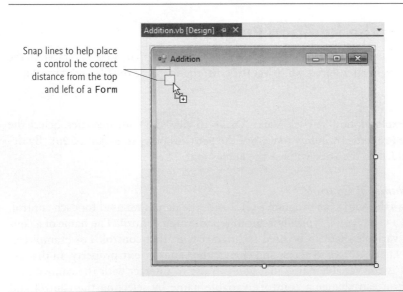

Snap lines to help place a control the correct distance from the top and left of a **Form**

Fig. 3.11 | Snap lines for positioning a Label near the upper-left corner of the Form.

lines indicate the recommended minimum distance that you should place the control from the top and left of the Form. After releasing this Label, set its Name property to number1Label and its Text property to Enter first integer:.

Look-and-Feel Observation 3.1

A Label used to describe the purpose of a control should use sentence-style capitalization—only the first word should be capitalized—and end with a colon.

Control Naming Convention

You'll notice that, by convention, each variable name we create for a control ends with the control's type. For example, the variable name number1Label ends with Label. For example, the **Enter first integer:** Label's name could be number1Label.

Good Programming Practice 3.4

Appending the control's type to the end of the variable name for a control. This helps you know the control's type when reading your code.

Creating the *number2Label*

Next, drag another Label onto the Form. Set its Name property to number2Label and its Text property to Enter second integer:. Drag the Label near the top of the Form and to the right of number1Label as shown in Fig. 3.12.

Look-and-Feel Observation 3.2

Align the bottoms of a group of descriptive Labels if they're arranged horizontally. Align the left or right sides of a group of descriptive Labels if they're arranged vertically.

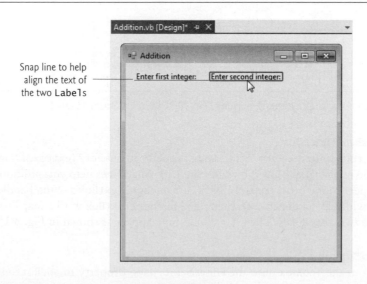

Fig. 3.12 | Snap line for aligning the text of two Labels.

Creating the *number1TextBox*

Next, drag a TextBox from the **Toolbox** onto the Form. Set its Name property to number1TextBox. Drag the TextBox below the number1Label as shown in Fig. 3.13. Snap lines help you align the left sides of the TextBox and Label, and help you position the TextBox the recommended distance from the Label.

Look-and-Feel Observation 3.3

Place each descriptive Label *either above or to the left of the control that it identifies.*

Look-and-Feel Observation 3.4

A descriptive Label *and the control it identifies should be aligned on the left if they're arranged vertically. The text in a descriptive* Label *and the text in the control it identifies should be aligned on the bottom if they're arranged horizontally.*

Snap lines to help align the TextBox with the left side of the Label and to position the TextBox the recommended distance below the Label

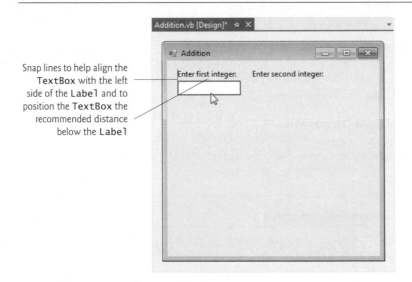

Fig. 3.13 | Snap lines for positioning number1TextBox below number1Label.

Creating the *number2TextBox*

Drag another TextBox onto the Form. Set its Name property to number2TextBox. Drag the TextBox below the number2Label as shown in Fig. 3.14. Snap lines help you position the TextBox with respect to the other controls. Next, use number2TextBox's sizing handles to make it the same width as number2Label, then resize number1TextBox until a snap line appears between the two TextBoxes. The GUI should now appear as shown in Fig. 3.15.

Creating the *addButton*

Drag a Button from the **Toolbox** onto the Form. Set its Name property to addButton and its Text property to Add. Drag the Button below the number1TextBox so that the two controls are aligned at the left side and the Button is the recommended distance from the

TextBox. Then use the Button's sizing handles to resize the Button as shown in Fig. 3.16. Snap lines help you size the Button so that it aligns with the right side of number2TextBox.

 Look-and-Feel Observation 3.5
*A Button's text should use **book-title capitalization**—each significant word should start with an uppercase letter. The text should be concise, but meaningful to the user.*

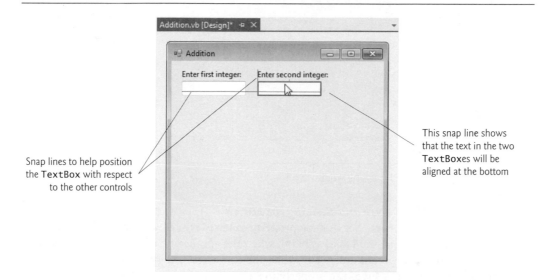

Snap lines to help position the TextBox with respect to the other controls

This snap line shows that the text in the two TextBoxes will be aligned at the bottom

Fig. 3.14 | Snap lines for positioning number2TextBox below number2Label.

Fig. 3.15 | GUI after resizing number2TextBox.

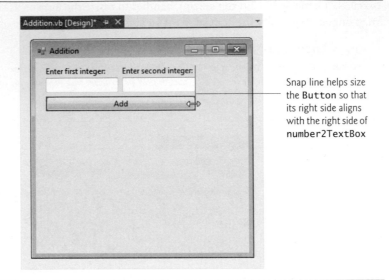

Snap line helps size the **Button** so that its right side aligns with the right side of `number2TextBox`

Fig. 3.16 | Snap line for sizing `addButton`.

Creating the `resultLabel` and Resizing the `Form`

Drag a `Label` onto the `Form`. Set its `Name` property to `resultLabel` and delete the value of the `Text` property so that the `Label` is blank when the app begins executing—remember that we'll set this text programmatically when the user clicks the **Add** button to add the numbers. Set the `Label`'s `AutoSize` property to `False` so that you'll be able to size the `Label`. Set the `Label`'s **BorderStyle** property to **Fixed3D** to give the `Label` a three-dimensional appearance. We use this style to highlight the fact that the `Label` displays the program's results. Set the `Label`'s `TextAlign` property to **MiddleLeft** as shown in Fig. 3.17. This centers the text vertically on the `Label`, so that the distance between the `Label`'s text and its top and bottom borders is balanced. Then use the `Label`'s sizing handles to resize the `Label` as shown in Fig. 3.18. Snap lines help you size the `Label` so that it aligns with the right side of `addButton`. Finally, click the `Form` and use its resizing handles to resize the window so that it appears as shown in Fig. 3.10.

Fig. 3.17 | Setting a `Label`'s `TextAlign` property to `MiddleLeft`.

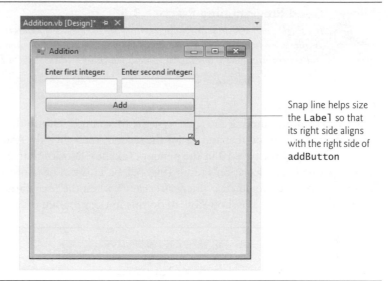

Fig. 3.18 | Snap line for sizing `resultLabel`.

 Look-and-Feel Observation 3.6
Place controls that display output below and/or to the right of a Form's input controls.

 Look-and-Feel Observation 3.7
Distinguish output Labels from descriptive Labels by setting each output Label's Border-Style property to Fixed3D (see resultLabel in Fig. 3.10).

Creating the **addButton_Click** *Event Handler*

Recall from Section 3.2.2 that double clicking any control creates that control's default event handler. For a Button, the default event is the Click event. Double click the add-Button now to create its addButton_Click event handler. The IDE automatically switches to the code editor window. The IDE automatically names the event handler with the control's name (addButton), an underscore (_) and the name of the event that the method handles (Click). Notice that the first line of the method ends with

```
Handles addButton.Click
```

This indicates that the method will be called when the user clicks the addButton, which raises a Click event.

Entering the Code from Fig. 3.7 into the **addButton_Click** *Event Handler*

You can now enter the code in the event handler to read the numbers, perform the calculation and display the result. To ensure that your line numbers match with those shown in Fig. 3.7, enter the comments on lines 1–2 of Fig. 3.7 and split the first line of the method definition as shown in lines 5–6.

Good Programming Practice 3.5

If a single statement must be split across lines, choose breaking points that make sense, such as after a comma in a comma-separated list or after an operator in a lengthy expression. If a statement is split across two or more lines, indent all subsequent lines with one level of indentation.

Testing the Program

When you're done entering the code, test the program to ensure that it works correctly. Enter 45 for the first number and 72 for the second, then click the **Add** Button. The result should be 117. Now, type 10 in the number1TextBox. Notice that the resultLabel still shows the previous calculation's result (Fig. 3.19). This can be confusing to the app user. For this reason, we should clear the resultLabel when the user starts typing a new number in either TextBox. We show how to do this in the program of Section 3.7.

resultLabel showing incorrect result after user enters 10 in number1TextBox and before user clicks **Add**

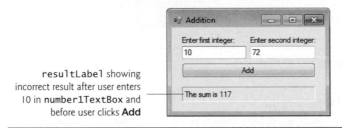

Fig. 3.19 | Addition program showing old result as new numbers are entered.

3.5 Memory Concepts

Variable names, such as number1, number2 and total, correspond to locations in the computer's memory. Every variable has a **name**, **type**, **size** and **value**. In the addition program of Fig. 3.7, when the statement (line 12)

```
number1 = number1TextBox.Text ' get the first number entered
```

executes, the data input by the user in number1TextBox is placed into a memory location to which the name number1 has been assigned by the compiler. Suppose the user enters the characters 45. This input is returned by number1TextBox.Text and assigned to number1. The program places the Integer value 45 into location number1, as shown in Fig. 3.20. Whenever a value is placed in a memory location, this value replaces the value previously stored in that location. The previous value is lost.

number1   45

Fig. 3.20 | Memory location showing the name and value of variable number1.

Suppose that the user then enters the characters 72 in number2TextBox. Line 13

```
number2 = number2TextBox.Text ' get the second number entered
```

places the Integer value 72 into location number2, and memory appears, as shown in Fig. 3.21.

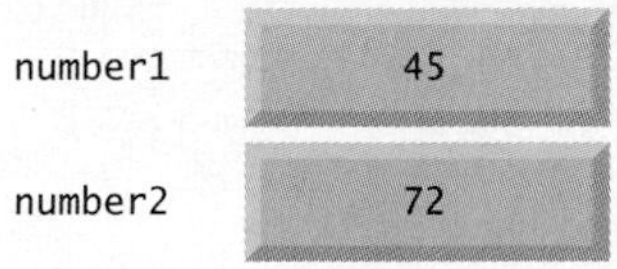

number1	45
number2	72

Fig. 3.21 | Memory locations after values for variables number1 and number2 have been input.

Once the program has obtained values for number1 and number2, it adds these values and places their total into variable total. The statement (line 14)

```
total = number1 + number2 ' add the two numbers
```

performs the addition and replaces total's previous value. After total is calculated, memory appears, as shown in Fig. 3.22. The values of number1 and number2 appear *exactly* as they did before they were used in the calculation of total. Although these values were used when the computer performed the calculation, they remain unchanged. As this illustrates, when a value is *read* from a memory location, the value is retained in memory.

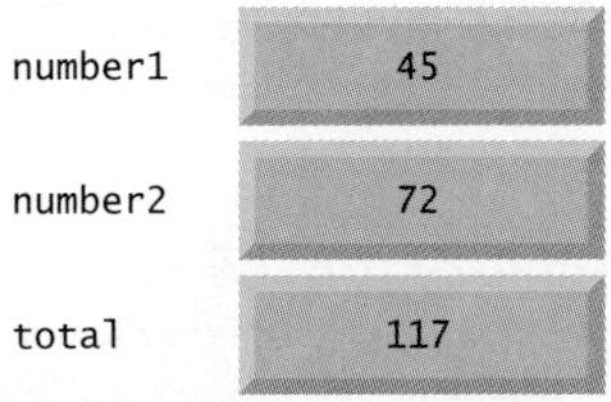

number1	45
number2	72
total	117

Fig. 3.22 | Memory locations after an addition operation.

3.6 Arithmetic

Programs often perform arithmetic calculations. The **arithmetic operators** are summarized in Fig. 3.23. Note the use of various special symbols not used in algebra. For example, the **asterisk** (*) indicates multiplication, and the keyword **Mod** represents the **Mod operator** (also known as the **modulus** or **modulo operator**), which we'll discuss shortly. Most of the arithmetic operators in Fig. 3.23 are binary operators, because each operates on two operands. For example, the expression sum + value contains the binary operator + and the two operands sum and value. Visual Basic also provides **unary operators** that take only one operand. For example, unary versions of plus (+) and minus (–) are provided, so that you can write expressions such as +9 and –19.

Division Operators

Visual Basic has separate operators for **integer division** (the backslash, \) and **floating-point division** (the forward slash, /). Integer division takes two Integer operands and yields an Integer result; for example, the expression 7\4 evaluates to 1, and the expression 17\5 evaluates to 3. Any fractional part in an Integer division result simply is *truncated*

Visual Basic operation	Arithmetic operator	Algebraic expression	Visual Basic expression
Addition	+	$f + 7$	f + 7
Subtraction	−	$p - c$	p - c
Multiplication	*	bm	b * m
Division (floating point)	/	x / y or $\frac{x}{y}$ or $x \div y$	x / y
Division (integer)	\	none	v \ u
Modulus	Mod	$r \bmod s$	r Mod s
Exponentiation	^	q^p	q ^ p
Unary minus	−	$-e$	-e
Unary plus	+	$+g$	+g

Fig. 3.23 | Arithmetic operators.

(that is, discarded)—no *rounding* occurs. When **floating-point numbers** (that is, numbers that contain a decimal point, such as 2.3456 and –845.7840) are used with the integer division operator, *the numbers are first rounded to the nearest whole number*, *then* divided. This means that, although 7.1\4 evaluates to 1 as expected, the statement 7.7\4 evaluates to 2, because 7.7 is *rounded* to 8 *before* the division occurs. To divide floating-point numbers *without* rounding the operands (which is normally what you want to do), use the floating-point division operator.

Common Programming Error 3.4
Using the integer division operator (\) when the floating-point division operator (/) is expected (that is, when one or both of the operands is a floating-point value) can lead to incorrect results.

Error-Prevention Tip 3.2
Ensure that each integer division operator has only integer operands.

Common Programming Error 3.5
The integer division operator does not allow division by zero, nor does the floating-point division operator when used with Decimal *values (introduced in Chapter 5). If your code divides by zero, a runtime error occurs. By default, this error terminates the app.*

Mod Operator

The Mod operator yields the *remainder* after division. The expression x Mod y yields the remainder after x is divided by y. Thus, 7 Mod 4 yields 3, and 17 Mod 5 yields 2. You use this operator mostly with Integer operands, but it also can be used with other types. When you add 1 to 59 you normally expect the result to be 60. But in an app that keeps time, adding 1 to 59 *seconds* should cause the seconds to reset to zero and the *minutes* to be incremented by 1. The Mod operator is helpful in this situation. In later chapters, we consider other interesting apps of the Mod operator, such as determining whether one number is a multiple of another.

Arithmetic Expressions in Straight-Line Form

Arithmetic expressions must be entered into the computer in **straight-line form.** Thus, expressions such as "a divided by b" must be written as a / b, so that all constants, variables and operators appear in a straight line. The algebraic notation

$$\frac{a}{b}$$

is *not* acceptable to compilers.

Parentheses for Grouping Subexpressions

Parentheses are used in Visual Basic expressions in the same manner as in algebraic expressions. For example, to multiply a times the quantity b + c, write a * (b + c).

Rules of Operator Precedence

Operators in arithmetic expressions are applied in a precise sequence determined by the **rules of operator precedence** (Fig. 3.24), which are similar to those in algebra. Operators in the same row of the table have the same level of precedence. When we say operators are evaluated from left to right, we're referring to the operators' **associativity.** All binary operators associate from left to right. If there are multiple operators, each with the same precedence, the order in which the operators are applied is determined by the operators' associativity.

Operator(s)	Operation	Order of evaluation (precedence)
^	Exponentiation	Evaluated first. If there are several such operators, they're evaluated from left to right.
+, -	Sign operations (unary)	Evaluated second. If there are several such operators, they're evaluated from left to right.
*, /	Multiplication and Division	Evaluated third. If there are several such operators, they're evaluated from left to right.
\	Integer division	Evaluated fourth. If there are several such operators, they're evaluated from left to right.
Mod	Modulus	Evaluated fifth. If there are several such operators, they're evaluated from left to right.
+, -	Addition and Subtraction (binary)	Evaluated sixth. If there are several such operators, they're evaluated from left to right.

Fig. 3.24 | Precedence of arithmetic operators.

Operators in expressions contained within a pair of parentheses are evaluated before those that are outside the parentheses. Parentheses can be used to group expressions and change the order of evaluation to occur *in any sequence you desire.* With **nested parentheses,** the operators contained in the innermost pair of parentheses are applied first.

Not all expressions with several pairs of parentheses contain *nested* parentheses. For example, although the expression

```
a * (b + c) + c * (d + e)
```

contains multiple sets of parentheses, none are nested. Rather, these sets are said to be "on the same level." Appendix A contains a complete operator-precedence chart.

Sample Algebraic and Visual Basic Expressions

Now consider several expressions in light of the rules of operator precedence. Each example lists an algebraic expression and its Visual Basic equivalent. The following is an example of an arithmetic mean (average) of five terms:

Algebra: $m = \dfrac{a + b + c + d + e}{5}$

Visual Basic: m = (a + b + c + d + e) / 5

The parentheses are required, because division has *higher* precedence than addition. The entire quantity (a + b + c + d + e) is to be divided by 5. If the parentheses are erroneously omitted, we obtain a + b + c + d + e / 5, which evaluates as

$$a + b + c + d + \dfrac{e}{5}$$

The following is the equation of a straight line:

Algebra: $y = mx + b$

Visual Basic: y = m * x + b

No parentheses are required. The multiplication is applied first, because multiplication has a *higher* precedence than addition.

Evaluation of a More Complex Expression

To develop a better understanding of the rules of operator precedence, consider how the expression $y = ax^2 + bx + c$ is evaluated:

```
y  =  a  *  x  ^  2  +  b  *  x  +  c
         2     1     4     3     5
```

The circled numbers under the statement indicate the order in which Visual Basic applies the operators. In Visual Basic, x^2 is represented as x ^ 2, where the ^ is the exponentiation operator. The exponentiation is applied first. The multiplication operators are evaluated next in left-to-right order (that is, they associate from left to right). The addition operators are evaluated next from left to right.

Now, suppose that a, b, c and x in the preceding expression are initialized as follows: a = 2, b = 3, c = 7 and x = 5. Figure 3.25 illustrates the order in which the operators are applied.

Redundant Parentheses

As in algebra, it's acceptable to place unnecessary parentheses in an expression to make the expression clearer—these are called **redundant parentheses**. For example, many people might parenthesize the preceding assignment statement for clarity as

```
y = (a * x ^ 2) + (b * x) + c
```

Error-Prevention Tip 3.3
When you are uncertain about the order of evaluation in a complex expression, you can use parentheses to force the order, as you would in an algebraic expression, or you can break complex expressions into several simpler ones. Doing so can help avoid subtle bugs.

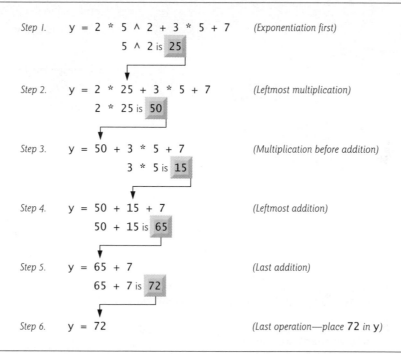

Fig. 3.25 | Order in which operations are evaluated.

3.7 Decision Making: Equality and Relational Operators

This section introduces Visual Basic's **If...Then** statement, which allows a program to make a decision based on the truth or falsity of some expression. The expression in an If...Then statement is called a **condition**. If the condition *is* met (that is, the condition is true), the statement in the If...Then statement's body executes. If the condition *is not* met (that is, the condition is false), the body statement does *not* execute. Conditions in If...Then statements can be formed by using the **equality operators** and **relational operators** (also called **comparison operators**), which are summarized in Fig. 3.26. The relational and equality operators all have the same level of precedence and associate from left to right.

Comparing Integers with the Equality and Relational Operators
The Comparison program uses six If...Then statements to compare two numbers you enter. If the condition in any of these statements is true, the statement associated with that If...Then executes. The values you enter are stored in variables number1 and number2, respectively. Then the comparisons are performed and the results are displayed in a multiline TextBox. Figure 3.27 shows the program and sample outputs.

Standard algebraic equality operator or relational operator	Visual Basic equality or relational operator	Example of Visual Basic condition	Meaning of Visual Basic condition
Equality operators			
=	=	x = y	x is equal to y
≠	<>	x <> y	x is not equal to y
Relational operators			
>	>	x > y	x is greater than y
<	<	x < y	x is less than y
≥	>=	x >= y	x is greater than or equal to y
≤	<=	x <= y	x is less than or equal to y

Fig. 3.26 | Equality and relational operators.

```
1   ' Fig. 3.27: Comparison.vb
2   ' Comparing integers with the equality and relational operators.
3   Public Class Comparison
4       ' compares two integers using the relational and equality operators
5       Private Sub compareButton_Click(sender As Object,
6           e As EventArgs) Handles compareButton.Click
7
8           ' declare Integer variables to store user input
9           Dim number1 As Integer
10          Dim number2 As Integer
11
12          number1 = number1TextBox.Text ' get first number entered by user
13          number2 = number2TextBox.Text ' get second number entered by user
14
15          If number1 = number2 Then ' number1 is equal to number2
16              resultTextBox.AppendText(number1 & " = " & number2)
17          End If
18
19          If number1 <> number2 Then ' number1 is not equal to number2
20              resultTextBox.AppendText(number1 & " <> " & number2)
21          End If
22
23          If number1 < number2 Then ' number1 is less than number2
24              resultTextBox.AppendText(vbCrLf & number1 & " < " & number2)
25          End If
26
27          If number1 > number2 Then ' number1 is greater than number2
28              resultTextBox.AppendText(vbCrLf & number1 & " > " & number2)
29          End If
30
```

Fig. 3.27 | Comparing integers with the equality and relational operators. (Part 1 of 2.)

```
31              ' number1 is less than or equal to number2
32              If number1 <= number2 Then
33                 resultTextBox.AppendText(vbCrLf & number1 & " <= " & number2)
34              End If
35
36              ' number1 is greater than or equal to number2
37              If number1 >= number2 Then
38                 resultTextBox.AppendText(vbCrLf & number1 & " >= " & number2)
39              End If
40        End Sub ' compareButton_Click
41
42        ' clears resultTextBox when the user begins typing in number1TextBox
43        Private Sub number1TextBox_TextChanged(sender As Object,
44           e As EventArgs) Handles number1TextBox.TextChanged
45
46           resultTextBox.Clear() ' clears the resultTextBox
47        End Sub ' number1TextBox_TextChanged
48
49        ' clears resultTextBox when the user begins typing in number2TextBox
50        Private Sub number2TextBox_TextChanged(sender As Object,
51           e As EventArgs) Handles number2TextBox.TextChanged
52
53           resultTextBox.Clear() ' clears the resultTextBox
54        End Sub ' number2TextBox_TextChanged
55   End Class ' Comparison
```

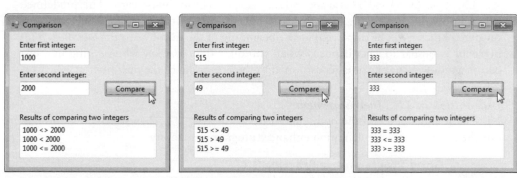

Fig. 3.27 | Comparing integers with the equality and relational operators. (Part 2 of 2.)

Getting the Values Entered By the User

Lines 9–10 declare the variables that are used in the compareButton_Click event handler. The comment that precedes the declarations indicates the purpose of the variables in the program. Lines 12–13 get the numbers that the user entered and assign the values to Integer variables number1 and number2, respectively.

The If...Then Statement

The If...Then statement in lines 15–17 compares the values of the variables number1 and number2 for equality. If the values are equal, the statement in line 16 outputs a string indicating that the two numbers are equal. The keywords **End If** (line 17) end the body of the If...Then statement. Assignment and the equality operator both use the = symbol.

When a condition is expected (such as after the If keyword in an If...Then statement), the = is used as an equality operator.

Displaying Text in a Multiline *TextBox*

In this program, we display several lines of text in a TextBox. To enable this functionality, we set the TextBox's MultiLine property to True in the Properties window. We also use the TextBox's **AppendText method**, which enables us to add more text to what is already displayed in a TextBox. The statement in line 16 is known as a **method call** because it "calls" a method (that is, method AppendText of class TextBox) to ask the method to perform its task. Sometimes you give a method values—known as **arguments**—that the method uses while performing its task. In line 16 of Fig. 3.27, the *expression* number1 & " = " & number2 in parentheses is the argument to method AppendText.

In line 16, if number1 contains the value 333 and number2 contains the value 333, the expression inside the parentheses following AppendText evaluates as follows: number1 is converted to a string and concatenated with the string " = ", then number2 is converted to a string and concatenated with the resulting string from the first concatenation. At this point, the string "333 = 333" is appended to the TextBox's Text property by method AppendText. As the program proceeds through the remaining If...Then statements (lines 19–39), additional strings are appended by the resultTextBox.AppendText statements. For example, when given the value 333 for number1 and number2, the conditions in lines 32 and 37 also are true, resulting in the third output of Fig. 3.27.

Lines 24, 28, 33 and 38 also append the value vbCrLf to the TextBox. This predefined value, known as a constant, positions the **output cursor** (the location where the next output character will be displayed) at the beginning of the next line in the TextBox. This behavior is similar to what happens when you press the *Enter* key when typing in a text editor window—the cursor is repositioned to the beginning of the next line.

Indentation in *If...Then* Statements

Notice the indentation of the body statements within the If...Then statements throughout the program. Such indentation enhances program readability.

Good Programming Practice 3.6

Visual Basic indents the statements in the body of an If...Then statement to emphasize the body statements and enhance program readability.

Handling the *TextChanged* Events for *number1TextBox* and *number2TextBox*

After comparing two numbers and clicking the **Compare** Button, the resultTextBox shows the results of comparing the two values. If the user wishes to compare different values and starts typing in number1TextBox or number2TextBox, the previous results will still be displayed in the resultTextBox. This can be confusing to the program's user. To prevent this problem, you can handle number1TextBox's and number2TextBox's TextChanged events and use them to clear the contents of the resultTextBox. The **TextChanged event** is a TextBox's default event. Lines 43–47 and 50–54 show the TextChanged event handlers for number1TextBox and number2TextBox, respectively. These methods are called when the user types in the corresponding TextBoxes. In both cases, we call the resultTextBox's **Clear method**, which removes the text that's currently displayed in the TextBox. You can also clear a `Label`'s or `TextBox`'s `Text` property by assigning it the value `String.Empty`, which represents a string that does not contain any characters.

Building the GUI

Use the techniques you learned in Section 3.4 to build the GUI for the `Comparison` program. Figure 3.28 shows the GUI with all of its variable names. To allow the `resultText-Box` to display multiple lines, set its `MultiLine` property to `True`. In the Windows Forms designer, double click the `compareButton` to create its event handler. To create the `Text-Changed` event handlers for the `number1TextBox` and `number2TextBox`, double click each one in the Windows Forms designer—`TextChanged` is the default event for a `TextBox`.

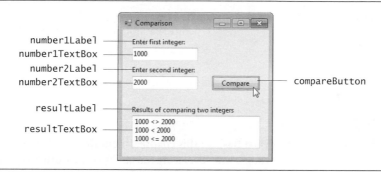

Fig. 3.28 | Comparison program GUI with variable names.

Entering the Code; Introducing the *Parameter Info Window*

Enter the code from Fig. 3.27 into the three event handlers to complete the app. When you're typing line 16, the IDE displays the *Parameter Info* window (Fig. 3.29) as you type the opening left parenthesis character, `(`, after `resultTextBox.AppendText`. This window contains information about the method and the information that the method needs to perform its task—its so-called parameter (methods can have several parameters). In this case, the *parameter info* window shows that the method requires you to give it the text to append to the current contents of the `TextBox`. The information you provide when you call the method is the method's argument.

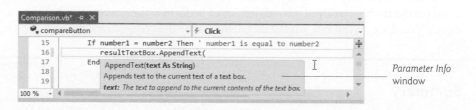

Fig. 3.29 | *Parameter Info* window for the `TextBox`'s `AppendText` method.

Testing the Program

Be sure to test your program. Enter the values shown in the sample outputs of Fig. 3.27 to ensure that the program is working properly.

Operator Precedence

Figure 3.30 shows the precedence of the operators introduced in this chapter. The operators are displayed from top to bottom in *decreasing* order of precedence.

Operators	Type
^	exponentiation
+ -	sign operations (unary)
* /	multiplication and floating-point division
\	Integer division
Mod	modulus
+ -	addition and subtraction (binary)
= <> < <= > >=	equality and relational

Fig. 3.30 | Precedence of the operators introduced in this chapter.

3.8 Wrap-Up

You learned many features of Visual Basic in this chapter, including displaying data on Labels, inputting data from TextBoxes and declaring variables of primitive type Integer. You used GUIs to build simple interactive programs. We demonstrated how to use event handling to respond to a Form's Load event, a Button's Click event and a TextBox's Text-Changed event. You learned how to position, size and align controls using the IDE's Windows Forms designer. We explained how values are stored in and retrieved from variables in memory. You learned how to use arithmetic operators to perform calculations, and the order in which Visual Basic applies these operators (that is, the rules of operator precedence and associativity). We demonstrated how Visual Basic's If...Then statement allows a program to perform actions based on a condition. You learned how to create conditions using the equality and relational operators.

In the next chapter, we continue our discussion of control statements . We demonstrate creating apps using pseudocode, an informal language that helps you develop programs. We study how to specify and vary the order in which statements are executed—this is called **flow of control**. You'll learn how to use control statements to select between alternative actions based on the truth or falsity of a condition, or to perform actions repeatedly based on a condition. You'll see several case studies that demonstrate the types of repetition.

Summary

Section 3.1 Introduction
- Graphical user interfaces (GUIs) allow users to interact visually with programs.
- A GUI (pronounced "GOO-ee") gives a program a distinctive look-and-feel.
- GUI controls can display information on the screen or enable users to interact with an app via the mouse, keyboard or another form of input.
- The .NET framework provides many predefined controls.

Section 3.2 Programmatically Displaying Text in a `Label`

- Most programmers use a combination of visual programming and conventional programming.

Section 3.2.1 Analyzing the Program

- A single-quote character (') indicates that the remainder of the line is a comment.
- The compiler ignores comments.
- Classes are logical groupings of methods and data that simplify program organization.
- Every Windows Forms app consists of at least one class containing one or more methods.
- Keywords like `Public` and `Class` are reserved for use by Visual Basic.
- An identifier is a series of characters consisting of letters, digits and underscores (_). Identifiers cannot begin with a digit and cannot contain spaces.
- Visual Basic keywords and identifiers are not case sensitive.
- Whitespace (spaces, tabs and blank lines) makes programs easier to read.
- GUIs are event driven. When the user interacts with a GUI component, the interaction—known as an event—causes the program to perform a task by calling a method. Common events include clicking a `Button`, selecting an item from a menu, closing a window and moving the mouse.
- A method that performs a task in response to an event is called an event handler, and the overall process of responding to events is known as event handling.
- A `Form`'s `Load` event occurs just before a `Form` is displayed on the screen.
- The keyword `Sub` begins a method declaration; `End Sub` closes it.
- Indentation improves program readability.
- A series of characters between double quotation marks is called a string.
- The assignment operator (=) can be used to give a new value to a property.
- The dot separator (.) is used to programmatically access a control's properties and methods.

Section 3.2.2 Modifying `ASimpleApp` to Programmatically Change the `Label`'s Text Property

- To load an existing project, select **FILE > Open Project...** in the IDE and locate the project's `.sln` file, or double click the `.sln` file in Windows Explorer.
- To view the code for a `Form`: Right click the `Form` and select **View Code**; right click the `.vb` file in the **Solution Explorer** and select **View Code**; or select **Code** from the **View** menu.
- Syntax-color highlighting helps you visually differentiate program elements in the IDE.
- The IDE will often update your code to conform to various Visaul Basic code conventions.
- Double clicking any control creates that control's default event handler (if it does not already exist) and switches to code view. For a `Form`, the default is the `Load` event handler.
- To improve readability, long statements may be split over several lines. In earlier versions of Visual Basic, you were required to use the line-continuation character (_) to do this. When used, the line-continuation character *must* be preceded by a space.
- As you begin typing code, *IntelliSense* lists keywords, class names, members of a class and other features that start with the same characters you've typed so far.
- *IntelliSense* highlights the most commonly used item that matches the characters typed, then displays a tool tip with information about that item. You can either type the complete item name, double click the item name in the list or press the *Tab* or *Space* key to complete the name.
- Once you type a dot (.) after a variable name, the *IntelliSense* window shows the members that can be used on the right of the dot.

- While the *IntelliSense* window is displayed, pressing the *Ctrl* key makes the window transparent so you can see the code behind it. You can display *IntelliSense* by pressing *Ctrl* and the *Spacebar*.

- To run a program, select **DEBUG > Start Debugging** (or press *F5* or the toolbar button ▶). When you run a program, the IDE first compiles it. You can also compile the program without running it by selecting **BUILD > Rebuild Solution**. This creates a new file with the project's name and a .exe file-name extension, which indicates that the file is executable.

- When you type a line of code and press the *Enter* key, the IDE responds either by applying syntax-color highlighting or by generating a syntax error, which indicates a violation of Visual Basic's rules for creating correct programs.

- When a syntax error occurs, the IDE places a blue squiggle below the error and provides a description of the error in the **Error List** window. You can double click an error message in the **Error List** to jump to the line of code that caused the error. For some errors, the IDE shows the **Error Correction Options** drop-down list and allows you to simply click a link to fix the error.

Section 3.3 Addition Program
- A Label's text can be changed programmatically by modifying the Label's Text property.

- Labels that direct the user to take a specific action are called prompts.

- A TextBox's Text property can be used to change the text that's displayed in a TextBox or to get information the user types in a TextBox.

- The user clicks a Button to trigger a specific action. The text displayed on a Button is specified using its Text property.

- Variable declarations begin with keyword Dim and specify identifiers for variables. All variables must be declared before they can be used in a program.

- Types defined as part of the Visual Basic language, such as Integer, are known as primitive types and their type names are keywords.

- A variable name can be any valid identifier.

- The assignment operator (=) is used to give a value to a variable. The expression to the right of the = is always evaluated first before the assignment occurs.

- The string concatenation operator, &, is a binary operator that joins two strings together, resulting in a new, longer string. If one of the operands is a number, the program creates a string representation of the number before performing the concatenation.

Section 3.4 Building the Addition Program
- You can rename a control by modifying its (Name) property.

- Snap lines help you position a control with respect to the Form's edges and other controls.

- Set a Label's BorderStyle property to Fixed3D to give the Label a three-dimensional appearance.

- For a Button, the default event is the Click event.

Section 3.5 Memory Concepts
- Every variable has a name, type, size and value.

- A value placed in a memory location replaces the value previously stored there.

- When a value is read from a memory location, the value is retained unmodified.

Section 3.6 Arithmetic
- Most arithmetic operators are binary operators—they take two operands.

- Unary operators take only one operand. Unary versions of plus (+) and minus (–) are provided, so that you can write expressions such as +9 and –19.

- Integer division (\) takes two Integer operands and yields an Integer result. Any fractional part in an Integer division result is truncated. When floating-point numbers are used with the integer division operator, the numbers are rounded to the nearest whole number, then divided. To divide floating-point numbers without rounding, use the floating-point division operator (/).

- The Mod operator yields the remainder after division.

- Parentheses are used in Visual Basic expressions in the same manner as in algebraic expressions.

- Operators in arithmetic expressions are applied in a precise sequence determined by the rules of operator precedence, which are similar to those in algebra.

- Multiple operators with the same precedence are applied in the order determined by the operators' associativity. Binary operators associate from left to right.

- Operators in expressions contained in parentheses are evaluated before those that are outside the parentheses. Parentheses can be used to change the order of evaluation. With nested parentheses, the operators contained in the innermost pair of parentheses are applied first.

- As in algebra, it's acceptable to place redundant parentheses in an expression to make the expression clearer.

Section 3.7 Decision Making: Equality and Relational Operators

- The If...Then statement allows a program to make a decision based on a condition. If the condition is true, the body statements execute; otherwise, they do not.

- Conditions can be formed by using the equality operators and relational operators. These operators all have the same level of precedence and associate from left to right.

- Assignment and the equality operator both use the = symbol. When a condition is expected, = represents the equality operator.

- To display several lines of text in a TextBox, set its MultiLine property to True.

- TextBox method AppendText adds more text to what is already displayed in a TextBox.

- A method call asks a method to perform its task. Sometimes a method receives values, known as arguments, from its caller—it uses these arguments while performing its task.

- A TextBox's TextChanged event occurs when the text in a TextBox changes. This is the default event for a TextBox.

- TextBox method Clear removes the text that's currently displayed in a TextBox.

- The IDE displays the *Parameter Info* window as you type the opening left parenthesis character, (, in a method call. This window contains information about the method and the information that the method needs to perform its task—its so-called parameters.

Terminology

_ line-continuation character 100
. dot separator 98
* multiplication operator 113
+ addition operator 113
- subtraction operator 113
/ floating-point division operator 113
\ integer division operator 113
& string concatenation operator 105

= assignment operator 98
action 98
AppendText method of a TextBox 120
arithmetic operator 113
argument 120
assignment statement 104
associativity of operators 115
asterisk (*) indicating multiplication 113

binary operator 105
body of a method declaration 97
book-title capitalization 109
BorderStyle property of a Label 110
Button class 103
case sensitive 97
class 96
Class...End Class keywords 96
Clear method of a TextBox 120
comment 96
comparison operators 117
component 94
condition 117
declaration 103
Dim keyword 103
End Class keywords 98
End If keywords 119
End Sub keywords 97
equality operators (=, <>) 117
Error List window 101
event 97
event driven 97
event handler 97
.exe file extension 101
executable file 101
File Name property of a file in the **Solution Explorer** 99
Fixed3D value for BorderStyle property 110
floating-point number 113
flow of control 122
Handles keyword 97
identifier 96
If...Then selection statement 117
Integer primitive type 103
IntelliSense 100
keyword 96
Load event of a Form 97
member of a class 100
method 96

method call 120
MiddleLeft value for TextAlign property 110
Mod (modulus, modulo) operator 113
Name property of a control 105
nested parentheses 115
operand 105
operator precedence 115
output cursor 120
Parameter Info window 121
primitive types 104
procedure 97
prompt 103
property name 98
Public keyword 96
raise an event 97
redundant parentheses 116
relational operators (<, >, <=, >=) 117
rules of operator precedence 115
runtime error 104
sentence-style capitalization 107
single quote character (') 96
snap line 106
statement 98
straight-line form 115
string 98
string literal 98
Sub...End Sub keywords 97
syntax-color highlighting 99
Text property of a TextBox 103
TextBox class 103
TextChanged event 120
unary operator 113
variable 103
variable name 112
variable size 112
variable type 112
variable value 112
whitespace 97
widget 94

Self-Review Exercises

3.1 Answer each of the following questions:

a) The Form's _____ property specifies the text that's displayed in the Form's title bar.

    1. Title   2. Text

    3. (Name)   4. Name

b) Property _____ specifies how text is aligned within a Label's boundaries.

    1. Alignment   2. AlignText

    3. Align   4. TextAlign

c) A `Button`'s text should use _____ capitalization.
    1. book-title   2. complete
    3. no   4. sentence-style

d) An output `Label` should _____.
    1. be distinguishable from other `Label`s
    2. initially have an empty `Text` property or a default value (e.g., 0)
    3. use `Fixed3D` for the `BorderStyle` property
    4. All of the above

e) A `Button`'s _____ property sets the text on the face of the `Button`.
    1. `Name`   2. `Text`
    3. `Title`   4. `Face`

f) If there are errors in an app, they appear in a window known as the _____.
    1. **Task List**   2. **Output**
    3. **Properties**   4. **Error List**

g) When a value is placed into a memory location, the value _____ the previous value in that location.
    1. copies   2. replaces
    3. adds itself to   4. moves

h) When a value is read from memory, that value is _____.
    1. overwritten   2. replaced with a new value
    3. moved to a new location in memory   4. not overwritten

i) Arithmetic expressions in must be written _____ to facilitate entering apps into the computer.
    1. using parentheses   2. on multiple lines
    3. in straight-line form   4. None of the above

j) The expression to the right of an assignment operator (=) is evaluated _____ the assignment occurs.
    1. before   2. after
    3. at the same time   4. None of the above

3.2 State whether each of the following is *true* or *false*. If *false*, explain why.

a) Comments cause the computer to print the text after the ' on the screen when the program executes.

b) All variables must be declared before they can be used in a Visual Basic program.

c) Visual Basic considers the variable names `number` and `NuMbEr` to be different.

d) The arithmetic operators `*`, `/`, `+` and `-` all have the same level of precedence.

e) A string of characters contained between double quotation marks is called a phrase or phrase literal.

f) Integer division yields an `Integer` result.

Answers to Self-Review Exercises

3.1   a) 2. b) 4. c) 1. d) 4. e) 2. f) 4. g) 2. h) 4. i) 3. j) 1.

3.2   a)   False. Comments do not cause any action to be performed when the program executes. They're used to document programs and improve their readability. b) True. c) False. Identifiers are not case sensitive, so these variable names are identical. d) False. The operators `*` and `/` are on the same level of precedence, and the operators `+` and `-` are on a lower level of precedence. e) False. A string of characters is called a string or string literal. f) True.

Quick Quiz

3.3 Answer each of the following questions:

a) A Label's BorderStyle property can be set to _____.

   1. Fixed3D
         2. Single
   3. 3D
         4. All of the above

b) A(n) _____ helps the user understand a control's purpose.

   1. Button
         2. descriptive Label
   3. output Label
         4. title bar

c) A _____ is a control in which the user can enter data from a keyboard.

   1. Button
         2. TextBox
   3. Label
         4. PictureBox

d) A descriptive Label uses _____.

   1. sentence-style capitalization
         2. book-title capitalization
   3. a colon at the end of its text
         4. Both 1 and 3

e) A(n) _____ represents a user action, such as clicking a Button.

   1. statement
         2. event
   3. app
         4. function

f) Code that performs the functionality of an app _____.

   1. normally is provided by the programmer
   2. can never be in the form of an event handler
   3. always creates a graphical user interface
   4. is always generated by the IDE

g) Comments _____.

   1. help improve program readability
   2. are preceded by the single-quote character
   3. are ignored by the compiler
         4. All of the above

h) A(n) _____ contains code that performs a specific task.

   1. variable
         2. method
   3. operand
         4. identifier

i) Visual Basic keywords are _____.

   1. identifiers
         2. reserved words
   3. case sensitive
         4. properties

j) An example of a whitespace character is a _____ character.

   1. space
         2. tab
   3. newline
         4. All of the above

k) Parentheses added to an expression simply to make it easier to read are known as _____ parentheses.

   1. necessary
         2. redundant
   3. embedded
         4. nested

l) The _____ operator performs integer division.

   1. \
         2. +
   3. Mod
         4. ^

m) Every variable has a _____.

   1. name
         2. value
   3. type
         4. All of the above

n) Variable declarations in event handlers begin with the keyword _____.
   1. `Declare`   2. `Dim`
   3. `Sub`   4. `Integer`

o) Entering a value in a TextBox causes a _____ event.
   1. `TextAltered`   2. `ValueChanged`
   3. `ValueEntered`   4. `TextChanged`

p) Variables that store integer values should be declared as an _____.
   1. `Integer`   2. `Int`
   3. `IntVariable`   4. None of the above

q) The data type in a variable declaration is immediately preceded by keyword _____.
   1. `IsA`   2. `Type`
   3. `Dim`   4. `As`

Exercises

3.4 Write Visual Basic statements that accomplish each of the following tasks:
  a) Display the message `"Hello"` in `resultTextBox`.
  b) Assign the product of `hourlySalary` and `hoursWorked` to variable `earnings`.
  c) State that a program performs a sample payroll calculation (that is, use text that helps to document a program).

3.5 *(What does this code do?)* This code modifies variables `number1`, `number2` and `result`. What are the final values of these variables?

```
1  Dim number1 As Integer
2  Dim number2 As Integer
3  Dim result As Integer
4
5  number1 = 5 * (4 + 6)
6  number2 = 2 ^ 2
7  result = number1 \ number2
```

3.6 *(What's wrong with this code?)* Find the error(s) in the following code, which uses variables to perform a calculation.

```
1  Dim number1 As Integer
2  Dim number2 As Integer
3  Dim result As Integer
4
5  number1 = (4 * 6 ^ 4) / (10 Mod 4 - 2)
6  number2 = (16 \ 3) ^ 2 * 6 + 1
7  result = number1 - number2
```

3.7 *(Temperature Converter App)* Write an app that converts a Celsius temperature, *C*, to its equivalent Fahrenheit temperature, *F*. Figure 3.31 displays the completed app. Use the following formula:

$$F = \frac{9}{5}C + 32$$

  a) *Creating the app.* Create a new Windows Forms app named `TemperatureConverter`. Rename its `Form1.vb` file as `TemperatureConverter.vb`. Set the Form's Font property to Segoe UI 9pt and its Text property to `Temperature Converter`.

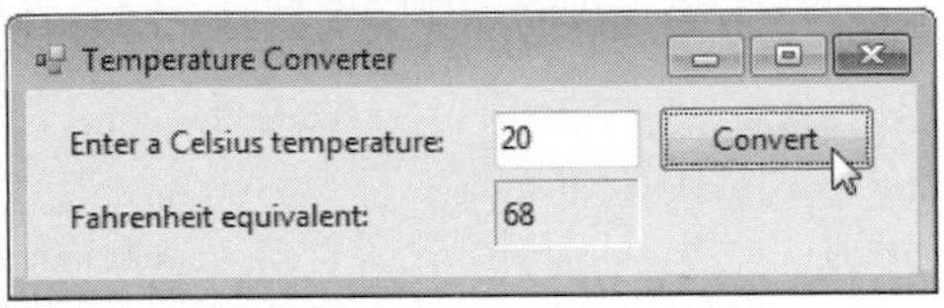

Fig. 3.31 | Completed **Temperature Converter**.

    b) *Coding the Click event handler.* Perform the conversion in the **Convert** Button's Click event handler. Display the Fahrenheit equivalent of the Celsius temperature.

    c) *Clearing the result.* When the user starts typing in the **Enter a Celsius temperature:** TextBox, use the TextBox's TextChanged event to clear the previous result. You can do this by assigning the value String.Empty to the output Label's Text property. String.Empty is equivalent to a string literal with no characters—that is, "".

    d) *Running the app.* Select **DEBUG > Start Debugging** to run your app. Enter the value 20 into the **Enter a Celsius temperature:** TextBox and click the **Convert** Button. Verify that the value 68 is displayed in the output Label. Enter other Celsius temperatures; click the **Convert** Button after each. Verify that the proper Fahrenheit equivalent is displayed each time.

3.8 *(Simple Calculator App)* Write a simple calculator app (Fig. 3.32). The calculator allows a user to enter two integers in the TextBoxes. There are four Buttons labeled +, -, / and *. When the user clicks one of these Buttons, the app performs that operation on the integers in the TextBoxes and displays the result. The calculator also should clear the calculation result when the user enters new input.

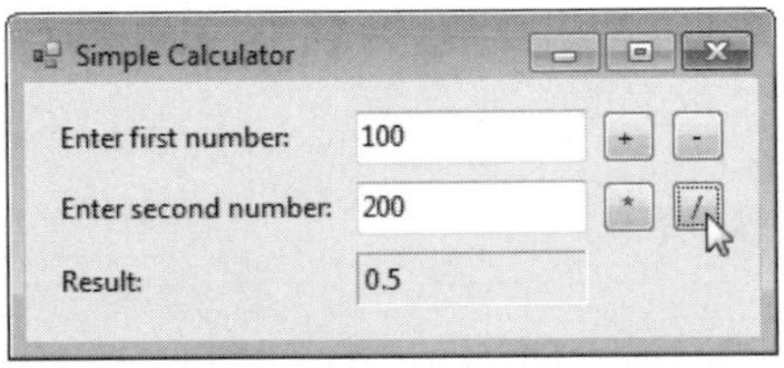

Fig. 3.32 | Result of **Simple Calculator** app.

    a) *Creating the app.* Create a new Windows Forms app named SimpleCalculator. Rename its Form1.vb file as SimpleCalculator.vb. Set the Form's Font property to Segoe UI 9pt and its Text property to Simple Calculator.

    b) *Coding the addition Click event handler.* This event handler should add the two numbers and display the result.

    c) *Coding the subtraction Click event handler.* This event handler should subtract the second number from the first number and display the result.

    d) *Coding the multiplication Click event handler.* This event handler should multiply the two numbers and display the result.

    e) *Coding the division Click event handler.* This event handler should divide the first number by the second number and display the result.

    f) *Clearing the result.* Write event handlers for the TextBoxes' TextChanged events. Write code to clear resultLabel after the user enters new input into either TextBox.

    g) *Running the app.* Run your app. Enter a first number and a second number, then verify that each of the Buttons works by clicking each and viewing the output.

3.9 *(Average Calculator App)* Write an app that takes three numbers as input in TextBoxes, stores the three integers in variables, then calculates and displays the average of the numbers. The output is displayed in a Label. Figure 3.33 shows the completed app.

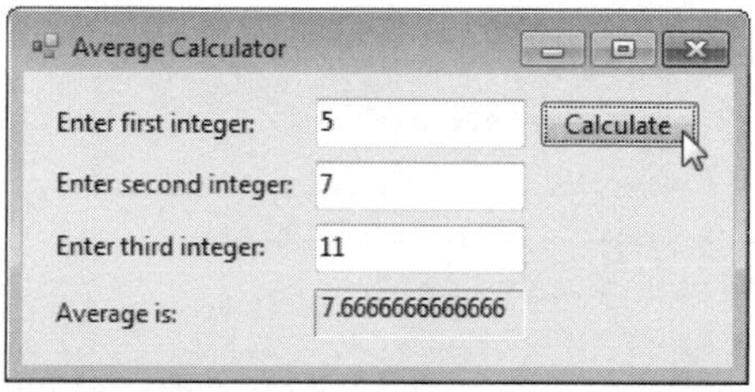

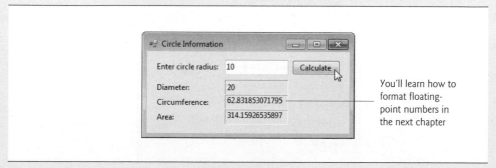

Fig. 3.33 | Result of **Average Calculator** app.

  a) *Creating the app.* Create a new Windows Forms app named AverageCalculator. Rename its Form1.vb file as AverageCalculator.vb. Set the Form's Font property to Segoe UI 9pt and its Text property to Average Calculator.
  b) *Coding the Click event handler.* Perform the average calculation in the **Calculate** Button's Click event handler. Display the average in the resultLabel.
  c) *Clearing the result.* Write event handlers for the TextBoxes' TextChanged events. Write code to clear resultLabel after the user enters new input into any of the TextBoxes.
  d) *Running the app.* Select **DEBUG > Start Debugging** to run your app. Enter three integers, then verify that the average is calculated properly.

Solve Exercises 3.10–3.15 using the same techniques as in Exercises 3.7–3.9.

3.10 *(Diameter, Circumference and Area)* Write an app that inputs from the user the radius of a circle and displays the circle's diameter, circumference and area. Use the following formulas (r is the radius): *diameter* = $2r$, *circumference* = $2\pi r$, *area* = πr^2. Use the predefined constant Math.PI from class Math for π. Figure 3.34 shows the completed app.

You'll learn how to format floating-point numbers in the next chapter

Fig. 3.34 | Completed **Circle Information** app.

3.11 *(Multiples)* Write an app that reads two integers and determines and prints whether the first is a multiple of the second. For example, if the user inputs 15 and 3, the first number is a multiple of the second. If the user inputs 2 and 4, the first number is not a multiple of the second. [*Hint:* Use the Mod operator.] Figure 3.35 shows the completed app.

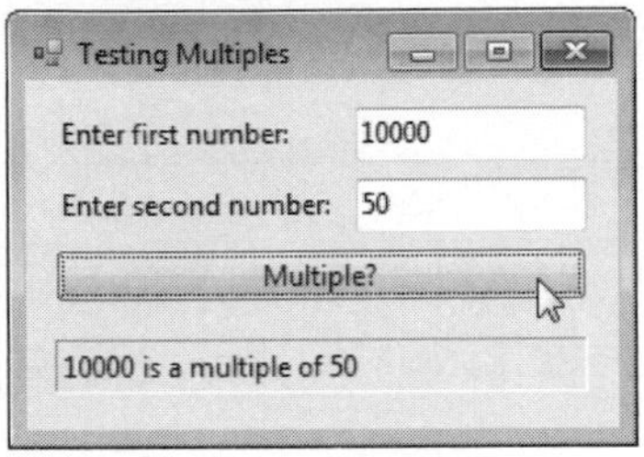

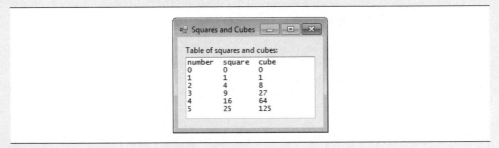

Fig. 3.35 | Completed **Testing Multiples** app.

3.12 *(Displaying Tabular Data)* Write an app that calculates the squares and cubes of the numbers from 0 to 5 and displays the resulting values in table format as shown in Figure 3.36. Set the TextBox's MultiLine property to True and its Font property to the fixed-width font Lucida Console. You can use the Visual Basic constant vbTab to create the tabular output by placing tabs between each column. In Chapter 4, we study repetition, which will make this much easier.

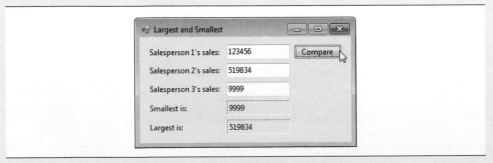

Fig. 3.36 | Displaying tabular data in a TextBox.

3.13 *(Find the Largest and Smallest Sales Figures)* Write an app that reads integers representing the total sales for three sales people then determines and prints the largest and the smallest integers in the group. Figure 3.37 shows the completed app.

![Completed Largest and Smallest app showing Salesperson 1's sales: 123456, Salesperson 2's sales: 519834, Salesperson 3's sales: 9999, Smallest is: 9999, Largest is: 519834, with a Compare button]

Fig. 3.37 | Completed **Largest and Smallest** app.

3.14 *(Concatenating Strings)* Write an app that reads a first name and a last name from the user as two separate inputs and concatenates the first name and last name, separating them by a space. Display the concatenated name in a Label. You can store the user input in variables of type String, a primitive type used to represent string data. Figure 3.38 shows the completed app. You can create variables of type `String` just as you created variables of type `Integer`, except using the keyword `String`:

```
Dim firstName As String
Dim lastName As String
```

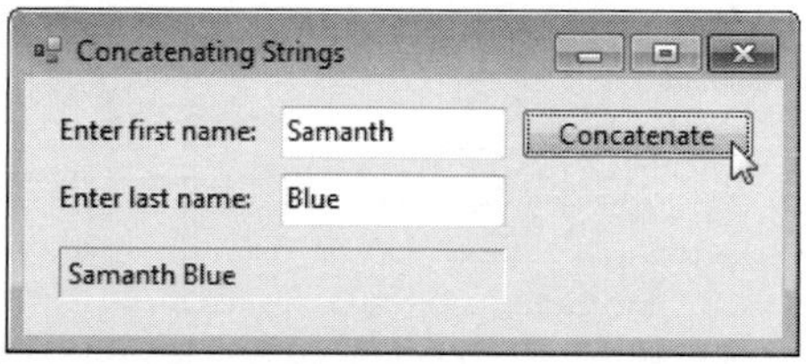

Fig. 3.38 | Completed **Concatenating Strings** app.

3.15   *(Digit Extraction)* Write an app that allows the user to enter a five-digit number into a `TextBox`. The app then separates the number into its individual digits and displays each digit in a separate `Label`. The app should look and behave similarly to Figure 3.39. [*Hint:* You can use the `Mod` operator to extract the ones digit from a number. For instance, 12345 `Mod` 10 is 5. You can use integer division (\) to "peel off" digits from a number. For instance, 12345 \ 100 is 123. This allows you to treat the 3 in 12345 as a ones digit. Now you can isolate the 3 by using the `Mod` operator. Apply this technique to the rest of the digits.]

Fig. 3.39 | Digit Extractor app GUI.

Making a Difference Exercises

3.16   *(CO2 Emissions Calculator)* Whenever your vehicle is using fuel, it produces tailpipe emissions including GHGs (Greenhouse Gases). CO2 is a primary GHG, and the amount of CO2 your vehicle generates depends on the amount and type of fuel used. For every litre of gasoline used, about 2.3 kg of CO2 is produced; for every litre of diesel fuel, about 2.7 kg of CO2 is produced.

Vehicle technology also influences the level of CO2 emissions from a vehicle. For example, a modern diesel vehicle is inherently more fuel efficient than its gasoline equivalent. And for the same distance travelled, a modern diesel vehicle can reduce CO2 emissions by about 20 percent compared with those from a similar gasoline vehicle, even though the per-litre CO2 emissions are higher. Hybrid gasoline-electric vehicles can also reduce CO2 emissions through increased fuel efficiency and reduced fuel use. [Reference: http://oee.nrcan.gc.ca]

Develop an application to estimate annual CO2 emissions, calculated by multiplying the vehicle's estimated annual fuel use by a conversion factor for the type of fuel used.

Figure 3.40 shows the complete application.

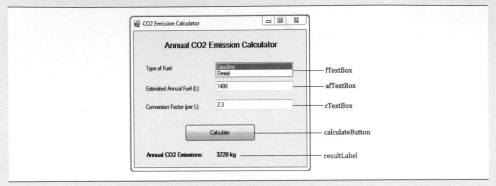

Fig. 3.40 | Annual CO2 emissions Calculator

3.17   *(Fuel Consumption Calculator)* Develop an application to estimate annual fuel use and fuel cost based on an annual driving distance (km) with a mix of percent city driving and percent highway driving. The following formula can be used to calculate estimated annual fuel use and assess potential savings when comparing vehicles:

Annual fuel use (in litres) = $(d \times c \times r)/100 + (d \times h \times s)/100$

d - Annual distance travelled (km)

c - Fraction of city driving.

r - City fuel consumption rating (L/100 km).

h - Fraction of highway driving.

s - Highway fuel consumption rating (L/100 km).

Figure 3.41 shows the completed application.

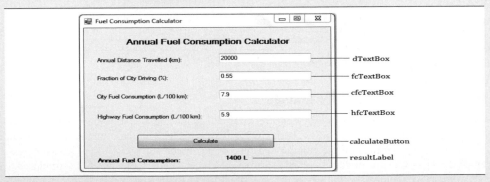

Fig. 3.41 | Annual Fuel Consumption Calculator

Introduction to Problem Solving and Control Statements

4

Let's all move one place on.
—Lewis Carroll

The wheel is come full circle.
—William Shakespeare

How many apples fell on Newton's head before he took the hint?
—Robert Frost

Objectives

In this chapter you'll learn:

- Basic problem-solving techniques.
- To develop algorithms through the process of top-down, stepwise refinement.
- To use the `If...Then` and `If...Then...Else` selection statements to choose among alternative actions.
- To use the `Do While...Loop`, `While...End While` and `Do Until...Loop` repetition statements to execute statements in an app repeatedly.
- To use the compound assignment operators to abbreviate assignment operations.
- To use counter-controlled repetition.
- To use nested control statements.
- To use the debugger to locate logic errors in an app.

4.1 Introduction

Before writing an app to solve a problem, you should have a thorough understanding of the problem and a carefully planned approach. When writing an app, it's also important to know the available building blocks and to use proven program-construction principles. In this chapter and the next, we present the theory and principles of programming with control statements. We introduce the If...Then, If...Then...Else, Do While...Loop, While...End While and Do Until...Loop statements—five of the building blocks that allow you to specify the logic required for methods to perform their tasks. We introduce the ListBox control and use it to display and process data, such as a list of grades in a class-average app. We also demonstrate how to "stack" and "nest" control statement to solve problems. The chapter concludes with an introduction to the Visual Studio debugger. You'll learn how to view the values of variables during a app's execution, how to step through code one statement at a time and how the debugger can help you locate logic errors in your apps.

4.2 Algorithms

Any computing problem can be solved by executing a series of actions in a specific order. A **procedure** for solving a problem, in terms of

    1. the **actions** to be executed and

    2. the **order** in which these actions are to be executed

is called an **algorithm**. The following example demonstrates the importance of getting the order right.

Consider the "rise-and-shine algorithm" followed by one junior executive for getting out of bed and going to work: (1) get out of bed, (2) take off pajamas, (3) take a shower, (4) get dressed, (5) eat breakfast and (6) carpool to work. This routine prepares the executive for a productive day at the office.

However, suppose that the same steps are performed in a slightly different order: (1) get out of bed, (2) take off pajamas, (3) get dressed, (4) take a shower, (5) eat breakfast, (6) carpool to work. In this case, our junior executive shows up for work soaking wet.

Specifying the order in which statements (actions) execute in an app is called **program control**. This chapter investigates program control using **control statements**.

> **Software Engineering Observation 4.1**
>
> *Experience has shown that the most difficult part of solving a problem on a computer is developing the algorithm for the solution. Once a correct algorithm has been specified, the process of producing a working app from the algorithm is normally straightforward.*

4.3 Pseudocode Algorithm

Pseudocode is an informal language that helps you develop algorithms. It's similar to everyday English; it's convenient and user friendly, but *not* an actual computer programming language. The pseudocode we present is particularly useful for developing algorithms that will be converted to Visual Basic apps.

Pseudocode algorithms are not executed on computers. Rather, they help you "think out" an app before writing it in a programming language. You can easily convert a carefully prepared pseudocode algorithm to a corresponding Visual Basic app.

Pseudocode normally describes only the *actions* that occur after you convert an algorithm from pseudocode to Visual Basic and run the app on a computer. Such actions typically include input, output, calculations and decisions.

4.4 Control Structures

Normally, statements in an app are executed one after another in the order in which they're written. This is called **sequential execution**. A **transfer of control** occurs when an executed statement does *not* directly follow the previously executed statement.

During the 1960s, it became clear that the indiscriminate use of transfers of control was causing difficulty for software development groups. A key problem was the **GoTo statement,** which allows you to specify a transfer of control to one of a wide range of possible destinations in a program. The excessive use of GoTo statements caused programs to become quite unstructured and hard to follow—such disorganized programs were referred to as "spaghetti code." Since then, the notion of **structured programming** has become almost synonymous with "GoTo elimination."

Research demonstrated that all programs could be written in terms of only three types of **control structures**—the **sequence structure**, the **selection structure** and the **repetition structure**. The term "control structures" comes from the field of computer science. When we introduce Visual Basic's implementation of control structures, we'll refer to them as "control statements."

Sequence Structure

Unless directed otherwise, the computer executes statements *sequentially*. The UML **activity diagram** in Fig. 4.1 illustrates a sequence structure that performs two calculations in order. You can have as many actions as you want in a sequence structure. Anywhere a single action may be placed, you may place several actions in sequence.

The two statements in Fig. 4.1 involve adding a grade to a `total` variable and adding the value 1 to a `counter` variable. Such statements might appear in a program that takes the average of several student grades. To calculate an average, the total of the grades being

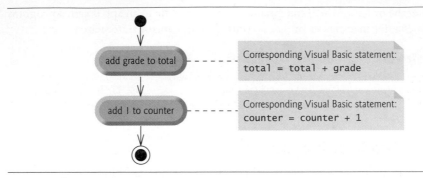

Fig. 4.1 | Sequence-structure activity diagram.

averaged is divided by the number of grades. A counter variable would be used to keep track of the number of values being averaged.

UML Activity Diagrams

Like pseudocode, activity diagrams help you develop and represent algorithms. An activity diagram models the **workflow** (also called the **activity**) of a portion of a software system. A workflow may include a portion of an algorithm, such as the sequence structure in Fig. 4.1. Activity diagrams are composed of special-purpose symbols, such as the **action state symbol** (a rectangle with its left and right sides replaced with arcs curving outward), the **diamond symbol** and the **small circle symbol**; these symbols are connected by **transition arrows**, which represent the flow of the activity.

Activity diagrams clearly show how control structures operate. The sequence-structure activity diagram in Fig. 4.1 contains two **action states** that represent actions to perform. Each action state contains an **action expression**—"add grade to total" or "add 1 to counter"—that specifies a particular *action* to perform. Other actions might include *calculations* or *input/output operations*. The arrows represent **transitions** that indicate the *order* in which the actions occur—the program that implements the activities illustrated by the activity diagram in Fig. 4.1 first adds grade to total, then adds 1 to counter.

The **solid circle symbol** located at the top of the activity diagram represents the activity's **initial state**—the *beginning* of the workflow before the corresponding program performs the activities. The solid circle surrounded by a hollow circle at the bottom of the activity diagram represents the **final state**—the *end* of the workflow after the corresponding program performs its activities.

Figure 4.1 also includes rectangles with the upper-right corners folded over. These are called **notes** in the UML. Notes are optional comments that describe the purpose of symbols in the diagram. A **dotted line** connects each note with the element the note describes.

Each activity diagram contains *one* initial state and *one* final state, which represent the control statement's entry point and exit point, respectively. These **single-entry/single-exit control statements** make it easy to build programs—the control statements are "attached" to one another by "connecting" the exit point of one control statement to the entry point of the next (which we accomplish simply by following one control statement immediately by another). This is similar to stacking building blocks, so we call it **control-statement stacking**. There is only one other way to connect control statements, and that is through **control-statement nesting**, where one control statement is placed *inside* another.

Selection Statements

Visual Basic provides three types of selection statements. You'll soon see examples of each.

- The `If...Then` selection statement either performs (selects) an action (or sequence of actions) if a condition is *true*, or *skips* the action (or sequence of actions) if the condition is *false*. The `If...Then` statement is called a **single-selection statement** because it selects or ignores a single action (or a sequence of actions). Actually, you saw this statement used in Fig. 3.27.

- The `If...Then...Else` selection statement performs an action (or sequence of actions) if a condition is *true*, and performs a *different* action (or sequence of actions) if the condition is *false*. The `If...Then...Else` statement is called a **double-selection statement** because it selects between *two* different actions (or sequences of actions).

- The `Select...Case` selection statement performs one of *many* possible actions (or sequences of actions), depending on the value of an expression. For this reason, the `Select...Case` statement is called a **multiple-selection statement**.

By providing various selection statements, the designers of Visual Basic make it more convenient for you to express certain types of algorithms. Theoretically, however, you need *only one* selection statement that enables you to make a decision—`If...Then`.

Repetition Statements

Visual Basic provides seven types of repetition statements (also called **looping statements** or **loops**) that enable programs to perform statements repeatedly based on the value of a condition. You'll soon see examples of each.

- The `Do While...Loop` and `While...End While` **repetition statements** execute a set of statements while a condition—known as the **loop-continuation condition**—remains *true*. If the condition is initially *false*, the set of statements does *not* execute.

- The `Do Until...Loop` repetition statement executes a set of statements until a condition—known as the **loop-termination condition**—becomes *true*. If the condition is initially *true*, the set of statements does *not* execute.

- The `Do...Loop While` repetition statement executes a set of statements while its loop-continuation condition remains *true*. The set of statements is *guaranteed* to execute at least once.

- The `Do...Loop Until` repetition statement executes a set of statements until its loop-termination condition becomes *true*. The set of statements is *guaranteed* to execute at least *once*.

- The `For...Next` repetition statement executes a set of statements a specified number of times—this is known as *counter-controlled* (or *definite*) *repetition*.

- The `For Each...Next` repetition statement (introduced in Chapter 7) performs a set of statements for every element of a so-called array or collection of values.

The words `If`, `Then`, `Else`, `End`, `Select`, `Case`, `While`, `Do`, `Until`, `Loop`, `For`, `Next` and `Each` are all keywords. By providing many repetition statements, the designers of Visual Basic make it more convenient for you to express certain types of algorithms. Theoretically, however, you need *only one* repetition statement that enables you to loop zero or more times based on the truth or falsity of a condition—both Do While...Loop and While...End While allow you to do this. In this book, we typically use the Do While...Loop, For...Next and For Each... Next repetition statements.

4.5 If...Then Selection Statement

A selection statement chooses among alternative courses of action. Suppose that the passing grade on an examination is 60 (out of 100). Then the pseudocode statement

> *If student's grade is greater than or equal to 60 then*
> *Display "Passed"*

determines whether the condition "student's grade is greater than or equal to 60" is *true* or *false*. If the condition is *true*, then "Passed" is displayed, and the next pseudocode statement in order is "performed" (remember that pseudocode is not a real programming language). If the condition is *false*, the display statement is ignored, and the next pseudocode statement in order is "performed."

The preceding pseudocode *If* statement may be written in Visual Basic as

```
If studentGrade >= 60 Then
    resultLabel.Text = "Passed" ' display "Passed"
End If
```

The code corresponds closely to the pseudocode, showing the usefulness of pseudocode as a program-development tool. The statement in the body of the If...Then statement displays the string "Passed" in resultLabel.

Whitespace
The compiler ignores whitespace, such as spaces, tabs and blank lines used for indentation and vertical spacing, unless the whitespace is contained in strings. Some whitespace is required, however, such as the space between variable names and keywords. You can insert extra whitespace characters to enhance app readability.

Single Line If... Then statement
The preceding If...Then selection statement also could be written on a single line as

```
If studentGrade >= 60 Then resultLabel.Text = "Passed"
```

In the multiple-line format, all statements (there can be many) in the If...Then's body execute if the condition is *true*. In the single-line format, only the statement immediately after the Then keyword executes if the condition is *true*.

UML Activity Diagram for the If... Then Selection Statement
Figure 4.2 is an activity diagram for the single-selection If...Then statement. It contains what is perhaps the most important symbol in an activity diagram—the diamond, or **decision symbol**, which indicates that a decision is to be made. A decision symbol indicates that the workflow will continue along a path determined by the symbol's associated **guard conditions**, which can be *true* or *false*. Each transition arrow emerging from a decision symbol has a guard condition (specified in square brackets above or next to the transition arrow). If a particular guard condition is true, the workflow enters the action state to which that transition arrow points. Exactly *one* of the guard conditions associated with a decision

symbol must be *true* when a decision is made. In Fig. 4.2, if the grade is greater than or equal to 60, the app displays "Passed" on the screen, then transitions to the final state of this activity. If the grade is less than 60, the program immediately transitions to the final state without displaying a message.

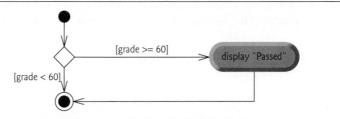

Fig. 4.2 | If...Then single-selection statement activity diagram.

4.6 If...Then...Else Selection Statement

The If...Then...Else selection statement allows you to specify that a *different* action (or sequence of actions) is to be performed when the condition is *true* than when the condition is *false*. For example, the pseudocode statement

> *If student's grade is greater than or equal to 60 then*
>   *Display "Passed"*
> *Else*
>   *Display "Failed"*

displays "Passed" if the student's grade is greater than or equal to 60, and displays "Failed" if the student's grade is less than 60. In either case, after the display occurs, the next pseudocode statement in sequence is "performed."

The preceding pseudocode *If...Else* statement may be written in Visual Basic as

```
If studentGrade >= 60 Then
    resultLabel.Text = "Passed" ' display "Passed"
Else
    resultLabel.Text = "Failed" ' display "Failed"
End If
```

The body of the **Else** clause is indented so that it lines up with the body of the If clause.

UML Activity Diagram for the If...Then...Else Selection Statement
Figure 4.3 illustrates the flow of control in the If...Then...Else statement.

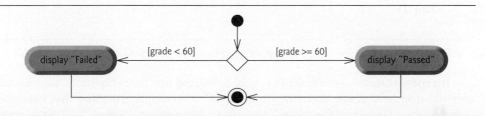

Fig. 4.3 | If...Then...Else double-selection statement activity diagram.

4.7 Nested If...Then...Else Selection Statements

Nested If...Then...Else statements test for multiple conditions by placing If...Then ...Else statements *inside* other If...Then...Else statements. For example, the pseudocode in Fig. 4.4 displays "A" for exam grades greater than or equal to 90, "B" for grades in the range 80–89, "C" for grades in the range 70–79, "D" for grades in the range 60–69 and "F" for all other grades. The pseudocode may be written in Visual Basic as shown in Fig. 4.5.

```
 1   If student's grade is greater than or equal to 90 then
 2       Display "A"
 3   Else
 4       If student's grade is greater than or equal to 80 then
 5           Display "B"
 6       Else
 7           If student's grade is greater than or equal to 70 then
 8               Display "C"
 9           Else
10               If student's grade is greater than or equal to 60 then
11                   Display "D"
12               Else
13                   Display "F"
```

Fig. 4.4 | Pseudocode for nested If...Then...Else statements that display a letter grade based on a numeric grade value.

```
 1   If studentGrade >= 90 Then
 2       resultLabel.Text = "A" ' display "A"
 3   Else
 4       If studentGrade >= 80 Then
 5           resultLabel.Text = "B" ' display "B"
 6       Else
 7           If studentGrade >= 70 Then
 8               resultLabel.Text = "C" ' display "C"
 9           Else
10               If studentGrade >= 60 Then
11                   resultLabel.Text = "D" ' display "D"
12               Else
13                   resultLabel.Text = "F" ' display "F"
14               End If
15           End If
16       End If
17   End If
```

Fig. 4.5 | nested If...Then...Else statements that correspond to the pseudocode in Fig. 4.4.

If studentGrade is greater than or equal to 90, the first four conditions are *true*, but only the statement at line 2 executes (causing "A" to be displayed). After that statement executes, the Else part of the "outer" If...Then...Else statement (line 3–17) is skipped, and the program proceeds with the next statement after the last End If.

ElseIf

Most programmers prefer to write the nested If...Then...Else statements from Fig. 4.5 using the **ElseIf** keyword as shown in Fig. 4.6. Both forms are equivalent, but the latter is popular because it avoids deeply indenting the code and makes it more readable. In nested If...Then...Else statements, if you type Else If on one line, the Visual Basic editor will automatically convert it to ElseIf and indent the code as in Fig. 4.6.

```
 1   If grade >= 90 Then
 2       resultLabel.Text = "A" ' display "A"
 3   ElseIf grade >= 80 Then
 4       resultLabel.Text = "B" ' display "B"
 5   ElseIf grade >= 70 Then
 6       resultLabel.Text = "C" ' display "C"
 7   ElseIf grade >= 60 Then
 8       resultLabel.Text = "D" ' display "D"
 9   Else
10       resultLabel.Text = "F" ' display "F"
11   End If
```

Fig. 4.6 | Nested If...Then...Else statements from Fig. 4.5 reimplemented using ElseIf.

4.8 Repetition Statements

A **repetition statement** (also called a looping statement, an iteration statement or a loop) allows you to specify that an action should be repeated, depending on the value of a *loop-continuation condition* or a *loop-termination condition*. The pseudocode statements

> *While there are more items on my shopping list*
>   *Put next item in cart*
>   *Cross it off my list*

describe the repetitive actions on a shopping trip. The loop-continuation condition "there are more items on my shopping list" can be *true* or *false*. If it's *true*, the actions "Put next item in cart" and "Cross it off my list" are performed. These actions execute repeatedly while the condition remains *true*. The statement(s) contained in the *While* repetition statement constitute the body of the *While*. Eventually, the condition becomes *false* (when the last remaining item on the shopping list has been purchased and crossed off the list). Then, the repetition terminates, and the first statement after the repetition statement executes.

*Performing a Calculation in a **Do While...Loop** Repetition Statement*
Consider an app segment designed to find the first power of 3 larger than 100. Suppose that the Integer variable product is initialized to 3. When the following Do While...Loop statement finishes executing, product contains the result:

```
Do While product <= 100
    product = product * 3 ' compute next power of 3
Loop
```

When the Do While...Loop statement begins execution, product is 3. The body statement repeatedly multiplies product by 3, so it takes on the values 3, 9, 27, 81 and 243, successively. When product becomes 243, the condition product <= 100 becomes false. This *ter-*

minates the repetition with 243 as product's final value. Then, execution continues with the next statement after the keyword Loop. If the condition in a Do While...Loop is initially false, the body statement(s) do not execute.

UML Activity Diagram for the **Do While...Loop** *Repetition Statement*

The activity diagram of Fig. 4.7 illustrates the preceding Do While...Loop statement's flow of control. Once again, the symbols in the diagram (besides the initial state, transition arrows, a final state and three notes) represent an action state and a decision. This diagram also introduces the UML's **merge symbol**, which joins two activity flows into one. The UML represents *both* the merge symbol *and* the decision symbol as diamonds (this can be confusing). In this diagram, the merge symbol *joins* the transitions from the initial state and the action state, so they *both* flow into the decision that determines whether the loop should begin (or continue) executing. The decision and merge symbols can be distinguished by the number of incoming and outgoing transition arrows. A decision symbol has *one* transition arrow pointing *to* the diamond and *two* or more transition arrows pointing out *from* the diamond to indicate possible transitions from that point. In addition, each transition arrow pointing out of a decision symbol has a guard condition next to it (exactly *one* of which must be *true* when a decision is made). A merge symbol has *two* or more transition arrows pointing *to* the diamond and only *one* transition arrow pointing *from* the diamond, to indicate multiple activity flows merging to continue the activity. The transition arrows associated with a merge symbol do *not* have guard conditions.

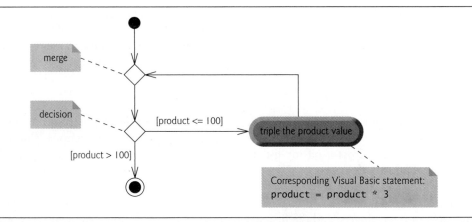

Fig. 4.7 | Do While...Loop repetition statement activity diagram.

Figure 4.7 clearly shows the repetition of the preceding Do While...Loop statement. The transition arrow emerging from the action state connects back to the merge, which transitions back to the decision that's tested each time through the loop until the guard condition product > 100 becomes true. Then the Do While...Loop statement exits (reaches its final state) and control passes to the next statement in sequence.

Common Programming Error 4.1

Failure to provide the body of a Do While...Loop statement with an action that eventually causes the loop-continuation condition to become false is a logic error. Normally, such a repetition statement never terminates, resulting in a logic error called an "infinite loop."

Error-Prevention Tip 4.1
Whereas syntax errors are caught by the compiler, logic errors affect the program only at execution time. A fatal logic error causes a program to fail and terminate prematurely (or "hang" in an infinite loop). A nonfatal logic error does not terminate a program's execution but causes the program to produce incorrect results.

`While...End While` *Repetition Statement*

The `While...End While` repetition statement behaves identically to the `Do While...Loop` repetition statement, so their activity diagrams are also identical. The following `While...End While` statement reimplements the preceding `Do While...Loop`:

```
While product <= 100
   product = product * 3 ' compute next power of 3
End While
```

`Do Until...Loop` *Repetition Statement*

Unlike the preceding repetition statements, the `Do Until...Loop` repetition statement executes its body statement(s) repeatedly as long as the condition (known as the **loop-termination condition**) evaluates to *false*. You can write the preceding `Do While...Loop` statement as a `Do Until...` Loop statement as follows:

```
Do Until product > 100
   product = product * 3 ' compute next power of 3
Loop
```

The activity diagram of Fig. 4.7 also illustrates the flow of control in the preceding statement; however, we focus on the *leftmost* guard condition—`product > 100`—the *loop-termination condition* for our control statement. Because we're using a `Do Until...Loop` statement, the statement's action is performed when the statement's loop-termination condition is *false* (that is, `product` is less than or equal to 100). When the loop-termination condition (`product > 100`, the leftmost guard condition) is *true*, the statement exits. If the condition in a `Do Until...Loop` is *initially true*, the body statement(s) do *not* execute. In general, you can use a `Do While...Loop` statement with the condition expressed differently (in this case `product <= 100`), rather than using a `Do Until...Loop`.

4.9 Compound Assignment Operators

The **compound assignment operators** enable you to *abbreviate* assignment statements. For example, the statement

```
value = value + 3
```

which mentions the variable `value` on *both* sides of the assignment, can be abbreviated with the **addition assignment operator, +=** as

```
value += 3
```

The `+=` operator adds the value of the *right* operand to the value of the *left* operand and stores the result in the *left* operand's variable. Figure 4.8 summarizes the compound assignment operators.

Compound assignment operator	Sample expression	Explanation	Assigns
Assume: c = 4, d = "He"			
+=	c += 7	c = c + 7	11 to c
-=	c -= 3	c = c - 3	1 to c
*=	c *= 4	c = c * 4	16 to c
/=	c /= 2	c = c / 2	2 to c
\=	c \= 3	c = c \ 3	1 to c
^=	c ^= 2	c = c ^ 2	16 to c
&=	d &= "llo"	d = d & "llo"	"Hello" to d

Fig. 4.8 | Compound assignment operators.

The variable on the left side of an assignment operator must be an *lvalue* ("left value")—a modifiable variable or property that can appear on the *left* side of an assignment statement. We'll learn how to declare constants in Section 6.10—constants *cannot* be *lvalues*.

The =, +=, -=, *=, /=, \=, ^= and &= operators are always applied *last* in an expression. When an assignment (=) is evaluated, the expression to the *right* of the operator is always evaluated first, then the value is assigned to the *lvalue* on the *left*. When a compound assignment is evaluated, the appropriate operator is applied to the *lvalue*'s original value and the value to the operator's *right*, then the resulting value is assigned to the *lvalue* on the *left*.

Demonstrating the ^= Compound Assignment Operator

Figure 4.9 calculates a power of 2 using the exponentiation assignment operator. In line 8, we take advantage of a Visual Basic feature that allows variable initialization to be incorporated into a declaration. In this case, we initialize variable exponent to the value of exponentTextBox's Text property. Lines 12 and 17 each raise variable result to the value of variable exponent. The results of these two calculations are identical as shown in the sample output.

```
1    ' Fig. 4.9: PowerOf2.vb
2    ' Calculates 2 raised to the exponent entered by the user.
3    Public Class PowerOf2
4       ' calculates 2 raised to the exponent entered by the user.
5       Private Sub calculateButton_Click(sender As Object,
6          e As EventArgs) Handles calculateButton.Click
7
8          Dim exponent As Integer = exponentTextBox.Text ' get the exponent
9          Dim result As Integer ' stores the calculation result
10
11         result = 2 ' number to raise to a power
12         result ^= exponent ' same as result = result ^ exponent
```

Fig. 4.9 | Exponentiation using a compound assignment operator. (Part 1 of 2.)

```
13        resultLabel.Text = "result = 2" & vbCrLf &
14          "result ^= " & exponent & ": " & result & vbCrLf & vbCrLf
15
16        result = 2 ' reset result to 2 for next calculation
17        result = result ^ exponent ' same as result ^= exponent
18        resultLabel.Text &= "result = 2" & vbCrLf &
19          "result = result ^ " & exponent & ": " & result
20     End Sub ' calculateButton_Click
21
22     ' clear results when user types in the exponentTextBox
23     Private Sub exponentTextBox_TextChanged(sender As Object,
24       e As EventArgs) Handles exponentTextBox.TextChanged
25       resultLabel.Text = String.Empty ' clears the resultLabel's text
26     End Sub ' exponentTextBox_TextChanged
27  End Class ' PowerOf2
```

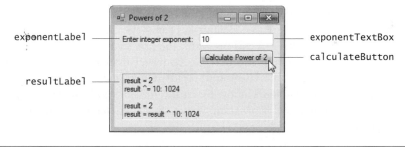

Fig. 4.9 | Exponentiation using a compound assignment operator. (Part 2 of 2.)

4.10 Formulating Algorithms: Counter-Controlled Repetition

To illustrate how algorithms are developed, we solve a problem that averages student grades. Consider the following problem statement:

> *A class of students took a quiz. The grades (integers in the range 0 to 100) for this quiz are available to you. Determine the class average on the quiz.*

The class average is equal to the sum of the grades divided by the number of students. The algorithm for solving this problem on a computer must input each grade, keep track of the total of all grades input, perform the averaging calculation and display the result.

GUI for the Class-Average App

Figure 4.10 shows this's GUI. For this example, we introduce the **ListBox control**, which we use to display the grades the user enters and to manipulate those grades to perform the class-average calculation. Each grade that the user enters into the program by pressing the **Submit Grade** Button is placed in the ListBox. We calculate the class average when the user presses the **Calculate Average** Button. We also provide a **Clear Grades** Button to remove all the grades from the ListBox and clear the results, so the user can enter a new set of grades.

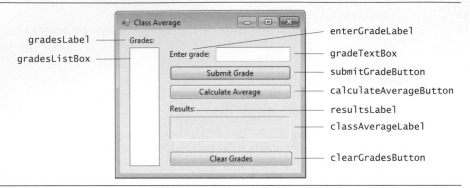

Fig. 4.10 | GUI for the class-average problem.

Setting the *Form's* Default Button

When you execute this program, notice that the **Submit Grade** Button has a blue highlight around it. This Button is the Form's **default Button**—the one that will be pressed when the user presses the *Enter* key. In this program, the user can type a value in the TextBox and press *Enter* to press the **Submit Grade** Button rather than clicking it with the mouse. This convenience feature enables the user to rapidly enter grades. You can specify a Form's default Button in the **Properties** window by setting the Form's **AcceptButton property** to the appropriate Button. For this program, we set the AcceptButton property to the submitGradeButton.

Pseudocode Algorithm with Counter-Controlled Repetition

Let's use pseudocode to list the actions to execute and specify the order of execution for calculating the class average. After the user enters the grades and presses the **Calculate Average** Button, we use **counter-controlled repetition** to get the grades from the ListBox and process them one at a time. This technique uses a variable called a **counter** (or **control variable**) to specify the number of times that a set of statements will execute. This is also called **definite repetition** because the number of repetitions is known *before* the loop begins executing. In this example, repetition terminates when the counter exceeds the number of grades in the ListBox. Figure 4.11 presents a fully developed pseudocode algorithm and Fig. 4.12 presents the app that implements the algorithm. In the next section, you'll learn how to develop pseudocode algorithms and convert them to Visual Basic. (In Exercise 4.15, you'll use counter-controlled repetition to output a table of values.)

---

1 *Set total to zero*
2 *Set grade counter to zero*
3
4 *While grade counter is less than the number of grades*
5   *Get the next grade*
6   *Add the grade into the total*
7   *Add one to the grade counter*

Fig. 4.11 | Pseudocode algorithm that uses counter-controlled repetition to solve the class-average problem. (Part 1 of 2.)

8
9   *If the grade counter is not equal to zero then*
10   *Set the class average to the total divided by the number of grades*
11   *Display the class average*
12   *Else*
13   *Display "No grades were entered"*

Fig. 4.11 | Pseudocode algorithm that uses counter-controlled repetition to solve the class-average problem. (Part 2 of 2.)

Note the references in the pseudocode algorithm (Fig. 4.11) to a total and a counter. A total is a variable used to accumulate the sum of several values. A counter is a variable used to count—in this case, the grade counter records the number of grades entered by the user. It's important that variables used as totals and counters have appropriate initial values before they're used. Counters usually are initialized to 0 or 1, depending on their use. Totals generally are initialized to 0. Numeric variables are initialized to 0 when they're declared, unless another value is assigned to the variable in its declaration.

Software Engineering Observation 4.2

Many algorithms can be divided logically into an initialization phase *that initializes the program variables, a* processing phase *that inputs data values and adjusts program variables accordingly and a* termination phase *that calculates and displays the results.*

In the pseudocode, we add 1 to the grade counter only in the body of the loop (line 7). If the user does not enter any grades, the condition *"grade counter is less than the number of grades"* (line 4) will be *false* and grade counter will be zero when we reach the part of the algorithm that calculates the class average. We test for the possibility of *division by zero*—a logic error that, if undetected, would cause the app to fail.

Error-Prevention Tip 4.2

When performing division by an expression whose value could be zero, explicitly test for this case and handle it appropriately in your program. Such handling could be as simple as displaying an error message. Sometimes more sophisticated processing is required, such as using the exception-handling techniques introduced in Chapter 7.

Implementing Counter-Controlled Repetition

The ClassAverage class (Fig. 4.12) defines the Click event handlers for the submitGradeButton, calculateAverageButton and clearGradesButton. The calculateAverageButton_Click method (lines 19–49) implements the class-averaging algorithm described by the pseudocode in Fig. 4.11.

Method submitGradeButton_Click

When the user presses the **Submit Grade** Button, method submitGradeButton_Click (lines 5–16) obtains the value the user typed and places it in the gradesListBox. Line 9 first ensures that the gradeTextBox is *not empty* by comparing its Text property to the constant String.Empty. This prevents the app from inserting an empty string in the ListBox, which would cause the app to *fail* when it attempts to process the grades. This is the beginning of our efforts to validate data entered by the user. In later chapters, we'll ensure that the data is *in range* (for example, an Integer representing a month needs to be in the range 1–12) and that data meets various other criteria. For this program, we assume that the user enters *only* Integer values—*noninteger* values could cause the program to fail when the grades are processed.

```vbnet
1   ' Fig. 4.12: ClassAverage.vb
2   ' Counter-controlled repetition: Class-average problem.
3   Public Class ClassAverage
4      ' place a grade in the gradesListBox
5      Private Sub submitGradeButton_Click(sender As Object,
6         e As EventArgs) Handles submitGradeButton.Click
7
8         ' if the user entered a grade
9         If gradeTextBox.Text <> String.Empty Then
10           ' add the grade to the end of the gradesListBox
11           gradesListBox.Items.Add(gradeTextBox.Text)
12           gradeTextBox.Clear() ' clear the gradeTextBox
13        End If
14
15        gradeTextBox.Focus() ' gives the focus to the gradeTextBox
16     End Sub ' submitGradeButton_Click
17
18     ' calculates the class average based on the grades in gradesListBox
19     Private Sub calculateAverageButton_Click(sender As Object,
20        e As EventArgs) Handles calculateAverageButton.Click
21
22        Dim total As Integer ' sum of grades entered by user
23        Dim gradeCounter As Integer ' counter for grades
24        Dim grade As Integer ' grade input by user
25        Dim average As Double ' average of grades
26
27        ' initialization phase
28        total = 0 ' set total to zero before adding grades to it
29        gradeCounter = 0 ' prepare to loop
30
31        ' processing phase
32        Do While gradeCounter < gradesListBox.Items.Count
33           grade = gradesListBox.Items(gradeCounter) ' get next grade
34           total += grade ' add grade to total
35           gradeCounter += 1 ' add 1 to gradeCounter
36        Loop
37
38        ' termination phase
39        If gradeCounter <> 0 Then
40           average = total / gradesListBox.Items.Count ' calculate average
41
42           ' display total and average (with two digits of precision)
43           classAverageLabel.Text = "Total of the " & gradeCounter &
44              " grade(s) is " & total & vbCrLf & "Class average is " &
45              String.Format("{0:F}", average)
```

Fig. 4.12 | Counter-controlled repetition: Class-average problem. (Part 1 of 2.)

```
46          Else
47              classAverageLabel.Text = "No grades were entered"
48          End If
49      End Sub ' calculateAverageButton_Click
50
51      ' clear grades from gradeListBox and results from classAverageLabel
52      Private Sub clearGradesButton_Click(sender As Object,
53          e As EventArgs) Handles clearGradesButton.Click
54
55          gradesListBox.Items.Clear() ' removes all items from gradesListBox
56          classAverageLabel.Text = String.Empty ' clears classAverageLabel
57      End Sub ' clearGradesButton_Click
58  End Class ' ClassAverage
```

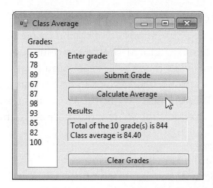

Fig. 4.12 | Counter-controlled repetition: Class-average problem. (Part 2 of 2.)

If the gradeTextBox is not empty, line 11 uses the ListBox's **Items property** to add the grade to the ListBox. This property keeps track of the values in the ListBox. To place a new item in the ListBox, call the Items property's Add method, which adds the new item at the end of the ListBox. Line 12 then clears the value in the gradeTextBox so the user can enter the next grade. Line 15 calls the gradeTextBox's **Focus** method, which makes the TextBox the **active control**—the one that will respond to the user's interactions. This allows the user to immediately start typing the next grade, without clicking the TextBox.

Method calculateAverageButton_Click; Introducing Type Double and Floating-Point Numbers

Method calculateAverageButton_Click (lines 19–49) uses the algorithm in Fig. 4.11 to calculate the class average and display the results. Lines 22–24 declare variables total, gradeCounter and grade to be of type Integer. Line 25 declares variable average to be of type Double. Although each grade is an Integer, the average calculation uses division, so it's likely to produce a number with a *fractional result*. Such numbers (like 84.4) contain decimal points and are called **floating-point numbers**. Type **Double** is typically used to store floating-point numbers. All the floating-point numbers you type in a program's source code (such as 7.33 and 0.0975) are treated as Double values by default and are known as **floating-point literals**. Values of type Double are represented approximately in memory. For precise calculations, such as those used in financial calculations, Visual Basic provides type Decimal (discussed in Section 5.4).

Variable total accumulates the sum of the grades entered. Variable gradeCounter helps us determine when the loop at lines 32–36 should terminate. Variable grade stores the most recent grade value obtained from the ListBox (line 33). Variable average stores the average grade (line 40).

Local Variables

The declarations (in lines 22–25) appear in the body of method calculateAverage-Button_Click. Variables declared in a method body are called *local variables* and can be used only from their declaration until the end of the method declaration. A local variable declared in a control statement can be used only until the end of that control statement. A local variable's declaration must appear *before* the variable is used in that method. A local variable cannot be accessed *outside* the method in which it's declared.

Looping Through the **ListBox** Items

The assignments (in lines 28–29) initialize total and gradeCounter to 0. Line 32 indicates that the Do While...Loop statement should continue looping (also called **iterating**) while gradeCounter's value is less than the ListBox's number of items. ListBox property Items keeps track of the ListBox's items. You can access the number of items via the expression gradesListBox.Items.**Count**. While this condition remains *true*, the Do While... Loop statement repeatedly executes the statements in its body (lines 33–35).

Accessing a **ListBox** Item

Line 33 reads a grade from the ListBox and assigns it to the variable grade. Each value in the ListBox's Items property has a position number associated with it—this is known as the item's **index**. For example, in the sample output of Fig. 4.12, the grade 65 is at index 0, 78 is at index 1, 89 is at index 2, and so on. The index of the last item is always one less than the total number of items represented by the ListBox's Items.Count property. To get the value at a particular index, we use the expression:

```
gradesListBox.Items(gradeCounter)
```

in which gradeCounter's current value is the index.

Adding **grade** to **total** and Incrementing **gradeCounter**

Line 34 adds the new grade entered by the user into the variable total using the += compound assignment operator. Line 35 adds 1 to gradeCounter to indicate that the program has processed another grade and is ready to input the next grade from the user. Incrementing gradeCounter eventually causes the loop to terminate when the condition gradeCounter < gradesListBox.Items.Count becomes false.

Displaying the Average

When the loop terminates, the If...Then...Else statement at lines 39–48 executes. Line 39 determines whether any grades have been entered. If so, line 40 performs the averaging calculation using the floating-point division operator (/) and stores the result in Double variable average. If we used the integer division operator (\), the class average would *not* be as precise because any *fractional part* of the average would be *discarded*. For example, 844 divided by 10 is 84.4, but with integer division the result would be 84. Lines 43–45 display the results in the classAverageLabel. If no grades were entered, line 47 displays a message in the classAverageLabel.

Method `clearGradesButton_Click`

When the user presses the **Clear Grades** Button, method `clearGradesButton_Click` (lines 52–57) prepares for the user to enter a new set of grades. First, line 55 removes the grades from the `gradesListBox` by calling the `Item`'s property's **Clear method**. Then, line 56 clears the text on the `classAverageLabel`.

Control Statement Stacking

In this example, we see that control statements may be stacked on top of one another (that is, placed in sequence) just as a child stacks building blocks. The `Do While...Loop` statement (lines 32–36) is followed in sequence by an `If...Then...Else` statement (lines 39–48).

Formatting for Floating-Point Numbers

The statement in lines 43–45 outputs the class average. In this example, we decided to display the class average rounded to the nearest hundredth and to output the average with exactly two digits to the right of the decimal point. To do so, we used the expression

```
String.Format("{0:F}", average)
```

which indicates that `average`'s value should be displayed as a number with a specific number of digits to the *right* of the decimal point—called a **fixed-point number**. This is an example of **formatted output**, in which you control how a number appears for display purposes. The `String` class's **Format method** performs the formatting. The first argument to the method (`"{0:F}"`) is the format string, which acts as a placeholder for the value being formatted. The numeric value that appears before the colon (in this case, 0) indicates which of `Format`'s arguments will be formatted—0 specifies the first argument *after* the format string passed to `Format`, namely `average`. As you'll see in later examples, additional values can be inserted into the string to specify other arguments. The value after the colon (in this case, F) is known as a **format specifier**, which indicates how a value is to be formatted. The format specifier **F** indicates that a fixed-point number should be rounded to *two decimal places* by default. The entire placeholder (`{0:F}`) is replaced with the formatted value of variable `average`. You can change the number of decimal places to display by placing an integer value after the format specifier—for example, the string `"{0:F3}"` rounds the number to three decimal places.

4.11 Formulating Algorithms: Nested Control Statements

We've seen that control statements can be stacked on top of one another (in sequence). We now examine the only other structured way that control statements can be combined—by *nesting* one control statement *inside* another.

Problem Statement and Notes

Consider the following problem statement:

> *A college offers a course that prepares students for the state real estate broker licensing exam. Last year, 10 of the students who completed this course took the exam. The college wants to know how well its students did. You've been asked to write a program to summarize the results. You've been given a list of the 10 students. Next to each name is written a "P" if the student passed the exam and an "F" if the student failed the exam.*
>
> *Your program should analyze the results of the exam as follows:*

1. *Input each exam result (that is, a "P" or an "F").*
2. *Count the number of passes and the number of failures.*
3. *Display a summary of the exam results, indicating the number of students who passed and the number who failed.*
4. *If more than eight students passed the exam, display the message "Bonus to Instructor."*

After reading the problem statement carefully, we make the following observations:

1. The program must process exam results for 10 students. A *counter-controlled loop* can be used because the number of test results is known in advance.

2. Each exam result is a *string*—either a "P" or an "F." When the program reads an exam result, it must determine whether the result is a "P" or an "F." We test for a "P" in our algorithm. If the input is not a "P," we *assume* it's an "F." Exercise 4.13 considers the consequences of this assumption. For instance, consider what happens when the user enters a lowercase "p" or a "$."

3. Two *counters* store the exam results—one counts the number of students who passed the exam and the other counts the number of students who failed.

4. After the program has processed all the exam results, it must determine whether *more than eight* students passed the exam, and, if so, bonus the instructor.

GUI for the Licensing-Exam Analysis App

Figure 4.13 shows this app's GUI. Each result is placed in the ListBox when the user presses the **Submit Result** Button. We process all 10 results when the user presses the **Analyze Results** Button. We also provide a **Clear Results** Button to reset the GUI so the user can enter a new set of results. As in the previous example, we used the Form's AcceptButton property to set the **Submit Result** Button as the default Button. We disabled the **Analyze Results** Button initially by setting its **Enabled** property to False.

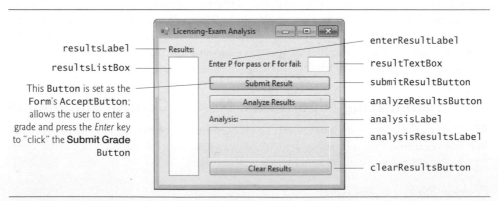

Fig. 4.13 | GUI for the licensing-exam analysis problem.

Developing the Pseudocode Algorithm with Top-Down, Stepwise Refinement: The Top and the First Refinement

We approach this program with **top-down, stepwise refinement**, a technique for developing well-structured algorithms. We begin with a pseudocode representation of the **top**—a single statement that conveys the overall function of the program:

Analyze exam results and decide if the instructor should receive a bonus

The top is a *complete* representation of a program. Unfortunately, the top rarely conveys enough *detail* from which to write a program, so we conduct the refinement process. We *divide* the top into a series of *smaller* tasks and list them in the order in which they must be performed, resulting in the following **first refinement**:

> *Initialize variables*
> *Input the 10 exam results, and count passes and failures*
> *Display a summary of the exam results and decide if the instructor should*
> *   receive a bonus*

Proceeding to the Second Refinement
To proceed to the **second refinement**, we commit to specific variables. In this example, counters are needed to record the passes and failures. A counter controls the looping process and a variable stores the user input. The pseudocode statement

> *Initialize variables*

can be refined as follows:

> *Initialize passes to zero*
> *Initialize failures to zero*
> *Initialize student to zero*

Only the counters for the number of passes, number of failures and number of students need to be initialized before they're used. The variable we use to store each value the user enters does not need to be initialized because the assignment of its value does *not* depend on its previous value, as is the case for the counter variables.

The pseudocode statement

> *Input the 10 exam results, and count passes and failures*

requires a repetition statement (that is, a loop) that successively inputs the result of each exam. We know in advance that there are 10 exam results, so *counter-controlled looping* is appropriate. Inside the loop (that is, *nested* inside the loop), a *double-selection statement* will determine whether each exam result is a pass or a failure and will increment the appropriate counter. The refinement of the preceding pseudocode statement is then

> *While student counter is less than or equal to 10*
> *   Get the next exam result*
>
> *   If the student passed then*
> *   Add one to passes*
> *   Else*
> *   Add one to failures*
>
> *   Add one to student counter*

Note the use of *blank lines* to set off the *If...Else* control statement to improve readability.

The pseudocode statement

> *Display a summary of the exam results and decide if the instructor should*
> *   receive a bonus*

may be refined as follows:

Display the number of passes
Display the number of failures

If more than eight students passed then
  Display "Bonus to instructor!"

Complete Second Refinement of Pseudocode

The complete second refinement of the pseudocode appears in Fig. 4.14. Blank lines are also used to set off the *While* loop (lines 5–13) for readability. This pseudocode is now sufficiently refined for conversion to Visual Basic.

Software Engineering Observation 4.3

Each refinement, including the top, is a complete *version of the algorithm; only the level of detail in each refinement varies.*

1	*Initialize passes to zero*
2	*Initialize failures to zero*
3	*Initialize student to zero*
4	
5	*While student counter is less than or equal to 10*
6	*Get the next exam result*
7	
8	*If the student passed then*
9	*Add one to passes*
10	*Else*
11	*Add one to failures*
12	
13	*Add one to student counter*
14	
15	*Display the number of passes*
16	*Display the number of failures*
17	
18	*If more than eight students passed then*
19	*Display "Bonus to instructor!"*

Fig. 4.14 | Pseudocode for examination-results problem.

Class Analysis

The app that implements the pseudocode algorithm and the sample outputs are shown in Fig. 4.15. We defined the Click event handlers for the submitResultButton, analyzeResultsButton and clearResultsButton. The analyzeResultsButton_Click method (lines 24–55) implements the class-averaging algorithm described by the pseudocode in Fig. 4.14.

```
1    ' Fig. 4.15: Analysis.vb
2    ' Nested control statements: Examination-results problem.
3    Public Class Analysis
```

Fig. 4.15 | Nested control statements: Examination-results problem. (Part 1 of 3.)

```vb
 4     ' place a result in the resultsListBox
 5     Private Sub submitResultButton_Click(sender As Object,
 6        e As EventArgs) Handles submitResultButton.Click
 7
 8        If resultsListBox.Items.Count < 10 Then
 9           ' add the grade to the end of the resultsListbox
10           resultsListBox.Items.Add(resultTextBox.Text)
11           resultTextBox.Clear() ' clear the resultTextBox
12           resultTextBox.Focus() ' select the resultTextBox
13        End If
14
15        ' determine whether to prevent the user from entering more results
16        If resultsListBox.Items.Count = 10 Then
17           submitResultButton.Enabled = False ' disables submitResultButton
18           resultTextBox.Enabled = False ' disables resultTextBox
19           analyzeResultsButton.Enabled = True ' enable analyzeResultsButton
20        End If
21     End Sub ' submitResultButton_Click
22
23     ' analyze the results
24     Private Sub analyzeResultsButton_Click(sender As Object,
25        e As EventArgs) Handles analyzeResultsButton.Click
26
27        ' initializing variables in declarations
28        Dim passes As Integer = 0 ' number of passes
29        Dim failures As Integer = 0 ' number of failures
30        Dim student As Integer = 0 ' student counter
31        Dim result As String ' one exam result
32
33        ' process 10 students using counter-controlled loop
34        Do While student < 10
35           result = resultsListBox.Items(student) ' get a result
36
37           ' nested control statement
38           If result = "P" Then
39              passes += 1 ' increment number of passes
40           Else
41              failures += 1 ' increment number of failures
42           End If
43
44           student += 1 ' increment student counter
45        Loop
46
47        ' display exam results
48        analysisResultsLabel.Text =
49           "Passed: " & passes & vbCrLf & "Failed: " & failures & vbCrLf
50
51        ' raise tuition if more than 8 students passed
52        If passes > 8 Then
53           analysisResultsLabel.Text &= "Bonus to instructor!"
54        End If
55     End Sub ' analyzeResultsButton_Click
56
```

Fig. 4.15 | Nested control statements: Examination-results problem. (Part 2 of 3.)

```
57     ' clears the resultsListBox and analysisResultsLabel
58     Private Sub clearResultsButton_Click(sender As Object,
59        e As EventArgs) Handles clearResultsButton.Click
60
61        resultsListBox.Items.Clear() ' removes all items
62        analysisResultsLabel.Text = String.Empty ' clears the text
63        submitResultButton.Enabled = True ' enables submitResultButton
64        resultTextBox.Enabled = True ' enables resultTextBox
65        analyzeResultsButton.Enabled = False ' disables analyzeResultsButton
66        resultTextBox.Focus() ' select the resultTextBox
67     End Sub ' clearResultsButton_Click
68  End Class ' Analysis
```

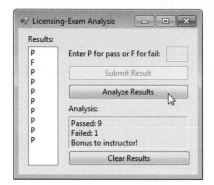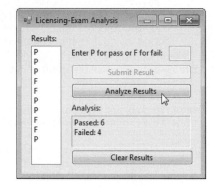

Fig. 4.15 | Nested control statements: Examination-results problem. (Part 3 of 3.)

Method *submitResultButton_Click*

When the user presses **Submit Result**, method submitResultButton_Click (lines 5–21) executes. The problem statement specified that the user can enter only 10 results, so we need to keep track of the number of results that have been entered. Since the ListBox property Items keeps track of the ListBox's total number of items, we use its Count property in line 8 to determine whether 10 results have been entered. If not, line 10 adds the next result to the ListBox, line 11 clears the TextBox and line 12 gives the TextBox the focus so the user can enter the next result. The last result entered could have been the 10th result (line 16). If so, lines 17–18 disable the submitResultButton and the resultTextBox by setting their Enabled properties to False. This prevents the user from interacting with these two controls, so the user cannot enter more than 10 results. Line 19 enables analyzeResultsButton by setting its Enabled property to True so the user can tell the program to analyze the results.

Method *analyzeResultsButton_Click*

Method analyzeResultsButton_Click (lines 24–55) uses the algorithm in Fig. 4.14 to calculate the class average and display the results. Lines 28–31 declare the variables the algorithm uses to process the examination results. Several of these declarations incorporate *variable initialization*—passes, failures and student are all initialized to 0.

The Do While...Loop statement (lines 34–45) loops 10 times. During each iteration, the loop inputs and processes one exam result from the ListBox. The If...Then...Else statement (lines 38–42) for processing each result is nested in the Do While...Loop statement. If the result is "P", the If...Then...Else statement increments passes; otherwise, it assumes the `result` is "F" and increments `failures`. Strings are *case sensitive* by default—uppercase and lowercase letters are *different*. Only "P" represents a passing grade. In Exercise 4.13, we ask you to enhance the program by processing lowercase inputs such as "p" and "f".

Line 44 increments `student` before the loop condition is tested again at line 34. After 10 values have been processed, the loop terminates and lines 48–49 display the number of `passes` and `failures`. The `If...Then` statement at lines 52–54 determines whether more than eight students passed the exam and, if so, displays "Bonus to instructor!". In the first sample execution, the condition at line 52 is `True`—more than eight students passed the exam, so the program outputs the bonus message.

Method `clearResultsButton_Click`

When the user presses the **Clear Results** Button, method `clearResultsButton_Click` (lines 58–67) prepares for the user to enter a new set of results. Line 61 removes the results from the `resultsListBox` by calling the `Item` property's `Clear` method. Line 62 clears the text on the `analysisResultsLabel`. Lines 63 and 64 *enable* the `submitResultButton` and the `resultTextBox` by setting their `Enabled` properties to `True`—the user can now interact with these controls again. Line 65 *disables* the `analyzeResultsButton` by setting its `Enabled` property to `False` so the user cannot click it. Line 66 gives the focus to the `resultTextBox` so the user can begin typing the next result immediately.

4.12 Using the Debugger: Locating a Logic Error

You'll now begin learning about the Visual Basic 2012 Express tools that can help you find and correct logic errors (also called **bugs**). Such errors *do not* prevent a program from compiling successfully, but can cause a running program to produce incorrect results. Visual Studio includes a tool called a **debugger** that can be used to monitor the execution of your programs so you can locate and remove *logic* errors. A program must successfully compile before it can be used in the debugger. Some of the debugger's features include:

- *suspending program execution* so you can *step through* the program one statement at a time
- *examining* and *setting* variable values
- *watching* the values of variables and expressions
- viewing the *order* in which methods are called

To illustrate some of the debugger's capabilities, let's use a modified version of the class-average program from Fig. 4.12. In the modified version (located in the `Debugging` folder with this chapter's examples), the condition in line 32 uses the `<=` rather than the `<` operator. This bug causes the loop in `calculateAverageButton_Click` to execute its statements one extra time. The program fails at line 33 when it attempts to access a grade that does *not* exist. The modified event handler is shown in Fig. 4.16.

```
18    ' calculates the class average based on the grades in gradesListBox
19    Private Sub calculateAverageButton_Click(sender As Object,
20      e As EventArgs) Handles calculateAverageButton.Click
21
```

Fig. 4.16 | Modified `calculateAverageButton_Click` event handler that contains a logic error. (Part 1 of 2.)

```
22     Dim total As Integer ' sum of grades entered by user
23     Dim gradeCounter As Integer ' counter for grades
24     Dim grade As Integer ' grade input by user
25     Dim average As Double ' average of grades
26
27     ' initialization phase
28     total = 0 ' set total to zero before adding grades to it
29     gradeCounter = 0 ' prepare to loop
30
31     ' processing phase
32     Do While gradeCounter <= gradesListBox.Items.Count
33         grade = gradesListBox.Items(gradeCounter) ' get next grade
34         total += grade ' add grade to total
35         gradeCounter += 1 ' add 1 to gradeCounter
36     Loop
37
38     ' termination phase
39     If gradeCounter <> 0 Then
40         average = total / gradesListBox.Items.Count ' calculate average
41
42         ' display total and average (with two digits of precision)
43         classAverageLabel.Text = "Total of the " & gradeCounter &
44             " grade(s) is " & total & vbCrLf & "Class average is " &
45             String.Format("{0:F}", average)
46     Else
47         classAverageLabel.Text = "No grades were entered"
48     End If
49 End Sub ' calculateAverageButton_Click
```

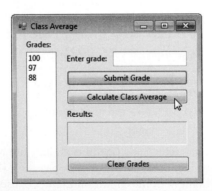

Fig. 4.16 | Modified `calculateAverageButton_Click` event handler that contains a logic error. (Part 2 of 2.)

The Off-By-One Logic Error

Execute this program with **Debug > Start Debugging** (or by pressing *F5* or the toolbar button ▶). Enter several grades and press the **Calculate Class Average** Button. The program does not display the class average. Rather, you get a dialog showing a runtime error known as an `InvalidArgument`. This indicates that the argument in parentheses at line 33 (grade-Counter) is invalid—in this case, it's *out of range*. As you'll soon see, gradeCounter's value is one higher than the index of the last grade in the gradesListBox, so the program attempts to *get a value that does not exist*. This *logic error*—commonly known as an **off-by-one error**—is frequently caused by using the incorrect relational operator in a loop's condition. The debugger also highlights the line of code (line 33) that caused the problem.

In the following steps, you'll use various debugger commands to examine the values of the variables used in the calculateAverageButton_Click event handler and to study the flow of control in the Do While...Loop repetition statement. This will help us locate and correct the logic error.

4.12.1 Breakpoints and Running the Program

Breakpoints are markers that you can set at any *executable* line of code. When a running program reaches a breakpoint, *execution pauses*, allowing you to examine the values of variables to help determine whether logic errors exist. For example, you can examine the value of a variable that stores a calculation's result to determine whether the calculation was performed correctly. You can also examine the value of an expression. Once the debugger pauses program execution, you can use various debugger commands to execute the program *one statement at a time*—this is called *single stepping* or simply *stepping*. We'll examine the code in the averageButton_Click event handler. Before proceeding, if you ran the program to cause the logic error, stop the debugger by selecting **Debug > Stop Debugging**.

Inserting a Breakpoint
To insert a breakpoint, left click in the **margin indicator bar** (the gray margin at the left of the code window in Fig. 4.17) next to line 28, or right click in line 28 and select **Breakpoint > Insert Breakpoint**. Additionally, you can click a line of code then press *F9* to toggle a breakpoint on and off for that line of code. You may set as many breakpoints as you like. A solid circle appears in the margin indicator bar where you clicked and the entire code statement is highlighted, indicating that a breakpoint has been set.

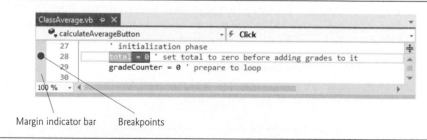

Fig. 4.17 | Breakpoint set at line 28.

Running the Program in Debug Mode
After setting breakpoints in the code editor, select **Debug > Start Debugging** (or press the *F5* key) to rebuild the program and begin the debugging process. Enter the grades 100, 97 and 88, then press the **Calculate Class Average** button. When the debugger reaches line 28 (the line that contains the breakpoint), it suspends execution and enters **break mode** (Fig. 4.18). At this point, the IDE becomes the *active window*. The yellow arrow to the left of line 28—called the **instruction pointer**—indicates that this line contains the next statement to execute. The IDE also *highlights* the line as well to emphasize the line that is about to execute.

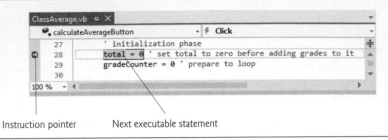

Instruction pointer   Next executable statement

Fig. 4.18 | Program execution suspended at the first breakpoint.

4.12.2 *Data Tip* Box

In break mode, you can place the mouse cursor over any variable and its value will be displayed in a *Data Tip* box (Fig. 4.19). This can help you spot logic errors.

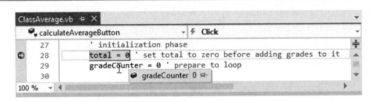

Fig. 4.19 | *Data Tip* box displays value of variable gradeCounter.

4.12.3 Locals Window

In break mode, you can also explore the values of a method's local variables using the debugger's **Locals** window (Fig. 4.20). To view the **Locals** window, select **Debug > Windows > Locals**. Recall that all variables in Visual Basic get initialized, so even though lines 28–29 have not executed yet, variables total and gradeCounter currently have the value 0 (the default for Integer variables). In Fig. 4.20, we call out only the variables declared in lines 22–25.

 Good Programming Practice 4.1

Explicitly initialize variables rather than relying on default initialization. This makes your programs more readable and easier to understand.

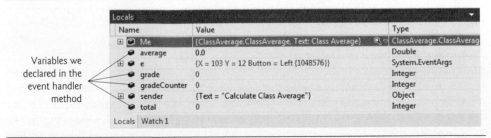

Fig. 4.20 | Locals window showing the values of the variables in the event-handler method calculateAverageButton_Click.

4.12.4 Using the Step Over Command to Execute Statements

You'll now execute the program one statement at a time using the debugger's **Step Over command.** You can access this command by selecting **Debug > Step Over,** by pressing *F10* or by pressing the **Step Over** command's toolbar icon (⨌). Do this *twice* now. The instruction pointer arrow now points to the Do While…Loop statement's first line. If you position the mouse over the word Count in gradesListBox.Items.Count (Fig. 4.21), you can see in the *Data Tip* window that the number of items in the ListBox is 3. Similarly, you can place the mouse over variable gradeCounter to see that its value is currently 0.

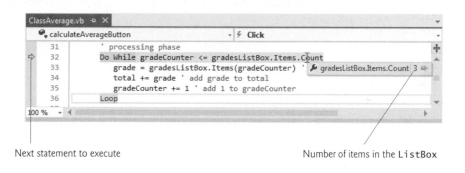

Next statement to execute   Number of items in the ListBox

Fig. 4.21 | Stepping over a statement in the calculateAverageButton_Click method.

At this point in the program's execution, the user *cannot* add more items to the ListBox because we've *disabled* the TextBox and Button that allow the user to enter a grade, so gradesListBox.Items.Count will remain as 3. Thus, the loop should execute the statements at lines 33–35 a total of three times to process the three grades.

First Iteration of the Loop
Since gradeCounter's value is less than or equal to 3, the condition in line 32 is *true*. Thus, when you use the **Step Over** command again, the instruction pointer moves to line 33 in the loop's body. Now use the **Step Over** command to execute line 33. The first item in the ListBox (100) is assigned to variable grade, which you can see in the *Data Tip* box and in the **Locals** window. Whenever a variable's value is modified as a result of the last statement to execute, the **Locals** window highlights that value in red.

Now, **Step Over** lines 34 and 35 to add the grade to the total and to add 1 to the gradeCounter. The instruction pointer is now aimed at line 36. When you use the **Step Over** command now, the instruction pointer moves back to the top of the loop so the condition can be tested again.

Second Iteration of the Loop
Variable gradeCounter's value is now 1, so the condition is *still true*, thus the loop's body will execute again. Use the **Step Over** command *five* times to step through this iteration of the loop, which adds the grade 97 to the total, increments gradeCounter to 2 and positions the instruction counter at the top of the loop.

Third Iteration of the Loop

Variable gradeCounter's value is now 2, so the condition is *still true*, thus the loop's body will execute again so we can process the last grade. Use the **Step Over** command five times to step through this iteration of the loop, which adds the grade 88 to the total, increments gradeCounter to 3 and positions the instruction counter at the top of the loop.

Fourth Iteration of the Loop

At this point, we've processed all three grades and the loop should terminate. However, gradeCounter's value is 3, which is less than *or equal to* 3. The condition is *still* true—even though we are done processing the three grades. Thus, the loop will attempt to process another grade, even though one does not exist. This is the logic error. When you **Step Over** line 33 again, you get the error.

Fixing the Logic Error

Stepping through the program in this manner enables you to see that the loop's body executes *four* times when it should only execute *three* times. So we can focus on the loop's condition as the source of the logic error, because the condition determines when the loop should stop executing. To correct the error, click **Break** in the dialog that appeared, then stop the debugger by selecting **Debug > Stop Debugging**, then edit the code by changing the <= operator in line 32 to a < operator. You can then test the program again to ensure that it's executing properly. To execute the program without the breakpoints, you can:

1. *Disable each breakpoint* by right clicking in the line of code with the breakpoint and selecting **Breakpoint > Disable Breakpoint**, then run the program;

2. *Remove each breakpoint* by right clicking the breakpoint and selecting **Delete Breakpoint**, then run the program; or

3. *Execute the program without debugging* by pressing *Ctrl + F5*.

4.13 Wrap-Up

This chapter presented basic problem-solving techniques that you use to build apps. We demonstrated how to develop an algorithm in pseudocode, evolving it through several refinements until it's ready to be translated to Visual Basic code that can be executed. This process is called top-down, stepwise refinement.

You learned that only three types of control structures—sequence, selection and repetition—are needed to develop an algorithm. We demonstrated the If...Then single-selection statement and the If...Then...Else double-selection statement. The If...Then statement is used to execute an action (or sequence of actions) based on a condition—if the condition is true, the statements execute; if it's false, the statements are skipped. The If...Then...Else double-selection statement is used to execute one set of statements if a condition is *true*, and another set if the condition is false.

We discussed the Do While...Loop and While...End While repetition statements that execute sets of statements repeatedly as long as a loop-continuation condition remains true. We discussed the Do Until...Loop repetition statement, where a set of statements executes repeatedly as long as a loop-termination condition remains false. You studied the UML activity diagrams that represent each control statement presented in the chapter.

We introduced compound assignment operators, which can be used for abbreviating assignment statements. We used control-statement stacking to compute a class average with counter-controlled repetition then display the results, and we used control-statement nesting to analyze and make decisions based on a set of exam results. You also learned how to use the debugger to view the values of variables during program execution and to step through a program to help locate a logic error. In Chapter 5, Problem Solving and Control Statements: Part 2, we present additional selection and repetition statements.

Summary

Section 4.2 Algorithms
- Computing problems are solved by executing actions in a specific order.
- An algorithm is a procedure for solving a problem in terms of the actions to be executed and the order in which these actions are to be executed.
- Program control refers to the task of ordering a program's statements correctly.

Section 4.3 Pseudocode Algorithm
- Pseudocode is an informal language that helps you develop algorithms and "think out" an app before attempting to write it in a programming language.
- Carefully prepared pseudocode can be converted easily to a corresponding Visual Basic app.

Section 4.4 Control Structures
- Normally, statements in an app execute sequentially in the order in which they're written.
- Various Visual Basic statements enable you to specify that the next statement to be executed might not be the next one in sequence. This is called a transfer of control.
- All apps can be written in terms of the sequence, selection and repetition structures.
- The sequence structure is built into Visual Basic. Unless directed otherwise, the computer executes Visual Basic statements one after the other in the order in which they're written.
- A UML activity diagram models the workflow (also called the activity) of a software system.
- Like pseudocode, activity diagrams help you develop and represent algorithms.
- An action state is represented as a rectangle with its left and right sides replaced by arcs curving outward. An action expression appears inside the action state.
- The arrows in an activity diagram represent transitions that indicate the order in which the actions represented by action states occur.
- The solid circle in an activity diagram represents the initial state—the beginning of the workflow before the program performs the modeled actions.
- The solid circle surrounded by a hollow circle in an activity diagram represents the final state—the end of the workflow after the program performs its actions.
- UML notes are optional explanatory remarks that describe the purpose of symbols in the diagram. A dotted line connects each note with the element that it describes.
- Single-entry/single-exit control statements make it easy to build apps.
- In control-statement stacking, the control statements are attached to one another by connecting the exit point of one control statement to the entry point of the next.
- In control-statement nesting, one control statement is placed inside another.

- The If...Then single-selection statement selects or ignores an action (or group of actions) based on the truth or falsity of a condition.

- The If...Then...Else double-selection statement selects between two different actions (or groups of actions) based on the truth or falsity of a condition.

- A multiple-selection statement selects among many different actions or groups of actions.

- The Do While...Loop and While...End While repetition statements execute a set of statements while a loop-continuation condition remains true. If the condition is initially false, the set of statements does not execute.

- The Do Until...Loop repetition statement executes a set of statements until a loop-termination condition becomes true. If the condition is initially true, the set of statements does not execute.

- The Do...Loop While repetition statement executes a set of statements while its loop-continuation condition remains true. The set of statements is guaranteed to execute at least once.

- The Do...Loop Until repetition statement executes a set of statements until a loop-termination condition becomes true. The set of statements is guaranteed to execute at least once.

- The For...Next repetition statement executes a set of statements a specified number of times.

- The For Each...Next repetition statement performs a set of statements for every element of a an array or collection of values.

Section 4.5 If...Then Selection Statement
- Syntax errors are caught by the compiler. Logic errors affect the app only at execution time. Fatal logic errors cause an app to fail and terminate prematurely. Nonfatal logic errors do not terminate an app's execution but cause the app to produce incorrect results.

- The diamond or decision symbol in an activity diagram indicates that a decision is to be made. A decision symbol indicates that the workflow will continue along a path determined by the symbol's associated guard conditions, which can be true or false.

- Each transition arrow emerging from a decision symbol has a guard condition (specified in square brackets above or next to the transition arrow). If a particular guard condition is true, the workflow enters the action state to which that transition arrow points.

Section 4.6 If...Then...Else Selection Statement
- The If...Then...Else selection statement allows you to specify that a different action (or sequence of actions) is to be performed when the condition is true than when the condition is false.

Section 4.7 Nested If...Then...Else Selection Statements
- Nested If...Then...Else statements test for multiple conditions by placing If...Then...Else statements inside other If...Then...Else statements.

- Keyword ElseIf can be used in nested If...Then...Else statements to make them more readable.

Section 4.8 Repetition Statements
- The UML's merge symbol joins two flows of activity into one flow of activity. The UML represents both the merge symbol and the decision symbol as diamonds.

- The Do While...Loop repetition statement allows you to specify that an action is to be repeated while a specific condition remains true.

- Eventually, the loop-continuation condition in a Do While...Loop statement becomes false. At this point, the repetition terminates, and continues with the next statement in sequence.

- Failure to provide the body of a Do While...Loop statement with an action that eventually causes the loop-continuation condition to become false is a logic error. Normally, such a repetition statement never terminates, resulting in an error called an "infinite loop."

- The `While...End While` repetition statement operates identically to `Do While...Loop`.
- Statements in the body of a `Do Until...Loop` are executed repeatedly as long as the loop-termination condition evaluates to false.

Section 4.9 Compound Assignment Operators
- Visual Basic provides the compound assignment operators +=, -=, *=, /=, \=, ^= and &= for abbreviating assignment statements.

Section 4.10 Formulating Algorithms: Counter-Controlled Repetition
- Many algorithms can be divided logically into an initialization phase, a processing phase and a termination phase.
- The `ListBox` control can be used to display a list of values that your program manipulates.
- A `Form`'s default `Button` is the one that will be pressed when the user presses the *Enter* key and is specified by setting the `Form`'s `AcceptButton` property to the appropriate `Button`.
- Counter-controlled repetition uses a variable called a counter (or control variable) to specify the number of times that a set of statements will execute. Counter-controlled repetition also is called definite repetition because the number of repetitions is known before the loop begins executing.
- Variables used as totals and counters should be initialized before they're used. Counters usually are initialized to 0 or 1, depending on their use. Totals generally are initialized to 0.
- Numeric variables are initialized to 0 when they're declared, unless another value is assigned to the variable in its declaration.
- A `ListBox`'s `Items` property keeps track of the values in the `ListBox`. To place a new item in a `ListBox`, call the `Items` property's `Add` method.
- Calling a control's `Focus` method makes the control the active control—the one that will respond to the user's interactions.
- Type `Double` is typically used to store floating-point numbers. Floating-point literals in an app's source code are treated as `Double` values by default.
- Local variables can be used only from their declaration until the end of the method declaration or control statement in which they're declared. A local variable's declaration must appear before the variable is used in that method.
- `ListBox` property `Items.Count` keeps track of the `ListBox`'s number of items.
- Each value in a `ListBox` has a position number associated with it—this is known the item's index.
- For a `ListBox`, calling the `Item`'s property's `Clear` method removes all the items in the `ListBox`.
- Formatted output allows you to control how a number appears for display purposes. The `String` class's `Format` method performs formatting.
- In the format string "{0:F}", the numeric value that appears before the colon indicates which of `Format`'s arguments will be formatted—0 specifies the first argument *after* the format string passed to `Format`. The F is as a format specifier which indicates that a fixed-point number should be rounded to two decimal places by default.

Section 4.11 Formulating Algorithms: Nested Control Statements
- Control statements can be stacked or nested within one another.
- Top-down, stepwise refinement is a technique for developing algorithms.
- The top is a single statement that conveys the overall function of the app. As such, the top is a complete representation of an app.

- Through the process of refinement, we divide the top into a series of smaller tasks, listed in the order in which they must be performed. Each refinement, including the top, is a complete specification of the algorithm; only the level of detail in each refinement varies.

- You terminate the top-down, stepwise refinement process when the pseudocode algorithm is specified in sufficient detail for the pseudocode to be converted to a Visual Basic app.

Section 4.12 Using the Debugger: Locating a Logic Error

- Logic errors are also called bugs. Such errors do not prevent an app from compiling successfully, but can cause a running app to produce incorrect results.

- Visual Studio's debugger can be used to monitor the execution of your apps so you can locate and remove logic errors.

- An off-by-one error is often caused by using the incorrect relational operator in a loop condition.

- Breakpoints can be set at any executable line of code.

- Once the debugger pauses app execution, you can use various debugger commands to execute the app one statement at a time—this is called "single stepping" or simply "stepping."

- To insert a breakpoint, left click in the margin indicator bar or select **Breakpoint > Insert Breakpoint**. You can also click a line of code then press *F9* to toggle a breakpoint on and off.

- After setting breakpoints in the code editor, select **Debug > Start Debugging** (or press the *F5* key) to rebuild the app and begin the debugging process.

- When the debugger reaches a breakpoint, it suspends execution and enters break mode. A yellow instruction-pointer arrow in the IDE indicates the next statement to execute.

- While in break mode, you can place the mouse cursor over any variable and its value will be displayed in a *Data Tip* box. You can also explore the values of a method's local variables using the debugger's **Locals** window. To view the **Locals** window, select **Debug > Windows > Locals**.

- To execute an app one statement at a time, use the **Step Over** command. You can access this command by selecting **Debug > Step Over** or by pressing the **Step Over** command's toolbar icon (↷).

Terminology

Self-Review Exercises

4.1   Answer each of the following questions.

    a) _____ refer(s) to the task of ordering an apps's statements correctly.

        1. Actions   2. Program control

        3. Control structures   4. Visual programming

    b) A(n) _____ is a plan for solving a problem in terms of the actions to be executed and the order in which these actions are to be executed.

        1. chart   2. control structure

        3. algorithm   4. ordered list

    c) _____ is an informal language that helps you develop algorithms.

        1. Pseudocode   2. VB-Speak

        3. Notation   4. None of the above

d) Pseudocode _____.

1. usually describes only declarations
2. is executed on computers
3. usually describes only executable lines of code
4. usually describes declarations and executable lines of code

e) All Visual Basic apps can be written in terms of _____ types of control structures.

1. one
2. two
3. three
4. four

f) The process of app statements executing one after another in the order in which they are written is called _____.

1. transfer of control
2. sequential execution
3. workflow
4. None of the above

g) Which of the following If...Then statements correctly displays that a student received an A on an exam if the score was 90 or above?

1.
```
If studentGrade <> 90 Then
    displayLabel.Text = "Student received an A"
End If
```
2.
```
If studentGrade > 90 Then
    displayLabel.Text = "Student received an A"
End If
```
3.
```
If studentGrade = 90 Then
    displayLabel.Text = "Student received an A"
End If
```
4.
```
If studentGrade >= 90 Then
    displayLabel.Text = "Student received an A"
End If
```

h) The symbol _____ is not a Visual Basic operator.

1. *
2. ^
3. %
4. <>

i) If...Then...Else is a _____-selection statement.

1. single
2. double
3. triple
4. nested

j) Placing an If...Then...Else statement inside another If...Then...Else statement is an example of _____.

1. nesting If...Then...Else statements
2. stacking If...Then...Else statements
3. creating sequential If...Then...Else statements
4. None of the above

k) The *= operator _____.

1. squares the value of the right operand and stores the result in the left operand
2. adds the value of the right operand to the value of the left operand and stores the result in the left operand
3. creates a new variable and assigns the value of the right operand to that variable
4. multiplies the value of the left operand by the value of the right operand and stores the result in the left operand

l) If number is initialized with the value 5, what value will number contain after the expression number -= 3 executes?

1. 3
2. 5
3. 7
4. 2

m) Method `String.Format` is used to _____.

1. create constants
2. control how text is formatted
3. format Visual Basic statements
4. All of the above

n) An app enters break mode when _____.

1. **Debug > Start** is selected
2. a breakpoint is reached
3. there is a syntax error
4. None of the above.

o) The body of a `Do While...Loop` statement executes _____.

1. at least once
2. never
3. while its condition is true
4. while its condition is false

p) The UML represents both the merge symbol and the decision symbol as _____.

1. rectangles with rounded sides
2. diamonds
3. small black circles
4. ovals

q) A `Do Until...Loop` repetition statement differs from a `Do While...Loop` repetition statement in _____.

1. that a `Do While...Loop` repetition statement loops as long as the loop-continuation condition remains `False`, whereas a `Do Until...Loop` repetition statement loops as long as the loop-continuation condition remains `True`
2. that a `Do Until...Loop` repetition statement loops as long as the loop-termination condition remains `False`, whereas a `Do While...Loop` repetition statement loops as long as the loop-continuation condition remains `True`
3. that a `Do Until...Loop` repetition statement always executes at least once
4. no way. There is no difference between the `Do Until...Loop` and `Do While...Loop` repetition statements

r) Statements in the body of a `Do Until...Loop` execute repeatedly for as long as the _____ remains `False`.

1. loop-continuation condition
2. do-loop condition
3. loop-termination condition
4. until-loop condition

s) Counter-controlled repetition is also called _____ because the number of repetitions is known before the loop begins executing.

1. definite repetition
2. known repetition
3. sequential repetition
4. counter repetition

4.2 State whether each of the following is *true* or *false*. If *false*, explain why.
a) It's difficult to convert pseudocode into a Visual Basic program.
b) Sequential execution refers to statements in a program that execute one after another.
c) The `If...Then` statement is called a single-selection statement.
d) Pseudocode closely resembles actual Visual Basic code.
e) The `Do While` statement is terminated with the keywords `End While`.

4.3 Write two different Visual Basic statements that each add 1 to `Integer` variable `number`.

4.4 Write a statement or a set of statements to accomplish each of the following:
a) Sum the odd integers between 1 and 15 using a `While` statement. Use `Integer` variables `sum` and `count`.
b) Sum the squares of the even integers between 1 and 15 using a `Do While...Loop` repetition statement. Use `Integer` variables `sum` and `count` and initialize them to 0 and 2, respectively.
c) Display the numbers from 5 to 1 in `resultListBox` using a `Do Until...Loop` and `Integer` counter variable `counterIndex`. Initialize `counterIndex` to 5.
d) Repeat Exercise 4.4 (c) using a `Do While...Loop` statement.

4.5 Write a Visual Basic statement to accomplish each of the following tasks:
a) Declare variables sum and number to be of type Integer.
b) Assign 1 to variable number.
c) Assign 0 to variable sum.
d) Total variables number and sum, and assign the result to variable sum.
e) Display "The sum is: " followed by the value of variable sum in resultLabel.

4.6 Combine the statements that you wrote in Exercise 4.5 into an app that calculates and displays the sum of the Integers from 1 to 10. Use a Do While...Loop statement to loop through the calculation and increment statements. The loop should terminate when the value of control variable number becomes 11.

4.7 Identify and correct the error(s) in each of the following (you may need to add code):
a) The following loop should total the values from 1 to 50. Assume that value is 50.

```
Do While value >= 0
    sum += value
Loop
```

b) The following code should display the squares of 1 to 10 in resultListBox.

```
Dim number As Integer = 1

Do While number < 10
    resultListBox.Items.Add(number ^ 2)
End While
```

c) This segment should display the integers from 888 to 1000 in resultListBox. Initialize variable value to 888.

```
Dim value As Integer = 888

Do While value <= 1000
    value -= 1
Loop
```

4.8 State whether each of the following is *true* or *false*. If the answer is *false*, explain why.
a) Pseudocode is part of the Visual Basic programming language.
b) The body of a Do While...Loop is executed only if the loop-continuation test is false.
c) The body of a While...End While is executed only if the loop-continuation test is false.
d) The body of a Do Until...Loop is executed only if the loop-termination condition is false.

Answers to Self-Review Exercises

4.1 a) 2. b) 3. c) 1. d) 3. e) 3. f) 2. g) 4. h) 3. i) 2. j) 1. k) 4. l) 4. m) 2. n) 2. o) 3. p) 2. q) 2. r) 3. s) 1.

4.2 a) False. Pseudocode normally converts easily into Visual Basic code. b) True. c) True. d) True. e) False. It's terminated with the keyword Loop.

4.3
```
number = number + 1
number += 1
```

4.4 a)
```
Dim sum As Integer = 0
Dim count As Integer = 1

While count <= 15
    sum += count
    count += 2
End While
```

b) `Dim sum As Integer = 0`
   `Dim count As Integer = 2`

   `Do While count <= 15`
   `    sum += count ^ 2`
   `    count += 2`
   `Loop`

c) `Dim counterIndex As Integer = 5`

   `Do Until counterIndex < 1`
   `    resultListBox.Items.Add(counterIndex)`
   `    counterIndex -= 1`
   `Loop`

d) `Dim counterIndex As Integer = 5`

   `Do While counterIndex >= 1`
   `    resultListBox.Items.Add(counterIndex)`
   `    counterIndex -= 1`
   `Loop`

4.5 a) `Dim sum As Integer`
   `Dim number As Integer`
b) `number = 1`
c) `sum = 0`
d) `sum += number` or `sum = sum + number`
e) `resultLabel.Text = "The sum is: " & sum`

4.6 See the code below:

```
1   ' Ex. 4.6: CalculateSum.vb
2   ' Calculates the sum of the integers from 1 to 10.
3   Public Class CalculateSum
4       ' performs the calculation
5       Private Sub CalculateSum_Load(sender As Object,
6           e As EventArgs) Handles MyBase.Load
7
8           Dim sum As Integer
9           Dim number As Integer
10
11          sum = 0
12          number = 1
13
14          Do While number <= 10
15              sum += number
16              number += 1
17          Loop
18
19          resultLabel.Text = "The sum is: " & sum
20      End Sub ' CalculateSum_Load
21  End Class ' CalculateSum
```

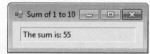

4.7 a) Error: Repetition condition never becomes false, resulting in an infinite loop.

```
While value >= 0
    sum += value
    value -= 1
End While
```

b) Errors: The counter is never incremented, resulting in an infinite loop. The repetition condition uses the wrong relational operator. Keywords End While are used instead of keyword Loop.

```
Dim number As Integer = 1

Do While number <= 10
    resultListBox.Items.Add(number ^ 2)
    number += 1
Loop
```

c) Error: The values are never displayed and are decremented instead of incremented.

```
value = 888

While value <= 1000
    resultListBox.Items.Add(value)
    value += 1
End While
```

4.8 a) False. Pseudocode is not part of the Visual Basic programming language.
b) False. The loop condition must evaluate to true for the body to be executed.
c) False. The loop condition must evaluate to true for the body to be executed.
d) True.

Quick Quiz

4.9 Answer each of the following questions.
a) The _____ operator returns False if the left operand is larger than the right operand.

1. =	2. <
3. <=	4. All of the above

b) A _____ occurs when an executed statement does not directly follow the previously executed statement in the written app.

1. transition	2. flow
3. logical error	4. transfer of control

c) The If...Then statement is called a _____ statement because it selects or ignores one action (or group of actions).

1. single-selection	2. multiple-selection
3. double-selection	4. repetition

d) The three types of control structures are sequence, selection and _____.

1. repeat	2. looping
3. redo	4. repetition

e) In an activity diagram, a rectangle with curved sides represents _____.

1. a complete algorithm	2. a comment
3. an action	4. the termination of the app

f) The If...Then...Else selection statement ends with the keywords _____.

1. End If Then Else	2. End If Else
3. End Else	4. End If

g) The _____ operator assigns the result of adding the left and right operands to the left operand.

1. +   2. =+
3. +=   4. None of the above

h) The _____ statement executes until its loop-termination condition becomes `True`.

1. `Do While...Loop`   2. `Do Until...Loop`
3. `Do`   4. `Loop`

i) The _____ statement executes until its loop-continuation condition becomes `False`.

1. `Do While...Loop`   2. `Do Until...Loop`
3. `Do`   4. `Do While`

j) A(n) _____ loop occurs when a condition in a `Do While...Loop` never becomes `False`.

1. infinite   2. undefined
3. nested   4. indefinite

k) A _____ is a variable that helps control the number of times that a set of statements executes.

1. repeater   2. counter
3. loop   4. repetition control statement

l) The _____ control allows users to add and view items in a list.

1. `ListItems`   2. `SelectBox`
3. `ListBox`   4. `ViewBox`

m) In a UML activity diagram, a(n) _____ symbol joins two flows of activity into one flow of activity.

1. merge   2. combine
3. action state   4. decision

n) Property _____ maintains all the values in a `ListBox`.

1. `All`   2. `List`
3. `ListItemValues`   4. `Items`

o) Items's method _____ deletes all the values in a `ListBox`.

1. `Remove`   2. `Delete`
3. `Clear`   4. `Del`

p) Items's method _____ adds an item to a `ListBox`.

1. `Include`   2. `Append`
3. `Add`   4. None of the above

Exercises

Selection Statement Exercises

4.10   What does this code do? Assume that the user entered the marks value 75 into `marksTextBox`.

```
1   Dim marks As Integer
2   marks = marksTextBox.Text
3   If marks < 0 Then
4       marksLabel.Text = "Enter a marks greater than or equal to zero."
5   ElseIf marks >= 90 Then
6       marksLabel.Text = "A"
7   ElseIf marks >= 80 Then
8       marksLabel.Text = "B"
```

```
 9    ElseIf marks >= 70 Then
10        marksLabel.Text = "C"
11    ElseIf marks >= 60 Then
12        marksLabel.Text = "D"
13    Else
14        marksLabel.Text = "F"
15    End If
```

4.11 *(Wage Calculator with Tax Calculations)* Develop an app that calculates an employee's earnings, as shown in Fig. 4.22. The user should provide the hourly wage and number of hours worked per week. When the Calculate Button is clicked, the employee's gross earnings should display in the **Gross earnings:** TextBox. **The Less FWT:** TextBox should display the amount deducted for federal taxes and the **Net earnings:** TextBox should display the difference between the gross earnings and the federal tax amount. You can use the format specifier C with String method Format, to format the result as currency.

Assume that overtime is calculated for hours over 48 hours worked, overtime wages are 2 times the hourly wage and federal taxes are 30% of gross earnings. The **Clear** Button should clear all fields. Set the TextAlign properties of the Labels that show the results to MiddleRight so that the values are aligned at their decimal points. In the next chapter, we'll introduce the data type Decimal for financial calculations.

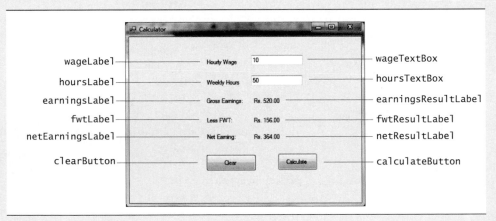

Fig. 4.22 | Wage Calculator

4.12 *(Credit Checker App)* Develop an app (as shown in Fig. 4.23) that determines whether a department-store customer has exceeded the credit limit on a charge account. Each customer enters an account number (an Integer), a balance at the beginning of the month (a Double), the total of all items charged this month (a Double), the total of all credits applied to the customer's account this month (a Double), and the customer's allowed credit limit (a Double). The app should input each of these facts, calculate the new balance (= *beginning balance – credits + charges*), display the new balance and determine whether the new balance exceeds the customer's credit limit. You can use the format "{0:C}" with String method Format, to format the result as currency (see Fig. 4.23). If the customer's credit limit is exceeded, display a message (in messageLabel at the bottom of the Form) informing the customer of this fact; otherwise, display the customer's remaining credit amount. If the user presses the **Clear Fields** Button, the app should clear the TextBoxes and Labels. In the next chapter, we'll introduce the data type Decimal for financial calculations.

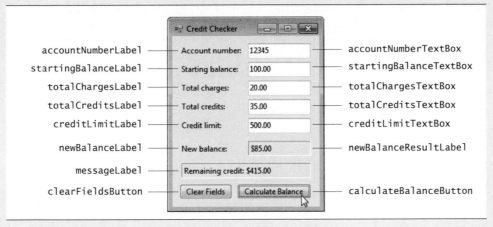

Fig. 4.23 | Credit Checker GUI.

Repetition Statement Exercises

4.13   *(Enhanced Exam Analysis App)* Modify the app of Fig. 4.15 to process the four Strings: "P", "p", "F" and "f". If any other String input is encountered, increment a counter that tracks the number of invalid inputs. Display a message indicating the number of invalid inputs. Test your new app.

4.14   *(Miles Per Gallon App)* Drivers are concerned with the mileage obtained by their automobiles. One driver has kept track of several tankfuls of gasoline by recording the miles driven and the gallons used for each tankful. Each time the user enters the miles driven and gallons used (both as Doubles) for a tankful and presses the **Calculate MPG** Button, the app should calculate the miles per gallon then display the miles driven, gallons used and miles per gallon in ListBoxes as shown in Fig. 4.24. The app should also display the total miles per gallon. (Be careful—this is not the average of the miles per gallon for each tankful.) All average calculations should produce floating-point results. Avoid division by zero—if the user enters zero for the number of gallons, inform the user that the input value for gallons must be greater than zero.

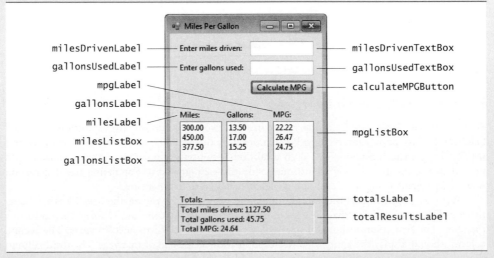

Fig. 4.24 | Miles Per Gallon GUI.

4.15 *(Table of Powers App)* Write an app that displays a table of numbers from 1 to an upper limit, along with each of those numbers raised to the power 2 ($n ^ 2$), to the power 3 ($n ^ 3$), to the power 4 ($n ^ 4$) and to the power 5 ($n ^ 5$). The user specifies the upper limit, and the results are displayed in a ListBox, as in Fig. 4.25.

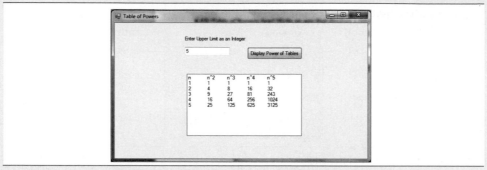

Fig. 4.25 | Table of Powers GUI.

4.16 *(Using the Debugger: Odd Numbers App)* The **Odd Numbers** app should display all of the odd integers between one and the number input by the user. Open the **Odd Numbers** app from the ex04_16 folder located with this chapter's examples. Run the app. Note that an infinite loop occurs after you enter a value into the **Upper limit:** TextBox and click the **Display** Button. Select **Debug > Stop Debugging** to close the running app. Use the debugger to find and fix the error(s) in the app. Figure 4.26 displays the correct output for the app.

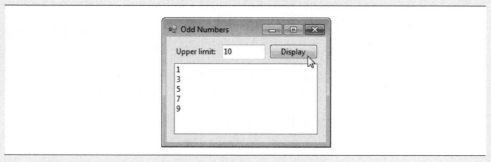

Fig. 4.26 | Correct output for the **Odd Numbers** app.

Making a Difference Exercises

4.17 *(World Population Calculator)* Darwin's first two observations in the exposition of Natural Selection involve population ecology: Populations have the potential to increase exponentially, but usually they remain constant in size. Both conditions are observed in nature and are associated with the balance of (births + immigrations) minus (deaths + emigrations). Population size depends on how many (births + immigrations) minus (deaths + emigrations) there are.

Write an app that calculates world population growth each year for the next 75 years, using the simplifying assumption that the current growth rate will stay constant. Display the results in a ListBox. The first column should display the year from year 2013 to next 75 years. The second column should display the anticipated world population at the end of that year. The third column should display the numerical increase in the world population that would occur that year. Using your results, determine the year in which the population would be double what it is today, if this year's growth rate were to persist. [Note: Current World population is 6,973,738,433. Hint: Use Double variables because Integer variables can store values only up to approximately two billion.] Fig. 4.27 shows the application GUI for the world population for the next 75 years.

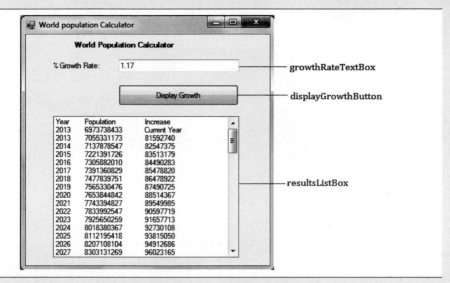

Fig. 4.27 | World Population Calculator

4.18 *(Encryption-Decryption)* In cryptography, encryption is the process of encoding messages in such a way that eavesdroppers or hackers cannot read it, but authorized parties can. In an encryption scheme, the message or information is encrypted using an encryption algorithm, turning it into an unreadable ciphertext. This is usually done with the use of an encryption key, which specifies how the message is to be encoded. Any adversary that can see the ciphertext should not be able to determine anything about the original message. An authorized party, however, is able to decode the ciphertext using a decryption algorithm that usually requires a secret decryption key that adversaries do not have access to. Develop an app to encrypt and decrypt a four-digit integer and encrypt it as follows: Replace each digit with the result of adding 9 to the digit and getting the remainder after dividing the new value by 10. Then swap the first digit with the fourth, and swap the second digit with the third. Decryption of the ciphertext should be done in the reverse order of encryption.

Fig. 4.28 shows the GUI for encryption and decryption.

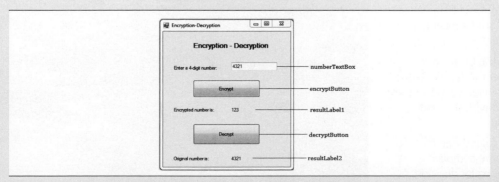

Fig. 4.28 | Encryption-Decryption

5

Problem Solving and Control Statements: Part 2

Who can control his fate?
—William Shakespeare

The used key is always bright.
—Benjamin Franklin

Not everything that can be counted counts, and not every thing that counts can be counted.
—Albert Einstein

Objectives

In this chapter you'll learn:

- Problem solving with additional control statement building blocks.

- The essentials of counter-controlled repetition.

- To use the `For...Next`, `Do...Loop While` and `Do...Loop Until` repetition statements.

- To perform multiple selection using the `Select...Case` selection statement.

- To use the `Exit` statement to break out of a repetition statement.

- To use the `Continue` statement to terminate the current iteration of a loop and proceed with the next iteration.

- To use logical operators to form more complex conditions for decision making.

5.1 Introduction

Chapter 4 began our introduction to the types of building blocks that are available for problem solving. We used those building blocks with proven program-construction techniques. In this chapter, we continue our study of control statements. We demonstrate the For...Next, Select...Case, Do...Loop While and Do...Loop Until control statements. We explore the essentials of counter-controlled repetition and demonstrate nested repetition statements. We use a Select...Case multiple-selection statement to count the number of A, B, C, D and F grades in a set of letter grades entered by the user. We introduce the Exit program control statement for terminating a control statement immediately, and we introduce the Continue program control statement for terminating the current iteration of a repetition statement. Finally, we discuss the logical operators, which enable you to form more powerful conditional expressions in control statements.

5.2 For...Next Repetition Statement

In Chapter 4, we introduced counter-controlled repetition with the Do While...Loop statement. Counter-controlled repetition requires:

1. the name of a control variable (or loop counter) that's used to determine whether the loop continues to iterate

2. the initial value of the control variable

3. the increment (or decrement) by which the control variable is modified each time through the loop

4. the condition that tests for the final value of the control variable (that is, whether looping should continue).

The **For...Next** repetition statement specifies counter-controlled repetition details in a *single* line of code. In general, counter-controlled repetition should be implemented with For...Next. Figure 5.1 illustrates the power of the For...Next statement by displaying the even integers from 2 to 10. The ForCounter_Load event handler is called when you execute the program.

```vb
1   ' Fig. 5.1: ForCounter.vb
2   ' Counter-controlled repetition with the For…Next statement.
3   Public Class ForCounter
4      ' display the even Integers from 2 to 10
5      Private Sub ForCounter_Load(sender As Object,
6         e As EventArgs) Handles MyBase.Load
7
8         ' initialization, repetition condition and
9         ' incrementing are all included in the For...Next statement
10        For counter As Integer = 2 To 10 Step 2
11           ' append counter value to outputLabel's Text property
12           outputLabel.Text &= counter & " " ' display counter
13        Next
14     End Sub ' ForCounter_Load
15  End Class ' ForCounter
```

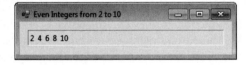

Fig. 5.1 | Counter-controlled repetition with the For...Next statement.

When the For...Next statement (lines 10–13) is reached, the control variable counter is declared as an Integer and initialized to 2, thus addressing the first two elements of counter-controlled repetition—the control variable's *name* and its *initial value*. Next, the *implied* loop-continuation condition counter <= 10 is tested. The **To** keyword is required in the For...Next statement. The optional **Step** keyword specifies the *increment*, that is, the amount that's added to counter after each time the For...Next body is executed. If Step and the value following it are omitted, the increment defaults to 1. You typically omit the Step portion for increments of 1. The increment of a For...Next statement could be *negative*, in which case it's called a *decrement*, and the loop actually counts *downward*. If the implied loop-continuation condition is *initially false* (for example, if the initial value is *greater* than the final value and the increment is positive), the For...Next's body is *not* performed. Instead, execution proceeds with the first statement after the For...Next.

Error-Prevention Tip 5.1

Use a For...Next loop for counter-controlled repetition. Off-by-one errors (which occur when a loop is executed for one more or one less iteration than is necessary) tend to disappear, because the initial and terminating values are clear.

First Iteration of the Loop

In Fig. 5.1, the initial value of `counter` is 2, so the implied loop-continuation condition (`counter <= 10`) is true, and the `counter`'s value 2 is appended to `outputLabel`'s `Text` property (line 12). The required `Next` keyword (line 13) marks the end of the `For...Next` repetition statement. When `Next` is reached, variable `counter` is incremented by the `Step` value (2), and the implied loop-continuation test is performed again.

Second and Subsequent Iterations of the Loop

Now, the control variable is equal to 4. This value still does not exceed the final value, so the program performs the body statement again. This process continues until the `counter` value 10 has been displayed and the control variable `counter` is incremented to 12, causing the implied loop-continuation test to fail and the loop to terminate. The program continues by performing the first statement after the `For...Next` statement (line 14).

Good Programming Practice 5.1

Some programmers place the control variable name after `Next` as in `Next counter`. This is particularly useful in nested `For...Next` statements to identify the statement to which the `Next` belongs.

5.2.1 For...Next Statement Header Components

Figure 5.2 takes a closer look at the `For...Next` statement of Fig. 5.1. The first line of the `For...Next` statement sometimes is called the `For...Next` header. It specifies each of the items needed for counter-controlled repetition with a control variable.

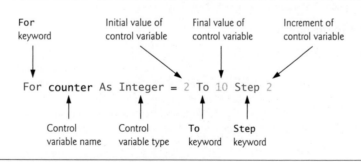

Fig. 5.2 | For...Next header components.

5.2.2 General Form of a For...Next Statement

The general form of the `For...Next` statement is

```
For initialization To finalValue Step increment
   statement
Next
```

where the *initialization* expression initializes the loop's control variable, *finalValue* determines whether the loop should continue executing and *increment* specifies the amount the control variable should be incremented (or decremented) each time through the loop.

5.2.3 Declaring the Control Variable Before a For...Next Statement

In Fig. 5.1, the counter variable is declared and initialized *in* the For...Next header. The counter variable may be declared *before* the For...Next statement. For example, the code in Fig. 5.1 could have been written as

```
Dim counter As Integer
For counter = 2 To 10 Step 2
    outputLabel.Text &= counter & " "
Next
```

Although both forms are correct, declaring the control variable in the For...Next header is clearer and more concise. The difference between the two forms is that if the *initialization* expression in the For...Next statement header declares the control variable (as we've done in Fig. 5.1), the control variable can be used *only* in the body of the For...Next statement—it will be unknown outside the For...Next statement. This restricted use of the control-variable name is known as the variable's scope, which specifies *where* the variable can be used in a program. If the control variable is declared *before* the For...Next control statement, it can be used from the point of declaration, inside the control statement's body and *after* the control statement as well.

5.2.4 Using Expressions in the For...Next Statement's Header

The starting value, ending value and increment portions of a For...Next statement can contain arithmetic expressions. The expressions are evaluated *once* (when the For...Next statement *begins* executing) and used as the starting value, ending value and increment of the For...Next statement's header. For example, assume that x = 2 and y = 10. The header

```
For j As Integer = x To 4 * x * y Step y \ x
```

is equivalent to the header

```
For j As Integer = 2 To 80 Step 5
```

Common Programming Error 5.1

Counter-controlled loops should not be controlled with Double *or* Single *variables. Values of these types are represented only* approximately *in the computer's memory. This can lead to imprecise counter values and inaccurate tests for termination.*

5.2.5 For...Next Statement UML Activity Diagram

The activity diagram of the For...Next statement in Fig. 5.1 is shown in Fig. 5.3. This activity diagram makes it clear that the initialization occurs only *once* and that incrementing occurs *after each* execution of the body statement.

5.2.6 Local Type Inference

In each For...Next statement presented so far, we declared the control variable's type in the For...Next statement's header. For any local variable that's initialized in its declaration, the variable's type can be determined based on its initializer value—this is known as local type inference. Recall that a local variable is any variable declared in the body of a method. For example, in the declaration

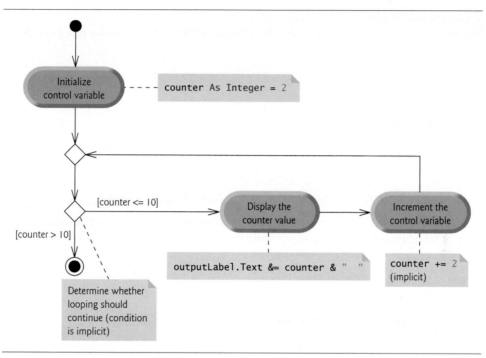

Fig. 5.3 | For...Next repetition statement activity diagram.

```
Dim x = 7
```

the compiler *infers* that the variable x should be of type Integer, because the compiler assumes that whole-number values, like 7, are Integer values. In the declaration

```
Dim y = -123.45
```

the compiler *infers* that the variable y should be of type Double, because the compiler assumes that floating-point literals, like -123.45, are Double values.

Literal Type Characters
In the declaration

```
Dim z = 987.65D
```

the compiler *infers* that the variable z should be of type Decimal, because the value 987.65 is followed by the literal type character D, which indicates that the value is of type Decimal. Some common literal type characters include C for Char ("T"C), F for Single (123.45F), S for Short (123S) and L for Long (123L).[1]

---

1. The complete list of literal type characters can be found in Section 2.4 of the Visual Basic Language specification, which is installed on your computer with Visual Studio. By default, you can find it in C:\Program Files (x86)\Microsoft Visual Studio 11.0\VB\Specifications\1033.

Type Inference in For...Next Statements
You can also use local type inference with control variables in the header of a For...Next statement. For example, the For...Next header

```
For counter As Integer = 1 To 10
```

can be written as

```
For counter = 1 To 10
```

In this case, counter is *inferred* to be of type Integer because it's initialized with an Integer literal (1).

5.3 Examples Using the For...Next Statement

The following examples demonstrate different ways of varying the control variable in a For...Next statement. In each case, we write the appropriate For...Next header using *local type inference*.

a) Vary the control variable from 1 to 100 in increments of 1.

```
For i = 1 To 100 or For i = 1 To 100 Step 1
```

b) Vary the control variable from 100 to 1 in *decrements* of 1.

```
For i = 100 To 1 Step -1
```

c) Vary the control variable from 7 to 77 in increments of 7.

```
For i = 7 To 77 Step 7
```

d) Vary the control variable from 20 to 2 in *decrements* of 2.

```
For i = 20 To 2 Step -2
```

e) Vary the control variable over the sequence of the following values: 2, 5, 8, 11, 14, 17, 20.

```
For i = 2 To 20 Step 3
```

f) Vary the control variable over the sequence of the following values: 99, 88, 77, 66, 55, 44, 33, 22, 11, 0.

```
For i = 99 To 0 Step -11
```

5.4 App: Interest Calculator

Consider the following problem statement:

A person invests $1000.00 in a savings account. Assuming that all the interest is left on deposit, calculate and print the amount of money in the account at the end of each year for up to 10 years. Allow the user to specify the principal amount, the interest rate and the number of years. To determine these amounts, use the following formula:

$$a = p \, (1 + r)^n$$

where

> *p is the original amount invested (that is, the principal)*
> *r is the annual interest rate (for example, .05 stands for 5%)*

n is the number of years
a is the amount on deposit at the end of the nth year.

This problem involves a loop that performs the indicated calculation for each of the years that the money remains on deposit. Figure 5.4 shows the GUI for this app. We introduce the **NumericUpDown** control, which limits a user's choices to a specific range of values—this helps to avoid data entry errors. In this program, we use the control to allow the user to choose a number of years from 1 to 10. The control's **Minimum** property specifies the starting value in the range. Its **Maximum** property specifies the ending value in the range. Its **Value** property specifies the current value displayed in the control. You can also use this property programmatically to obtain the current value displayed. The control provides up and down arrows that allow the user to scroll through the control's range of values. In this example, we use 1 as the minimum value, 10 as the maximum value and 1 as the initial value for this control. The **Increment** property specifies by how much the current number in the NumericUpDown control changes when the user clicks the control's up (for incrementing) or down (for decrementing) arrow. We use the Increment property's default value, 1. When the user changes the value in a NumericUpDown control, a **Value-Changed** event occurs. If you double click the yearsNumericUpDown control in *design mode*, the IDE generates the event handler yearsNumericUpDown_ValueChanged to handle the ValueChanged event. The **Interest Calculator** program is shown in Fig. 5.5.

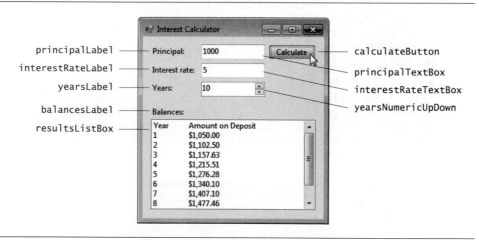

Fig. 5.4 | GUI for the **Interest Calculator** app.

```
1    ' Fig. 5.5: InterestCalculator.vb
2    ' Compound interest calculation using For...Next.
3    Public Class InterestCalculator
4       ' handles Calculate Button's Click event
5       Private Sub calculateButton_Click(sender As Object,
6          e As EventArgs) Handles calculateButton.Click
7
```

Fig. 5.5 | Compound interest calculation using For...Next. (Part 1 of 2.)

```vb
 8        ' store the principal and the interest rate
 9        Dim principal As Decimal = Val(principalTextBox.Text)
10        Dim rate As Decimal = Val(interestRateTextBox.Text)
11
12        ' display the output header
13        resultsListBox.Items.Add(
14            "Year" & vbTab & "Amount on Deposit")
15        Dim amount As Decimal ' amount on deposit after each year
16
17        ' calculate amount after each year and add to resultListBox
18        For yearCounter As Integer = 1 To yearsNumericUpDown.Value
19            amount = principal * ((1 + rate / 100) ^ yearCounter)
20            resultsListBox.Items.Add(yearCounter & vbTab &
21                String.Format("{0:C}", amount))
22        Next
23    End Sub ' calculateButton_Click
24
25    ' clear resultListBox when principal changes
26    Private Sub principalTextBox_TextChanged(sender As Object,
27        e As EventArgs) Handles principalTextBox.TextChanged
28        resultsListBox.Items.Clear() ' empty ListBox when inputs change
29    End Sub ' principalTextBox_TextChanged
30
31    ' clear resultListBox when interest rate changes
32    Private Sub interestRateTextBox_TextChanged(
33        sender As Object,
34        e As EventArgs) Handles interestRateTextBox.TextChanged
35        resultsListBox.Items.Clear() ' empty ListBox when inputs change
36    End Sub ' interestRateTextBox_TextChanged
37
38    ' clear resultListBox when number of years changes
39    Private Sub yearsNumericUpDown_ValueChanged(sender As Object,
40        e As EventArgs) Handles yearsNumericUpDown.ValueChanged
41        resultsListBox.Items.Clear() ' empty ListBox when inputs change
42    End Sub ' yearsNumericUpDown_ValueChanged
43 End Class ' InterestCalculator
```

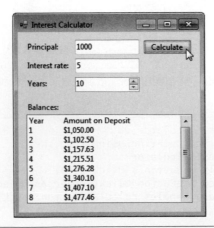

Fig. 5.5 | Compound interest calculation using For...Next. (Part 2 of 2.)

Decimal Variables

Lines 9–10 in the calculateButton_Click event handler declare and initialize two Decimal variables. Type **Decimal** should be used for *monetary calculations* such as those required in the **Interest Calculator** app. Line 9 declares principal as type Decimal. Variable principal is initialized to the value in principalTextBox and rate (line 10) is initialized to the value in interestRateTextBox. Line 15 declares amount as a Decimal. This variable stores the amount on deposit at the end of each year.

Using the Val Function to Convert Strings to Numbers

This app uses TextBoxes to read numeric input. Unfortunately, we cannot prevent users from accidentally entering nonnumeric input, such as letters and special characters like $ and @ in the TextBoxes. Lines 9–10 use the built-in **Val function** to prevent inputs like this from terminating the app. Previously, you've used the method Format, which is part of class String. When a method is not part of a class, it's called a function.

Function Val obtains a value from a String of characters, such as a TextBox's Text property. The value returned is *guaranteed* to be a number. We use Val because this app is not intended to perform arithmetic calculations with characters that are not numbers. Val reads its argument one character at a time until it encounters a character that's not a number. Once a nonnumeric character is read, Val returns the number it has read up to that point. Val ignores whitespace (for example, "33 5" will be converted to 335). Val recognizes the decimal point as well as plus and minus signs that indicate whether a number is positive or negative (such as -123). Val does not recognize such symbols as commas and dollar signs. If Val receives an argument that cannot be converted to a number (for example, "b35", which begins with a nonnumeric character, or an empty string), it returns 0.

Performing the Interest Calculations

The For...Next statement (lines 18–22) varies the control variable yearCounter from 1 to yearsNumericUpDown.Value in increments of 1. Line 19 performs the calculation from the problem statement

$$a = p \, (1 + r)^n$$

where *a* is the amount, *p* is the principal, *r* is the rate / 100 and *n* is the yearCounter.

Formatting Currency Output

Lines 20–21 display the amount on deposit at the end of each year in the resultsListBox. The text includes the current yearCounter value, a tab character (vbTab) to position to the second column and the result of the method call String.Format("{0:C}", amount). The C ("currency") format specifier indicates that its corresponding value (amount) should be displayed in *monetary format*—with a dollar sign to the left and commas in the proper locations. For example, the value 1334.50, when formatted using the C format specifier, will appear as "$1,334.50." This may differ based on locales throughout the world. Other commonly used format specifiers include:

- F for floating-point numbers—sets the number of decimal places to two (introduced in Section 4.10).

- N for numbers—separates every three digits with a *comma* and sets the number of decimal places to two.

- D for integers

A Warning About Function **Val**

Although the value returned by Val is *always* a number, it's not necessarily the value the user intended. For example, the user might enter the text $10.23 to represent a monetary amount, which Val evaluates to 0 without reporting an error. A common mistake like this causes the app to execute incorrectly. Visual Basic provides two ways to handle invalid input. One is to use string-processing capabilities to examine input. We discuss these throughout this book. The other form of handling invalid input is called *exception handling*, which you'll learn in Chapter 7.

5.5 Formulating Algorithms: Nested Repetition Statements

Consider the following problem statement:

> *Write a program that displays in a TextBox a filled square consisting solely of one type of character, such as the asterisk (*). The side of the square (1 to 20) and the character to be used to fill the square should be entered by the user.*

Your program should draw the square as follows:

1. Input the *fill character* and *side length* of the square.

2. Use a NumericUpDown control to strictly limit the side length to the exact range of allowed values.

3. Use repetition to draw the square by displaying only one fill character at a time.

After reading the problem statement, we make the following observations:

- The program must draw *side* rows, each containing *side* fill characters, where *side* is the value entered by the user. Counter-controlled repetition should be used.

- Four variables should be used—one that represents the side length of the square, one that represents (as a String) the fill character to be used, one that represents the row in which the next symbol should appear and one that represents the column in which the next symbol should appear.

GUI for the **Square of Characters** *App*

Figure 5.6 shows this app's GUI. We use a NumericUpDown control to allow the user to specify a side length in the range 1 to 20. The output is displayed in a TextBox with its MultiLine property set to True and its Font property set to the fixed-width font Lucida Console.

Evolving the Pseudocode

Let's proceed with top-down, stepwise refinement. We begin with a pseudocode representation of the top:

> *Display a square of fill characters*

Our first refinement is

> *Input the fill character*
> *Input the side of the square*
> *Display the square*

Here, too, even though we have a *complete* representation of the entire program, further refinement is necessary.

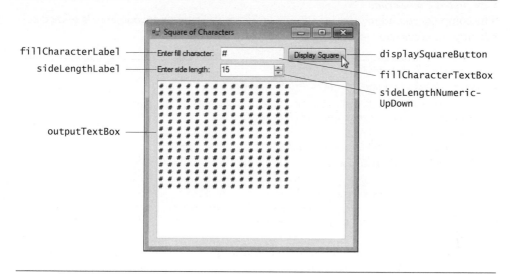

Fig. 5.6 | GUI for the **Square of Characters** app.

Displaying the Square

The pseudocode statement

> *Display the square*

can be implemented by using one loop nested inside another. In this example, it's known in advance that there are *side* rows of *side* fill characters each, so counter-controlled repetition is appropriate. One loop controls the row in which each fill character is to be displayed. A nested loop displays each fill character (one at a time) for that row. The refinement of the preceding pseudocode statement is

> *For row from 1 to the number of characters in a side*
>
> > *For column from 1 to the number of characters in a side*
> > *Display the fill character*
>
> *Move to the next line of output*

The outer *For* statement initializes *row* to 1 to prepare to display the square's first row and loops while the implied condition *row is less than or equal to the number of characters in a side* remains true—that is, for each row of the square. Within this *For* statement, the nested *For* statement initializes *column* to 1 to prepare to display the first fill character of the current row. The nested (or inner) loop executes while the implied condition *column is less than or equal to the number of characters in a side* remains true. Each iteration of the inner loop displays one fill character. After each row of characters, we move to the next line in the TextBox to prepare to display the next row of the square. At this point, the outer loop increments variable *row* by 1. If the outer loop's condition is still true, *column* is reset to 1, and the inner loop executes again, displaying another row of fill characters. Then, the outer loop increments *row* by 1 again. This process repeats until the value of *row* exceeds *side*, at which point the square of fill characters is complete.

Completed Pseudocode

The complete second refinement appears in Fig. 5.7. The pseudocode now is refined sufficiently for conversion to Visual Basic.

I	*Input the fill character*
2	*Input the side of the square*
3	
4	*For each row from 1 to the number of characters in a side*
5	
6	*For each column from 1 to the number of characters in a side*
7	*Display the fill character*
8	
9	*Move to the next line of output*

Fig. 5.7 | Second refinement of the pseudocode.

Visual Basic Code for the *Square of Characters App*

We implement the pseudocode algorithm in the displaySquareButton_Click event handler (Fig. 5.8, lines 5–25). The nested For...Next statements (lines 15–24) display the square of characters. The outer loop specifies which row is being displayed and the inner loop (lines 18–21) displays the current row of characters. We follow each fill character by a space (line 20) to make the output look more like a square. Line 23 in the outer loop moves the cursor to the next line in the TextBox to begin the next line of output.

```vb
 1   ' Fig. 5.8: SquareOfCharacters.vb
 2   ' Nested repetition statements used to display a square of characters.
 3   Public Class SquareOfCharacters
 4      ' display a square of characters
 5      Private Sub displaySquareButton_Click(sender As Object,
 6         e As EventArgs) Handles displaySquareButton.Click
 7
 8         outputTextBox.Clear() ' clears the output
 9
10         ' get the fill character and side length
11         Dim fillCharacter As String = fillCharacterTextBox.Text
12         Dim sideLength As Integer = sideLengthNumericUpDown.Value
13
14         ' this For...Next controls the row being displayed
15         For row As Integer = 1 To sideLength
16            ' this For...Next controls the column being displayed;
17            ' this loop is nested in the For...Next at lines 15-24
18            For column As Integer = 1 To sideLength
19               ' display fill character and a space
20               outputTextBox.AppendText(fillCharacter & " ")
21            Next column
22
23            outputTextBox.AppendText(vbCrLf) ' move to next line
24         Next row
25      End Sub ' displaySquareButton_Click
```

Fig. 5.8 | Nested repetition statements used to display a square of characters. (Part 1 of 2.)

```
26
27      ' clear outputTextBox when the fill character is changed by the user
28      Private Sub fillCharacterTextBox_TextChanged(
29         sender As Object, e As EventArgs) _
30         Handles fillCharacterTextBox.TextChanged
31         outputTextBox.Clear() ' clears the output
32      End Sub ' fillCharacterTextBox_TextChanged
33
34      ' clear outputTextBox when the side length is changed by the user
35      Private Sub sideLengthNumericUpDown_ValueChanged(
36         sender As Object, e As EventArgs) _
37         Handles sideLengthNumericUpDown.ValueChanged
38         outputTextBox.Clear() ' clears the output
39      End Sub ' sideLengthNumericUpDown_ValueChanged
40   End Class ' TextBox_TextChanged
```

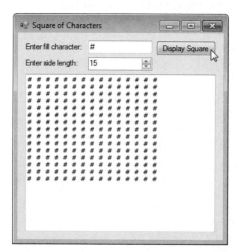
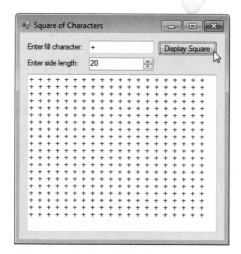

Fig. 5.8 | Nested repetition statements used to display a square of characters. (Part 2 of 2.)

5.6 Select...Case Multiple-Selection Statement

Occasionally, an algorithm contains a series of decisions that test a variable or expression separately for each value that the variable or expression might assume. The algorithm then takes different actions based on those values. The **Select...Case multiple-selection statement** handles such decision making. Figure 5.9 enhances the **Class Average** app of Fig. 4.12 by using a Select...Case statement to determine whether each grade is the equivalent of an A, B, C, D or F and to increment the appropriate grade counter. The program also displays a summary of the number of students who received each grade. An extra counter is used to display the number of students who received a perfect score of 100 on the exam. The GUI uses the same controls as in Fig. 4.12, but we've made the class-AverageLabel taller to display more output and resized the gradesListBox so that it extends to the bottom of the clearGradesButton.

```
1   ' Fig. 5.9: ClassAverage.vb
2   ' Counter-controlled repetition: Class-average problem.
3   Public Class ClassAverage
4      ' variables declared in the class, but not inside the class's methods
5      ' can be used in all of the class's methods
6      Dim aCount As Integer ' count of A grades
7      Dim bCount As Integer ' count of B grades
8      Dim cCount As Integer ' count of C grades
9      Dim dCount As Integer ' count of D grades
10     Dim fCount As Integer ' count of F grades
11     Dim perfectScoreCount As Integer ' count of perfect scores
12
13     ' places a grade in the gradesListBox
14     Private Sub submitGradeButton_Click(sender As Object,
15        e As EventArgs) Handles submitGradeButton.Click
16
17        Dim grade As Integer = Val(gradeTextBox.Text) ' get grade
18
19        ' add the grade to the end of the gradesListBox
20        gradesListBox.Items.Add(grade)
21        gradeTextBox.Clear() ' clear the gradeTextBox
22
23        ' add 1 to appropriate counter for specified grade
24        Select Case grade ' determine which grade was entered
25           Case 100 ' perfect score
26              perfectScoreCount += 1 ' increment perfectScoreCount
27              aCount += 1 ' increment aCount
28           Case 90 To 99 ' grade was between 90 and 99
29              aCount += 1 ' increment aCount
30           Case 80 To 89 ' grade was between 80 and 89
31              bCount += 1 ' increment bCount
32           Case 70 To 79 ' grade was between 70 and 79
33              cCount += 1 ' increment cCount
34           Case 60 To 69 ' grade was between 60 and 69
35              dCount += 1 ' increment dCount
36           Case Else ' grade was less than 60
37              fCount += 1 ' increment fCount
38        End Select
39
40        gradeTextBox.Focus() ' gives the focus to the gradeTextBox
41     End Sub ' submitGradeButton_Click
42
43     ' calculates the class average based on the grades in gradesListBox
44     Private Sub calculateAverageButton_Click(sender As Object,
45        e As EventArgs) Handles calculateAverageButton.Click
46
47        Dim total As Integer ' sum of grades entered by user
48        Dim gradeCounter As Integer ' counter for grades
49        Dim grade As Integer ' grade input by user
50        Dim average As Double ' average of grades
51
52        ' initialization phase
53        total = 0 ' set total to zero before adding grades to it
```

Fig. 5.9 | Counter-controlled repetition: Class-average problem. (Part 1 of 2.)

```
54          gradeCounter = 0 ' prepare to loop
55
56       ' processing phase
57       Do While gradeCounter < gradesListBox.Items.Count
58          grade = gradesListBox.Items(gradeCounter) ' get next grade
59          total += grade ' add grade to total
60          gradeCounter += 1 ' add 1 to gradeCounter
61       Loop
62
63       ' termination phase
64       If gradeCounter <> 0 Then
65          average = total / gradeCounter ' calculate average
66
67          ' display total and average (with two digits of precision)
68          classAverageLabel.Text = "Total of the " & gradeCounter &
69             " grade(s) is " & total & vbCrLf & "Class average is " &
70             String.Format("{0:F}", average) & vbCrLf & vbCrLf
71
72          ' display summary of letter grades
73          classAverageLabel.Text &=
74             "Letter grade summary:" & vbCrLf & "A: " & aCount &
75             vbCrLf & "B: " & bCount & vbCrLf & "C: " & cCount &
76             vbCrLf & "D: " & dCount & vbCrLf & "F: " & fCount &
77             vbCrLf & "Perfect scores: " & perfectScoreCount
78       Else
79          classAverageLabel.Text = "No grades were entered"
80       End If
81    End Sub ' calculateAverageButton_Click
82
83    ' clears grades from gradeListBox and results from classAverageLabel
84    Private Sub clearGradesButton_Click(sender As Object,
85       e As EventArgs) Handles clearGradesButton.Click
86
87       gradesListBox.Items.Clear() ' removes all items from gradesListBox
88       classAverageLabel.Text = String.Empty ' clears classAverageLabel
89    End Sub ' clearGradesButton_Click
90 End Class ' ClassAverage
```

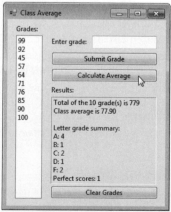

Fig. 5.9 | Counter-controlled repetition: Class-average problem. (Part 2 of 2.)

Instance Variables

For the first time in this example, we declare a variable in the class, but *outside* all of the class's event-handling methods. Such variables—called **instance variables**—are special because they can be used by *all* of the class's methods. They also retain their values, so a value set by one method in the class can be used by another method. We do this so that we can increment the letter-grade counters declared in lines 6–11 in the submitGrade-Button_Click event handler, then use those variables' values to display a grade report in the calculateAverageButton_Click event handler. The variable perfectScoreCount (line 11) counts the number of students who received a perfect score of 100 on the exam.

Method **submitGradeButton_Click**

In this version of the program, we no longer check whether the user entered a grade before pressing the **Submit Grade** Button. Instead, we now use the Val function to convert the user's input into a number. If the TextBox is empty, 0 will be added to the ListBox.

Lines 24–38 in submitGradeButton_Click use a Select...Case statement to determine which counter to increment. A grade in the range 90–100 represents an A, 80–89 represents a B, 70–79 represents a C, 60–69 represents a D and 0–59 represents an F. We assume that the user enters a grade in the range 0–100.

Line 24 begins the Select...Case statement. The expression following the keywords Select Case (in this case, grade) is called the **controlling expression**. It's compared in order with each Case. If a matching Case is found, the code in the Case executes, then program control proceeds to the first statement after the Select...Case statement (line 40).

The first Case (line 25) determines whether the value of grade is equal to 100. If so, the statements in lines 26–27 execute, incrementing both aCount (because a grade of 100 is an A) and perfectScoreCount. A Case statement can specify multiple actions—here we increment both aCount and perfectScoreCount. The next Case statement (line 28) determines whether grade is between 90 and 99, inclusive. In this case, only aCount is incremented (line 29). Keyword To in a Case specifies a range; lines 30–35 use this keyword to present a series of similar Cases. Each case increments the appropriate counter.

If *no match* occurs between the controlling expression's value and a Case label, the optional **Case Else** (lines 36–37) executes. We use the Case Else in this example to process all controlling-expression values that are less than 60—that is, all failing grades. If no match occurs and the Select...Case does not contain a Case Else, program control simply continues with the first statement after the Select...Case. Case Else commonly is used to deal with *invalid* values. In this example, we assume all values entered by the user are in the range 0–100. When used, the Case Else must be the last Case. The required **End Select** keywords (line 38) terminate the Select...Case statement.

Common Programming Error 5.2
Duplicate Case statements are logic errors. At runtime, the first matching Case executes.

Common Programming Error 5.3
If the value on the left side of keyword To in a Case statement is larger than the value on the right side, the Case is ignored during program execution; this is typically a logic error. The compiler issues a warning in this case.

Error-Prevention Tip 5.2

Provide a Case Else *in* Select...Case *statements. Cases not handled in a Se-lect...Case statement are ignored unless a* Case Else *is provided. Including a* Case Else *statement can facilitate the processing of exceptional conditions.*

Types of **Case** Statements

Case statements also can use relational operators to determine whether the controlling expression satisfies a condition. For example

    Case Is < 0

uses keyword **Is** along with the relational operator, <, to test for values less than 0.

Multiple values can be tested in a Case statement by separating the values with commas, as in

    Case 0, 5 To 9

which tests for the value 0 or values in the range 5–9. Also, Cases can be used to test String values.

Select...Case Statement UML Activity Diagram

Figure 5.10 shows the UML activity diagram for the general Select...Case statement.

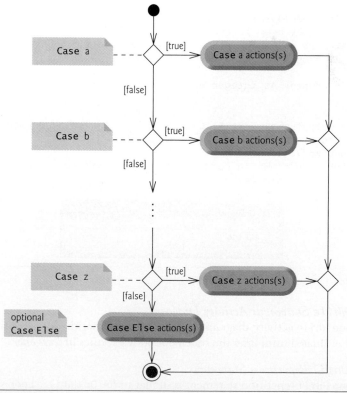

Fig. 5.10 | Select...Case multiple-selection statement UML activity diagram.

5.7 Do...Loop While and Do...Loop Until Repetition Statements

The **Do...Loop While** repetition statement is similar to the While...End While statement and Do While...Loop statement. In the While...End While and Do While...Loop statements, the loop-continuation condition is tested at the *beginning* of the loop, *before* the body of the loop is performed, so these are referred to as *pre-test loops*. The Do...Loop While statement tests the loop-continuation condition *after* the loop body is performed, so it's referred to as a *post-test loop*. In a Do...Loop While statement, the loop body is always executed *at least once*. When a Do...Loop While statement terminates, execution continues with the statement after the Loop While clause. The program in Fig. 5.11 uses a Do...Loop While statement to output the even integers from 2 to 10.

Lines 10–13 demonstrate the Do...Loop While statement. When program control enters the loop, lines 11–12 execute, displaying the value of counter (at this point, 2), then incrementing counter by 2. Then the loop-continuation condition in line 13 is evaluated. Variable counter is 4, which is less than or equal to 10, so the Do...Loop While statement executes lines 11–12 again. In the fifth iteration of the statement, line 11 outputs the value 10, and line 12 increments counter to 12. At this point, the loop-continuation condition in line 13 evaluates to false, and the program exits the Do...Loop While statement.

```
1   ' Fig. 5.11: DoLoopWhile.vb
2   ' Do...Loop While repetition statement.
3   Public Class DoLoopWhile
4      ' display the even Integers from 2 to 10
5      Private Sub DoLoopWhile_Load(sender As Object,
6         e As EventArgs) Handles MyBase.Load
7
8         Dim counter As Integer = 2 ' initialize counter
9
10        Do
11           outputLabel.Text &= counter & "  " ' display counter value
12           counter += 2 ' increment counter
13        Loop While counter <= 10
14     End Sub ' DoLoopWhile_Load
15  End Class ' DoLoopWhile
```

Even Integers from 2 to 10

```
2 4 6 8 10
```

Fig. 5.11 | Do...Loop While repetition statement.

Do...Loop While *Statement Activity Diagram*

The Do...Loop While activity diagram (Fig. 5.12) shows that the loop-continuation condition is not evaluated until *after* the statement body executes *at least once*.

Do...Loop Until *Repetition Statement*

The **Do...Loop Until** repetition statement is similar to the Do Until...Loop statement, except that the loop-termination condition is tested *after* the loop body is performed; therefore, the loop body executes *at least once*. When a Do...Loop Until terminates, execution continues with the statement after the Loop Until clause. The following code uses a Do...Loop Until statement to reimplement the Do...Loop While statement of Fig. 5.11

```
Do
    outputLabel.Text &= counter & "  " ' display counter value
    counter += 2 ' increment counter
Loop Until counter > 10
```

The Do...Loop Until statement activity diagram is the same as the one in Fig. 5.12. The loop-termination condition (counter > 10) is not evaluated until *after* the loop body executes *at least once*. If this condition is true, the statement exits. If the condition is false (that is, the condition counter <= 10 is true), the loop continues executing.

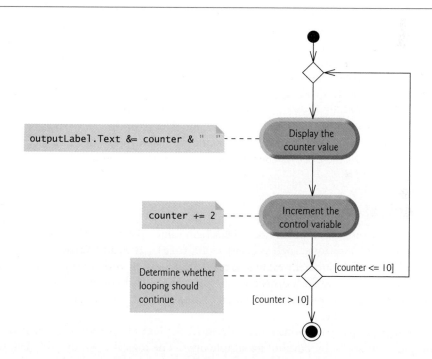

Fig. 5.12 | Do...Loop While repetition statement activity diagram.

5.8 Using Exit to Terminate Repetition Statements

There are many forms of the **Exit** statement, designed to terminate different types of repetition statements. When the **Exit Do** statement executes in a Do While...Loop, Do...Loop While, Do Until...Loop or Do...Loop Until statement, the program terminates that repetition statement and continues execution with the first statement after the repetition statement. Similarly, the **Exit For** statement and the **Exit While** statement cause immediate exit from For...Next and While...End While loops, respectively. The **Exit Select** statement causes immediate exit from a Select...Case statement.

5.9 Using Continue in Repetition Statements

A Continue statement terminates *only the current iteration* of a repetition statement and continues execution with the next iteration of the loop. The **Continue Do** statement can be executed in a Do While...Loop, Do...Loop While, Do Until...Loop or Do...Loop Until statement. Similarly, the **Continue For** statement and **Continue While** statement can be used in For...Next and While...End While statements, respectively.

When Continue For is encountered in a For...Next statement, execution continues with the statement's increment expression, then the program evaluates the loop-continuation test. When Continue is used in another type of repetition statement, the program evaluates the loop-continuation (or loop-termination) test immediately after the Continue statement executes. If a control variable's increment occurs in the loop body after the Continue statement, the increment is skipped.

Exit *and* Continue *in Nested Control Statements*

Exit and Continue also can be used in nested control statements. For instance, Exit For or Continue For can be used in a While...End While statement, as long as that statement is nested in a For...Next statement. In such an example, the Exit or Continue statement would be applied to the proper control statement based on the keywords used in the Exit or Continue statement—in this example, the For keyword is used, so the For...Next statement's flow of control will be altered. If there are nested loops of the same type (for example, a For...Next statement within a For...Next statement), the statement that immediately surrounds the Exit or Continue statement is the one affected.

5.10 Logical Operators

A condition is an expression that results in a Boolean value—**True** or **False**. So far, we've studied only **simple conditions**, such as count <= 10, total > 1000 and number <> -1. Each selection and repetition statement evaluated only *one* condition with *one* of the operators >, <, >=, <=, = and <>. To make a decision that relied on the evaluation of *multiple* conditions, we performed these tests in separate statements or in nested If...Then or If...Then...Else statements.

To handle multiple conditions more efficiently, the logical operators can be used to form complex conditions by combining simple ones. The logical operators are And, Or, AndAlso, OrElse, Xor and Not.

Logical *And Operator*

Suppose we wish to ensure that two conditions are *both* True in a program before a certain path of execution is chosen. In such a case, we can use the logical **And** operator as follows:

```
If gender = "F" And age >= 65 Then
    seniorFemales += 1
End If
```

This If...Then statement contains *two* simple conditions. The condition gender = "F" determines whether a person is female and the condition age >= 65 determines whether a person is a senior citizen. The two simple conditions are evaluated first, because the precedences of = and >= are both higher than the precedence of And. The If...Then statement then considers the combined condition

```
gender = "F" And age >= 65
```

This condition evaluates to True if and only if *both* simple conditions are True. When this combined condition is True, the seniorFemales count is incremented by 1. However, if either or both simple conditions are False, the program skips the increment and proceeds to the statement following the If...Then statement. The readability of the preceding combined condition can be improved by adding redundant (that is, unnecessary) parentheses:

```
(gender = "F") And (age >= 65)
```

Figure 5.13 illustrates the effect of using the And operator with two expressions. The table lists all four possible combinations of True and False values for *expression1* and *expression2*. Such tables often are called **truth tables**. Expressions that include relational operators, equality operators and logical operators evaluate to True or False.

expression1	expression2	expression1 And expression2
False	False	False
False	True	False
True	False	False
True	True	True

Fig. 5.13 | Truth table for the logical And operator.

Logical Or Operator (Also Called the Logical Inclusive Or Operator)
Now let's consider the **Or** operator. Suppose we wish to ensure that *either or both* of two conditions are True before we choose a certain path of execution. We use the Or operator as in the following program segment:

```
If (semesterAverage >= 90 Or finalExam >= 90) Then
    resultLabel.Text = "Student grade is A"
End If
```

This statement also contains *two* simple conditions. The condition semesterAverage >= 90 is evaluated to determine whether the student deserves an "A" in the course because of an outstanding performance throughout the semester. The condition finalExam >= 90 is evaluated to determine whether the student deserves an "A" in the course because of an outstanding performance on the final exam. The If...Then statement then considers the combined condition

```
(semesterAverage >= 90 Or finalExam >= 90)
```

and awards the student an "A" if *either or both* of the conditions are True. The text "Student grade is A" is displayed, unless *both* of the conditions are False. Figure 5.14 shows the Or operator's truth table. The And operator has a higher precedence than Or.

expression1	expression2	expression1 Or expression2
False	False	False
False	True	True
True	False	True
True	True	True

Fig. 5.14 | Truth table for the logical Or operator.

Logical *AndAlso* and *OrElse* Operators

The logical AND operator with short-circuit evaluation (AndAlso) and the logical inclusive OR operator with short-circuit evaluation (OrElse) are similar to the And and Or operators, respectively, with one exception—an expression containing AndAlso or OrElse operators is evaluated only until its truth or falsity is known. For example, the expression

```
(gender = "F" AndAlso age >= 65)
```

stops evaluating immediately if gender is not equal to "F" (that is, the entire expression is False); the second expression is irrelevant because the first condition is False. Evaluation of the second condition occurs if and only if gender is equal to "F" (that is, the entire expression could still be True if the condition age >= 65 is True). This performance feature for the evaluation of AndAlso and OrElse expressions is called short-circuit evaluation.

 Performance Tip 5.1

In expressions using operator AndAlso, if the separate conditions are independent of one another, place the condition most likely to be False as the leftmost condition. In expressions using operator OrElse, make the condition most likely to be True the leftmost condition. Each of these suggestions can reduce a program's execution time.

Logical *Xor* Operator

A condition containing the logical exclusive OR (Xor) operator is True if and only if one of its operands results in a True value and the other results in a False value. If both operands are True or both are False, the entire condition is False. Figure 5.15 presents a truth table for the logical exclusive OR operator (Xor). This operator always evaluates *both* of its operands—there's no short-circuit evaluation.

expression1	expression2	expression1 Xor expression2
False	False	False
False	True	True
True	False	True
True	True	False

Fig. 5.15 | Truth table for the logical exclusive OR (Xor) operator.

Logical *Not* Operator

The **Not** (logical negation) operator enables you to "reverse" the meaning of a condition. Unlike the logical operators And, AndAlso, Or, OrElse and Xor, which each combine *two* conditions, the logical negation operator is a unary operator, requiring only one operand. The logical negation operator is placed before a condition to choose a path of execution if the original condition (without the logical negation operator) is False. The logical negation operator is demonstrated by the following program segment:

```
If Not (value = 0) Then
   resultLabel.Text = "The value is " & value
End If
```

The parentheses around the condition value = 0 are necessary because the logical negation operator (Not) has a higher precedence than the equality operator. Figure 5.16 provides a truth table for the logical negation operator.

In most cases, you can avoid using logical negation by expressing the condition differently with relational or equality operators. This flexibility helps you express conditions more naturally. For example, the preceding statement can be written as follows:

```
If value <> 0 Then
   resultLabel.Text = "The value is " & value
End If
```

expression	Not expression
False	True
True	False

Fig. 5.16 | Truth table for operator Not (logical negation).

5.11 App: Dental Payment Calculator

To demonstrate some of the logical operators, let's consider the following problem:

A dentist's office administrator wishes to create an app that employees can use to bill patients. The app must allow users to enter the patient's name and specify which services were performed during the visit. The app will then calculate the total charges. If a user attempts to calculate a bill before any services are specified, or before the patient's name is entered, an error message will be displayed informing the user that necessary input is missing.

GUI for the Dental Payment Calculator App

In the **Dental Payment Calculator** app, you'll use two new GUI controls—CheckBoxes and a message dialog—to assist the user in entering data. The CheckBoxes allow the user to select which dental services were performed. Programs often use **message dialogs** to display important messages to the user.

A **CheckBox** is a small square that either is blank or contains a check mark. A CheckBox is known as a **state button** because it can be in the "on" state or the "off" state—a CheckBox may also have an "indeterminate" state, which we do not cover in this book. When a CheckBox is selected, a check mark appears in the box. Any number of CheckBoxes can be selected at a time, including none at all. The text that appears alongside a CheckBox is called the **CheckBox label** and is specified with the Text property. If the CheckBox is "on" (checked), its **Checked property** has the Boolean value True; otherwise, it's False ("off"). The app's GUI is shown in Fig. 5.17 and the code is shown in Fig. 5.18.

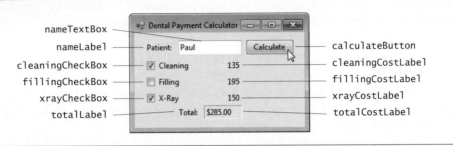

Fig. 5.17 | GUI for **Dental Payment Calculator** app.

```
 1    ' Fig. 5.18: DentalPayment.vb
 2    ' Dental Payment Calculator displays bill amount for a dental visit.
 3    Public Class DentalPayment
 4       ' calculate the bill amount
 5       Private Sub calculateButtonClick(sender As Object,
 6          e As EventArgs) Handles calculateButton.Click
 7
 8          ' if no name entered or no CheckBoxes checked, display message
 9          If (nameTextBox.Text = String.Emtpy) OrElse
10             (Not cleaningCheckBox.Checked AndAlso
11              Not xrayCheckBox.Checked AndAlso
12              Not fillingCheckBox.Checked) Then
13
14             totalCostLabel.Text = String.Empty ' clear totalCostLabel
15
16             ' display an error message in a dialog
17             MessageBox.Show(
18                "Please enter a name and check at least one item",
19                "Missing Information", MessageBoxButtons.OK,
20                MessageBoxIcon.Error)
21          Else ' add prices
22             ' total contains amount to bill patient
23             Dim total As Decimal = 0
24
25             ' if patient had a cleaning
26             If cleaningCheckBox.Checked Then
27                total += Val(cleaningCostLabel.Text)
28             End If
29
30             ' if patient had a cavity filled
31             If fillingCheckBox.Checked Then
32                total += Val(fillingCostLabel.Text)
33             End If
```

Fig. 5.18 | **Dental Payment Calculator** displays bill amount for a dental visit. (Part 1 of 2.)

```
34
35              ' if patient had an X-Ray taken
36          If xrayCheckBox.Checked Then
37              total += Val(xrayCostLabel.Text)
38          End If
39
40              ' display the total
41              totalCostLabel.Text = String.Format("{0:C}", total)
42          End If
43      End Sub ' calculateButtonClick
44  End Class ' DentalPayment
```

Fig. 5.18 | **Dental Payment Calculator** displays bill amount for a dental visit. (Part 2 of 2.)

Using Logical Operators

Recall from the problem statement that an error message should be displayed if the user does not enter a name or select at least one CheckBox. When the user presses the **Calculate** Button, lines 9–12 test these possibilities using logical operators Not, OrElse and AndAlso. The compound condition is split into two parts. If the condition in line 9 is True, the user did not enter a name, so an error message should be displayed. Short-circuit evaluation occurs with the OrElse operator, so the rest of the condition (lines 10–12) is ignored. If the user entered a name, then lines 10–12 check all three CheckBoxes. The expression

```
    Not cleaningCheckBox.Checked
```

is True if the cleaningCheckBox is not checked—the Checked property has the value False and the Not operator returns True. If all three CheckBoxes are unchecked, the compound condition in lines 10–12 is True, so an error message should be displayed.

Calculating the Total of the Selected Services

If the user entered a name and selected at least one CheckBox, lines 21–42 calculate the total of the selected dental services. Each condition in lines 26, 31 and 36 uses the value of one of the CheckBox's Checked properties as the condition. If a given CheckBox's Checked property is True, the body statement gets the value from the corresponding price Label, converts it to a number and adds it to the total. Then, line 41 displays the result in the totalCostLabel.

Displaying an Error Message Dialog

Class MessageBox creates message dialogs. We use a message dialog in lines 17–20 to display an error message to the user if the condition in lines 9–12 is True. MessageBox method Show displays the dialog. This method takes four arguments. The first is the String that's displayed in the message dialog. The second is the String that's displayed in the message dialog's title bar. The third and fourth are predefined constants that specify the Button(s) and the icon to show on the dialog, respectively.

Figure 5.19 shows the message box displayed by lines 17–20. It includes an **OK** button that allows the user to dismiss (that is, close) the message dialog by clicking the button. The program *waits* for the dialog to be closed before executing the next line of code—this type of dialog is known as a **modal dialog**. You can also dismiss the message dialog by clicking the dialog's close box—the button with an **X** in the dialog's upper-right corner.

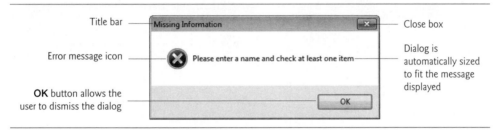

Title bar — Missing Information — Close box

Error message icon — Please enter a name and check at least one item — Dialog is automatically sized to fit the message displayed

OK button allows the user to dismiss the dialog — OK

Fig. 5.19 | Message dialog displayed by calling MessageBox.Show.

Summary of Operator Precedence

Figure 5.20 displays the precedence of the operators introduced so far. The operators are shown from top to bottom in decreasing order of precedence.

Operators	Type
^	exponentiation
+ -	unary plus and minus
* /	multiplicative operators
\	integer division
Mod	modulus
+ -	additive operators
&	concatenation
< <= > >= = <>	relational and equality
Not	logical NOT

Fig. 5.20 | Precedence of the operators discussed so far. (Part 1 of 2.)

Operators	Type
`And` `AndAlso`	logical AND
`Or` `OrElse`	logical inclusive OR
`Xor`	logical exclusive OR
`=` `+=` `-=` `*=` `/=` `\=` `^=` `&=`	assignment

Fig. 5.20 | Precedence of the operators discussed so far. (Part 2 of 2.)

5.12 Wrap-Up

In this chapter, we completed our introduction to the control statements that enable you to control the flow of execution. We demonstrated the `For...Next`, `Select...Case`, `Do...Loop While` and `Do...Loop Until` statements. Any algorithm can be developed using combinations of the sequence structure (that is, statements listed in the order in which they are to execute), the three types of selection statements—`If...Then`, `If...Then...Else` and `Select...Case`—and the seven types of repetition statements—`While...End While`, `Do While...Loop`, `Do Until...Loop`, `Do...Loop While`, `Do...Loop Until`, `For...Next` and `For Each...Next` (which we discuss in Chapter 7). We discussed how you can combine these building blocks using proven program-construction and problem-solving techniques. We showed how to use nested `For...Next` statements. We showed how to alter the flow of program control using the various `Exit` and `Continue` statements. You used the logical operators to form more complex conditional expressions in control statements. Chapter 6 discusses methods in greater depth and shows how to use them to organize larger programs as small, manageable pieces.

Summary

Section 5.2 For...Next Repetition Statement

- Counter-controlled repetition requires the name of a control variable, the initial value of the control variable, the increment (or decrement) by which the control variable is modified each time through the loop and the condition that tests for the final value of the control variable.

- The `For...Next` repetition statement specifies counter-controlled repetition details in a single line of code. In general, counter-controlled repetition should be implemented with `For...Next`.

- When the `For...Next` statement is reached, its control variable is initialized. Next, the *implied* loop-continuation condition is tested.

- The `To` keyword is required and is followed by the control variable's final value.

- The optional `Step` keyword specifies the increment. If `Step` and the value following it are omitted, the increment defaults to `1`.

- If the loop-continuation condition is initially false, the `For...Next`'s body is not performed.

- When `Next` is reached, the control variable is incremented by the `Step` value, and the implied loop-continuation test is performed again.

- The first line of the `For...Next` statement sometimes is called the `For...Next` header.

- The general form of the For...Next statement is

    ```
    For initialization To finalValue Step increment
        statement
    Next
    ```

    where the *initialization* expression initializes the loop's control variable, *finalValue* determines whether the loop should continue executing and *increment* specifies the amount the control variable should be incremented each time through the loop.

- When the *initialization* expression in the For...Next statement header declares the control variable, the control variable can be used only in the body of the For...Next statement.

- A variable's scope specifies where the variable can be used in a program.

- The starting value, ending value and increment portions of a For...Next statement can contain arithmetic expressions.

- Local type inference determines a local variable's type based on its initializer value.

- You can also use local type inference with the control variable of a For...Next statement.

- The literal type character D (123.45D) indicates that a literal numeric value is of type Decimal. Other common literal type characters include C for Char ("T"C), F for Single (123.45F), S for Short (123S) and L for Long (123L).

Section 5.4 App: Interest Calculator

- The NumericUpDown control limits a user's choices to a range of values specified by its Minimum and Maximum properties. The Value property specifies the current value displayed in the control and can be used to obtain the current value. The Increment property specifies by how much the current number in the control changes when the user clicks the control's up or down arrow.

- When the user changes the value in a NumericUpDown control, a ValueChanged event occurs.

- Type Decimal should be used for monetary calculations.

- The built-in Val function obtains a value from a String of characters. The value returned is guaranteed to be a number. Val ignores whitespace. Val recognizes the decimal point as well as plus and minus signs that indicate whether a number is positive or negative. If Val receives an argument that cannot be converted to a number, it returns 0.

- The C ("currency") format specifier indicates that its corresponding value should be displayed in monetary format—with a dollar sign to the left and commas in the proper locations. This may differ based on your locale throughout the world.

- Other commonly used format specifiers include F for floating-point numbers (sets the number of decimal places to two), N for numbers (separates every three digits with a comma and sets the number of decimal places to two) and D for integers.

Section 5.6 Select...Case Multiple-Selection Statement

- A variable that's declared in the class, but outside all of the class's methods is called an instance variable. Such variables are special because they can be used by all of the class's methods.

- The Select...Case multiple-selection statement tests a variable or expression for each value that the variable or expression might assume, then takes different actions based on those values.

- The expression following the keywords Select Case is called the controlling expression. It's compared in order with each Case. If a matching Case is found, its code executes, then program control proceeds to the first statement after the Select...Case statement.

- Cases may contain single values, multiple values or ranges of values. Keyword To specifies a range.

- If no match occurs between the controlling expression's value and a Case, the optional Case Else executes. If there's not a Case Else, program control simply continues with the first statement after the Select...Case. When used, the Case Else must be the last Case.

- The required End Select keywords terminate the Select...Case statement.

- Case statements can use relational operators to determine whether the controlling expression satisfies a condition. Case Is < 0 tests for values less than 0.

- Multiple values can be tested in a Case statement by separating the values with commas.

Section 5.7 *Do...Loop While and Do...Loop Until Repetition Statements*

- The Do...Loop While repetition statement tests the loop-continuation condition after the loop body is performed—the loop body is always executed at least once.

- The Do...Loop Until repetition statement test the loop-termination condition after the loop body is performed—the loop body executes at least once.

Section 5.8 *Using Exit to Terminate Repetition Statements*

- When the Exit Do statement executes in a Do While...Loop, Do...Loop While, Do Until...Loop or Do...Loop Until statement, that repetition statement terminates and the program continues execution with the first statement after the repetition statement. Exit For and Exit While cause immediate exit from For...Next and While...End While loops, respectively.

Section 5.9 *Using Continue in Repetition Statements*

- A Continue statement terminates only the current iteration of a repetition statement and continues execution with the next iteration of the loop. Continue Do statement can be executed in a Do While...Loop, Do...Loop While, Do Until...Loop or Do...Loop Until statement. Continue For and Continue While can be used in For...Next and While...End While statements, respectively.

- Continue For causes a For...Next statement to increment the control variable, then evaluate the loop-continuation test. When Continue is used other repetition statements, the program evaluates the loop-continuation (or loop-termination) test immediately.

- Exit and Continue also can be used in nested control statements.

Section 5.10 *Logical Operators*

- A condition is an expression that results in a Boolean value—True or False.

- The logical operators can be used to form complex conditions.

- Operator And evaluates a complex condition to true if and only if both of its operands are true.

- Operator Or evaluates a complex condition to true unless both of its operands are false.

- Operator And has a higher precedence than the Or operator.

- The operators AndAlso and OrElse are similar to the And and Or operators, but an expression containing AndAlso or OrElse uses short-circuit evaluation.

- A condition containing the logical exclusive OR (Xor) operator is true if and only if one of its operands results in a true value and the other results in a false value. If both operands are true or both are false, the entire condition is false.

- The Not operator enables you to "reverse" the meaning of a condition.

Section 5.11 *App: Dental Payment Calculator*

- A CheckBox is known as a state button because it can be in the "on" state or the "off" state.

- When a CheckBox is selected, a check mark appears in the box. Any number of CheckBoxes can be selected at a time.

- The text that appears alongside a CheckBox is called the CheckBox label.
- If a CheckBox is "on" (checked), its Checked property is True; otherwise, it's False ("off").
- MessageBox method Show displays a message dialog, which is typically used to display an important message to the user. The method's four arguments are the message String, the String that's displayed in the dialog's title bar and predefined constants that specify the Button(s) and the icon to show on the dialog, respectively.
- A program waits for a message dialog to be closed before executing the next line of code—this type of dialog is known as a modal dialog.

Terminology

And (logical AND) operator 200
AndAlso (logical AND with short-circuit evaluation) operator 202
C format specifier 189
C literal type character 185
Case Else clause 196
CheckBox control 203
Checked property of CheckBox control 204
close a dialog 206
Continue statement 200
controlling expression in a Select...Case 196
D format specifier 189
D literal type character 185
Decimal primitive type 189
decrement a control variable 181
dismiss (hide) a dialog 206
Do...Loop Until repetition statement 198
Do...Loop While repetition statement 198
End Select keywords 196
Exit statement 199
F literal type character 185
False keyword 200
final value of a control variable 181
For...Next header 183
For...Next repetition statement 182
increment a control variable 181
Increment property of NumericUpDown 187
initial value of a control variable 181
instance variable 196
Is keyword 197
L literal type character 185

local type inference 184
logical operator 200
Maximum property of NumericUpDown 187
message dialog 203
MessageBox class 206
Minimum property of NumericUpDown 187
modal dialog 206
N format specifier 189
name of a control variable 181
Next keyword 183
Not (logical NOT) operator 203
NumericUpDown control 187
off-by-one error 182
Or (logical inclusive OR) operator 201
OrElse (logical inclusive OR with short-circuit evaluation) operator 202
S literal type character 185
scope 184
Select...Case multiple-selection statement 193
short-circuit evaluation 202
Show method of class MessageBox 206
simple condition 200
state button 203
Step keyword in a For...Next statement 182
To keyword in a For...Next statement 182
True keyword 200
truth table 201
Val function 189
Value property of NumericUpDown 187
ValueChanged event of NumericUpDown 187
Xor (exclusive OR) operator 202

Self-Review Exercises

5.1 State whether each of the following is *true* or *false*. If *false*, explain why.
  a) The Case Else is required in the Select...Case selection statement.
  b) The expression x > y And a < b is true if either x > y is true or a < b is true.
  c) An expression containing the Or operator is true if either or both of its operands are true.

d) The expression x <= y AndAlso y > 4 is true if x is less than or equal to y and y is greater than 4.

e) Logical operator Or performs short-circuit evaluation.

f) The Exit Do, Exit For and Exit While statements, when executed in a repetition statement, cause immediate exit from only the current iteration of the repetition statement.

g) The Do...Loop While statement tests the loop-continuation condition *before* the loop body is performed.

h) The Or operator has a *higher* precedence than the And operator.

5.2 Answer each of the following questions.

a) Which property specifies whether a CheckBox is selected?
   1. Selected   2. Checked
   3. Clicked   4. Check

b) Call the _____ method of class MessageBox to display a message dialog.
   1. Display   2. Message
   3. Open   4. Show

c) A unary operator _____.
   1. requires exactly one operand   2. requires two operands
   3. must use the AndAlso keyword   4. can have no operands

d) The _____ operator is used to ensure that two conditions are both true.
   1. Xor   2. AndAlso
   3. Also   4. OrElse

e) The Do...Loop While statement body repeats when the loop-continuation condition _____.
   1. is False after the body executes   2. is False before the body executes
   3. is True after the body executes   4. is True before the body executes

f) An infinite loop occurs when the loop-continuation condition in a Do While...Loop or Do...Loop While statement _____.
   1. never becomes True   2. never becomes False
   3. is False   4. is tested repeatedly

g) The Do...Loop Until statement checks the loop-termination condition _____.
   1. for False after the body executes   2. for False before the body executes
   3. for True after the body executes   4. for True before the body executes

h) Counter-controlled repetition _____ the control variable after each iteration.
   1. increments   2. initializes
   3. decrements   4. Either answer 1 or 3

i) What aspect of the control variable determines whether looping should continue?
   1. name   2. initial value
   3. type   4. final value

j) If the Step is omitted, the increment of a For...Next statement defaults to _____.
   1. 1   2. -1
   3. 0   4. Either answer 1 or 2

k) The value before the To keyword in a For...Next statement specifies the _____.
   1. initial value of the counter variable   2. final value of the counter variable
   3. increment   4. number of times the statement iterates

l) Which of the following is the appropriate For...Next header for varying the control variable over the following sequence of values: 25, 20, 15, 10, 5?

   1. `For i As Integer = 5 To 25 Step 5`   2. `For i As Integer = 25 To 5 Step -5`

   3. `For i As Integer = 5 To 25 Step -5`   4. `For i As Integer = 25 To 5 Step 5`

m) Which of the following statements describes the For...Next header shown below?

   `For i As Integer = 81 To 102`

   1. Vary the control variable from 81 to 102 in increments of 1.

   2. Vary the control variable from 81 to 102 in increments of 0.

   3. Vary the control variable from 102 to 81 in increments of –1.

   4. Vary the control variable from 81 to 102 in increments of 2.

n) `Select Case` is a _____-selection statement.

   1. multiple   2. double

   3. single   4. None of the above

o) When does the `Case Else` body execute?

   1. Every time a `Select Case` statement executes.

   2. When more than one `Case` matches the controlling expression.

   3. When the controlling expression does not match any other cases.

   4. None of the above.

p) A `Case` that handles all values larger than a specified value must precede the > operator with keyword _____.

   1. `Select`   2. `Is`

   3. `Case`   4. `All`

q) Use a(n) _____ to separate multiple conditions in a Case statement.

   1. period   2. asterisk

   3. comma   4. colon

r) The _____ property determines by how much the current number in a `NumericUp-Down` control changes when the user clicks the up arrow or the down arrow.

   1. `Amount`   2. `Step`

   3. `Increment`   4. `Next`

s) Which For...Next header alters the control variable from 0 to 50 in increments of 5?

   1. `For i = 0 To 50 Step 50`   2. `For 0 To 50 Step 5`

   3. `For i = 0 To 50 Step = 5`   4. `For i = 0 To 50 Step 5`

5.3 Write a statement or a set of statements to accomplish each of the following:

a) Sum the odd integers between 1 and 99 using a For...Next statement. Assume that the `Integer` variables `sum` and `count` have been declared.

b) Write a statement that exits a `Do While...Loop` statement.

c) Display in `outputTextBox` the integers from 1 to 20, using a `Do...Loop While` loop and the counter variable `counter`. Display only five integers per line. [*Hint:* Use the expression `counter Mod 5` to determine when five values have been displayed. When the value of this expression is 0, move to the next line; otherwise, display a tab character.]

d) Repeat part c, using a For...Next statement.

Answers to Self-Review Exercises

5.1   a) False. The `Case Else` is optional. b) False. *Both* of the simple conditions must be true for the entire expression to be true. c) True. d) True. e) False. Logical operator `Or` always evaluates both of its operands. f) False. The `Exit Do`, `Exit For` and `Exit While` statements, when executed in a repetition statement, cause immediate exit from the repetition statement. The `Continue Do`, `Continue For` and `Continue While` statements, when executed in a repetition statement, cause immediate exit from the current iteration of the repetition statement. g) False. The `Do...Loop While` statement tests the loop-continuation condition *after* the loop body is performed. h) False. The `And` operator has higher precedence than the `Or` operator.

5.2   a) 2. b) 4. c) 1. d) 2. e) 3. f) 2. g) 3. h) 4. i) 4. j) 1. k) 1. l) 2. m) 1. n) 1. o) 3. p) 2. q) 3. r) 3. s) 4.

5.3
a)
```
sum = 0
For count = 1 To 99 Step 2
  sum += count
Next
```
b)
```
Exit Do
```
c)
```
Dim counter As Integer = 1

Do
    outputTextBox.AppendText(counter)

    If counter Mod 5 = 0 Then
        outputTextBox.AppendText(vbCrLf)
    Else
        outputTextBox.AppendText(vbTab)
    End If

    counter += 1
Loop While counter <= 20
```
d)
```
For counter = 1 To 20
    outputTextBox.AppendText(counter)

    If counter Mod 5 = 0 Then
        outputTextBox.AppendText(vbCrLf)
    Else
        outputTextBox.AppendText(vbTab)
    End If
Next
```

Quick Quiz

5.4   Answer each of the following questions.
a) How many `CheckBoxes` in a GUI can be selected at once?
1. 0   2. 1
3. 4   4. any number
b) The first argument passed to method `MessageBox.Show` is _____.
1. the text displayed in the dialog's title bar
2. a constant representing the `Buttons` displayed in the dialog
3. the text displayed inside the dialog
4. a constant representing the icon that appears in the dialog

c) _____ are used to create complex conditions.

    1. Assignment operators   2. Activity diagrams

    3. Logical operators   4. Formatting codes

d) Operator `AndAlso` _____.

    1. performs short-circuit evaluation   2. is not a keyword

    3. is a comparison operator   4. None of the above.

e) A `CheckBox` is selected when its `Checked` property is set to _____.

    1. `On`   2. `True`

    3. `Selected`   4. `Checked`

f) The condition *expression1* `AndAlso` *expression2* evaluates to `True` if _____.

    1. *expression1* is `True` and *expression2* is `False`

    2. *expression1* is `False` and *expression2* is `True`

    3. both *expression1* and *expression2* are `True`

    4. both *expression1* and *expression2* are `False`

g) The condition *expression1* `OrElse` *expression2* evaluates to `False` if _____.

    1. *expression1* is `True` and *expression2* is `False`

    2. *expression1* is `False` and *expression2* is `True`

    3. both *expression1* and *expression2* are `True`

    4. both *expression1* and *expression2* are `False`

h) The condition *expression1* `Xor` *expression2* evaluates to `True` if _____.

    1. *expression1* is `True` and *expression2* is `False`

    2. *expression1* is `False` and *expression2* is `True`

    3. both *expression1* and *expression2* are `True`

    4. Both answers 1 and 2

i) The condition `Not(`*expression1* `AndAlso` *expression2*`)` evaluates to `True` if _____.

    1. *expression1* is `True` and *expression2* is `False`

    2. *expression1* is `False` and *expression2* is `True`

    3. both *expression1* and *expression2* are `False`

    4. All of the above.

j) A(n) _____ occurs when a loop-continuation condition in a `Do...Loop While` never becomes `False`.

    1. infinite loop   2. counter-controlled loop

    3. control statement   4. nested control statement

k) The _____ statement executes at least once and continues executing until its loop-termination condition becomes `True`.

    1. `Do While...Loop`   2. `Do...Loop Until`

    3. `Do...Loop While`   4. `Do Until...Loop`

l) The _____ statement executes at least once and continues executing until its loop-continuation condition becomes `False`.

    1. `Do...Loop Until`   2. `Do Until...Loop`

    3. `Do While...Loop`   4. `Do...Loop While`

m) A `Do...Loop Until` repetition statement's loop-termination condition is evaluated _____.

    1. only the first time the body executes   2. before the body executes

    3. after the body executes   4. None of the above

n) If its continuation condition is initially `False`, a `Do...Loop While` statement _____.
   1. never executes
   2. executes while the condition is `False`
   3. executes only once
   4. None of the above.

o) The `For...Next` header specifies _____.
   1. control variable and initial value
   2. increment or decrement
   3. loop-continuation condition
   4. All of the above.

p) The _____ is optional in a `For...Next` when the control variable's increment is 1.
   1. keyword `To`
   2. initial value of the control variable
   3. keyword `Step`
   4. final value of the control variable

q) The _____ is used to determine whether a `For...Next` loop continues to iterate.
   1. initial value of the control variable
   2. keyword `For`
   3. keyword `Step`
   4. final value of the control variable

r) In a `For...Next`, the control variable is incremented (or decremented) _____.
   1. when keyword `Next` is reached
   2. when keyword `To` is reached
   3. before the loop body executes
   4. None of the above.

s) `NumericUpDown` properties _____ and _____ specify the range of values that users can select.
   1. `Maximum, Minimum`
   2. `Top, Bottom`
   3. `High, Low`
   4. `Max, Min`

t) The `For...Next` header _____ can be used to vary the control variable over the odd numbers in the range 1–9.
   1. `For i = 1 To 9 Step 1`
   2. `For i = 1 To 9 Step 2`
   3. `For i = 1 To 9 Step -1`
   4. `For i = 1 To 9 Step -2`

u) Which of the following is a syntax error?
   1. Having duplicate `Case` statements in the same `Select Case` statement.
   2. Having a `Case` statement in which the value to the left of a `To` keyword is larger than the value to the right.
   3. Preceding a `Case` statement with the `Case Else` statement in a `Select Case` statement.
   4. Using keyword `Is` in a `Select Case` statement.

v) Keyword _____ is used to specify a range in a `Case` statement.
   1. `Also`
   2. `Between`
   3. `To`
   4. `From`

w) If the value on the left of the `To` keyword in a `Case` statement is larger than the value on the right, _____.
   1. a syntax error occurs
   2. the body of the `Case` statement executes
   3. the body of the `Case` statement never executes
   4. the statement causes a runtime error

x) The expression following the keywords `Select Case` is called a _____.
   1. guard condition
   2. controlling expression
   3. selection expression
   4. case expression

Exercises

5.5 *(Retail Sales Calculator App)* An online retailer sells five products whose retail prices are as follows: Product 1, $2.98; product 2, $4.50; product 3, $9.98; product 4, $4.49 and product 5, $6.87. Write an app that reads a series of pairs of numbers as follows:

  a) product number;
  b) quantity sold.

Your program should use a Select...Case statement to determine the retail price for each product. It should calculate and display the total retail value of all products sold in an output Label as shown in Fig. 5.21. Keep the total retail value up to date as the user enters values. [*Hint:* Create instance variables to store the quantity sold of each product so the values are maintained between calls to the event handler.]

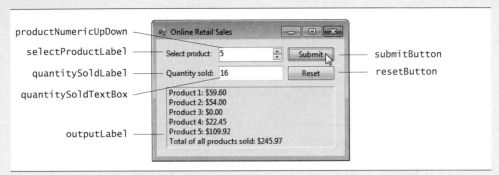

Fig. 5.21 | Online Retail Sales GUI.

5.6 (*Table of Decimal, Octal, Hexadecimal and Binary Equivalents*) Write a program that displays in a TextBox a table of the binary, octal, and hexadecimal equivalents of the decimal numbers in the range 1–255. If you are not familiar with these number systems, read Appendix C, Number Systems, first. Set the TextBox's MultiLine property to True and its ScrollBars property to Vertical so that you can scroll through the results. Figure 5.21 shows the app's GUI.

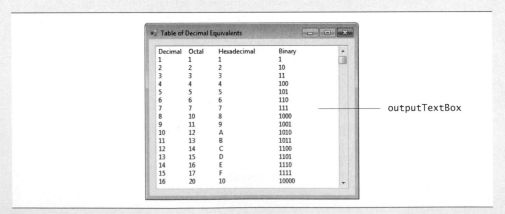

Fig. 5.22 | Table of Decimal Equivalents GUI.

5.7 (*Triangles of Asterisks*) Write a program that displays the following patterns separately, one below the other in a TextBox. Use For...Next loops to generate the patterns. All asterisks (*) should be displayed one at a time by the statement outputTextBox.AppendText("*") (this causes the asterisks to display side by side). The statement outputTextBox.AppendText(vbCrLf) can be used to position to the next line, and a statement of the form outputTextBox.AppendText(" ") can be used to display spaces for the last two patterns. There should be no other output statements in the program. [*Hint:* The last two patterns require that each line begin with an appropriate number of blanks.]

Maximize your use of repetition (with nested For...Next statements) and minimize the number of output statements. Set the TextBox's Font property to Lucida Console, its MultiLine property to True and its ScrollBars property to Vertical so that you can scroll through the results.

```
(a)              (b)              (c)              (d)
*                **********       **********                *
**               *********        *********                **
***              ********         ********                 ***
****             *******          *******                  ****
*****            ******           ******                   *****
******           *****            *****                    ******
*******          ****             ****                     *******
********          ***              ***                     ********
*********          **               **                     *********
**********          *                *                     **********
```

5.8   Assume that nameTextBox is a TextBox and that otherCheckBox is a CheckBox next to which is another TextBox called otherTextBox, in which the user should specify a value. What does this code segment do?

```
1    If (nameTextBox.Text = "George" AndAlso
2        (otherCheckBox.Checked = True OrAlso
3        otherTextBox.Text = "")) Then
4        MessageBox.Show("Please enter a name or value",
5            "Input Error", MessageBoxButtons.OK,
6            MessageBoxIcon.Error)
7    End If
```

5.9   *(Using the Debugger: Sibling Survey App)* This app is located in the Debugging folder with this chapter's examples. The **Sibling Survey** app displays the siblings selected by the user in a dialog. If the user checks either the **Brother(s)** or **Sister(s)** CheckBox and the **No Siblings** CheckBox, the user is asked to verify the selection. Otherwise, the user's selection is displayed in a MessageBox. While testing this app, you noticed that it does not execute properly. Use the debugger to find and correct the logic error(s) in the code. Figure 5.23 shows the correct output for the app. For message dialogs that do not represent errors, this program uses MessageBoxIcon.Information rather than MessageBox-Icon.Error.

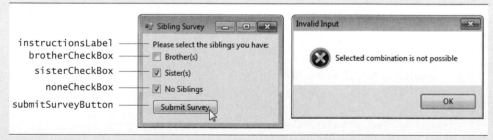

Fig. 5.23 | Correct output for the **Sibling Survey** app.

5.10   *(Arithmetic Calculator App)* Write an app that allows the user to enter a series of numbers and manipulate them. The app should provide users with the option of adding or multiplying the numbers. Users should enter each number in a TextBox. After entering each number, the user clicks an **Enter** Button, and the number is inserted in a ListBox. If the result of a previous calculation is displayed, the **Enter** Button's event handler should clear the result, clear the ListBox and disable the **Add** and **Multiply** Buttons. It should then insert the current number in the **Operands list:** ListBox. When the ListBox contains at least two numbers, the event handler should enable the **Add** and **Multiply** Buttons. The GUI should behave as shown in Figure 5.24.

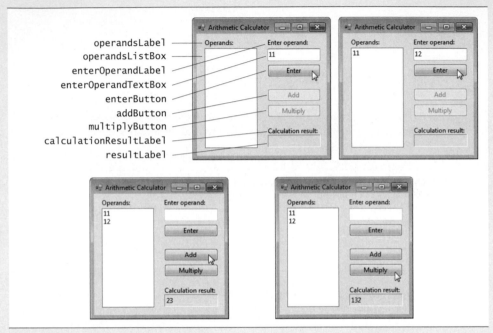

Fig. 5.24 | Arithmetic Calculator GUI.

5.11 *(What does this code do?)* What is the result of the following code?

```
1   Dim y As Integer
2   Dim x As Integer
3   Dim mysteryValue As Integer
4   x = 1
5   mysteryValue = 0
6   Do
7       y = x ^ 2
8       displayListBox.Items.Add(y)
9       mysteryValue += 1
10      x += 2
11  Loop While y <= 200
12  resultLabel.Text = mysteryValue
```

5.12 *(Using the Debugger: Factorial App)* This app is located in the Debugging folder with this chapter's examples. The **Factorial** app calculates the factorial of an integer input by the user. The factorial of an integer is the product of the integers from one to that number. For example, the factorial of 3 is 6 ($1 \times 2 \times 3$). While testing the app, you noticed that it did not execute correctly. Use the debugger to find and correct the logic error(s) in the app. Figure 5.25 displays the correct output for the **Factorial** app.

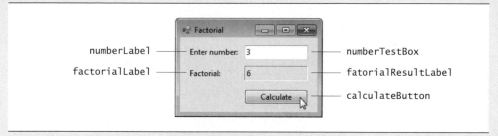

Fig. 5.25 | Correct output for the **Factorial** app.

5.13   *(Present Value Calculator App)* A bank wants to show its customers how much they would need to invest now (that is, the "present value") to achieve a specified financial goal (that is, the "future value") in 5, 10, 15, 20, 25 or 30 years. Users must provide their financial goal (the amount of money desired after the specified number of years have elapsed), an interest rate and the length of the investment in years. Create an app that calculates and displays the principal (initial amount to invest) needed to achieve the user's financial goal. Your app should allow the user to invest money for 5, 10, 15, 20, 25 or 30 years. For example, a customer who wants to reach the financial goal of $15,000 over a period of 5 years when the interest rate is 6.6% will need to invest $10,896.96, as shown in Fig. 5.26. Use the same GUI for this app as the one in Fig. 5.5. The formula to calculate the present value is:

$$p = a / (1 + r)^n$$

where

1. p is the amount needed to achieve the future value

2. a is the future-value amount

3. r is the annual interest rate (for example, .05 is equivalent to 5%)

4. n is the number of years the money will be invested.

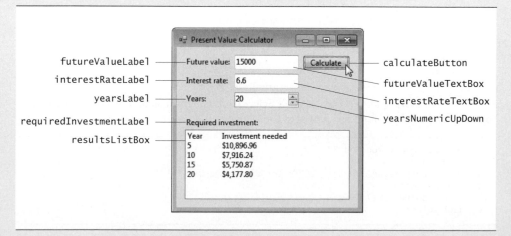

Fig. 5.26 | Future Value Calculator GUI.

5.14 *(What does this code do?)* What is the value of the result after the following code executes?

```
1  Dim power As Integer = 5
2  Dim number As Integer = 2
3  Dim result As Integer = number
4  For i As Integer = 1 To (power - 1)
5     result *= number
6  Next
```

5.15 *(Using the Debugger: Savings Calculator App)* This app is located in the Debugging folder with this chapter's examples. The **Savings Calculator** app calculates the amount that the user will have on deposit after one year. The app gets the initial amount on deposit from the user, and assumes that the user will add $100 to the account every month for the entire year. No interest is added to the account. While testing the app, you noticed that the amount calculated by the app was incorrect. Use the debugger to locate and correct any logic error(s). Figure 5.27 displays the correct output for this app.

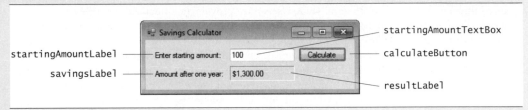

Fig. 5.27 | Correct output for the **Savings Calculator** app.

5.16 *(What does this code do?)* What is the output of the following code, if marksTextBox is 65?

```
1  Private Sub resultsButton_Click_1(ByVal sender As System.Object,
2     ByVal e As System.EventArgs) Handles resultsButton.Click
3     Select Case Val(marksTextBox.Text)
4        Case Is > 70
5           resultsLabel.Text = "First Class With Distinction."
6        Case 60 To 70
7           resultsLabel.Text = "First Class."
8        Case Is > 50
9           resultsLabel.Text = "Second Class."
10       Case Else
11          resultsLabel.Text = "Sorry, you have failed."
12    End Select
13 End Sub
```

5.17 *(What's wrong with this code?)* This **Select Case** statement should determine whether an Integer is divisible by 5. Find the error(s) in the following code:

```
1  Select Case value Mod 5
2     Case 0
3        outputLabel.Text = "It is not divisible by 5"
4     Case Else
5        outputLabel.Text = "It is divisible by 5"
6  End Select
```

5.18   *(Using the Debugger: Discount Calculator App)* This app is located in the Debugging folder with this chapter's examples. The **Discount Calculator** app determines the discount the user receives, based on how much money the user spends. A 15% discount is received for purchases over $200, a 10% discount is received for purchases between $150 and $200, a 5% discount is received for purchases between $100 and $149 and a 2% discount is received for purchases between $50 and $99. While testing your app, you notice that the app is not calculating the discount properly for some values. Use the debugger to find and fix the logic error(s) in the app. Figure 5.28 displays the correct output for the app.

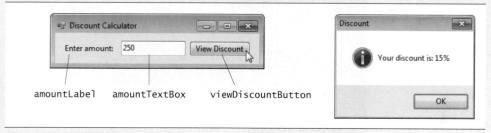

Fig. 5.28 | Correct output for the **Discount Calculator** app.

Making a Difference Exercise

5.19   *(Family's Budget Calculator)* Develop an application for a family annual budget calculator, which reads as inputs: the family's total annual income – includes income from all the sources after deducting income taxes; expenses such as housing – includes mortgage payments and property taxes, home repairs, furnishings, and utilities; food – includes both dining away from home, and money spent on groceries eaten at home; health care – Includes insurance payments and regular medical checkups; tranportation - includes car leases, car loans, gasoline and maintenance, as well as any budgeted money for public transportation; education – includes school fees, reading materials and school educational tours; lifestyle -includes family trips, clothing, etc. The application should display the budget that can be reserved under each heading. Fig. 5.29 shows the app's GUI.

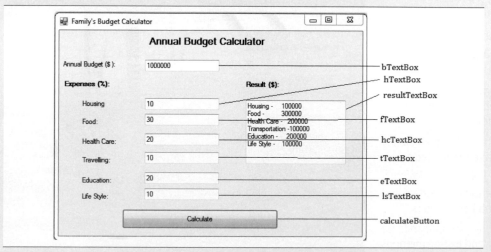

Fig. 5.29 | Annual Budget Calculator

6

Methods

The greatest invention of the nineteenth century was the invention of the method of invention.
—Alfred North Whitehead

Form ever follows function.
—Louis Henri Sullivan

O! call back yesterday, bid time return.
—William Shakespeare

Answer me in one word.
—William Shakespeare

There is a point at which methods devour themselves.
—Frantz Fanon

Objectives

In this chapter you'll:

■ Construct programs modularly from methods.

■ Create new methods.

■ Pass information between methods.

■ Learn simulation techniques that employ random-number generation.

■ Understand how the visibility of identifiers is limited to specific regions of programs.

■ Use method overloading and `Optional` parameters.

■ Use debugger commands for entering and exiting methods and for continuing program execution.

6.1 Introduction

Experience has shown that the best way to develop and maintain a large program is to construct it from small, simple pieces—a technique known as **divide and conquer**. In this chapter, we formalize our discussion of methods and use them to facilitate the design, implementation, operation and maintenance of larger programs.

We'll take a brief diversion into simulation techniques with random-number generation and develop a version of a popular casino dice game that uses most of the programming techniques you've learned to this point in the book. In addition, we'll introduce two techniques for declaring constants in your programs.

You'll learn that applications can have more than one method with the same name. This technique, called *overloading*, is used for convenience and clarity when implementing methods that perform similar tasks using different types or numbers of arguments.

6.2 Classes and Methods

Typical programs consist of one or more classes. These classes are composed of smaller pieces called methods, instance variables and (as you'll learn in Chapter 9) properties. You combine new classes with the prepackaged classes available in the .NET Framework Class Library and in various other class libraries. The .NET Framework Class Library provides a rich collection of classes and methods for performing:

- common mathematical calculations
- error checking
- building sophisticated GUI applications
- graphics
- string and character manipulations
- input/output operations
- XML processing

- database manipulations
- creating applications for the web
- many other useful operations.

Each of the preceding topics is covered in this book or in its online chapters. Earlier chapters presented various GUI controls, each of which is defined as a class in the .NET Framework Class Library. You can create your own customized classes and methods (beginning in Chapter 9) to meet the unique requirements of a particular app.

Software Engineering Observation 6.1

When possible, use .NET Framework classes and methods instead of writing new classes and methods. This reduces program-development time and can help prevent errors.

You write methods to define specific tasks that a program may use one or more times during its execution. Although the same method can be executed from multiple points in a program, the actual statements that define the method are written only once.

A method is invoked (that is, made to perform its task) by a method call. The method call specifies the method name and provides information (as arguments) that the **callee** (that is, the method being called) requires to do its job. When the method completes its task, it returns control to the caller (that is, the calling method). In some cases, the method also returns a result to the caller.

A common analogy for calling methods and returning results is communication among bosses and workers in a business. A boss (the caller) asks a worker (the callee) to perform a task and return (that is, report) the results when the task is done. The boss does not need to know how the worker performs the designated task. The worker might call other workers—the boss would be unaware of this. This **hiding of implementation details** promotes good software engineering. Figure 6.1 depicts a Boss method communicating with worker methods Worker1, Worker2 and Worker3. In this example Worker1 also acts as a "boss" method to Worker4 and Worker5.

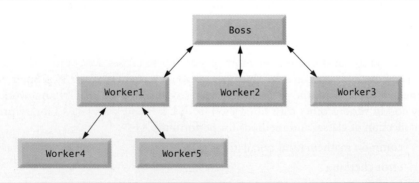

Fig. 6.1 | Boss-method/worker-method relationship.

There are several motivations for dividing code into methods.

- First, the divide-and-conquer approach makes program development more manageable.

- A second motivation is *software reusability*—the ability to use existing methods as building blocks for new programs. When proper naming and definition conventions are applied, programs can be created from standardized pieces that accomplish specific tasks, minimizing the need for customized code.

- A third motivation is to avoid repeating code in a program—when code is packaged as a method, the code can be executed from various points in a program simply by calling the method. This also makes the code easier to modify and debug.

6.3 Subroutines: Methods That Do Not Return a Value

The programs presented earlier in the book each contain at least one event-handler method that's called in response to an event and performs the program's tasks. An event-handling method is a **subroutine**—a method that performs a task but *does not* return a value. A **function** is a method that performs a task then *does* return a value to the calling method. In Section 6.4, we'll reimplement this section's example by using a function.

To demonstrate a subroutine, we'll create a **Wage Calculator** app. Consider the following problem statement:

> *Employees' weekly salaries are based on the number of hours they worked and their hourly wage. Create an app that accepts this information for one employee then calculates and displays the employee's total (gross) earnings. Assume a standard work week of 40 hours. The wages for 40 or fewer hours are calculated by multiplying the hourly wage by the number of hours worked. Hours over 40 hours are considered "overtime" and earn "time and a half." Salary for time and a half is calculated by multiplying the employee's hourly wage by 1.5 and multiplying the result of that calculation by the number of overtime hours worked. The overtime pay is added to the user's gross earnings for the regular 40 hours of work to calculate the total earnings for that week.*

Figure 6.2 shows a sample output with the labeled control names, and Fig. 6.3 shows the completed code. The program uses the method `DisplayPay` (lines 25–41) to calculate and display an employee's pay based on the hours worked and the hourly wage.

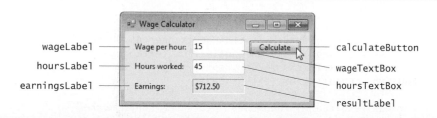

Fig. 6.2 | GUI for the **Wage Calculator** app.

```
1    ' Fig. 6.3: WageCalculator.vb
2    ' Calculating and displaying an employee's pay using a method.
3    Public Class WageCalculator
4       Const HOURS_IN_A_WEEK As Integer = 168 ' total hours in one week
5       Const HOUR_LIMIT As Integer = 40 ' maximum hours before overtime
```

Fig. 6.3 | Calculating and displaying an employee's pay using a method. (Part 1 of 2.)

```
6
7     ' calculate and display the employee's pay
8     Private Sub calculateButton_Click(sender As Object,
9        e As EventArgs) Handles calculateButton.Click
10
11       ' get hours worked and hourly wage
12       Dim hoursWorked As Double = Val(hoursTextBox.Text)
13       Dim hourlyWage As Decimal = Val(wageTextBox.Text)
14
15       ' determine whether hoursWorked is less than or equal to 168
16       If hoursWorked <= HOURS_IN_A_WEEK Then
17          DisplayPay(hoursWorked, hourlyWage) ' calls DisplayPay
18       Else
19          MessageBox.Show("Hours worked must be less than or equal to 168",
20             "Invalid Value", MessageBoxButtons.OK, MessageBoxIcon.Error)
21       End If
22    End Sub ' calculateButton_Click
23
24    ' calculate and display wages
25    Sub DisplayPay(hours As Double, wages As Decimal)
26       Dim earnings As Decimal ' stores the total earnings
27
28       ' determine wage amount
29       If hours <= HOUR_LIMIT Then
30          ' earnings for regular wages
31          earnings = hours * wages
32       Else
33          ' regular wages for first HOUR_LIMIT hours
34          earnings = HOUR_LIMIT * wages
35
36          ' time and a half for overtime
37          earnings += ((hours - HOUR_LIMIT) * (1.5 * wages))
38       End If
39
40       resultLabel.Text = String.Format("{0:C}", earnings)
41    End Sub ' DisplayPay
42
43    ' clear resultLabel when user enters new hourly wage
44    Private Sub wageTextBox_TextChanged(sender As Object,
45       e As EventArgs) Handles wageTextBox.TextChanged
46       resultLabel.Text = String.Empty ' clear the Label
47    End Sub ' wageTextBox_TextChanged
48
49    ' clear resultLabel when user enters new hours worked
50    Private Sub hoursTextBox_TextChanged(sender As Object,
51       e As EventArgs) Handles hoursTextBox.TextChanged
52       resultLabel.Text = String.Empty ' clear the Label
53    End Sub ' hoursTextBox_TextChanged
54 End Class ' WageCalculator
```

Fig. 6.3 | Calculating and displaying an employee's pay using a method. (Part 2 of 2.)

The program contains four method declarations. Lines 8–22 define the event-handler method calculateButton_Click, the method that executes when the user clicks the **Cal-**

culate Button. Lines 25–41 define method DisplayPay, a subroutine that executes when it's called from line 17 of method calculateButton_Click. Lines 44–53 define methods wageTextBox_TextChanged and hoursTextBox_TextChanged, which each clear the resultLabel when the user enters a new value in the corresponding TextBox.

Declaring Constants for Values That Do Not Change

Keyword **Const** (lines 4–5) declares a constant—a value that cannot be changed after it's initialized. Constants enhance program readability by providing descriptive identifiers for values that do not change. In this program, we want to ensure that the user does not enter a number of hours greater than the total number of hours in a week (that is, 168). This value never changes, so we declare HOURS_IN_A_WEEK as a Const. Similarly, recall from the problem statement that overtime pay is calculated for hours worked over 40 hours. This "hour limit" does not change during the program's execution, so we also declared HOUR_LIMIT as a Const. Using constants eliminates so-called **magic numbers**. For example, repeatedly mentioning the hour limit 40 gives the number 40 an artificial significance and can be confusing when the program includes other 40s that have nothing to do with the hour limit.

Method DisplayPay

When the user clicks the **Calculate** Button, lines 12–13 get the values entered by the user. Line 16 ensures that the hoursWorked is less than or equal to HOURS_IN_A_WEEK. If so, line 17 calls subroutine DisplayPay (lines 25–41), which causes it to execute.

When DisplayPay is called, the program makes a copy of the value of each argument—hoursWorked and hourlyWage—and program control transfers to the method's first line. The method receives the copied values and stores them in the parameters hours and wages. Then lines 29–38 calculate the earnings (accounting for overtime, if necessary) and store the result in Decimal variable earnings. Finally, line 40 displays earnings, using the currency format. When End Sub (line 41) is encountered, program control returns to the next statement in the calling method, calculateButton_Click. In this case, the end of the event handler is reached and the program now waits for the next user interaction.

The first line of method DisplayPay (line 25) shows that DisplayPay declares a Double parameter hours and a Decimal parameter wages. These parameters hold the values passed to DisplayPay so that they can be accessed within this method. The entire declaration of method DisplayPay appears within the body of class WageCalculator.

Subroutine Declarations

The format of a subroutine declaration is

> **Sub** *method-name(parameter-list)*
> *declarations and statements*
> **End Sub**

Keyword Sub indicates that this method will perform a task but will *not* return (that is, give back) any information to its **calling method** when it completes its task. You've already used methods that return information—for example, you used String method Format to create formatted representations of various String and numeric data. When Format completes its task, it returns a formatted String for use in the program.

Method Naming

The *method-name* follows keyword Sub. By convention, method names begin with an uppercase letter and all subsequent words in the name begin with a capital letter.

Parameters and the Parameter List

The parentheses after the method name are used to indicate any **parameters**—additional information that's required by the method to perform its task. An empty set of parentheses indicates that a method does not require any additional information and does not need any parameters. If there are parameters, they're placed in a **parameter-list**—specified by the set of parentheses following the method's name. A method can specify multiple parameters by separating each from the next with a comma—this is known as a *comma-separated list*. Each parameter has a variable name and a type. We refer to the part of the method that contains the keyword Sub, the method name and the parameter list as the **method header**.

Arguments in Method Calls

There must be one argument in the method call for each parameter in the method declaration. (We'll see an exception to this when we study Optional parameters in Section 6.12.) The type of each argument must be *consistent* with its corresponding parameter's type; that is, the compiler must be able to implicitly convert the value of the argument to a value of the parameter's type. For example, a parameter of type Double could receive an argument value of 7.35, 22 or –0.03546, but not "hello", because a Double variable cannot contain a String. If a method does not receive any values, the parameter list is *empty* (that is, the method name is followed by an *empty set of parentheses*).

Body of a Method

The *declarations and statements* (for example, lines 26–40 of Fig. 6.3) in the method declaration form the method body, which contains code that performs actions, generally by manipulating or processing the method's parameters and by calling other methods. After the statements execute, the method has completed its task. The body of a method declared with Sub must be terminated with keywords End Sub. Control returns to the next statement in the caller when execution reaches End Sub in the called method. The method body is also referred to as a **block**—a group of declarations and executable statements. The bodies of control statements are also blocks. For an If...Else...End If statement, the If part and the Else part are each separate blocks. For a Select...Case statement, each Case is a block. The bodies of repetition statements are also blocks.

Common Programming Error 6.1
Declaring a variable in the method's body with the same name as one of the method's parameters is a compilation error.

Software Engineering Observation 6.2
Method names tend to be verbs because methods typically perform actions. By convention, method names begin with an uppercase first letter. For example, a method that sends an e-mail message might be named SendMail. An exception to this is an event handler's name, which typically starts with the variable name of the control that generates the event.

6.4 Functions: Methods That Return a Value

As mentioned in Section 6.3, a function is a method that **returns a value** to the caller. Figure 6.4 reimplements the **Wage Calculator** app of Fig. 6.3 using the function CalculatePay (lines 27–43) to calculate and return an employee's pay based on the hours worked and hourly wage.

```vb
 1    ' Fig. 6.4: WageCalculator.vb
 2    ' Calculating an employee's pay using a function that returns a value.
 3    Public Class WageCalculator
 4       Const HOURS_IN_A_WEEK As Integer = 168 ' total hours in one week
 5       Const HOUR_LIMIT As Integer = 40 ' maximum hours before overtime
 6
 7       ' calculate and display the employee's pay
 8       Private Sub calculateButton_Click(sender As Object,
 9          e As EventArgs) Handles calculateButton.Click
10
11          ' get hours worked and hourly wage
12          Dim hoursWorked As Double = Val(hoursTextBox.Text)
13          Dim hourlyWage As Decimal = Val(wageTextBox.Text)
14
15          ' determine whether hoursWorked is less than or equal to 168
16          If hoursWorked <= HOURS_IN_A_WEEK Then
17             ' call CalculatePay Function
18             Dim totalPay As Decimal = CalculatePay(hoursWorked, hourlyWage)
19             resultLabel.Text = String.Format("{0:C}", totalPay)
20          Else
21             MessageBox.Show("Hours worked must be less than or equal to 168",
22                "Invalid Value", MessageBoxButtons.OK, MessageBoxIcon.Error)
23          End If
24       End Sub ' calculateButton_Click
25
26       ' calculate employee's wages
27       Function CalculatePay(hours As Double, wages As Decimal) As Decimal
28          Dim earnings As Decimal ' stores the total earnings
29
30          ' determine wage amount
31          If hours <= HOUR_LIMIT Then
32             ' earnings for regular wages
33             earnings = hours * wages
34          Else
35             ' regular wages for first HOUR_LIMIT hours
36             earnings = HOUR_LIMIT * wages
37
38             ' time and a half for overtime
39             earnings += ((hours - HOUR_LIMIT) * (1.5 * wages))
40          End If
41
42          Return earnings ' returns the total earnings back to the caller
43       End Function ' CalculatePay
44
```

Fig. 6.4 | Calculating an employee's pay using a function that returns a value. (Part 1 of 2.)

```
45      ' clear resultLabel when user enters new hourly wage
46      Private Sub wageTextBox_TextChanged(sender As Object,
47         e As EventArgs) Handles wageTextBox.TextChanged
48         resultLabel.Text = String.Empty ' clear the Label
49      End Sub ' wageTextBox_TextChanged
50
51      ' clear resultLabel when user enters new hours worked
52      Private Sub hoursTextBox_TextChanged(sender As Object,
53         e As EventArgs) Handles hoursTextBox.TextChanged
54         resultLabel.Text = String.Empty ' clear the Label
55      End Sub ' hoursTextBox_TextChanged
56   End Class ' WageCalculator
```

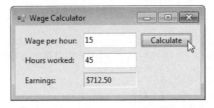

Fig. 6.4 | Calculating an employee's pay using a function that returns a value. (Part 2 of 2.)

When the user clicks the **Calculate** Button, lines 12–13 get the entered values. Line 16 ensures that the hoursWorked is less than or equal to the total number of hours in a week. If so, line 18 calls CalculatePay, which causes it to execute. At this point, the program copies the values of each argument—hoursWorked and hourlyWage—and program control transfers to CalculatePay's first line. The method receives the copied values and stores them in the parameters hours and wages. Then lines 31–40 calculate the earnings and store the result in the Decimal variable earnings. The **Return** statement (line 42) terminates the method and gives the value of earnings to the calling method. The result is returned to the point in line 18 where CalculatePay was called, where it's assigned to variable totalPay. Then line 19 displays totalPay's value.

Function Declarations

The format of a function declaration is

```
Function method-name(parameter-list) As return-type
   declarations and statements
End Function
```

The *method-name*, *parameter-list*, and *declarations and statements* in a function declaration behave like the corresponding elements in a subroutine declaration. In the function header, the *return-type* indicates the type of the value returned from the function to its caller. The statement

```
Return expression
```

can occur anywhere in a function body and returns the value of *expression* to the caller. When a Return statement executes, control returns immediately to the point at which that function was invoked.

> **Common Programming Error 6.2**
> *Failure to return a value from a function (for example, by forgetting to provide a* Return
> *statement) causes the function to return the default value for the return-type, possibly pro-*
> *ducing incorrect output.*

6.5 Implicit Argument Conversions

An important feature of argument passing is **implicit argument conversion**—in which Visual Basic converts an argument's value to the type that the method expects to receive in its corresponding parameter. Widening and narrowing conversions are supported. A **widening conversion** occurs when an argument is converted to a parameter of another type that can hold *more* data, whereas a **narrowing conversion** occurs when there's potential for *data loss* during the conversion (that is, a conversion to a parameter of a type that holds a *smaller* amount of data). Figure 6.5 lists the widening conversions that occur between primitive types.

Type	Conversion types
Boolean	No possible widening conversions to other primitive types
Byte	UShort, Short, UInteger, Integer, ULong, Long, Decimal, Single or Double
Char	String
Date	No possible widening conversions to other primitive types
Decimal	Single or Double
Double	No possible widening conversions to other primitive types
Integer	Long, Decimal, Single or Double
Long	Decimal, Single or Double
SByte	Short, Integer, Long, Decimal, Single or Double
Short	Integer, Long, Decimal, Single or Double
Single	Double
String	No possible widening conversions to other primitive types
UInteger	ULong, Long, Decimal, Single or Double
ULong	Decimal, Single or Double
UShort	UInteger, Integer, ULong, Long, Decimal, Single or Double

Fig. 6.5 | Widening conversions between primitive types.

For example, the Math class's Sqrt method (which returns the square root of it's argument) can be called with an Integer argument, even though the method is defined with a Double parameter. The statement

```
resultLabel.Text = Math.Sqrt(4)
```

correctly evaluates Math.Sqrt(4) and displays the value 2. The Integer argument 4 is implicitly converted to the Double value 4.0 before the argument is passed to Math.Sqrt. In this case, the argument does not precisely correspond to the parameter type in the method declaration, so an *implicit widening conversion* changes the value to the proper type before the method is called. *Narrowing conversions* can also be performed on arguments passed to methods. For example, if a `Double` variable containing the value `4.0` were passed to a method expecting an `Integer` variable, the value would be converted to `4`. Some *implicit narrowing conversions* can cause runtime errors. In the next section, we discuss measures you can take to avoid such errors. In Chapter 7, we introduce *exception handling*, which can be used to handle the errors caused by *failed* narrowing conversions.

Conversions also occur for expressions containing values of two or more types. In such expressions, the values' original types are maintained, while *temporary* copies of the values are converted for use in the expression. Each value is converted to the "widest" type in the expression (that is, widening conversions are made until the values are of the same type as the "widest" type). For example, if `doubleValue` is of type `Double` and `integerValue` is of type `Integer`, when the expression

```
doubleValue + integerValue
```

is evaluated, the value of `integerValue` is converted to type `Double` (the widest type in the expression), then added to `doubleValue`, producing a `Double` result.

6.6 Option Strict and Data-Type Conversions

Several options are provided for controlling the way the compiler handles types. These options can help you eliminate errors such as those caused by *narrowing conversions*.

Option Explicit

Option Explicit—which is set to **On** by default and has been enabled in the programs we created in Chapters 2–5—requires you to declare all variables *before* they're used in a program. This eliminates various errors. For example, when **Option Explicit** is set to **Off**, the compiler interprets misspelled variable names as *new variables* and implicitly declares them to be of type `Object`. (Class **Object** is the base type of all types. We'll discuss class `Object` in more detail in Chapter 10.) This creates subtle errors that can be difficult to debug. It's recommended that you leave this option set to **On**.

Option Strict

A second option, which defaults to **Off**, is **Option Strict**. *This option increases program clarity and reduces debugging time.* When set to **On**, Option Strict causes the compiler to check all conversions and requires you to perform **explicit conversions**—that is, using a cast operator or a method to force a conversion to occur—for all *narrowing conversions* or conversions that might cause program *termination* (for example, conversion of a `String`, such as `"hello"`, to type `Integer`).

Option Infer

Option Infer, which defaults to **On**, enables the compiler to *infer a variable's type* based on its intializer value. For example, in the statement

```
Dim x = 7 ' compiler infers that x is an Integer
```

the compiler infers that x is an `Integer` because the initializer value is an `Integer` literal.

Setting **Option Explicit**, **Option Strict** *and* **Option Infer**

You can set **Option Explicit**, **Option Strict** and **Option Infer** for all future projects as follows.

1. Select **TOOLS > Options...** to display the **Options** dialog (Fig. 6.6).

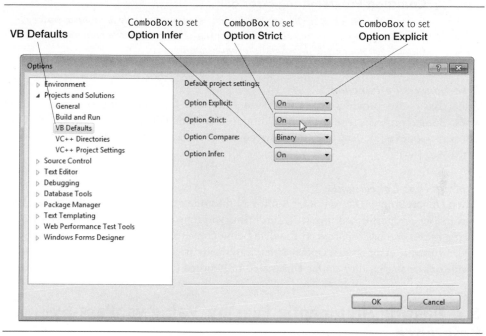

Fig. 6.6 | Modifying **Option Strict**, **Option Infer** and **Option Explicit**.

2. Under **Projects and Solutions**, select **VB Defaults** and choose the appropriate value in each option's ComboBox.

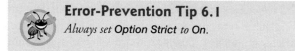

Error-Prevention Tip 6.1

Always set **Option Strict** *to* **On**.

Class **Convert**

Class **Convert**'s methods *explicitly* convert data from one primitive type to another. The name of each conversion method is the word To, typically followed by the name of the type to which the method converts its argument. For instance, to convert the String stored in numberTextBox.Text to type Double, we use the statement

```
Dim number As Double = Convert.ToDouble(numberTextBox.Text)
```

If numberTextBox does not contain a String that can be converted to a Double value, a FormatExcepton will occur. For now we assume that the user enters valid values that can be properly converted. In Chapter 7, you'll learn how to process *exceptions* when they occur. Some other commonly used Convert methods include **ToInt32** (to convert to an Integer), **ToDecimal** (to convert to a Decimal) and **ToString** (to convert to a String). Each method can receive arguments of any of the primitive types.

Many of the primitive types have a Parse method that you can use to convert a String to a value of that primitive type. For instance, method **Double.Parse** also converts a String representation of a number to a value of type Double.

> **Common Programming Error 6.3**
> *With Option Strict set to On, Strings cannot be assigned directly to numeric variables and numeric values cannot be assigned to Strings. Doing so causes a compilation error. Instead, you must explicitly perform the conversions in code.*

Type-Conversion Functions

Visual Basic also provides **type-conversion functions** for converting between built-in types. Some common type-conversion functions include **CChar** (convert to Char), **CDec** (convert to Decimal), **CInt** (convert to Integer), **CDbl** (convert to Double) and **CStr** (convert to String).

Implicit Type Conversions

When **Option Strict** is **Off** (as it has been for all the code examples so far in this book), type conversions are performed implicitly, and thus you may not realize that a *dangerous narrowing conversion* has occurred. If the data being converted is incompatible with the new type, a runtime error occurs. **Option Strict** draws your attention to *narrowing conversions* at compile time so that they can be eliminated or handled properly.

6.7 Passing Arguments: Pass-by-Value vs. Pass-by-Reference

Arguments are passed in one of two ways—pass-by-value or pass-by-reference. When an argument is passed by value, the program makes a *copy* of the argument's value and passes the copy to the called method. With pass-by-value, changes to the called method's copy *do not* affect the original variable's value in the caller. In contrast, when an argument is passed by reference, the called method *can* access and modify the caller's original data directly. Figure 6.7 demonstrates passing value-type arguments by value and by reference. The program passes the values of variables, number1, number2 and number3, in different ways to methods SquareByValue (lines 45–53) and SquareByReference (lines 56–64). For the purpose of the following discussion, we assume that the user enters the value 2 in the TextBox then presses the **Square** Button.

Keyword ByVal and Method SquareByValue

Keyword ByVal in the method header of SquareByValue (line 45) indicates that the argument should be passed by value. A parameter declared with keyword ByVal is known as a **value parameter**. By default, all parameters in Visual Basic are passed by value, so keyword ByVal is *not* required. When number1 is passed to SquareByValue (line 15), a copy of the value stored in number1 (that is, 2) is passed to the method. Therefore, the value of number1 in the calling method, squareButton_Click, is *not* modified when parameter number is squared in method SquareByValue (line 49)—only the local copy stored in the method's number parameter gets modified.

```vb
 1    ' Fig. 6.7: ValueAndReferencePassing.vb
 2    ' ByVal and ByRef used to pass value-type arguments.
 3    Public Class ValueAndReferencePassing
 4       ' call methods SquareByValue and SquareByReference
 5       Private Sub squareButton_Click(sender As Object,
 6          e As EventArgs) Handles squareButton.Click
 7          ' get user input and convert it to an Integer value
 8          Dim number1 As Integer = Convert.ToInt32(squareTextBox.Text)
 9
10          outputTextBox.AppendText(
11             "Passing a value-type argument by value:" & vbCrLf)
12          outputTextBox.AppendText(String.Format(
13             "Before calling SquareByValue, number1 is {0}{1}",
14             number1, vbCrLf))
15          SquareByValue(number1)   ' passes number1 by value
16          outputTextBox.AppendText(String.Format(
17             "After returning from SquareByValue, number1 is {0}{1}{1}",
18             number1, vbCrLf))
19
20          Dim number2 As Integer = Convert.ToInt32(squareTextBox.Text)
21
22          outputTextBox.AppendText(
23             "Passing a value-type argument by reference:" & vbCrLf)
24          outputTextBox.AppendText(String.Format(
25             "Before calling SquareByReference, number2 is {0}{1}",
26             number2, vbCrLf))
27          SquareByReference(number2) ' passes number2 by reference
28          outputTextBox.AppendText(String.Format(
29             "After returning from SquareByReference, number2 is {0}{1}{1}",
30             number2, vbCrLf))
31
32          Dim number3 As Integer = Convert.ToInt32(squareTextBox.Text)
33
34          outputTextBox.AppendText("Passing a value-type argument" &
35             " by reference, but in parentheses:" & vbCrLf)
36          outputTextBox.AppendText(String.Format("Before calling " &
37             "SquareByReference using parentheses, number3 is {0}{1}",
38             number3, vbCrLf))
39          SquareByReference((number3)) ' passes number3 by value
40          outputTextBox.AppendText(String.Format("After returning from " &
41             "SquareByReference, number3 is {0}", number3))
42       End Sub ' squareButton_Click
43
44       ' squares number by value (note ByVal keyword)
45       Sub SquareByValue(ByVal number As Integer)
46          outputTextBox.AppendText(String.Format(
47             "After entering SquareByValue, number is {0}{1}",
48             number, vbCrLf))
49          number *= number
50          outputTextBox.AppendText(String.Format(
51             "Before exiting SquareByValue, number is {0}{1}",
52             number, vbCrLf))
53       End Sub ' SquareByValue
```

Fig. 6.7 | ByVal and ByRef used to pass value-type arguments. (Part 1 of 2.)

```
54
55      ' squares number by reference (note ByRef keyword)
56      Sub SquareByReference(ByRef number As Integer)
57        outputTextBox.AppendText(String.Format(
58          "After entering SquareByReference, number is {0}{1}",
59          number, vbCrLf))
60        number *= number
61        outputTextBox.AppendText(String.Format(
62          "Before exiting SquareByReference, number is {0}{1}",
63          number, vbCrLf))
64      End Sub ' SquareByReference
65
66      ' clear the outputTextBox when squareTextBox's value changes
67      Private Sub squareTextBox_TextChanged(sender As Object,
68        e As EventArgs) Handles squareTextBox.TextChanged
69        outputTextBox.Text = String.Empty
70      End Sub ' squareTextBox_TextChanged
71    End Class ' ValueAndReferencePassing
```

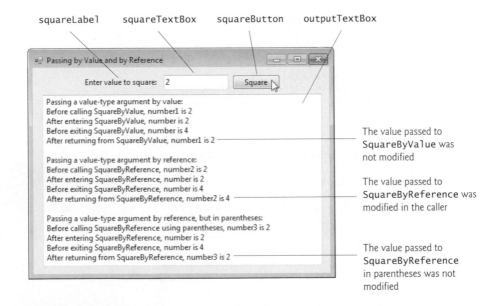

Fig. 6.7 | ByVal and ByRef used to pass value-type arguments. (Part 2 of 2.)

*Keyword **ByRef** and Method **SquareByReference***

Method SquareByReference uses **keyword ByRef** (line 56) to receive its parameter by reference. A parameter declared with keyword ByRef is known as a **reference parameter**. When squareButton_Click calls SquareByReference (line 27), a reference to the variable number2 is passed, which gives SquareByReference direct access to the original variable in the caller. Any changes that SquareByReference makes to its parameter actually modify the original variable's value. Thus, the value stored in number2 after SquareByReference finishes executing is the same as the final value of the method's number parameter.

Preventing a Reference Parameter from Being Modified in the Caller
When an argument is enclosed in an additional set of parentheses, as in line 39, the expression within the parentheses is evaluated and the result of that expression is passed to the method. In line 39, the inner set of parentheses evaluates number3, returns its value (that is, 2) and passes this *value* to the method, *even* if the method header includes keyword ByRef. Thus, the value of number3 does not change after it's passed to SquareByReference (line 39) enclosed in an additional set of parentheses.

*Reusing Values in **String** Method **Format***
In lines 17 and 29, we use the format specifier "{0}{1}{1}" as part of the format String. The values inside the braces indicate which arguments after the format String should replace each placeholder. Using {1} twice indicates that the second argument after the format String (that is, vbCrLf) should be inserted into the formatted String twice. This allows us to skip a line in the output.

6.8 Scope of Declarations

You've seen declarations of various entities, such as classes, methods, variables and parameters. Declarations introduce names that are used to refer to such entities. A declaration's scope is the portion of the program that can refer to the declared entity by its name without qualification—that is, without preceding the entity with a variable name or class name and a dot (.) separator. Such an entity is said to be "in scope" for that portion of the program. This section introduces several important scope issues. The Visual Basic language specification does not use formal names to describe scopes. We've chosen our own descriptive names for clarity.

The basic scopes are:

1. **Block scope**—The scope of a variable declared in a block is from the *point of the declaration* to the *end of the block* (for example, a variable declared in a control statement's body is in scope only until the end of that control statement).

2. **Method scope**—The scope of a method's local-variable declaration or parameter is from the *point at which the declaration appears* to the *end of that method*. This is similar to block scope. Variables with method scope do not retain their values between method calls and are reinitialized each time the method in which they're declared is invoked.

3. **Class scope**—The scope of a member that's declared in the class's body, but *outside* the bodies of the class's methods is the *entire body of the class*. This enables a class's methods to use *all* of the class's members. (You'll learn in Chapter 9 that Shared methods of a class can access *only* the class's Shared members.)

Lifetime of a Variable
Although a variable may not be in scope, it may still exist. A variable's **lifetime** is the period during which the variable *exists in memory*. Some variables exist briefly, some are created and destroyed repeatedly, and others are maintained through the program's execution. Variables normally exist as long as the construct in which they're declared exists—for instance, a local variable of a method will exist as the call to that method is still executing.

Fund Raiser *App*

To demonstrate scoping issues, let's create a **Fund Raiser** app. Consider the following problem statement:

> *An organization is hosting a fund raiser to collect donations. A portion of each donation is used to cover the operating expenses of the organization—the rest of the donation goes to the charity. Create an app that allows the organization to keep track of the total amount of money raised. The app should deduct 17% of each donation to cover operating expenses—the remaining 83% is given to the charity. The app should display the amount of each donation after the 17% for operating expenses is deducted—it also should display the total amount raised for the charity (that is, the total amount donated less operating expenses) for all donations so far.*

The user inputs the amount of a donation into a TextBox and clicks the **Donate** Button to calculate the net amount of the donation that the charity receives after operating expenses have been deducted. In addition, the total amount of money raised for the charity is updated and displayed. Figure 6.8 shows the app's GUI and the code in Fig. 6.9 demonstrates scoping issues.

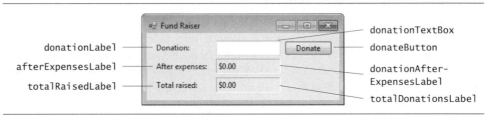

Fig. 6.8 | GUI for the **Fund Raiser** app.

```
 1  ' Fig. 6.9: FundRaiser.vb
 2  ' Calculate total donations after operating expenses.
 3  Public Class FundRaiser
 4      ' stores total of all donations after expenses
 5      Dim totalRaised As Decimal = 0
 6
 7      ' calculate and display donation amount and total donations
 8      Private Sub donateButton_Click(sender As Object,
 9          e As EventArgs) Handles donateButton.Click
10
11          ' get donation amount
12          Dim donation As Decimal =
13              Convert.ToDecimal(Val(donationTextBox.Text))
14
15          ' obtain donation amount after operating costs deduction
16          Dim afterCosts As Decimal = CalculateDonation(donation)
17
18          ' display amount of donation after costs
19          donationAfterExpensesLabel.Text = String.Format("{0:C}", afterCosts)
20
21          ' update total amount of donations received
22          totalRaised += afterCosts
```

Fig. 6.9 | Scoping rules in a class. (Part 1 of 2.)

```
23
24            ' display total amount collected for charity
25            totalDonationsLabel.Text = String.Format("{0:C}", totalRaised)
26        End Sub ' donateButton_Click
27
28        ' calculates donation amount after operating expenses
29        Function CalculateDonation(donatedAmount As Decimal) As Decimal
30            ' 17% of donation is used to cover operating costs
31            Const COSTS As Decimal = 0.17D
32
33            ' calculate amount of donation after operating expenses
34            Return donatedAmount * (1D - COSTS)
35        End Function ' CalculateDonation
36
37        ' clear donationAfterExpensesLabel when user enters new donation amount
38        Private Sub donationTextBox_TextChanged(sender As Object,
39            e As EventArgs) Handles donationTextBox.TextChanged
40            donationAfterExpensesLabel.Text = String.Empty
41        End Sub ' donationTextBox_TextChanged
42    End Class ' FundRaiser
```

Fig. 6.9 | Scoping rules in a class. (Part 2 of 2.)

Instance Variable *totalRaised*

Line 5 declares instance variable totalRaised to store the total amount of money raised for charity. This variable is initialized when the Form first loads and retain its value while the app executes (that is, it's not created each time a method is invoked). Instance variables have class scope, so all methods in class FundRaiser have access to this variable and can modify its value.

Method *donateButton_Click and Local Variables*

Lines 12–13 in the event-handler method donateButton_Click declare and initialize variable donation, which stores the current donation amount. Identifiers, such as donation, that are declared inside a method (but outside a control statement) have *method scope*. This scope begins at the identifier's declaration and ends at the last statement of the method. Identifiers with method scope cannot be referenced outside of the method in which they're declared. A method's parameters also have method scope.

Identifiers declared inside control statements (such as inside an If...Then statement) have *block scope*, which begins at the identifier's declaration and ends at the enclosing block's final statement (for example, Else or End If).

Variables with method or block scope are called **local variables**—they cannot be referenced outside the method or block in which they're declared. If a local variable has the same name as a variable with class scope, the local variable hides the class-scope variable (for example, an instance variable) in the block or method. Any expression containing the variable name uses the local variable's value and not the class-scope variable's value. Section 9.10 shows how to access the class-scope variable in this case.

Line 16 calls method CalculateDonation with the amount of the donation (donation). The result of this call—the net amount that goes to charity after the deduction for operating costs—is assigned to local variable afterCosts. The donation amount after operating costs is formatted as currency and displayed (line 19).

Line 22 updates instance variable totalRaised, which stores the total amount given to the charity after the operating costs have been deducted. Even though totalRaised is not declared in this event handler, the variable is in scope because it's an instance variable of class FundRaiser. Line 25 displays the total amount raised for charity so far.

Method CalculateDonation

Method CalculateDonation (lines 29–35) subtracts the operating cost from the donation amount (donatedAmount) then returns the Decimal result (line 34). Let's consider the limits of method scope. In line 34, temporarily replace donatedAmount with the variable donation, which is declared as a local variable in method donateButton_Click (line 12). The jagged line under donation indicates an error. Variables with method scope can be accessed and modified only in the method in which they're declared. The error message displayed when you rest the mouse pointer on the jagged line indicates that donation is not declared—its "local" to method donateButton_Click, so CalculateDonation cannot "see" donation's declaration. Be sure to replace donation with donatedAmount in line 34.

GUI Controls are Instance Variables

You might be wondering why we've been able to use the GUI controls in all the methods of our classes. When you create a GUI control in the designer, the IDE automatically declares an instance variable with the name you choose for the control. This declaration is placed in a separate file—*YourClassName*.Designer.vb—that's automatically compiled together with *YourClassName*.vb. All of the instance variables in your class's Designer.vb file can be used by your Form class's methods to interact with the GUI. You can view the Designer.vb file by clicking the **Show all files** Button in the **Solution Explorer**, then expanding the node for *YourClassName*.vb.

6.9 Case Study: Random-Number Generation

We now take a brief and hopefully entertaining diversion into a popular programming app—simulation and game playing. In this and the next section, we develop a game-playing program with multiple methods. The program employs many of the control statements presented thus far in the book and introduces several new concepts. The element of chance can be introduced through class **Random**.

*Using Keyword **New** to Create a **Random** Object*

To this point, you've actually been interacting with many objects. Each control you drag onto the Form using the Windows Forms Designer is an object of that control's class—for example, in Fig. 6.3, hoursTextBox is an object of class TextBox. Each of these objects is created for you by the Windows Forms Designer in the Desinger.vb file that's associated with the class in a Windows Forms app. When you want to use objects of most non-GUI classes, you need to create those objects yourself. In the statement

```
Dim randomObject As New Random()
```

Variable randomObject is initialized with the result of the **object-creation expression** New Random(). **New** creates a new object of the class specified to its right (that is, Random). The variable randomObject now said to "refer to an object of class Random."

The class name is followed by a set of parentheses. As you'll learn in Chapter 9, those parentheses in combination with a class name represent a call to a **constructor**—a special method that's used to initialize an object's data when the object is created. You'll see that arguments can be placed in the parentheses to specify initial values for the object's data. In the preceding statement, we simply leave the parentheses empty. When there are no arguments to be placed in the parentheses, the parentheses can be omitted.

*Class **Random** and Method **Next***

We can now use variable randomObject to call methods of class Random. The statement

```
Dim randomNumber As Integer = randomObject.Next()
```

declares Integer variable randomNumber and assigns to it the value returned by calling Random method **Next**. To interact with an object of a class, you use the variable name that refers to the object followed by a *dot separator (.)* and the method or property name, just as you've done many times with GUI controls.

Method Next generates a positive Integer value greater than or equal to zero and less than the constant **Int32.MaxValue** (2,147,483,647). If Next truly produces values at random, every value in this range has an equal chance (or probability) of being chosen when Next is called. The values returned by Next are actually **pseudorandom numbers**, or a sequence of values produced by a complex mathematical calculation. This calculation requires a **seed value** to begin the chain of calculations. If the seed value is *different* each time the program is run, the series of values will be *different* as well (so that the generated numbers are indeed random). When we create a Random object, the seed is based on the current time. Alternatively, we can pass a seed value as an argument in the parentheses after New Random. Using the current time of day as the seed value is effective because the time is likely to change for each Random object we create.

The range of values produced by Next is often different from what's needed in a particular app. For example, a program that simulates coin tossing might require only 0 for "heads" and 1 for "tails." A program that simulates the rolling of a six-sided die would require random integers in the range 1–6. Similarly, a program that randomly predicts the next type of spaceship (out of four possibilities) that flies across the horizon in a video game might require random integers from 1 to 4.

6.9.1 Scaling and Shifting of Random Numbers

By passing an argument to method Next as follows

```
value = 1 + randomObject.Next(6)
```

we can produce integers in the range 1–6. When a *single* argument is passed to Next, the values returned by Next will be in the range from 0 to (but not including) the value of that argument. This is called **scaling**. The number 6 is the **scaling factor**. We **shift** the range of numbers produced by adding 1 to our previous result, so that the return values are between 1 and 6 rather than 0 and 5.

To simplify the process of specifying a range of random numbers, you can pass two arguments to Next. For example, the preceding statement also could be written as

```
value = randomObject.Next(1, 7)
```

We must use 7 as the second argument to produce integers in the range from 1–6. The first argument indicates the *minimum value* in our desired range, whereas the second is equal to *1 + the maximum value desired*. Figure 6.10 demonstrates the use of class Random and method Next by simulating 20 rolls of a six-sided die and showing the value of each roll. All the values are in the range from 1 to 6, inclusive.

```vb
1   ' Fig. 6.10: RandomIntegers.vb
2   ' Random integers from 1 to 6 created by calling Random method Next.
3   Public Class RandomIntegers
4      ' display 20 random integers
5      Private Sub RandomIntegers_Load(sender As Object,
6         e As EventArgs) Handles MyBase.Load
7
8         Dim randomObject As New Random() ' create Random object
9         Dim randomNumber As Integer
10
11        ' generate 20 random numbers between 1 and 6
12        For i = 1 To 20
13           randomNumber = randomObject.Next(1, 7)
14           outputTextBox.AppendText(randomNumber & "    ")
15
16           If i Mod 5 = 0 Then ' is i a multiple of 5?
17              outputTextBox.AppendText(vbCrLf) ' move to next line of output
18           End If
19        Next
20     End Sub ' RandomIntegers_Load
21  End Class ' RandomIntegers
```

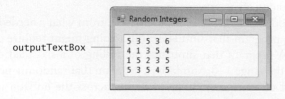

Fig. 6.10 | Random integers from 1 to 6 created by calling **Random** method Next.

6.9.2 Randomly Selecting Images

The program in Fig. 6.11 uses class Random to simulate rolling four six-sided dice and displays in PictureBox controls corresponding images for each die value. We use some of the functionality from this program in another example (Fig. 6.14) to demonstrate that the numbers generated by Next indeed occur with approximately equal likelihood.

```vb
1   ' Fig. 6.11: RollDice.vb
2   ' Rolling four dice and displaying corresponding images.
3   Public Class RollDice
4      Dim randomObject As New Random() ' create Random object
5
6      ' display results of four rolls
7      Private Sub rollButton_Click(sender As Object, _
8         e As EventArgs) Handles rollButton.Click
9         ' method randomly assigns a face to each die
10        DisplayDie(die1PictureBox)
11        DisplayDie(die2PictureBox)
12        DisplayDie(die3PictureBox)
13        DisplayDie(die4PictureBox)
14     End Sub ' rollButton_Click
15
16     ' get a random die image
17     Sub DisplayDie(diePictureBox As PictureBox)
18        ' generate random integer in range 1 to 6
19        Dim face As Integer = randomObject.Next(1, 7)
20
21        ' retrieve specific die image from resources
22        Dim pictureResource = My.Resources.ResourceManager.GetObject( _
23           String.Format("die{0}", face))
24
25        ' convert pictureResource to type Image and display in PictureBox
26        diePictureBox.Image = CType(pictureResource, Image)
27     End Sub ' DisplayDie
28   End Class ' RollDice
```

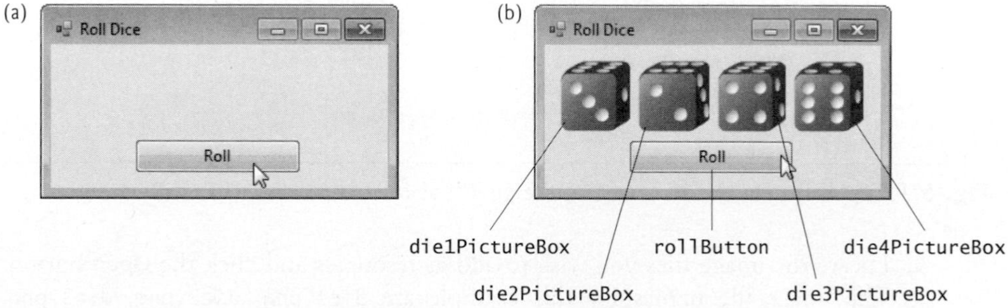

Fig. 6.11 | Rolling four dice and displaying corresponding images.

Displaying Random Images in a PictureBox

The event handler rollButton_Click (Fig. 6.11, lines 7–14) calls method DisplayDie four times (lines 10–13), once for each PictureBox on the Form. Calling DisplayDie causes four dice to appear as if they were being rolled each time **Roll** is clicked. The images do not appear until the user clicks **Roll** the first time.

Method `DisplayDie` (lines 17–27) specifies the correct image for the face value calculated by method `Next` (line 19). We declare `randomObject` as an instance variable (line 4) of class `RollDice`. This allows the same `Random` object to be used each time `DisplayDie` executes. The code in lines 22–26 sets the `Image` property (line 26) of the `PictureBox` that's passed as an argument.

Embedding Image as Resources in a Project

In this example, we embedded the images into the project as resources. This causes the compiler to include the images in the app's executable file and enables the app to access the images through the `My` namespace, which provides many capabilities that make common programming tasks easier. Namespaces organize classes into groups by functionality. For example, namespace `System.Windows.Forms` in the Framework Class Library contains the controls you've been using in your GUIs. Embedded images make it easy to move an app to another location or computer. The images used in this example are located with this chapter's examples in the `Images` folder. To add images to the project as resources:

1. After creating your project, double click **My Project** in the **Solution Explorer** to display the project's properties.

2. Click the **Resources** tab.

3. At the top of the **Resources** tab click the down arrow next to the **Add Resource** button and select **Add Existing File…** (Fig. 6.12) to display the **Add** existing file to resources dialog.

Fig. 6.12 | Preparing to add images to the project as resources.

4. Locate the image files you wish to add as resources and click the **Open** button. The image file names for this example are `die1.png`, `die2.png`, `die3.png`, `die4.png`, `die5.png` and `die6.png`.

5. Save your project.

The files now appear in a folder named **Resources** in the **Solution Explorer**. We'll use this technique in most examples that display images. For more details on the `My` namespace visit `msdn.microsoft.com/library/5btzf5yk.aspx`.

Using Embedded Images

To use an image (or any other resource) in the project's resources, you use the method `My.Resources.ResourceManager.GetObject`, which takes as an argument the resource name as it appears in the **Resources** tab (for example, `"die1"`) and returns the resource as an `Object`. Lines 22–23 invoke `GetObject` with the result of the expression

```
String.Format("die{0}", face)
```

which builds the name of the resource by placing the random number `face` at the end of the word `"die"`. You must convert this `Object` to type `Image` to assign it to the `Picture-Box`'s `Image` property. Line 26 uses the `CType` function to perform the conversion. `CType` converts its first argument to the type specified in its second argument. A conversion performed with the `CType` function is also known as a cast **operation** or more simply as cast.

The `My` namespace also provides direct access to the resources you define with expressions of the form `My.Resources.resourceName`, where *resourceName* is the name you provided to the resource when you created it. When using such an expression, the resource returned already has the appropriate type. For example, `My.Resources.die1` is an `Image` object representing the `die1.png` image.

6.9.3 Rolling Dice Repeatedly and Displaying Statistics

The next app allows you to repeatedly roll 12 dice to show that the numbers generated by class `Random` occur with approximately equal frequencies. The program displays the cumulative frequencies of each face, and each roll's faces are displayed using `PictureBoxes`. The GUI is shown in Fig. 6.13 and the app code is shown in Fig. 6.14.

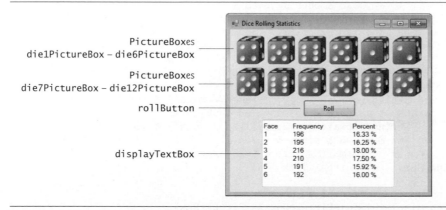

Fig. 6.13 | GUI for **Dice Rolling Statistics** app.

```
1    ' Fig. 6.14: DiceStatistics.vb
2    ' Rolling 12 dice with frequency chart.
3    Public Class DiceStatistics
4       Dim randomObject As New Random() ' generate random number
5       Dim ones As Integer = 0 ' count of die face 1
6       Dim twos As Integer = 0 ' count of die face 2
```

Fig. 6.14 | Rolling 12 dice with frequency chart. (Part 1 of 3.)

```vb
 7      Dim threes As Integer = 0 ' count of die face 3
 8      Dim fours As Integer = 0 ' count of die face 4
 9      Dim fives As Integer = 0 ' count of die face 5
10      Dim sixes As Integer = 0 ' count of die face 6
11
12      ' display result of twelve rolls
13      Private Sub rollButton_Click(sender As Object,
14         e As EventArgs) Handles rollButton.Click
15
16         ' display 12 randomly selected die faces
17         DisplayDie(die1PictureBox)
18         DisplayDie(die2PictureBox)
19         DisplayDie(die3PictureBox)
20         DisplayDie(die4PictureBox)
21         DisplayDie(die5PictureBox)
22         DisplayDie(die6PictureBox)
23         DisplayDie(die7PictureBox)
24         DisplayDie(die8PictureBox)
25         DisplayDie(die9PictureBox)
26         DisplayDie(die10PictureBox)
27         DisplayDie(die11PictureBox)
28         DisplayDie(die12PictureBox)
29
30         Dim total As Integer = ones + twos + threes + fours + fives + sixes
31
32         ' display frequencies of faces
33         displayTextBox.Text =
34            "Face" & vbTab & "Frequency" & vbTab & "Percent" & vbCrLf &
35            "1" & vbTab & ones & vbTab & vbTab &
36            String.Format("{0:P2}", ones / total) & vbCrLf &
37            "2" & vbTab & twos & vbTab & vbTab &
38            String.Format("{0:P2}", twos / total) & vbCrLf &
39            "3" & vbTab & threes & vbTab & vbTab &
40            String.Format("{0:P2}", threes / total) & vbCrLf &
41            "4" & vbTab & fours & vbTab & vbTab &
42            String.Format("{0:P2}", fours / total) & vbCrLf &
43            "5" & vbTab & fives & vbTab & vbTab &
44            String.Format("{0:P2}", fives / total) & vbCrLf &
45            "6" & vbTab & sixes & vbTab & vbTab &
46            String.Format("{0:P2}", sixes / total)
47      End Sub ' rollButton_Click
48
49      ' display a single die image
50      Sub DisplayDie(diePictureBox As PictureBox)
51         Dim face As Integer = randomObject.Next(1, 7)
52
53         ' retrieve specific die image from resources
54         Dim pictureResource = My.Resources.ResourceManager.GetObject(
55            String.Format("die{0}", face))
56
57         ' convert pictureResource to image type and load into PictureBox
58         diePictureBox.Image = CType(pictureResource, Image)
59
```

Fig. 6.14 | Rolling 12 dice with frequency chart. (Part 2 of 3.)

```
60                    ' maintain count of die faces
61                    Select Case face
62                       Case 1 ' die face 1
63                          ones += 1
64                       Case 2 ' die face 2
65                          twos += 1
66                       Case 3 ' die face 3
67                          threes += 1
68                       Case 4 ' die face 4
69                          fours += 1
70                       Case 5 ' die face 5
71                          fives += 1
72                       Case 6 ' die face 6
73                          sixes += 1
74                    End Select
75                 End Sub ' DisplayDie
76              End Class ' DiceStatistics
```

Fig. 6.14 | Rolling 12 dice with frequency chart. (Part 3 of 3.)

Figure 6.13 shows the program after the user has clicked **Roll** 100 times. If the values produced by method Next are indeed random, the frequencies of the face values (1–6) should be approximately the same (as the figure illustrates).

To show that the faces occur with approximately equal likelihood, the program maintains statistics. We declare as instance variables counters for each face value in lines 5–10. Lines 33–46 display the frequency of each face as percentages using the **P** format specifier. P2 displays percentages with two digits to the right of the decimal point. The more you roll the dice, the closer each percentage should get to 16.66%.

As the program output demonstrates, method Next can be used to effectively simulate the rolling of a six-sided die. Over the course of many die rolls, each of the possible faces in the range 1–6 appears with equal likelihood, or approximately one-sixth of the time. *No* Case Else is provided in the Select...Case statement (lines 61–74), because we know that the values generated are in the range 1–6. In Chapter 7, we show how to replace the entire Select...Case statement in this program with a single line of code.

Click the **Roll** Button several times and observe the results. A *different* sequence of random numbers is obtained each time the program is executed, causing the resulting frequencies to vary. When the Button has the *focus*, you can hold down the *Enter* key to rapidly "press" the button and roll the dice.

6.10 Case Study: A Game of Chance

A popular game of chance is the dice game "craps." The rules of the game are as follows:

> *A player rolls two dice. Each die has six faces. Each face contains 1, 2, 3, 4, 5 or 6 spots. After the dice have come to rest, the sum of the spots on the two upward faces is calculated. If the sum is 7 or 11 on the first throw, the player wins. If the sum is 2, 3 or 12 on the first throw (called "craps"), the player loses (that is, the "house" wins). If the sum is 4, 5, 6, 8, 9 or 10 on the first throw, that sum becomes the player's "point." To win, players must continue rolling the dice until they "make their point" (that is, roll their point value). The player loses by rolling a 7 before making the point.*

Craps GUI

Figure 6.15 shows the GUI for the **Craps** app. This program introduces the **GroupBox** control and uses it to display the user's point. A GroupBox is used to group related controls. Within the GroupBox pointGroupBox, we add two PictureBoxes, which are controls that display images. You can drag and drop a GroupBox onto the Form the same way you would any other control. When adding other controls to a GroupBox (such as the two Picture-Boxes in this example), drag and drop the controls within the bounds of the GroupBox on the Form. We set the GroupBox's **Text property** to **Point**. This is the text that displays in the upper-left corner of the GroupBox. We'll modify this text programmatically to display the user's point value. If you leave the Text property blank, the GroupBox displays as a simple border without any text. The statusLabel control is attached to the bottom of the Form. This is known as "docking" the control. When a control is docked to the bottom of a Form, the control becomes as wide as the Form and always remains at the bottom, even if the Form is resized. You can dock a control to the Top, Bottom, Left, Right or Center of a Form by selecting the appropriate value for the control's **Dock property** in the **Properties** window. The app in Fig. 6.16 simulates the game of craps.

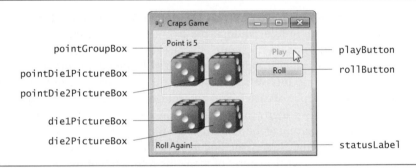

Fig. 6.15 | GUI for the **Craps** app.

```
1   ' Fig. 6.16: Craps.vb
2   ' Craps game using class Random.
3   Public Class Craps
4       ' die-roll constants
5       Enum DiceNames
6           SNAKE_EYES = 2
7           TREY = 3
8           LUCKY_SEVEN = 7
9           CRAPS = 7
10          YO_LEVEN = 11
11          BOX_CARS = 12
12      End Enum
13
14      Dim myPoint As Integer ' total point if not 2, 3, 12, 7 or 11
15      Dim myDie1 As Integer ' die 1 face
16      Dim myDie2 As Integer ' die 2 face
17      Dim randomObject As New Random() ' generate random number
```

Fig. 6.16 | Craps game using class Random. (Part 1 of 4.)

```
18
19      ' begins new game and determines point
20      Private Sub playButton_Click(sender As Object, _
21         e As EventArgs) Handles playButton.Click
22
23         ' initialize variables for new game
24         myPoint = 0
25         pointGroupBox.Text = "Point"
26         statusLabel.Text = String.Empty
27
28         ' remove point-die images
29         pointDie1PictureBox.Image = Nothing
30         pointDie2PictureBox.Image = Nothing
31
32         Dim sum As Integer = RollDice() ' roll dice and calculate sum
33
34         ' check die roll
35         Select Case sum
36            Case DiceNames.LUCKY_SEVEN, DiceNames.YO_LEVEN
37               rollButton.Enabled = False ' disable Roll button
38               statusLabel.Text = "You Win!!!"
39            Case DiceNames.SNAKE_EYES, DiceNames.TREY, DiceNames.BOX_CARS
40               rollButton.Enabled = False ' disable Roll button
41               statusLabel.Text = "Sorry. You Lose."
42            Case Else
43               myPoint = sum ' store the point value
44               pointGroupBox.Text = "Point is " & sum
45               statusLabel.Text = "Roll Again!"
46               DisplayDie(pointDie1PictureBox, myDie1)
47               DisplayDie(pointDie2PictureBox, myDie2)
48               playButton.Enabled = False ' disable Play button
49               rollButton.Enabled = True ' enable Roll button
50         End Select
51      End Sub ' playButton_Click
52
53      ' determines outcome of next roll
54      Private Sub rollButton_Click(sender As Object, _
55         e As EventArgs) Handles rollButton.Click
56
57         Dim sum As Integer = RollDice() ' roll dice and calculate sum
58
59         ' check outcome of roll
60         If sum = myPoint Then ' win
61            statusLabel.Text = "You Win!!!"
62            rollButton.Enabled = False ' disable Roll button
63            playButton.Enabled = True ' enable Play button
64         ElseIf sum = DiceNames.CRAPS Then ' lose
65            statusLabel.Text = "Sorry. You Lose."
66            rollButton.Enabled = False ' disable Roll button
67            playButton.Enabled = True ' enable Play button
68         End If
69      End Sub ' rollButton_Click
70
```

Fig. 6.16 | Craps game using class Random. (Part 2 of 4.)

```
71      ' display die image
72      Sub DisplayDie(diePictureBox As PictureBox, _
73         face As Integer)
74
75         ' retrieve specific die image from resources
76         Dim pictureResource = My.Resources.ResourceManager.GetObject( _
77            String.Format("die{0}", face))
78
79         ' convert pictureResource to image type and load into PictureBox
80         diePictureBox.Image = CType(pictureResource, Image)
81      End Sub ' DisplayDie
82
83      ' generate random die rolls
84      Function RollDice() As Integer
85         ' determine random integer
86         myDie1 = randomObject.Next(1, 7) ' choose value from 1 to 6
87         myDie2 = randomObject.Next(1, 7) ' choose value from 1 to 6
88
89         ' display rolls
90         DisplayDie(die1PictureBox, myDie1) ' display first die
91         DisplayDie(die2PictureBox, myDie2) ' display second die
92
93         Return myDie1 + myDie2 ' return sum
94      End Function ' RollDice
95   End Class ' Craps
```

a) Before first roll

b) Lost on first roll

c) Won on first roll

d) Point is 5 after first roll

Fig. 6.16 | Craps game using class Random. (Part 3 of 4.)

e) Lost by rolling 7 before 5.

f) Point is 6 after first roll

g) Continue rolling to make a 6

h) Won by rolling 6 before 7

Fig. 6.16 | Craps game using class Random. (Part 4 of 4.)

Game Play
Click the **Play** Button to play the game. You roll two dice on the first and all subsequent rolls. If you do not win or lose on the first roll, the **Play** Button is *disabled* and the **Roll** Button is *enabled*. You can then click the **Roll** Button to continue playing the game until you win or lose. At this point, the **Roll** Button is *disabled* and the **Play** Button is *enabled*.

The screen captures depict several sample games. Figure 6.16(a) displays the Form before the game has begun. The remaining outputs show several games:

- Figure 6.16(b) shows a game in which the user rolled a 3 and lost on the first roll.

- Figure 6.16(c) shows a game in which the user rolled an 11 and won on the first roll.

- Figure 6.16(d) and (e) show a game in which the user rolled a 5 on the first roll, then lost on the second roll by rolling a 7.

- Finally, Fig. 6.16(f)–(h) show a game in which the user rolled a 6 on the first roll, rolled a 10 on the second roll, then won on the third roll by rolling a 6 again.

Enumerations and Constants
The program includes our first **enumeration**—declared with **Enum...End Enum** in lines 5–12. Enumerations enhance program readability by providing descriptive identifiers for groups of related constant numbers. Enumerations help you ensure that values are consistent throughout a program. (Recall that keyword **Const** creates a single constant identifier

and that such an identifier must be initialized in its declaration.) In this case, we create an Enum of descriptive names for the various dice combinations in craps (that is, SNAKE_EYES, TREY, LUCKY_SEVEN, CRAPS, YO_LEVEN and BOX_CARS). Multiple enumeration members can have the same value—in this example, LUCKY_SEVEN and CRAPS both have the value 7. We use two identifiers for program clarity; on the first roll, a seven causes the player to win (LUCKY_SEVEN), and on subsequent rolls, a seven causes the player to lose (CRAPS). You are not required to provide initializer values for the constants in an Enum. If you do not, the initial value of the first constant will be zero and all others will be initialized to one higher than the preceding constant in the list.

Method playButton_Click

After the declarations for several instance variables (lines 14–17), lines 20–51 declare method playButton_Click to handle playButton's Click event. When the user clicks the **Play** button, method playButton_Click sets up a new game by initializing several values (lines 24–26). Line 26 clears the status Label's Text property.

Setting the Image property of pointDie1PictureBox and pointDie2PictureBox to Nothing (lines 29–30) causes the PictureBoxes to appear blank. Method playButton_Click executes the game's first roll by calling RollDice (line 32). Function RollDice (lines 84–94) generates two random numbers and calls method DisplayDie (lines 72–81) to display the corresponding die images in the PictureBoxes that represent the current roll of the dice.

The Select...Case statement (lines 35–50) analyzes the roll returned by RollDice to determine how play should continue (that is, by terminating the game with a win or loss, or by enabling subsequent rolls). If the user does not win or lose on the first roll, the GroupBox's text is set to display the point value (line 44) and the proper images are displayed in the GroupBox's PictureBoxes (lines 46–47). Depending on the value of the roll, Buttons **Roll** and **Play** become either enabled or disabled (lines 37, 40 and 48–49). Disabling a Button means that no action will be performed when the Button is clicked. Recall that a control can be enabled and disabled by setting its Enabled property to True or False, respectively.

Method rollButton_Click

If the button **Roll** is enabled, clicking it invokes method rollButton_Click (lines 54–69), which executes an additional roll of the dice. Method rollButton_Click then analyzes the roll, letting users know whether they've won or lost.

6.11 Method Overloading

There are several ways to declare methods with variable-length sets of parameters. Method overloading allows you to create methods with the *same* name but *different* signatures—that is, there are different numbers and/or types of parameters, or they're listed in a different order (by type). A method's signature *does not* include its return type. When you call an overloaded method, the compiler selects the proper method by examining the number, types and order (by type) of the arguments. Often, method overloading is used to create several methods with the same name that perform *similar* tasks on *different* types of data.

Figure 6.17 uses overloaded method Square to calculate the square of both an Integer and a Double. If the compiler looked only at method names during compilation, the code in Fig. 6.17 would be ambiguous—the compiler would not know how to differentiate between the two Square methods. The compiler uses a process known as **overload resolution** to determine which method to call. This process first searches for all methods that *could* be used on the basis of the number and type of arguments that are present. Although it might seem that only one method would match, it's important to remember that values are converted as necessary when they're passed as arguments. Once all matching methods are found, the compiler then selects the closest match.

```vb
1   ' Fig. 6.17: MethodOverloading.vb
2   ' Using overloaded methods.
3   Public Class MethodOverloading
4      ' call overloaded functions
5      Private Sub MethodOverloading_Load(sender As Object,
6         e As EventArgs) Handles MyBase.Load
7
8         ' call the overloaded Square methods and display the results
9         outputLabel.Text =
10           "The square of Integer 7 is " & Square(7) & vbCrLf &
11           "The square of Double 7.5 is " & Square(7.5)
12     End Sub ' MethodOverloading_Load
13
14     ' method Square takes an Integer and returns an Integer
15     Function Square(value As Integer) As Integer
16        Return Convert.ToInt32(value ^ 2)
17     End Function ' Square
18
19     ' method Square takes a Double and returns a Double
20     Function Square(value As Double) As Double
21        Return value ^ 2
22     End Function ' Square
23  End Class ' MethodOverloading
```

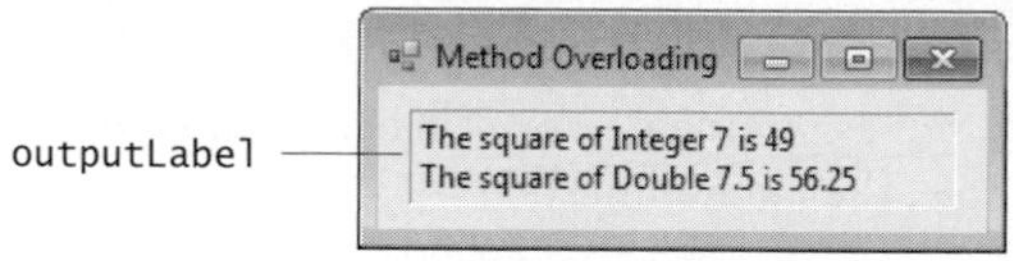

Fig. 6.17 | Using overloaded methods.

Line 10 calls method Square with the argument 7. The compiler treats whole-number literals as Integers by default. So line 10 calls the version of method Square that has an Integer parameter (lines 15–17). Similarly, line 11 calls method Square with the argument 7.5. The compiler treats floating-point literals as Double values by default, line 11 calls the version of method Square that has a Double parameter (lines 20–22).

The call to method Convert.ToInt32 in line 16 *explicitly* converts its argument to type Integer. This is required to prevent compilation errors. The exponent (^) operator expects operands of type Double and *implicitly* converts its operands to that type. Recall that we're now using **Option Strict**, so *implicit* conversions from Double (the result type of the ^ operator) to Integer (the return type of the method) are no longer allowed.

Notes on Method Overloading

Overloaded methods need not have the same number of parameters. The *order* of the parameters (by type) is important to the compiler. For example, if the declaration of method AddMixedTypes begins with

```
Function AddMixedTypes(a As Integer,
    b As Double) As Integer
```

and an overloaded version of the method begins with

```
Function AddMixedTypes(a As Double,
    b As Integer) As Integer
```

the compiler considers these two AddMixedTypes methods to be distinct.

Also, methods cannot be distinguished *only* by their return types. For example, if you modify method Square in line 20 of Fig. 6.17 so that its parameter is of type Integer rather than type Double, you'll receive the following compilation error:

```
Public Function Square(value As Integer) As Integer' and
    'Public Function Square(value As Integer) As Double' cannot
    overload each other because they differ only by return types.
```

6.12 Optional Parameters

Methods can have **optional parameters**. Declaring a parameter as **Optional** allows the calling method to *vary* the number of arguments to pass. An Optional parameter specifies a *default value* that's assigned to the parameter if the optional argument is omitted.

You can create methods with one or more Optional parameters. All Optional parameters *must* be placed to the right of the method's non-Optional parameters—that is, at the end of the parameter list.

Common Programming Error 6.4

Declaring a non-Optional parameter to the right of an Optional parameter is a compilation error.

When a parameter is declared as Optional, the caller has the *option* of passing that particular argument. For example, the method header

```
Function Power(base As Integer,
    Optional exponent As Integer = 2) As Integer
```

specifies the last parameter exponent as Optional. Any call to Power must pass at least an argument for the parameter base, or a compilation error occurs. Optionally, a second argument (for the exponent parameter) can be passed to Power. Consider the following calls to Power:

```
Power()
Power(10)
Power(10, 3)
```

The first call generates a syntax error because a minimum of one argument is required for this method. The second call is valid because one argument (10) is being passed—the Optional exponent is not specified in the method call. The last call is also valid—10 is passed as the one required argument and 3 is passed as the Optional argument.

In the call that passes only one argument (10), parameter exponent defaults to 2, which is the value specified in the method header. Optional parameters must specify a **default value** by using an equal (=) sign followed by the value. For example, the header for Power sets 2 as the *default value* for exponent. Default values can be used only with parameters declared as Optional.

Figure 6.19 demonstrates an optional parameter. The program calculates the result of raising a base value to an exponent. Method Power (lines 23–33) specifies that its second parameter is Optional. If the user does not specify an exponent, the Optional argument is omitted, and the default parameter value, 2, is used.

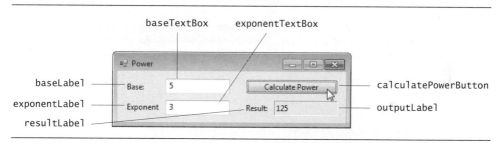

Fig. 6.18 | GUI for the **Power** app.

```
1    ' Fig. 6.19: Power.vb
2    ' Optional argument demonstration with method Power.
3    Public Class Power
4        ' reads input and displays result
5        Private Sub calculatePowerButton_Click(sender As Object,
6            e As EventArgs) Handles calculatePowerButton.Click
7
8            Dim value As Integer ' stores the result
9
10           ' call version of Power depending on power input
11           If exponentTextBox.Text <> String.Empty Then
12               value = Power(Convert.ToInt32(baseTextBox.Text),
13                   Convert.ToInt32(exponentTextBox.Text))
14           Else
15               value = Power(Convert.ToInt32(baseTextBox.Text))
16               exponentTextBox.Text = Convert.ToString(2)
17           End If
18
19           outputLabel.Text = Convert.ToString(value)
20       End Sub ' calculatePowerButton_Click
21
22       ' use iteration to calculate power
23       Function Power(base As Integer,
24           Optional exponent As Integer = 2          ) As Integer
25
26           Dim result As Integer = 1 ' initialize total
27
```

Fig. 6.19 | Optional argument demonstration with method Power. (Part I of 2.)

```
28          For i = 1 To exponent ' calculate power
29             result *= base
30          Next
31
32          Return result ' return result
33       End Function ' Power
34
35       ' clear outputLabel when user changes the base value
36       Private Sub baseTextBox_TextChanged(sender As Object,
37          e As EventArgs) Handles baseTextBox.TextChanged
38          outputLabel.Text = String.Empty
39       End Sub ' baseTextBox_TextChanged
40
41       ' clear outputLabel when user changes the exponent value
42       Private Sub exponentTextBox_TextChanged(sender As Object,
43          e As EventArgs) Handles exponentTextBox.TextChanged
44          outputLabel.Text = String.Empty
45       End Sub ' exponentTextBox_TextChanged
46    End Class ' Power
```

a) Calculating the cube of 5

b) Calculating 8 squared with the default exponent of 2

When the exponent is left blank, the program uses method Power's Optional parameter value (2) and automatically displays that value so the user sees the exponent that was used in the calculation

c) Calculating 8 squared with the exponent 2 explicitly specified

Fig. 6.19 | Optional argument demonstration with method Power. (Part 2 of 2.)

In this example, we use TextBoxes to input data from the user. When the user clicks the **Calculate Power** Button, line 11 determines whether exponentTextBox contains a value. If the condition is true (as in Fig. 6.19(a)), the values in the TextBoxes are converted to Integers using method Convert.ToInt32 then passed to Power (lines 12–13). Otherwise, baseTextBox's value is converted to an Integer and passed as the required argument to Power in line 15. An example of this is shown in Fig. 6.19(b), where we clicked the **Calculate Power** Button without entering an exponent value. The second argument, 2, is provided by the compiler (using the default value of the Optional argument) and is not visible to you in the call. Line 16 displays the default exponent value (2) in exponentTextBox, for clarity (Fig. 6.19(c)).

6.13 Using the Debugger: Debugging Commands

We now present additional debugging commands from the **Debug** toolbar (Fig. 6.20) that provide convenient access to commands in the **DEBUG** menu. If the **Debug** toolbar isn't visible in the IDE when you're running in debug mode, select **VIEW > Toolbars > Debug**.

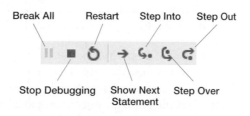

Fig. 6.20 | Debugging controls on Visual Studio's **Debug** toolbar.

Now that you've learned more about methods, we'll demonstrate the **Step Into** and **Step Out** commands that can be used to view the code for a called method as it executes and returns from the method to the caller, respectively. In addition, we'll show how to continue program execution from a breakpoint.

To begin, open the **Wage Calculator** app from Fig. 6.3. Next, set a breakpoint at the call to method DisplayPay (line 17) by clicking in the margin indicator bar (Fig. 6.21). Start the debugger to begin executing the **Wage Calculator** app. Enter the value 7.50 in the **Wage per hour:** TextBox, and enter 35 in the **Hours worked:** TextBox, then click the **Calculate** Button. The debugger enters *break mode* at line 17, indicating that method DisplayPay will execute next—the IDE highlights in yellow.

```
WageCalculator.vb  ⊬ ✕  WageCalculator.vb [Design]
  calculateButton                         ⏣ Click
    13          Dim hourlyWage As Decimal = Val(wageTextBox.Text)
    14
    15          ' determine whether hoursWorked is less than or equal to 168
    16          If hoursWorked <= HOURS_IN_A_WEEK Then
    17              DisplayPay(hoursWorked, hourlyWage) ' calls DisplayPay Function
At WageCalculator.vb, line 17 character 10 ('WageCalculator.calculateButton_Click(Object, EventArgs)', line 10)
100 %  ▾ ◂
```

Fig. 6.21 | Setting a breakpoint at line 17.

Using the Step Into Command
When the debugger is in *break mode* and the next statement to execute represents a method call, you can use the **Step Into** command (⇘) to transfer control to the called method, so that you can use other debugging commands to step through the method's statements and confirm that the method is executing correctly. If the next statement to execute is *not* a method call, then the **Step Into** command has the *same effect* as the **Step Over** command—that is, the debugger executes the current statement and pauses at the next statement to execute. Click the **Step Into** command now to transfer control to method DisplayPay (Fig. 6.22).

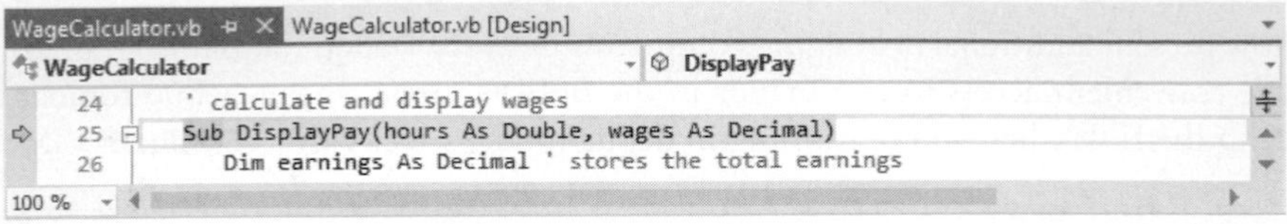

Fig. 6.22 | IDE showing that `DisplayPay` is about to execute.

Executing the Statements in Method DisplayPay

As you learned in Section 4.12, you can use the **Step Over** command to execute statements *one at a time*. If you wish to execute several statements without repeatedly clicking the **Step Over** command, you'll want to tell the debugger to continue to a later point in a method's (or the program's) execution. There are two ways to do this. One is to simply *right click* the statement where you'd like to continue *step-by-step execution*, then select **Run to Cursor** from the menu that appears. The debugger will execute the statements up to, but *not* including, that statement. When an app is running in the debugger, the **Start** (▶) command becomes the **Continue** command. If you set another breakpoint then click **Continue**, the debugger will execute statements until it reaches the next breakpoint. If there aren't any breakpoints, the program will simply execute until it completes or until the event handler that you're debugging finishes executing—at which point the program waits for the next user interaction.

Set a breakpoint now at line 40 in method `DisplayPay` by clicking in the *margin indicator bar*, then click **Continue** to execute the code in method `DisplayPay` up to, but not including, line 40. The next executable statement is now line 40. Click **Continue** again to complete the call to `DisplayPay` and complete the execution of the event handler `calculateButton_Click`. At this point, the program waits for the next user interaction.

Using the Step Out Command

Often, in lengthy methods, you'll want to look at a few key lines of code and then continue debugging the caller's code. The **Step Out** command (↪) is useful for such situations, where you do not want to continue stepping through the entire method line by line.

To demonstrate this feature, first remove the breakpoint at line 40. Then, enter new values in the **Wage per hour:** and **Hours worked:** TextBoxes and click the **Calculate** Button. When the debugger enters break mode at line 17, **Step Into** the `DisplayPay` method. At this point you can step through some of the code in method `DisplayPay`. Before you reach the end of the method, click the **Step Out** command to execute the remaining statements in the method and return control to line 17, where the method was called. Click the **Stop Debugging** command to end the debugging session.

6.14 Wrap-Up

In this chapter, you studied methods in greater depth. You learned the difference between subroutines and functions, and when to use each. You learned how to declare named constants using both enumerations and with the `Const` keyword. You learned about how arguments can be implicitly converted to the type of their corresponding parameters. We demonstrated **Option Strict**, which causes the compiler to check all conversions and requires you to perform an *explicit* conversion for all *narrowing conversions* that could cause data loss or program termination. You saw how to use class Random to generate random numbers that can be used for simulations and game playing. You also learned about the scope of instance variables and local variables in classes and methods, respectively. You learned that multiple methods in one class can be overloaded by providing methods with the *same* name and *different* signatures. Such methods can be used to perform the same or similar tasks using different types or different numbers of parameters. You learned how to specify Optional parameters with default values that are passed to a method if a corresponding argument is not provided in a method call. Finally, we demonstrated the **Step Into**, **Continue** and **Step Out** debugging commands, which help you follow the flow of control through the various methods in your programs.

In Chapter 7, you'll learn how to maintain lists and tables of data in arrays. You'll also see a more elegant implementation of the dice-rolling app of Fig. 6.14.

Summary

Section 6.1 Introduction
- Experience has shown that the best way to develop and maintain a large program is to construct it from small, simple pieces—a technique known as divide and conquer.

Section 6.2 Classes and Methods
- Typical programs consist of one or more classes. You combine new classes with "prepackaged" classes available in the .NET Framework Class Library and in various other class libraries.

- You can create your own customized classes and methods to meet the unique requirements of a particular app.

- Methods define specific tasks that a program may use one or more times during its execution.

- Although the same method can be executed from multiple points in a program, the actual statements that define the method are written only once.

- Hiding implementation details promotes good software engineering.

- A method is invoked by a method call. The method call specifies the method name and provides arguments that the method requires to do its job.

- When a method completes its task, it returns control to the calling method. In some cases, the method also returns a result to the caller.

Section 6.3 Subroutines: Methods That Do Not Return a Value
- A subroutine is a method that performs a task but does not return a value. It's declared with the keywords Sub...End Sub.

- Keyword Const declares a constant—a value that cannot change after it's initialized. Constants enhance program readability by providing descriptive identifiers for values that do not change.

- When a method is called, by default the program makes a copy of the value of each argument (if any) and program control transfers to the method's first line. The method receives the copied values and stores them in its parameters.

- When End Sub is encountered, program control returns to the next statement in the calling method.

- Keyword Sub indicates that a method will perform a task but will not return any information to its calling method when it completes its task.

- By convention, method names begin with an uppercase letter and all subsequent words in the name begin with a capital letter.
- In a method declaration, the parentheses after the name indicate any parameters required by the method to perform its task. Empty parentheses indicate that a method does not have parameters.
- A method can specify multiple parameters by separating each from the next with a comma.
- Each parameter has a variable name and a type.
- There must be one argument in the method call for each non-optional parameter in the method declaration.
- The type of each argument must be consistent with its corresponding parameter's type.
- The declarations and statements in the method declaration form the method body.
- The method body is also referred to as a block. The bodies of control statements are also blocks.

Section 6.4 Functions: Methods That Return a Value
- A function is a method that performs a task then returns a value to the calling method.
- A function is declared with the keywords Function...End Function.
- A Return statement terminates a function and gives a value back to the calling method.
- In a Function's header, the return type indicates the type of the value returned from the function.

Section 6.5 Implicit Argument Conversions
- Implicit argument conversion converts an argument's value to the type that a method expects to receive in its corresponding parameter.
- A widening conversion occurs when an argument is converted to a parameter of another type that can hold more data, whereas a narrowing conversion occurs when there's potential for data loss during the conversion.
- Implicit conversions also occur for expressions containing values of two or more types.

Section 6.6 Option Strict and Data-Type Conversions
- Option Explicit, which defaults to On, requires you to declare all variables before they're used in a program.
- Option Strict, which defaults to Off, increases program clarity and reduces debugging time. When set to On, Option Strict causes the compiler to check all conversions and requires you to perform explicit conversions for all narrowing conversions or conversions that might cause program termination.
- Option Infer, which defaults to On, enables the compiler to infer a variable's type based on its initializer value.
- Class Convert's methods explicitly convert data from one primitive type to another.
- Many of the primitive types have a Parse method that you can use to convert a String to a value of that primitive type.
- Visual Basic also provides type-conversion functions for converting between built-in types.

Section 6.7 Passing Arguments: Pass-by-Value vs. Pass-by-Reference
- Arguments are passed in one of two ways—pass-by-value or pass-by-reference.
- When an argument is passed by value, the program makes a copy of the argument's value and passes the copy to the called method. Changes to the called method's copy do not affect the original variable's value in the caller.

- When an argument is passed by reference, the called method can access and modify the caller's original data directly.
- Keyword ByVal in a method header indicates that the argument is be passed by value.
- Keyword ByRef indicates that the argument is passed by reference.

Section 6.8 Scope of Declarations
- A declaration's scope is the portion of the program that can refer to the declared entity by its name without qualification.
- The scope of a variable declared in a block is from the declaration point to the end of the block.
- The scope of a method's local-variable declaration or parameter is from the point at which the declaration appears to the end of that method.
- Variables with method scope do not retain their values between method calls and are reinitialized each time the method in which they're declared is invoked.
- The scope of a class's members is the entire body of the class. This enables methods of a class to use all of the class's members.
- A variable's lifetime is the period during which the variable exists in memory.
- Variables with method or block scope are called local variables, because they cannot be referenced outside the method or block in which they're declared.
- If a local variable has the same name as a variable with class scope, the local variable hides the class-scope variable in the block or method.

Section 6.9 Case Study: Random-Number Generation
- A Random variable is initialized with the result of an object-creation expression. New creates a new object of the class specified to the right of the New keyword.
- Random method Next generates a positive Integer value greater than or equal to zero and less than the constant Int32.MaxValue (2,147,483,647).
- The values returned by Next are actually pseudorandom numbers.

Section 6.9.1 Scaling and Shifting of Random Numbers
- By passing an argument to method Next you can produce integers in the range 0 up to, but not including, the argument value. The argument is the scaling factor. You can also shift the range of numbers produced by adding a value to the result.
- You can pass two arguments to Next to produce values from the first argument up to, but not including, the second argument.

Section 6.9.2 Randomly Selecting Images
- You can embed images into a project as resources. This causes the compiler to embed the images in the app's executable file and enables the app to access the images through the My namespace.
- To use an image in the project's resources, you use the method My.Resources.ResourceManager.GetObject, which takes as an argument the resource name as it appears in the **Resources** tab and returns the resource as an Object. Then, convert this Object to type Image using the CType function.

Section 6.10 Case Study: A Game of Chance
- A GroupBox is used to group related controls. When adding other controls to a GroupBox, drag and drop the controls within the bounds of the GroupBox.
- A GroupBox's Text property displays in the upper-left corner of the GroupBox.

- You can dock a control to the Top, Bottom, Left, Right or Center of a Form by selecting the appropriate value for the control's Dock property in the **Properties** window.

- An enumeration—declared with Enum...End Enum—enhances program readability by providing descriptive identifiers for groups of related constant numbers.

Section 6.11 Method Overloading

- Method overloading allows you to create multiple methods with the same name but different signatures—that is, the parameters have different numbers and/or types, or they're listed in a different order (by type). A method's signature does not include its return type.

- When an overloaded method is called, the compiler selects the proper method by examining the number, types and order (by type) of the arguments.

Section 6.12 Optional Parameters

- Declaring a parameter as Optional allows the calling method to vary the number of arguments to pass. An Optional parameter specifies a default value that's assigned to the parameter if the optional argument is omitted.

- All Optional parameters must be placed to the right of the method's nonoptional parameters.

Section 6.13 Using the Debugger: Debugging Commands

- The **Step Into** and **Step Out** debugger commands can be used to view the code for a called method as it executes and return from the method to the caller, respectively.

- If the next statement to execute is not a method call, then the **Step Into** command has the same effect as the **Step Over** command.

- If you wish to execute several statements without repeatedly clicking the **Step Over** command, you can right click the statement where you'd like to continue step-by-step execution, then select **Run to Cursor** from the menu that appears. The debugger will execute the statements up to, but not including, that statement.

- When an app is running in the debugger, the **Start Debugging** (▶) command becomes the **Continue** command. If you click **Continue** while in break mode, the debugger will execute statements until it reaches the next breakpoint. If there aren't any, the program will simply execute until it completes or until the event handler that you're debugging finishes executing.

Terminology

Self-Review Exercises

6.1   Answer each of the following questions.

    a)   Programmers normally use _____.

       1. programmer-defined methods   2. preexisting methods

       3. both programmer-defined and preex-   4. neither programmer-defined nor pre-
          isting methods   existing methods

    b)   The _____ statement in a Function sends a value back to the calling method.

       1. Return   2. Back

       3. End   4. None of the above

    c)   Arguments passed to a method can be _____.

       1. constants   2. expressions

       3. variables   4. All of the above

    d)   The _____ is a comma-separated list of declarations in a method header.

       1. argument list   2. parameter list

       3. value list   4. variable list

    e)   During debugging, the _____ command executes the remaining statements in the current method and returns program control to the place where the method was called.

       1. Step Into   2. Step Out

       3. Step Over   4. Steps

f) The debugger command _____ behaves like the **Step Over** command when the next statement to execute does not contain a method call.
   1. **Step Into**
   2. **Step Out**
   3. **Step Over**
   4. **Steps**

g) Instance variables have _____ scope.
   1. block
   2. method
   3. class
   4. None of the above

h) Variables with either method scope or block scope are called _____.
   1. instance variables
   2. local variables
   3. class variables
   4. hidden variables

i) When **Option Strict** is set to On, you must explicitly perform _____.
   1. narrowing conversions
   2. widening conversions
   3. all type conversions
   4. no conversions

j) The methods in class _____ are used to perform explicit conversions.
   1. Strict
   2. Change
   3. Convert
   4. Conversion

k) The statement _____ returns a number in the range from 8 to 300.
   1. randomObject.Next(8, 300)
   2. randomObject.Next(8, 301)
   3. 1 + randomObject.Next(8, 300)
   4. None of the above

l) The statement _____ returns a number in the range 15 to 35.
   1. randomObject.Next(15, 36)
   2. randomObject.Next(15, 35)
   3. 10 + randomObject.Next(5, 26)
   4. Both 1 and 3

m) Use keyword _____ to define groups of related constants.
   1. ReadOnly
   2. Enum
   3. Constants
   4. Enumeration

n) The constants defined in an Enum _____.
   1. may use repeated values
   2. can be accessed using the Enum's name followed by the member access operator
   3. are not required to declare a value
   4. All of the above

o) To clear the image in a PictureBox, set its Image property to _____.
   1. "" (double quotes)
   2. Nothing
   3. None
   4. Empty

6.2 State whether each of the following is *true* or *false*. If *false*, explain why.
   a) Conversion of a data item from type Single to type Double is an example of a widening conversion.
   b) Variables of type Char cannot be converted to type Integer.
   c) **Option Explicit** causes the compiler to check all conversions and requires you to perform an explicit conversion for all narrowing conversions that could cause data loss or program termination.
   d) When an argument is passed by value, the program makes a copy of the argument's value and passes the copy to the called method.

6.3 Give the method header for each of the following:
   a) Method Hypotenuse, which takes two double-precision, floating-point arguments, side1 and side2, and returns a double-precision, floating-point result.
   b) Method Smallest, which takes three integers, x, y and z, and returns an integer.
   c) Method Instructions, which does not take any arguments and does not return a value.

d) Method `IntegerToSingle`, which takes an integer argument, `number`, and returns a floating-point result.

6.4 Find the error in each of the following program segments and explain how the error can be corrected:

a)
```
Function Sum(x As Integer, y As Integer) As Integer
    Dim result As Integer
    result = x + y
End Function ' Sum
```

b)
```
Sub Display(value As Double)
    Dim value As Double
    resultLabel.Text = Convert.ToString(value)
End Sub ' Display
```

c)
```
Sub Product()
    Dim a As Integer = 6
    Dim b As Integer = 5
    Dim result As Integer = a * b
    resultLabel.Text = "Result is " & result
    Return result
End Sub ' Product
```

Answers to Self-Review Exercises

6.1 a) 3. b) 1. c) 4. d) 2. e) 2. f) 1. g) 3. h) 2. i) 1. j) 3. k) 2. l) 4. m) 2. n) 4. o) 2.

6.2 a) True. b) False. Type `Char` variables can be converted to type `Integer` with a narrowing conversion. c) False. **Option Strict** causes the compiler to check all conversions and requires you to perform an explicit conversion for all narrowing conversions that could cause data loss or program termination. **Option Explicit** forces you to explicitly declare all variables before they're used in a program. d) True.

6.3

a)
```
Function Hypotenuse(side1 As Double, _
    side2 As Double) As Double
```

b)
```
Function Smallest(x As Integer, _
    y As Integer, z As Integer) As Integer
```

c)
```
Sub Instructions()
```

d)
```
Function IntegerToSingle(number As Integer) As Single
```

6.4

a) Error: The method is supposed to return an `Integer`, but does not.
Correction: Replace the method body with
```
Return x + y
```
or add the following statement at the end of the method body:
```
Return result
```

b) Error: Parameter `value` is redefined in the method declaration.
Correction: Delete the declaration `Dim value As Double`.

c) Error: The method returns a value, but is declared as a subroutine.
Correction: Change the method to a function with return type `Integer` or remove the `Return` statement.

Quick Quiz

6.5 Answer each of the following questions.

a) A method defined with keyword `Sub` _____.

1. must specify a return type   2. does not accept arguments

3. returns a value   4. does not return a value

b) The technique of developing large applications from small, manageable pieces is known as _____.

1. divide and conquer
2. returning a value
3. click and mortar
4. a building-block algorithm

c) What's the difference between Sub and Function methods?

1. Sub methods return values, Function methods do not.
2. Function methods return values, Sub methods do not.
3. Sub methods accept parameters, Function methods do not.
4. Function methods accept parameters, Sub methods do not.

d) What occurs after a method call is made?

1. Control is given to the called method. After the method is run, the app continues execution at the point where the method call was made.
2. Control is given to the called method. After the method is run, the app continues execution with the statement after the called method's definition.
3. The statement before the method call is executed.
4. The app terminates.

e) Functions can return _____ value(s).

1. zero
2. exactly one
3. one or more
4. any number of

f) Which of the following must be true when making a method call?

1. The number of arguments in the method call must match the number of parameters in the method header.
2. The argument types must be compatible with their corresponding parameter types.
3. Both a and b
4. None of the above

g) Which of the following statements correctly returns the variable value from a Function?

1. Return Dim value
2. Return value As Integer
3. value Return
4. Return value

h) The debugging command _____ executes the next statement in the app. If the next statement to execute contains a method call, the called method executes in its entirety.

1. Step Into
2. Step Out
3. Step Over
4. Steps

i) The first line of a method (including the keyword Sub or Function, the method name, the parameter list and possibly a return type) is known as the method _____.

1. body
2. title
3. caller
4. header

j) When **Option Strict** is set to On, variables _____.

1. are passed by value
2. are passed by reference
3. might need to be converted explicitly to a different type to avoid errors
4. are used only within the block in which they're declared

k) A variable declared inside a class, but outside a method, is called a(n) _____.

1. local variable
2. hidden variable
3. instance variable
4. constant variable

l) When **Option Strict** is _____, the implicit conversion from a Decimal to an Integer results in an error.

1. On
2. True
3. Off
4. False

m) Keyword _____ indicates pass-by-reference.

   1. `ByReference`   2. `ByRef`

   3. `Ref`   4. `Reference`

n) With _____, changes made to a parameter variable's value do not affect the value of the variable in the calling method.

   1. **Option Strict**   2. pass-by-value

   3. pass-by-reference   4. None of the above

o) Instance variables _____.

   1. can be accessed by a method in the same class   2. have class scope

   3. Neither of the above   4. Both of the above

p) Assigning a "smaller" type to a "larger" type is a _____ conversion.

   1. narrowing   2. shortening

   3. widening   4. lengthening

q) A `Single` value can be implicitly converted to _____ when **Option Strict** is `On`.

   1. `Integer`   2. `Double`

   3. Neither of the above   4. Both of the above

r) A `Random` object can generate pseudorandom numbers of type _____.

   1. `Integer`   2. `Single`

   3. `Char`   4. Both 1 and 3

s) Constant identifiers within enumerations _____ be assigned the same numeric value.

   1. cannot   2. can

   3. must   4. should

t) The `Next` method of class `Random` can be called using _____.

   1. one argument   2. no arguments

   3. two arguments   4. All of the above

u) The statement _____ assigns `value` a random number in the range 5–20.

   1. `value = randomObject.Next(5, 21)`   2. `value = randomObject.Next(4, 20)`

   3. `value = randomObject.Next(5, 20)`   4. `value = randomObject.Next(4, 21)`

v) The values returned by the methods of class `Random` are _____ numbers.

   1. pseudorandom   2. completely random

   3. ordered   4. None of the above

w) The second argument passed to class `Random`'s `Next` method is _____.

   1. equal to the maximum value you wish to be generated

   2. equal to one more than the maximum value you wish to be generated

   3. equal to one less than the maximum value you wish to be generated

   4. equal to the minimum value you wish to be generated

Exercises

6.6 *(Find the Smallest and Largest Values)* Write an app that allows the user to enter three `Double` values, then determines and displays the smallest and largest values. Provide methods `Minimum` and `Maximum` that each receive three `Double` values and return a `Double` result.

6.7 *(Find the Smallest and Largest Values)* Class `Math` provides methods `Min` and `Max` to determine the smaller or larger of two values, respectively. Reimplement your methods `Minimum` and `Maximum` from Exercise 6.6 so that they use `Math.Min` and `Math.Max`, respectively.

6.8 *(Gas Pump)* A gas pump calculates the cost of gas at a local gas station. The station charges $2.69 per gallon for regular grade gas, $2.79 per gallon for special grade gas and $2.89 per gallon for super grade gas. Create an app that simulates the functionality of the gas pump. The user enters the number of gallons to purchase and clicks the desired grade (each grade is represented by a Button whose Text properties are set to **Regular**, **Special** and **Super**). Each Button's Click event handler calls a method to compute the total cost from the number of gallons entered and the selected grade. [*Note:* Use the Text property of each Button to pass the selected grade to your method.]

6.9 *(Lottery Number Generator)* A lottery commission offers four different lottery games to play: Three-number, Four-number, Five-number and Five-number + 1 lotteries. Each game has independent numbers. Develop an app that randomly picks numbers for all four games and displays the generated numbers in a GUI. Declare a method that generates a random number based on a range given, and returns the random number as a String. The games are played as follows:
   a) Three-number lotteries require players to choose three numbers in the range 0–9.
   b) Four-number lotteries require players to choose four numbers in the range 0–9.
   c) Five-number lotteries require players to choose five numbers in the range 1–39.
   d) Five-number + 1 lotteries require players to choose five numbers in the range 1–49 and an additional number in the range 1–42.

6.10 *(Sales Commissions)* Develop an app that calculates a salesperson's commission from the number of items sold. Assume that all items have a fixed price of $10 per unit. Use a Select...Case statement to implement the following sales-commission schedule:
   a) Up to 50 items sold = 6% commission
   b) Between 51 and 100 items sold = 7% commission
   c) Between 101 and 150 items sold = 8% commission
   d) More than 150 items sold = 9% commission

Create an app that inputs the number of items sold and contains a **Calculate** Button. When this Button is clicked, three methods should be called—one to calculate gross sales, one to calculate the commission percentage based on the commission schedule above and one to calculate the salesperson's earnings. Earnings are defined as gross sales multiplied by commission percentage, divided by 100 (because we're working with a percentage value). The data returned by these three methods should be displayed in the GUI.

6.11 *(Parking Charges)* A parking garage charges a $2.00 minimum fee to park for up to three hours. The garage charges an additional $0.50 per hour for each hour *or part thereof* in excess of three hours. The maximum charge for any given 24-hour period is $10.00. Assume that no car parks for longer than 24 hours at a time. Write a program that calculates and displays the parking charges for each customer who parked a car in this garage yesterday. You should enter in a TextBox the hours parked for each customer. The program should display the charge for the current customer. The program should use the method CalculateCharges to determine the charge for each customer. Use the techniques described in the chapter to read the Double value from a TextBox. [*Note:* You may need to use methods Convert.ToDouble and Convert.ToDecimal when doing calculations with the number of hours and charges, respectively.]

6.12 *(Coin Tossing)* Write an app that simulates coin tossing. Let the program toss the coin each time the user presses the **Toss** button. Count the number of times each side of the coin appears. Display the results. The program should call a separate method Flip, which takes no arguments and returns False for tails and True for heads. Use the head and tail images provided in the Images folder with this chapter's examples. [*Note:* If the program simulates the coin tossing realistically, each side of the coin should appear approximately half the time.]

6.13   *(Temperature Converter App)* Write an app that performs temperature conversions. The app should perform two types of conversions: degrees Fahrenheit to degrees Celsius, and degrees Celsius to degrees Fahrenheit. To convert degrees Fahrenheit to degrees Celsius, use this formula:

```
celsius = (5 / 9) * (fahrenheit - 32)
```

To convert degrees Celsius to degrees Fahrenheit, use this formula:

```
fahrenheit = (9 / 5) * celsius + 32
```

Create Functions to perform each conversion, using the formulas above. The user should provide the temperature to convert. Allow the user to enter a number. Provide separate Buttons that allow the use to convert the number entered into Fahrenheit and Celsius, respectively.

6.14   *(What Does This Code Do?)* What does the following code do? Assume that this method is invoked by using Mystery(90, 120).

```
1  Sub Mystery(number1 As Integer, number2 As Integer)
2      Dim x As Integer
3      Dim y As Double
4      x = number1 + number2
5      y = x / 3
6      If y <= 60 Then
7          resultLabel.Text = "<= 60"
8      Else
9          resultLabel.Text = "Result is " & y
10     End If
11 End Sub ' Mystery
```

6.15   *(What's Wrong With This Code?)* Find the error(s) in the following code, which should take an Integer value as a parameter and return the value of the parameter multiplied by itself.

```
1  Function numSquare(number As Integer) As Integer
2      Dim result As Integer
3      result = number * number
4  End Function ' square
```

6.16   *(Quiz Average App)* Develop an app that computes a student's average quiz score for all of the quiz scores entered. The user enters each grade and presses a Button to submit it. Use instance variables to keep track of the sum of all the quiz scores entered and the number of quiz scores entered. After the user enters each grade, display the number of quizzes taken and the average for all grades entered so far.

6.17   *(What Does This Code Do?)* What's displayed in displayLabel when the user clicks the enter Button?

```
1  Public Class ScopeTest
2      Dim value2 As Integer = 5
3      Private Sub enterButton_Click(sender As Object, _
4          e As EventArgs) Handles enterButton.Click
5          Dim value1 As Integer = 15
6          Dim value2 As Integer = 10
```

```
7            Test(value1)
8            displayLabel.Text = value1.ToString()
9        End Sub ' enterButton_Click
10       Sub Test(ByRef value1 As Integer)
11           value1 += value2
12       End Sub ' Test
13    End Class ' ScopeTest
```

6.18 *(What is Missing With This Code?)* Find the missing statement(s) in the following code (the method should assign the value 90 to the variable result). Assume that Option Strict is set to On.

```
1    Sub Sum()
2        Dim numberWords As String = "6"
3        Dim number As Integer = 15
4        Dim result As Integer
5        result = numberWords * number
6    End Sub ' Sum
```

6.19 *(Guess the Number App)* Develop an app that generates a random number and prompts the user to guess the number. When the user clicks the **New Game** Button, the app chooses a number in the range 1 to 100 at random. The user enters guesses into the **Guess:** TextBox and clicks the **Enter** Button. If the guess is correct, the game ends, and the user can start a new game. If the guess is not correct, the app should indicate whether the guess is higher or lower than the correct number. Use instance variables for a Random object and to store the randomly generated number in the range of 1 to 100. If a guess is correct, display **Correct!** in the output Label, then disable the **Enter** Button and enable the **New Game** Button. If a guess is higher than the correct answer, display **Too high...** in the output Label. If a guess is lower than the correct answer, display **Too low...** in the output Label. For the user's convenience, give the **Guess:** TextBox the focus after each guess is processed.

Making a Difference Exercises

As computer costs decline, it becomes feasible for every student, regardless of economic circumstance, to have a computer and use it in school. This creates exciting possibilities for improving the educational experience of all students worldwide as suggested by the next two exercises. [*Note:* Check out initiatives such as the One Laptop Per Child Project (one.laptop.org). Also, research "green" laptops—and note the key "going green" characteristics of these devices. Look into the Electronic Product Environmental Assessment Tool (www.epeat.net) which can help you assess the "greenness" of desktops, notebooks and monitors to help you decide which products to purchase.]

6.20 *(Computer-Assisted Instruction)* The use of computers in education is referred to as *computer-assisted instruction* (*CAI*). Write a program that will help an elementary school student learn multiplication. Use a Random object to produce two positive one-digit integers. The program should then prompt the user with a question, such as

```
How much is 6 times 7?
```

The student then inputs the answer. Next, the program checks the student's answer. If it's correct, display the message "Very good!" and ask another multiplication question. If the answer is wrong, display the message "No. Please try again." and let the student try the same question repeatedly until the student finally gets it right. A separate function should be used to generate each new question. This function should be called once when the app begins execution and each time the user answers the question correctly.

6.21 *(Computer-Assisted Instruction: Reducing Student Fatigue)* One problem in CAI environments is student fatigue. This can be reduced by varying the computer's responses to hold the student's attention. Modify the program of Exercise 6.20 so that various comments are displayed for each answer as follows:

Possible responses to a correct answer:

```
Very good!
Excellent!
Nice work!
Keep up the good work!
```

Possible responses to an incorrect answer:

```
No. Please try again.
Wrong. Try once more.
Don't give up!
No. Keep trying.
```

Use random-number generation to choose a number from 1 to 4 that will be used to select one of the four appropriate responses to each correct or incorrect answer. Use a Select...Case statement to issue the responses.

7

Arrays

Now go, write it before them in a table, and note it in a book.
—Isaiah 30:8

With sobs and tears he sorted out
Those of the largest size …
—Lewis Carroll

Attempt the end, and never stand to doubt;
Nothing's so hard, but search will find it out.
—Robert Herrick

Begin at the beginning, … and go on till you come to the end: then stop.
—Lewis Carroll

To go beyond is as wrong as to fall short
—Confucius

Objectives

In this chapter you'll learn:

- How arrays are used to store, sort and search lists and tables of values.

- To declare, initialize and refer to elements of arrays.

- To pass arrays to methods.

- To use the **For Each...Next** statement to iterate through all the elements of an array.

- To use the elements of arrays as counters.

- To declare and manipulate rectangular arrays.

7.1 Introduction

This chapter introduces basic concepts of *data structures*—collections of related data items. Arrays are simple data structures consisting only of data items of the *same* type. Arrays normally are "static" entities, in that they typically remain the same size once they're created, although they can be resized (as we show in Section 7.16). We discuss arrays that can represent lists and tables of values. We begin by creating and accessing arrays. We then perform various array manipulations, including summing the elements of an array, using arrays to summarize survey results, searching arrays for specific values and sorting arrays so their elements are in ascending order. We also introduce the For Each...Next repetition statement and use it to process the elements of an array.

7.2 Arrays

An array is a group of variables (called elements) containing values that all have the *same* type. To refer to a particular element, we specify the array's *name* and the *position number* of the element to which we refer. All arrays are objects of class **System.Array** and thus have that class's methods and properties (msdn.microsoft.com/library/system.array).

Figure 7.1 shows a logical representation of a *one-dimensional* integer array called c that represents a list of values. This array contains 12 elements, any one of which can be referred to by giving the name of the array followed by the position number of the element in parentheses (). The first element in every array is the zeroth element. Thus, the names of array c's elements are c(0), c(1), c(2), ..., c(11) and so on. The highest position number in array c is 11 (also called the array's **upper bound**), which is 1 less than the number of elements in the array (12).

Accessing Array Elements

The position number in parentheses more formally is called an index and must be a nonnegative integer or integer expression. If a program uses an expression as an index, the ex-

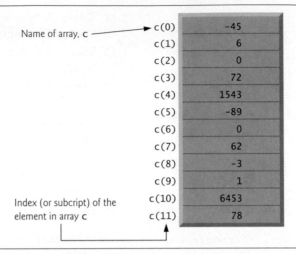

Fig. 7.1 | Array consisting of 12 elements.

pression is evaluated first to determine the index. For example, if variable value1 is equal to 5, and variable value2 is equal to 6, then the statement

```
c(value1 + value2) += 2
```

adds 2 to array element c(11). The name of an array element can be used on the left side of an assignment statement to place a new value into an array element.

Let's examine array c (Fig. 7.1) more closely. The array's name is c. Its 12 elements are referred to as c(0) through c(11)—pronounced as "c sub zero" through "c sub 11," where "sub" derives from "subscript," which is another word for index. The value of c(0) is –45, the value of c(1) is 6, the value of c(7) is 62 and the value of c(11) is 78. Values stored in arrays can be used in calculations. For example, to determine the total of the values contained in the first three elements of array c and then store the result in variable sum, we would write

```
sum = c(0) + c(1) + c(2)
```

To divide the value of c(6) by 2 using Integer division and assign the result to the variable result, we'd write

```
result = c(6) \ 2
```

Array Length
Every array "knows" its own length (that is, number of elements), which is determined by the array's **Length** property, as in:

```
c.Length
```

7.3 Declaring and Allocating Arrays
The following statement can be used to declare the array in Fig. 7.1:

```
Dim c(11) As Integer
```

The parentheses that follow the variable name indicate that c is an array. Arrays can be declared to contain elements of *any* type; *every* element of the array is of that type. For example, every element of an Integer array contains an Integer value.

The number in parentheses in the array declaration helps the compiler allocate memory for the array c. In the preceding declarations, the number 11 defines the array's upper bound. **Array bounds** determine what indices can be used to access an element in the array. Here the array bounds are 0 and 11. The bound 0 is implicit in the preceding statement and is *always* the lower bound of every array. An index outside these bounds cannot be used to access elements in the array c; otherwise, a runtime error known as an exception occurs. We discuss how to deal with this exception in Section 7.6.

The actual size of the array is one larger (12) than the specified upper bound. We can also *explicitly* specify the array bounds, as in

```
Dim c(0 To 11) As Integer
```

The *explicit array bounds* indicate that the lower bound of the array is 0 and the upper bound is 11. The *size* of the array is still 12. Because the lower bound must *always* be 0, we do not include "0 To" when declaring an array's bounds in this book.

Initializer Lists

You can follow an array declaration with an equal sign and an **initializer list** in braces, { and }, to specify the initial values of the array's elements. For instance,

```
Dim numbers() As Integer = {1, 2, 3, 6}
```

declares and allocates an array containing *four* Integer values. The compiler determines the array bounds from the number of elements in the initializer list—you *cannot* specify the upper bound of the array when an initializer list is present. You can also use *local type inference* to determine an array's type from an initializer list. So, the preceding declaration can be written as:

```
Dim numbers = {1, 2, 3, 6}
```

Default Initialization

When you do not provide an initializer list, the elements in the array are initialized to the default value for the array's type—0 for numeric primitive data-type variables, False for Boolean variables and Nothing for String and other class types.

7.4 Initializing the Values in an Array

Figure 7.2 creates two five-element integer arrays and sets their element values, using an initializer list and a For...Next statement that calculates the element values, respectively. The arrays are displayed in tabular format in the outputTextBox.

Line 10 combines the declaration and initialization of array1 into one statement. The compiler *implicitly* allocates the array based on the number of values in the initializer list. Line 13 declares and allocates array2, whose size is determined by the expression array1.GetUpperBound(0). Array method **GetUpperBound** returns the index of the *last* element in the array. The value returned by method GetUpperBound is one less than the value of the array's Length property. For *one-dimensional arrays*, the argument passed to GetUpperBound is always 0—in Section 7.14, we'll discuss other arguments for GetUpperBound.

```
1   ' Fig. 7.2: InitializeArrays.vb
2   ' Initializing array elements with an array initializer and a For...Next
3   Public Class InitalizeArrays
4      ' initialize and display two arrays' contents
5      Private Sub InitalizeArrays_Load(sender As Object,
6         e As EventArgs) Handles MyBase.Load
7
8         ' initializer list specifies the number of elements
9         ' and the value of each element
10        Dim array1() As Integer = {32, 27, 64, 18, 95}
11
12        ' allocate array2 based on length of array1
13        Dim array2(array1.GetUpperBound(0)) As Integer
14
15        ' set values in array2 by a calculation
16        For i = 0 To array2.GetUpperBound(0)
17           array2(i) = 2 + 2 * i ' generate 2, 4, 6, ..., 10
18        Next
19
20        outputTextBox.AppendText(
21           "Index " & vbTab & "Array1" & vbTab & "Array2" & vbCrLf)
22
23        ' display values for both arrays side by side
24        For i = 0 To array1.GetUpperBound(0)
25           outputTextBox.AppendText(
26              i & vbTab & array1(i) & vbTab & array2(i) & vbCrLf)
27        Next
28     End Sub ' InitalizeArrays_Load
29  End Class ' InitalizeArrays
```

outputTextBox ——

Index	Array1	Array2
0	32	2
1	27	4
2	64	6
3	18	8
4	95	10

Fig. 7.2 | Initializing array elements with an array initializer and a For...Next statement.

In this example, array1.GetUpperBound(0) returns 4, which is then used to specify the upper bound of array2, so array1 and array2 have the *same* upper bound (4) and the *same* length (5). This makes it easy to display the arrays' contents side-by-side.

The For statement in lines 16–18 initializes the elements in array2 to the even integers 2, 4, 6, 8 and 10. These numbers are generated by multiplying each successive value of the loop counter by 2 and adding 2 to the product. The For statement in lines 24–27 displays the values from the two arrays side-by-side in a TextBox.

7.5 Summing the Elements of an Array

Often, the elements of an array represent a series of related values that are used in a calculation. For example, if the elements of an array represent students' exam grades, the instructor might wish to total the elements of the array, then calculate the class average for the exam. Figure 7.3 sums the values contained in the 10-element integer array values and displays the result in sumLabel.

```
1   ' Fig. 7.3: SumArray.vb
2   ' Computing the sum of the elements in an array.
3   Public Class SumArray
4      ' use a loop to sum the elements in an array
5      Private Sub SumArray_Load(sender As Object,
6         e As EventArgs) Handles MyBase.Load
7
8         Dim values() As Integer = {85, 77, 91, 44, 65, 72, 99, 84, 95, 100}
9         Dim total As Integer = 0
10
11        ' sum the array element values
12        For i = 0 To values.GetUpperBound(0)
13           total += values(i)
14        Next
15
16        sumLabel.Text = Convert.ToString(total)
17     End Sub ' SumArray_Load
18  End Class ' SumArray
```

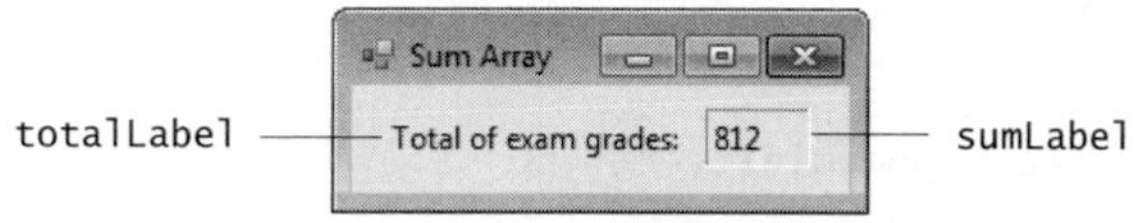

totalLabel ——— Total of exam grades: 812 ——— sumLabel

Fig. 7.3 | Computing the sum of the elements in an array.

Line 8 declares, allocates and initializes the 10-element array values. Line 13, in the body of the For statement, performs the addition. Alternatively, the values supplied as initializers for array could have been read into the app. For example, the user could enter the values through a TextBox, or the values could be read from a file on disk. Information about reading values from a file can be found in Chapter 8, Files.

7.6 Using Arrays to Analyze Survey Results

Our next example uses arrays to summarize data collected in a survey. Consider the following problem statement:

> Twenty students were asked to rate on a scale of 1 to 5 the quality of the food in the student cafeteria, with 1 being "awful" and 5 being "excellent." Place the 20 responses in an integer array and determine the frequency of each rating.

This is a typical array-processing app (Fig. 7.4). We wish to summarize the number of responses of each type (that is, 1–5). Array responses (lines 9–10) is a 20-element integer array containing the students' survey responses.

The frequency Array

We use the *six-element* array frequency (line 13) to count the number of occurrences of each response. Each element is used as a counter for one of the possible types of survey

```vb
1  ' Fig. 7.4: StudentPoll.vb
2  ' Using arrays to summarize poll results.
3  Public Class StudentPoll
4     ' summarize and display poll results
5     Private Sub StudentPoll_Load(sender As Object,
6        e As EventArgs) Handles MyBase.Load
7
8        ' student response array (more typically, input at run time)
9        Dim responses() As Integer =
10          {1, 2, 5, 4, 3, 5, 2, 1, 3, 3, 1, 4, 3, 3, 3, 2, 3, 3, 2, 14}
11
12       ' response frequency array (indices 0 through 5)
13       Dim frequency(5) As Integer
14
15       ' count frequencies
16       For answer = 0 To responses.GetUpperBound(0)
17          Try
18             frequency(responses(answer)) += 1
19          Catch ex As IndexOutOfRangeException
20             MessageBox.Show(String.Format("{0}{1}responses({2}) = {3}",
21                ex.Message, vbCrLf, answer, responses(answer)),
22                "IndexOutOfRangeException",
23                MessageBoxButtons.OK, MessageBoxIcon.Error)
24          End Try
25       Next
26
27       outputTextBox.AppendText("Rating" & vbTab & "Frequency" & vbCrLf)
28
29       ' display output, ignore element 0 of frequency
30       For rating = 1 To frequency.GetUpperBound(0)
31          outputTextBox.AppendText(
32             rating & vbTab & frequency(rating) & vbCrLf)
33       Next
34    End Sub ' StudentPoll_Load
35 End Class ' StudentPoll
```

a) **MessageBox** that's displayed by lines 20–23 when the app processes the **responses** array's last element, which causes an attempt to access a non-existent element in array **frequency**

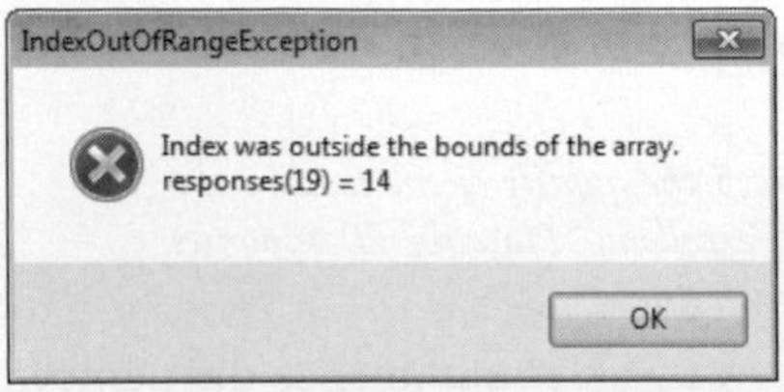

b) Results of the **Student Poll** app summarize only 19 of the 20 values in the **responses** array, because the invalid value 14 was ignored

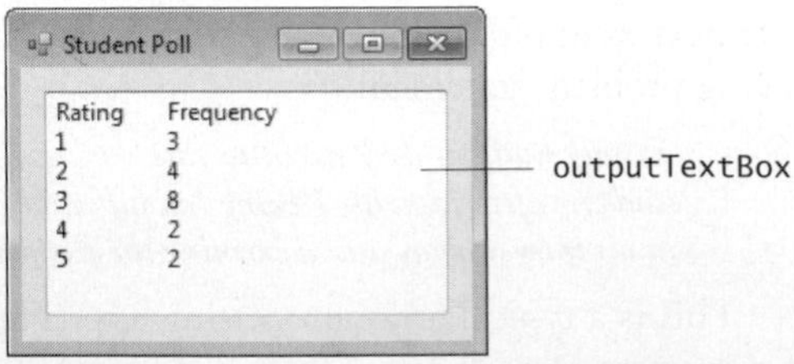

Fig. 7.4 | Using arrays to summarize poll results.

responses—frequency(1) counts the number of students who rated the food as 1, frequency(2) counts the number of students who rated the food as 2, and so on. The results are displayed in outputTextBox.

Summarizing the Results

The For statement (lines 16–25) reads the responses from the array responses one at a time and increments one of the five counters in the frequency array (frequency(1) to frequency(5); we ignore frequency(0) because the survey responses are limited to the range 1–5). The key statement in the loop appears in line 18. This statement increments the appropriate frequency counter as determined by the value of responses(answer).

Let's step through the first few iterations of the For statement:

- When the counter answer is 0, responses(answer) is the value of responses(0) (that is, 1—see line 10). In this case, frequency(responses(answer)) is interpreted as frequency(1), and the counter frequency(1) is incremented by one. To evaluate the expression, we begin with the value in the *innermost* set of parentheses (answer, currently 0). The value of answer is plugged into the expression, and the next set of parentheses (responses(answer)) is evaluated. That value is used as the index for the frequency array to determine which counter to increment (in this case, frequency(1)).

- The next time through the loop answer is 1, responses(answer) is the value of responses(1) (that is, 2—see line 10), so frequency(responses(answer)) is interpreted as frequency(2), causing frequency(2) to be incremented.

- When answer is 2, responses(answer) is the value of responses(2) (that is, 5—see line 10), so frequency(responses(answer)) is interpreted as frequency(5), causing frequency(5) to be incremented, and so on.

Regardless of the number of responses processed in the survey, only a six-element array (in which we ignore element zero) is required to summarize the results, because all the correct response values are between 1 and 5, and the index values for a six-element array are 0–5. In the output in Fig. 7.4, the frequency column summarizes only 19 of the 20 values in the responses array—the last element of the array responses contains an *incorrect* response that was *not* counted.

Exception Handling: Processing the Incorrect Response

The last value in the responses array is *intentionally* an *incorrect* response with the value 14. When a Visual Basic app executes, array element indices are checked for *validity*—all indices must be greater than or equal to 0 and less than the array's length—this is known as **bounds checking**. Any attempt to access an element *outside* that range of indices results in a runtime error that's known as an IndexOutOfRangeException. When 14 is used as an index for the frequency array an IndexOutOfRangeException occurs.

An **exception** indicates a problem that occurs while an app executes. The name "exception" suggests that the problem occurs *infrequently*—if the "rule" is that a statement normally executes correctly, then the problem represents the "exception to the rule." **Exception handling** enables you to create **fault-tolerant programs** that can resolve (or handle) exceptions. In many cases, this allows an app to continue executing as if no problems were encountered. For example, the **Student Poll** app still displays results (Fig. 7.4(b)), even though one of the responses was out of range. More severe problems might prevent an app from continuing normal execution, instead requiring the app to notify the user of the problem, then terminate. When the runtime or a method detects a problem, such as an invalid array index or an invalid method argument, it **throws** an exception—that is, an exception occurs.

The *Try Statement*

To handle an exception, place any code that might throw an exception in a **Try statement** (lines 17–24). The **Try block** (lines 17–18) contains the code that might *throw* an exception, and the **Catch block** (lines 19–23) contains the code that *handles* the exception if one occurs. You can have many Catch blocks to handle different types of exceptions that might be thrown in the corresponding Try block. When line 18 correctly increments an element of the frequency array, lines 19–23 are ignored. The End Try keywords terminate a Try statement.

Executing the *Catch Block*

When the app encounters the value 14 in the responses array, it attempts to add 1 to frequency(14), which does *not* exist—the frequency array has *only* six elements. Because array bounds checking is performed at *execution time*, line 18 throws an IndexOutOfRangeException to notify the app of this problem. At this point the Try block terminates and the Catch block begins executing—if you declared any variables in the Try block, they're now *out of scope* and are *not accessible* in the Catch block.

The Catch block declares an exception parameter (ex) and a type (IndexOutOfRangeException)—the Catch block can handle exceptions of the specified type. Inside the Catch block, you can use the parameter's identifier to interact with a caught exception object.

Entering a *Try Statement in the Code Editor*

When you create a Try statement in your own code, you begin by typing Try and pressing *Enter*. The IDE then generates the following code:

```
Try

Catch ex As Exception

End Try
```

which can catch *any* type of exception thrown in the Try block. We changed Exception to IndexOutOfRangeException—the type of exception that might occur in line 18.

Message *Property of the Exception Parameter*

When lines 19–23 *catch* the exception, the app displays a MessageBox indicating the problem that occurred. Line 21 uses the exception object's **Message property** to get the error message that's stored in the exception object and display it in the MessageBox. Once the user dismisses the MessageBox, the exception is considered handled and the app continues with the next statement after the End Try keywords. In this example, Next (line 25) causes the app to continue with line 16. Chapter 16 includes a detailed treatment of exception handling.

7.7 Die-Rolling App with an Array of Counters

In Chapter 6, we used a series of counters in our die-rolling app to track the number of occurrences of each face on a six-sided die. We indicated that we can do what we did in

Fig. 6.14 in a more elegant way than using a Select...Case statement to write the dice-rolling app. An array version of this app is shown in Fig. 7.5. This new version uses the same GUI as the app in Fig. 6.14.

```
1   ' Fig. 7.5: DiceStatistics.vb
2   ' Rolling 12 dice with frequency chart.
3   Public Class DiceStatistics
4      Dim randomObject As New Random() ' generates random numbers
5      Dim frequency(6) As Integer ' create 7-element array
6
7      ' display result of twelve rolls
8      Private Sub rollButton_Click(sender As Object,
9         e As EventArgs) Handles rollButton.Click
10
11        ' display 12 randomly selected die faces
12        DisplayDie(die1PictureBox)
13        DisplayDie(die2PictureBox)
14        DisplayDie(die3PictureBox)
15        DisplayDie(die4PictureBox)
16        DisplayDie(die5PictureBox)
17        DisplayDie(die6PictureBox)
18        DisplayDie(die7PictureBox)
19        DisplayDie(die8PictureBox)
20        DisplayDie(die9PictureBox)
21        DisplayDie(die10PictureBox)
22        DisplayDie(die11PictureBox)
23        DisplayDie(die12PictureBox)
24
25        Dim total As Double = 0
26
27        ' total the die faces (used in percentage calculations)
28        For i = 1 To frequency.GetUpperBound(0)
29           total += frequency(i)
30        Next
31
32        ' display frequencies of faces
33        displayTextBox.Text =
34           "Face" & vbTab & "Frequency" & vbTab & "Percent" & vbCrLf
35
36        ' output frequency values--ignore element 0
37        For i = 1 To frequency.GetUpperBound(0)
38           displayTextBox.Text &= i & vbTab & frequency(i) &
39              vbTab & vbTab & String.Format("{0:P2}",
40              frequency(i) / total) & vbCrLf
41        Next
42     End Sub ' rollButton_Click
43
44     ' display a single die image
45     Sub DisplayDie(diePictureBox As PictureBox)
46        Dim face As Integer = randomObject.Next(1, 7)
47
```

Fig. 7.5 | Rolling 12 dice with frequency chart. (Part 1 of 2.)

```
48              ' retrieve specific die image from resources
49              Dim pictureResource = My.Resources.ResourceManager.GetObject(
50                  String.Format("die{0}", face))
51
52              ' convert pictureResource to image type and load into PictureBox
53              diePictureBox.Image = CType(pictureResource, Image)
54
55              frequency(face) += 1 ' increment appropriate frequency counter
56          End Sub ' DisplayDie
57      End Class ' DiceStatistics
```

a) Freqencies after two rolls of the 12 dice

b) Frequencies after many rolls of the 12 dice

Fig. 7.5 | Rolling 12 dice with frequency chart. (Part 2 of 2.)

Lines 61–74 of Fig. 6.14 are replaced by line 55 of Fig. 7.5, which uses face's value as the index for array frequency to determine which element should be incremented during each iteration of the loop. The random number calculation at line 46 produces numbers from 1 to 6 (the values for a six-sided die); thus, the frequency array must have seven elements so we can use the index values 1–6. We ignore frequency element 0. Lines 37–41 replace lines 35–46 from Fig. 6.14. We can loop through array frequency; therefore, we do not have to enumerate each line of text to display in the TextBox, as we did in Fig. 6.14. Recall from Section 6.9 that the more you roll the dice, the closer each percentage should get to 16.66%, as shown in Fig. 7.5(b).

7.8 Case Study: Flag Quiz

Let's create an app that tests a student's knowledge of the flags of various countries. Consider the following problem statement:

> *A geography instructor would like to quiz students on their knowledge of the flags of various countries. The instructor has asked you to write an app that displays a flag and allows the student to select the corresponding country from a list. The app should inform the user of whether the answer is correct and display the next flag. The app should display a flag randomly chosen from those of Australia, Brazil, China, Italy, Russia, South Africa, Spain and the United States. When the app executes, a given flag should be displayed only once.*

The app uses arrays to store information. One array stores the country names. Another stores Boolean values that help us determine whether a particular country's flag has already been displayed, so that no flag is displayed more than once during a quiz.

Flag Quiz *GUI*

Figure 7.6 shows the app's GUI. The flag images should be added to the project as image resources—you learned how to do this in Section 6.9. The images are located in the Images folder with this chapter's examples. This app introduces the **ComboBox control**, which presents options in a *drop-down list* that opens when you click the *down arrow* at the right side of the control. A ComboBox combines features of a TextBox and a ListBox. You can click the down arrow to display a list of predefined items. If you choose an item from this list, that item is displayed in the ComboBox. If the list contains more items than the drop-down list can display at one time, a *vertical scrollbar* appears. You may also type into the ComboBox control to locate an item. In this app, the user selects an answer from the ComboBox, then clicks the **Submit** Button to check if the selected country name is correct for the currently displayed flag.

Fig. 7.6 | GUI for the **Flag Quiz** app.

ComboBox property **DropDownStyle** determines the ComboBox's appearance. Value **DropDownList** specifies that the ComboBox is *not editable* (you *cannot* type text in its TextBox). In this ComboBox style, if you press the key that corresponds to the first letter of an item in the ComboBox, that item is selected and displayed in the ComboBox. If multiple items start with the same letter, pressing the key *repeatedly* cycles through the corresponding items. Set the ComboBox's DropDownStyle property to DropDownList. Then, set the ComboBox's **MaxDropDownItems** property to 4, so that the drop-down list displays a maximum of four items at one time. We do this to demonstrate that a vertical scrollbar is added to the drop-down list to allow users to scroll through the remaining items. We show how to programmatically add items to the ComboBox shortly. Figure 7.7 shows the app's code.

```
1    ' Fig. 7.7: FlagQuiz.vb
2    ' Using an array of Strings to represent quiz answers.
3    Public Class FlagQuiz
4       ' String array stores country names
5       Dim countries() As String = {"Australia", "Brazil", "China", "Italy",
6          "Russia", "South Africa", "Spain", "United States"}
7       Dim randomObject As New Random()
```

Fig. 7.7 | Using an array of Strings to represent quiz answers. (Part 1 of 3.)

```
 8
 9    ' Boolean array tracks which flags have been displayed
10    Dim used(countries.GetUpperBound(0)) As Boolean ' all False by default
11
12    Dim count As Integer = 1 ' number of flags shown
13    Dim country As String ' current flag's country
14
15    ' handles Flag Quiz Form's Load event
16    Private Sub FlagQuizForm_Load(sender As Object,
17       e As EventArgs) Handles MyBase.Load
18
19       ' display country names in ComboBox
20       countriesComboBox.DataSource = countries
21
22       DisplayFlag() ' display first flag in PictureBox
23    End Sub ' FlagQuizForm_Load
24
25    ' handles Submit Button's Click event
26    Private Sub submitButton_Click(sender As Object,
27       e As EventArgs) Handles submitButton.Click
28
29       ' verify user's answer
30       If countriesComboBox.Text = country Then
31          MessageBox.Show("Correct!", "Correct Answer")
32       Else
33          MessageBox.Show("The correct answer is " & country,
34             "Incorrect Answer")
35       End If
36
37       ' inform user if quiz is over
38       If count >= countries.Length Then ' quiz is over
39          countriesComboBox.Enabled = False
40          submitButton.Enabled = False
41       Else ' quiz is not over
42          DisplayFlag() ' display next flag
43          countriesComboBox.SelectedIndex = 0 ' select first ComboBox entry
44          count += 1 ' update number of flags shown
45       End If
46    End Sub ' submitButton_Click
47
48    ' return an unused random number
49    Function GetUniqueRandomNumber() As Integer
50       Dim randomNumber As Integer
51
52       Do ' generate random numbers until unused flag is found
53          randomNumber = randomObject.Next(0, used.Length)
54       Loop Until used(randomNumber) = False
55
56       used(randomNumber) = True ' indicate that flag has been used
57       Return randomNumber ' return index for new flag
58    End Function ' GetUniqueRandomNumber
59
```

Fig. 7.7 | Using an array of Strings to represent quiz answers. (Part 2 of 3.)

```
60      ' display random flag in PictureBox
61    Sub DisplayFlag()
62        ' unique index ensures that a flag is used no more than once
63        Dim randomNumber As Integer = GetUniqueRandomNumber()
64
65        country = countries(randomNumber) ' get country name
66
67        ' get image resource--remove spaces from country name
68        Dim pictureResource = My.Resources.ResourceManager.GetObject(
69            country.Replace(" ", ""))
70        flagPictureBox.Image = CType(pictureResource, Image) ' display flag
71    End Sub ' DisplayFlag
72  End Class ' FlagQuiz
```

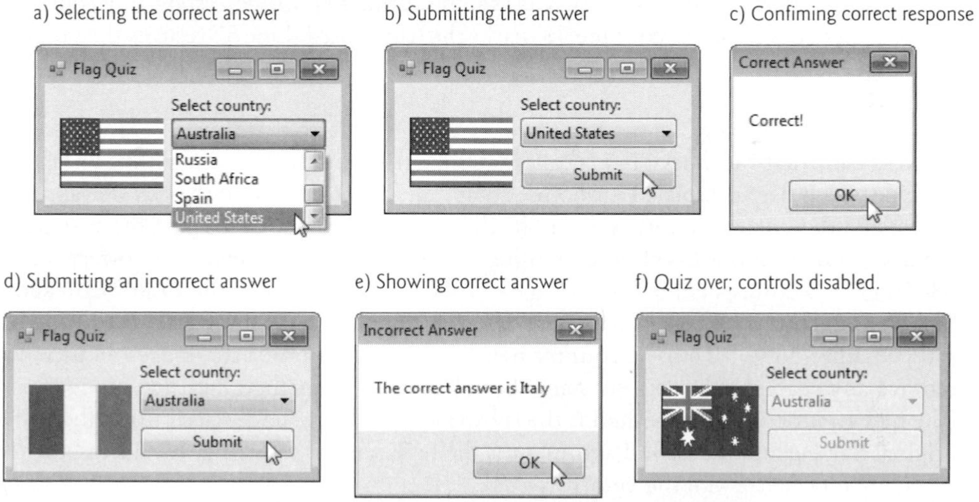

a) Selecting the correct answer   b) Submitting the answer   c) Confiming correct response

d) Submitting an incorrect answer   e) Showing correct answer   f) Quiz over; controls disabled.

Fig. 7.7 | Using an array of Strings to represent quiz answers. (Part 3 of 3.)

Instance Variables

Lines 5–6 create and initialize the array of Strings called countries. Each element is a String containing a country's name. The compiler determines the array's size (in this case, eight elements) based on the number of items in the initializer list. Line 7 creates the Random object that's used in method GetUniqueRandomNumber (lines 49–58). Line 10 creates the Boolean array used, which helps us determine which countries have already been displayed in the quiz. We specify the upper bound of the array used by getting the upper bound of the array countries. By default, each of used's elements is set to False. Variable count (line 12) keeps track of the number of flags displayed so far, and variable country (line 13) stores the name of the country that corresponds to the currently displayed flag.

Method *FlagQuizForm_Load*

When the app loads, method FlagQuiz_Load executes. ComboBox property **DataSource** (line 20) specifies the source of the items displayed in the ComboBox. In this case, the source is array countries. Line 22 calls method DisplayFlag (declared in lines 61–71) to display the first flag.

Method submitButton_Click

When you click the **Submit** Button, method submitButton_Click (lines 26–46) determines whether the selected answer is correct and displays an appropriate message (lines 30–35). If all the flags have been displayed, line 38 indicates that the quiz is over and lines 39–40 disable the ComboBox and Button. Otherwise, the quiz continues. Line 42 calls method DisplayFlag to display the next flag. Line 43 uses ComboBox property **Selected-Index** to select the item at index 0 in the ComboBox—ComboBoxes are indexed from 0 like arrays.

Method GetUniqueRandomNumber

Method GetUniqueRandomNumber (lines 49–58) uses a Do...Loop Until statement to choose a random number in the bounds of the used array. The loop performs this task until the value at used(randomNumber) is False, indicating that the corresponding country's flag has not yet been displayed. Line 56 marks the flag as used. Line 57 returns the random number.

Method DisplayFlag

Method DisplayFlag (lines 61–71) calls method GetUniqueRandomNumber (line 63) to determine which flag to display. Line 65 uses that value as the index into the countries array and stores the current country's name in the variable country. This variable is used in method submitButton_Click to determine whether the selected answer is correct. Lines 68–70 get the corresponding flag's image resource and display it in the flagPictureBox. Some of the country names in the countries array contain spaces. However, the image resource names do not. To use a country name to load the appropriate image resource, we remove any spaces in the country name by calling String method **Replace** on country. The first argument to this method is the substring that should be replaced throughout the original String and the second argument is the replacement substring. In this case, we're replacing each space with the empty String ("").

7.9 Passing an Array to a Method

To pass an array argument to a method, specify the name of the array without using parentheses. For example, if array hourlyTemperatures has been declared as

```
Dim hourlyTemperatures(24) As Integer
```

the method call

```
DisplayDayData(hourlyTemperatures)
```

passes array hourlyTemperatures to method DisplayDayData.

Every array object "knows" its own upper bound (that is, the value returned by the method GetUpperBound), so when you pass an array object to a method, you do not need to pass the upper bound of the array as a separate argument.

For a method to receive an array through a method call, the method's parameter list must specify that an array will be received. For example, the method header for Display-DayData might be written as

```
Sub DisplayDayData(temperatureData() As Integer)
```

indicating that `DisplayDayData` expects to receive an `Integer` array in parameter `temper-atureData`. When you pass an array to method `DisplayDayData`, a *copy* of the array's *reference* is passed and the method can change the original array's element values.

Individual array elements can be passed by value or by reference like simple variables of that type. For instance, array element values of primitive types, such as `Integer`, can be passed either by value or by reference, depending on the method definition. To pass an array element to a method, use the indexed name of the array element as an argument in the method call. Figure 7.8 demonstrates the difference between passing an entire array and passing an array element. The results are displayed in `outputTextBox`—you should read these results *before* studying the app.

```vb
 1    ' Fig. 7.8: PassArray.vb
 2    ' Passing arrays and individual array elements to methods.
 3    Public Class PassArray
 4       ' invoke methods to demonstrate passing arrays
 5       ' and array elements to methods
 6       Private Sub PassArray_Load(sender As Object,
 7          e As EventArgs) Handles MyBase.Load
 8
 9          Dim array1() As Integer = {1, 2, 3, 4, 5}
10
11          outputTextBox.AppendText(
12             "EFFECTS OF PASSING AN ENTIRE ARRAY BY REFERENCE:" & vbCrLf &
13             vbCrLf & "The values of the original array are:" & vbCrLf)
14
15          ' display original elements of array1
16          For i = 0 To array1.GetUpperBound(0)
17             outputTextBox.AppendText(vbTab & array1(i))
18          Next
19
20          ModifyArray(array1) ' array is passed by reference
21          outputTextBox.AppendText(vbCrLf &
22             "The values of the modified array are:" & vbCrLf)
23
24          ' display modified elements of array1
25          For i = 0 To array1.GetUpperBound(0)
26             outputTextBox.AppendText(vbTab & array1(i))
27          Next
28
29          outputTextBox.AppendText(vbCrLf & vbCrLf &
30             "EFFECTS OF PASSING AN ARRAY ELEMENT BY VALUE:" & vbCrLf &
31             vbCrLf & "array1(3) before ModifyElementByVal: " &
32             array1(3) & vbCrLf)
33
34          ModifyElementByVal(array1(3)) ' array element passed by value
35          outputTextBox.AppendText("array1(3) after ModifyElementByVal: " &
36             array1(3) & vbCrLf)
37          outputTextBox.AppendText(vbCrLf & "EFFECTS OF PASSING AN " &
38             "ARRAY ELEMENT BY REFERENCE: " & vbCrLf & vbCrLf &
39             "array1(3) before ModifyElementByRef: " & array1(3) & vbCrLf)
40
```

Fig. 7.8 | Passing arrays and individual array elements to methods. (Part 1 of 2.)

```
41          ModifyElementByRef(array1(3)) ' array element passed by reference
42          outputTextBox.AppendText("array1(3) after ModifyElementByRef: " &
43             array1(3))
44       End Sub ' PassArray_Load
45
46       ' method modifies array it receives (note ByVal)
47       Sub ModifyArray(ByVal arrayParameter() As Integer)
48          For j = 0 To arrayParameter.GetUpperBound(0)
49             arrayParameter(j) *= 2 ' double the array element
50          Next
51       End Sub ' ModifyArray
52
53       ' method modifies integer passed to it
54       ' original is not modified (note ByVal)
55       Sub ModifyElementByVal(ByVal element As Integer)
56          outputTextBox.AppendText(
57             "Value received in ModifyElementByVal: " & element & vbCrLf)
58          element *= 2 ' double the array element
59          outputTextBox.AppendText(
60             "Value calculated in ModifyElementByVal: " & element & vbCrLf)
61       End Sub ' ModifyElement
62
63       ' method modifies integer passed to it
64       ' original is modified (note ByRef)
65       Sub ModifyElementByRef(ByRef element As Integer)
66          outputTextBox.AppendText(
67             "Value received in ModifyElementByRef: " & element & vbCrLf)
68          element *= 2 ' double the array element
69          outputTextBox.AppendText(
70             "Value calculated in ModifyElementByRef: " & element & vbCrLf)
71       End Sub ' ModifyElementByRef
72    End Class ' PassArray
```

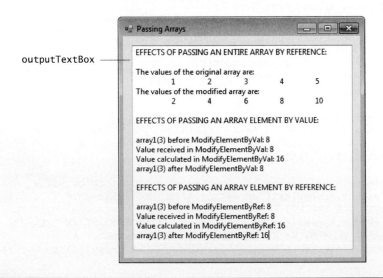

Fig. 7.8 | Passing arrays and individual array elements to methods. (Part 2 of 2.)

The For...Next statement in lines 16–18 displays the five elements of integer array array1 (line 9). Line 20 passes array1 to method ModifyArray (lines 47–51), which then multiplies each element by 2 (line 49). To illustrate that array1's elements were modified in the called method, the For...Next statement in lines 25–27 displays the five elements of array1. As the output indicates, the elements of array1 are indeed modified by ModifyArray.

Lines 29–32 display the value of array1(3) before the call to ModifyElementByVal. Line 34 invokes method ModifyElementByVal (lines 55–61) and passes array1(3). When array1(3) is passed by value, the Integer value in position 3 of array array1 (now an 8) is copied and passed to method ModifyElementByVal, where it becomes the value of parameter element. Method ModifyElementByVal then multiplies element by 2 (line 58). The parameter element of ModifyElementByVal is a *local variable* that's destroyed when the method terminates. Thus, when control is returned to Main, the unmodified value of array1(3) is displayed.

Lines 37–43 demonstrate the effects of method ModifyElementByRef (lines 65–71). This method performs the same calculation as ModifyElementByVal, multiplying element by 2. In this case, array1(3) is passed by reference, meaning that the value of array1(3) displayed (lines 42–43) is the *same* as the value calculated in the method (that is, the original value in the caller is modified by the called method).

7.10 For Each...Next Repetition Statement

The **For Each...Next** repetition statement iterates through the values in a data structure, such as an array, *without* using a loop counter. For Each...Next behaves like a For...Next statement that iterates through the range of indices from 0 to the value returned by Get-UpperBound(0). Instead of a counter, For Each...Next uses a variable to represent the value of each element.

In this example, we'll use the For Each...Next statement to determine the minimum value in a one-dimensional array of grades. The GUI for the app is shown in Fig. 7.9 and the code is shown in Fig. 7.10.

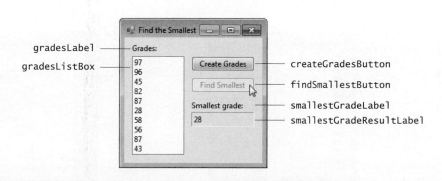

Fig. 7.9 | GUI for the **Find the Smallest** app.

```vb
1    ' Fig. 7.10: FindTheSmallest.vb
2    ' Using a For Each...Next loop to find the smallest value in an array.
3    Public Class FindTheSmallest
4       Dim gradesArray(9) As Integer ' create 10-element array
5       Dim randomNumber As New Random()
6
7       ' creates random generated numbers
8       Private Sub createGradesButton_Click(sender As Object,
9          e As EventArgs) Handles createGradesButton.Click
10
11         gradesListBox.Items.Clear() ' clear gradesListBox
12         smallestGradeResultLabel.Text = String.Empty ' clear Label
13
14         ' create 10 random numbers and append to output
15         For i = 0 To gradesArray.GetUpperBound(0)
16            gradesArray(i) = randomNumber.Next(100)
17            gradesListBox.Items.Add(gradesArray(i))
18         Next
19
20         findSmallestButton.Enabled = True ' enable Find Smallest button
21      End Sub ' createGradesButton_Click
22
23      ' finds smallest randomly generated number
24      Private Sub findSmallestButton_Click(sender As Object,
25         e As EventArgs) Handles findSmallestButton.Click
26
27         Dim lowGrade As Integer = 100 ' start with the maximum grade value
28
29         ' use For Each...Next to find the minimum grade
30         For Each grade In gradesArray
31            If grade < lowGrade Then
32               lowGrade = grade ' current grade is the lowest one so far
33            End If
34         Next
35
36         smallestGradeResultLabel.Text = Convert.ToString(lowGrade)
37         findSmallestButton.Enabled = False ' disable Find Smallest button
38      End Sub ' findSmallestButton_Click
39   End Class ' FindTheSmallest
```

a) Generating random grade values

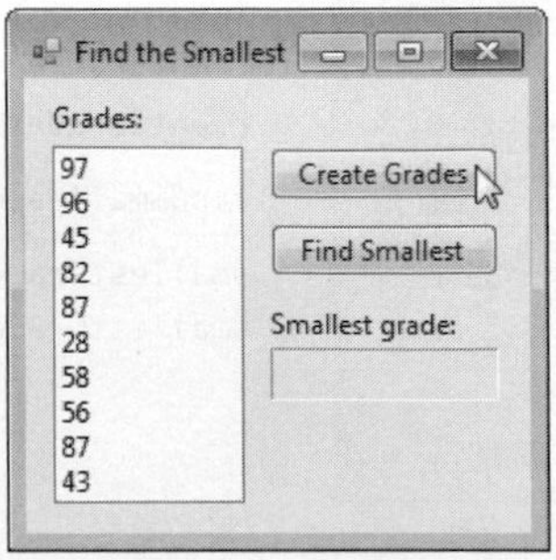

b) Finding the smallest grade

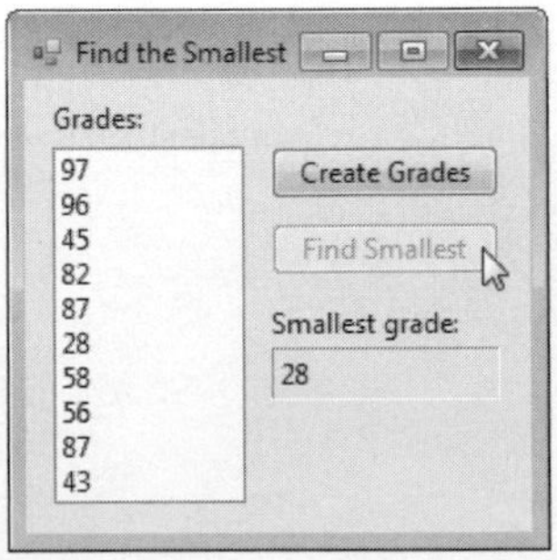

Fig. 7.10 | Using a For Each...Next loop to find the smallest value in an array.

When the user clicks the **Create Grades** Button, method createGradesButton_Click (lines 8–21) creates 10 random grade values in the range 0–99 and places them in the gradesListBox. When the user clicks the **Find Smallest** Button, method findSmallestButton_Click (lines 24–38) uses a For Each...Next statement to find the lowest grade.

The header of the For Each repetition statement (line 30) specifies an Integer variable (grade) and an array (gradesArray). The type of variable grade is determined from the type of the elements in gradesArray, though you can also declare the variable's type explicitly as in

```
For Each grade As Integer In gradesArray
```

The For Each statement iterates through *all* the elements in gradesArray, *sequentially* assigning each value to variable grade. The values are compared to variable lowGrade (line 31), which stores the lowest grade in the array.

The repetition of the For Each...Next statement begins with the element whose index is zero, iterating through *all* the elements. In this case, grade takes on the *successive values* that are stored in gradesArray and displayed in the gradesListBox. When all the grades have been processed, lowGrade is displayed (line 36). Although many array calculations are handled best with a counter, For Each is useful when you wish to process *all* of an array's elements and do not need to access the index values in the loop's body.

7.11 Sorting an Array with Method Sort of Class Array

Sorting data (that is, arranging the data in ascending or descending order) is one of the most popular computing applications. For example, a bank sorts all checks by account number, so that it can prepare individual bank statements at the end of each month. Telephone companies sort their lists of accounts by last name and, within last-name listings, by first name, to make it easy to find phone numbers.

Arrays have the methods and properties of class Array in namespace System. Class Array provides methods for creating, modifying, sorting and searching arrays. By default, Array method **Sort** sorts an array's elements into *ascending* order. The next app (GUI in Fig. 7.11 and code in Fig. 7.12) demonstrates method Sort by sorting an array of 10 randomly generated elements (which may contain duplicates).

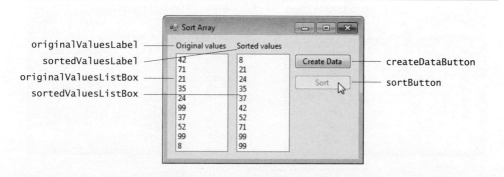

Fig. 7.11 | GUI for the **Sort Array** app.

```vb
 1   ' Fig. 7.12: SortArray.vb
 2   ' Sorting an array with method Array.Sort.
 3   Public Class SortArray
 4      Dim integerArray(9) As Integer ' create 10-element array
 5      Dim randomNumber As New Random()
 6
 7      ' creates random generated numbers
 8      Private Sub createDataButton_Click(sender As Object,
 9         e As EventArgs) Handles createDataButton.Click
10
11         originalValuesListBox.Items.Clear() ' clear originalValuesListBox
12         sortedValuesListBox.Items.Clear() ' clear sortedValuesListBox
13
14         ' create 10 random numbers and add to originalValuesListBox
15         For i = 0 To integerArray.GetUpperBound(0)
16            integerArray(i) = randomNumber.Next(100)
17            originalValuesListBox.Items.Add(integerArray(i))
18         Next
19
20         sortButton.Enabled = True ' enable Sort button
21      End Sub ' createDataButton_Click
22
23      ' sorts randomly generated numbers
24      Private Sub sortButton_Click(sender As Object,
25         e As EventArgs) Handles sortButton.Click
26
27         Array.Sort(integerArray) ' sort array integerArray
28
29         ' display sorted numbers in sortedValuesListBox
30         For i = 0 To integerArray.GetUpperBound(0)
31            sortedValuesListBox.Items.Add(integerArray(i))
32         Next
33
34         sortButton.Enabled = False ' disable Sort button
35      End Sub ' sortButton_Click
36   End Class ' SortArray
```

a) Generating random values

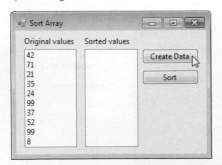

b) Sorting the values

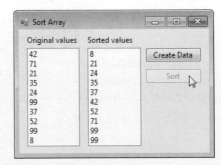

Fig. 7.12 | Sorting an array with method Array.Sort.

Method `createDataButton_Click` (lines 8–21) assigns 10 random values to the elements of `integerArray` and displays the contents of the array in the `originalValuesListBox`. Method `sortButton_Click` (lines 24–35) sorts `integerArray` by calling `Array.Sort`, which takes an array as its argument and sorts the elements in the array in *ascending* order.

Sorting in Descending Order

To sort an array in *descending* order, first call method `Sort` to sort the array, then call `Array.Reverse` with the array as an argument to reverse the order of the elements in the array. Exercise 7.14 asks you to modify this app to display an array's values in both ascending and descending order.

7.12 Searching an Array with Linear Search

Often it's necessary to determine whether an array contains a value that matches a certain **key value.** The process of locating a particular element value in an array is called **searching.** In this section and the next, we use two searching techniques—the simple **linear search** and the more efficient **binary search**.

Our next app (Fig. 7.14) demonstrates a *linear search*—implemented at lines 39–48—to search a 20-element array that's filled with random values created when the user clicks the **Create Data** Button. The loop at lines 43–48 compares each element of an array with a **search key** (stored in variable `searchKey`). The user types the search key in the **Enter integer search key:** TextBox and clicks the **Search** Button to start the search. If the search key is found, the index of the matching element is stored in variable `index` (line 45) and the loop terminates (line 46). If the search key is not found, `index` will still be –1 (its initial value). The value –1 is a good choice to indicate that the search key is not found because –1 is not a valid index number. If the elements of the array being searched are unordered, it's just as likely that the value will be found in the front half of the array as in the back half, so on average the method will have to compare the search key with *half* the elements of the array. The GUI for this app is shown in Fig. 7.13 and the code is shown in Fig. 7.14.

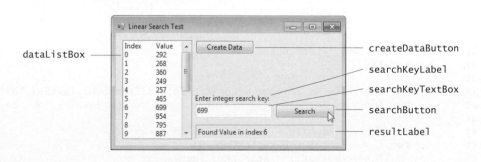

Fig. 7.13 | GUI for the **Linear Search Test** app.

Other Array Methods for Searching Arrays

Class `Array` provides a method `IndexOf` that performs the same operation as the linear search in Fig. 7.14. Class `Array` also provides methods such as `Find` and `FindAll`, which search the array for element(s) that meet certain criteria. The criteria can be more general than simply searching for an element. For instance, the FindAll method allows you to search for all elements in an Integer array that have values in a specified range.

```vb
 1   ' Fig. 7.14: LinearSearchTest.vb
 2   ' Linear search of an array.
 3   Public Class LinearSearchTest
 4      Dim searchData(19) As Integer ' create 20-element array
 5      Dim randomNumber As New Random()
 6
 7      ' create random data and display it
 8      Private Sub createDataButton_Click(sender As Object,
 9         e As EventArgs) Handles createDataButton.Click
10
11         ' create random array elements
12         For i = 0 To searchData.GetUpperBound(0)
13            searchData(i) = randomNumber.Next(1000)
14         Next
15
16         ' display array elements
17         dataListBox.Items.Add("Index" & vbTab & "Value")
18
19         For i = 0 To searchData.GetUpperBound(0)
20            dataListBox.Items.Add(i & vbTab & searchData(i))
21         Next
22
23         searchKeyTextBox.Clear() ' clear search key text box
24         searchButton.Enabled = True ' enable search button
25      End Sub ' createDataButton_Click
26
27      ' search array for search key
28      Private Sub searchButton_Click(sender As Object,
29         e As EventArgs) Handles searchButton.Click
30
31         ' if search key text box is empty, display
32         ' message and exit method
33         If searchKeyTextBox.Text = String.Empty Then
34            MessageBox.Show("You must enter a search key.", "Error",
35               MessageBoxButtons.OK, MessageBoxIcon.Error)
36            Exit Sub ' terminates the method call immediately
37         End If
38
39         Dim searchKey As Integer = Convert.ToInt32(searchKeyTextBox.Text)
40         Dim index As Integer = -1 ' stores index of found value (or -1)
41
42         ' statement iterates linearly through array
43         For i = 0 To searchData.GetUpperBound(0)
44            If searchData(i) = searchKey Then
45               index = i
46               Exit For ' terminate loop because value was found
47            End If
48         Next
```

Fig. 7.14 | Linear search of an array. (Part 1 of 2.)

```
49
50          If index >= 0 Then
51              resultLabel.Text = "Found Value in index " & index
52          Else
53              resultLabel.Text = "Value Not Found"
54          End If
55      End Sub ' searchButton_Click
56  End Class ' LinearSearchTest
```

a) Creating
random values
to search

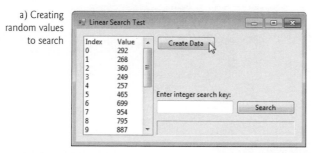

b) Searching for a value that is in the array

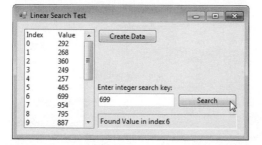

c) Searching for a value that is not in the array

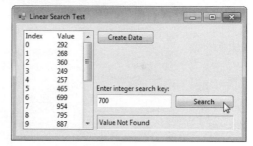

Fig. 7.14 | Linear search of an array. (Part 2 of 2.)

7.13 Searching a Sorted Array with Array Method BinarySearch

Linear searches work well for small or unsorted arrays, but, for large unsorted arrays, linear searching is inefficient. If the array is *sorted*, the high-speed binary search technique can be used with class Array's **BinarySearch method**. Our app that demonstrates method BinarySearch is nearly identical to the one in Fig. 7.14, so we show only the differences here. The complete code is located in the Fig07_15 folder with this chapter's examples. The sample outputs are shown in Fig. 7.15. The GUI for this app is identical to the one in Fig. 7.13.

As in Fig. 7.14, the user clicks the **Create Data** Button to generate random values. For method BinarySearch to perform correctly, the array *must* have been sorted. Method createDataButton_Click uses the following call to Array method Sort before displaying the values in the dataListBox:

```
Array.Sort(searchData) ' sort array to enable binary searching
```

In method `searchButton_Click`, we replaced lines 40–48 of Fig. 7.14 with

```
Dim index As Integer = Array.BinarySearch(searchData, searchKey)
```

which uses `Array` method `BinarySearch` to perform a binary search for a key value. The method receives two arguments—the *sorted* integer array `searchData` (the array to search) and integer `searchKey` (the search key). If the value is found, method `BinarySearch` returns the index of the search key; otherwise, it returns a negative number.

a) Creating random values to search

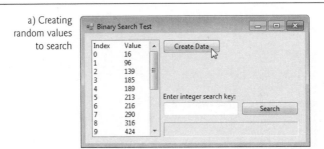

b) Searching for a value that is in the array

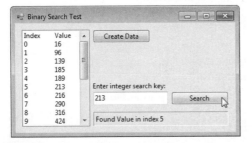

c) Searching for a value that is not in the array

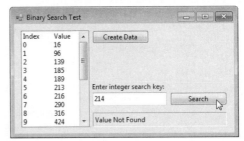

Fig. 7.15 | Binary search of an array.

7.14 Rectangular Arrays

The arrays we've studied so far are **one-dimensional** arrays—they contain a list of values and use only *one* index to access each element. In this section, we introduce **multidimensional** arrays, which require two or more indices to identify particular elements. We concentrate on **two-dimensional** arrays—also known as **rectangular arrays**—which are often used to represent **tables** of values consisting of data arranged in **rows** and **columns** (Fig. 7.16). Each row is the same size, and each column is the same size (hence the term "rectangular"). To identify a particular table element, we specify two indices—by convention, the first identifies the element's row, the second the element's column. Figure 7.16 illustrates a rectangular array, a, containing three rows and four columns. A rectangular array with *m* rows and *n* columns is called an *m*-by-*n* array; the array in Fig. 7.16 is a 3-by-4 array.

Every element in array a is identified in Fig. 7.16 by an element name of the form a(i, j), where a is the name of the array and i and j are the indices that uniquely identify the row and column, respectively, of each element in array a. Array indices are *zero based*, so the names of the elements in row 0 all have a *first* index of 0; the names of the elements in column 3 all have a *second* index of 3.

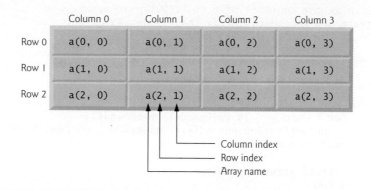

Fig. 7.16 | Two-dimensional array with three rows and four columns.

Declaring and Initializing Rectangular Arrays

A two-dimensional rectangular array numbers with two rows and two columns can be declared and initialized with

```
Dim numbers(1, 1) As Integer ' numbers in a 2 by 2 array
numbers(0, 0) = 1 ' leftmost element in row 0
numbers(0, 1) = 2 ' rightmost element in row 0
numbers(1, 0) = 3 ' leftmost element in row 1
numbers(1, 1) = 4 ' rightmost element in row 1
```

Alternatively, the initialization can be written on one line, as shown with and without local type inference below:

```
Dim numbers = {{1, 2}, {3, 4}}
Dim numbers(,) As Integer = {{1, 2}, {3, 4}}
```

In the second declaration, the comma in (,) indicates that numbers is a two-dimensional array. The values are grouped by row in braces, with 1 and 2 initializing numbers(0, 0) and numbers(0, 1), respectively, and 3 and 4 initializing numbers(1, 0) and numbers(1, 1), respectively. The compiler determines the number of rows by counting the number of subinitializer lists (represented by the sets of data in *curly braces*) in the main initializer list. Then the compiler determines the number of columns in each row by counting the number of initializer values in the subinitializer list for that row. The subinitializer lists must have the same number of elements for each row.

Manipulating a Rectangular Array

The app in Fig. 7.17 initializes rectangular array values and uses nested For...Next loops to traverse the array (that is, to manipulate every array element). The contents of the array are displayed in outputTextBox.

```
1  ' Fig. 7.17: RectangularArray.vb
2  ' Initializing and displaying a rectangular array.
3  Public Class RectangularArray
```

Fig. 7.17 | Initializing and displaying a rectangular array (Part 1 of 2.).

```
4      ' display the contents of a rectangular array
5      Private Sub RectangularArray_Load(sender As Object,
6         e As EventArgs) Handles MyBase.Load
7
8         Dim values(,) As Integer = {{1, 2, 3}, {4, 5, 6}}
9
10        ' output elements of the values array
11        For row = 0 To values.GetUpperBound(0)
12           For column = 0 To values.GetUpperBound(1)
13              outputTextBox.AppendText(values(row, column) & vbTab)
14           Next column
15
16           outputTextBox.AppendText(vbCrLf)
17        Next row
18     End Sub ' RectangularArray_Load
19  End Class ' RectangularArray
```

outputTextBox

| 1 | 2 | 3 |
| 4 | 5 | 6 |

Fig. 7.17 | Initializing and displaying a rectangular array (Part 2 of 2.).

The app declares rectangular array `values` (line 8) and uses an initializer list to determine the number of rows, number of columns and initial values of the array's elements. The initializer list contains two sublists. The number of sublists determines the number of rows in the array. The compiler uses the number of elements in the first sublist to determine the number of columns in each row. All subsequent sublists *must* have the *same* number of initializers as the first sublist; otherwise, a compilation error occurs. The first sublist initializes row 0 of the array to the values 1, 2 and 3; the second sublist initializes row 1 of the array to the values 4, 5 and 6.

The nested For...Next statements in lines 11–17 display the elements of rectangular array `values`. The outer For...Next statement traverses the rows; the inner For...Next statement traverses the columns within a row. Each For...Next statement calls method `GetUpperBound` to obtain the upper bound of the dimension it traverses. `GetUpperBound` with the argument 0 (line 11) returns the number of rows. `GetUpperBound` with the argument 1 (line 12) returns the number of columns in each row.

7.15 Case Study: Maintaining Grades Using a Rectangular Array

We now present a substantial case study using rectangular arrays. Consider the following problem statement:

> *An instructor gives three tests to a class of 10 students. The grades on these tests are integers in the range from 0 to 100. The instructor has asked you to develop an app to keep track of each student's average and the class average. The instructor has also asked that there be a choice to view the grades as either numbers or letters. Letter grades should be calculated according to the following grading system:*

90–100	*A*
80–89	*B*
70–79	*C*
60–69	*D*
Below 60	*F*

The app should allow a user to input each student's three test grades, then compute each student's average and the class average for all grades entered so far. The app should display numeric grades by default. It should also display a grade distribution chart showing how many of the numeric grades fall into the ranges 0–9, 10–19, ... 90–99 and 100.

We'll use a rectangular array with 10 rows and three columns to store the student grades. This app uses most of the programming concepts you've learned up to now in this book. Figure 7.19 shows sample outputs for the **Grade Report** app.

a) **Grade Report** window after the user has entered the first student's grades and is about to submit them.

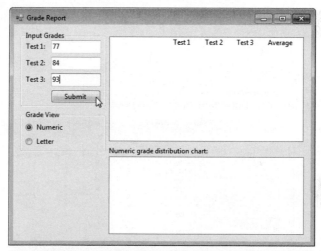

b) **Grade Report** window after five students' grades have been entered.

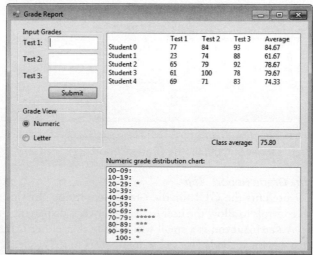

Fig. 7.18 | Sample outputs for the **Grade Report** app. (Part 1 of 2.)

c) **Grade Report** window after the user has entered all 10 students' grades.

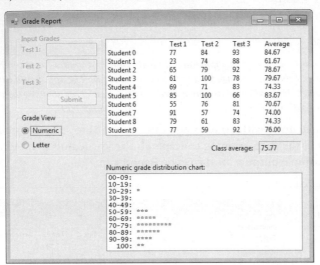

d) **Grade Report** window after the user has entered all 10 students' grades and clicked the **Letter** RadioButton to display letter grades.

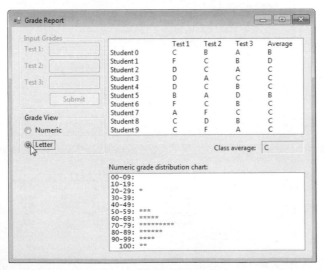

Fig. 7.18 | Sample outputs for the **Grade Report** app. (Part 2 of 2.)

GUI for the Grade Report App

Figure 7.19 presents the GUI for the **Grade Report** app. In this app, we introduce RadioButton controls to allow the user to select between displaying grades in numeric or letter format. A **RadioButton** is a small white circle that either is blank or contains a small dot. When a RadioButton is selected, a dot appears in the circle. A RadioButton is known as a state button because it can be in only the "on" (True) state or the "off" (False) state. You've previously used the CheckBox state buttons (introduced in Chapter 5).

RadioButtons are similar to CheckBoxes, but RadioButtons normally appear as a group—only one RadioButton in the group can be selected at a time. Like car radio preset buttons, which can select *only one* station at a time, RadioButtons represent a set of options in which only one option can be selected at a time—also known as **mutually exclusive options**. By default, all RadioButtons become part of the same group. To separate them into several groups, each group must be in a different container (typically a GroupBox).

A RadioButton's Boolean **Checked** property indicates whether the RadioButton is checked (contains a small dot) or unchecked (blank). If the RadioButton is checked, the Checked property returns True; otherwise, it returns False.

A RadioButton also generates an event when its checked state changes. Event **CheckedChanged** occurs when a RadioButton is either selected or deselected. We use this event to switch between the numeric grade and letter grade views in the gradesListBox.

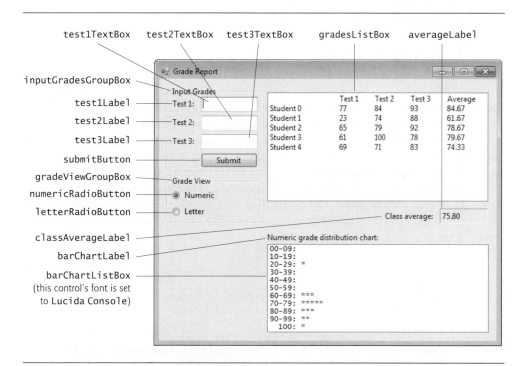

Fig. 7.19 | GUI for the **Grade Report** app

Grade Report *App*

Over the next several figures we'll discuss the **Grade Report** app's code. Due to the size of this app, we've split the source code into several small figures.

Figure 7.20 declares class GradeReport's instance variables and Load event handler. The rectangular array grades (line 4) has 10 rows and 3 columns to store the grades for 10 students and three exams per student. Variable studentCount (line 5) keeps track of the number of students processed so far. After 10 students are processed, the app disables the input TextBoxes and **Submit** Button. The GradeReport_Load event handler (lines 8–13) displays the column heads in the gradesListBox.

```
 1    ' Fig. 7.20: GradeReport.vb
 2    ' Grade report using a rectangular array.
 3    Public Class GradeReport
 4       Dim grades(9, 2) As Integer ' stores 10 students' grades on 3 tests
 5       Dim studentCount As Integer = 0 ' number of students entered
 6
 7       ' display heading in gradeListBox
 8       Private Sub GradeReport_Load(sender As Object,
 9          e As EventArgs) Handles MyBase.Load
10          ' headings row for gradesListBox
11          gradesListBox.Items.Add(vbTab & vbTab & "Test 1" & vbTab &
12             "Test 2" & vbTab & "Test 3" & vbTab & "Average")
13       End Sub
14
```

Fig. 7.20 | Grade Report app: Instance variables and method GradeReport_Load.

Method submitButton_Click

When the user enters three grades, then presses the **Submit Button**, method submit-Button_Click (Fig. 7.21) processes the three grades and displays the current class average and a bar chart showing the grade distribution for all grades entered so far. Lines 20–22 get the three grades from the TextBoxes and assign them to the elements of the grades array in row studentCount. Lines 25–37 build a String representing the current student's grades and average. Lines 28–37 loop through the current row of the grades array and append either a letter grade or numeric grade, based on whether the letterRadioButton's Checked property is True. If so, line 32 calls method LetterGrade to get the letter representation of the numeric grade. Otherwise, line 35 appends the numeric grade. Line 40 calls method CalculateStudentAverage to obtain the current student's average for the three exams.

```
15       ' process one student's grades
16       Private Sub submitButton_Click(sender As Object,
17          e As EventArgs) Handles submitButton.Click
18
19          ' retrieve the student's grades
20          grades(studentCount, 0) = Convert.ToInt32(test1TextBox.Text)
21          grades(studentCount, 1) = Convert.ToInt32(test2TextBox.Text)
22          grades(studentCount, 2) = Convert.ToInt32(test3TextBox.Text)
23
24          ' begin creating String containing the student's grades and average
25          Dim output As String = "Student " & studentCount & vbTab
26
27          ' append each test grade to the output
28          For column = 0 To grades.GetUpperBound(1)
29             ' if the Letter RadioButton is checked
30             If letterRadioButton.Checked = True Then
31                ' append letter grade to the output
32                output &= vbTab & LetterGrade(grades(studentCount, column))
```

Fig. 7.21 | Grade Report app: Method submitButton_Click. (Part 1 of 2.)

```
33              Else
34                  ' append number grade to the output
35                  output &= vbTab & grades(studentCount, column)
36              End If
37          Next
38
39          ' append the student's test average to the output
40          output &= vbTab & CalculateStudentAverage(studentCount)
41
42          gradesListBox.Items.Add(output) ' add output to the ListBox
43          studentCount += 1 ' update number of students entered
44          averageLabel.Text = CalculateClassAverage() ' display class average
45          DisplayBarChart() ' display the current grade distribution
46
47          ' clear the input TextBoxes and set focus to first TextBox
48          test1TextBox.Clear()
49          test2TextBox.Clear()
50          test3TextBox.Clear()
51          test1TextBox.Focus()
52
53          ' limit number of students
54          If studentCount = grades.GetUpperBound(0) + 1 Then
55              inputGroupBox.Enabled = False ' disable GroupBox's controls
56          End If
57      End Sub ' submitButton_Click
58
```

Fig. 7.21 | **Grade Report** app: Method submitButton_Click. (Part 2 of 2.)

Line 42 displays the information for the current student. Line 43 updates the student count. Line 44 and 45 call the methods CalculateClassAverage and DisplayBarChart to determine the current class average and to display a grade distribution chart based on the grades that have been entered so far. Lines 48–51 prepare the user interface to receive the next student's grades by clearing the TextBoxes and giving the focus to the test1-TextBox. Finally, lines 54–56 check whether grades have been entered for 10 students. If so, line 55 sets the inputGradeGroupBox's Enabled property to False, which *disables* all the controls in the GroupBox, preventing the user from entering more grades.

Method *RadioButton_CheckChanged: Handling Multiple Events with One Event Handler*

At any time, the user can select the **Numeric** or **Letter** RadioButton to change how the grades are displayed in the gradesListBox. When the selected RadioButton changes, method RadioButton_CheckedChanged (Fig. 7.22) is called. In this example, we handle both RadioButton's CheckedChanged events with the same event handler. To do this, double click the **Numeric** RadioButton, then rename the event handler to RadioButton_Checked-Changed. Next, add letterRadioButton.CheckedChanged to the Handles clause of the event handler (lines 62–63). Now this method is called when the CheckChanged event occurs for either RadioButton. In this case, as long as at least one student has been processed, line 67 calls method DisplayGrades to update the presentation of the grades in gradesListBox.

```
59     ' handles Numeric and Letter RadioButtons' CheckChanged events
60     Private Sub RadioButton_CheckedChanged(sender As Object,
61        e As EventArgs) _
62        Handles numericRadioButton.CheckedChanged,
63           letterRadioButton.CheckedChanged
64
65        ' if there are grades to display, call DisplayClassGrades
66        If studentCount > 0 Then
67           DisplayClassGrades()
68        End If
69     End Sub ' RadioButton_CheckedChanged
70
```

Fig. 7.22 | **Grade Report** app: Method `RadioButton_CheckedChanged`.

Method CalculateStudentAverage

Method `CalculateStudentAverage` (Fig. 7.23) processes one row of the grades array to determine the corresponding student's average. The method returns a `String` containing either the letter grade for that student's average or the numeric value, depending on whether the `letterRadioButton`'s Checked property is True.

```
71     ' calculates a student's test average
72     Function CalculateStudentAverage(row As Integer) As String
73        Dim gradeTotal As Integer = 0 ' student's total grade
74
75        ' sum the grades for the student
76        For column = 0 To grades.GetUpperBound(1)
77           gradeTotal += grades(row, column)
78        Next
79
80        Dim studentAverage As String = String.Empty ' output string
81
82        ' calculate the student's test average
83        If letterRadioButton.Checked = True Then
84           studentAverage =
85              LetterGrade(gradeTotal / (grades.GetUpperBound(1) + 1))
86        Else
87           studentAverage = String.Format("{0:F}",
88              (gradeTotal / (grades.GetUpperBound(1) + 1)))
89        End If
90
91        Return studentAverage ' return the student's average
92     End Function ' CalculateStudentAverage
93
```

Fig. 7.23 | **Grade Report** app: Method `CalculateStudentAverage`.

Method CalculateClassAverage

Method `CalculateClassAverage` (Fig. 7.24) processes the grades array to determine the class average for all the grades entered so far. The method returns a `String` containing either the letter grade for the class average or the numeric value, depending on whether the `letterRadioButton`'s Checked property is True.

```
94      ' calculates the class average
95      Function CalculateClassAverage() As String
96         Dim classTotal As Integer = 0 ' class's total grade
97
98         ' loop through all rows that currently contain grades
99         For row = 0 To studentCount - 1
100           ' loop through all columns
101           For column = 0 To grades.GetUpperBound(1)
102              classTotal += grades(row, column) ' add grade to total
103           Next column
104        Next row
105
106        Dim classAverage As String = String.Empty ' output string
107
108        ' if the Letter RadioButton is checked, return letter grade
109        If letterRadioButton.Checked = True Then
110           classAverage = LetterGrade(classTotal /
111              (studentCount * (grades.GetUpperBound(1) + 1)))
112        Else ' return numeric grade
113           classAverage = String.Format("{0:F}", (classTotal /
114              (studentCount * (grades.GetUpperBound(1) + 1))))
115        End If
116
117        Return classAverage ' return the class average
118     End Function ' CalculateClassAverage
119
```

Fig. 7.24 | **Grade Report** app: Method `CalculateClassAverage`.

Method *LetterGrade*

Method `LetterGrade` (Fig. 7.25) receives a numeric grade and returns the corresponding letter grade as a `String`.

```
120     ' determines a letter grade corresponding to a numeric grade
121     Function LetterGrade(grade As Double) As String
122        Dim output As String ' the letter grade to return
123
124        ' determine the correct letter grade
125        Select Case grade
126           Case Is >= 90
127              output = "A"
128           Case Is >= 80
129              output = "B"
130           Case Is >= 70
131              output = "C"
132           Case Is >= 60
133              output = "D"
134           Case Else
135              output = "F"
136        End Select
```

Fig. 7.25 | **Grade Report** app: Method `LetterGrade`. (Part 1 of 2.)

```
137
138        Return output ' return the letter grade
139     End Function ' LetterGrade
140
```

Fig. 7.25 | Grade Report app: Method LetterGrade. (Part 2 of 2.)

Method *DisplayClassGrades*

Method DisplayClassGrades (Fig. 7.26) displays the student grades and averages in the gradesListBox. Line 143 clears the ListBox's current contents and lines 146–147 display the column heads in the ListBox. Lines 150–169 processes the grades array to display all the grades entered so far, displaying letter grades if letterRadioButton's Checked property is True. Line 172 updates the class average and displays the result in averageLabel.

```
141     ' display the grades for all students entered
142     Sub DisplayClassGrades()
143        gradesListBox.Items.Clear() ' clear the ListBox
144
145        ' add the header to the ListBox
146        gradesListBox.Items.Add(vbTab & vbTab & "Test 1" & vbTab &
147           "Test 2" & vbTab & "Test 3" & vbTab & "Average")
148
149        ' loop through all the rows
150        For row = 0 To studentCount - 1
151           Dim output As String = "Student " & row & vbTab
152
153           ' loop through all the columns
154           For column = 0 To grades.GetUpperBound(1)
155              If letterRadioButton.Checked = True Then
156                 ' add letter grade to output string
157                 output &= vbTab & LetterGrade(grades(row, column))
158              Else
159                 ' add number grade to output string
160                 output &= vbTab & (grades(row, column))
161              End If
162           Next column
163
164           ' add the student's average to the output
165           output &= vbTab & CalculateStudentAverage(row)
166
167           ' add the output to the ListBox
168           gradesListBox.Items.Add(output)
169        Next row
170
171        ' update the class average
172        averageLabel.Text = CalculateClassAverage()
173     End Sub ' DisplayClassGrades
174
```

Fig. 7.26 | Grade Report app: Method DisplayClassGrades.

Method `DisplayBarChart`

Many apps present data to users in a visual or graphical format. For example, numeric values are often displayed as bars in a bar chart. In such a chart, longer bars represent proportionally larger numeric values (see Fig. 7.18). Method `DisplayBarChart` (Fig. 7.27) displays a graphical summary of the grade distribution by creating a bar chart that shows how many numeric grades fall into each of the ranges 0–9, 10–19, … 90–99 and 100.

```
175     ' display a bar chart of the grade distribution
176     Sub DisplayBarChart()
177         barChartListBox.Items.Clear() ' remove current items
178
179         ' stores frequency of grades in each range of 10 grades
180         Dim frequency(10) As Integer
181
182         ' for each grade, increment the appropriate frequency
183         For row = 0 To studentCount - 1
184           For column = 0 To grades.GetUpperBound(1)
185               frequency(grades(row, column) \ 10) += 1
186           Next column
187         Next row
188
189         ' for each grade frequency, display bar of asterisks
190         For count = 0 To frequency.GetUpperBound(0)
191             Dim bar As String ' stores the label and bar
192
193             ' create bar label ( "00-09: ", ..., "90-99: ", "100: " )
194             If count = 10 Then
195                 bar = String.Format("{0, 5:D}: ", 100)
196             Else
197                 bar = String.Format("{0, 2:D2}-{1, 2:D2}: ",
198                     count * 10, count * 10 + 9)
199             End If
200
201             ' append bar of asterisks
202             For stars = 1 To frequency(count)
203                 bar &= ("*")
204             Next
205
206             barChartListBox.Items.Add(bar) ' display bar
207         Next count
208     End Sub ' DisplayBarChart
209 End Class ' GradeReport
```

Fig. 7.27 | Grade Report app: Method `DisplayBarChart`.

Lines 180–187 summarize the number of grades in each range using the elements of the 11-element array `frequency`. Next, lines 190–207 build a `String` containing the range of values represented by the current bar (lines 194–199) and a bar of asterisks representing the number of grades that fall into that range (lines 202–204). Line 206 then displays this `String` in the `barCharListBox`. The format `Strings` in lines 195 and 197 use field widths to control the number of characters in which each value is output. The format specifier `{0, 5:D}` (line 195) indicates that an integer value will be displayed in a field of 5 characters right justified by default. So, if the number contains *fewer* than 5 characters, it will be preceded by an appropriate number of spaces. The format specifier {0, 2:D2} (line 197) indicates that an integer will be displayed in a field of 2 characters. The D2 forces the number to use two character positions—single digit numbers are preceded by a leading 0.

7.16 Resizing an Array with the ReDim Statement

An array's size cannot be changed, so a new array must be created if you need to change the size of an existing array. The **ReDim** statement "resizes" an array at execution time by creating a *new* array and assigning it to the specified array variable. The old array's memory is eventually reclaimed by the runtime. Figure 7.28 demonstrates the ReDim statement.

```
1   ' Fig. 7.28: ReDimTest.vb
2   ' Resize an array using the ReDim statement.
3   Public Class ReDimTest
4      ' demonstrate ReDim
5      Private Sub ReDimTest_Load(sender As Object,
6         e As EventArgs) Handles MyBase.Load
7
8         ' create and initialize two 5-element arrays
9         Dim values1() As Integer = {1, 2, 3, 4, 5}
10        Dim values2() As Integer = {1, 2, 3, 4, 5}
11
12        ' display array length and the elements in array
13        outputTextBox.AppendText(
14           "The original array has " & values1.Length & " elements: ")
15        DisplayArray(values1)
16
17        ' change the size of the array without the Preserve keyword
18        ReDim values1(6)
19
20        ' display new array length and the elements in array
21        outputTextBox.AppendText("New array (without Preserve) has " &
22           values1.Length & " elements: ")
23        DisplayArray(values1)
24
25        ' change the size of the array with the Preserve keyword
26        ReDim Preserve values2(6)
27        values2(6) = 7 ' assign 7 to array element 6
28
29        ' display new array length and the elements in array
30        outputTextBox.AppendText("New array (with Preserve) has " &
31           values2.Length & " elements: ")
32        DisplayArray(values2)
33     End Sub
34
35     ' display array elements
36     Sub DisplayArray(array() As Integer)
37        For Each number In array
38           outputTextBox.AppendText(number & "   ")
39        Next
```

Fig. 7.28 | Resize an array using the ReDim statement. (Part 1 of 2.)

```
40
41            outputTextBox.AppendText(vbCrLf)
42        End Sub ' DisplayArray
43    End Class ' ReDimTest
```

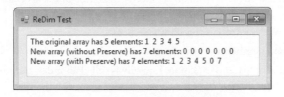

Fig. 7.28 | Resize an array using the `ReDim` statement. (Part 2 of 2.)

Line 9 creates and initializes a five-element array `values1`. Line 10 creates a second array named `values2` containing the same data. Lines 13–15 display the size and elements of `values1`. Line 18 uses a `ReDim` statement to change the upper bound of `values1` to 6, so that the array now contains seven elements. The `ReDim` statement contains keyword `ReDim`, followed by the name of the array to be "resized" and the new upper bound in parentheses. Lines 21–23 then display the size and elements of `values1` again. The output of Fig. 7.28 shows that after the `ReDim` statement executes, the size of `values1` is changed to 7 and the value of each element is reinitialized to the default value of the type of the array element (that is, 0 for `Integers`). To save the original data stored in an array, follow the `ReDim` keyword with the optional **Preserve** keyword. Line 26 uses `Preserve` in the `ReDim` statement to indicate that the existing array elements are to be *preserved* in the now larger array after the array is resized. If the new array is *smaller* than the original array, the existing elements that are outside the bounds of the new array are *discarded*. If the new array is *larger* than the original array, all the existing elements are preserved in the now larger array, and the *extra elements are initialized to the default value* of the type of the array element. For example, after line 26 executes, the value of `values2(5)` is 0. Line 27 assigns the value 7 to `values2(6)`, so that the now larger array `values2` contains elements 1, 2, 3, 4, 5, 0 and 7. Lines 30–32 display the size and elements of `values2`.

7.17 Wrap-Up

This chapter began our discussion of data structures, using arrays to store data in and retrieve data from lists and tables of values. We demonstrated how to declare an array, initialize an array and refer to individual elements of an array. We showed how to pass arrays to methods. We discussed how to use the `For Each...Next` statement to iterate through the values in an array without using an index. We used method `Sort` of class `Array` to sort an array and method `BinarySearch` of class `Array` to search a sorted array efficiently for a specific value. We explained how to declare and manipulate rectangular arrays. Finally, we demonstrated how to use the `ReDim` statement to dynamically change an array's size. In the next chapter, you'll learn how to write data to and read data from files.

Summary

Section 7.2 Arrays

- An array is a group of variables (called elements) containing values that all have the same type.
- All arrays are objects of and have the methods and properties of class System.Array.
- To refer to a particular element in an array, specify the name of the array and the position number of the element.
- The first element in every array is the zeroth element.
- The highest position number in a array is alwas 1 less than the number of elements in the array.
- The position number in parentheses more formally is called an index and must be a nonnegative integer or integer expression.
- The name of an array element can be used on the left side of an assignment statement to place a new value into an array element.
- Every array "knows" its own length via its Length property.

Section 7.3 Declaring and Allocating Arrays

- In an array declaration, the parentheses that follow the variable name indicate the variable represents an array.
- Arrays can be declared to contain elements of any type; every element of the array is of that type.
- The number in parentheses in the array declaration represents the array's upper bound and helps the compiler allocate memory for the array.
- You can follow an array declaration with an equal sign and an initializer list in braces, { and }, to specify the initial values of the array's elements. The compiler determines the array bounds from the number of elements in the initializer list.
- When you do not provide an initializer list, the elements in the array are initialized to the default value for the array's type—0 for numeric primitive data-type variables, False for Boolean variables and Nothing for String and other class types.

Section 7.4 Initializing the Values in an Array

- Array method GetUpperBound returns the index of the last element in an array. The value returned by method GetUpperBound is one less than the value of the array's Length property.

Section 7.5 Summing the Elements of an Array

- Often, the elements of an array represent a series of related values that are used in a calculation.

Section 7.6 Using Arrays to Analyze Survey Results

- Arrays can be used as sets of counters.
- When an expression contains nested parentheses, its evaluation begins with the value in the innermost set of parentheses.
- When an app is executed, array element indices are checked for validity—all indices must be greater than or equal to 0 and less than the length of the array. If an attempt is made to use an invalid index to access an element, an IndexOutOfRangeException exception occurs.

Section 7.8 Case Study: Flag Quiz

- The ComboBox control presents options in a drop-down list that opens when you click the down arrow at the right side of the control. A ComboBox combines features of a TextBox and a ListBox.

- A `ComboBox` usually appears as a `TextBox` with a down arrow to its right. You can click the down arrow to display a list of predefined items. If you choose an item from this list, that item is displayed in the `ComboBox`.

- You may also type into the `ComboBox` control to locate an item.

- `ComboBox` property `DropDownStyle` determines the `ComboBox`'s appearance. Value `DropDownList` specifies that the `ComboBox` is not editable. In this `ComboBox` style, if you press the key that corresponds to the first letter of a `ComboBox` item, that item is selected and displayed in the `ComboBox`.

- Property `MaxDropDownItems` specifies the maximum number of items to display at once. A vertical scrollbar is added to the drop-down list to allow users to scroll through the remaining items.

- `ComboBox` property `DataSource` specifies the source of the items displayed in the `ComboBox`.

- `String` method `Replace` receives two arguments—the substring that should be replaced throughout the original `String` and the the replacement substring.

Section 7.9 Passing an Array to a Method
- To pass an array argument to a method, specify the name of the array without using parentheses.

- Every array object "knows" its own upper bound, so when you pass an array object to a method, you do not need to pass the upper bound of the array as a separate argument.

- For a method to receive an array through a method call, the method's parameter list must specify that an array will be received.

- When you pass an array to a method, the method receives a copy of the array's reference and can change the original array's element values.

- To pass an array element to a method, use the indexed name of the array element as an argument in the method call. An individual element can be passed by value or by reference.

Section 7.10 For Each...Next Repetition Statement
- The `For Each...Next` repetition statement iterates through the values in a data structure, such as an array, without using a loop counter.

- When used with one-dimensional arrays, `For Each...Next` behaves like a `For...Next` statement that iterates through the range of indices from 0 to the value returned by `GetUpperBound(0)`.

- Instead of a counter, `For Each...Next` uses a variable to represent the value of each element.

- The header of a `For Each` repetition statement specifies a variable and an array. The type of variable is determined from the type of the elements in the array.

- The `For Each` statement iterates through all the elements in the array, sequentially assigning each value to the variable specified in the header.

Section 7.11 Sorting an Array with Method **Sort** of Class **Array**
- Sorting data is one of the most popular computing applications.

- Class `Array` provides methods for creating, modifying, sorting and searching arrays.

- `Array` method `Sort` sorts an array's elements into ascending order.

- To sort an array in descending order, first call method `Sort` to sort the array, then call `Array.Reverse` with the array as an argument to reverse the order of the elements in the array.

Section 7.12 Searching an Array with Linear Search
- The process of locating a particular element value in an array is called searching.

- A linear search iterates through all the elements of an array, comparing each element with a search key. If the elements of the array being searched are unordered, it's just as likely that the value will be found in the front half of the array as in the back half, so on average the method will have to compare the search key with half the elements of the array.

- Class Array's IndexOf method performs a linear search. Class Array also provides methods such as Find and FindAll, which search the array for element(s) that meet certain criteria.

Section 7.13 Searching a Sorted Array with **Array** Method **BinarySearch**

- Linear searches work well for small or unsorted arrays. The high-speed binary search technique is better for sorted arrays.

- Array method BinarySearch performs a binary search for a key value. The method receives a sorted array and a search key and returns the index of the search key; otherwise, it returns a negative number.

Section 7.14 Rectangular Arrays

- One-dimensional arrays are arrays that contain a list of values.

- Multidimensional arrays require two or more indices to identify particular elements.

- Two-dimensional (rectangular) arrays are often used to represent tables of values arranged in rows and columns. Each row is the same size, and each column is the same size.

- To identify a particular table element, we specify two indices—by convention, the first identifies the element's row, the second the element's column.

- Every element in a rectangular array is identified by an element name of the form a(i, j), where a is the name of the array and i and j are the indices that uniquely identify the row and column, respectively, of each element in array a.

- A rectangular array is declared by placing two bounds separated by a comma in the parentheses that follow the variable name.

- If an initializer list is used, then the parentheses must contain only the comma. The initializer list must have sublists to represent each row and all sublists must have the same number of columns. The compiler determines the number of columns in each row by counting the number of initializer values in the subinitializer list for that row.

- Rectangular arrays are often manipulated with nested For...Next loops.

- For a rectangular array, method GetUpperBound with the argument 0 returns the number of rows. GetUpperBound with the argument 1 returns the number of columns in each row.

Section 7.15 Case Study: Maintaining Grades Using a Rectangular Array

- A RadioButton is a small white circle that either is blank or contains a small dot. When a RadioButton is selected, a dot appears in the circle. A RadioButton is known as a state button because it can be in only the "on" (True) state or the "off" (False) state.

- RadioButtons are similar to CheckBoxes, but RadioButtons normally appear as a group—only one RadioButton in the group can be selected at a time—also known as mutually exclusive options.

- To separate RadioButtons into several groups, each group must be in a different container (typically a GroupBox).

- A RadioButton's Boolean Checked property indicates whether the RadioButton is checked (contains a small dot) or unchecked (blank). If the RadioButton is checked, the Checked property returns True; otherwise, it returns False.

- A CheckedChanged event occurs when a RadioButton is either selected or deselected.

- Many apps present data to users in a visual or graphical format. For example, numeric values are often displayed as bars in a bar chart. In such a chart, longer bars represent proportionally larger numeric values.

Section 7.16 Resizing an Array with the `ReDim` *Statement*

- The `ReDim` statement enables you to dynamically change an array's size. It "resizes" an array by creating a new array and assigning it to the specified variable.

- A `ReDim` statement contains keyword `ReDim`, followed by the name of the array to be "resized" and the new upper bound in parentheses. The value of each element is reinitialized to the default value of the type of the array element.

- To save the original data stored in an array, follow the `ReDim` keyword with the optional `Preserve` keyword. If the new array is smaller than the original array, the existing elements that are outside the bounds of the new array are discarded. If the new array is larger than the original array, all the existing elements are preserved in the now larger array, and the extra elements are initialized to the default value of the type of the array element.

Terminology

array 273
array bounds 275
Array class 273
binary search 293
BinarySearch method of class Array 295
bounds checking 279
Catch block 280
Checked property of the RadioButton
    control 301
CheckedChanged event of the RadioButton
    control 301
column in a rectangular array 296
ComboBox control 283
DataSource property of a ComboBox 285
DropDownList value of property
    DropDownStyle 283
DropDownStyle property of ComboBox 283
element of an array 273
exception 279
exception handling 279
fault-tolerant program 279
For Each...Next statement 289
GetUpperBound method of class Array 275
index of an array 273
initializer list 275
key value 293
length of an array 274
Length property of class Array 274

linear search 293
m-by-*n* array 296
MaxDropDownItems property of ComboBox
    control 283
Message property of an exception 280
multidimensional array 296
mutually exclusive options and
    RadioButtons 301
one-dimensional array 296
Preserve keyword 309
RadioButton control 300
rectangular array 296
ReDim statement 308
Replace method of class String 286
Reverse method of class Array 293
row in a rectangular array 296
search key 293
searching 293
SelectedIndex property of a ComboBox 286
sorting 291
Sort method of class Array 291
table of values 296
two-dimensional array 296
throw an exception 280
Try block 280
Try statement 280
upper bound 273
zeroth element 273

Self-Review Exercises

7.1   Answer each of the following questions:

    a) The number that refers to a particular element of an array is called its _____.

        1. value   2. size

        3. indexed array name   4. index

b) The indexed array name of one-dimensional array `units`'s element 2 is _____.

   1. `units{2}`   2. `units(2)`

   3. `units[0,2]`   4. `units[2]`

c) An array's length is _____.

   1. one more than the array's last index   2. one less than the array's last index

   3. the same as the array's last index   4. returned by method `GetUpperBound`

d) Property _____ specifies the source of the data displayed in a `ComboBox`.

   1. `ComboData`   2. `Source`

   3. `DataList`   4. `DataSource`

e) `ComboBox` property _____ is 0 when the first `ComboBox` item is selected.

   1. `SelectedIndex`   2. `SelectedValue`

   3. `Index`   4. `SelectedNumber`

f) The process of ordering the elements of an array is called _____ the array.

   1. allocating   2. sorting

   3. declaring   4. initializing

g) Which of the following sorts array `averageRainfall`?

   1. `Array(averageRainfall).Sort()`   2. `Sort.Array(averageRainfall)`

   3. `Sort(averageRainfall)`   4. `Array.Sort(averageRainfall)`

h) Arrays that use two indices are referred to as _____ arrays.

   1. single-dimensional   2. two-dimensional

   3. `double`   4. one-dimensional

i) The expression _____ creates an `Integer` array of two rows and five columns.

   1. `Dim a(2, 5) As Integer`   2. `Dim a(1, 5) As Integer`

   3. `Dim a(1, 4) As Integer`   4. `Dim a(2, 4) As Integer`

j) The _____ event is raised when a `RadioButton` is either selected or deselected.

   1. `CheckedChanged`   2. `Changed`

   3. `SelectedChanged`   4. None of the above

k) When one `RadioButton` in a container is selected, _____.

   1. others can be selected at the same time   2. a logic error will occur

   3. all others will be deselected   4. Both 1 and 2

l) Typically, _____ statements are used to iterate over each element in a two-dimensional array.

   1. `Do While...Loop`   2. nested `For...Next`

   3. `Do...Loop Until`   4. nested `Do...Loop While`

7.2 State whether each of the following is *true* or *false*. If *false*, explain why.

a) An array can store many different types of values.

b) An array index normally should be of type `Double`.

c) Method `GetUpperBound` returns the highest numbered index in an array.

d) To determine the number of elements in an array, use the `NumberOfElements` property.

e) The linear search works well for unsorted arrays.

Answers to Self-Review Exercises

7.1   a) 4. b) 2. c) 1. d) 4. e) 1. f) 2. g) 4. h) 2. i) 3. j) 1. k) 3. l) 2.

7.2   a)   False. An array can store only values of the same type. b) False. An array index must be a nonnegative integer or integer expression. c) True. d) False. To determine the number of elements in an array, we can use the `Length` property. e) True.

Quick Quiz

7.3   Answer each of the following questions:

a) Arrays can be declared to hold values of _____.

    1. type `Double`   2. type `Integer`

    3. type `String`   4. any data type

b) An array's elements are related by the fact that they have the same name and _____.

    1. constant value   2. index

    3. type   4. value

c) Method _____ returns an array's highest index.

    1. `GetUpperBound`   2. `GetUpperLimit`

    3. `GetHighestIndex`   4. `GetUpperIndex`

d) The first element in every array is the _____.

    1. index   2. zeroth element

    3. length of the array   4. smallest value in the array

e) The initializer list can _____.

    1. be used to determine the size of the array

    2. contain a comma-separated list of initial values for the array elements

    3. be empty

    4. All of the above

f) Which method call sorts array `words` in ascending order?

    1. `Array.Sort(words)`   2. `words.SortArray()`

    3. `Array.Sort(words, 1)`   4. `Sort(words)`

g) The `ComboBox` control combines a `TextBox` control with a _____ control.

    1. `DateTimePicker`   2. `ListBox`

    3. `NumericUpDown`   4. `Label`

h) Property _____ contains the size of an array.

    1. `Elements`   2. `ArraySize`

    3. `Length`   4. `Size`

i) When declaring an array, a(n) _____ is required inside parentheses in order to indicate that the array is two-dimensional.

    1. comma   2. asterisk

    3. period   4. apostrophe

j) In a _____ array each row contains the same number of columns.

    1. data   2. rectangular

    3. tabular   4. All of the above

k) In an *m*-by-*n* array, the *m* stands for _____.

    1. the number of columns in the array   2. the total number of array elements

    3. the number of rows in the array   4. the number of elements in each row

l) Which of the following creates an `Integer` array of five rows and three columns?

    1. `Dim values(5, 3) As Integer`   2. `Dim values(4, 2 ) As Integer`

    3. `Dim values(4, 3) As Integer`   4. `Dim values(5, 2) As Integer`

m) Use a _____ to group `RadioButtons` on a Form.

    1. `GroupBox` control   2. `ComboBox` control

    3. `ListBox` control   4. None of the above

n) The _____ property is set to True when a RadioButton is selected.
   1. Selected
   2. Chosen
   3. On
   4. Checked

o) Two-dimensional arrays are often used to represent _____.
   1. a pie chart
   2. distances
   3. lines
   4. tables

p) Which of the following statements creates Integer array values with three rows and three columns?
   1. Dim array()() As Integer = {{1, 2, 3}, {4, 5, 6}, {7, 8, 9}}
   2. Dim array() As Integer = {{1, 2, 3}, {4, 5, 6}, {7, 8, 9}}
   3. Dim array(,) As Integer = {{1, 2, 3}, {4, 5, 6}, {7, 8, 9}}
   4. All of the above

Exercises

7.4 Write statements to accomplish each of the following tasks:
   a) Display the value of element 6 of array numbers.
   b) Using a For...Next statement, assign the value 8 to each of the five elements of one-dimensional Integer array values.
   c) Total the 100 elements of floating-point array results.
   d) Copy 11-element array source into the first portion of 34-element array sourceCopy.
   e) Determine the smallest and largest values in 99-element floating-point array data.

7.5 *(Salary Survey App)* Use a one-dimensional array to solve the following problem: A company pays its salespeople on a commission basis. The salespeople receive $200 per week, plus 9% of their gross sales for that week. For example, a salesperson who grosses $5,000 in sales in a week receives $200 plus 9% of $5,000, a total of $650. Write an app (using an array of counters) that determines how many of the salespeople earned salaries in each of the following ranges (assuming that each salesperson's salary is truncated to an integer amount): $200–299, $300–399, $400–499, $500–599, $600–699, $700–799, $800–899, $900–999 and over $999.

Allow the user to enter the sales for each employee in a TextBox. The user clicks the **Calculate** Button to calculate the salesperson's salary. When the user is done entering this information, clicking the **Show Totals** Button displays how many of the salespeople earned salaries in each of the above ranges.

7.6 *(Cafeteria Survey App)* Twenty students were asked to rate, on a scale from 1 to 10, the quality of the food in the student cafeteria, with 1 being "awful" and 10 being "excellent." Allow the user input to be entered using a ComboBox. Use an Integer array to store the frequency of each rating. Display the frequencies as a bar chart in a ListBox.

7.7 *(What Does This Code Do?)* This function declares numbers as its parameter. What does it return if number() = {1, 2, 3, 4}?

```
1   Function Mystery(numbers() As Integer) As Integer()
2      Dim length As Integer = numbers.Length - 1
3      Dim tempArray(length) As Integer
4      For i As Integer = length To 0 Step -1
5         tempArray(length - i) = numbers(i) * number(i)
6      Next
7      Return tempArray
8   End Function ' Mystery
```

7.8   *(What's Wrong with This Code?)* The code that follows uses a For…Next loop to multiply the elements of an array. Find the error(s) in the following code:

```
1   Sub ProductArray()
2      Dim product As Integer
3      Dim numbers() As Integer = {4, 5, 7, 2, 18}
4      For counter As Integer = 0 To numbers.Length
5         product *= numbers(counter)
6      Next
7   End Sub ' ProductArray
```

7.9   *(Road Sign Test App)* Write an app that tests the user's knowledge of road signs. Your app should display a random sign image and ask the user to select the sign name from a ComboBox (similar to the **Flag Quiz** app). You can find the images in the Images folder with this chapter's examples.

7.10   *(Enhanced Cafeteria Survey App)* A school cafeteria is giving an electronic survey to its students to improve their lunch menu. Create an app that uses a rectangular array to store votes for the survey. The app should display four food items in a ComboBox. Provide **Like** and **Dislike** RadioButtons to allow students to indicate whether they like or dislike a particular food. The user selects an item from the ComboBox, clicks the appropriate RadioButton and presses the **Submit** Button to submit the vote. Display a report that's updated as each new set of responses is entered. Use a rectangular Integer array named votes, with four rows and two columns to summarize the results. Each row corresponds to a food item in the ComboBox. The columns store the number of "like" and "dislike" votes, respectively.

7.11   *(What Does This Code Do?)* What is returned by the following code? Assume that Get-StockPrices is a Function that returns a 2-by-7 array, with the first row containing the stock price at the beginning of the day and the last row containing the stock price at the end of the day, for each day of the week.

```
1   Function Mystery() As Integer()
2      Dim prices(1, 7) As Integer
3      prices = GetStockPrices()
4      Dim result(6) As Integer
5      For i As Integer = 0 To 6
6         result(i) = prices(1, i) - prices(0, i)
7      Next
8      Return result
9   End Function ' Mystery
```

7.12   *(What's Wrong with This Code?)* Find the error(s) in the following code. The TwoDArrays procedure should create a two-dimensional array and initialize all its values to five.

```
1   Sub TwoDArrays()
2      Dim array(4, 4) As Integer
3      ' assign 5 to all cell values
4      For i As Integer = 0 To 4
5         array(i, i) = 5
6      Next
7   End Sub ' TwoDArrays
```

7.13 *(Duplicate Elimination)* Use a one-dimensional array to solve the following problem: Read in 20 numbers, each of which is between 10 and 100, inclusive. As each number is read, display it in numbersEnteredListBox and, if it's not a duplicate of a number already read, display it in uniqueValuesListBox. Provide for the "worst case" (in which all 20 numbers are different). Use the smallest possible array to solve this problem.

7.14 *(Sorting in Ascending and Descending Order)* Modify the sorting example of Fig. 7.12 so that it displays the "Original values," "Values sorted in ascending order" and "Values sorted in descending order"; your app should display in the last two columns the values sorted in ascending and descending order, respectively.

7.15 *(Telephone-Number Word Generator)* Standard telephone keypads contain the digits zero through nine. The numbers two through nine each have three letters associated with them (Fig. 7.29). Many people find it difficult to memorize phone numbers, so they use the correspondence between digits and letters to develop seven-letter words that correspond to their phone numbers. For example, a person whose telephone number is 686-2377 might use the correspondence indicated in Fig. 7.29 to develop the seven-letter word "NUMBERS." Every seven-letter word corresponds to exactly one seven-digit telephone number. A restaurant wishing to increase its takeout business could surely do so with the number 825-3688 (that is, "TAKEOUT").

Digit	Letters	Digit	Letters
2	A B C	6	M N O
3	D E F	7	P R S
4	G H I	8	T U V
5	J K L	9	W X Y

Fig. 7.29 | Telephone keypad digits and letters.

Every seven-letter phone number corresponds to many different seven-letter combinations. Unfortunately, most of these represent unrecognizable juxtapositions of letters. It's possible, however, that the owner of a barbershop would be pleased to know that the shop's telephone number, 424-7288, corresponds to "HAIRCUT." A veterinarian with the phone number 738-2273 would be pleased to know that the number corresponds to the letters "PETCARE." An automotive dealership would be pleased to know that the dealership number, 639-2277, corresponds to "NEW-CARS."

Write an app that allows the user to enter a seven-digit number in a TextBox, and displays every possible seven-letter word combination corresponding to that number in a multiple line scrollable TextBox when the user clicks the **Generate Words** button. There are 2,187 (3^7) such combinations. Avoid phone numbers with the digits 0 and 1.

7.16 *(Airline Reservations System)* A small airline has just purchased a computer for its new automated reservations system. You've been asked to develop the new system. You are to write an app to assign seats on each flight of the airline's only plane (capacity: 10 seats).

Your app should display RadioButtons that allow the user to choose **First Class** or **Economy**. If the user selects **First Class**, your app should assign a seat in the first-class section (seats 1–5). If the user types **Economy**, your app should assign a seat in the economy section (seats 6–10). Your app should then display a boarding pass indicating the person's seat number and whether it's in the first-class or economy section of the plane.

Use a one-dimensional array of type Boolean to represent the plane's seating chart. All the elements of the array are initially False to indicate that the seats are empty. As each seat is assigned, set the corresponding elements of the array to True to indicate that the seat is no longer available.

Your app should never assign a seat that has already been assigned. When the economy section is full, your app should ask the person if it's acceptable to be placed in the first-class section (and vice versa). If yes, make the appropriate seat assignment. If no, display the message "Next flight leaves in 3 hours."

Making a Difference Exercise

7.17   *(Polling)* The Internet and the web are enabling more people to network, join a cause, voice opinions, and so on. The presidential candidates in 2008 used the Internet intensively to get out their messages and raise money for their campaigns. In this exercise, you'll write a simple polling app that allows users to rate five social-consciousness issues from 1 (least important) to 10 (most important). Pick five causes that are important to you (for example, political issues, global environmental issues). Use a one-dimensional array topics (of type String) to store the five causes. To summarize the survey responses, use a 5-row, 10-column two-dimensional array responses (of type Integer), each row corresponding to an element in the topics array. When the app runs, it should ask the user to rate each issue. Have your friends and family respond to the survey. Then have the app display a summary of the results, including:

    a)   A tabular report with the five topics down the left side and the 10 ratings across the top, listing in each column the number of ratings received for each topic.

    b)   To the right of each row, show the average of the ratings for that issue.

    c)   Which issue received the highest point total? Display both the issue and the point total.

    d)   Which issue received the lowest point total? Display both the issue and the point total.

8

Files

Consciousness ... does not appear to itself chopped up in bits. ... A "river" or a "stream" are the metaphors by which it is most naturally described.
—William James

I can only assume that a "Do Not File" document is filed in a "Do Not File" file.
—Senator Frank Church,
Senate Intelligence Subcommittee
Hearing, 1975

Objectives

In this chapter you'll learn:

■ To use file processing to implement a business app.

■ To create, write to and read from files.

■ To become familiar with sequential-access file processing.

■ To use classes `StreamWriter` and `StreamReader` to write text to and read text from files.

■ To organize GUI commands in menus.

■ To manage resources with `Using` statements and the Finally block of a `Try` statement.

8.1 Introduction

Variables and arrays offer only *temporary* storage of data in memory—the data is *lost*, for example, when a local variable "goes out of scope" or when the app terminates. By contrast, files (and databases, which we cover in Chapter 12) are used for *long-term retention* of large (and often *vast*) amounts of data, even after the app that created the data terminates, so data maintained in files is often called **persistent data**. Computers store files on **secondary storage devices**, such as magnetic disks, optical disks (like CDs, DVDs and Blu-ray Discs™), USB flash drives and magnetic tapes. In this chapter, we explain how to create, write to and read from data files. We continue our treatment of GUIs, explaining how to organize commands in menus and showing how to use the Windows Forms Designer to rapidly create menus. We also discuss resource management—as apps execute, they often *acquire* resources, such as memory and files, that need to be *returned* to the system so they can be *reused* at a later point. We show how to *ensure* that resources are properly returned to the system when they're no longer needed.

8.2 Data Hierarchy

Ultimately, all data items that computers process are reduced to combinations of 0s and 1s. This occurs because it's simple and economical to build electronic devices that can assume two stable states—one represents 0 and the other represents 1. It's remarkable that the impressive functions performed by computers involve only the most fundamental manipulations of 0s and 1s!

Bits
The smallest data item that computers support is called a **bit**, short for "**binary digit**"—a digit that can assume either the value 0 or the value 1. Computer circuitry performs various simple bit manipulations, such as examining the value of a bit, setting the value of a bit and reversing a bit (from 1 to 0 or from 0 to 1). For more information on the binary number system, see Appendix C, Number Systems.

Characters

Programming with data in the low-level form of bits is cumbersome. It's preferable to program with data in forms such as **decimal digits** (that is, 0, 1, 2, 3, 4, 5, 6, 7, 8 and 9), **letters** (that is, the uppercase letters A–Z and the lowercase letters a–z) and **special symbols** (that is, $, @, %, &, *, (,), -, +, ", :, ?, / and many others). Digits, letters and special symbols are referred to as **characters**. The set of all characters used to write programs and represent data items on a particular computer is called that computer's **character set**. Because computers process only 0s and 1s, every character in a computer's character set is represented as a pattern of 0s and 1s. **Bytes** are composed of eight bits. Visual Basic uses the **Unicode character set**, in which each character is typically composed of *two* bytes (and hence 16 bits). You create programs and data items with characters; computers manipulate and process these characters as patterns of bits.

Fields

Just as characters are composed of bits, fields are composed of characters. A **field** is a group of characters that conveys meaning. For example, a field consisting of uppercase and lowercase letters can represent a person's name.

Data Hierarchy

Data items processed by computers form a **data hierarchy** (Fig. 8.1), in which data items become larger and more complex in structure as we progress up the hierarchy from bits to characters to fields to larger data aggregates.

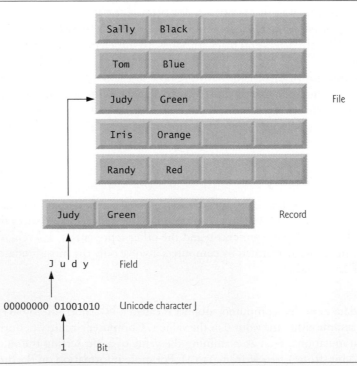

Fig. 8.1 | Data hierarchy (assuming that files are organized into records).

Records

Typically, a **record** is composed of several related fields. In a payroll system, for example, a record for a particular employee might include the following fields:

1. Employee identification number
2. Name
3. Address
4. Hourly pay rate
5. Number of exemptions claimed
6. Year-to-date earnings
7. Amount of taxes withheld

In the preceding example, each field is associated with the *same* employee. A data file can be implemented as a group of related records.[1] A company's payroll file normally contains one record for each employee. Companies typically have many files, some containing millions, billions or even trillions of characters of information.

To facilitate the retrieval of specific records from a file, at least one field in each record can be chosen as a **record key**, which identifies a record as belonging to a particular person or entity and distinguishes that record from all others. For example, in a payroll record, the employee identification number normally would be the record key.

Sequential Files

There are many ways to organize records in a file. A common organization is called a **sequential file** in which records typically are stored in order by a record-key field. In a payroll file, records usually are placed in order by employee identification number.

Databases

Most businesses use many different files to store data. For example, a company might have payroll files, accounts receivable files (listing money due from clients), accounts payable files (listing money due to suppliers), inventory files (listing facts about all the items handled by the business) and many other files. Related files often are stored in a **database**. A collection of programs designed to create and manage databases is called a **database management system (DBMS)**. You'll learn about databases in Chapter 12 and you'll do additional work with databases in Chapter 13, Web App Development with ASP.NET, and online Chapters 24–25.

8.3 Files and Streams

Visual Basic views a file simply as a sequential **stream** of bytes (Fig. 8.2). Depending on the operating system, each file ends either with an **end-of-file marker** or at a specific byte number that's recorded in a system-maintained administrative data structure for the file. You open a file from a Visual Basic app by creating an object that enables communication

---

1. In some operating systems, a file is viewed as nothing more than a collection of bytes, and any organization of the bytes in a file (such as organizing the data into records) is a view created by the programmer.

between an app and a particular file, such as an object of class `StreamWriter` to write text to a file or an object of class `StreamReader` to read text from a file.

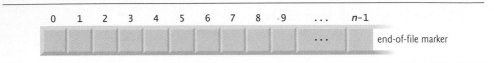

Fig. 8.2 | Visual Basic's view of an n-byte file.

8.4 Test-Driving the Credit Inquiry App

A credit manager would like you to implement a **Credit Inquiry** app that enables the credit manager to separately search for and display account information for customers with

- debit balances—customers who owe the company money for previously received goods and services
- credit balances—customers to whom the company owes money
- zero balances—customers who do not owe the company money

The app reads records from a text file then displays the contents of each record that matches the type selected by the credit manager, whom we shall refer to from this point forward simply as "the user."

Opening the File
When the user initially executes the **Credit Inquiry** app, the `Buttons` at the bottom of the window are *disabled* (Fig. 8.3(a))—the user *cannot* interact with them until a file has been selected. The company could have several files containing account data, so to begin processing a file of accounts, the user selects **Open…** from the app's custom **File** menu (Fig. 8.3(b)), which you'll create in Section 8.6. This displays an **Open** dialog (Fig. 8.3(c)) that allows the user to specify the *name* and *location* of the file from which the records will be read. In our case, we stored the file in the folder `C:\DataFiles` and named the file `Accounts.txt`. The left side of the dialog allows the user to locate the file on disk. The user can then select the file in the right side of the dialog and click the **Open** `Button` to submit the file name to the app. The **File** menu also provides an **Exit** menu item that allows the user to terminate the app.

a) Initial GUI with `Buttons` disabled until the user selects a file from which to read records

Fig. 8.3 | GUI for the **Credit Inquiry** app. (Part 1 of 2.)

b) Selecting the **Open...** menu item from the **File** menu displays the **Open** dialog in part (c)

c) The **Open** dialog allows the user to specify the location and name of the file

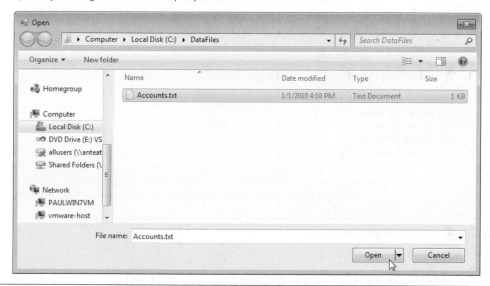

Fig. 8.3 | GUI for the **Credit Inquiry** app. (Part 2 of 2.)

Displaying Accounts with Debit, Credit and Zero Balances

After selecting a file name, the user can click one of the Buttons at the bottom of the window to display the records that match the specified account type. Figure 8.4(a) shows the accounts with debit balances. Figure 8.4(b) shows the accounts with credit balances. Figure 8.4(c) shows the accounts with zero balances.

a) Clicking the **Debit Balances** Button displays the accounts with *positive* balances (that is, the people who owe the company money)

Fig. 8.4 | GUI for **Credit Inquiry** app. (Part 1 of 2.)

b) Clicking the **Credit Balances** Button displays the accounts with *negative* balances (that is, the people to whom the company owes money)

Negative currency values are displayed in parentheses by default

c) Clicking the **Zero Balances** Button displays the accounts with zero balances (that is, the people who do not have a balance because they've already paid or have not had any recent transactions)

Fig. 8.4 | GUI for **Credit Inquiry** app. (Part 2 of 2.)

8.5 Writing Data Sequentially to a Text File

Before we can implement the **Credit Inquiry** app, we must create the file from which that app will read records. Our first app builds the sequential file containing the account information for the company's clients. For each client, the app obtains through its GUI the client's account number, first name, last name and balance—the amount of money that the client owes to the company for previously purchased goods and services. The data obtained for each client constitutes a "record" for that client. In this app, the account number is used as the record key—files are often maintained in order by their record keys. For simplicity, this app assumes that the user enters records in account number order.

GUI for the Create Accounts *App*

The GUI for the **Create Accounts** app is shown in Fig. 8.5. This app introduces the **Menu-Strip** control which enables you to place a menu bar in your window. It also introduces **ToolStripMenuItem** controls which are used to create menus and menu items. We show how use the IDE to build the menu and menu items in Section 8.6. There you'll see that the menu and menu item variable names are generated by the IDE and begin with capital letters. Like other controls, you can change the variable names in the **Properties** window by modifying the **(Name)** property.

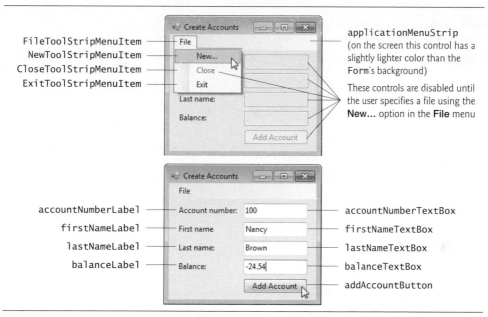

Fig. 8.5 | GUI for the **Create Accounts** app.

*Interacting with the **Create Accounts** App*

When the user initially executes this app, the **Close** menu item, the TextBoxes and the **Add Account** Button are *disabled* (Fig. 8.6(a))—the user can interact with these controls only after specifying the file into which the records will be saved. To begin creating a file of accounts, the user selects **File > New...** (Fig. 8.6(b)), which displays a **Save As** dialog (Fig. 8.6(c)) that allows the user to specify the name and location of the file into which the records will be placed. The **File** menu provides two other menu items—**Close** to close the file so the user can create another file and **Exit** to terminate the app. After the user specifies a file name, the app opens the file and *enables* the controls, so the user can begin entering account information. Figure 8.6(d)–(h) shows the sample data being entered for five accounts. The app does not depict how the records are stored in the file. This is a text file, so after you close the app, you can open the file in any text editor to see its contents. Figure 8.6(j) shows the file's contents in **Notepad**.

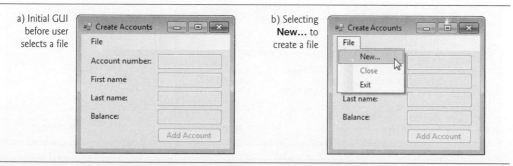

Fig. 8.6 | User creating a text file of account information. (Part I of 3.)

c) **Save As** dialog displayed when user selects **New...** from the **File** menu. In this case, the user is naming the file `Accounts.txt` and placing the file in the `C:\DataFiles` folder.

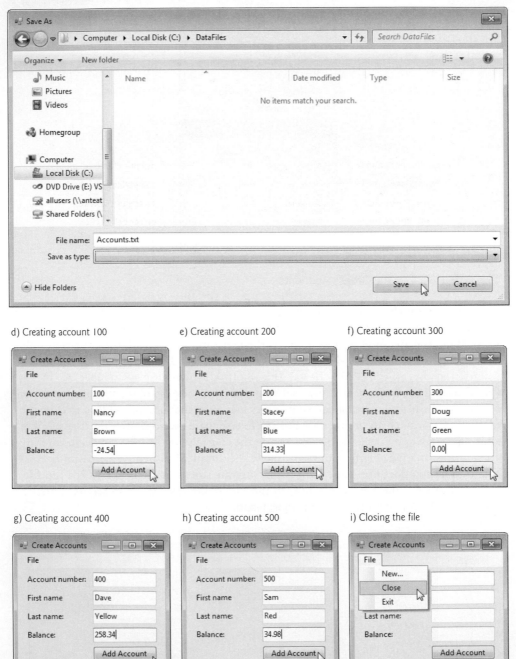

d) Creating account 100 e) Creating account 200 f) Creating account 300

g) Creating account 400 h) Creating account 500 i) Closing the file

Fig. 8.6 | User creating a text file of account information. (Part 2 of 3.)

j) The `Accounts.txt` file
open in **Notepad** to show
how the records were
written to the file. Note the
comma separators between
the data items

```
Accounts.txt - Notepad
File  Edit  Format  View  Help
100,Nancy,Brown,-24.54
200,Stacey,Blue,314.33
300,Doug,Green,0.00
400,Dave,Yellow,258.34
500,Sam,Red,34.98
```

Fig. 8.6 | User creating a text file of account information. (Part 3 of 3.)

8.5.1 Class CreateAccounts

Let's now study the declaration of class `CreateAccounts`, which begins in Fig. 8.7. Framework Class Library classes are grouped by functionality into **namespaces**, which make it easier for you to find the classes needed to perform particular tasks. Line 3 is an **Imports statement**, which indicates that we're using classes from the **System.IO namespace**. This namespace contains stream classes such as **StreamWriter** (for text output) and **StreamReader** (for text input). Line 6 declares `fileWriter` as an instance variable of type `StreamWriter`. We'll use this variable to interact with the file that the user selects.

```
1   ' Fig. 8.7: CreateAccounts.vb
2   ' App that creates a text file of account information.
3   Imports System.IO ' using classes from this namespace
4
5   Public Class CreateAccounts
6       Dim fileWriter As StreamWriter ' writes data to text file
7
```

Fig. 8.7 | App that creates a text file of account information.

You must import `System.IO` before you can use the namespace's classes. In fact, *all namespaces except System must be imported into a program to use the classes in those namespaces. Namespace System is imported by default into every program.* Classes like `String`, `Convert` and `Math` that we've used frequently in earlier examples are declared in the `System` namespace. So far, we have *not* used `Imports` statements in any of our programs, but we *have* used many classes from namespaces that *must* be imported. For example, all of the GUI controls you've used so far are classes in the `System.Windows.Forms` namespace.

So why were we able to compile those programs? When you create a project, each Visual Basic project type automatically imports several namespaces that are commonly used with that project type. You can see the namespaces (Fig. 8.8) that were automatically imported into your project by right clicking the project's name in the **Solution Explorer** window, selecting **Properties** from the menu and clicking the **References** tab. The list appears under **Imported namespaces:**—each namespace with a checkmark is automatically imported into the project. This app is a Windows Forms app. The `System.IO` namespace is not imported by default. To import a namespace, you can either use an `Imports` statement (as in line 3 of Fig. 8.7) or you can scroll through the list in Fig. 8.8 and check the checkbox for the namespace you wish to import.

Fig. 8.8 | Viewing the namespaces that are pre-Imported into a Windows Forms app.

8.5.2 Opening the File

When the user selects **File > New...**, method `NewToolStripMenuItem_Click` (Fig. 8.9) is called to handle the **New...** menu item's `Click` event. This method opens the file. First, line 12 calls method `CloseFile` (Fig. 8.11, lines 102–111) in case the user previously opened another file during the current execution of the app. `CloseFile` closes the file associated with this app's `StreamWriter`.

```
8      ' create a new file in which accounts can be stored
9      Private Sub NewToolStripMenuItem_Click(sender As Object,
10         e As EventArgs) Handles NewToolStripMenuItem.Click
11
12         CloseFile() ' ensure that any prior file is closed
13         Dim result As DialogResult ' stores result of Save dialog
14         Dim fileName As String ' name of file to save data
15
16         ' display dialog so user can choose the name of the file to save
17         Using fileChooser As New SaveFileDialog()
18            result = fileChooser.ShowDialog()
19            fileName = fileChooser.FileName ' get specified file name
20         End Using ' automatic call to fileChooser.Dispose() occurs here
21
22         ' if user did not click Cancel
23         If result <> Windows.Forms.DialogResult.Cancel Then
24            Try
25               ' open or create file for writing
26               fileWriter = New StreamWriter(fileName, True)
27
28               ' enable controls
29               CloseToolStripMenuItem.Enabled = True
30               addAccountButton.Enabled = True
31               accountNumberTextBox.Enabled = True
32               firstNameTextBox.Enabled = True
```

Fig. 8.9 | Using the `SaveFileDialog` to allow the user to select the file into which records will be written. (Part 1 of 2.)

```
33                    lastNameTextBox.Enabled = True
34                    balanceTextBox.Enabled = True
35              Catch ex As IOException
36                 MessageBox.Show("Error Opening File", "Error",
37                    MessageBoxButtons.OK, MessageBoxIcon.Error)
38              End Try
39           End If
40        End Sub ' NewToolStripMenuItem_Click
41
```

Fig. 8.9 | Using the `SaveFileDialog` to allow the user to select the file into which records will be written. (Part 2 of 2.)

Next, lines 17–20 of Fig. 8.9 display the **Save As** dialog and get the file name specified by the user. First, line 17 creates the `SaveFileDialog` object (namespace `System.Windows.Forms`) named `fileChooser`. Line 18 calls its **ShowDialog** method to display the `SaveFileDialog` (Fig. 8.6(c)). This dialog prevents the user from interacting with any other window in the app until the user closes it by clicking either **Save** or **Cancel**, so it's a *modal dialog*. The user selects the location where the file should be stored and specifies the file name, then clicks **Save**. Method `ShowDialog` returns a **DialogResult** enumeration constant specifying which button (**Save** or **Cancel**) the user clicked to close the dialog. This is assigned to the `DialogResult` variable `result` (line 18). Line 19 uses `SaveFileDialog` property **FileName** to obtain the location and name of the file.

8.5.3 Managing Resources with the Using Statement

Lines 17–20 introduce the **Using** statement, which simplifies writing code in which you obtain, use and release a resource. In this case, the resource is a `SaveFileDialog`. Windows and dialogs are limited system resources that occupy *memory* and should be returned to the system (to free up that memory) as soon as they're no longer needed. In all our previous apps, this happens when the app terminates. In a long-running app, if resources are not returned to the system when they're no longer needed, a **resource** leak occurs and the resources are not available for use in this or other apps. Objects that represent such resources typically provide a `Dispose` method that *must* be called to return the resources to the system. The `Using` statement in lines 17–20 creates a `SaveFileDialog` object, uses it in lines 18–19, then automatically calls its `Dispose` method to release the object's resources as soon as `End Using` is reached, thus guaranteeing that the resources are returned to the system and the memory they occupy is freed up (even if an exception occurs).

Line 23 tests whether the user clicked **Cancel** by comparing `result` to the constant `Windows.Forms.DialogResult.Cancel`. If not, line 26 creates a `StreamWriter` object that we'll use to write data to the file. The two arguments are a `String` representing the location and name of the file, and a `Boolean` indicating what to do if the file already exists. If the file doesn't exist, this statement creates the file. If the file does exist, the second argument (`True`) indicates that new data written to the file should be *appended* at the end of the file's current contents. If the second argument is `False` and the file already exists, *the file's contents will be discarded* and new data will be written starting at the *beginning* of the file. Lines 29–34 enable the **Close** menu item and the `TextBoxes` and `Button` that are used to enter records into the app. Lines 35–37 catch an **IOException** if there's a problem opening the file. If so, the app displays an error message. If no exception occurs, the file is opened for writing. Most file-processing operations have the potential to throw exceptions, so such operations are typically placed in Try statements.

8.5.4 Adding an Account to the File

After typing information in each TextBox, the user clicks the **Add Account** Button, which calls method addAccountButton_Click (Fig. 8.10) to save the data into the file. If the user entered a valid account number (that is, an integer greater than zero), lines 56–59 write the record to the file by invoking the StreamWriter's **WriteLine** method, which writes a sequence of characters to the file and positions the output cursor to the beginning of the next line in the file. We separate each field in the record with a comma in this example (this is known as a **comma-delimited text file**), and we place each record on its own line in the file. If an IOException occurs when attempting to write the record to the file, lines 64–66 Catch the exception and display an appropriate message to the user. Similarly, if the user entered invalid data in the accountNumberTextBox or balanceTextBox lines 67–69 catch the **FormatException**s thrown by class Convert's methods and display an appropriate error message. Lines 73–77 clear the TextBoxes and return the focus to the account-NumberTextBox so the user can enter the next record.

```vb
42      ' add an account to the file
43      Private Sub addAccountButton_Click(sender As Object,
44          e As EventArgs) Handles addAccountButton.Click
45
46          ' determine whether TextBox account field is empty
47          If accountNumberTextBox.Text <> String.Empty Then
48              ' try to store record to file
49              Try
50                  ' get account number
51                  Dim accountNumber As Integer =
52                      Convert.ToInt32(accountNumberTextBox.Text)
53
54                  If accountNumber > 0 Then ' valid account number?
55                      ' write record data to file separating fields by commas
56                      fileWriter.WriteLine(accountNumber & "," &
57                          firstNameTextBox.Text & "," &
58                          lastNameTextBox.Text & "," &
59                          Convert.ToDecimal(balanceTextBox.Text))
60                  Else
61                      MessageBox.Show("Invalid Account Number", "Error",
62                          MessageBoxButtons.OK, MessageBoxIcon.Error)
63                  End If
64              Catch ex As IOException
65                  MessageBox.Show("Error Writing to File", "Error",
66                      MessageBoxButtons.OK, MessageBoxIcon.Error)
67              Catch ex As FormatException
68                  MessageBox.Show("Invalid account number or balance",
69                      "Format Error", MessageBoxButtons.OK, MessageBoxIcon.Error)
70              End Try
71          End If
```

Fig. 8.10 | Writing an account record to the file. (Part 1 of 2.)

```
72
73          accountNumberTextBox.Clear()
74          firstNameTextBox.Clear()
75          lastNameTextBox.Clear()
76          balanceTextBox.Clear()
77          accountNumberTextBox.Focus()
78       End Sub ' addAccountButton_Click
79
```

Fig. 8.10 | Writing an account record to the file. (Part 2 of 2.)

8.5.5 Closing the File and Terminating the App

When the user selects **File > Close**, method CloseToolStripMenuItem_Click (Fig. 8.11, lines 81–91) calls method CloseFile (lines 102–111) to close the file. Then lines 85–90 *disable* the controls that should not be available when a file is not open.

```
80       ' close the currently open file and disable controls
81       Private Sub CloseToolStripMenuItem_Click(sender As Object,
82          e As EventArgs) Handles CloseToolStripMenuItem.Click
83
84          CloseFile() ' close currently open file
85          CloseToolStripMenuItem.Enabled = False
86          addAccountButton.Enabled = False
87          accountNumberTextBox.Enabled = False
88          firstNameTextBox.Enabled = False
89          lastNameTextBox.Enabled = False
90          balanceTextBox.Enabled = False
91       End Sub ' CloseToolStripMenuItem_Click
92
93       ' exit the app
94       Private Sub ExitToolStripMenuItem_Click(sender As Object,
95          e As EventArgs) Handles ExitToolStripMenuItem.Click
96
97          CloseFile() ' close the file before terminating app
98          Application.Exit() ' terminate the app
99       End Sub ' ExitToolStripMenuItem_Click
100
101      ' close the file
102      Sub CloseFile()
103         If fileWriter IsNot Nothing Then
104            Try
105               fileWriter.Close() ' close StreamWriter
106            Catch ex As IOException
107               MessageBox.Show("Error closing file", "Error",
108                  MessageBoxButtons.OK, MessageBoxIcon.Error)
109            End Try
110         End If
111      End Sub ' CloseFile
112   End Class ' CreateAccounts
```

Fig. 8.11 | Closing the file and terminating the app.

When the user clicks the **Exit** menu item, method ExitToolStripMenuItem_Click (lines 94–99) responds to the menu item's Click event by exiting the app. Line 97 closes the StreamWriter and the associated file, then line 98 terminates the app. The call to method Close (line 105) is located in a Try block. Method **Close** throws an IOException if the file cannot be closed properly. In this case, it's important to notify the user that the information in the file or stream might be corrupted.

8.6 Building Menus with the Windows Forms Designer

In the test-drive of the **Credit Inquiry** app (Section 8.4) and in the overview of the **Create Accounts** app (Section 8.5), we demonstrated how menus provide a convenient way to organize the commands that you use to interact with an app without "cluttering" its user interface. Menus contain groups of related commands. When a command is selected, the app performs a specific action (for example, select a file to open, exit the app, etc.).

Menus make it simple and straightforward to locate an app's commands. They can also make it easier for users to use apps. For example, many apps provide a **File** menu that contains an **Exit** menu item to *terminate* the app. If this menu item is always placed in the **File** menu, then users become accustomed to going to the **File** menu to terminate an app. When they use a new app and it has a **File** menu, they'll already be familiar with the location of the **Exit** command.

The menu that contains a menu item is that menu item's **parent menu**. In the **Create Accounts** app, **File** is the parent menu that contains three menu items—**New...**, **Close** and **Exit**.

Adding a *MenuStrip* to the *Form*
Before you can place a menu on your app, you must provide a MenuStrip to organize and manage the app's menus. Double click the MenuStrip control in the **Toolbox**. This creates a menu bar (the MenuStrip) across the top of the Form (below the title bar; Fig. 8.12) and places a MenuStrip icon in the **component tray** (the gray area) at the bottom of the designer. You can access the MenuStrip's properties in the **Properties** window by clicking the MenuStrip icon in the component tray. We set the MenuStrip's **(Name)** property to applicationMenuStrip.

Adding a *ToolStripMenuItem* to *MenuStrip*
You can now use **Design** mode to create and edit menus for your app. To add a menu, click the **Type Here** TextBox (Fig. 8.12) in the menu bar and type the menu's name. For the **File** menu, type &File (we'll explain the & in a moment) then press *Enter*. This creates a ToolStripMenuItem that the IDE automatically names FileToolStripMenuItem. Additional **Type Here** TextBoxes appear, allowing you to add menu items to the menu or add more menus to the menu bar (Fig. 8.13). Most menus and menu items provide **access shortcuts** (or **keyboard shortcuts**) that allow users to open a menu or select a menu item by using the keyboard. For example, most apps allow you to open the **File** menu by typing *Alt* + *F*. The letter that's used as the shortcut is underlined in the GUI when you press the *Alt* key. To specify the shortcut key, type an ampersand (&) before the character to be underlined—so &File underlines the **F** in **File**.

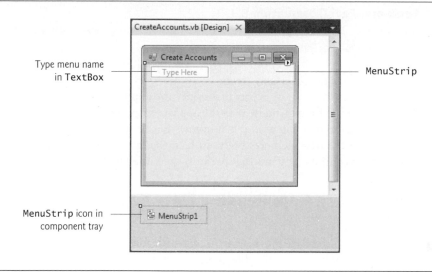

Fig. 8.12 | Editing menus in Visual Studio.

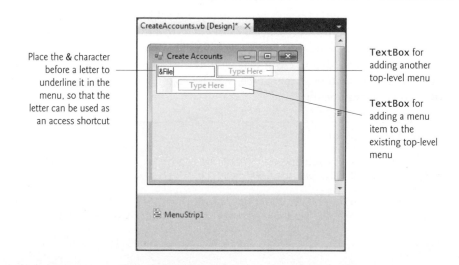

Fig. 8.13 | Adding ToolStripMenuItems to a MenuStrip.

Adding Menu Items to the File Menu

To add the **New...**, **Close** and **Exit** menu items to the **File** menu, type &New..., &Close and E&xit (one at a time) into the TextBox that appears below the **File** menu. When you press *Enter* after each, a new TextBox appears below that item so you can add another menu item. Placing the & before the x in Exit makes the x the access key—x is commonly used as the access key for the **Exit** menu item. The menu editor automatically names the Tool-StripMenuItems for the **New...**, **Close** and **Exit** menu items as NewToolStripMenuItem, CloseToolStripMenuItem and ExitToolStripMenuItem, respectively.

Look-and-Feel Observation 8.1

*By convention, place an ellipsis (...) after the name of a menu item that, when selected, displays a dialog (e.g. **New**...).*

Creating Event Handlers for the Menu Items

Like Buttons, menu items have Click events that notify the app when an item is selected. To create the event handler for a menu item so the app can respond when the menu item is selected, double click the menu item in the Windows Forms Designer then insert your event handling code in the new method's body. In fact, the same event-handler method can be used for Buttons and menu items that perform the same task.

8.7 Credit Inquiry App: Reading Data Sequentially from a Text File

Now that we've presented the code for creating the file of accounts, let's develop the code for the **Credit Inquiry** app which reads that file. Much of the code in this example is similar to the **Create Accounts** app, so we'll discuss only the unique aspects of the app.

8.7.1 Implementing the Credit Inquiry App

The declaration of class CreditInquiry begins in Fig. 8.14. Line 4 imports the System.IO namespace, which contains the StreamReader class that we'll use to read from the text file in this example. Line 7 declares the instance variable fileName in which we store the file name selected by the user (that is, credit manager) in the **Open** dialog (Fig. 8.3(c)). Lines 9–13 declare the enumeration AccountType, which creates constants that represent the types of accounts that can be displayed.

```
1   ' Fig. 8.14: CreditInquiry.vb
2   ' Read a file sequentially and display contents based on
3   ' account type specified by user (credit, debit or zero balances).
4   Imports System.IO ' using classes from this namespace
5
6   Public Class CreditInquiry
7      Private fileName As String ' name of file containing account data
8
9      Enum AccountType ' constants representing account types
10        CREDIT
11        DEBIT
12        ZERO
13     End Enum ' AccountType
14
```

Fig. 8.14 | Declaring the fileName instance variable and creating the AccountType enumeration that's used to specify the type of account to display.

8.7.2 Selecting the File to Process

When the user selects **File > Open**..., the event handler OpenToolStripMenuItem_Click (Fig. 8.15, lines 16–33) executes. Line 22 creates an **OpenFileDialog**, and line 23 calls its

ShowDialog method to display the **Open** dialog, in which the user selects the file to open. Line 24 stores the selected file name in **fileName**.

```
15      ' opens a file in which accounts are stored
16      Private Sub OpenToolStripMenuItem_Click(sender As Object,
17         e As EventArgs) Handles OpenToolStripMenuItem.Click
18
19         Dim result As DialogResult ' stores result of Open dialog
20
21         ' create dialog box enabling user to open file
22         Using fileChooser As New OpenFileDialog()
23            result = fileChooser.ShowDialog()
24            fileName = fileChooser.FileName ' get specified file name
25         End Using ' automatic call to fileChooser.Dispose() occurs here
26
27         ' if user did not click Cancel, enable Buttons
28         If result <> Windows.Forms.DialogResult.Cancel Then
29            creditBalancesButton.Enabled = True
30            debitBalancesButton.Enabled = True
31            zeroBalancesButton.Enabled = True
32         End If
33      End Sub ' OpenToolStripMenuItem_Click
34
35      ' exit the app
36      Private Sub ExitToolStripMenuItem_Click(sender As Object,
37         e As EventArgs) Handles ExitToolStripMenuItem.Click
38
39         Application.Exit() ' terminate the app
40      End Sub ' ExitToolStripMenuItem_Click
41
```

Fig. 8.15 | Event handlers for the **Open...** and **Exit** menu items.

8.7.3 Specifying the Type of Records to Display

When the user clicks the **Credit Balances**, **Debit Balances** or **Zero Balances** Button, the app invokes the corresponding event-handler method—creditBalancesButton_Click (Fig. 8.16, lines 43–47), debitBalancesButton_Click (lines 50–54) or zeroBalancesButton_Click (lines 57–61). Each of these methods calls method DisplayAccounts (Fig. 8.17), passing a constant from the AccountType enumeration as an argument. Method DisplayAccounts then displays the matching accounts.

```
42      ' display accounts with credit balances
43      Private Sub creditBalancesButton_Click(sender As Object,
44         e As EventArgs) Handles creditBalancesButton.Click
45
46         DisplayAccounts(AccountType.CREDIT) ' displays credit balances
47      End Sub ' creditBalancesButton_Click
48
```

Fig. 8.16 | Each Button event handler calls method DisplayAccounts and passes the appropriate AccountType as an argument to specify which accounts to display. (Part 1 of 2.)

```
49      ' display accounts with debit balances
50      Private Sub debitBalancesButton_Click(sender As Object,
51         e As EventArgs) Handles debitBalancesButton.Click
52
53         DisplayAccounts(AccountType.DEBIT) ' displays debit balances
54      End Sub ' debitBalancesButton_Click
55
56      ' display accounts with zero balances
57      Private Sub zeroBalancesButton_Click(sender As Object,
58         e As EventArgs) Handles zeroBalancesButton.Click
59
60         DisplayAccounts(AccountType.ZERO) ' displays zero balances
61      End Sub ' zeroBalancesButton_Click
62
```

Fig. 8.16 | Each `Button` event handler calls method `DisplayAccounts` and passes the appropriate `AccountType` as an argument to specify which accounts to display. (Part 2 of 2.)

8.7.4 Displaying the Records

Method `DisplayAccounts` (Fig. 8.17, lines 64–104) receives as an argument an `AccountType` constant specifying the type of accounts to display. The method reads the entire file one record at a time until the end of the file is reached, displaying a record only if its balance matches the type of accounts specified by the user.

Opening the File
Line 65 declares the `StreamReader` variable `fileReader` that will be used to interact with the file. Line 72 opens the file by passing the `fileName` instance variable to the `StreamReader` constructor.

```
63      ' display accounts of specified type
64      Sub DisplayAccounts(accountType As AccountType)
65         Dim fileReader As StreamReader = Nothing
66
67         ' read and display file information
68         Try
69            accountsTextBox.Text = "The accounts are:" & vbCrLf
70
71            ' open file for reading
72            fileReader = New StreamReader(fileName)
73
74            ' read file and display lines that match the balance type
75            Do While Not fileReader.EndOfStream ' while not end of file
76               Dim line As String = fileReader.ReadLine() ' read line
77               Dim fields() As String = line.Split(","c) ' split into fields
78
```

Fig. 8.17 | Method `DisplayAccounts` opens the file, reads one record at a time, displays the record if it matches the selected `AccountType` and closes the file when all records have been processed. (Part 1 of 2.)

```
79                        ' get data from fields array
80                        Dim accountNumber As Integer = Convert.ToInt32(fields(0))
81                        Dim firstName As String = fields(1)
82                        Dim lastName As String = fields(2)
83                        Dim balance As Decimal = Convert.ToDecimal(fields(3))
84
85                        If ShouldDisplay(balance, accountType) Then
86                            accountsTextBox.AppendText(accountNumber & vbTab &
87                                firstName & vbTab & lastName & vbTab &
88                                String.Format("{0:C}", balance) & vbCrLf)
89                        End If
90                    Loop
91                Catch ex As IOException
92                    MessageBox.Show("Cannot Read File", "Error",
93                        MessageBoxButtons.OK, MessageBoxIcon.Error)
94                Finally ' ensure that file gets closed
95                    If fileReader IsNot Nothing Then
96                        Try
97                            fileReader.Close() ' close StreamReader
98                        Catch ex As IOException
99                            MessageBox.Show("Error closing file", "Error",
100                                MessageBoxButtons.OK, MessageBoxIcon.Error)
101                        End Try
102                    End If
103                End Try
104        End Sub ' DisplayAccounts
105
106        ' determine whether to display given account based on the balance
107        Function ShouldDisplay(balance As Double,
108            type As AccountType) As Boolean
109
110            If balance < 0 AndAlso type = AccountType.CREDIT Then
111                Return True ' record should be displayed
112            ElseIf balance > 0 AndAlso type = AccountType.DEBIT Then
113                Return True ' record should be displayed
114            ElseIf balance = 0 AndAlso type = AccountType.ZERO Then
115                Return True ' record should be displayed
116            End If
117
118            Return False ' record should not be displayed
119        End Function ' ShouldDisplay
120    End Class ' Credit Inquiry
```

Fig. 8.17 | Method `DisplayAccounts` opens the file, reads one record at a time, displays the record if it matches the selected `AccountType` and closes the file when all records have been processed. (Part 2 of 2.)

Reading and Processing Records

The company could have many separate files containing account information. So this app does not know in advance how many records will be processed. In file processing, we receive an indication that the end of the file has been reached when we've read the entire contents of a file. For a `StreamReader`, this is when its **EndOfStream** property returns True (line 75).

As long as the end of the file has not been reached, line 76 uses the StreamReader's **ReadLine method** (which returns a String) to read one line of text from the file. Recall from Section 8.5 that a each line of text in the file represents one "record" and that the record's fields are delimited by commas. To access the record's data, we need to break the String into its separate fields. This is known as **tokenizing** the String. Line 77 breaks the line of text into fields using String method **Split**, which receives a *delimiter* as an argument. In this case, the delimiter is the *character literal* `","c`—indicating that the delimiter is a comma. A character literal looks like a String literal that contains one character and is followed immediately by the letter c. Method Split returns an array of Strings representing the tokens, which we assign to array variable fields.

Preparing to Display the Record

Lines 80–83 assign the tokens to the local variables accountNumber, firstName, lastName and balance. Line 85 calls method ShouldDisplay (lines 107–119) to determine whether the current record should be displayed. If so, lines 86–88 display the record. If the balance is *negative*, the currency format specifier (C) formats the value in *parentheses* (Fig. 8.4(b)). Method ShouldDisplay receives the balance and the AccountType as arguments. If the balance represents the specified AccountType, the method returns True and the record will be displayed by method DisplayAccounts; otherwise, it returns False and the record will not be displayed.

Ensuring that the File is Closed Properly

When performing file processing, exceptions can occur. In this example, if the app is unable to open the file or unable to read from the file, IOExceptions will occur. For this reason, file-processing code normally appears in a Try block. Regardless of whether an app experiences exceptions while processing a file, the app should close the file when it's no longer needed. Suppose we put the statement that closes the StreamReader after the Do While...Loop at line 91. If no exceptions occur, the Try block executes normally and the file is closed. However, if an *exception* occurs, the Try block terminates immediately—*before* the StreamReader can be closed. We could duplicate the statement that closes the StreamReader in the Catch block, but this would make the code more difficult to modify and maintain. We could also place the statement that closes the StreamReader after the Try statement; however, if the Try block terminated due to a Return statement, code following the Try statement would never execute.

To address these problems, Visual Basic's exception-handling mechanism provides the optional **Finally block**, which—if present—is *guaranteed to execute* regardless of whether the Try block executes successfully or an exception occurs. This makes the Finally block an ideal location in which to place *resource release code* for resources that are acquired and manipulated in the corresponding Try block (such as files). By placing the statement that closes the StreamReader in a Finally block, we ensure that the file will always be closed properly.

Local variables in a Try block cannot be accessed in the corresponding Finally block. For this reason, variables that must be accessed in both a Try block and its corresponding Finally block should be declared before the Try block, as we did with the StreamReader variable (line 65).

Relationship Between the **Using** *and* **Try** *Statements*

In Section 8.5.3, we discussed how a Using statement manages resources. The Using statement is actually a shorthand notation for a Try statement with a Finally block. For example, the Using statement in Fig. 8.15 (lines 22–25) is equivalent to the following code

```vb
Dim fileChooser As New OpenFileDialog()
Try
    result = fileChooser.ShowDialog()
    fileName = fileChooser.FileName ' get specified file name
Finally
    fileChooser.Dispose()
End Try
```

8.8 Wrap-Up

In this chapter, you learned how to use file processing to create and manipulate persistent data. You learned that data is stored as 0s and 1s, and that combinations of these values are used to form bytes, fields, records and eventually files. Next, you learned how to use sequential-access file processing to manipulate records in text files. We began by creating a text-file of accounts using a StreamWriter. We then used a StreamReader to read the contents of the file into a separate app for processing.

In Chapter 9, we show you how to create your own classes and how to use those classes to create objects in your apps. In particular, we present an Account class that could represent a bank account, Card and DeckOfCards classes that could be used to implement a card game, and a Time class that represents the time in 24-hour clock format.

Summary

Section 8.1 Introduction

- Variables and arrays offer only temporary storage of data—the data is lost, for example, when a local variable "goes out of scope" or when the app terminates.

- Files and databases are used for long-term retention of large (and often *vast*) amounts of data, even after the app that created the data terminates.

- Data maintained in files is often called persistent data.

- Computers store files on secondary storage devices.

Section 8.2 Data Hierarchy

- All data items that computers process are reduced to combinations of 0s and 1s.

- The smallest data item that computers support is called a bit and has the value 0 or 1.

- Digits, letters and special symbols are referred to as characters. The set of all characters used to write programs and represent data items on a particular computer is called that computer's character set. Every character in a computer's character set is represented as a pattern of 0s and 1s.

- A byte is composed of eight bits.

- Characters in Visual Basic are Unicode characters composed of two bytes each.

- A field is a group of characters that conveys meaning.

- A record is composed of related fields.

- A data file can be implemented as a group of related records
- Typically, at least one field in each record is chosen as a record key, which uniquely identifies a record as belonging to a particular person or entity and distinguishes that record from all others.
- The most common type of file organization is a sequential file, in which records typically are stored in order by record-key field.
- Related files often are stored in a database. A collection of programs designed to create and manage databases is called a database management system (DBMS).

Section 8.3 Files and Streams
- Visual Basic views a file as a sequential stream of bytes.
- Visual Basic imposes no structure on files. You must structure files to meet the requirements of your apps.

Section 8.5 Writing Data Sequentially to a Text File
- The MenuStrip control enables you to place a menu bar in your window.
- ToolStripMenuItem controls are used to create menus and menu items.

Section 8.5.1 Class CreateAccounts
- Framework Class Library classes are grouped by functionality into namespaces.
- An Imports statement indicates that you're using classes from a particular namespace.
- The System.IO namespace contains stream classes such as StreamWriter and StreamReader.
- All namespaces except System must be imported into an app to use the classes in those namespaces. Namespace System is imported by default into every app.
- Each Visual Basic project type imports several commonly used namespaces.

Section 8.5.2 Opening the File
- A SaveFileDialog object's ShowDialog method displays a modal dialog that allows the user to specify the location and name of a file. The method returns a DialogResult enumeration constant specifying which button (**Save** or **Cancel**) the user clicked to close the dialog.
- SaveFileDialog property FileName returns the location and name of the selected file.

Section 8.5.3 Managing Resources with the Using Statement
- The Using statement simplifies writing code in which you obtain, use and release a resource.
- Objects which represent resources that should be returned to the system typically provide a Dispose method that must be called to return the resources.
- When End Using is reached, the Using statement automatically calls the Dispose method of the object created in the statement's first line.
- The StreamWriter constructor receives two arguments—a String representing the location and name of the file, and a Boolean indicating what to do if the file already exists. If the file doesn't exist, it's created. If the file does exist, a second argument of True indicates that new data written to the file should be appended to the end of the file's current contents. If the second argument is False and the file already exists, the file's contents will be discarded and new data will be written starting at the beginning of the file.
- Most file-processing operations have the potential to throw IOExceptions, so such operations are typically placed in Try statements.

Section 8.5.4 Adding an Account to the File
- `StreamWriter` method `WriteLine` writes a sequence of characters to a file and positions the output cursor to the beginning of the next line in the file.

Section 8.5.5 Closing the File and Terminating the App
- `StreamWriter` method `Close` closes the stream and the corresponding file.

Section 8.6 Building Menus with the Windows Forms Designer
- Menus contain groups of related commands that, when selected, cause the app to perform specific actions.
- A `MenuStrip` organizes an app's menus. You can access the `MenuStrip`'s properties in the **Properties** window by clicking the `MenuStrip` icon in the component tray.
- You can use **Design** mode to create and edit menus for your app.
- To specify the shortcut key for a menu or menu item, type an ampersand (&) before the character to be underlined in the menu or menu item's name.
- Like `Buttons`, menu items have `Click` events that notify the app when an item is selected.

Section 8.7 Credit Inquiry App: Reading Data Sequentially from a Text File
- `OpenFileDialog` method `ShowDialog` display an **Open** dialog, in which the user can select the file to open. The method returns a `DialogResult` enumeration constant specifying which button (**Open** or **Cancel**) the user clicked to close the dialog.
- `OpenFileDialog` property `FileName` returns the location and name of the selected file.
- A `StreamReader` reads text from the file specified as the argument to the object's constructor.
- `StreamReader` property `EndOfStream` returns `True` if the end of the file has been reached.
- `StreamReader` method `ReadLine` returns one line of text from a file as a `String`.
- `String` method `Split` receives a delimiter as an argument and tokenizes a `String`, using the delimiter to separate the tokens. Method `Split` returns an array of `Strings` representing the tokens.
- Visual Basic's exception-handling mechanism provides the optional `Finally` block, which—if present—is guaranteed to execute regardless of whether the `Try` block executes successfully or an exception occurs. The `Finally` block is an ideal location in which to place resource release code for resources such as files that are acquired and manipulated in the corresponding `Try` block.
- Local variables in a `Try` block cannot be accessed in the corresponding `Finally` block.
- The `Using` statement is a shorthand notation for a `Try` statement with a `Finally` block.

Terminology

Self-Review Exercises

8.1 Answer each of the following questions:

a) The smallest data item a computer can process is called a _____.

   1. database   2. byte

   3. file   4. bit

b) A group of related records is stored in a _____.

   1. file   2. field

   3. bit   4. byte

c) Data maintained in a file is called _____.

   1. persistent data   2. bits

   3. secondary data   4. databases

d) Methods from the _____ class can be used to write data to a file.

   1. StreamReader   2. WriteFile

   3. StreamWriter   4. None of the above

e) Namespace _____ provides the classes and methods you need to perform file processing.

   1. System.IO   2. System.Files

   3. System.Stream   4. System.Windows.Forms

f) Sometimes a group of related files is called a _____.

   1. field   2. database

   3. collection   4. byte

g) A(n) _____ allows the user to select a file to open.

   1. CreateFileDialog   2. OpenFileDialog

   3. MessageBox   4. None of the above

h) Digits, letters and special symbols are referred to as _____.

   1. constants   2. Integers

   3. characters   4. None of the above

i) StreamReader method _____ reads a line from a file.

   1. ReadLine   2. Read

   3. ReadAll   4. ReadToNewline

j) A _____ contains information that's read in the order it was written.
   1. sequential-access file
   2. `StreamWriter`
   3. `StreamReader`
   4. None of the above

k) Methods from class _____ can be used to read data from a file.
   1. `StreamWriter`
   2. `FileReader`
   3. `StreamReader`
   4. None of the above.

Answers to Self-Review Exercises

8.1   a) 4. b) 1. c) 1. d) 3. e) 1. f) 2. g) 2. h) 3. i) 1. j) 1. k) 3.

Exercises

8.2   *(Enhanced Class Average App)* The class average app of Fig. 4.12 allowed the user to enter a set of grades then calculate and display the total of the grades and the class average. Create an app that enables the user to select a file in which to store grades. The app should allow the user to write any number of grades into that file and it should write one grade per line. Next, modify the app of Fig. 4.12 to allow the user to specify the location and name of a file containing grades. The app should read the grades from the file, then display the total of the grades and the class average.

8.3   *(Enhanced Student Poll App)* Figure 7.4 contains an array of survey responses that's hard-coded into the app. Suppose we wish to process survey results that are stored in a file. First, create an app that enables the user to write survey responses to a file. Use a `StreamWriter` to create a file called `SurveyResponses.txt` and write each response on a separate line. Modify the code in Fig. 7.4 to read the survey responses from `SurveyResponses.txt` by using a `StreamReader`. The app should continue to read responses until it reaches the end of file. The results should be output to the Text-Box.

8.4   *(Telephone-Number Word Generator)* Modify the telephone-number word generator that you created in Exercise 7.15 to write to a file every possible seven-letter word combination corresponding to a telephone number.

8.5   *(Writing a Grade Report to a File)* Modify the Grade Report app in Section 7.15 to provide an option that allows the user to write the entire grade report to a file. The report should include all of the information in the `gradesListBox`, the class average and the grade distribution chart from the `barChartListBox`. To get the data from the `ListBoxes`, use each `ListBox`'s `Items` collection. For example, to output the first line in the `gradesListBox`, you'd write the value of the expression `gradesListBox.Items(0).ToString()` to the file.

8.6   *(Reading Grades into a Two-Dimensional Array)* Modify your solution to Exercise 8.5 to allow the user to read the grades from a text file, rather than entering them via the GUI. Assume that the file contains 10 lines of text and that each line contains three grades.

9

Object-Oriented Programming: Classes and Objects

Nothing can have value without being an object of utility.
—Karl Marx

Your public servants serve you right.
—Adlai E. Stevenson

Objectives

In this chapter you'll:

- Declare a class and use it to create an object.
- Implement a class's behaviors as methods.
- Implement a class's attributes as instance variables and properties.
- Use a constructor to ensure that an object's attributes are initialized.
- Use properties to ensure that only valid data is placed in attributes.
- Construct new classes that reuse existing classes via composition.
- Implement classwide information with **Shared** class variables.
- Use the **Object Browser** to discover the capabilities of the classes in the .NET Framework Class Library.

Outline

9.1 Introduction

We introduced the basic terminology and concepts of object-oriented programming in Section 1.6. Many apps consist of one or more classes, each containing one or more methods. If you become part of a development team in industry, you may work on apps that contain hundreds, or even thousands, of classes. In this chapter, we motivate the notion of classes with real-world examples and use complete working apps to demonstrate creating your own classes and manipulating objects of those classes.

9.2 Classes, Objects, Methods and Instance Variables

We begin with a real-world analogy to help you understand classes and their contents. Suppose you want to drive a car and make it go faster by pressing its accelerator pedal. What must happen before you can do this? Well, before you can drive a car, someone has to design it. A car typically begins as engineering drawings, similar to the blueprints used to design a house. These engineering drawings include the design for an accelerator pedal to make the car go faster. The accelerator pedal "hides" the complex mechanisms that actually make the car go faster, just as the brake pedal "hides" the mechanisms that slow the car and the steering wheel "hides" the mechanisms that turn the car. This "hiding" enables people with little or no knowledge of how automotive hardware works to easily drive a car.

Unfortunately, you cannot drive a car's engineering drawings. Before you can drive a car, the car must be built from the engineering drawings that describe it. A completed car has an *actual* accelerator pedal to make it go faster, but even that's not enough—the car will not accelerate on its own, so the driver must *press* the accelerator pedal.

Now let's use our car example to introduce some key programming concepts. Performing a task in a program requires a method. The method describes the mechanisms that actually perform its tasks. The method hides these mechanisms from its user, just as the accelerator pedal of a car hides from the driver the mechanisms that make the car go faster. We begin by creating a program unit called a *class* to house a method, just as a car's engineering drawings house the design of an accelerator pedal. In a class, you provide one or more methods that are designed to perform the class's tasks. For example, the class in the next section represents a bank account and contains methods to deposit money in the account, withdraw money from the account and inquire what the current balance is.

Just as you cannot drive an engineering drawing of a car, you cannot "drive" a class. Just as someone has to build a car from its engineering drawings before you can actually drive it, *you must build an object of a class before you can get a program to perform the tasks the class describes how to do.*

When you drive a car, pressing its gas pedal sends a message to the car to perform a task—that is, to go faster. Similarly, you send **messages** to an object—each message is a method call that tells one of the object's methods to perform its task. Any program code that interacts with any objects of a particular class (from outside those objects) is known as a **client** of that class—objects provide services to the class's clients.

We've used the car analogy to introduce classes, objects and methods. In addition to the capabilities a car provides, it also has many *attributes*, such as its color, the number of doors, the amount of gas in its tank, its current speed and its odometer reading. Like the car's capabilities, its attributes are represented as part of a car's design in its engineering diagrams. As you drive a car, these attributes are always associated with the car. For example, each car *knows* how much gas is in its *own* gas tank, but *not* how much is in the tanks of *other* cars. Similarly, an object has attributes that are carried with it as it's used in a program. These attributes are specified in the object's class. For example, a bank account object has a balance attribute that represents the amount of money in the account. Each bank account object knows the balance in the account it represents, but *not* the balances of *other* accounts. Attributes are specified by a class's instance variables.

9.3 Account Class

We begin with a business example that consists of classes `Account` and `AccountTest`. The `Account` class (declared in file `Account.vb` of Fig. 9.2) represents a bank account that has a balance—an actual bank account class would include other information, such as name, address, telephone number and account number. The `AccountTest` class (Fig. 9.3) creates and uses an object of class `Account`. The classes are placed in separate files for clarity, but it's possible to place them in the same file. The GUI for the `AccountTest` app is shown in Fig. 9.1. When the program initially executes, it creates an `Account` object and displays its initial balance in the `accountBalanceValueLabel`. The user can enter a deposit or withdrawal amount in the `inputTextBox`, then press the **Deposit** Button to make a deposit or the **Withdraw** Button to make a withdrawal. After each operation, the `accountBalanceValueLabel` is updated with the new balance.

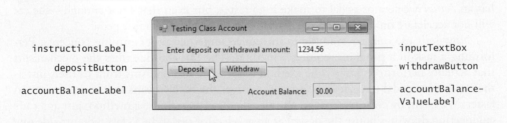

Fig. 9.1 | GUI for the app that tests class `Account`.

Adding a Class to a Project

For each example in this chapter, you'll add a class to your project. To do this, right click the project name in the **Solution Explorer** and select **Add > Class...** from the menu that appears. In the **Add New Item** dialog that appears, enter the name of your new file—in this case Account.vb—then click the **Add** Button. A new file will be added to your project with an empty Account class. Add the code from Fig. 9.2 to this file.

Account Class Declaration

The Account class declaration (Fig. 9.2) begins at line 3. The keyword **Public** is an **access modifier**. Only Public classes can be reused in other projects. Every class declaration contains keyword **Class** followed immediately by the class's name. Every class's body ends with the keywords **End Class**, as in line 49.

```
 1   ' Fig. 9.2: Account.vb
 2   ' Account class for maintaining a bank account balance.
 3   Public Class Account
 4      Private balanceValue As Decimal ' instance variable stores the balance
 5
 6      ' constructor initializes balanceValue
 7      Public Sub New(Optional initialBalance As Decimal = 0D)
 8         ' if initialBalance is less than 0, throw an exception
 9         If initialBalance < 0D Then
10            Throw New ArgumentOutOfRangeException(
11               "Initial balance must be greater than or equal to 0.")
12         End If
13
14         balanceValue = initialBalance ' initialize balanceValue
15      End Sub ' New
16
17      ' deposit money to the account
18      Public Sub Deposit(depositAmount As Decimal)
19         ' if depositAmount is less than or equal to 0, throw an exception
20         If depositAmount <= 0D Then
21            Throw New ArgumentOutOfRangeException(
22               "Deposit amount must be positive.")
23         End If
24
25         balanceValue += depositAmount ' add depositAmount to balanceValue
26      End Sub ' Deposit
27
28      ' withdraw money from the account
29      Public Sub Withdraw(withdrawalAmount As Decimal)
30         ' if withdrawalAmount is greater than Balance, throw an exception
31         If withdrawalAmount > Balance Then  ' invokes lines 45-47
32            Throw New ArgumentOutOfRangeException(
33               "Withdrawal amount must be less than or equal to balance.")
34         ElseIf withdrawalAmount <= 0D Then
35            Throw New ArgumentOutOfRangeException(
36               "Withrawal amount must be positive.")
37         End If
38
```

Fig. 9.2 | Account class for maintaining a bank account balance. (Part 1 of 2.)

```
39            ' subtract withdrawalAmount from balanceValue
40            balanceValue -= withdrawalAmount
41        End Sub ' Withdraw
42
43        ' return the current balance
44        Public ReadOnly Property Balance As Decimal
45            Get
46                Return balanceValue
47            End Get
48        End Property ' Balance
49    End Class ' Account
```

Fig. 9.2 | Account class for maintaining a bank account balance. (Part 2 of 2.)

Account *Class Instance Variables*

Class Account contains one Decimal instance variable—balanceValue (line 4)—that represents the Account's balance. In earlier examples, we declared instance variables with the keyword Dim. Here, we use the **Private member-access modifier**. Class members declared with member access modifier Private are accessible *only* within the class, which gives the class complete control over how those members are used. This is known as **encapsulating** the data in the class. Class members declared with member-access modifier Public are accessible wherever the program has a *reference* to an Account object.

Instance variables declared with Dim default to Private access. For clarity, every instance variable and method definition should be preceded by a member access modifier. We'll explicitly use Private rather than Dim to indicate that our instance variables are Private.

Account *Class Constructor and Throwing Exceptions*

When you create an object of a class, the class's **constructor** is called to initialize the object. *A constructor call is required for every object that's created.* By default, the compiler provides a **default constructor** with no parameters in any class that does not explicitly include a constructor. Alternatively, you can provide a **parameterless constructor** that contains code and takes no parameters, or that takes only Optional parameters so you can call it with no arguments. If you provide *any* constructors for a class, the compiler will *not* provide a default constructor for that class.

Constructors must be named New and are generally declared Public—Private constructors are beyond the scope of the book. Constructors are implemented as Sub procedures, *because they cannot return values.* Like methods, they *can* be overloaded.

Class Account defines a constructor (lines 7–15). It declares one Optional parameter with a default value of 0D (line 7) that represents the Account's initial balance. Because the *only* parameter is Optional, this constructor also serves as the class's parameterless constructor—it can be called with no arguments. Lines 9–12 validate the initialBalance parameter's value. If it's greater than or equal to 0, line 14 assigns initialBalance to the balanceValue instance variable. We assume that an Account cannot have a negative initial balance, so if initialBalance is negative, the constructor **throws an exception** of type **ArgumentOutOfRangeException** (lines 10–11), which notifies the client code that an invalid argument was passed to the constructor. As you learned in Chapter 7, you can use Try...Catch to catch exceptions and attempt to recover from them, which we'll do in Fig. 9.3. The **Throw statement** (Fig. 9.2, lines 10–11) creates a new object of type ArgumentOutOfRangeException. The parentheses following the class name indicate a call to the constructor, which receives an error message String as its argument. After the exception object is created, the Throw statement immediately terminates the constructor (line 14 is *not* executed) and the exception is returned to the code that attempted to create the Account object.

Method Deposit

Method Deposit (lines 18–26) receives a deposit amount as an argument and attempts to add that amount to the balance. A deposit amount must be positive, so lines 20–23 check whether depositAmount is less than or equal to 0 and, if so, throw an Argument-OutOfRangeException with an appropriate error message. This terminates the Deposit method (line 25 is *not* executed) and returns the exception to the caller. If depositAmount is greater than 0, line 25 adds it to the balanceValue.

Method Withdraw

Method Withdraw (lines 29–41) receives a withdrawal amount as an argument and attempts to subtract that amount from the balance. A withdrawal amount must be a positive number that's less than or equal to the Account's balance. If the withdrawalAmount is not valid, lines 32–33 or 35–36 throw an ArgumentOutOfRangeException with an appropriate error message. If withdrawalAmount is valid, line 40 subtracts it from balanceValue.

Property Balance

A class's methods *can* manipulate the class's Private instance variables, but *clients cannot*. Classes often provide **Public properties** that allow clients to assign values to (*set*) or obtain the values of (*get*) Private instance variables. Each property contains a **Set accessor** (to modify the variable's value) and/or a **Get accessor** (to retrieve the variable's value).

For the Account class, we'd like the client code to be able to get the Account's balance, but *not* modify it—all modifications should be performed by methods Deposit and Withdraw. A property is defined with the **Property...End Property keywords**. A property that can be used *only to get* a value is declared as a **ReadOnly property** and provides *only* a Get accessor.

Lines 44–48 define class Account's Public ReadOnly property named Balance. Client code can use this property to obtain the current account balance. We also use the property inside the class at line 31 in method Withdraw when we check whether the withdrawalAmount is greater than the current balance. When the compiler sees Balance used in a way that needs a value, it invokes the property's Get accessor (lines 45–47). When you type the first line of this property then press *Enter*, the IDE will automatically insert an empty Get accessor (**Get...End Get**) and the End Property keywords. You can then type the Return statement at line 46 to complete the Get accessor's declaration. Later in this chapter, we'll declare properties with *both* Get and Set accessors. If you type the first line of a property without the ReadOnly keyword, then the IDE will generate empty Get *and* Set accessors for you.

Class AccountTest

The AccountTest class declaration (Fig. 9.3) creates the Account object account as an instance variable (line 4). The variable's type is Account—the class we declared in Fig. 9.2. Each new class you create becomes a new *type* that can be used to declare variables and create objects. You can declare new class types as needed; this is one reason why Visual Basic is known as an **extensible language**.

```vb
 1  ' Fig. 9.3: AccountTest.vb
 2  ' Create and manipulate an Account object.
 3  Public Class AccountTest
 4     Private account As New Account() ' create an Account object
 5
 6     ' display the initial account balance when program executes
 7     Private Sub AccountTest_Load(sender As Object,
 8        e As EventArgs) Handles MyBase.Load
 9
10        accountBalanceValueLabel.Text =
11           String.Format("{0:C}", account.Balance)
12     End Sub ' AccountTest_Load
13
14     ' process a deposit
15     Private Sub depositButton_Click(sender As Object,
16        e As EventArgs) Handles depositButton.Click
17
18        Try
19           ' get deposit amount
20           Dim depositAmount As Decimal =
21              Convert.ToDecimal(inputTextBox.Text)
22           account.Deposit(depositAmount) ' make the deposit
23           accountBalanceValueLabel.Text =
24              String.Format("{0:C}", account.Balance)
25        Catch ex As ArgumentOutOfRangeException
26           MessageBox.Show("Deposit amount must be positive.",
27              "Error", MessageBoxButtons.OK, MessageBoxIcon.Error)
28        End Try
29
30        inputTextBox.Clear() ' clear the inputTextBox
31        inputTextBox.Focus() ' allow user to type in the inputTextBox
32     End Sub ' depositButton_Click
33
34     ' process a withdrawal
35     Private Sub withdrawButton_Click(sender As Object,
36        e As EventArgs) Handles withdrawButton.Click
37
38        Try
39           ' get withdrawal amount
40           Dim withdrawalAmount As Decimal =
41              Convert.ToDecimal(inputTextBox.Text)
42           account.Withdraw(withdrawalAmount) ' make the withdrawal
43           accountBalanceValueLabel.Text =
44              String.Format("{0:C}", account.Balance)
45        Catch ex As ArgumentOutOfRangeException
46           MessageBox.Show("Withdrawal amount must be greater than 0 " &
47              "and less than or equal to the account balance.",
48              "Error", MessageBoxButtons.OK, MessageBoxIcon.Error)
49        End Try
```

Fig. 9.3 | Create and manipulate an Account object. (Part 1 of 2.)

```
50
51          inputTextBox.Clear() ' clear the inputTextBox
52          inputTextBox.Focus() ' allow user to type in the inputTextBox
53       End Sub ' withdrawButton_Click
54    End Class ' AccountTest
```

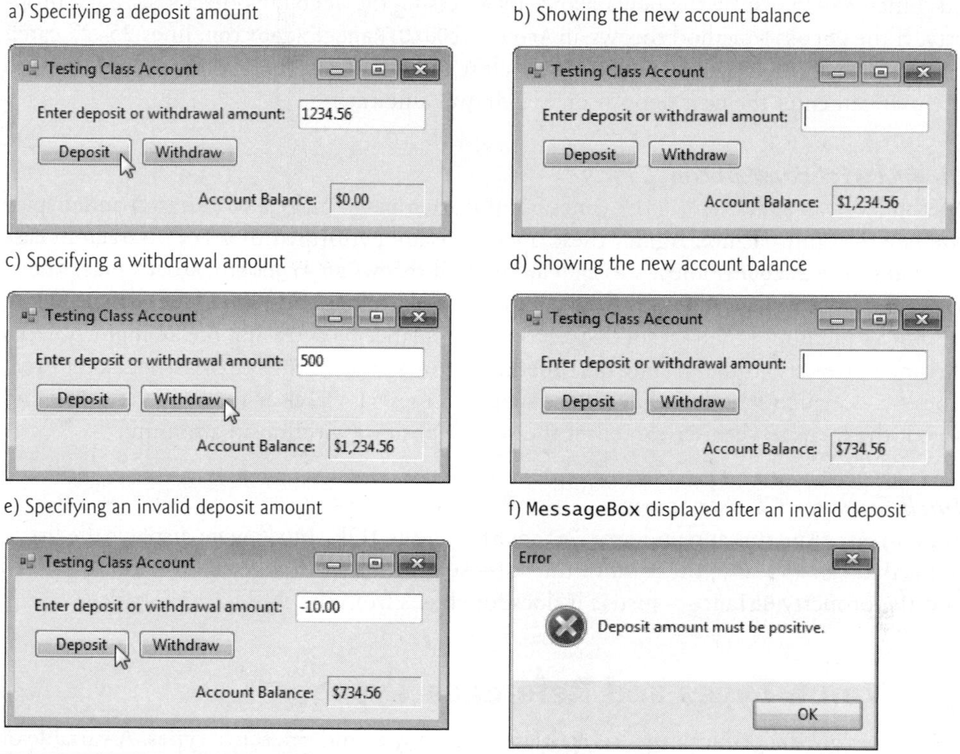

a) Specifying a deposit amount   b) Showing the new account balance

c) Specifying a withdrawal amount   d) Showing the new account balance

e) Specifying an invalid deposit amount   f) MessageBox displayed after an invalid deposit

Fig. 9.3 | Create and manipulate an Account object. (Part 2 of 2.)

Object-Creation Expressions

Variable account is initialized (Fig. 9.3, line 4) with the result of the **object-creation expression** New Account(). New creates a new object of the class specified to the right of the New keyword (that is, Account). The class name is followed by *parentheses*, which together with the class name represent a call to class's constructor. In this example, we left the parentheses empty. Because we don't pass an argument, the default value 0D is used for the Account's initial balance (because of the Optional parameter in line 7 of Fig. 9.2). When there are no arguments, the parentheses can be omitted, though we include them for clarity. Although Visual Basic is *not* case sensitive, it *does* allow you to create objects (for example, account) with the "same" name as their class (e.g. Account)—we do this throughout the book.

Method AccountTest_Load

Method AccountTest_Load (Fig. 9.3, lines 7–12) displays the account object's initial balance in the accountBalanceValueLabel by using the expression account.Balance to access the account object's Balance property. The property returns the current value of the account object's instance variable balanceValue.

Method deposit*Button_Click*

Method depositButton_Click (lines 15–32) attempts to make a deposit and display the new account balance. These operations are performed in a Try...Catch in case the call to the account object's Deposit method throws an ArgumentOutOfRangeException. Lines 20–21 get the user input. Line 22 passes that value to the account object's Deposit method. Lines 23–24 display the new balance by accessing the account object's Balance property. If the Deposit method throws an ArgumentOutOfRangeException, lines 25–27 catch it and display a MessageBox. Lines 30–31 clear the inputTextBox and give it the focus so the user can enter the next deposit or withdrawal amount.

Method withdraw*Button_Click*

Method withdrawButton_Click (lines 35–53) attempts to make a withdrawal and display the new account balance. Again, these operations are performed in a Try...Catch in case the call to the account object's Withdraw method throws an ArgumentOutOfRangeException. Lines 40–41 get the user input. Line 42 passes that value to the account object's Withdraw method. Lines 43–44 display the new balance by accessing the account object's Balance property. If the Withdrawal method throws an ArgumentOutOfRangeException, lines 45–48 catch it and display a MessageBox. Lines 51–52 clear the inputTextBox and give it the focus so the user can enter the next deposit or withdrawal amount.

IntelliSense for Class *Account*

When you create this app and type "account." in the IDE, *IntelliSense* displays the list of items that can appear to the right of the dot—such as the methods Deposit and Withdraw and the property Balance—just as it does for classes from the .NET framework.

9.4 Value Types and Reference Types

Data types are divided into two categories—**value types** and **reference types**. A variable of a value type (such as Integer) contains a single *value* of that type. For example, Fig. 9.4 shows an Integer variable named count that contains the value 7.

```
Dim count As Integer = 7
```

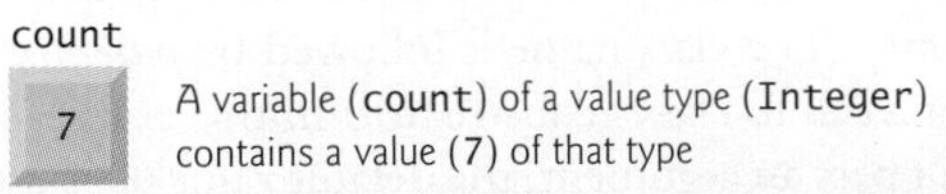

count

| 7 | A variable (count) of a value type (Integer) contains a value (7) of that type |

Fig. 9.4 | Value type variable and its value.

By contrast, a variable of a reference type (sometimes called a **reference**) contains the *address* where an object is stored in memory. Such a variable is said to **refer to an object**. The actual object to which the variable refers can contain many individual pieces of data (that is, its instance variables). Line 4 of Fig. 9.3 created an Account object in memory and stored the object's location in reference variable account of type Account. Figure 9.5 shows the relationship between the variable account and the Account object. The Account object is shown with its balanceValue instance variable.

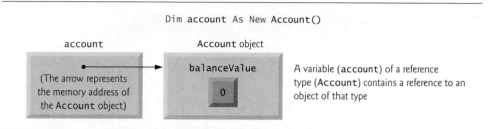

Fig. 9.5 | Reference type variable.

Reference Type Variables Initialized to *Nothing*

A reference type variable is initialized by default to the value Nothing if you do not initialize it in its declaration to refer to an object. When you attempt to use a variable that contains Nothing to interact with an object, you'll receive a NullReferenceException.

Most Primitive Types are Value Types

Visual Basic's primitive types are value types, except for the reference type String (which actually represents the **String** class in the .NET framework). The primitive value types include the **integral types** (Byte, SByte, Short, UShort, Integer, UInteger, Long and ULong), the **floating-point types** (Single and Double) and types Boolean, Date, Decimal and Char. Appendix B lists the primitive types with their sizes and ranges of values.

9.5 Case Study: Card Shuffling and Dealing Simulation

Next, we show how to create and manipulate an array of objects. The elements of an array can be of either value types or reference types. This section uses *random number generation* and an array of references to objects representing playing cards, to develop a class that simulates card shuffling and dealing. You can then use this class to implement apps that play specific card games. First, we develop class Card (Fig. 9.7), which represents a playing card that has a face (for example, "Ace", "Two", "Three", ..., "Jack", "Queen", "King") and a suit (for example, "Hearts", "Diamonds", "Clubs", "Spades"). Next, we develop the DeckOfCards class (Fig. 9.8), which creates a deck of 52 playing cards in which each element is a Card object. We then build a test app DeckOfCardsTest (Fig. 9.9) that demonstrates class DeckOfCards's card shuffling and dealing capabilities.

GUI for the Card Shuffling and Dealing Simulation

Figure 9.6 shows the app's GUI. At any time, the user can click the **Shuffle** Button to shuffle the deck of cards. Each time the user clicks the **Deal** Button, five cards are dealt and displayed as images in PictureBoxes. When only two cards remain in the deck, the last three PictureBoxes are left empty.

Class *Card*

Class Card (Fig. 9.7) contains two String instance variables—face and suit—that store *references* to the face name and suit name for a specific Card. The constructor for the class (lines 8–11) receives two Strings that it uses to initialize face and suit. Method ToString (lines 14–16) creates a String consisting of the face of the card, the String " of " and the suit of the card.

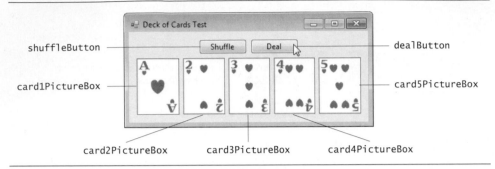

Fig. 9.6 | GUI for the card shuffling and dealing simulation.

```
 1   ' Fig. 9.7: Card.vb
 2   ' Card class represents a playing card.
 3   Public Class Card
 4      Private face As String ' face of card ("Ace", "Two", ...)
 5      Private suit As String ' suit of card ("Hearts", "Diamonds", ...)
 6
 7      ' two-argument constructor initializes card's face and suit
 8      Public Sub New(cardFace As String, cardSuit As String)
 9         face = cardFace ' initialize face of card
10         suit = cardSuit ' initialize suit of card
11      End Sub ' New
12
13      ' return String representation of Card, Overrides defined in Ch 10
14      Public Overrides Function ToString() As String
15         Return face & " of " & suit
16      End Function ' ToString
17   End Class ' Card
```

Fig. 9.7 | Card class represents a playing card.

Composition
A class can have references to objects of other classes as members. This is called **composition** and is sometimes referred to as a *has-a* relationship. In this example, an object of class Card needs to know the face and suit of the Card, so a Card object has two references to String objects.

Method ToString
Method **ToString** (lines 14–16) takes no arguments and returns a String representation of a Card. Method ToString must be declared as shown in line 14 and is the standard method used to create a String representation of *any* object. For most classes, you should declare method ToString to return information that matches the unique requirements of your class. We discuss the keyword Overrides in detail in Chapter 10.

Class DeckOfCards
Class DeckOfCards (Fig. 9.8) creates an instance variable array named deck, which consists of 52 Card objects (line 5). This is another example of composition—a DeckOfCards *has*

an array of 52 Cards. Like primitive-type array declarations, the declaration of an array of objects includes the name of the array variable (deck) and its upper bound in parentheses, followed by the keyword As and the type of the array elements. Class DeckOfCards also declares an Integer instance variable currentCard (line 6) representing the next Card to be dealt from the deck array.

```vb
 1   ' Fig. 9.8: DeckOfCards.vb
 2   ' DeckOfCards class represents a deck of playing cards.
 3   Public Class DeckOfCards
 4      Private Const NUMBER_OF_CARDS As Integer = 52 ' number of cards
 5      Private deck(NUMBER_OF_CARDS - 1) As Card ' array of Card objects
 6      Private currentCard As Integer ' index of next Card to be dealt
 7      Private Shared randomNumbers As New Random() ' random number generator
 8
 9      ' constructor fills deck of Cards
10      Public Sub New()
11         Static faces() As String = {"Ace", "Two", "Three", "Four", "Five",
12            "Six", "Seven", "Eight", "Nine", "Ten", "Jack", "Queen", "King"}
13         Static suits() As String = {"Hearts", "Diamonds", "Clubs", "Spades"}
14         currentCard = 0 ' set currentCard so first Card dealt is deck(0)
15
16         ' populate deck array with Card objects
17         For count = 0 To deck.GetUpperBound(0)
18            deck(count) = New Card(faces(count Mod 13), suits(count \ 13))
19         Next
20      End Sub ' New
21
22      ' shuffle deck of Cards with simple one-pass algorithm
23      Public Sub Shuffle()
24         ' after shuffling, dealing should start at deck(0) again
25         currentCard = 0 ' reinitialize currentCard
26
27         ' for each Card, pick another random Card and swap them
28         For first = 0 To deck.GetUpperBound(0)
29            ' select a random number between 0 and 51
30            Dim second As Integer = randomNumbers.Next(NUMBER_OF_CARDS)
31
32            ' swap current Card with randomly selected Card
33            Dim temp As Card = deck(first) ' store copy of deck(first)
34            deck(first) = deck(second) ' move deck(second) to deck(first)
35            deck(second) = temp ' move original deck(first) to deck(second)
36         Next
37      End Sub ' Shuffle
38
39      ' deal one Card
40      Public Function DealCard() As Card
41         ' determine whether Cards remain to be dealt
42         If currentCard <= deck.GetUpperBound(0) Then
43            Dim lastCard As Integer = currentCard ' store current card number
44            currentCard += 1 ' increment current card number
45            Return deck(lastCard)
```

Fig. 9.8 | DeckOfCards class represents a deck of playing cards. (Part 1 of 2.)

```
46          Else
47              Return Nothing ' no more cards to deal
48          End If
49      End Function ' DealCard
50  End Class ' DeckOfCards
```

Fig. 9.8 | `DeckOfCards` class represents a deck of playing cards. (Part 2 of 2.)

The parameterless constructor (lines 10–20) initializes the deck of cards. When first created, the deck array's elements are Nothing by default, so the constructor uses a For statement (lines 17–19) to fill the deck array with Cards. This statement initializes control variable count to 0 and loops while count is less than or equal to deck.GetUpperBound(0), causing count to take on each integer value from 0 to 51 (the deck array's indices). Each Card is initialized with two Strings—one from array faces (which contains the Strings "Ace" through "King") and one from array suits (which contains the Strings "Hearts", "Diamonds", "Clubs" and "Spades"). The calculation count Mod 13 *always* results in a value from 0 to 12 (the 13 indices of the faces array in lines 11–12), and the calculation count \ 13 *always* results in a value from 0 to 3 (the four indices of the suits array in line 13). When the deck array is initialized, it contains the Cards with faces "Ace" through "King" in order for each suit—Hearts then Diamonds then Clubs then Spades.

Static *Local Variables*

The arrays faces (line 11–12) and suits (line 13) are declared with the keyword Static. A **Static** local variable is initialized *only* the first time you call the method or constructor in which the variable is declared. It *retains* its value when the method or constructor finishes executing. The next time you call the method or constructor, the Static local variable contains the value it had when the function last exited. We declared arrays faces and suits as Static so they're created and initialized *only* the first time the DeckOfCards constructor is called—regardless of the number of DeckOfCards objects you create. This improves performance.

Method *Shuffle*

Method Shuffle (lines 23–37) shuffles the Cards in the deck. The method loops through all 52 Cards (array indices 0 to 51). For each Card, a number between 0 and 51 is picked randomly to select another Card (line 30). Next, the current Card object and the randomly selected Card object are swapped in the array (lines 33–35). The extra variable temp temporarily stores one of the two Card objects being swapped. The swap cannot be performed with only the two statements

```
deck(first) = deck(second)
deck(second) = deck(first)
```

For example, if deck(first) is the "Ace" of "Spades" and deck(second) is the "Queen" of "Hearts", after the first assignment, *both* array elements contain the "Queen" of "Hearts" and the "Ace" of "Spades" is *lost*—hence, the extra variable temp is needed. After the For loop terminates, the Card objects are randomly ordered. Only 52 swaps are made in a single pass of the entire array, and the array of Card objects is shuffled!

[*Note:* It's recommended that you use a so-called *unbiased* shuffling algorithm for real card games. Such an algorithm ensures that all possible shuffled card sequences are equally

likely to occur. A popular unbiased shuffling algorithm is the *Fisher-Yates algorithm*—
`en.wikipedia.org/wiki/Fisher%E2%80%93Yates_shuffle`. This page also shows how to
implement the algorithm in several programming languages.]

Method DealCard

Method `DealCard` (lines 40–49) deals one `Card` in the array. Recall that `currentCard` indicates the index of the next `Card` to be dealt (that is, the `Card` at the top of the deck).
Thus, line 42 compares `currentCard` to the upper bound (51) of the deck array. If the
deck is not empty (that is, `currentCard` is less than or equal to 51), line 43 assigns `currentCard` (the index of the card that will be returned) to temporary variable `lastCard`, line
44 increments `currentCard` to prepare for the next call to `DealCard` and line 45 returns
`deck(lastCard)`, which represents the top card of the deck for this call to `DealCard`. Otherwise, `DealCard` returns `Nothing` to indicate that all the cards have been dealt.

Shuffling and Dealing Cards

Figure 9.9 demonstrates the card shuffling and dealing capabilities of class `DeckOfCards`
(Fig. 9.8). The images used in this example are located in the `CardImages` folder with this
chapter's examples and were added to the project as resources. Line 4 of Fig. 9.9 creates a
`DeckOfCards` object named deck.

```
 1    ' Fig. 9.9: DeckOfCardsTest.vb
 2    ' Card shuffling and dealing app.
 3    Public Class DeckOfCardsTest
 4       Private deck As New DeckOfCards() ' create the deck of cards
 5
 6       ' shuffle the deck when user clicks the Shuffle Button
 7       Private Sub shuffleButton_Click(sender As Object,
 8          e As EventArgs) Handles shuffleButton.Click
 9
10          deck.Shuffle() ' shuffles the deck
11          card1PictureBox.Image = Nothing ' clear image
12          card2PictureBox.Image = Nothing ' clear image
13          card3PictureBox.Image = Nothing ' clear image
14          card4PictureBox.Image = Nothing ' clear image
15          card5PictureBox.Image = Nothing ' clear image
16          dealButton.Enabled = True ' allow user to click the Deal Button
17          MessageBox.Show("Deck is shuffled")
18       End Sub ' shuffleButton_Click
19
20       ' deal five cards
21       Private Sub dealButton_Click(sender As Object,
22          e As EventArgs) Handles dealButton.Click
23
24          card1PictureBox.Image = GetCardImage(deck.DealCard())
25          card2PictureBox.Image = GetCardImage(deck.DealCard())
26          card3PictureBox.Image = GetCardImage(deck.DealCard())
27          card4PictureBox.Image = GetCardImage(deck.DealCard())
28          card5PictureBox.Image = GetCardImage(deck.DealCard())
29       End Sub ' dealButton_Click
30
```

Fig. 9.9 | Card shuffling and dealing app. (Part 1 of 2.)

```
31    ' return an image for the Card argument
32    Private Function GetCardImage(card As Card) As Image
33       If card IsNot Nothing Then
34          ' retrieve specific card image from resources
35          Dim pictureResource = My.Resources.ResourceManager.GetObject(
36             card.ToString().Replace(" ", ""))
37          Return CType(pictureResource, Image) ' return Image
38       Else
39          dealButton.Enabled = False ' disable the Deal Button
40          Return Nothing ' no more cards
41       End If
42    End Function ' GetCardImage
43 End Class ' DeckOfCardsTest
```

a) When the app begins executing, clicking **Deal** before **Shuffle** deals cards from the unshuffled deck

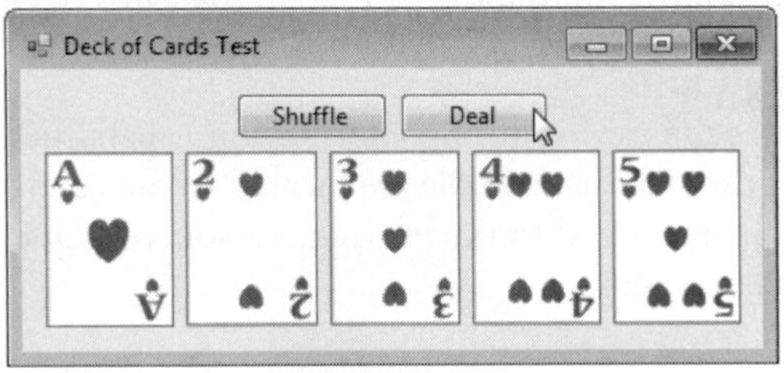

b) Clicking **Shuffle** shuffles the deck, then displays a dialog indicating that the deck is shuffled; after the deck is shuffled, the card images are cleared so we can start displaying cards from the beginning of the shuffled deck

c) Clicking **Deal** after shuffling deals five cards from the shuffled deck

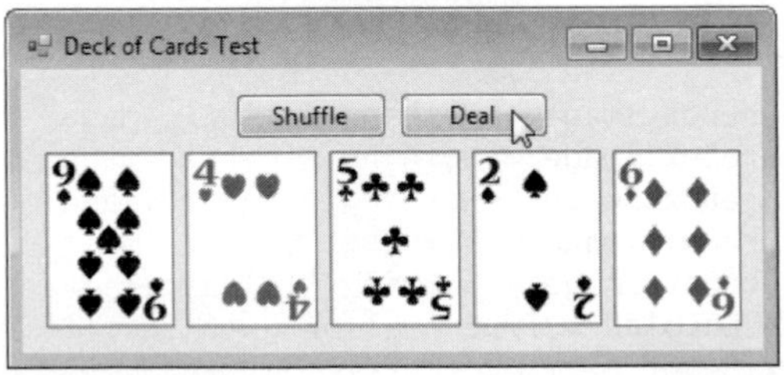

Fig. 9.9 | Card shuffling and dealing app. (Part 2 of 2.)

Method *shuffleButton_Click*

Recall that the DeckOfCards constructor creates the 52 Card objects in order by suit and then by face within each suit. When you click the **Shuffle** Button, line 10 invokes deck's Shuffle method to randomly rearrange the Card objects. Then, lines 11–15 clear the card images, line 16 enables the **Deal** Button and line 17 displays a MessageBox indicating that the deck is shuffled.

Method *dealButton_Click*

Each time you click the **Deal** Button, lines 24–28 call the deck's DealCard method repeatedly to deal five Cards. Each Card is passed to method GetCardImage, which returns the corresponding image for that Card.

Method *GetCardImage*

The Private method GetCardImage (lines 32–42) receives a Card as an argument. Private methods are called **utility methods**, or **helper methods**, because they can be called *only* by other methods of the class to support their operation. If the card parameter's value is not Nothing (line 33), the method uses the Card's String representation to locate the corresponding Image resource. Line 36 calls the Card's ToString method to get the String representation of the face and suit. This String contains spaces (for example, "Ace of Spades"); however, the names of the image resources do not. So line 36 also calls the String method Replace to replace all spaces in the String returned by ToString with the empty String. Thus, if the Card's ToString method returned "Ace of Spades", then the name of the image resource would be "AceofSpades". Line 37 returns the Image for the card. If the card parameter is Nothing, then line 39 disables the **Deal** Button and line 40 returns Nothing to indicate that there's no Image to display.

9.6 Case Study: Time Class

We now discuss a Time class with three Integer instance variables—hourValue, minuteValue and secondValue—representing the time in *universal-time (24-hour clock) format*.

GUI for Testing Class *Time's* Properties

The GUI for this app is shown in Fig. 9.10. You can set the hour, minute and second using the three TextBoxes. If you specify an *invalid* value, an *exception* occurs. The app catches the exception and displays an appropriate message in a MessageBox. You can also press the **Increment Second** Button to add one second to the time. When you update the time, the app displays the new values of the hour, minute and second in the output1Label and displays the standard and universal times in the output2Label.

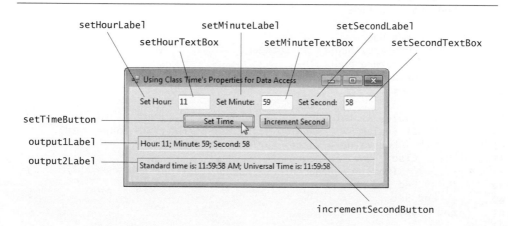

Fig. 9.10 | GUI for testing class Time's properties.

Time Class Declaration

The app consists of classes Time (Fig. 9.11) and TimeTest (Fig. 9.12). Class Time declares properties Hour (Fig. 9.11, lines 29–41), Minute (lines 44–56) and Second (lines 59–71) to control access to instance variables hourValue, minuteValue and secondValue, respectively. Each of *these* properties contains a Get accessor and a Set accessor. The Set accessors perform validation to ensure that the corresponding instance variables are set to valid values; otherwise, they throw an *exception* and the corresponding instance variable is *not* modified. Each Get accessor returns the appropriate instance variable's value.

```vb
1   ' Fig. 9.11: Time.vb
2   ' Time class with Hour, Minute and Second properties.
3   Public Class Time
4      ' declare Integer instance variables for the hour, minute and second
5      Private hourValue As Integer ' 0 - 23
6      Private minuteValue As Integer ' 0 - 59
7      Private secondValue As Integer ' 0 - 59
8
9      ' Time constructor with hour, minute and second as optional parameters
10     Public Sub New(Optional h As Integer = 12,
11        Optional m As Integer = 0, Optional s As Integer = 0)
12        SetTime(h, m, s) ' call SetTime with three arguments
13     End Sub ' New
14
15     ' Time constructor: another Time object supplied
16     Public Sub New(t As Time)
17        SetTime(t.hourValue, t.minuteValue, t.secondValue)
18     End Sub ' New
19
20     ' set a new time value using universal time, check validity of the data
21     Public Sub SetTime(h As Integer, m As Integer, s As Integer)
22
23        Hour = h ' Set accessor validates the hour
24        Minute = m ' Set accessor validates the minute
25        Second = s ' Set accessor validates the second
26     End Sub ' SetTime
27
28     ' property Hour
29     Public Property Hour() As Integer
30        Get ' return hourValue
31           Return hourValue
32        End Get
33
34        Set(value As Integer) ' set hourValue
35           If (value >= 0 AndAlso value < 24) Then ' in range 0-23?
36              hourValue = value ' value is valid
37           Else ' invalid hour
38              Throw New ArgumentOutOfRangeException("hour must be 0-23")
39           End If
40        End Set
41     End Property ' Hour
42
43     ' property Minute
44     Public Property Minute() As Integer
45        Get ' return minuteValue
46           Return minuteValue
47        End Get
```

Fig. 9.11 | Time class with Hour, Minute and Second properties. (Part 1 of 2.)

```vbnet
48
49          Set(value As Integer) ' set minuteValue
50             If (value >= 0 AndAlso value < 60) Then ' in range 0-59?
51                minuteValue = value ' value is valid
52             Else ' invalid minute
53                Throw New ArgumentOutOfRangeException("minute must be 0-59")
54             End If
55          End Set
56       End Property ' Minute
57
58       ' property Second
59       Public Property Second() As Integer
60          Get ' return secondValue
61             Return secondValue
62          End Get
63
64          Set(value As Integer) ' set secondValue
65             If (value >= 0 AndAlso value < 60) Then ' in range 0-59?
66                secondValue = value ' value is valid
67             Else  ' invalid second
68                Throw New ArgumentOutOfRangeException("second must be 0-59")
69             End If
70          End Set
71       End Property ' Second
72
73       ' return Time as a String in universal-time (24-hour clock) format
74       Public Function ToUniversalString() As String
75          Return String.Format("{0}:{1:D2}:{2:D2}", Hour, Minute, Second)
76       End Function ' ToUniversalString
77
78       ' return Time as a String in standard-time (12-hour clock) format
79       Public Overrides Function ToString() As String
80          Dim suffix As String ' AM or PM suffix
81          Dim standardHour As Integer ' a standard hour in the range 1-12
82
83          ' determine whether the 12-hour clock suffix should be AM or PM
84          If Hour < 12 Then
85             suffix = "AM"
86          Else
87             suffix = "PM"
88          End If
89
90          ' convert hour from universal-time format to standard-time format
91          If (Hour = 12 OrElse Hour = 0) Then
92             standardHour = 12 ' noon or midnight
93          Else
94             standardHour = Hour Mod 12 ' 1 through 11, AM or PM
95          End If
96
97          Return String.Format("{0}:{1:D2}:{2:D2} {3}",
98             standardHour, Minute, Second, suffix)
99       End Function ' ToString
100   End Class ' Time
```

Fig. 9.11 | Time class with Hour, Minute and Second properties. (Part 2 of 2.)

Time Class Constructors

Like methods, constructors of a class can be *overloaded*. To do so, you provide a separate constructor declaration with the *same* name (New) for each version but *different* numbers, types and/or orders of parameters (that is, different signatures). Class Time of Fig. 9.11 includes two overloaded constructors (lines 10–18) that provide various ways to initialize Time objects. Each constructor calls method SetTime to set the hour, minute and second values. In line 17, notice that we access the argument Time object's Private instance variables directly with the expressions t.hourValue, t.minuteValue and t.secondValue. *When one object of a class has a reference to another object of the* same *class, the first object can access all of the second object's data, methods and properties (including those that are* Private*).*

The compiler invokes the appropriate constructor by matching the number, types and order of the arguments specified in the constructor call with the number, types and order of the parameters specified in each constructor method declaration. The following statements demonstrate how these overloaded constructors can be used:

```
Dim time1 As New Time() ' use default hour, minute and second
Dim time2 As New Time(2) ' use default minute and second
Dim time3 As New Time(21, 34) ' use default second
Dim time4 As New Time(12, 25, 42) ' all arguments supplied
Dim time5 As New Time(time4) ' copy another Time object
```

The first four statements call the constructor in lines 10–13 using varying numbers of arguments. The last statement calls the constructor in lines 16–18.

Common Programming Error 9.1

A constructor can call other class methods that use instance variables not yet initialized. Using instance variables before they've been initialized can lead to logic errors.

Method SetTime

Method SetTime (lines 21–26) receives three parameters representing the hour, minute and second. Rather than validating the hour, minute and second values in both method SetTime *and* in the properties, method SetTime simply assigns its arguments to the corresponding properties (lines 23–25). Assigning a value to a property invokes the property's Set accessor, which, in turn, validates the value. Coding SetTime this way ensures that we do not duplicate the validation code. Only the properties in this class actually modify the instance variables, so if one is set incorrectly, we can focus on debugging its corresponding property to correct the problem.

Properties Hour, Minute and Second

Properties Hour, Minute and Second are *read-write properties*—they include both Get and Set accessors. These enable clients of class Time to get the values of the class's instance variables and modify them in a controlled manner, respectively. Because we want client code to be able to both *get* and set the hour, minute and second, we could have declared the instance variables Public. However, using Public instance variables in a class is dangerous—other parts of the program could accidentally or maliciously set Public instance variables to *invalid* values, producing potentially disastrous results. Public access to instance variables should be accomplished through properties. The properties also can be used throughout class Time as well.

> ### Software Engineering Observation 9.1
> *Access all of your class's instance variables through their corresponding properties, even inside the class definition. This makes your class easier to maintain, modify and debug.*

Method ToUniversalString

Method ToUniversalString (lines 74–76) takes no arguments and returns a String in universal-time format, consisting of the Hour property value, two digits for the Minute property value and two digits for the Second property value. For example, if the time were 1:30:07 PM, method ToUniversalString would return the String "13:30:07". Format specifier D2 formats a single-digit integer value with a leading 0.

Method ToString

Method ToString (lines 79–99) takes no arguments and returns a String in standard-time format, consisting of the Hour, Minute and Second property values separated by colons and followed by AM or PM (for example, 1:27:06 PM). Lines 84–88 determine the proper AM or PM suffix. Lines 91–95 determine the proper formatting for the hour—hours from 0 to 11 display with AM, hours from 12 to 23 display with PM, hour 0 displays as 12 (midnight), hours 1–12 display as is and hours 13–23 display as 1–11 (PM).

Using the Time Class

Class TimeTest (Fig. 9.12) provides a GUI for testing class Time. The GUI contains three text boxes in which the user can enter values for the Time object's Hour, Minute and Second properties, respectively. Class TimeTest creates an object of class Time (line 4) using *default arguments* and assigns its reference to variable time.

```
1   ' Fig. 9.12: TimeTest.vb
2   ' Accessing data via properties.
3   Public Class TimeTest
4      Dim time As New Time() ' construct Time with zero arguments
5
6      ' invoked when user clicks the Add 1 to Second button
7      Private Sub addSecondButton_Click(sender As Object,
8         e As EventArgs) Handles incrementSecondButton.Click
9
10        time.Second = (time.Second + 1) Mod 60 ' add 1 to Second
11
12        ' add one minute if 60 seconds have passed
13        If time.Second = 0 Then
14           time.Minute = (time.Minute + 1) Mod 60 ' add 1 to Minute
15
16           ' add one hour if 60 minutes have passed
17           If time.Minute = 0 Then
18              time.Hour = (time.Hour + 1) Mod 24 ' add 1 to Hour
19           End If
20        End If
21
22        UpdateDisplay() ' update the TextBoxes and output Labels
23     End Sub ' addSecondButton_Click
```

Fig. 9.12 | Accessing data via properties. (Part 1 of 3.)

```vbnet
24
25          ' set time based on TextBox values
26          Private Sub setTimeButton_Click(sender As Object,
27             e As EventArgs) Handles setTimeButton.Click
28
29             ' ensure that hour, minute and second are in range
30             Try
31                If setHourTextBox.Text <> String.Empty Then
32                   time.Hour = Convert.ToInt32(setHourTextBox.Text)
33                End If
34
35                If setMinuteTextBox.Text <> String.Empty Then
36                   time.Minute = Convert.ToInt32(setMinuteTextBox.Text)
37                End If
38
39                If setSecondTextBox.Text <> String.Empty Then
40                   time.Second = Convert.ToInt32(setSecondTextBox.Text)
41                End If
42             Catch ex As ArgumentOutOfRangeException
43                MessageBox.Show("The hour, minute or second was out of range",
44                   "Out of Range", MessageBoxButtons.OK, MessageBoxIcon.Error)
45             End Try
46
47             UpdateDisplay() ' update the TextBoxes and output Labels
48          End Sub ' setTimeButton_Click
49
50          ' update time display
51          Private Sub UpdateDisplay()
52             setHourTextBox.Text = Convert.ToString(time.Hour)
53             setMinuteTextBox.Text = Convert.ToString(time.Minute)
54             setSecondTextBox.Text = Convert.ToString(time.Second)
55             output1Label.Text = ("Hour: " & time.Hour & "; Minute: " &
56                time.Minute & "; Second: " & time.Second)
57             output2Label.Text = ("Standard time is: " & time.ToString() &
58                "; Universal Time is: " & time.ToUniversalString())
59          End Sub ' UpdateDisplay
60       End Class ' TimeTest
```

a) Setting the time to 11:59:58 AM

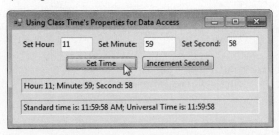

Fig. 9.12 | Accessing data via properties. (Part 2 of 3.)

b) Incrementing the time to 11:59:59 AM

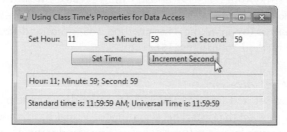

c) Incrementing the time to 12:00:00 PM

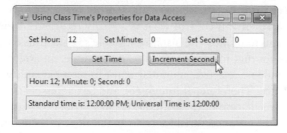

d) Attempting to set an invalid hour causes an `ArgumentOutOfRangeException`

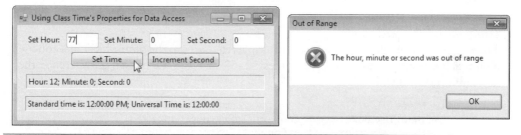

Fig. 9.12 | Accessing data via properties. (Part 3 of 3.)

Method *addSecondButton_Click*

The GUI contains an **Increment Second** Button that enables the user to increment the Second property value by 1 without having to use the corresponding text box. Method addSecondButton_Click (lines 7–23) uses properties to determine and set the new time, ensuring that the values for the hour, minute and second are updated properly. For example, 23:59:59 becomes 00:00:00 when the user presses **Increment Second**. Line 22 calls method UpdateDisplay (lines 51–59) to update the TextBoxes and the output Labels with the new time.

Method *setTimeButton_Click*

Method setTimeButton_Click (lines 26–48) checks each TextBox to ensure that it's not empty. For each TextBox that's not empty, the method sets the corresponding property of the Time object to the value in the TextBox. If any of the Time object's properties throws an exception, lines 43–44 display a MessageBox indicating that one of the values was out of range.

Method `UpdateDisplay`

Method `UpdateDisplay` (lines 51–59) updates the TextBoxes with the current values of the `Time` object's `Hour`, `Minute` and `Second` properties. Then, lines 57–58 display the time in *standard-time format* (by invoking `Time` method `ToString`) and *universal-time format* (by invoking `Time` method `ToUniversalString`).

Notes on **Set** and **Get** Accessors

Although providing `Set` and `Get` *accessors* appears to be the *same* as making the instance variables `Public`, this is *not* the case. This is another of Visual Basic's subtleties that makes the language so attractive from a software-engineering standpoint. If an instance variable is `Public`, it can be read or written by *any* method in the program. If an instance variable is `Private`, a `Public` `Get` accessor seems to allow other methods to read the data at will. However, the `Get` accessor can control what is actually returned. A `Public` `Set` accessor can scrutinize attempts to modify the instance variable's value, thus ensuring that the new value is appropriate for that instance variable. For example, an attempt to set the day of the month to 37 would be rejected, and an attempt to set a person's weight to a negative value would be rejected. Therefore, although `Set` and `Get` accessors provide access to `Private` data, the implementation of these methods can restrict access to that data.

The declaration of instance variables as `Private` does not guarantee data integrity. You must provide *validity checking*—Visual Basic provides only the framework with which you can design better programs.

Using the **With** Statement

The `With` statement allows you to make multiple references to the same object in a concise manner. For example, we can replace lines 52–58 of Fig. 9.12 (which all reference the same object, `time`) with

```
With time
    setHourTextBox.Text = Convert.ToString(.Hour)
    setMinuteTextBox.Text = Convert.ToString(.Minute)
    setSecondTextBox.Text = Convert.ToString(.Second)
    output1Label.Text = ("Hour: " & .Hour & "; Minute: " &
        .Minute & "; Second: " & .Second)
    output2Label.Text = ("Standard time is: " & .ToString() &
        "; Universal Time is: " & .ToUniversalString())
End With
```

These lines of code are collectively known as a **With statement block**. At the beginning of the block, we specify the object (`time`) that we'll be using in the block. The `With` statement allows you to access an object's members in the block *without* having to specify the name of the object before the dot separator—for example, `.Hour()` instead of `time.Hour`.

9.7 Class Scope

A class's instance variables, properties and methods have **class scope**. Within this scope, a class's members are accessible to all of the class's other members and can be referenced simply by name. Outside a class's scope, class members cannot be referenced directly by name. Those class members that are visible (such as `Public` members) can be accessed through a variable that refers to an object of the class (for example, `time.Hour`). In Section 9.12, you'll see that `Public Shared` members are accessed through the class name.

9.8 Object Initializers

Object initializers use the `With` keyword to allow you to create an object and initialize its properties in the same statement. This is useful when a class does not provide an appropriate constructor to meet your needs. For example, the `Time` class used in this section (from Fig. 9.11) does not provide constructors that can receive only the minute and second, or only the second, as arguments. To use object initializers, you follow the object creation expression with the `With` keyword and an **object initializer list**—a comma-separated list in curly braces ({ }) of properties and their values as in the following statements:

```
Dim timeObject1 As New Time() With {.Minute = 33, .Second = 12}
Dim timeObject2 As New Time() With {.Minute = 45}
```

The `With` keyword indicates that the new object is used to access the properties specified in the object-initializer list. Each property name must be preceded by the dot separator (`.`) and can appear only *once* in the object-initializer list. The object-initializer list cannot be empty and cannot contain properties that are declared as `Shared` (Section 9.12), `Const` (Section 9.13) or `ReadOnly` (Section 9.13).

The first of the preceding statements creates a `Time` object (`timeObject1`) and initializes it with class `Time`'s parameterless constructor. The object initializer then executes the property initializers in the *order in which they appear*. In this case, the time is set to `12:33:12`. Recall that an object intializer first calls the class's constructor. The parameterless `Time` constructor initializes the time to noon (`12:00:00`). The object initializer then sets each specified property to the supplied value. In this case, the `Minute` property is set to 33 and the `Second` property is set to 12. The `Hour` property retains its default value. Of course, the `Set` accessors of the properties still *validate* the values in the object-initializer list.

The second of the preceding statements uses an object intializer to create a new `Time` object (`timeObject2`) and set only its `Minute` property. The time is set to `12:45:00`. First, the `Time` constructor initializes the time to noon (`12:00:00`). Then, the object initializer sets the `Minute` property to 45. The `Hour` and `Second` properties retain their default values.

9.9 Auto-Implemented Properties

The properties we declared in class `Time` each perform *validation* to ensure that the hour, minute and second always contain valid values. For properties that do not have any additional logic in their `Set` and `Get` accessors, there's a feature called **auto-implemented properties**—that allows you to write one line of code and have the compiler to generate the property's code for you. For example, if the `Time` class's `Hour` property did not require validation in Fig. 9.11, we could have replaced line 5 and lines 29–41 with

```
Public Property Hour As Integer
```

The compiler would then generate a `Private` instance variable of type `Integer` named `_Hour` and the following property code:

```
Public Property Hour As Integer
   Get
      Return _Hour
   End Get

   Set(value As Integer)
      _Hour = value
   End Set
End Property
```

You can also assign an initial value to an auto-implemented property in its declaration, just as you can for a class's instance variables.

Auto-implemented properties are provided as a convenience feature for "simple" properties like the one described above. In general, however, you should perform validation in a property's Set accessor. Doing so requires *you* to define the property *and* its corresponding instance variable.

9.10 Using Me to Access the Current Object

Every object of a class shares *one copy* of the class's method declarations. We've seen that an object's methods can manipulate the object's data. But how do methods know *which* object's instance variables to manipulate? Every object can *access itself* through its **Me reference**. On every call to a non-Shared method, the compiler passes an object's Me reference as an *implicit* argument. The Me reference can then be used to access a particular object's members *implicitly* (by the compiler) or *explicitly* (which is rarely needed). (Section 9.12 introduces Shared class members and explains why the Me reference is *not* implicitly passed to Shared methods.)

Accessing Shadowed Instance Variables with Me
When a method has a parameter or local variable with the same name as one of the class's instance variables, the instance variable is "hidden" until the method terminates execution—this is called **shadowing**. You can use the Me reference to access the shadowed instance variable. Assume that we have a Time class with hour, minute and second instance variables. The following Time class constructor's parameters *shadow* (have the same name as) the class's instance variables, so we use Me to access each shadowed instance variable:

```
Public Sub New(hour As Integer,
   minute As Integer, second As Integer)

   Me.hour = hour ' initializes instance variable hour
   Me.minute = minute ' initializes instance variable minute
   Me.second = second ' initializes instance variable second
End Sub ' New
```

The identifiers qualified with "Me." represent the instance variables. The unqualified identifiers represent the constructor's parameters.

9.11 Garbage Collection

Every object you create uses various system resources, including the memory that holds the object itself. These resources must be *returned* to the system when they're no longer needed to avoid **resource leaks**. The Common Language Runtime (CLR) performs automatic **garbage collection** to *reclaim* the memory occupied by objects that are no longer in use. When there are no more references to an object, it's **marked for garbage collection** by the CLR. The memory for such an object can be reclaimed when the CLR executes its **garbage collector**, which is responsible for reclaiming the memory of objects that are no longer used, so that the memory can be used for other objects. Resources like memory that are allocated and reclaimed by the CLR are known as **managed resources**.

Other types of resource leaks can occur. For example, an app may open a file on disk to modify the file's contents. If the app does *not* close the file, other apps may not be allowed to use the file until the app that opened the file finishes. An app that no longer needs a file should close it immediately so that other programs can access it. Resources like files that *you* must manage are known as **unmanaged resources** (because they're not managed by the CLR). Such resources are typically scarce and should be released as soon as they're no longer needed by a program.

The Using statement (which you learned about in Chapter 8) specifies a list of resources and disposes of them at the end of the Using statement, indicated by the End Using keywords. This statement ensures the disposal of its resources regardless of how the code in the Using statement terminates.

9.12 Shared Class Members

Each object has its *own* copy of the instance variables of its class. In certain cases, all objects of a class should share *only one* copy of a particular variable. A **Shared class variable** represents **classwide information**—all objects of the class share the same variable, no matter how many objects of the class have been instantiated. Together, a class's instance variables and Shared variables are know as the class's **fields**.

*Motivation for **Shared** Variables*
Let's use a video game example to explain the need for Shared classwide data. Suppose we have a video game in which Martians attack other space creatures. A Martian tends to be brave and willing to attack when it's aware that at least four other Martians are present. If fewer than five Martians are present, all Martians become cowardly. For this reason, each Martian must know the martianCount. We could endow class Martian with a martianCount instance variable. If we were to do this, then every Martian would have a separate *copy* of the instance variable, and every time we create a Martian, we would have to update the instance variable martianCount in *every* Martian. The redundant copies waste space, and updating those copies is time consuming. Worse yet, while we're updating the individual copies of martianCount, there will be periods of time during which some of these copies have not yet been updated, so we could have inconsistent bravery behavior among the Martians. Instead, we declare martianCount to be Shared so that it's classwide data. Each Martian can then see the martianCount as if it were instance data of that Martian, but Visual Basic maintains only *one* copy of the Shared martianCount to save space. We also save time, in that the Martian constructor increments only the Shared martianCount—there's only *one* copy, so we do not have to increment separate copies of martianCount for each Martian object. This also prevents inconsistent bravery behavior among the Martians.

*Class **Employee** with **Shared** Variables*

Our next example uses class Employee (Fig. 9.13) to demonstrate a Private Shared class variable and a Public Shared Property to access that value. The Shared class variable countValue is initialized to zero by default (line 6). It maintains a count of the number of Employee objects that have been created.

```vb
1   ' Fig. 9.13: Employee.vb
2   ' Class Employee uses Shared variable.
3   Public Class Employee
4      Private firstNameValue As String ' employee first name
5      Private lastNameValue As String ' employee last name
6      Private Shared countValue As Integer ' Employee objects in memory
7
8      ' Employee constructor
9      Public Sub New(first As String, last As String)
10        firstNameValue = first
11        lastNameValue = last
12        countValue += 1 ' increment shared count of employees
13     End Sub ' New
14
15     ' return first name
16     Public ReadOnly Property FirstName() As String
17        Get
18           Return firstNameValue
19        End Get
20     End Property ' FirstName
21
22     ' return last name
23     Public ReadOnly Property LastName() As String
24        Get
25           Return lastNameValue
26        End Get
27     End Property ' LastName
28
29     ' property Count
30     Public Shared ReadOnly Property Count() As Integer
31        Get
32           Return countValue
33        End Get
34     End Property ' Count
35  End Class ' Employee
```

Fig. 9.13 | Class Employee uses Shared variable.

When Employee objects exist, Shared member countValue can be used in any Employee method or property—in this example, the constructor increments countValue (line 12). If no objects of class Employee exist, member countValue can be referenced through the Shared ReadOnly Property Count (lines 30–34)—you do *not* have to create an Employee object to call the Get method of a Shared Property. We declared property Count as ReadOnly so that client code cannot modify countValue.

Scope of *Shared* Members

Shared class members have class scope. A class's Public Shared members can be accessed via the class name using the dot separator (for example, *ClassName.sharedMemberName*), as in lines 8, 13 and 18 of Fig. 9.14. A class's Private Shared members can be accessed by clients only indirectly through the class's non-Private methods and properties. Shared class members are available as soon as the class is loaded into memory at execution time; they exist for the duration of program execution, *even when no objects of that class exist*. To allow clients to access a Private Shared class member when no objects of the class exist, you must provide a non-Private Shared method or property, like Count (Fig. 9.13).

Testing *Shared* Variables

Class SharedTest (Fig. 9.14) demonstrates the Shared members of Fig. 9.13. Lines 7–8 of Fig. 9.14 use class Employee's ReadOnly Shared Property Count to obtain the current value of countValue. No Employee objects exist yet, so countValue is 0. We access Count using the expression Employee.Count. Line 10 then creates an Employee object, causing countValue to be incremented by 1. Lines 11–13 output the Employee's name and use ReadOnly Shared Property Count to display the updated countValue (now 1). Line 15 creates a second Employee object, then lines 16–19 output the Employee's name and use ReadOnly Shared Property Count to display the updated countValue (now 2). Lines 22–23 set the Employee objects' references to Nothing, so that employee1 and employee2 no longer refer to the Employee objects. This "marks" the objects for garbage collection, because there are no more references to these objects in the program. The garbage collector *can* now reclaim the objects' memory, but it's *not guaranteed when (or if)* this will occur. *When a program terminates, all memory used by that program is returned to the system.*

```
1   ' Fig. 9.14: SharedTest.vb
2   ' Demonstrate Shared members.
3   Public Class SharedTest
4      Private Sub SharedTest_Load(sender As Object,
5         e As EventArgs) Handles MyBase.Load
6
7         outputTextBox.AppendText("Employees before instantiation: " &
8            Employee.Count & vbCrLf) ' Count is a Shared property
9
10        Dim employee1 As New Employee("Susan", "Baker") ' call constructor
11        outputTextBox.AppendText(vbCrLf & "Created employee: " &
12           employee1.FirstName & " " & employee1.LastName & vbCrLf &
13           "Current number of Employees is: " & Employee.Count & vbCrLf)
14
15        Dim employee2 As New Employee("Bob", "Blue") ' call constructor
16        outputTextBox.AppendText(vbCrLf & "Created employee: " &
17           employee2.FirstName & " " & employee2.LastName & vbCrLf &
18           "Current number of Employees is: " & Employee.Count &
19           vbCrLf & vbCrLf)
20
21        outputTextBox.AppendText("Marking employees for garbage collection")
22        employee1 = Nothing ' mark employee1 for garbage collection
```

Fig. 9.14 | Demonstrate Shared members. (Part 1 of 2.)

```
23          employee2 = Nothing ' mark employee2 for garbage collection
24       End Sub ' SharedTest_Load
25    End Class ' SharedTest
```

a) Showing the number of **Employees** before and after **Employee** objects are created

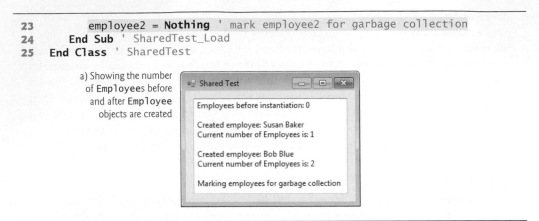

Fig. 9.14 | Demonstrate **Shared** members. (Part 2 of 2.)

Shared Members and the Me Reference

Shared methods and properties do not have access to the **Me** reference, which can be used to directly access only non-**Shared** class members. **Shared** class members exist *independently* of any class objects and even when there are no objects of that class. Like other methods and properties, **Shared** methods and properties *can* use a reference to an object to access that object's non-**Shared** members.

Shared Constructors

Shared variables are often initialized to their default values or to other values in their declarations. When a **Shared** variable requires initialization that cannot be accomplished in its declaration (such as complex calculations or constructor arguments), you can perform the initialization in a **Shared constructor**. Such a constructor is preceded by the **Shared** modifier and can be used to initialize only the class's **Shared** variables. A **Shared** constructor is implicitly **Public**, must be declared with no parameters and is guaranteed to execute before a program creates any objects of the class or accesses any **Shared** class members. A class can have both a **Shared** constructor and a non-**Shared** parameterless constructor.

9.13 Const and ReadOnly Fields

Some data needs to be modifiable and some does not. Constants are fields whose values cannot change during program execution. To create a constant in a class, declare an identifier as either **Const** or **ReadOnly**. Neither type of constant can be modified once initialized—the compiler will flag as an error any attempt to do so.

Const

A **Const** identifier *must be initialized at compile time in its declaration and can be initialized only to constant values*, such as integers, floating-point numbers, string literals, characters and other **Const** values. For example, in Fig. 9.8, we used the following **Const** declaration:

```
    Private Const NUMBER_OF_CARDS As Integer = 52 ' number of cards
```

to create a constant representing the number of cards in a deck of playing cards.

ReadOnly

In some cases, a constant's value is not known until *execution time*—either because the constant is initialized with a non-constant value (such as a variable), or because the constant must be initialized with a (possibly) different value on a per-object basis. For example, in a large company, each employee typically has a unique employee ID that does not change. Such a value would be initialized by a constructor at the time you create each Employee object. An identifier declared as ReadOnly can be initialized *either* in its declaration *or* in the class's constructor(s). The following declaration creates an employeeID constant that might be part of an Employee class:

```
Private ReadOnly employeeID As Integer ' unique employee ID
```

To initialize the constant employee-by-employee, you can use the constructor:

```
Public Sub New(ID As Integer)
    employeeID = ID ' initialize constant with constructor argument
End Sub
```

Accessing Public Constants from Client Code

Consts are implicitly Shared. If you have a Public Const value, client code can access it with the class name followed by the dot separator and the Const's name. Each object of a class with a ReadOnly constant has a *separate copy* of the constant, unless you explicitly declare the constant as Shared. If you have a Public ReadOnly constant in your class, client code can access it via a reference to an object of that class.

9.14 Shared Methods and Class Math

Class Math provides a collection of Shared methods that enable you to perform common mathematical calculations. For example, you can calculate the square root of 900.0 with the Shared method call

```
Math.Sqrt(900.0)
```

which evaluates to and returns 30.0. Method Sqrt takes an argument of type Double and returns a result of type Double. We do *not* create a Math object before calling method Sqrt. All Math class methods are Shared and are therefore called by preceding the name of the method with the class name Math and a dot (.) separator. Figure 9.15 summarizes several Math class methods. In the figure, x and y are of type Double. Methods Min, Max and Abs have overloaded versions for several types. Methods Floor and Ceiling each provide an overloaded version for type Decimal.

Method	Description	Example
Abs(x)	returns the *absolute value* of x	Abs(23.7) is 23.7 Abs(0) is 0 Abs(-23.7) is 23.7
Ceiling(x)	*rounds x* to the smallest integer not less than x	Ceiling(9.2) is 10.0 Ceiling(-9.8) is -9.0

Fig. 9.15 | Common Math class methods. (Part 1 of 2.)

Method	Description	Example
Floor(x)	rounds x to the largest integer *not greater than x*	Floor(9.2) is 9.0 Floor(-9.8) is -10.0
Max(x, y)	returns the *larger* value of x and y (overloaded for each of the primitive numeric types)	Max(2.3, 12.7) is 12.7 Max(-2.3, -12.7) is -2.3
Min(x, y)	returns the *smaller* value of x and y (overloaded for each of the primitive numeric types)	Min(2.3, 12.7) is 2.3 Min(-2.3, -12.7) is -12.7
Pow(x, y)	calculates x raised to the *power y* (x^y)	Pow(2.0, 7.0) is 128.0 Pow(9.0, .5) is 3.0
Sqrt(x)	returns the *square root* of x	Sqrt(9.0) is 3.0 Sqrt(2.0) is 1.4142135623731

Fig. 9.15 | Common Math class methods. (Part 2 of 2.)

Math Class Constants *PI and E*

Class Math also declares two commonly used mathematical constants: **Math.PI** and **Math.E**. These values are declared in class Math with the modifiers Public and Const. The constant Math.PI represents π (3.14159265358979323846)—the ratio of a circle's circumference to its diameter. The constant Math.E (2.7182818284590452354) is the base value for natural logarithms (calculated with Shared Math method Log).

9.15 Object Browser

Visual Studio's **Object Browser** lists all the class libraries that are available to the app, including the Framework Class Library classes and programmer-defined classes. You use the **Object Browser** to learn about the functionality provided by specific classes. To open the **Object Browser**, right click any class, method or property in the code editor and select **Go To Definition**. If the source code for the selected type is available (for example, it's another class in the same project), the source code opens rather than the **Object Browser**.

Figure 9.16 shows the **Object Browser** after right clicking the class Random in line 7 of Fig. 9.8 and selecting **Go To Definition**. Figure 9.17 shows the **Object Browser** after the user selects method Next of class Random in Fig. 9.16. The **Object Browser** lists all non-Private members provided by class Random in the upper-right portion of the window, which offers you instant access to information regarding the services of the selected class. This is an excellent way to learn more about the classes you're using.

9.16 Wrap-Up

This chapter investigated the object-oriented programming concepts of classes, objects, methods, constructors, properties, instance variables and Shared class members. We presented several complete class declarations consisting of Private data, overloaded constructors for initialization flexibility, properties for manipulating the class's data, and methods that performed the services provided by each class.

Classes available to the app are listed here   Selected class's non-`Private` members are listed here   Details of a particular member are listed here (or a summary of the class if a specific member is not selected)

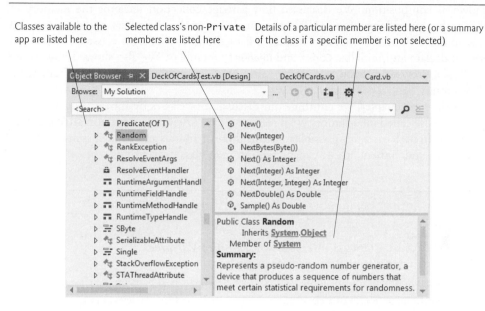

Fig. 9.16 | **Object Browser** for class Random.

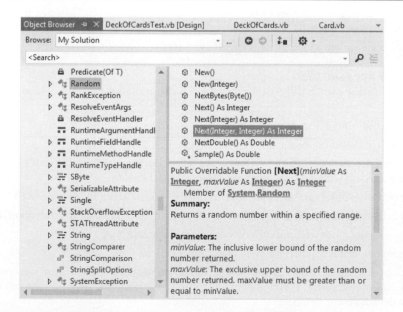

Fig. 9.17 | **Object Browser** for class Random's Next method.

You learned how to initialize the properties of an object with an object-initializer list. You saw that a class can have references to objects of other classes as members—a concept known as composition. We discussed how garbage collection reclaims the memory of objects that are no longer needed. We motivated Shared class members, and demonstrated how to declare and use Shared variables and methods in your own classes. You learned how to declare and initialize Const and ReadOnly members. We also showed how to use the **Object Browser** to learn the functionality provided by the classes of the Framework Class Library.

In the next chapter, we continue our discussion of classes by introducing a form of software reuse called inheritance. We'll see that classes often share common attributes and behaviors. In such cases, it's possible to define those attributes and behaviors in a common "base" class and "inherit" those capabilities into new class declarations.

Summary

Section 9.2 Classes, Objects, Methods and Instance Variables

- Performing a task in a program requires a method.
- In a class, you provide one or more methods that are designed to perform the class's tasks.
- You must build an object of a class before a program can perform the class's tasks.
- Each message sent to an object is a method call that tells a method to perform its task.
- Any code that interacts with any object of a particular class is known as a client of that class—objects provide services to the class's clients.
- An object has attributes that are carried with it as it's used in a program. These attributes are specified in the object's class.
- Attributes are specified by the class's instance variables.

Section 9.3 Account Class

- To add a class to a project, right click the project name in the **Solution Explorer** and select **Add > Class...**.
- The keyword Public is an access modifier.
- Only Public classes can be reused in other projects.
- Every class declaration contains keyword Class followed immediately by the class's name. Every class's body ends with the keywords End Class.
- Private class members are accessible only within the class in which they are declared.
- Public class members are accessible wherever the program has a reference to an object of the class.
- Instance variables declared with Dim default to Private access.
- A constructor call is required for every object that's created.
- The compiler provides a default constructor with no parameters in any class that does not explicitly declare a constructor. If you provide any constructors for a class, the compiler will not provide a default one.
- You can provide a parameterless constructor that contains code and takes no parameters, or that takes only Optional parameters so you can call it with no arguments.
- Constructors must be named New and be implemented as Sub procedures.
- Constructors can be overloaded.
- A Throw statement immediately returns its exception argument to the caller.

- Classes often provide `Public` properties that allow clients to assign values to (set) or obtain the values of (get) `Private` instance variables. Each property typically contains a `Set` accessor (to modify the variable's value) and a `Get` accessor (to retrieve the variable's value).

- A property is defined with the `Property...End Property` keywords.

- A `ReadOnly` property provides only a `Get` accessor.

- Each class you create becomes a new type that can be used to declare variables and create objects.

- An object-creation expression creates a new object of the class specified to the right of `New` and calls the object's constructor.

Section 9.4 Value Types and Reference Types
- A variable of a value type (such as `Integer`) contains a single value of that type.

- A variable of a reference type (sometimes called a reference) contains the location where an object is stored in memory. Such a variable is said to refer to an object.

- A reference-type variable is initialized by default to the value `Nothing` if you do not initialize it to refer to an object.

- Except for the reference type `String`, Visual Basic's primitive types are value types.

Section 9.5 Case Study: Card Shuffling and Dealing Simulation
- The elements of an array can be of either value types or reference types.

- A class can have references to objects of other classes as members. This is called composition and is sometimes referred to as the *has-a* relationship.

- `Private` methods are called utility methods, or helper methods, because they can be called only by other methods of the class to support their operation.

- Method `ToString` takes no arguments and returns a `String` representation of an object.

- `String` method `Replace` replaces substrings in a `String`. All occurrences of the method's first `String` argument are replaced with its second `String` argument.

Section 9.6 Case Study: Time Class
- Constructors can be overloaded. The compiler invokes the appropriate constructor by matching the number, types and order of the arguments in the constructor call with the number, types and order of the parameters specified in each constructor's declaration.

- When one object of a class has a reference to another object of the same class, the first object can access all of the second object's data, methods and properties (including those that are `Private`).

- Assigning a value to a property invokes the property's `Set` accessor.

- `Private` instance variables do not guarantee data integrity. You must provide validity checking.

- The `With` statement allows you to access an object's members inside the statement without having to specify the name of the object before the dot separator.

Section 9.7 Class Scope
- A class's instance variables and methods have class scope. Within this scope, a class's members are accessible to all of the class's members and can be referenced simply by name.

Section 9.8 Object Initializers
- Object initializers use the `With` keyword to allow you to create an object and initialize its properties in the same statement. To use an object initializer, follow the object creation expression with the `With` keyword and an object initializer list in curly braces (`{ }`) containing the properties to initialize and their values.

- Each property name must be preceded by the dot separator (.) and can appear only once in the object-initializer list.
- An object-initializer list cannot be empty and cannot contain properties that are declared Shared, Const or ReadOnly.

Section 9.9 Auto-Implemented Properties
- For properties that do not have any additional logic in their Set and Get accessors, auto-implemented properties allow you to write one line of code and have the compiler to generate the property's instance variable and accessors.

Section 9.10 Using Me to Access the Current Object
- Every object can access itself through the Me reference. On every method call, the compiler passes an object's Me reference as an implicit argument to each of the object's non-Shared methods.
- When a method has a parameter or local variable with the same name as one of the class's instance variables, the instance variable is shadowed until the method terminates execution.
- Shadowed class members can be accessed via the Me reference.

Section 9.11 Garbage Collection
- Every object you create uses various system resources, such as memory. These resources must be returned to the system when they're no longer needed to avoid resource leaks.
- The Common Language Runtime (CLR) performs automatic garbage collection to reclaim the memory occupied by objects that are no longer in use.

Section 9.12 Shared Class Members
- A Shared class variable represents classwide information—all objects of the class share the same variable. Together, a class's instance variables and Shared variables are know as the class's fields.
- Shared class members have class scope.
- A class's Public Shared members can be accessed by clients via the class name and a dot separator.
- A class's Private Shared class members can be accessed by clients only indirectly through the class's non-Private methods and properties.
- Shared class members are available as soon as the class is loaded into memory at execution time; they exist for the duration of program execution, even when no objects of that class exist.
- Shared methods and properties do not have access to the Me reference.
- A Shared constructor is implicitly Public, must be declared with no parameters, can initialize only the class's Shared variables and is guaranteed to execute before a program creates any objects of the class or accesses any Shared class members.

Section 9.13 Const and ReadOnly Members
- Constants are values that cannot change during program execution.
- An identifier declared as Const must be initialized in its declaration. Const fields can be initialized only to constant values.
- An identifier declared as ReadOnly can be initialized either in its declaration *or* in the class's constructor(s). Constant fields with values that cannot be determined at compile time must be declared ReadOnly.

Section 9.14 Shared Methods and Class Math
- Class Math provides a collection of Shared methods that enable you to perform common mathematical calculations.

- Class Math also declares two commonly used mathematical constants: Math.PI and Math.E. These values are declared in class Math with the modifiers Public and Const.

Section 9.15 Object Browser
- Visual Studio's **Object Browser** lists all the libraries that are available to an app, including the Framework Class Library classes and programmer-defined classes. You use the **Object Browser** to learn about the functionality provided by specific classes. To open the **Object Browser**, right click any class, method or property in the code editor and select **Go To Definition**.

Terminology

access modifier 349
ArgumentOutOfRangeException class 350
auto-implemented property 369
Class...End Class keywords 349
class scope 368
classwide information 371
client of a class 348
composition 356
Const keyword 374
constructor 350
default constructor 350
encapsulation 350
extensible language 352
field of a class 371
floating-point type 355
garbage collector 371
Get accessor of a Property 351
Get...End Get keywords 351
has-a relationship 356
helper method 361
integral type 355
managed resource 371
marked for garbage collection 371
Math.E 376
Math.PI 376
Me reference 370
message (send to an object) 348
Object Browser 376

object-creation expression 353
object initializer 369
object initializer list 369
parameterless constructor 350
Private member-access modifier 350
Property...End Property keywords 351
Public keyword 349
Public property 351
ReadOnly keyword 375
ReadOnly property 351
refer to an object 354
reference 354
reference type 354
resource leak 371
Set accessor of a Property 351
shadowing an instance variable 370
Shared class variable 371
Shared constructor 374
Static local variable 358
String class 355
throw an exception 350
Throw statement 350
ToString method 356
unmanaged resource 371
utility method 361
value type 354
With statement 368
With statement block 368

Self-Review Exercises

9.1   Answer each of the following questions:
- a) Properties can contain both _____ accessors.
    1. Return and Value   2. Get and Value
    3. Get and Set   4. Return and Set
- b) Instance variable declarations should be preceded by which of the following keywords?
    1. Dim   2. Private
    3. Public   4. Any of the above

c) Instance variables are considered _____ by default.

1. `Private`
2. `Public`
3. `Dimensional`
4. None of the above

9.2 Fill in the blanks in each of the following:

a) A(n) _____ variable represents classwide information.

b) The keyword _____ specifies that an object or variable is not modifiable after it's initialized at runtime.

c) A method declared `Shared` cannot access _____ class members.

9.3 State whether each of the following is *true* or *false*. If *false*, explain why.

a) The `Me` reference allows an object to access its own non-`Shared` members.

b) A `Shared` member of a class can be referenced when no object of that type exists.

c) `ReadOnly` variables must be initialized in a declaration.

d) An object initializer first calls the class's constructor, then assigns the specified property values.

9.4 Write code to accomplish following: Suppose class `Book` defines properties `Title`, `Author` and `Year`. Use an object initializer to create an object of class `Book` and initialize its properties.

Answers to Self-Review Exercises

9.1 a) 3. b) 2. c) 1.

9.2 a) `Shared`. b) `ReadOnly`. c) non-`Shared`.

9.3 a) True. b) True. c) False. They can also be initialized in the class's constructors. d) True.

9.4 `New Book() With {.Title = "Visual Basic 2012 How to Program",`
`.Author = "Deitel", .Year = 2013}`

Quick Quiz

9.5 Answer each of the following questions:

a) Keyword _____ introduces a class definition.

1. `NewClass`
2. `ClassDef`
3. `VBClass`
4. `Class`

b) Keyword _____ is used to create an object.

1. `CreateObject`
2. `Instantiate`
3. `Create`
4. `New`

c) The _____ is used to retrieve the value of an instance variable.

1. `Get` accessor of a property
2. `Retrieve` method of a class
3. `Client` method of a class
4. `Set` accessor of a property

d) An important difference between constructors and other methods is that _____.

1. constructors cannot specify a return data type
2. constructors cannot specify any parameters
3. other methods are implemented as `Sub` procedures
4. constructors can assign values to instance variables

e) A class can yield many _____, just as a primitive data type can yield many values.

1. names
2. objects (instances)
3. values
4. types

f) Instance variables declared Private are not accessible _____.
   1. outside the class   2. by other methods of the same class
   3. inside the same class   4. All of the above.

g) A class definition ends with the keyword(s) _____.
   1. Class End   2. End Class
   3. EndClass   4. End

h) A(n) _____ language is one that can be "extended" with new data types.
   1. data   2. extensible
   3. typeable   4. None of the above.

i) Variables can be initialized _____.
   1. when they are declared   2. to their default values
   3. in a constructor   4. All of the above

j) A(n) _____ can ensure that a value is appropriate for a data member before the data member is assigned that value.
   1. Get accessor   2. Access accessor
   3. Modify accessor   4. Set accessor

Exercises

9.6   *(Invoice Class)* Create a class called Invoice that a hardware store might use to represent an invoice for an item sold at the store. An Invoice should include four pieces of information as instance variables—a part number (type String), a part description (type String), a quantity of the item being purchased (type Integer) and a price per item (type Integer). Your class should have a constructor that initializes the four instance variables. Provide a property for each instance variable. If the quantity is not positive, it should be set to 0. If the price per item is not positive, it should be set to 0. Use validation in the properties for these instance variables to ensure that they remain positive. In addition, provide a method named DisplayInvoiceAmount that calculates and displays the invoice amount (that is, multiplies the quantity by the price per item). Write an app that demonstrates class Invoice's capabilities.

9.7   *(Employee Class)* Create a class called Employee that includes three pieces of information as instance variables—a first name (type String), a last name (type String) and a monthly salary (type Integer). Your class should have a constructor that initializes the three instance variables. Provide a property for each instance variable. The property for the monthly salary should ensure that its value remains positive—if an attempt is made to assign a negative value, throw an exception. Write an app that demonstrates class Employee's capabilities. Create two Employee objects and display each object's *yearly* salary. Then give each Employee a 10% raise and display each Employee's yearly salary again.

9.8   *(DateInformation Class)* Create a class called DateInformation that includes three pieces of information as instance variables—a month (type Integer), a day (type Integer) and a year (type Integer). Your class should provide properties that enable a client of the class to Get and Set the month, day and year values. The Set accessors should perform validation and throw exceptions for invalid values. Your class should have a constructor that initializes the three instance variables and uses the class's properties to set each instance variable's value. Provide a method ToString that returns the month, day and year separated by forward slashes (/). Write an app that demonstrates class DateInformation's capabilities.

9.9   *(Savings Account Class)* Create class SavingsAccount. Use a Shared class variable to store the annualInterestRate for all SavingsAccounts. Each object of the class contains a Private instance variable savingsBalance indicating the amount the saver currently has on deposit. Provide the CalculateMonthlyInterest method to calculate the monthly interest by multiplying the savingsBalance by the annualInterestRate divided by 12; this interest should be added to savingsBalance and returned to the method caller. Provide a Shared method ModifyInterestRate that sets the annualInterestRate to a new value. Write an app to test class SavingsAccount. Instantiate two SavingsAccount objects, saver1 and saver2, with balances of $2000.00 and $3000.00, respectively. Set annualInterestRate to 4%, then calculate the monthly interest and display the amounts of interest earned and the new balances for each of the savers. Then set the annualInterestRate to 5% and calculate the next month's interest and display the amounts of interest earned and the new balances for each of the savers.

9.10 *(Square Class)* Write a class that implements a Square shape. Class Square should contain a Side property for accessing Private data. Provide a constructor that takes a side length as a value. Also provide the following ReadOnly properties:

    a) Perimeter returns 4 × Side.
    b) Area returns Side × Side.
    c) Diagonal returns the square root of the expression (2 × Side²).

The Perimeter, Area and Diagonal properties should not have corresponding instance variables; rather, their Get accessors should use the Side property's value in calculations that return the desired values. Write an app to test your new Square class.

9.11 *(Enhancing Class Time)* Write a GUI app that's similar to Fig. 9.12, but with two more buttons—**Add 1 to Minute** and **Add 1 to Hour**. Modify class Time of Fig. 9.11 to provide a Tick method that increments the time by one second. Also provide methods IncrementMinute to increment the minute and method IncrementHour to increment the hour. The Tick method, the IncrementMinute method and the IncrementHour method should be called when you click the **Add 1 to Second** button, the **Add 1 to Minute** button and the **Add 1 to Hour** button, respectively. Be sure to test the following cases:

    a) incrementing into the next minute.
    b) incrementing into the next hour.
    c) incrementing into the next day (that is, 11:59:59 PM to 12:00:00 AM).

9.12 *(Modifying the Internal Data Representation of a Class)* It would be perfectly reasonable for the Time class of Fig. 9.11 to represent the time internally as the number of seconds since midnight rather than the three integer values hourValue, minuteValue and secondValue. Clients could use the same Public methods and properties and get the same results. Modify the Time class of Fig. 9.11 to implement the Time as the number of seconds since midnight and show that no change is visible to the clients of the class by using the modified Time class with the TimeTest class of Fig. 9.12.

9.13 *(Account Information App)* A bank wants you to create a GUI app that will allow bank employees to view the clients' information. The app interface should have four Labels and four TextBoxes, which are used to display first name, last name, account number and account balance, respectively. The interface should also have two Buttons, **Previous** and **Next**, which allow the bank manager to search through each client's information backward and forward, respectively. Create a Customer class to represent the client with first name, last name, account number and account balance. When the GUI app is loaded, create an array of Customer objects, then display the first client's information to the manager. [*Hint:* Use object initializers in the array's initializer list to create each Customer object.] If the current client is the first in the array, the last client in the array is displayed when the manager clicks the **Previous** button. If the current client is the last in the array, the first client in the array is displayed when the manager clicks the **Next** button.

9.14 *(Project: Evaluating Poker Hands)* The card shuffling and dealing app in Section 9.5 can be used as the foundation for a Poker-game program. Study the different types of Poker hands at en.wikipedia.org/wiki/List_of_poker_hands. Create a class called PokerHand that can hold five

Cards and provides appopriate properties and methods to help evaluate a hand. You might also need to modify class Card with ReadOnly properties that return the Face and Suit of a Card. Modify the card shuffling and dealing program to evaluate the dealt hand and display the type of hand. [*Instructor Note:* No solution is provided for this exercise.]

Making a Difference Exercises

9.15   *(Target-Heart-Rate Calculator)* While exercising, you can use a heart-rate monitor to see that your heart rate stays within a safe range suggested by your trainers and doctors. According to the American Heart Association (AHA) (www.americanheart.org/presenter.jhtml?identifier=4736), the formula for calculating your *maximum heart rate* in beats per minute is 220 minus your age in years. Your *target heart rate* is a range that's 50–85% of your maximum heart rate. [*Note:* These formulas are estimates provided by the AHA. Maximum and target heart rates may vary based on the health, fitness and gender of the individual. **Always consult a physician or qualified health care professional before beginning or modifying an exercise program.**] Create a class called HeartRates. The class's instance variables should include the person's first name, last name and date of birth (consisting of separate attributes for the month, day and year of birth). Your class should have a constructor that receives this data as parameters. For each instance variable provide a property with a Get and a Set accessor. The class also should include a method that calculates and returns the person's age (in years), a method that calculates and returns the person's maximum heart rate and a method that calculates and returns the person's target heart rate. Write an app that prompts for the person's information, instantiates an object of class HeartRates and displays the information from that object— including the person's first name, last name and date of birth—then calculates and displays the person's age in (years), maximum heart rate and target-heart-rate range. To perform the age calculation, you can get today's date with DateTime.Today, which returns the date as a DateTime that has Month, Day and Year properties.

9.16   *(Computerization of Health Records)* A health care issue that has been in the news lately is the computerization of health records. This possibility is being approached cautiously because of sensitive privacy and security concerns, among others. Computerizing health records could make it easier for patients to share their health profiles and histories among their various health care professionals. This could improve the quality of health care, help avoid drug conflicts and erroneous drug prescriptions, reduce costs and in emergencies, could save lives. In this exercise, you'll design a "starter" HealthProfile class for a person. The class attributes should include the person's first name, last name, gender, date of birth (consisting of separate attributes for the month, day and year of birth), height (in inches) and weight (in pounds). Your class should have a constructor that receives this data. For each instance variable provide a property with a Get and Set accessor. The class also should include methods that calculate and return the user's age in years, maximum heart rate and target-heart-rate range (see Exercise 9.15), and body mass index (BMI; see Exercise 3.16). Write an app that prompts for the person's information, instantiates an object of class HealthProfile for that person and displays the information from that object—including the person's first name, last name, gender, date of birth, height and weight—then calculates and displays the person's age in years, BMI, maximum heart rate and target-heart-rate range. It should also display the "BMI values" chart from Exercise 3.16.

10

Object-Oriented Programming: Inheritance and Polymorphism

Say not you know another entirely, till you have divided an inheritance with him.
—Johann Kasper Lavater

This method is to define as the number of a class the class of all classes similar to the given class.
—Bertrand Russell

A philosopher of imposing stature doesn't think in a vacuum. Even his most abstract ideas are, to some extent, conditioned by what is or is not known in the time when he lives.
—Alfred North Whitehead

Objectives

In this chapter you'll learn:

- What inheritance is and how it promotes software reuse.
- To use keyword `Inherits` to create a derived class that inherits attributes and behaviors from a base class.
- To use access modifier `Protected` to give derived-class methods access to base-class members.
- How constructors are used in inheritance hierarchies.
- What polymorphism is and how it makes systems extensible and maintainable.
- To distinguish between abstract and concrete classes.

10.1 Introduction

This chapter continues our discussion of object-oriented programming by introducing **inheritance**, a form of software reuse in which a new class is created quickly and easily by absorbing an existing class's members and customizing them with new or modified capabilities. With inheritance, you can save time during program development and build better software by *reusing* proven, high-quality classes. Enormous numbers of these classes are available in **class libraries** provided by Microsoft and independent software vendors.

When creating a class, rather than declaring completely new members, you can designate that the new class *inherits* the members of an existing class. The existing class is called the **base class**, and the new class is the **derived class**.

A derived class can add its own instance variables, Shared variables, properties and methods, and it can customize methods and properties it inherits. Therefore, a derived class is *more specific* than its base class and represents a more *specialized group of objects*.

We explain and demonstrate **polymorphism**, which enables you to conveniently program "in the general" rather than "in the specific." As we send method calls in this general way, the specific objects "do the right thing." You'll see that polymorphism simplifies programming with classes and makes it easy to extend systems with new capabilities.

10.2 Base Classes and Derived Classes

Inheritance enables an *is-a* relationship. In an *is-a* relationship, an object of a derived class also can be treated as an object of its base class. For example, a car *is a* vehicle. Figure 10.1 lists several simple examples of base classes and derived classes—base classes tend to be *more general* and derived classes tend to be *more specific*. Base-class objects *cannot* be treated as objects of their derived classes—although all cars are vehicles, *not* all vehicles are cars (the other vehicles could be trucks, planes or bicycles, for example).

Because every derived-class object *is an* object of its base class, and one base class can have *many* derived classes, the set of objects represented by a base class is typically larger than the set of objects represented by any of its derived classes. For example, the *base class*

Base class	Derived classes
Student	A GraduateStudent *is a* Student
	An UndergraduateStudent *is a* Student
Shape	A Circle *is a* Shape
	A Triangle *is a* Shape
Loan	A CarLoan *is a* Loan
	A HomeImprovementLoan *is a* Loan
BankAccount	A CheckingAccount *is a* BankAccount
	A SavingsAccount *is a* BankAccount

Fig. 10.1 | Inheritance examples.

Vehicle represents *all* vehicles, including cars, trucks, boats, bicycles and so on. By contrast, *derived class* Car represents a smaller, more specific subset of vehicles.

CommunityMember *Inheritance Hierarchy*
Figure 10.2 shows a sample UML class diagram of an **inheritance hierarchy**. A college community has thousands of community members, including employees, students and alumni. Employees are either faculty members or staff members. Faculty members are either administrators (such as deans and department chairpersons) or teachers. The hierarchy could contain many other classes. For example, students can be graduate or undergraduate students. Undergraduate students can be freshmen, sophomores, juniors or seniors.

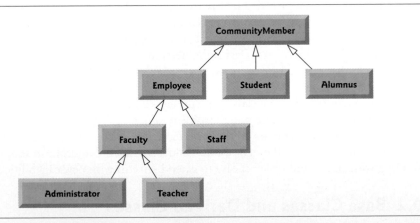

Fig. 10.2 | Inheritance hierarchy for university CommunityMembers.

Each arrow in the inheritance hierarchy represents an *is-a* relationship. As we follow the arrows *upward* in this class hierarchy, we can state, for instance, that "an Employee *is a* CommunityMember" and "a Teacher *is a* Faculty member." A direct base class is the class from which a derived class explicitly inherits. An indirect base class is inherited from two or more levels up in the class hierarchy. So, class CommunityMember is the *direct* base class of Employee, Student and Alumnus, and is an *indirect* base class of all the other classes in the diagram. Starting from the bottom of the diagram, you can follow the arrows and apply the *is-a* relationship up to the topmost base class. For example, an Administrator *is a* Faculty member, *is an* Employee and *is a* CommunityMember.

Shape Inheritance Hierarchy

Now consider the Shape hierarchy in Fig. 10.3. It begins with base class Shape, which is inherited by derived classes TwoDimensionalShape and ThreeDimensionalShape—Shapes are either TwoDimensionalShapes or ThreeDimensionalShapes. The third level of the hierarchy contains more specific types of TwoDimensionalShapes and ThreeDimensionalShapes. As in Fig. 10.2, we can follow the arrows from the derived classes at the bottom of the diagram to the topmost base class in this class hierarchy to identify several *is-a* relationships. For example, a Triangle *is a* TwoDimensionalShape and *is a* Shape, while a Sphere *is a* ThreeDimensionalShape and *is a* Shape. Shape is a *direct base class* of classes TwoDimensionalShape and ThreeDimensionalShape, and is an *indirect base class* of all the classes on the third level.

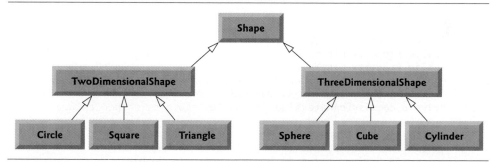

Fig. 10.3 | Inheritance hierarchy for Shapes.

10.3 Business Case Study: Commission Employees Class Hierarchy

In this section, we use a business-oriented inheritance hierarchy containing types of employees in a company's payroll app to discuss the relationship between a base class and its derived class. All employees of the company have a lot in common, but *commission employees* (who will be represented as objects of a base class) are paid a percentage of their sales, while *base-salaried commission employees* (who will be represented as objects of a derived class) receive a percentage of their sales *plus* a base salary. First, we present *base class* CommissionEmployee. Next, we create a *derived class* BasePlusCommissionEmployee that inherits from class CommissionEmployee. Then we present an app that creates a BasePlusCommissionEmployee object and demonstrates that it has all the capabilities of the base class *and* the derived class, but calculates its earnings differently.

10.3.1 Creating Base Class CommissionEmployee

Consider class CommissionEmployee (Fig. 10.4). The Public services of class CommissionEmployee include:

- a constructor (lines 11–20)

- properties FirstName (line 4), LastName (line 5), SocialSecurityNumber (line 6), GrossSales (lines 23–36) and CommissionRate (lines 39–52)

- methods CalculateEarnings (lines 55–57) and ToString (lines 60–66).

The class also declares Private instance variables grossSalesValue and commissionRateValue (lines 7–8) to represent the employee's gross sales and commission rate. Recall that the compiler automatically generates a Private instance variable for each *auto-implemented property*, so a CommissionEmployee actually has *five* Private instance variables.

The Set accessors of properties GrossSales and CommissionRate *validate* their arguments before assigning the values to instance variables grossSalesValue and commissionRateValue, respectively. Properties FirstName, LastName and SocialSecurityNumber are *auto-implemented* in this example, because we're not providing any validation code in their Set accessors. We could validate the first and last names—perhaps by ensuring that they're of a reasonable length. The social security number could be validated to ensure that it contains nine digits, with or without dashes (for example, 123-45-6789 or 123456789).

```vb
1   ' Fig. 10.4: CommmissionEmployee.vb
2   ' CommissionEmployee base class.
3   Public Class CommissionEmployee
4      Public Property FirstName() As String ' auto-implemented
5      Public Property LastName() As String ' auto-implemented
6      Public Property SocialSecurityNumber() As String ' auto-implemented
7      Private grossSalesValue As Decimal ' gross weekly sales
8      Private commissionRateValue As Double ' commission percentage
9
10     ' five-argument constructor
11     Public Sub New(first As String, last As String,
12        ssn As String, sales As Decimal, rate As Double)
13
14        ' implicit call to class Object's constructor occurs here
15        FirstName = first
16        LastName = last
17        SocialSecurityNumber = ssn
18        GrossSales = sales ' validate and store gross sales
19        CommissionRate = rate ' validate and store commission rate
20     End Sub ' New
21
22     ' property GrossSales
23     Public Property GrossSales() As Decimal
24        Get
25           Return grossSalesValue
26        End Get
27
28        Set(sales As Decimal)
29           If sales >= 0D Then ' validate gross sales
30              grossSalesValue = sales ' valid
31           Else
32              Throw New ArgumentOutOfRangeException(
33                 "Gross sales must be greater than or equal to 0")
34           End If
35        End Set
36     End Property ' GrossSales
37
```

Fig. 10.4 | CommissionEmployee base class. (Part 1 of 2.)

```vbnet
38        ' property CommissionRate
39        Public Property CommissionRate() As Double
40          Get
41              Return commissionRateValue
42          End Get
43
44          Set(rate As Double)
45              If rate > 0.0 AndAlso rate < 1.0 Then ' validate rate
46                  commissionRateValue = rate ' valid
47              Else
48                  Throw New ArgumentOutOfRangeException(
49                      "Interest rate must be greater than 0 and less than 1")
50              End If
51          End Set
52        End Property ' CommissionRate
53
54        ' calculate earnings
55        Public Overridable Function CalculateEarnings() As Decimal
56          Return Convert.ToDecimal(CommissionRate) * GrossSales
57        End Function ' CalculateEarnings
58
59        ' return String representation of CommissionEmployee object
60        Public Overrides Function ToString() As String
61          Return "commission employee: " & FirstName & " " & LastName &
62              vbCrLf & "social security number: " & SocialSecurityNumber &
63              vbCrLf & "gross sales: " & String.Format("{0:C}", GrossSales) &
64              vbCrLf & "commission rate: " &
65              String.Format("{0:F}", CommissionRate)
66        End Function ' ToString
67    End Class ' CommissionEmployee
```

Fig. 10.4 | CommissionEmployee base class. (Part 2 of 2.)

All Classes Inherit Directly or Indirectly from *Object* (from Namespace *System*)

You use inheritance to create new classes from existing ones. Every class except Object inherits from an existing class. When you do not explicitly specify the base class for a new class, the compiler implicitly assumes that the class **Inherits** from Object. The class hierarchy begins with class Object (in namespace System), which *every* class directly or indirectly extends (or "inherits from"). So, the beginning of class CommissionEmployee could be written as

```vbnet
Public Class CommissionEmployee
    Inherits Object
```

You typically do not include "Inherits Object" in your code, since it's implied. Class CommissionEmployee inherits the methods of class Object—class Object does not have any fields. One of the methods inherited from class Object is ToString, so *every* class has a ToString method that returns a String representation of the object on which it's called. We discuss the default behavior of method ToString momentarily.

CommissionEmployee Constructor

Constructors are *not* inherited, so class CommissionEmployee does not inherit class Object's constructor. However, class CommissionEmployee's constructor (lines 11–20) calls Object's constructor *implicitly*. In fact, the first task of *any* derived-class constructor is to call its *direct* base class's constructor, either explicitly or implicitly (if no constructor call is specified), to ensure that the instance variables declared in the base class are initialized properly. The syntax for calling a base-class constructor *explicitly* is discussed in Section 10.3.2. If the code does not include an explicit call to the base-class constructor, Visual Basic implicitly calls the base class's default or parameterless constructor. The comment in line 14 of Fig. 10.4 indicates where the implicit call to the base class Object's default constructor occurs (you do not need to write the code for this call). Object's default constructor does nothing. Even if a class does not have constructors, the default constructor that the compiler implicitly creates for the class will call the base class's default or parameterless constructor. After the implicit call to Object's constructor occurs, lines 15–19 assign values to the class's properties.

Method `CalculateEarnings` and Declaring Methods `Overridable`

Method CalculateEarnings (lines 55–57) calculates a CommissionEmployee's earnings. Line 56 multiplies the CommissionRate by the GrossSales and returns the result. A base-class method must be declared **Overridable** if a derived class should be allowed to **override** the method with a version more appropriate for that class. When we create class Base-PlusCommissionEmployee, we'll want to override (redefine) CommissionEmployee's CalculateEarnings method to *customize* the earnings calculation for a BasePlus-CommissionEmployee. For this reason, we declared CalculateEarnings as Overridable in line 55. In BasePlusCommissionEmployee, we'll declare method CalculateEarnings with the keyword Overrides.

Method `ToString` and Overriding Base Class Methods

Method ToString (lines 60–66) returns a String containing information about the CommissionEmployee. The keyword **Overrides** (line 60) indicates that this method overrides (redefines) the version of ToString that was inherited from CommissionEmployee's base class (that is, Object). In class Object, method ToString is declared as:

```
Public Overridable Function ToString() As String
```

so that ToString can be overridden in any derived class.

If you do not override ToString in class CommissionEmployee, the default implementation inherited from class Object would return only "*ProjectName*.CommissionEmployee"—for this example, we named the project InheritanceTest.

10.3.2 Creating Derived Class `BasePlusCommissionEmployee`

Most of a BasePlusCommissionEmployee's capabilities are similar, if not identical, to the those of class CommissionEmployee (Fig. 10.4). Both classes require instance variables for the first name, last name, social security number, gross sales and commission rate, and properties and methods to manipulate that data. To create class BasePlusCommissionEmployee *without* using inheritance, we probably would have *copied* the code from class CommissionEmployee and *pasted* it into class BasePlusCommissionEmployee, then modified the new class to include a base salary instance variable, and the methods and properties that manipulate the base salary, including a new CalculateEarnings method. This *copy-and-paste approach* is often error prone and time consuming. Worse yet, it can spread many physical copies of the same code (including errors) throughout a system, creating a code-maintenance nightmare. Is there a way to "absorb" the instance variables and methods of one class in a way that makes them part of another class without duplicating code? Indeed there is—using the elegant object-oriented programming technique of inheritance.

Software Engineering Observation 10.1

With inheritance, the common instance variables and methods of all the classes in the hierarchy are declared only in a base class. When changes are required for these common features, you need to make the changes only in the base class—derived classes then inherit the changes. Without inheritance, the changes would need to be made to all the source-code files that contain copies of the code in question.

Declaring Class *BasePlusCommissionEmployee*

We now discuss the second part of our introduction to inheritance by declaring the derived class BasePlusCommissionEmployee (Fig. 10.5), which *inherits* most of its capabilities from class CommissionEmployee (line 4). A BasePlusCommissionEmployee *is a* CommissionEmployee (because inheritance passes on the capabilities of class CommissionEmployee), but class BasePlusCommissionEmployee also has

- instance variable baseSalaryValue (line 6)
- property BaseSalary (lines 19–32).

Also, BasePlusCommissionEmployee provides

- a constructor (lines 9–16)
- a customized version of method CalculateEarnings (lines 35–37)
- a customized version of method ToString (lines 40–43).

```vb
1   ' Fig. 10.5: BasePlusCommissionEmployee.vb
2   ' BasePlusCommissionEmployee inherits from class CommissionEmployee.
3   Public Class BasePlusCommissionEmployee
4      Inherits CommissionEmployee
5
6      Private baseSalaryValue As Decimal ' base salary per week
7
8      ' six-argument constructor
9      Public Sub New(first As String, last As String,
10        ssn As String, sales As Decimal,
11        rate As Double, salary As Decimal        )
12
13        ' use MyBase reference to call CommissionEmployee constructor
14        MyBase.New(first, last, ssn, sales, rate)
15        BaseSalary = salary ' validate and store base salary
16     End Sub ' New
17
18     ' property BaseSalary
19     Public Property BaseSalary() As Decimal
20        Get
21           Return baseSalaryValue
22        End Get
```

Fig. 10.5 | BasePlusCommissionEmployee class inherits from class CommissionEmployee. (Part 1 of 2.)

```
23
24          Set(salary As Decimal)
25             If salary >= 0D Then ' validate base salary
26                baseSalaryValue = salary ' valid
27             Else
28                Throw New ArgumentOutOfRangeException(
29                   "Base salary must be greater than or equal to 0")
30             End If
31          End Set
32       End Property ' BaseSalary
33
34       ' calculate earnings
35       Public Overrides Function CalculateEarnings() As Decimal
36          Return BaseSalary + MyBase.CalculateEarnings()
37       End Function ' CalculateEarnings
38
39       ' return String representation of BasePlusCommissionEmployee object
40       Public Overrides Function ToString() As String
41          Return "base-plus-" & MyBase.ToString() & vbCrLf &
42             "base salary: " & String.Format("{0:C}", BaseSalary)
43       End Function ' ToString
44    End Class ' BasePlusCommissionEmployee
```

Fig. 10.5 | BasePlusCommissionEmployee class inherits from class CommissionEmployee. (Part 2 of 2.)

Inheriting from Class *CommissionEmployee*

Keyword Inherits in line 4 of the class declaration indicates that class BasePlusCommissionEmployee inherits *all* of the Public members (*and,* as we'll soon see, Protected members if there were any) of class CommissionEmployee. We do *not* redeclare the base class's Private instance variables—these are nevertheless present (but hidden) in derived class objects. Even though they're present, they're declared Private in the base class, so as we'll see in a moment, we'll have to make a special provision to access this base-class information from the derived class. The CommissionEmployee constructor is *not* inherited. Thus, the Public services of BasePlusCommissionEmployee include its

- constructor (lines 9–16)
- the Public methods and properties inherited from class CommissionEmployee
- property BaseSalary (lines 19–32), which *cannot* be auto-implemented because it performs validation in its Set accessor
- method CalculateEarnings (lines 35–37)
- method ToString (lines 40–43).

BasePlusCommissionEmployee Constructor

Each derived-class constructor must implicitly or explicitly call its base-class constructor to ensure that the instance variables inherited from the base class are properly initialized. BasePlusCommissionEmployee's *six-argument constructor* (lines 9–16) explicitly calls class

CommissionEmployee's *five-argument constructor* (line 14) to initialize the base class portion of a BasePlusCommissionEmployee object (that is, the five instance variables from class CommissionEmployee). Line 14 uses the **base-class constructor call syntax**—keyword **MyBase**, followed by the dot (.) separator, followed by New and a set of parentheses containing the arguments to the base-class constructor—first, last, ssn, sales and rate. Then, line 15 initializes the BasePlusCommissionEmployee's base salary.

If the BasePlusCommissionEmployee constructor did not include line 14, Visual Basic would attempt to invoke class CommissionEmployee's parameterless or default constructor, which does not exist, so a compilation error would occur. The explicit base-class constructor call (line 14) must be the *first* statement in the derived-class constructor's body.

Overriding Method CalculateEarnings

Class BasePlusCommissionEmployee's CalculateEarnings method (lines 35–37) overrides class CommissionEmployee's CalculateEarnings method (Fig. 10.4, lines 55–57) to calculate the earnings of a base-salaried commission employee. The new version obtains the portion of the employee's earnings based on *commission alone* by calling CommissionEmployee's CalculateEarnings method with the expression MyBase.CalculateEarnings() (line 36). BasePlusCommissionEmployee's CalculateEarnings method then adds the BaseSalary to this value to calculate the total earnings of the derived-class employee. Note the syntax used to invoke an overridden base-class method from a derived class—place the keyword MyBase and a dot (.) separator before the base-class method name. By having BasePlusCommissionEmployee's CalculateEarnings method invoke CommissionEmployee's CalculateEarnings method to calculate part of a BasePlusCommissionEmployee object's earnings, we *avoid duplicating the code and reduce code-maintenance problems.*

Overriding Method ToString

BasePlusCommissionEmployee's ToString method (lines 40–43) overrides class CommissionEmployee's ToString method (Fig. 10.4, lines 60–66) to return a String representation that's appropriate for a BasePlusCommissionEmployee. The derived class creates part of a BasePlusCommissionEmployee object's String representation by concatenating "baseplus-" with the String returned by calling CommissionEmployee's ToString method via the expression MyBase.ToString() (Fig. 10.5, line 41). BasePlusCommissionEmployee's ToString method then concatenates the remainder of a BasePlusCommissionEmployee object's String representation (that is, the value of class BasePlusCommissionEmployee's base salary) before returning the String.

10.3.3 Testing Class BasePlusCommissionEmployee

Figure 10.6 tests class BasePlusCommissionEmployee. Lines 9–10 create a BasePlusCommissionEmployee object and pass "Bob", "Lewis", "333-33-3333", 5000, 0.04 and 300 to the constructor as the first name, last name, social security number, gross sales, commission rate and base salary, respectively. Lines 13–22 use BasePlusCommissionEmployee's properties to output the object's data. Notice that we're able to access *all* of the Public properties of classes CommissionEmployee *and* BasePlusCommissionEmployee here. Lines 25–26 calculate and display the BasePlusCommissionEmployee's earnings by calling its

CalculateEarnings method. Because this method is called on a BasePlusCommission-Employee object, the *derived-class version* of the method executes. Next, lines 29–31 modify the GrossSales, CommissionRate and BaseSalary properties. Lines 34–36 output the updated data—this time by calling the BasePlusCommissionEmployee's ToString method. Again, because this method is called on a BasePlusCommissionEmployee object, the *derived class version* of the method executes. Finally, lines 39–40 calculate and display the BasePlusCommissionEmployee's updated earnings.

```vb
1   ' Fig. 10.6: InheritanceTest.vb
2   ' Testing derived class BasePlusCommissionEmployee.
3   Public Class InheritanceTest
4      ' demonstrate class BasePlusCommissionEmployee
5      Private Sub InheritanceTest_Load(sender As Object,
6         e As EventArgs) Handles MyBase.Load
7
8         ' instantiate BasePlusCommissionEmployee object
9         Dim employee As New BasePlusCommissionEmployee(
10           "Bob", "Lewis", "333-33-3333", 5000D, 0.04, 300D)
11
12        ' get base-salaried commission employee data
13        outputTextBox.AppendText(
14           "Employee information obtained by properties:" & vbCrLf &
15           "First name is " & employee.FirstName & vbCrLf &
16           "Last name is " & employee.LastName & vbCrLf &
17           "Social Security Number is " & employee.SocialSecurityNumber &
18           vbCrLf & "Gross sales is " &
19           String.Format("{0:C}", employee.GrossSales) & vbCrLf &
20           "Commission rate is " &
21           String.Format("{0:F}", employee.CommissionRate) & vbCrLf &
22           "Base salary is " & String.Format("{0:C}", employee.BaseSalary))
23
24        ' display the employee's earnings
25        outputTextBox.AppendText(vbCrLf & vbCrLf & "Earnings: " &
26           String.Format("{0:C}", employee.CalculateEarnings()))
27
28        ' modify properties
29        employee.GrossSales = 10000D ' set gross sales
30        employee.CommissionRate = 0.05 ' set commission rate
31        employee.BaseSalary = 1000D ' set base salary
32
33        ' get new employee information
34        outputTextBox.AppendText(vbCrLf & vbCrLf &
35           "Updated employee information returned by ToString: " &
36           vbCrLf & employee.ToString())
37
38        ' display the employee's earnings
39        outputTextBox.AppendText(vbCrLf & vbCrLf & "Earnings: " &
40           String.Format("{0:C}", employee.CalculateEarnings()))
41     End Sub ' InheritanceTest_Load
42  End Class ' InheritanceTest
```

Fig. 10.6 | Testing derived class BasePlusCommissionEmployee. (Part 1 of 2.)

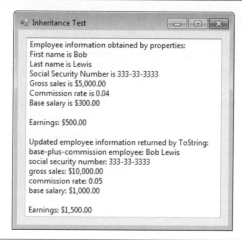

Fig. 10.6 | Testing derived class `BasePlusCommissionEmployee`. (Part 2 of 2.)

10.4 Constructors in Derived Classes

Creating a derived-class object begins a *chain of constructor calls* in which the derived-class constructor, *before* performing its own tasks, invokes its *direct* base class's constructor either explicitly (via the `MyBase` reference) or implicitly (calling the base class's default or parameterless constructor). Similarly, if the base class is derived from another class (as is *every* class except `Object`), the base-class constructor invokes the constructor of the next class up the hierarchy, and so on. The last constructor called in the chain is *always* the constructor for class `Object`. The original derived-class constructor's body finishes executing *last*.

Each base class's constructor initializes the base-class instance variables that are part of the derived-class object. For example, When a program creates a `BasePlusCommissionEmployee` object (Fig. 10.6, lines 9–10), the `BasePlusCommissionEmployee` constructor is called. That constructor, before executing its full body code, immediately calls `CommissionEmployee`'s constructor (Fig. 10.5, line 14), which in turn calls `Object`'s constructor. Class `Object`'s constructor has an empty body, so it immediately returns control to the `CommissionEmployee`'s constructor, which then initializes the `Private` instance variables of `CommissionEmployee` (Fig. 10.4, lines 15–19) that are part of the `BasePlusCommissionEmployee` object. When the `CommissionEmployee`'s constructor completes execution, it returns control to the `BasePlusCommissionEmployee`'s constructor, which initializes the `BasePlusCommissionEmployee` object's `baseSalaryValue` (via property `BaseSalary`; Fig. 10.5, line 15).

10.5 Protected Members

This section introduces the access modifier `Protected`. A base class's `Protected` members can be accessed *only* by members of that base class *and* by members of its derived classes.

In inheritance, `Public` members of the base class become `Public` members of the derived class, and `Protected` members of the base class become `Protected` members of the derived class. A base class's `Private` members are inherited but not directly accessible to its derived classes.

Derived-class methods can refer to Public and Protected members inherited from the base class simply by using the member names.

Derived-class methods cannot *directly* access Private members of their base class. A derived class *can* change the state of Private base-class instance variables only through Public *and* Protected methods provided in the base class and inherited by the derived class.

In most cases, it's better to use Private instance variables to encourage proper software engineering. Your code will be easier to maintain, modify and debug.

Using Protected instance variables creates several potential problems. First, the derived-class object can set an inherited variable's value directly without using a Set accessor. Therefore, a derived-class object can assign an *invalid* value to the variable.

Another problem with using Protected instance variables is that derived-class methods are more likely to be written so that they depend on the base class's data implementation. *In practice, derived classes should depend only on the base-class services (that is, non-Private methods and properties) and not on the base-class data implementation.* With Protected instance variables in the base class, all the derived classes of the base class may need to be modified if the base-class implementation changes. In such a case, the software is said to be **brittle**, because a small change in the base class can "break" derived-class implementations. You should be able to change the base-class implementation while still providing the same services to the derived classes. Of course, if the base-class services change, you must reimplement the derived classes.

Software Engineering Observation 10.2
Use the Protected access modifier on a method when a base class is to provide the method to its derived classes but not to other clients.

Software Engineering Observation 10.3
Declaring base-class instance variables Private (as opposed to Protected) enables the base-class implementation of these instance variables to change without affecting derived-class implementations.

10.6 Introduction to Polymorphism: A Polymorphic Video Game

Suppose we design a video game that manipulates objects of many different types, including objects of classes Martian, Venutian, Plutonian, SpaceShip and LaserBeam. Imagine that each class inherits from the common base class called SpaceObject, which contains method Draw. Each derived class implements this method in a manner appropriate to that class. A screen-manager program maintains a collection (for example, a SpaceObject array) of references to objects of the various classes. To refresh the screen, the screen manager periodically sends each object the same message, Draw. However, each object responds in a unique way. For example, a Martian object might *draw itself* in red with the appropriate number of antennae. A SpaceShip object might *draw itself* as a bright silver flying saucer. A LaserBeam object might *draw itself* as a bright red beam across the screen. The same message (in this case, Draw) sent to a variety of objects of classes in the same hierarchy has *many forms* of results, hence the term polymorphism.

A screen manager might use polymorphism to make the system **extensible** and facilitate adding new classes to a system with minimal modifications to the system's code. Suppose that we want to add Mercurian objects to our video game. To do so, we must build a class Mercurian that inherits from SpaceObject and provides its own Draw method implementation. When objects of class Mercurian appear in the SpaceObject collection, the screen-manager code invokes method Draw, exactly as it does for the other objects in the collection, *regardless* of their types. So the new Mercurian class simply *plugs right in* without any modification of the screen-manager code by the programmer. Thus, without modifying the system (other than to build new classes and modify the code that creates new objects), programmers can use polymorphism to include types that were not envisioned when the system was created.

10.7 Abstract Classes and Methods

When we think of a class type, we assume that programs will create objects of that type. In some cases, however, it's useful to declare classes for which you *never* intend to instantiate objects. Such classes are called **abstract classes**. Because they're typically used as base classes in inheritance hierarchies, we refer to them as **abstract base classes**. These classes *cannot* be used to instantiate objects, because, as you'll soon see, abstract classes are *incomplete*. We demonstrate abstract classes in Section 10.8.

The purpose of an abstract class is primarily to provide an appropriate base class from which other classes can *inherit* and thus *share a common design*. In the Shape hierarchy of Fig. 10.3, for example, derived classes inherit the notion of what it means to be a Shape—possibly including common properties such as Location, Color and Border-Thickness, and behaviors such as Draw, Move, Resize and ChangeColor. Classes that *can* be used to instantiate objects are called **concrete classes**. Such classes provide implementations of *every* method they declare (some of the implementations can be inherited). For example, we could derive concrete classes Circle, Square and Triangle from abstract base class TwoDimensionalShape. Similarly, we could derive concrete classes Sphere, Cube and Tetrahedron from abstract base class ThreeDimensionalShape. Abstract base classes are *too general* to create real objects—they specify only what's common among derived classes. We need to be more specific before we can create objects. For example, if you send the Draw message to abstract class TwoDimensionalShape, it knows that two-dimensional shapes should be *drawable*, but it does not know *what specific shape to draw*, so it cannot implement a real Draw method. Concrete classes provide the *specifics* that make it reasonable to instantiate objects.

Declaring Abstract Classes and Abstract Methods

You make a class abstract by declaring it with keyword MustInherit. An abstract class normally contains one or more **abstract methods**. An abstract method is declared with keyword MustOverride, as in

```
Public MustOverride Sub Draw() ' abstract method
```

MustOverride methods do not provide implementations. A class that contains *any* Must-Override methods must be declared as a MustInherit class even if it contains *some* concrete methods. Each concrete derived class of a MustInherit base class must provide concrete implementations of *all* the base class's MustOverride methods. Constructors and Shared methods cannot be overridden, so they cannot be declared MustOverride.

Common Programming Error 10.1

Attempting to instantiate an object of an abstract class is a compilation error.

Common Programming Error 10.2

Failure to implement a base class's abstract methods in a derived class is a compilation error unless the derived class is also declared MustInherit.

10.8 Case Study: Payroll System Class Hierarchy Using Polymorphism

Let's reexamine the CommissionEmployee–BasePlusCommissionEmployee hierarchy that we explored in Section 10.3. Now we use an abstract method and polymorphism to perform payroll calculations based on the type of employee. We create an enhanced employee hierarchy to solve the following problem:

> *A company pays its employees on a weekly basis. The employees are of three types: Salaried employees are paid a fixed weekly salary regardless of the number of hours worked, commission employees are paid a percentage of their sales, and base-plus-commission employees receive a base salary plus a percentage of their sales. The company wants to implement an app that performs its payroll calculations polymorphically.*

We use abstract (that is, MustInherit) class Employee to represent the *general concept* of an employee. The classes that inherit from Employee are SalariedEmployee and CommissionEmployee. Class BasePlusCommissionEmployee inherits from CommissionEmployee. The UML class diagram in Fig. 10.7 shows our polymorphic employee inheritance hierarchy. Abstract class name Employee is *italicized*, as per UML convention; concrete class names are *not* italicized.

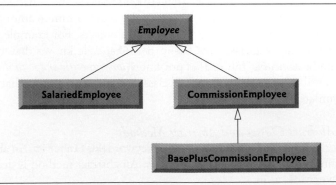

Fig. 10.7 | Employee hierarchy UML class diagram.

The following five sections implement the Employee class hierarchy. The first four show the *abstract base class* Employee and the *concrete derived classes* SalariedEmployee, CommissionEmployee, and the *indirectly derived concrete class* BasePlusCommissionEmployee. The last section shows a test program that builds objects of these classes and processes them polymorphically.

10.8.1 Abstract Base Class `Employee`

Abstract base class `Employee` declares the set of methods that a program can invoke on all employees. Each employee, regardless of the way his or her earnings are calculated, has a first name, a last name and a social security number. So `Public` properties `FirstName`, `LastName` and `SocialSecurityNumber` will appear in abstract base class `Employee`.

Class `Employee` also provides methods `CalculateEarnings` and `ToString`. Method `CalculateEarnings` certainly applies to all employees, but each *specific* earnings calculation depends on the employee's class. So we declare the method as `MustOverride` in base class `Employee` because a default implementation does not make sense for that method—there's not enough information to determine what amount `CalculateEarnings` should return for a *general* `Employee`. Each derived class `Overrides` `CalculateEarnings` with an appropriate *specific* implementation. In the test program, we'll maintain an array of `Employee` variables, each holding a reference to an `Employee` object. Of course, *there cannot be `Employee` objects because `Employee` is an abstract class*—thanks to inheritance, however, all objects of all derived classes of `Employee` may be thought of as `Employee` objects.

Although we cannot instantiate objects of abstract base classes, we *can* use abstract base class variables to refer to objects of *any* concrete classes derived from those abstract classes. Programs typically use such variables to manipulate derived-class objects polymorphically. The program we build in Fig. 10.13 iterates through an array of `Employee` variables and calls `CalculateEarnings` for each `Employee` object. These method calls are processed *polymorphically*. Including the abstract method `CalculateEarnings` in class `Employee` forces every directly derived concrete class of `Employee` to override `CalculateEarnings`.

Method `ToString` in class `Employee` returns a `String` containing the first name, last name and social security number of the employee. Each derived class of `Employee` will override method `ToString` to create a `String` representation of an object of that class that contains the employee's type (for example, `"salaried employee:"`) followed by the rest of the employee's information.

Fig. 10.8 shows the four classes of the hierarchy of Fig. 10.7 down the left side and methods `CalculateEarnings` and `ToString` across the top. For each class, the diagram shows the desired results of each method. We do not list base class `Employee`'s properties because they're *not* overridden in *any* of the derived classes—each of these properties is inherited and used "as is" by each of the derived classes.

Class `Employee` (Fig. 10.9) is a `MustInherit` class, meaning it can be used *only* as an abstract base class. The class includes

- a constructor that takes the first name, last name and social security number as arguments (lines 9–13)

- properties for the first name, last name and social security number (lines 4–6)

- method `ToString` (lines 16–19), which returns the `String` representation of an `Employee`

- `MustOverride` (abstract) method `CalculateEarnings` (line 22), which *must* be implemented by concrete derived classes.

	CalculateEarnings	ToString
Employee	MustOverride	*FirstName LastName* social security number: *SSN*
Salaried-Employee	*WeeklySalary*	salaried employee: *FirstName LastName* social security number: *SSN* weekly salary: *WeeklySalary*
Commission-Employee	*CommissionRate * GrossSales*	commission employee: *FirstName LastName* social security number: *SSN* gross sales: *GrossSales*; commission rate: *CommissionRate*
BasePlus-Commission-Employee	*(CommissionRate * GrossSales) + BaseSalary*	base-salaried commission employee: *FirstName LastName* social security number: *SSN* gross sales: *GrossSales*; commission rate: *CommissionRate*; base salary: *BaseSalary*

Fig. 10.8 | Polymorphic interface for the `Employee` hierarchy classes.

```vb
1   ' Fig. 10.9: Employee.vb
2   ' Employee abstract base class.
3   Public MustInherit Class Employee
4      Public Property FirstName() As String  ' auto-implemented
5      Public Property LastName() As String   ' auto-implemented
6      Public Property SocialSecurityNumber() As String ' auto-implemented
7
8      ' three-argument constructor
9      Public Sub New(first As String, last As String, ssn As String)
10        FirstName = first ' invoke auto-implemented property
11        LastName = last ' invoke auto-implemented property
12        SocialSecurityNumber = ssn ' invoke auto-implemented property
13     End Sub ' New
14
15     ' return String representation of Employee object
16     Public Overrides Function ToString() As String
17        Return String.Format("{0} {1}{2}{3} {4}", FirstName, LastName,
18           vbCrLf, "social security number:", SocialSecurityNumber)
19     End Function ' ToString
20
21     ' abstract method overridden by derived classes
22     Public MustOverride Function CalculateEarnings() As Decimal
23  End Class ' Employee
```

Fig. 10.9 | Employee abstract base class.

Why did we decide to declare `CalculateEarnings` as a `MustOverride` method? It simply does not make sense to provide an implementation of this method in class

Employee. We cannot calculate the earnings for a *general* Employee—we first must know the *specific* Employee type to determine the appropriate earnings calculation. By declaring this method MustOverride, we indicate that *every* concrete derived class *must* provide an appropriate CalculateEarnings implementation that Overrides the base class method, and that a program will be able to use base-class Employee variables to invoke method CalculateEarnings polymorphically for *every* type of Employee.

10.8.2 Concrete Derived Class SalariedEmployee

Class SalariedEmployee (Fig. 10.10) inherits from class Employee (line 4) and overrides CalculateEarnings (lines 33–35), which makes SalariedEmployee a *concrete* class. The class includes

- a constructor (lines 9–14) that takes a first name, a last name, a social security number and a weekly salary as arguments

- a WeeklySalary property that has a Get accessor (lines 18–20) to return weekly-SalaryValue's value and a Set accessor (lines 22–29) to assign a new nonnegative value to instance variable weeklySalaryValue

- a method CalculateEarnings (lines 33–35) to calculate a SalariedEmployee's earnings

- a method ToString (lines 38–42) that returns a String including the employee's type, namely, "salaried employee:", followed by employee-specific information produced by base class Employee's ToString method, and the value of Salaried-Employee's WeeklySalary property.

```vb
1   ' Fig. 10.10: SalariedEmployee.vb
2   ' SalariedEmployee class derived from class Employee
3   Public Class SalariedEmployee
4      Inherits Employee
5
6      Private weeklySalaryValue As Decimal ' employee's weekly salary
7
8      ' four-argument constructor
9      Public Sub New(first As String, last As String,
10        ssn As String, salary As Decimal)
11
12        MyBase.New(first, last, ssn) ' pass to Employee constructor
13        WeeklySalary = salary ' validate and store salary
14     End Sub ' New
15
16     ' property WeeklySalary
17     Public Property WeeklySalary() As Decimal
18        Get
19           Return weeklySalaryValue
20        End Get
21
22        Set(salary As Decimal)
23           If salary >= 0D Then ' validate salary
24              weeklySalaryValue = salary ' valid
```

Fig. 10.10 | SalariedEmployee class derived from class Employee. (Part 1 of 2.)

```
25              Else
26                  Throw New ArgumentOutOfRangeException(
27                      "Salary must be greater than or equal to 0")
28              End If
29          End Set
30      End Property ' WeeklySalary
31
32      ' calculate earnings; override abstract method CalculateEarnings
33      Public Overrides Function CalculateEarnings() As Decimal
34          Return WeeklySalary
35      End Function ' CalculateEarnings
36
37      ' return String representation of SalariedEmployee object
38      Public Overrides Function ToString() As String
39          Return String.Format(
40              "salaried employee: {0}{1}weekly salary: {2:C}",
41              MyBase.ToString(), vbCrLf, WeeklySalary)
42      End Function ' ToString
43  End Class ' SalariedEmployee
```

Fig. 10.10 | SalariedEmployee class derived from class Employee. (Part 2 of 2.)

Class SalariedEmployee's constructor passes the first name, last name and social security number to base class Employee's constructor (line 12). Method CalculateEarnings overrides abstract method CalculateEarnings of Employee with a concrete implementation that returns the SalariedEmployee's weekly salary.

SalariedEmployee's ToString method (lines 38–42) overrides Employee method ToString. If class SalariedEmployee did *not* override ToString, the class would have inherited Employee's ToString method. In that case, SalariedEmployee's ToString method would simply return the employee's full name and social security number, which does not *fully* represent a SalariedEmployee. To produce a complete String representation of a SalariedEmployee, the derived class's ToString method returns "salaried employee:" followed by the base-class Employee-specific information (that is, first name, last name and social security number) obtained by invoking the base class's ToString method (line 41)—a nice example of *code reuse*. The String representation of a Salaried-Employee also contains the employee's weekly salary obtained from the WeeklySalary property.

10.8.3 Concrete Derived Class CommissionEmployee

Class CommissionEmployee (Fig. 10.11) inherits from class Employee (line 4); therefore, CommissionEmployee no longer declares the properties that are declared in base class Employee. The class includes

- a constructor (lines 10–16) that takes a first name, a last name, a social security number, a sales amount and a commission rate

- Get accessors (lines 20–22 and 36–38) that retrieve the values of instance variables grossSalesValue and commissionRateValue, respectively

- Set accessors (lines 24–31 and 40–47) that assign validated new values to these instance variables

- method CalculateEarnings (lines 51–53) to calculate a CommissionEmployee's earnings

- method ToString (lines 56–60), which returns the employee's type, namely, "commission employee:" and employee-specific information, including the full name and social security number, and the values of properties GrossSales and CommissionRate.

The CommissionEmployee's constructor passes the first name, last name and social security number to the Employee constructor (line 13) to initialize Employee's Private instance variables. Method ToString calls base-class method ToString (line 59) to obtain the Employee-specific information (that is, first name, last name and social security number).

```vb
 1   ' Fig. 10.11: CommmissionEmployee.vb
 2   ' CommissionEmployee class derived from Employee.
 3   Public Class CommissionEmployee
 4      Inherits Employee
 5
 6      Private grossSalesValue As Decimal ' gross weekly sales
 7      Private commissionRateValue As Double ' commission percentage
 8
 9      ' five-argument constructor
10      Public Sub New(first As String, last As String,
11         ssn As String, sales As Decimal, rate As Double)
12
13         MyBase.New(first, last, ssn) ' pass to Employee constructor
14         GrossSales = sales ' validate and store gross sales
15         CommissionRate = rate ' validate and store commission rate
16      End Sub ' New
17
18      ' property GrossSales
19      Public Property GrossSales() As Decimal
20         Get
21            Return grossSalesValue
22         End Get
23
24         Set(sales As Decimal)
25            If sales >= 0D Then ' validate gross sales
26               grossSalesValue = sales ' valid
27            Else
28               Throw New ArgumentOutOfRangeException(
29                  "Gross sales must be greater than or equal to 0")
30            End If
31         End Set
32      End Property ' GrossSales
33
34      ' property CommissionRate
35      Public Property CommissionRate() As Double
36         Get
37            Return commissionRateValue
38         End Get
39
```

Fig. 10.11 | CommissionEmployee class derived from Employee. (Part 1 of 2.)

```vb
40      Set(rate As Double)
41          If rate > 0.0 AndAlso rate < 1.0 Then ' validate rate
42              commissionRateValue = rate ' valid
43          Else
44              Throw New ArgumentOutOfRangeException(
45                  "Interest rate must be greater than 0 and less than 1")
46          End If
47      End Set
48  End Property ' CommissionRate
49
50  ' calculate earnings
51  Public Overrides Function CalculateEarnings() As Decimal
52      Return Convert.ToDecimal(CommissionRate) * GrossSales
53  End Function ' CalculateEarnings
54
55  ' return String representation of CommissionEmployee object
56  Public Overrides Function ToString() As String
57      Return String.Format("commission employee: {0}{1}" &
58          "gross sales: {2:C}{1}commission rate: {3:F}",
59          MyBase.ToString(), vbCrLf, GrossSales, CommissionRate)
60  End Function ' ToString
61  End Class ' CommissionEmployee
```

Fig. 10.11 | CommissionEmployee class derived from Employee. (Part 2 of 2.)

10.8.4 Indirect Concrete Derived Class BasePlusCommissionEmployee

Class BasePlusCommissionEmployee (Fig. 10.12) inherits class CommissionEmployee (line 4) and therefore is an *indirect* derived class of class Employee. Class BasePlusCommission-Employee has

- a constructor (lines 9–16) that takes as arguments a first name, a last name, a social security number, a sales amount, a commission rate *and* a base salary—the first five are passed to the CommissionEmployee constructor (line 14) to initialize the inherited members

- a property BaseSalary whose Set accessor (lines 24–31) assigns a validated new value to instance variable baseSalaryValue, and whose Get accessor (lines 20–22) returns baseSalaryValue

- method CalculateEarnings (lines 35–37) which calculates a BasePlusCommissionEmployee's earnings—line 36 calls base-class CommissionEmployee's CalculateEarnings method to calculate the *commission-based portion* of the employee's earnings (another nice example of *code reuse*)

- method ToString (lines 40–43) which creates a String representation of a BasePlusCommissionEmployee that contains "base-plus-", followed by the String obtained by invoking base-class CommissionEmployee's ToString method (another nice example of *code reuse*), then the base salary.

Recall that CommissionEmployee's ToString method calls Employee's ToString method, so BasePlusCommissionEmployee's ToString initiates a *chain of method calls* that spans all three levels of the Employee hierarchy.

```vb
1    ' Fig. 10.12: BasePlusCommissionEmployee.vb
2    ' BasePlusCommissionEmployee derived from CommissionEmployee.
3    Public Class BasePlusCommissionEmployee
4       Inherits CommissionEmployee
5
6       Private baseSalaryValue As Decimal ' base salary per week
7
8       ' six-argument constructor
9       Public Sub New(first As String, last As String,
10         ssn As String, sales As Decimal,
11         rate As Double, salary As Decimal)
12
13         ' call CommissionEmployee constructor
14         MyBase.New(first, last, ssn, sales, rate)
15         BaseSalary = salary ' validate and store base salary
16      End Sub ' New
17
18      ' property BaseSalary
19      Public Property BaseSalary() As Decimal
20         Get
21            Return baseSalaryValue
22         End Get
23
24         Set(salary As Decimal)
25            If salary >= 0D Then ' validate base salary
26               baseSalaryValue = salary ' valid
27            Else
28               Throw New ArgumentOutOfRangeException(
29                  "Base salary must be greater than or equal to 0")
30            End If
31         End Set
32      End Property ' BaseSalary
33
34      ' calculate earnings
35      Public Overrides Function CalculateEarnings() As Decimal
36         Return BaseSalary + MyBase.CalculateEarnings()
37      End Function ' CalculateEarnings
38
39      ' return String representation of BasePlusCommissionEmployee object
40      Public Overrides Function ToString() As String
41         Return String.Format("base-plus-{0}{1}base salary: {2:C}",
42            MyBase.ToString(), vbCrLf, BaseSalary)
43      End Function ' ToString
44   End Class ' BasePlusCommissionEmployee
```

Fig. 10.12 | BasePlusCommissionEmployee derived from CommissionEmployee.

10.8.5 Demonstrating Polymorphic Processing

To test our Employee hierarchy, the program in Fig. 10.13 creates an object of each of the three concrete classes SalariedEmployee, CommissionEmployee and BasePlusCommissionEmployee. The program manipulates these objects, first via variables of each object's own type, then polymorphically, using an array of Employee variables. Lines 8–13 create an object of each of the three concrete Employee derived classes. Lines 16–26 display (*non-*

polymorphically) the String representation and earnings of each of these objects in outputTextBox1.

Creating an Array of Abstract Base Class *Employee* Variables

Lines 29–30 create and initialize array employees with three Employees. This statement is valid because, through inheritance, a SalariedEmployee *is an* Employee, a CommissionEmployee *is an* Employee and a BasePlusCommissionEmployee *is an* Employee. Therefore, we can assign the references of SalariedEmployee, CommissionEmployee and BasePlusCommissionEmployee objects to base-class Employee variables, even though Employee is a MustInherit (abstract) class.

Polymorphically Processing *Employees*

Lines 36–41 iterate through array employees and invoke methods ToString (line 39) and CalculateEarnings (line 40) with Employee variable currentEmployee, which is assigned the reference to a different Employee in the array during each iteration. The output

```vbnet
1   ' Fig. 10.13: PolymorphismTest.vb
2   ' Employee class hierarchy test program.
3   Public Class PolymorphismTest
4      Private Sub PolymorphismTest_Load(sender As Object,
5         e As EventArgs) Handles MyBase.Load
6
7         ' create derived-class objects
8         Dim salariedEmployee As New SalariedEmployee(
9            "John", "Smith", "111-11-1111", 800D)
10        Dim commissionEmployee As New CommissionEmployee(
11           "Sue", "Jones", "333-33-3333", 10000D, 0.06)
12        Dim basePlusCommissionEmployee As New BasePlusCommissionEmployee(
13           "Bob", "Lewis", "444-44-4444", 5000D, 0.04, 300D)
14
15        ' display each employee's info nonpolymorphically
16        outputTextBox1.AppendText(
17           "Employees processed individually:" & vbCrLf & vbCrLf &
18           String.Format("{0}{1}earned: {2:C}{1}{1}",
19              salariedEmployee.ToString(), vbCrLf,
20              salariedEmployee.CalculateEarnings()) &
21           String.Format("{0}{1}earned: {2:C}{1}{1}",
22              commissionEmployee.ToString(), vbCrLf,
23              commissionEmployee.CalculateEarnings()) &
24           String.Format("{0}{1}earned: {2:C}",
25              basePlusCommissionEmployee.ToString(), vbCrLf,
26              basePlusCommissionEmployee.CalculateEarnings()))
27
28        ' create three-element Employee array
29        Dim employees() As Employee = {salariedEmployee,
30           commissionEmployee, basePlusCommissionEmployee}
31
32        outputTextBox2.AppendText(
33           "Employees processed polymorphically:" & vbCrLf & vbCrLf)
34
```

Fig. 10.13 | Employee class hierarchy test program. (Part 1 of 2.)

```
35              ' polymorphically process each element in array employees
36          For Each currentEmployee In employees
37              outputTextBox2.AppendText(
38                  String.Format("{0}{1}earned {2:C}{1}{1}",
39                      currentEmployee.ToString(), vbCrLf,
40                      currentEmployee.CalculateEarnings()))
41          Next
42      End Sub ' PolymorphismTest_Load
43  End Class ' PolymorphismTest
```

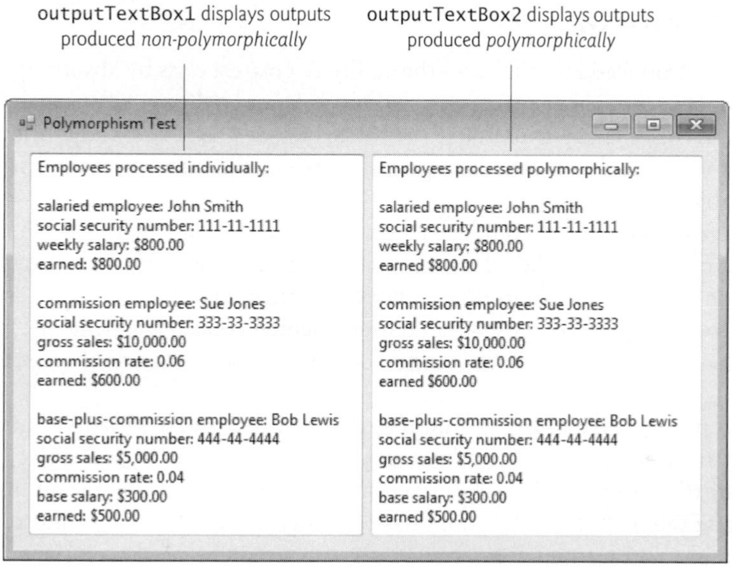

outputTextBox1 displays outputs
produced *non-polymorphically*

outputTextBox2 displays outputs
produced *polymorphically*

Polymorphism Test

Employees processed individually:

salaried employee: John Smith
social security number: 111-11-1111
weekly salary: $800.00
earned: $800.00

commission employee: Sue Jones
social security number: 333-33-3333
gross sales: $10,000.00
commission rate: 0.06
earned: $600.00

base-plus-commission employee: Bob Lewis
social security number: 444-44-4444
gross sales: $5,000.00
commission rate: 0.04
base salary: $300.00
earned: $500.00

Employees processed polymorphically:

salaried employee: John Smith
social security number: 111-11-1111
weekly salary: $800.00
earned: $800.00

commission employee: Sue Jones
social security number: 333-33-3333
gross sales: $10,000.00
commission rate: 0.06
earned: $600.00

base-plus-commission employee: Bob Lewis
social security number: 444-44-4444
gross sales: $5,000.00
commission rate: 0.04
base salary: $300.00
earned: $500.00

Fig. 10.13 | Employee class hierarchy test program. (Part 2 of 2.)

displayed in outputTextBox2 illustrates that the appropriate methods for each class are indeed invoked—you can compare the results in outputTextBox2 with the non-polymorphic results in outputTextBox1 to see that they're identical. All calls to methods ToString and CalculateEarnings are resolved *polymorphically* at execution time, based on the type of the object to which currentEmployee refers. This process is known as **late binding**. For example, line 39 explicitly invokes method ToString of the object to which currentEmployee refers. As a result of *late binding*, the proper ToString method to call is decided at *execution time* rather than at *compile time*.

10.9 Online Case Study: Interfaces

The book's Companion Website (www.pearsonhighered.com/deitel) provides an introduction to **interfaces**. An interface describes a set of methods that can be called on an object but it does *not* provide concrete implementations for the methods. Programmers can declare classes that **implement** (that is, declare the methods of) one or more interfaces. Each interface method must be declared in *all* the classes that implement the interface. Once a class implements an interface, all objects of that class have an *is-a* relationship with the interface type, and all objects of the class are guaranteed to provide the functionality described by the interface. This is true of all derived classes of that class as well.

Interfaces are particularly useful for assigning *common functionality to possibly unrelated classes*. This allows objects of unrelated classes to be processed polymorphically—objects of classes that implement the *same interface* can respond to the *same method calls*. To demonstrate creating and using interfaces, we modify our payroll app to create a general accounts payable app that can calculate payments due not only for company employees, but also for invoice amounts to be billed for purchased goods.

10.10 Wrap-Up

This chapter introduced inheritance—the ability to create a class by absorbing an existing class's members, customizing them as appropriate and adding new capabilities. You learned how to use the keyword `Inherits` to create a derived class using inheritance and how to override base-class methods to provide versions that are more appropriate for derived-class objects.

We discussed the access modifier `Protected`—derived-class methods can access `Protected` base-class members. We demonstrated the order in which constructors are called for objects of classes that are part of an inheritance hierarchy.

We introduced polymorphism—an object-oriented concept that enables you to write programs that handle, in a general manner, objects of a wide variety of classes related by inheritance.

Polymorphism makes programs more extensible. We began with an example of how polymorphism would allow a screen manager to display several "space" objects. We then discussed `MustOverride` methods (abstract methods that do not provide an implementation) and `MustInherit` classes (abstract classes that typically have one or more `MustOverride` methods). You learned that abstract classes cannot be used to instantiate objects, whereas concrete classes can. We showed how abstract classes are used at the top of an inheritance hierarchy. We introduced late binding, which enables the proper methods to be called when objects at various levels of an inheritance hierarchy are referenced at execution time via base class variables.

You're now familiar with classes, objects, encapsulation, inheritance and polymorphism—the essential aspects of object-oriented programming. In the next chapter, we introduce LINQ (Language Integrated Query), which enables you to write expressions that can retrieve information from a wide variety of data sources such as arrays, files, collections and databases. You'll see how to search, sort and "filter" data using LINQ.

Summary

Section 10.1 Introduction
- Inheritance is a form of software reuse in which a new class is created by absorbing an existing class's members and customizing them with new or modified capabilities.
- When creating a class, you can designate that the new class inherits the members of an existing class. The existing class is called the base class and the new class is the derived class.
- A direct base class is the specific base class from which a derived class inherits.

- An indirect base class is inherited from two or more levels up in the class hierarchy.

- A derived class is more specific than its base class and normally represents a more specialized group of objects.

- The class hierarchy begins with class Object (in namespace System), from which every class directly or indirectly inherits.

Section 10.2 Base Classes and Derived Classes

- An *is-a* relationship represents inheritance. In an *is-a* relationship, an object of a derived class also can be treated as an object of its base class, but not vice versa.

- Base classes tend to be more general and derived classes tend to be more specific.

- The set of objects represented by a base class is typically larger than the set of objects represented by any of its derived classes.

- The common aspects of a base class and its derived classes are expressed in the base class.

- A derived class can override (redefine) a base-class method with a customized implementation appropriate for the derived class.

Section 10.3.1 Creating Base Class CommissionEmployee

- A class that does not explicitly specify its base class inherits from Object.

- Class Object does not have any fields. One of the methods inherited from class Object is ToString, so every class has a ToString method. Method ToString is typically overridden to return a String representation of the contents of an object.

- The first task of any derived-class constructor is to call its direct base class's constructor, either explicitly or implicitly, to ensure that the base class instance variables are initialized properly.

- If a derived class constructor does not explicitly call the base class's constructor, the base class's default or parameterless constructor is called.

- If a class does not have constructors, the default constructor for the class will call the base class's default or parameterless constructor.

- A base-class method must be declared Overridable if a derived class should be allowed to override the method with a version more appropriate for that class.

- Keyword Overrides indicates that a method overrides an Overridable base class method.

Section 10.3.2 Creating Derived Class BasePlusCommissionEmployee

- Keyword Inherits indicates that a class inherits all of the Public members (and Protected members if there are any) of the specified base class.

- A base class's Private instance variables are present (but hidden) in derived class objects.

- To call a base class constructor explicitly, use the base-class constructor call syntax—keyword MyBase, followed by the dot (.) separator, followed by New and a set of parentheses containing the arguments to the base-class constructor. An explicit base-class constructor call must be the first statement in the derived-class constructor's body.

- To invoke an overridden base-class method from a derived class, place the keyword MyBase and a dot (.) separator before the base-class method name.

Section 10.3.3 Testing Class BasePlusCommissionEmployee

- When you call an Overridable base class method on a derived class object, the derived class version of the method executes. This is the basis of polymorphism.

Section 10.4 Constructors in Derived Classes

- Creating a derived-class object begins a chain of constructor calls in which the derived-class constructor, before performing its own tasks, invokes its direct base class's constructor. This process continues until class `Object`'s constructor is reached.

Section 10.5 Protected Members

- A base class's `Protected` members can be accessed only by that base class and its derived classes.

- In inheritance, `Public` members of the base class become `Public` members of the derived class, and `Protected` members of the base class become `Protected` members of the derived class.

- It's better to use `Private` instance variables (rather than `Protected` ones) to encourage proper software engineering.

Section 10.6 Introduction to Polymorphism: A Polymorphic Video Game

- The same message sent to a variety of objects has many forms of results, hence the term polymorphism.

- Polymorphism helps makes systems extensible. Without modifying a system (other than to build new classes and modify the code that creates new objects), you can use polymorphism to include types that were not envisioned when the system was created.

Section 10.7 Abstract Classes and Methods

- An abstract class is a base class from which other classes can inherit a common design. Abstract classes cannot be used to instantiate objects.

- Classes that can be used to instantiate objects are called concrete classes. Such classes provide implementations of every method they declare (some of the implementations can be inherited).

- A method with a parameter of an abstract base-class type can be passed an object of any concrete class that directly or indirectly inherits the base class specified as the parameter's type.

- You make a class abstract by declaring it with keyword `MustInherit`. An abstract class normally contains one or more abstract methods.

- A `MustOverride` method is an abstract method and does not provide an implementation.

- A class that contains any `MustOverride` methods must be declared as `MustInherit`.

- Each concrete derived class of a `MustInherit` base class must provide concrete implementations of all the base class's `MustOverride` methods.

- Constructors and `Shared` methods cannot be overridden, so they cannot be declared `MustOverride`.

Section 10.8 Case Study: Payroll System Class Hierarchy Using Polymorphism

- An abstract base class declares the "interface" to the hierarchy—that is, the set of methods and properties that a program can invoke on all objects of the abstract base class's derived classes.

- Although you cannot instantiate objects of an abstract class, you can use an abstract class to declare variables that can refer to objects of any concrete classes derived from the abstract class. Programs typically use such variables to manipulate derived-class objects polymorphically.

- `MustOverride` methods enable a class hierarchy designer to require that each derived concrete class provide concrete implementations of those methods.

- Polymorphic method calls are resolved at execution time via a process known as late binding.

- A base-class variable can be used to invoke only methods declared in the base class.

Terminology

abstract base class 399	inheritance 387
abstract class 399	inheritance hierarchy 388
abstract method 399	Inherits keyword 391
base class 387	interface 409
base-class constructor call syntax 395	*is-a* relationship 387
brittle software 398	late binding 409
class hierarchy 388	MustInherit keyword 399
class library 387	MustOverride keyword 399
concrete class 399	MyBase keyword 395
derived class 387	Overridable keyword 392
direct base class 388	override a base class method 392
extensible 399	Overrides keyword 392
implement an interface 409	polymorphism 387
indirect base class 388	Protected access modifier 397

Self-Review Exercises

10.1   Fill in the blanks in each of the following statements:

a) _____ is a form of software reusability in which new classes acquire the members of existing classes and enhance those classes with new capabilities.

b) A base class's _____ members can be accessed only in the base-class declaration and in derived-class declarations.

c) In a(n) _____ relationship, an object of a derived class can also be treated as an object of its base class.

d) A base class's _____ members are accessible anywhere that the app has a reference to an object of that base class or to an object of any of its derived classes.

e) When an object of a derived class is instantiated, a base class _____ is called implicitly or explicitly.

f) Derived-class constructors can call base-class constructors via the _____ keyword.

g) If a class contains at least one abstract method, the class must be declared _____.

h) Classes from which objects can be instantiated are called _____ classes.

i) With _____, you use base-class variables to invoke methods on base-class and derived-class objects and those objects "do the right thing."

j) Methods of a class that do not provide implementations must be declared using keyword _____.

10.2   State whether each of the following is *true* or *false*. If a statement is *false*, explain why.

a) Base-class constructors are not inherited by derived classes.

b) A Car class has *is-a* relationships with the SteeringWheel and Brakes classes.

c) When a derived class redefines a base-class method by using the same signature and return type, the derived class is said to overload that base-class method.

d) It's possible to treat base-class objects and derived-class objects similarly.

e) All methods in an abstract class must explicitly be declared as MustOverride methods.

f) It's a compilation error to invoke a derived-class-only method through a base-class variable.

g) If a base class declares a MustOverride method, a derived class must implement that method.

h) An object of a class that implements an interface may be thought of as an object of that interface type.

Answers to Self-Review Exercises

10.1   a) Inheritance. b) `Protected`. c) *is-a* or inheritance. d) `Public`. e) constructor. f) `MyBase`. g) `MustInherit`. h) concrete. i) polymorphism. j) `MustOverride`.

10.2   a) True. b) False. These are examples of *has-a* relationships. Class `Car` has an *is-a* relationship with class `Vehicle`. c) False. This is known as overriding, not overloading. d) True. e) False. An abstract class can include methods with implementations and `MustOverride` methods. f) True. g) False. Only a concrete derived class must implement the method. Not implementing the method in a derived class causes that class to be abstract (and it must explicitly be declared `MustInherit`). h) True.

Exercises

Discussion Exercises

10.3   *(Inheritance)* Justify with an example: "The set of objects represented by a base class is typically larger than the set of objects represented by any of its derived classes".

10.4   *(Derived Class)* What is an "is-a relationship"? With an example, explain why base-class objects cannot be treated as objects of their derived class.

10.5   *(Abstract & Concrete Class)* Explain with an example why an abstract class cannot be used to instantiate objects.

10.6   *(Protected Access)* What are the drawbacks of using `Protected` instance variables in the base class?

10.7   *(Shape Inheritance Hierarchy)* Draw a UML class diagram for an inheritance hierarchy for `Shape`. Use `Shape` as the base class of the hierarchy, which is inherited by derived classes `TwoDimensionalShape` and `ThreeDimensionalShape`—Shapes are either `TwoDimensionalShape`s or `ThreeDimensionalShape`s. The third level of the hierarchy contains more specific types of `TwoDimensionalShape`s like circle, triangle and square, and `ThreeDimensionalShape`s like sphere, cube and cylinder. After drawing the hierarchy, discuss the relationships that exist between the classes. You do not need to write any code for this exercise.

10.8   *(Class Object)* What is class `Object`? How does a system behave if a base class for a new class is not explicitly specified?

Programming Exercises

10.9   *(Account Inheritance Hierarchy)* Create an inheritance hierarchy that a bank might use to represent customer bank accounts. All customers at this bank can deposit (that is, credit) money into their accounts and withdraw (that is, debit) money from their accounts. More specific types of accounts also exist. Savings accounts, for instance, earn interest on the money they hold. Checking accounts, on the other hand, don't earn interest and charge a fee per transaction.

Create base class `Account` and derived classes `SavingsAccount` and `CheckingAccount` that inherit from class `Account`. Base class `Account` should include a `Private` instance variable of type `Decimal` to represent the account balance. The class should provide a constructor that receives an initial balance and uses it to initialize the instance variable with a `Public` property. The property should validate the initial balance to ensure that it's greater than or equal to 0.0. If not, the balance should be set to 0.0, and the `Set` accessor should throw an exception, indicating that the initial balance was invalid. The class should provide two `Public` methods. Method `Credit` should add an amount to the current balance. Method `Debit` should withdraw money from the `Account` and ensure that the debit amount does not exceed the `Account`'s balance. If it does, the balance should be left unchanged, and the method should throw an exception indicating that the debit amount exceeded the account balance. The class should also provide a Get accessor in property Balance that returns the current balance.

Derived class SavingsAccount should inherit the functionality of an Account, but also include a Double instance variable indicating the interest rate (percentage) assigned to the Account. Class SavingsAccount's constructor should receive the initial balance, as well as an initial value for the interest rate. SavingsAccount should provide Public method CalculateInterest that returns a Decimal indicating the amount of interest earned by an account. Method CalculateInterest should determine this amount by multiplying the interest rate by the account balance. [*Note:* SavingsAccount should inherit methods Credit and Debit without redefining them.]

Derived class CheckingAccount should inherit from base class Account and include a Decimal instance variable that represents the fee charged per transaction. CheckingAccount's constructor should receive the initial balance, as well as a parameter indicating a fee amount. Class CheckingAccount should redefine methods Credit and Debit so that they subtract the fee from the account balance whenever either transaction is performed successfully. CheckingAccount's versions of these methods should invoke the base-class Account version to perform the updates to an account balance. CheckingAccount's Debit method should charge a fee only if money is actually withdrawn (that is, the debit amount does not exceed the account balance).

After defining the classes in this hierarchy, write an app that creates objects of each class and tests their methods. Add interest to the SavingsAccount object by first invoking its CalculateInterest method, then passing the returned interest amount to the object's Credit method.

10.10 *(Payroll System Modification)* Modify the payroll system of Figs. 10.9–10.13 to include two additional Employee derived classes—class PieceWorker represents an employee who is paid based on the number of pieces of merchandise produced and class HourlyWorker who is paid by the hour and receives overtime pay (1.5 times the regular hourly wage) for hours worked in excess of 40 hours. Class PieceWorker should contain Private instance variables wageValue (to store the employee's wage per piece) and piecesValue (to store the number of pieces produced). Class HourlyWorker should contain Private instance variables hoursValue (to store the employee's hours worked) and wageValue (to store wage per hour). In each class, provide a concrete implementation of method CalculateEarnings. In class PieceWorker, the method should calculate the employee's earnings by multiplying the number of pieces produced by the wage per piece. In class HourlyWorker, the method should calculate the employee's earnings by multiplying the hourly wage times the hours worked for 40 or fewer hours. For any hours worked over 40, an HourlyWorker should receive 1.5 times the regular hourly wage. Create objects of each of the new classes and place them in the array of Employee variables. For each Employee, polymorphically display its String representation and earnings.

10.11 *(Shape Hierarchy)* Implement a portion of the Shape hierarchy shown in Fig. 10.3. You should implement the two-dimensional shapes Circle and Square and the three-dimensional shapes Sphere and Cube). Each TwoDimensionalShape should contain method GetArea to calculate the area of the two-dimensional shape. Each ThreeDimensionalShape should have methods GetArea and GetVolume to calculate the surface area and volume, respectively, of the three-dimensional shape. Use the following formulas for the area and volume of the various shapes:

  a) Area of a Square: Side * Side
  b) Area of a Circle: Math.PI * Radius * Radius, where Radius is the radius of the Circle
  c) Area of a Sphere: 4 * Math.PI * Radius * Radius where Radius is the radius of the Sphere
  d) Volume of a Sphere: (4 / 3) * Math.PI * Radius * Radius * Radius
  e) Area of a Cube: 6 * Side * Side
  f) Volume of a Cube: Side * Side * Side

Create a program that uses an array of Shape references to objects of each concrete class in the hierarchy. The program should display a String representation of each object. Each object's ToString method should display all of that object's data, its area and, for ThreeDimensionalShapes, its volume.

11

Introduction to LINQ

You shall listen to all sides and filter them from your self.
—Walt Whitman

The portraitist can select one tiny aspect of everything shown at a moment to incorporate into the final painting.
—Robert Nozick

Objectives

In this chapter you'll learn:

- Basic LINQ concepts.

- How to query an array using LINQ.

- How to sort an array in ascending or descending order using LINQ.

- How to perform transformations on the results of a LINQ query.

- How to select a portion of the properties for each object in a query result.

- How to create new objects as the result of a LINQ query.

- How a LINQ query executes only when you iterate over the results—a concept called deferred execution.

11.1 Introduction

Large amounts of data are often stored in a *database*—an organized collection of data. (We discuss databases in detail in Chapter 12, Databases and LINQ.) A *database management system (DBMS)* provides mechanisms for storing, organizing, retrieving and modifying data contained in the database. Today's most popular database systems are *relational databases*. A language called **Structured Query Language (SQL)**—pronounced "sequel"—is an international standard used with relational databases to perform **queries** (that is, to request information that satisfies given criteria) and to manipulate data. For years, programs that accessed a relational database passed SQL queries as `Strings` to the database management system then processed the results.

A logical extension of querying and manipulating data in databases is to perform similar operations on *any* sources of data, such as *arrays*, *collections* (like the `Items` collection of a `ListBox`) and *files*. Microsoft developed **LINQ (Language Integrated Query)** to enable you to write **query expressions** similar to SQL queries that retrieve information from a wide variety of data sources—not just relational databases—using a *common syntax* that's *built into* Visual Basic. This enables you to take advantage of the IDE's *IntelliSense* feature when writing LINQ queries—*IntelliSense* is *not* provided for SQL queries.

We use **LINQ to Objects** in this chapter to query the contents of arrays, selecting elements that satisfy a set of conditions—this is known as **filtering**. We also use LINQ to Objects to perform common array manipulations such as *sorting* an array. Figure 11.1 shows the types of LINQ queries we cover in this book and where and how we use them.

Types of LINQ and How We Use Them in This Book
LINQ to Objects   • Retrieve information from arrays (Chapter 11, Introduction to LINQ)   • Select GUI controls from a collection of controls in a Windows Forms app (Chapter 17, Strings and Characters: A Deeper Look)   • Query .NET collections using LINQ to Objects (Chapter 29, Data Structures and Generic Collections)
LINQ to SQL   • Retrieve information from a database and insert data into a database (Chapter 12, Databases and LINQ)

Fig. 11.1 | LINQ usage throughout the book. (Part 1 of 2.)

Types of LINQ and How We Use Them in This Book

- Retrieve information from a database to be used in a web-based app (Chapter 13, Web App Development with ASP.NET)
- Query and update a database (Chapter 25, Web Services)

LINQ to XML

- Query an XML document using LINQ to XML (Chapter 19, XML and LINQ to XML)
- Process XML returned by WCF services (Chapter 25, Web Services)

Fig. 11.1 | LINQ usage throughout the book. (Part 2 of 2.)

11.2 Querying an Array of Primitive-Type Elements Using LINQ

LINQ allows you to look at *collections* of data, extract information and manipulate data. In a LINQ query, you might want to locate all Employees whose salaries are in a specific *range* (Section 11.3). To respond to that query, LINQ has to *iterate* over the data, looking at *each* item to see if the Employee's salary is in range and, if so, *selecting* that item. You might also manipulate the data—for example, for each Employee in the result of the preceding query, you could increase the Employee's base salary by 4%.

You were introduced to *interfaces* in online Section 10.9. LINQ to Objects works with objects that implement the IEnumerable interface, which enables a program to *iterate* over a *collection* of data. In fact, the For Each...Next statement is specifically used to iterate over IEnumerable objects, such as arrays—arrays implement the IEnumerable interface. Any object of a class that implements the IEnumerable interface has an *is-a* relationship with IEnumerable—this is true for collections like the Items collection in a ListBox and other collections that we introduce in the *online* Chapter 29.

Figure 11.2 demonstrates querying the array of Integers named values (declared in line 9) in various ways using LINQ. Repetition statements that *filter* arrays focus on the process of getting the results—iterating through the elements and checking whether they satisfy the desired criteria. In contrast, LINQ specifies the *conditions* that selected elements must satisfy, not the *steps* necessary to get the results. The query in lines 20–22 specifies that the results should consist of all the Integers in the values array that are greater than 4. It does not specify *how* those results are obtained—nevertheless, the compiler generates all the necessary code.

```
1    ' Fig. 11.2: LINQWithArrayOfIntegers.vb
2    ' LINQ to Objects using an Integer array.
3    Public Class LINQWithArrayOfIntegers
4        ' test several LINQ queries
5        Private Sub LINQWithArrayOfIntegers_Load(ByVal sender As System.Object,
6            ByVal e As System.EventArgs) Handles MyBase.Load
```

Fig. 11.2 | LINQ to Objects using an Integer array. (Part 1 of 3.)

```
7
8        ' create an integer array
9        Dim values() As Integer = {2, 9, 5, 0, 3, 7, 1, 4, 8, 6}
10
11       ' display each element, separated by spaces
12       outputTextBox.AppendText(String.Format(
13          "Original array:{0}", vbCrLf))
14       For Each element In values
15          outputTextBox.AppendText("   " & element)
16       Next
17
18       ' LINQ query that obtains values greater than 4 from the array
19       Dim filtered =
20          From value In values
21          Where (value > 4)
22          Select value
23
24       ' display filtered results
25       outputTextBox.AppendText(String.Format(
26          "{0}{0}Array values greater than 4:{0}", vbCrLf))
27       For Each element In filtered
28          outputTextBox.AppendText("   " & element)
29       Next
30
31       ' use Order By clause to sort original array in ascending order
32       Dim sorted =
33          From value In values
34          Order By value
35          Select value
36
37       ' display sorted results
38       outputTextBox.AppendText(String.Format(
39          "{0}{0}Original array, sorted:{0}", vbCrLf))
40       For Each element In sorted
41          outputTextBox.AppendText("   " & element)
42       Next
43
44       ' sort the filtered results into descending order
45       Dim sortFilteredResults =
46          From value In filtered
47          Order By value Descending
48          Select value
49
50       ' display the sorted results
51       outputTextBox.AppendText(String.Format(
52          "{0}{0}Values greater than 4, descending order (chained):{0}",
53          vbCrLf))
54       For Each element In sortFilteredResults
55          outputTextBox.AppendText("   " & element)
56       Next
57
```

Fig. 11.2 | LINQ to Objects using an `Integer` array. (Part 2 of 3.)

```
58          ' filter original array and sort in descending order
59          Dim sortAndFilter =
60              From value In values
61              Where value > 4
62              Order By value Descending
63              Select value
64
65          ' display the filtered and sorted results
66          outputTextBox.AppendText(String.Format(
67              "{0}{0}Values greater than 4, descending order (one query):{0}",
68              vbCrLf))
69          For Each element In sortAndFilter
70              outputTextBox.AppendText("   " & element)
71          Next
72      End Sub ' LINQWithArrayOfIntegers_Load
73  End Class ' LINQWithArrayOfIntegers
```

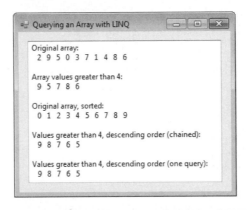

Fig. 11.2 | LINQ to Objects using an `Integer` array. (Part 3 of 3.)

Filtering the Elements of an Array

Our first LINQ query begins with a **From** clause (line 20), which specifies a **range variable** (value) and the data source to query (the array values). The range variable represents each item in the data source *successively*, much like the control variable in a For Each...Next statement. Introducing the range variable in the From clause at the beginning of the query allows the IDE to provide *IntelliSense* while you write the rest of the query—the IDE knows the *type* of the range variable (via *local type inference*), so it can display the methods and properties of the object.

If the condition in the **Where** clause (line 21) evaluates to True, the element is selected—that is, it's included in the collection of Integers that represents the *query results*. Here, the Integers in the array are included only if they're greater than 4.

For each item in the data source, the **Select** clause (line 22) determines what value appears in the results. In this case, it's the Integer that the range variable currently represents. The Select clause is usually placed at the end of the query for clarity, though it may be placed after the From clause and before other clauses, or omitted. If omitted, the range variable is *implicitly* selected. Later, you'll see that the Select clause can *transform* the selected items—for example, Select value * 2 in this example would have multiplied each selected value in the result by 2.

Displaying the Results of a LINQ Query
Lines 27–29 display the query results by iterating over them using a For Each...Next statement. This is possible because every LINQ query returns an IEnumerable object.

Sorting LINQ Query Results
The LINQ query in lines 33–35 selects the elements of the array values and returns an IEnumerable object containing a sorted copy of the elements. The **Order By** clause (line 34) sorts the query results in *ascending* order. The LINQ queries in lines 46–48 and 60–63 use the **Descending** modifier in the Order By clause to sort query results in *descending* order. An **Ascending** modifier also exists but is rarely used, because it's the default.

You can use the Order By clause only for values that can be compared to one another to determine their sorting order. In particular, the Order By clause supports values of any type that implements the IComparable interface, such as the primitive numeric types and String. Such types provide a CompareTo method that returns a negative, zero or positive value indicating whether one value is less than, equal to or greater than another value, respectively.

Chaining LINQ Queries
The query in lines 46–48 shows that you can *chain LINQ queries* by having one query operate on the results of another. In this case, the query sorts the results of the filtered query (lines 20–22) in *descending* order.

Combining the **Where** and **Order By** Clauses in a LINQ Query
The query in lines 60–63 uses the Where and Order By clauses to *filter* the elements of array values, looking for all values greater than 4, and sorts the results in *descending* order.

11.3 Querying an Array of Reference-Type Elements Using LINQ

LINQ is not limited to querying arrays of primitive types. It can be used with most data types. It cannot be used when a query does not have a defined meaning—for example, you cannot use Order By on objects that cannot be compared to one another to determine sorting order. Figure 11.3 presents class Employee and Fig. 11.4 uses LINQ to perform the following operations on an array of Employee objects:

- Select *all* Employees with salaries in the range $4000–6000 per month.
- Sort Employees by LastName *then* by FirstName for Employees that have the same LastName.
- Obtain the *first* Employee in the *sorted* collection of Employees.
- Select the *unique* LastNames.
- Select *just* the FirstName *and* LastName from each Employee object.

```vb
1   ' Fig. 11.3: Employee.vb
2   ' Employee class with FirstName, LastName and MonthlySalary properties.
3   Public Class Employee
4      Public Property LastName As String  ' employee's last name
5      Public Property FirstName As String ' employee's first name
6      Private monthlySalaryValue As Decimal ' monthly salary of employee
7
8      ' constructor initializes first name, last name and monthly salary
9      Public Sub New(ByVal first As String, ByVal last As String,
10        ByVal salary As Decimal)
11
12        FirstName = first ' calls FirstName property's Set accessor
13        LastName = last ' calls LastName property's Set accessor
14        MonthlySalary = salary ' calls MonthlySalary property's Set accessor
15     End Sub ' New
16
17     ' property that gets and sets the employee's monthly salary
18     Public Property MonthlySalary() As Decimal
19        Get
20           Return monthlySalaryValue
21        End Get
22
23        Set(ByVal value As Decimal)
24           If value >= 0 Then ' if salary is non-negative
25              monthlySalaryValue = value
26           Else
27              Throw New ArgumentOutOfRangeException(
28                 "Salary must be greater than or equal to 0")
29           End If
30        End Set
31     End Property ' MonthlySalary
32
33     ' return a String containing the employee's information
34     Public Overrides Function ToString() As String
35        Return String.Format("{0,-10} {1,-10} {2,10:C}",
36           FirstName, LastName, MonthlySalary)
37     End Function ' ToString
38  End Class ' Employee
```

Fig. 11.3 | Employee class with FirstName, LastName and MonthlySalary properties.

```vb
1   ' Fig. 11.4: LINQWithEmployeeArray.vb
2   ' LINQ to Objects using an array of Employee objects.
3   Public Class LINQWithEmployeeArray
4      Private Sub LINQWithEmployeeArray_Load(ByVal sender As System.Object,
5         ByVal e As System.EventArgs) Handles MyBase.Load
6
7         ' initialize array of employees
8         Dim employees() As Employee = {
9            New Employee("Jason", "Red", 5000D),
10           New Employee("Ashley", "Green", 7600D),
```

Fig. 11.4 | LINQ to Objects using an array of Employee objects. (Part 1 of 3.)

```
11          New Employee("Matthew", "Indigo", 3587.5D),
12          New Employee("James", "Indigo", 4700.77D),
13          New Employee("Luke", "Indigo", 6200D),
14          New Employee("Jason", "Blue", 3200D),
15          New Employee("Wendy", "Brown", 4236.4D)} ' end initializer list
16
17      ' display all employees
18      outputTextBox.AppendText(String.Format(
19          "Original array:{0}", vbCrLf))
20      For Each element In employees
21          outputTextBox.AppendText(
22              String.Format("   {0}{1}", element, vbCrLf))
23      Next
24
25      ' filter a range of salaries using AndAlso in a LINQ query
26      Dim between4K6K =
27          From employee In employees
28          Where (employee.MonthlySalary >= 4000D AndAlso
29              employee.MonthlySalary <= 6000D)
30          Select employee
31
32      ' display employees making between 4000 and 6000 per month
33      outputTextBox.AppendText(String.Format(
34          "{0}Employees earning in the range {1:C}-{2:C} per month:{0}",
35          vbCrLf, 4000, 6000))
36      For Each element In between4K6K
37          outputTextBox.AppendText(
38              String.Format("   {0}{1}", element, vbCrLf))
39      Next
40
41      ' order the employees by last name, then first name with LINQ
42      Dim nameSorted =
43          From employee In employees
44          Order By employee.LastName, employee.FirstName
45          Select employee
46
47      ' attempt to display the first result of the above LINQ query
48      outputTextBox.AppendText(String.Format(
49          "{0}First employee when sorted by name:{0}", vbCrLf))
50
51      If nameSorted.Count() > 0 Then
52          outputTextBox.AppendText(nameSorted.First().ToString() & vbCrLf)
53      Else
54          outputTextBox.AppendText("not found" & vbCrLf)
55      End If
56
57      ' use LINQ's Distinct clause to select unique last names
58      Dim lastNames =
59          From employee In employees
60          Select employee.LastName
61          Distinct
62
```

Fig. 11.4 | LINQ to Objects using an array of Employee objects. (Part 2 of 3.)

```
63        ' display unique last names
64        outputTextBox.AppendText(String.Format(
65           "{0}Unique employee last names:{0}", vbCrLf))
66        For Each element In lastNames
67           outputTextBox.AppendText(
68              String.Format("   {0}{1}", element, vbCrLf))
69        Next
70
71        ' use LINQ to select first and last names
72        Dim names =
73           From employee In employees
74           Select employee.FirstName, employee.LastName
75
76        ' display first and last names
77        outputTextBox.AppendText(String.Format(
78           "{0}Names only:{0}", vbCrLf))
79        For Each element In names
80           outputTextBox.AppendText(
81              String.Format("   {0}{1}", element, vbCrLf))
82        Next
83     End Sub ' LINQWithEmployeeArray_Load
84  End Class ' LINQWithEmployeeArray
```

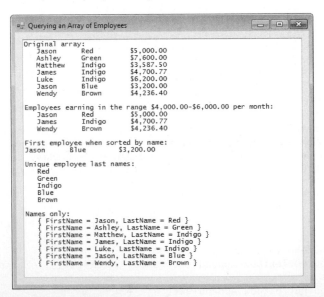

Fig. 11.4 | LINQ to Objects using an array of Employee objects. (Part 3 of 3.)

Filtering Employees Based on MonthlySalary

Lines 28–29 of Fig. 11.4 shows a Where clause that accesses the properties of the range variable employee. In this example, the compiler *infers* that the range variable is of type Employee because employees was declared as an array of Employees (lines 8–15). Any Boolean expression can be used in a Where clause. Lines 28–29 use AndAlso to combine conditions. Here, only employees that have a salary between $4,000 and $6,000 per month, inclusive, are included in the query result. Lines 36–39 display the query results.

Each element in the result is an `Employee` object, so when each element is *implicitly* converted to a `String` (line 38), `Employee`'s `ToString` method is called implicitly.

Sorting *Employees* by *LastName* and *FirstName*

Line 44 uses an `Order By` clause to sort the `Employees` in the result according to *multiple* properties specified in a comma-separated list. In this query, the employees are sorted *alphabetically* by last name. Each group of `Employees` that have the *same* last name is then sorted within the group by first name.

Using the *Count* and *First* Extension Methods

As we've mentioned, LINQ operates on `IEnumerable` objects. The `IEnumerable` interface contains the overloaded method `GetEnumerator`, which returns an object that can be used to iterate over a collection of data. Though `IEnumerable` declares only the overloaded `GetEnumerator` method, you can actually call *many* other methods on an `IEnumerable` object. In the IDE, when you type the name of an `IEnumerable` object (such as an array or the result of a LINQ query) then type the dot (.) separator, *IntelliSense* shows you a list of the methods and properties that can be used with that object. In the list, some of the method names are preceded by the icon ⚙. These are so-called **extension methods**. *Extension methods allow you to enhance the functionality of an existing class or interface without modifying the class's or interface's source code.* In fact, Microsoft has defined most LINQ capabilities as extension methods for the `IEnumerable` interface and you can call these directly on any `IEnumerable` object. For example, if you have an array of `Doubles` called `numbers` and you want to calculate the average of its values, you can simply call the `Average` extension method, as in `numbers.Average()`. You can also create your own extension methods, which is beyond the scope of this book. Some of `IEnumerable`'s 45 extension methods are shown in Fig. 11.5.

`IEnumerable` Extension Method	Description
Any	Determines if the `IEnumerable` object contains any elements.
Average	Calculates the average of the numbers in an `IEnumerable` object.
Cast	Converts the elements of an `IEnumerable` object to the specified type.
Contains	Determines if the `IEnumerable` object contains the specified value.
Count	Counts the number of elements in an `IEnumerable` object.
Distinct	Returns the unique items in an `IEnumerable` object.
ElementAt	Returns the element at the specified index in an `IEnumerable` object.
First	Returns the first element in an `IEnumerable` object.
Last	Returns the last element in an `IEnumerable` object.
Max	Finds the maximum element in an `IEnumerable` object.
Min	Finds the minimum element in an `IEnumerable` object.
Reverse	Reverses the elements in an `IEnumerable` object.
Sum	Calculates the sum of the numbers in an `IEnumerable` object.

Fig. 11.5 | Some common `IEnumerable` extension methods.

Line 51 of Fig. 11.4 introduces the **Count** extension method, which returns the *number of elements* in the result of the query at lines 43–45. The **First** extension method (line 52) returns the *first element* in the result—an Employee object in this example. If the result does not contain any elements, method First throws an InvalidOperationException. For this reason, we use extension method Count to ensure that the query result contains *at least one* item (line 51) before calling First.

You might wonder why Microsoft chose to use extension methods rather than simply including these methods directly in the IEnumerable interface. There are 45 extension methods for interface IEnumerable, so it would be costly to implement the interface for every class that wants to be an IEnumerable when you need only a few of the methods for your class. Separately, the extension methods for IEnumerable are implemented in such a manner that they are defined once and can be used on any IEnumerable object, so you do not need to customize these methods for your own classes.

Selecting Specific Properties of an Object

Line 60 uses the Select clause in a new way. Rather than selecting the range variable, we select each Employee's LastName property. So, the query result is a collection of only of the last names—which are String objects, rather than complete Employee objects. The **Distinct** clause (line 61) prevents duplicate values from appearing in the query results. In this case, it eliminates duplicate last names—*this occurs because the clauses in a LINQ query are applied in the order in which they appear, each using the results of the previous clause in the query.*

Creating Objects of Anonymous Types

The last LINQ query in the example (lines 73–74) selects only the properties FirstName and LastName from each Employee object. You can select *portions* of matching objects by specifying the properties to select in a comma-separated list. Only the *selected* properties can be accessed when iterating over the query results.

When you select a portion of an object's properties, the compiler *creates a new class* containing those properties—FirstName and LastName in this example—*and* the methods that are inherited by all classes from class Object. The new class does not have a name and cannot be used by you to create new objects—such classes are called **anonymous types**. In the anonymous type, the compiler *overrides* the inherited ToString method to return a String representation of the object in the form:

```
{ propertyName1 = value1, propertyName2 = value2, ... }
```

Local type inference allows you to use the *anonymous type*—the compiler can *infer* the anonymous type from the query in lines 73–74. In addition, the IDE provides *IntelliSense* support for the compiler-generated anonymous types. In the loop at lines 79–82, the compiler infers that the control variable's type is the anonymous type containing the FirstName and LastName properties and the methods inherited from class Object. If you type a dot (.) separator after the control variable's name (element) in line 81, the IDE displays the *IntelliSense* window (Fig. 11.6) showing the anonymous type's properties and methods.

When you execute this program, line 81 *implicitly* calls the anonymous type's ToString method to get the String representation of each element. You can see in the program's output that the ToString method of an anonymous type returns the property names and their values, enclosed in braces. You can create your own anonymous types, but this is beyond the scope of this book.

Fig. 11.6 | *IntelliSense* window for the anonymous type produced by the query in lines 73–74 of Fig. 11.4.

11.4 Deferred Execution and Transforming Query Results

LINQ uses a technique called **deferred execution**—*a query executes only when you iterate over the results, not when the query is defined.* This allows you to create a query *once* and execute it *many* times. This is similar to how methods are used. If you make any changes to the data in a LINQ query's data source, the next time you iterate over the query's results, the query will process the current data in the data source.

Figure 11.7 *filters* an array of Strings by searching for those that begin with "r". Initially the array (lines 8–9) contains two such Strings. Later in the program we modify the array then reexecute the LINQ query to demonstrate *deferred execution*. This example also demonstrates how to *transform* the items that match the Where clause—in this case, each matching String is converted to uppercase in the query result.

```
1    ' Fig. 11.7: DeferredExecution.vb
2    ' Demonstrating deferred execution and transforming objects.
3    Public Class DeferredExecution
4       Private Sub DeferredExecution_Load(ByVal sender As System.Object, _
5          ByVal e As System.EventArgs) Handles MyBase.Load
6
7          ' create an array of Strings
8          Dim colors() As String = _
9             {"aqua", "rust", "yellow", "red", "blue", "orange"}
10
11         ' select Strings starting with "r" and convert them to uppercase
12         Dim startsWithR = _
13            From color In colors
14            Where (color.StartsWith("r"))
15            Order By color
16            Select color.ToUpper()
17
18         ' display query results
19         For Each item In startsWithR
20            outputTextBox.AppendText(item & "      ")
21         Next
22
23         outputTextBox.AppendText(vbCrLf)
24
```

Fig. 11.7 | Demonstrating deferred execution and transforming objects. (Part 1 of 2.)

```
25              ' modify array elements to help demonstrate deferred execution
26              colors(4) = "ruby" ' change "blue" to "ruby"
27              colors(5) = "rose" ' change "orange" to "rose"
28
29              ' reexecute the query and display updated query results
30              For Each item In startsWithR
31                  outputTextBox.AppendText(item & "      ")
32              Next
33          End Sub ' DeferredExecution_Load
34      End Class ' DeferredExecution
```

Fig. 11.7 | Demonstrating deferred execution and transforming objects. (Part 2 of 2.)

Calling a Method of an Object in a LINQ Query's **Where** Clause

The query in lines 13–16 filters the colors array by using String method **StartsWith** in the Where clause (line 14) to determine whether each item in the array starts with the letter "r". Method StartsWith uses a case sensitive comparison to determine whether a String starts with the String in the method's argument. If the String starts with "r", the StartsWith method returns True and the element is included in the query results.

Transforming the Results

In Section 11.2, we mentioned that the Select clause can transform the selected items. The Select clause (line 16) transforms the Strings in the result by converting each String to uppercase using String method **ToUpper**.

Modifying the Array's Contents and Reexecuting the Query

We created the query only once (lines 13–16), yet iterating over the results (lines 19–21 and 30–32) gives two different lists of colors. This demonstrates LINQ's *deferred execution*. The first line of output (produced by lines 19–21) shows the two Strings that begin with "r" in the original array. Lines 26–27 replaced the Strings "blue" and "orange" in the original array with the Strings "ruby" and "rose". Notice that the second line of output (produced by lines 30–32) shows four matching Strings rather than two—*the changes to the data source were included when we reexecuted the query.*

11.5 LINQ Resource Center

This chapter introduced LINQ's basic capabilities and syntax. We use more advanced features of LINQ in later chapters. We've created a LINQ Resource Center that contains many links to additional information, including blogs by Microsoft LINQ team members, sample chapters, tutorials, videos, FAQs, resource sites and webcasts. Browse the LINQ Resource Center (www.deitel.com/LINQ/) to learn about this exciting technology.

11.6 Wrap-Up

This chapter used LINQ (Language Integrated Query) to query and manipulate data. We showed how to filter an array or collection using LINQ's Where clause, and how to sort the query results using the Order By clause. You used the Select clause to select specific properties of an object. We showed how to filter Strings starting with a specified character or series of characters by using String method StartsWith. We used the LINQ's Distinct clause to remove duplicates from the results of a LINQ query. You also learned about several extension methods for IEnumerable objects.

In Chapter 12, we begin our discussion of databases, which organize data so that it can be retained for long periods, yet selected and updated quickly. We introduce LINQ to SQL, which allows you to write LINQ queries that extract data from databases. You can then interact with the objects in the query results to insert data in, update data in and delete data from databases.

Summary

Section 11.1 Introduction

- Large amounts of data are often stored in a database—an organized collection of data.
- A database management system (DBMS) provides mechanisms for storing, organizing, retrieving and modifying data contained in the database.
- SQL is an international standard used with relational databases to perform queries and to manipulate data.
- Microsoft developed LINQ to enable you to write queries, similar to SQL, that retrieve information from a wide variety of data sources using a common syntax that's built into Visual Basic.
- The IDE provides *IntelliSense* support for LINQ queries.
- Selecting elements that satisfy a set of conditions is known as filtering.

Section 11.2 Querying an Array of Primitive-Type Elements Using LINQ

- LINQ to Objects works with objects that implement the IEnumerable interface, which enables a program to iterate over a collection of data.
- The For Each...Next statement is used to iterate over IEnumerable objects.
- Arrays implement the IEnumerable interface.
- In a LINQ query, the From clause specifies a range variable and the data source to query. The range variable represents each item in the data source.
- Introducing the range variable in the From clause at the beginning of the query allows the IDE to provide *IntelliSense* while you write the rest of the query.
- If the condition in the Where clause evaluates to True, the element is selected (included in the query results).
- For each item in the data source, the Select clause determines what value appears in the results.
- A LINQ query returns an IEnumerable object.
- The Order By clause sorts the query results in ascending order by default. The Descending modifier can be used in the Order By clause to sort query results in descending order. An Ascending modifier also exists but is rarely used, because it's the default.

- The Order By clause supports values of any type that implements the interface IComparable, such as the primitive numeric types and String. Such types provide a CompareTo method that returns a negative, zero or positive value indicating whether one value is less than, equal to or greater than another value, respectively.

- You can chain LINQ queries by having one query operate on the results of another.

Section 11.3 Querying an Array of Reference-Type Elements Using LINQ

- LINQ infers the type of a range variable based on the query's data source.

- Any Boolean expression can be used in a Where clause.

- An Order By clause can sort objects in the result according to multiple properties specified in a comma-separated list.

- Most LINQ capabilities are defined as extension methods for the IEnumerable interface. You can call these on any IEnumerable object.

- The Count extension method returns the number of elements in an IEnumerable object.

- The First extension method returns the first element in an IEnumerable object. If the result does not contain any elements, method First throws an InvalidOperationException.

- The Distinct clause prevents duplicate values from appearing in the query results.

- You can select portions of matching objects by specifying the properties to select in a comma-separated list. Only the selected properties can be accessed when iterating over the query results.

- When you select a portion of an object's properties, the compiler creates a new class containing only those properties and the methods that are inherited by all classes from class Object. The new class does not have a name and cannot be used by you to create new objects—such classes are called anonymous types. In the anonymous type, the compiler overrides the inherited ToString method to return a String representation of the object.

- Local type inference allows you to use an anonymous type.

- The IDE provides full *IntelliSense* support for the anonymous types generated by the compiler.

Section 11.4 Deferred Execution and Transforming Query Results

- LINQ uses deferred execution—a query executes only when you iterate over the results, not when the query is defined. This allows you to create a query once and execute it many times.

- If you make any changes to the data in a LINQ query's data source, the next time you iterate over the query's results, the query will process the current data in the data source.

- The Select clause can be used to transform the values in a query result.

- String method StartsWith determines whether a String starts with the String in the method's argument. Method StartsWith uses a case-sensitive comparison.

- String method ToUpper returns a String with uppercase letters.

Terminology

anonymous type 426
Ascending modifier of a LINQ Order By
    clause 421
Count extension method of IEnumerable 426
deferred execution 427
Descending modifier of a LINQ Order By
    clause 421
Distinct clause in a LINQ query 426

extension method 425
filter a collection using LINQ 417
First extension method of IEnumerable 426
From clause of a LINQ query 420
IEnumerable interface 418
Language-Integrated Query (LINQ) 417
LINQ to Objects 417
Order By clause of a LINQ query 421

Self-Review Exercises

11.1   Fill in the blanks in each of the following statements:
   a) Microsoft developed _____ to enable you to write queries, similar to SQL, that re-
       trieve information from a wide variety of data sources using a common syntax.
   b) Use the _____ extension method to determine the number of elements in the result
       of a LINQ query.
   c) The LINQ _____ clause is used for filtering.
   d) To get only unique results from a LINQ query, use the _____ clause.
   e) To sort the elements of a LINQ query, use the _____ clause.
   f) Selecting elements that satisfy a set of conditions is known as _____.
   g) In a LINQ query, the From clause specifies a(n) _____ and the data source to query.
   h) LINQ uses a technique called _____—a query executes only when you iterate over
       the results, not when the query is defined.

11.2   State whether each of the following is *true* or *false*. If *false*, explain why.
   a) The Select clause in a LINQ query is optional.
   b) LINQ to Objects queries can be used on any IEnumerable object.
   c) A key advantage of SQL queries over LINQ queries is that the SQL syntax is built into
       Visual Basic and the IDE provides *IntelliSense* for SQL.
   d) When you write a LINQ query, it immediately determines the results.
   e) LINQ specifies the conditions that selected elements must satisfy, not the steps neces-
       sary to get the results.
   f) The Order By clause of a LINQ query by default sorts the array in descending order.
   g) LINQ can query arrays of only primitive types.
   h) Most LINQ capabilities are methods of the IEnumerable interface.
   i) A LINQ query's results are the same regardless of the order in which the clauses appear.

Answers to Self-Review Exercises

11.1   a) LINQ. b) Count. c) Where. d) Distinct. e) Order By. f) filtering. g) range variable.
h) deferred execution.

11.2   a) True. b) True. c) False. LINQ's syntax is built into Visual Basic and the IDE provides
IntelliSense for LINQ, but not for SQL. d) False. The LINQ query executes when you iterate over
the query's result. e) True. f) False. The default order is ascending. g) False. You can query arrays of
any type with LINQ. h) False. Most LINQ capabilities are implemented as extension methods for
the IEnumerable interface. i) False. The order does matter—the clauses in a LINQ query are applied
in the order in which they appear and this can affect the result.

Exercises

Short Answer Exercises

11.3   What is Structured Query Language? How it is different from Language Integrated Query?

11.4   Write a LINQ query that selects values greater than 4 from an array that contains integer
values.

11.5 Write a LINQ query to sort values greater than 4 in descending order using the Descending modifier in the Order By clause.

11.6 Write a LINQ query that sorts all the Employees from the array in Fig. 11.4. Write a LINQ query to select all the employees with salaries in the range $4000 – $6000.

Programming Exercises

11.7 *(Querying an Array of Invoice Objects)* Use the class Invoice provided in the ex11_07 folder with this chapter's examples to create an array of Invoice objects. Use the sample data shown in Fig. 11.8. Class Invoice includes four properties—a PartNumber (type Integer), a PartDescription (type String), a Quantity of the item being purchased (type Integer) and a Price (type Decimal). Write an app that performs the following LINQ queries on the array of Invoice objects and displays the results:

a) Sort the Invoice objects by PartDescription.

b) Sort the Invoice objects by Price.

c) Select the PartDescription and Quantity and sort the results by Quantity.

d) Select from each Invoice the PartDescription and the value of the Invoice (that is, Quantity * Price). Order the results by the value of the invoice. Name the calculated column InvoiceTotal by using the expression

```
InvoiceTotal = item.Quantity * item.Price
```

where item is the name of the range variable in the LINQ query.

e) Using the results of the LINQ query in part (d), select the InvoiceTotals in the range $200 to $500.

Part number	Part description	Quantity	Price
83	Electric sander	7	57.98
24	Power saw	18	99.99
7	Sledge hammer	11	21.50
77	Hammer	76	11.99
39	Lawn mower	3	79.50
68	Screwdriver	106	6.99
56	Jig saw	21	11.00
3	Wrench	34	7.50

Fig. 11.8 | Sample data for Exercise 11.7.

11.8 *(Array Sorting App)* Modify the sorting example of Fig. 7.12 so that it lists three columns of data headed "Original values," "Values sorted in ascending order" and "Values sorted in descending order"; your program should display in the last two columns the values sorted in ascending and descending order, respectively. Use LINQ to sort the values.

11.9 *(Duplicate Word Removal)* Write an app that inputs a sentence from the user (assume no punctuation), then determines and displays the non-duplicate words in alphabetical order. Treat uppercase and lowercase letters the same. [*Hint:* You can use String method Split with no arguments, as in sentence.Split(), to break a sentence into an array of Strings containing the individual words. By default, Split uses spaces as delimiters. Use String method ToLower in the Select and Order By clauses of your LINQ query to obtain the lowercase version of each word.]

Databases and LINQ

Now go, write it before them in a table, and note it in a book, that it may be for the time to come for ever and ever.
—Isaiah 30:8

It is a capital mistake to theorize before one has data.
—Arthur Conan Doyle

Objectives

In this chapter you'll:

- Learn about the relational database model.

- Use an ADO.NET Entity Data Model to create classes for interacting with a database via LINQ to Entities.

- Use LINQ to retrieve and manipulate data from a database.

- Add data sources to projects.

- Use the IDE's drag-and-drop capabilities to display database tables in apps.

- Use data binding to move data seamlessly between GUI controls and databases.

- Create Master/Detail views that enable you to select a record and display its details.

12.1 Introduction

A **database** is an organized collection of data. A **database management system** (DBMS) provides mechanisms for storing, organizing, retrieving and modifying data. Today's most popular DBMSs manage *relational databases*, which organize data simply as tables with *rows* and *columns*.

Some popular proprietary DBMSs are Microsoft SQL Server, Oracle, Sybase and IBM DB2. PostgreSQL and MySQL are popular *open-source* DBMSs that can be downloaded and used *freely* by anyone. In this chapter, we use Microsoft's free **SQL Server Express**, which is installed with Visual Studio. It can also be downloaded separately from Microsoft (`www.microsoft.com/express/sql`).

SQL Server Express

SQL Server Express provides many features of Microsoft's full (fee-based) SQL Server product, but has some limitations, such as a maximum database size of 10GB. A SQL Server Express database file can be easily migrated to a full version of SQL Server—we did this with our `deitel.com` website once our database became too large for SQL Server Express. You can learn more about the SQL Server versions at `bit.ly/SQLServerEditions`. The version of SQL Server Express that's bundled with Visual Studio Express 2012 for Windows Desktop is called **SQL Server Express 2012 LocalDB**. It's meant for development and testing of apps on your computer.

Structured Query Language (SQL)

A language called **Structured Query Language** (SQL)—pronounced "sequel"—is an international standard used with relational databases to perform **queries** (that is, to request information that satisfies given criteria) and to manipulate data. For years, programs that accessed a relational database passed SQL queries as `strings` to the database management system, then processed the results.

LINQ to Entities and the ADO.NET Entity Framework

A logical extension of querying and manipulating data in databases is to perform similar operations on *any* sources of data, such as arrays, collections (like the `Items` collection of a `ListBox`) and files. Chapter 11 introduced *LINQ to Objects* and used it to manipulate data stored in arrays. **LINQ to Entities** allows you to manipulate data stored in a relational database—in our case, a SQL Server Express database. As with LINQ to Objects, the IDE provides *IntelliSense* for your LINQ to Entities queries.

The **ADO.NET Entity Framework** (commonly referred to simply as **EF**) enables apps to interact with data in various forms, including data stored in relational databases. You'll use the ADO.NET Entity Framework and Visual Studio to create a so-called *entity data model* that represents the database, then use LINQ to Entities to manipulate objects in the entity data model. Though, you'll manipulate data in a *SQL Server Express* database in this chapter, the ADO.NET Entity Framework works with *most* popular database management systems. Behind the scenes, the ADO.NET Entity Framework generates SQL statements that interact with a database.

This chapter introduces general concepts of relational databases, then implements several database apps using the ADO.NET Entity Framework, LINQ to Entities and the IDE's tools for working with databases. In later chapters, you'll see other practical database and LINQ to Entities apps, such as a web-based guestbook and a web-based bookstore. Databases are at the heart of most "industrial strength" apps.

LINQ to SQL vs. LINQ to Entities

In the previous edition of this book, we discussed LINQ to SQL. Microsoft stopped further development on LINQ to SQL in 2008 in favor of the newer and more powerful LINQ to Entities and the ADO.NET Entity Framework.

Online SQL Introduction

In prior editions of this book, this chapter included an introduction to SQL. We've moved this introduction to the book's website at `www.deitel.com/books/vb2012htp/`, because we now perform all of the database interactions using LINQ.

12.2 Relational Databases

A **relational database** organizes data in tables. Figure 12.1 illustrates a sample `Employees` table that might be used in a personnel system. The table stores the attributes of employees. Tables are composed of **rows** (also called **records**) and **columns** (also called **fields**) in which values are stored. This table consists of six rows (one per employee) and five columns (one per attribute). The attributes are the employee's ID, name, department, salary and location. The `ID` column of each row is the table's **primary key**—a column (or group of columns) requiring a *unique* value that cannot be duplicated in other rows. This guarantees that each primary key value can be used to identify *one* row. A primary key composed of two or more columns is known as a **composite key**. Good examples of primary-key columns in other apps are a book's ISBN number in a book information system or a part number in an inventory system—values in each of these columns must be unique. LINQ to Entities *requires every table to have a primary key* to support updating the data in tables. The rows in Fig. 12.1 are displayed in *ascending order* by primary key. But they could be listed in *descending order* or in no particular order at all.

Table Employees

	ID	Name	Department	Salary	Location
	23603	Jones	413	1100	New Jersey
	24568	Kerwin	413	2000	New Jersey
Row	34589	Larson	642	1800	Los Angeles
	35761	Myers	611	1400	Orlando
	47132	Neumann	413	9000	New Jersey
	78321	Stephens	611	8500	Orlando
	Primary key		Column		

Fig. 12.1 | Employees table sample data.

Each *column* represents a different data *attribute*. Some column values may be duplicated between rows. For example, three different rows in the Employees table's Department column contain the number 413, indicating that these employees work in the same department.

Selecting Data Subsets

You can use LINQ to Entities to define queries that *select subsets* of the data from a table. For example, a program might select data from the Employees table to create a query result that shows where each department is located, in ascending order by Department number (Fig. 12.2).

Department	Location
413	New Jersey
611	Orlando
642	Los Angeles

Fig. 12.2 | Distinct Department and Location data from the Employees table.

12.3 A Books Database

We now consider a simple Books database that stores information about some Deitel books. First, we overview the database's tables. A database's tables, their fields and the relationships among them are collectively known as a **database schema**. The ADO.NET Entity Framework uses a database's schema to define classes that enable you to interact with the database. Sections 12.5–12.8 show how to manipulate the Books database. The database file—Books.mdf—is provided with this chapter's examples. SQL Server database files have the .mdf ("master data file") file-name extension.

Authors *Table of the* Books *Database*

The database consists of three tables: Authors, Titles and AuthorISBN. The Authors table (described in Fig. 12.3) consists of three columns that maintain each author's unique ID number, first name and last name, respectively. Figure 12.4 contains the data from the Authors table.

Column	Description
AuthorID	Author's ID number in the database. In the Books database, this integer column is defined as an *identity* column, also known as an *autoincremented* column— for each row inserted in the table, the AuthorID value is increased by 1 automatically to ensure that each row has a unique AuthorID. This is the *primary key.*
FirstName	Author's first name (a string).
LastName	Author's last name (a string).

Fig. 12.3 | Authors table of the Books database.

AuthorID	FirstName	LastName
1	Paul	Deitel
2	Harvey	Deitel
3	Abbey	Deitel
4	Dan	Quirk
5	Michael	Morgano

Fig. 12.4 | Data from the Authors table of the Books database.

Titles *Table of the* Books *Database*

The Titles table (described in Fig. 12.5) consists of four columns that maintain information about each book in the database, including its ISBN, title, edition number and copyright year. Figure 12.6 contains the data from the Titles table.

Column	Description
ISBN	ISBN of the book (a string). The table's primary key. ISBN is an abbreviation for "International Standard Book Number"—a numbering scheme that publishers worldwide use to give every book a *unique* identification number.
Title	Title of the book (a string).
EditionNumber	Edition number of the book (an integer).
Copyright	Copyright year of the book (a string).

Fig. 12.5 | Titles table of the Books database.

ISBN	Title	EditionNumber	Copyright
0132151006	Internet & World Wide Web How to Program	5	2012
0132575663	Java How to Program	9	2012

Fig. 12.6 | Data from the Titles table of the Books database. (Part 1 of 2.)

ISBN	Title	EditionNumber	Copyright
013299044X	C How to Program	7	2013
0132990601	Simply Visual Basic 2010	4	2013
0133406954	Visual Basic 2012 How to Program	6	2014
0133379337	Visual C# 2012 How to Program	5	2014
0136151574	Visual C++ 2008 How to Program	2	2008
0133378713	C++ How to Program	9	2014
0132121360	Android for Programmers: An App-Driven Approach	1	2012

Fig. 12.6 | Data from the Titles table of the Books database. (Part 2 of 2.)

AuthorISBN *Table of the* Books *Database*

The AuthorISBN table (described in Fig. 12.7) consists of two columns that maintain ISBNs for each book and their corresponding authors' ID numbers. This table associates authors with their books. The AuthorID column is a foreign key—a column in this table that matches the primary-key column in another table (that is, AuthorID in the Authors table). The ISBN column is also a *foreign key*—it matches the primary-key column (that is, ISBN) in the Titles table. A database might consist of many tables. A goal when designing a database is to *minimize* the amount of *duplicated* data among the database's tables. Foreign keys, which are specified when a database table is created in the database, link the data in *multiple* tables. Together the AuthorID and ISBN columns in this table form a *composite primary key*. Every row in this table *uniquely* matches *one* author to *one* book's ISBN. Figure 12.8 contains the data from the AuthorISBN table of the Books database.

Column	Description
AuthorID	The author's ID number, a foreign key to the Authors table.
ISBN	The ISBN for a book, a foreign key to the Titles table.

Fig. 12.7 | AuthorISBN table of the Books database.

AuthorID	ISBN	AuthorID	ISBN
1	0132151006	*(continued)*	
1	0132575663	1	0133379337
1	013299044X	1	0136151574
1	0132990601	1	0133378713
1	0133406954	1	0132121360
(continued)		2	0132151006

Fig. 12.8 | Data from the AuthorISBN table of the Books database. (Part 1 of 2.)

AuthorID	ISBN	AuthorID	ISBN
2	0132575663	*(continued)*	
2	013299044X	2	0132121360
2	0132990601	3	0132151006
2	0133406954	3	0132990601
2	0133379337	3	0132121360
2	0136151574	3	0133406954
2	0133378713	4	0136151574
(continued)		5	0132121360

Fig. 12.8 | Data from the AuthorISBN table of the Books database. (Part 2 of 2.)

Every foreign-key value must appear as another table's primary-key value so the DBMS can ensure that the foreign key value is valid. For example, the DBMS ensures that the AuthorID value for a particular row of the AuthorISBN table (Fig. 12.8) is valid by checking that there is a row in the Authors table with that AuthorID as the primary key.

Foreign keys also allow *related* data in *multiple* tables to be *selected* from those tables—this is known as **joining** the data. There is a **one-to-many relationship** between a primary key and a corresponding foreign key (for example, one author can write many books and one book can be written by many authors). This means that a foreign key can appear *many* times in its own table but only *once* (as the primary key) in another table. For example, the ISBN 0132151006 can appear in several rows of AuthorISBN (because this book has several authors) but only once in Titles, where ISBN is the primary key.

*Entity-Relationship Diagram for the **Books** Database*
Figure 12.9 is an **entity-relationship (ER) diagram** for the Books database. This diagram shows the tables in the database and the relationships among them. The first compartment in each box contains the table's name. The names in italic font are *primary keys—AuthorID* in the Authors table, AuthorID and ISBN in the AuthorISBN table, and ISBN in the Titles table. Every row *must* have a value in the primary-key column (or group of columns), and the value of the key must be *unique* in the table; otherwise, the DBMS will report an error. The names AuthorID and ISBN in the AuthorISBN table are both italic—together these form a *composite primary key* for the AuthorISBN table.

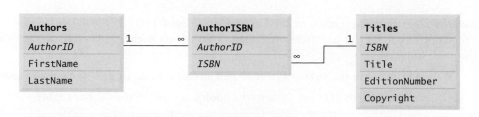

Fig. 12.9 | Entity-relationship diagram for the Books database.

The lines connecting the tables in Fig. 12.9 represent the *relationships* among the tables. Consider the line between the Authors and AuthorISBN tables. On the Authors end of the line, there's a 1, and on the AuthorISBN end, an infinity symbol (∞). This indicates a *one-to-many relationship*—for *each* author in the Authors table, there can be an *arbitrary number* of ISBNs for books written by that author in the AuthorISBN table (that is, an author can write *any* number of books). Note that the relationship line links the AuthorID column in the Authors table (where AuthorID is the primary key) to the AuthorID column in the AuthorISBN table (where AuthorID is a foreign key)—the line between the tables links the primary key to the matching foreign key.

The line between the Titles and AuthorISBN tables illustrates a *one-to-many relationship*—one book can be written by many authors. Note that the line between the tables links the primary key ISBN in table Titles to the corresponding foreign key in table AuthorISBN. The relationships in Fig. 12.9 illustrate that the sole purpose of the AuthorISBN table is to provide a **many-to-many relationship** between the Authors and Titles tables—an author can write *many* books, and a book can have *many* authors.

12.4 LINQ to Entities and the ADO.NET Entity Framework

When using the ADO.NET Entity Framework, you interact with the database via classes that the IDE generates from the database schema. You'll initiate this process by adding a new **ADO.NET Entity Data Model** to your project (as you'll see in Section 12.5.1).

Classes Generated in the Entity Data Model

For the Authors and Titles tables in the Books database, the IDE creates two classes *each* in the data model:

- The first class represents a row of the table and contains properties for each column in the table. Objects of this class—called **row objects**—store the data from individual rows of the table. The IDE uses the *singular* version of a table's *plural* name as the row class's name. For the Books database's Authors table, the row class's name is Author, and for the Titles table, it's Title.

- The second class represents the table itself. An object of this class stores a collection of row objects that correspond to all of the rows in the table. The table classes for the Books database are named Authors and Titles.

Once generated, the entity data model classes have full *IntelliSense* support in the IDE. Section 12.7 demonstrates queries that use the relationships among the Books database's tables to join data.

Relationships Between Tables in the Entity Data Model

You'll notice that we did not mention the Books database's AuthorISBN table. Recall that this table links:

- each author in the Authors table to that author's books in the Titles table, and
- each book in the Titles table to the book's authors in the Authors table.

Relationships between tables are taken into account in the entity data model's generated classes. For example, the Author row class contains a Titles **navigation property**, which you can use to get the Title objects that represent all the books written by that author. The IDE automatically adds the "s" to "Title" to indicate that this property represents a collection of Title objects. Similarly, the Title row class contains a navigation property named Authors, which you can use to get the Author objects that represent a given book's authors.

DbContext *Class*

A **DbContext** (namespace **System.Data.Entity**) manages the data flow between the program and the database. When the IDE generates the *entity data model's* row and table classes, it also creates a derived class of DbContext that is specific to the database being manipulated. For the Books database, this derived class has properties for the Authors and Titles tables. As you'll see, these can be used as data sources for manipulating data in LINQ queries and in GUIs. Any changes made to the data managed by the DbContext can be saved back to the database using the DbContext's **SaveChanges** method.

IQueryable(Of T) *Interface*

LINQ to Entities works through the **IQueryable(Of T)** interface, which inherits from the interface IEnumerable(Of T) introduced in Chapter 11. IEnumerable is a so-called *generic interface*—the notation Of T is a placeholder for a type. For example, an array of Integers implements the IEnumerable(Of Integer) interface. When a LINQ to Entities query on an IQueryable(Of T) object executes against the database, the results are loaded into objects of the corresponding entity data model classes for convenient access in your code.

Using Extension Methods to Manipulate IQueryable(Of T) *Objects*

Recall that extension methods add functionality to an existing class without modifying the class's source code. In Chapter 11, we introduced several LINQ extension methods, including First, Any, Count and Distinct. These methods, which are defined as static methods of class Enumerable (namespace System.Linq), can be applied to any object that implements the IEnumerable(Of T) interface, such as arrays, collections and the results of LINQ to Objects queries.

In this chapter, we use a combination of the LINQ query syntax and LINQ extension methods to manipulate database contents. The extension methods we use are defined as static methods of class **Queryable** (namespace System.Linq) and can be applied to any object that implements the IQueryable(Of T) interface—these include various entity data model objects and the results of LINQ to Entities queries.

12.5 Querying a Database with LINQ

In this section, we demonstrate how to *connect* to a database, *query* it and *display* the results of the query. There is little code in this section—the IDE provides *visual programming* tools and *wizards* that simplify accessing data in apps. These tools establish database connections and create the objects necessary to view and manipulate the data through Windows Forms GUI controls—a technique known as **data binding**.

For the examples in Sections 12.5–12.8, we'll create *one* solution that contains *several* projects. One will be a reusable *class library* containing the ADO.NET Entity Data Model for interacting with the Books database. The other projects will be Windows Forms apps that use the ADO.NET Entity Data Model in the class library to manipulate the database.

Our first example performs a simple query on the Books database from Section 12.3. We retrieve the entire Authors table, ordered by the authors' last name, then first name.

We then use data binding to display the data in a **DataGridView**—a control from namespace System.Windows.Forms that can display data from a data source in tabular format. The basic steps we'll perform are:

- Create the ADO.NET entity data model classes for manipulating the database.

- Add the entity data model object that represents the Authors table as a *data source*.

- Drag the Authors table data source onto the **Design** view to create a GUI for displaying the table's data.

- Add code to the Form's code-behind file to allow the app to interact with the database.

The GUI for the program is shown in Fig. 12.10. *All* of the controls in this GUI are automatically generated when we drag a *data source* that represents the Authors table onto the Form in **Design** view. The **BindingNavigator** toolbar at the top of the window is a collection of controls that allow you to navigate through the records in the DataGridView that fills the rest of the window. The BindingNavigator controls also allow you to add records, delete records, modify existing records and save your changes to the database. You can add a new record by pressing the **Add new** (✛) button, then entering the new author's first and last name. You can delete an existing record by selecting an author (either in the DataGridView or via the controls on the BindingNavigator) and pressing the **Delete** (✕) button. You can edit an existing record by clicking the first name or last name field for that record and typing the new value. To save your changes to the database, simply click the **Save Data** (💾) button. Empty values are *not* allowed in the Authors table of the Books database, so if you attempt to save a record that does not contain a value for both the first name and last name an exception occurs.

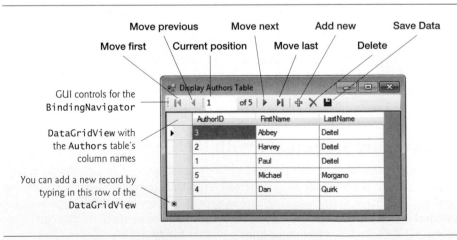

Fig. 12.10 | GUI for the **Display Authors Table** app.

12.5.1 Creating the ADO.NET Entity Data Model Class Library

This section presents the steps required to create the entity data model from an existing database. A *model* describes the data that you'll be manipulating—in our case, the data represented by the tables in the Books database.

Step 1: Creating a Class Library Project for the ADO.NET Entity Data Model
Select **FILE > New Project...** to display the **New Project** dialog, then select **Class Library** from the **Visual Basic** templates and name the project `BooksExamples`. Click **OK** to create the project, then delete the `Class1.vb` file from the **Solution Explorer.**

Step 2: Adding the ADO.NET Entity Data Model to the Class Library
To interact with the database, you'll add an ADO.NET entity data model to the class library project. This will also configure the connection to the database.

1. *Adding the ADO.NET Entity Data Model.* Right click the `BooksExamples` project in the **Solution Explorer**, then select **Add > New Item...** to display the **Add New Item** dialog (Fig. 12.11). From the **Data** category select **ADO.NET Entity Data Model** and name the model `BooksModel.edmx`—this file will contain the information about the entity data model you're about to create. Click **Add** to add the entity data model to the class library and display the **Entity Data Model Wizard** dialog.

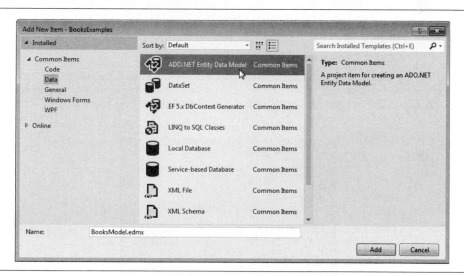

Fig. 12.11 | Selecting **ADO.NET Entity Data Model** in the **Add New Item** Dialog.

2. *Choosing the Model Contents.* The **Choose Model Contents** step in the **Entity Data Model Wizard** dialog (Fig. 12.12) enables you to specify the entity data model's contents. The model in these examples will consist of data from the Books database, so select **Generate from Database** and click **Next >** to display the **Choose Your Data Connection** step.

3. *Choosing the Data Connection.* In the **Choose Your Data Connection** step, click **New Connection...** to display the **Connection Properties** dialog (Fig. 12.13). (If the **Choose Data Source** dialog box appears, select **Microsoft SQL Server**, then click **OK**.) The **Data source:** TextBox should contain **Microsoft SQL Server Database File (SqlClient)**. (If it does not, click **Change...** to display a dialog where you can change the **Data source.**) Click **Browse...** to locate and select the `Books.mdf` file in the `Databases` directory included with this chapter's examples. You can click **Test Connection** to verify that the IDE can connect to the database through

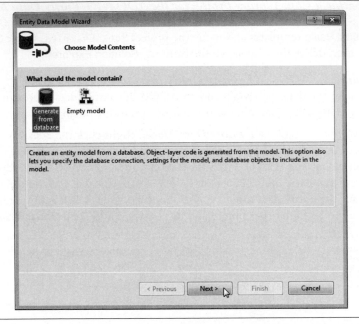

Fig. 12.12 | Entity Data Model Wizard dialog's Choose Model Contents step.

Fig. 12.13 | Connection Properties dialog.

SQL Server Express. Click **OK** to create the connection. Figure 12.14 shows the **Entity connection string** for the Books.mdf database. This string contains the information that the ADO.NET Entity Framework requires to connect to the database at runtime. Click **Next >**. A dialog will appear asking if you'd like to add the database file to your project. Click **Yes** to move to the next step.

Fig. 12.14 | Choose Your Data Connection step *after* selecting Books.mdf.

Error-Prevention Tip 12.1
SQL Server Express LocalDB allows only one program at a time to connect to a database file, so ensure that no other program is using the file before connecting to the database.

4. *Choosing the Database Objects to Include in the Model.* In the **Choose Your Database Objects and Settings** step, you'll specify the database parts to include in the entity data model. Select the **Tables** node as shown in Fig. 12.15, ensure that **Pluralize or singularize generated object names** is checked, then click **Finish**.

5. *Viewing the Entity Data Model Diagram in the Model Designer.* At this point, the IDE creates the entity data model and displays a diagram (Fig. 12.16) in the *model designer*. The diagram contains **Author** and **Title** *entities*—these represent *authors* and *titles* in the database and the properties of each. Notice that the IDE renamed the Title column of the Titles table as Title1 to avoid a naming conflict with the class Title that represents a row in the table. The line between the entities indicates a *relationship* between authors and titles—this relationship is implemented in the Books database as the AuthorISBN table. The asterisk (*) at each end of the line indicates a *many-to-many relationship*—an author can be an author for *many* titles and a title can have *many* authors. The **Navigation Properties** section in the **Author** entity contains the **Titles** property, which connects an author to all titles written by that author. Similarly, the **Navigation Properties** section in the **Title** entity contains the **Authors** property, which connects a title to all of its authors.

6. *Building the Class Library.* Select **BUILD > Build Solution** to build the class library that you'll reuse in the next several examples—this will compile the entity data model classes that were generated by the IDE. When you build the class library, the IDE generates the classes that you can use to interact with the database. These

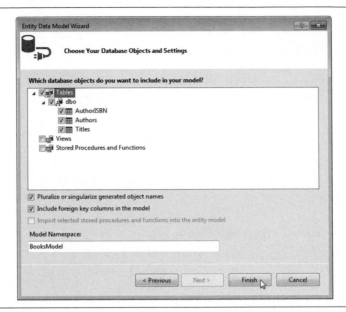

Fig. 12.15 | Selecting the database's tables to include in the ADO.NET Entity Data Model.

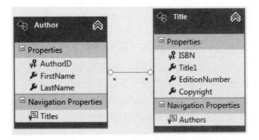

Fig. 12.16 | Entity data model diagram for the **Author** and **Title** entities.

include a class for each table you selected from the database and a derived class of `DbContext` named `BooksEntities` that enables you to programmatically interact with the database. [*Note:* Building the project causes the IDE to execute a script that creates and compiles the entity data model classes. A security warning dialog appears indicating that this script could harm your computer. Click **OK** to allow the script to execute. The warning is intended primarily for cases in which you download from the Internet Visual Studio templates that execute scripts.]

12.5.2 Creating a Windows Forms Project and Configuring It to Use the Entity Data Model

Recall that the next several examples will all be part of *one solution* containing *several projects*—the class library project with our *reusable model* and individual Windows Forms apps for each example. In this section, you'll create a new Windows Forms app and configure it to be able to use the entity data model that you created in the preceding section.

Step 1: Creating the Project

To add a new Windows Forms project to the existing solution:

1. Right click the solution name in **Solution Explorer** and select **Add > New Project...** to display the **Add New Project** dialog.

2. Select **Windows Forms Application**, name the project `DisplayTable` and click **OK**.

3. Change the name of the `Form1.vb` source file to `DisplayAuthorsTable.vb`. The IDE updates the Form's class name to match the source file. Set the Form's **Text** property to `Display Authors Table`.

4. Configure the solution so that this new project will execute when you select **DEBUG > Start Debugging** (or press *F5*). To do so, right click the `DisplayTable` project's name in the **Solution Explorer**, then select **Set as Startup Project**.

Step 2: Adding a Reference to the BooksExamples Class Library

To use the entity data model classes for data binding, you must first add a *reference* to the class library you created in Section 12.5.1—this allows the new project to use that class library. Each project you create typically contains references to several .NET class libraries (called *assemblies*) by default—for example, a Windows Forms project contains a reference to the `System.Windows.Forms` library. When you compile a class library, the IDE creates a `.dll` file (known as an *assembly*) containing the library's components. To add a reference to the class library containing the entity data model's classes:

1. Right click the `DisplayTable` project in the **Solution Explorer** and select **Add Reference....**

2. In the left column of the **Reference Manager** dialog that appears, select **Solution** to display the other projects in this solution, then in center of the dialog select `BooksExamples` and click **OK**. `BooksExamples` will be placed in the project's **References** node (which you can see when the **Show All Files** button is selected).

Step 3: Adding References to System.Data.Entity and EntityFramework

You'll also need references to the `System.Data.Entity` and `EntityFramework` libraries to use the ADO.NET Entity Framework. To add a reference to `System.Data.Entity`, repeat *Step 2* for adding a reference to the `BooksExamples` library, but in the left column of the **Reference Manager** dialog that appears, select **Assemblies** then locate `System.Data.Entity`, ensure that its checkbox is checked and click **OK**. `System.Data.Entity` should now appear in the projects **References** node.

The `EntityFramework` library was added by the IDE to the `BooksExamples` class library project when we created the entity data model, but the `EntityFramework` library is also required in *each* app that will use the entity data model. To add a reference to the `EntityFramework` library:

1. Right click the solution name in the **Solution Explorer** and select **Manage NuGet Packages for Solution...** to display the **Manage NuGet Packages** dialog.

2. In the dialog that appears, click **Manage** to display the **Select Projects** dialog, then select the `DisplayTable` project and click **OK**.

3. Click **Close** to close the **Manage NuGet Packages** dialog. `EntityFramework` should now appear in the projects **References** node.

Step 4: Adding the Connection String to the Windows *Forms App*

Each app that will use the entity data model also requires the *connection string* that tells the Entity Framework how to connect to the database. The connection string is stored in the BooksExamples class library's App.Config file. In the **Solution Explorer**, open the Books-Examples class library's App.Config file then copy the three lines that represent the connection string, which have the format:

```
<connectionStrings>
    Connection string information appears here
</connectionStrings>
```

Next, open the App.Config file in the DisplayTable project and paste the connection string information *after* the line containing </entityFramework> and *before* the line containing </configuration>. Save the App.Config file.

12.5.3 Data Bindings Between Controls and the Entity Data Model

You'll now use the IDE's drag-and-drop GUI design capabilities to create the GUI for interacting with the Books database. You must write a small amount of code to enable the *autogenerated* GUI to interact with the entity data model. You'll now perform the steps to display the contents of the Authors table in a GUI.

Step 1: Adding a Data Source for the **Authors** Table

To use the entity data model classes for data binding, you must first add them as a *data source*. To do so:

1. Select **VIEW > Other Windows > Data Sources** to display the **Data Sources** window at the left side of the IDE, then in that window click the **Add New Data Source...** link to display the **Data Source Configuration Wizard**.

2. The Entity Data Model classes are used to create *objects* representing the tables in the database, so we'll use an **Object** data source. In the dialog, select **Object** and click **Next >**. Expand the tree view as shown in Fig. 12.17 and ensure that **Author** is checked. An object of this class will be used as the *data source*.

3. Click **Finish**.

The Authors table in the database is now a data source from which a data bound GUI control can obtain data. In the **Data Sources** window (Fig. 12.18), you can see the Author class that you added in the previous step. Properties representing columns of the database's Authors table should appear below it, as well as a Titles navigation property representing the relationship between the database's Authors and Titles tables.

Step 2: Creating GUI Elements

Next, you'll use the **Design** view to create a DataGridView control that can display the Authors table's data. To do so:

1. Switch to **Design** view for the DisplayAuthorsTable class.

2. Click the **Author** node in the **Data Sources** window—it should change to a drop-down list. Open the drop-down by clicking the down arrow and ensure that the DataGridView option (which is the default) is selected—this is the GUI control that will be used to display and interact with the data.

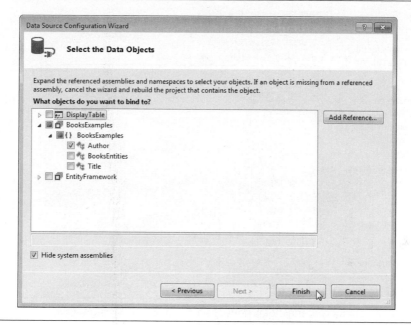

Fig. 12.17 | Selecting the Author class as the data source.

Fig. 12.18 | **Data Sources** window showing the Author class as a data source.

3. Drag the **Author** node from the **Data Sources** window onto the Form in **Design** view. You'll need to resize the Form to fit the DataGridView.

The IDE creates a DataGridView (Fig. 12.19) with column names representing *all* the properties for an Author, including the Titles navigation property. The IDE also creates a **BindingNavigator** that contains Buttons for *moving between entries, adding entries, deleting entries and saving changes to the database.* The IDE also generates a **BindingSource** (AuthorBindingSource), which handles the transfer of data between the *data source* and the *data-bound controls* on the Form. Nonvisual components such as the BindingSource and the nonvisual aspects of the BindingNavigator appear in the *component tray*—the gray region below the Form in **Design** view. The IDE names the BindingNavigator and BindingSource (AuthorBindingNavigator and AuthorBindingSource, respectively) based on the data source's name (Author). We use the default names for automatically generated components throughout this chapter to show exactly what the IDE creates.

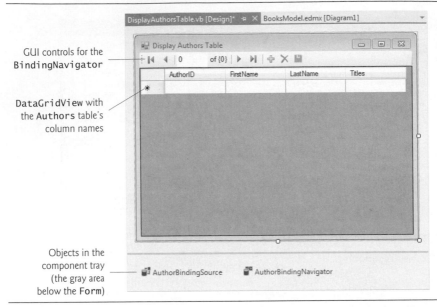

GUI controls for the
BindingNavigator

DataGridView with
the Authors table's
column names

Objects in the
component tray
(the gray area
below the Form)

Fig. 12.19 | Component tray holds nonvisual components in **Design** view.

To make the DataGridView occupy the *entire* window below the BindingNavigator, select the DataGridView, then use the **Properties** window to set the Dock property to Fill. You can stretch the window horizontally to see all the DataGridView columns. We do not use the Titles column in this example, so with the DataGridView selected, select the **Columns** property in the **Properties** window, then click the ellipsis button (...) to display the **Edit Columns** dialog. Select **Titles** in the **Selected Columns** list, then click **Remove** to remove that column.

Step 3: Connecting the Data Source to the *AuthorBindingSource*
The final step is to connect the data source to the AuthorBindingSource, so that the app can interact with the database. Figure 12.20 shows the code needed to *obtain* data from the database and to *save* any changes that the user makes to the data back into the database.

```
 1   ' Fig. 22.20: DisplayAuthorsTable.vb
 2   ' Displaying data from a database table in a DataGridView.
 3   Imports System.Data.Entity
 4   Imports System.Data.Entity.Validation
 5
 6   Public Class DisplayAuthorsTable
 7      ' Entity Framework DBContext
 8      Private dbcontext As New BooksExamples.BooksEntities()
 9
10      ' load data from database into DataGridView
11      Private Sub DisplayAuthorsTable_Load(sender As Object,
12         e As EventArgs) Handles MyBase.Load
```

Fig. 12.20 | Displaying data from a database table in a DataGridView. (Part 1 of 2.)

```
13
14          ' load Authors table ordered by LastName then FirstName
15          With dbcontext.Authors
16             .OrderBy(Function(currentAuthor) currentAuthor.LastName)
17             .ThenBy(Function(currentAuthor) currentAuthor.FirstName)
18             .Load()
19          End With
20
21          ' specify DataSource for AuthorBindingSource
22          AuthorBindingSource.DataSource = dbcontext.Authors.Local
23       End Sub ' DisplayAuthorsTable_Load
24
25       ' click event handler for the Save Button in the
26       ' BindingNavigator saves the changes made to the data
27       Private Sub AuthorBindingNavigatorSaveItem_Click(sender As Object,
28          e As EventArgs) Handles AuthorBindingNavigatorSaveItem.Click
29
30          Validate() ' validate the input fields
31          AuthorBindingSource.EndEdit() ' complete current edit, if any
32
33          ' try to save changes
34          Try
35             dbcontext.SaveChanges() ' write changes to database file
36          Catch ex As DbEntityValidationException
37             MessageBox.Show("FirstName and LastName must contain values",
38                "Entity Validation Exception")
39          End Try
40       End Sub ' AuthorBindingNavigatorSaveItem_Click
41    End Class ' DisplayAuthorsTable
```

Fig. 12.20 | Displaying data from a database table in a DataGridView. (Part 2 of 2.)

Creating the *DbContext* Object

As mentioned in Section 12.4, a DbContext object interacts with the database on the app's behalf. The BooksEntities class (a derived class of DbContext) was automatically generated by the IDE when you created the entity data model classes to access the Books database (Section 12.5.1). Line 8 creates an object of this class named dbcontext.

DisplayAuthorsTable_Load Event Handler

You can create the Form's Load event handler (lines 11–23) by double clicking the Form's title bar in **Design** view. In this app, we allow data to move between the DbContext and the database by using LINQ to Entities extension methods to extract data from the Books-Entities's Authors property (lines 15–19), which corresponds to the Authors table in the database. The expression

```
dbcontext.Authors
```

indicates that we wish to get data from the Authors table.

OrderBy Extension Method
The **OrderBy extension method** call

```
.OrderBy(Function(author) author.LastName)
```

indicates that the rows of the table should be retrieved in ascending order by the authors' last names. The argument to OrderBy is a **lambda expression** that defines a simple, **anonymous method**. Like other Visual Basic methods, a lambda expression begins with Function if it will return a value and Sub if it will not. This is followed by a *parameter list* in parentheses—author in this case, is an object of the Author entity data model class. The lambda expression *infers* the lambda parameter's type from dbcontext.Authors, which contains Author objects. The parameter list is followed by the body of the function. The value produced by the expression—a given author's last name—is implicitly returned by the lambda expression. The syntax shown here is for a *single-line lambda expression*. You do not specify a return type for a single-line lambda expression—the return type is inferred from the return value. You can also create *multiline lambda expressions* by placing the statements on separate lines between the Function...End Function or Sub...End Sub keywords. Multiline lambdas can optionally use the As clause to specify a return type, just as in a typical method definition. As we encounter lambda expressions in this chapter, we'll discuss the syntax we use. You can learn more about lambda expressions at

```
msdn.microsoft.com/en-us/library/bb531253.aspx
```

ThenBy Extension Method
When there are multiple authors with the *same* last name, we'd like them to be listed in ascending order by first name as well. The **ThenBy extension method** call

```
.ThenBy(Function(author) author.FirstName)
```

enables you to order results by an additional column. This is applied to the Author objects that have already been ordered by last name. We'll show similar LINQ query syntax shortly.

Load Extension Method
Finally, line 18 calls the **Load extension method** (defined in class **DbExtensions** from the namespace System.Data.Entity). This method executes the LINQ to Entities query and loads the results into memory. This data is tracked by the BookEntities DbContext in local memory so that any changes made to the data can eventually be saved into the database.

Setting the AuthorBindingSource's DataSource
Line 22 sets the AuthorBindingSource's **DataSource** property to the Local property of the dbcontext.Authors object. In this case, the Local property is an ObservableCollection(Author) that represents the query results that were loaded into memory by lines 15–19. When a BindingSource's DataSource property is assigned an **ObservableCollection(Of T)** (namespace System.Collections.ObjectModel), the GUI that's bound to

the BindingSource is notified of any changes to the data so the GUI can be updated accordingly. In addition, changes made by the user to the data in the GUI will be tracked so the DbContext can eventually save those changes to the database.

AuthorBindingNavigatorSaveItem_Click Event Handler: Saving Modifications to the Database

If the user modifies the data in the DataGridView, we'd also like to save the modifications in the database. By default, the BindingNavigator's **Save Data** Button (🖫) is disabled. To enable it, right click this Button's icon in the BindingNavigator and select **Enabled**. Then, double click the icon to create its Click event handler (lines 27–40).

Saving the data entered in the DataGridView back to the database is a three-step process. First, all controls on the form are *validated* by calling the DisplayTableForm's inherited Validate method (line 30)—if any control has an event handler for the Validating event, it executes. You typically handle this event to determine whether a control's contents are valid. Next, line 31 calls **EndEdit** on the AuthorBindingSource, which forces it to save any pending changes into the BooksEntities model *in memory*. Finally, line 35 calls SaveChanges on the BooksEntities object (dbcontext) to store any changes into the database. We placed this call in a Try statement, because the Authors table does not allow empty values for the first name and last name—these rules were configured when we originally created the database. When SaveChanges is called, any changes stored into the Authors table must satisfy the table's rules. If any of the changes do not, a **DBEntityValidationException** occurs.

12.6 Dynamically Binding Query Results

Now that you've seen how to display an entire database table in a DataGridView, we show how to perform several different queries and display the results in a DataGridView. This app only reads data from the entity data model, so we disabled the buttons in the BindingNavigator that enable the user to add and delete records.

The **Display Query Results** app (Fig. 12.21) allows the user to select a query from the ComboBox at the bottom of the window, then displays the results of the query.

a) Results of the "All titles" query, which shows the contents of the Titles table ordered by the book titles

ISBN	Title1	EditionNumber	Copyright
0132121360	Android for Programmers: An App-Driven Approach	1	2012
013299044X	C How to Program	7	2013
0133378713	C++ How to Program	9	2014
0132151006	Internet & World Wide Web How to Program	5	2012
0132575663	Java How to Program	9	2012
0132990601	Simply Visual Basic 2010	4	2013
0133406954	Visual Basic 2012 How to Program	6	2014
0133379337	Visual C# 2012 How to Program	5	2014
0136151574	Visual C++ 2008 How to Program	2	2008

Fig. 12.21 | Sample execution of the **Display Query Results** app. (Part 1 of 2.)

b) Results of the "Titles with 2014 copyright" query

	ISBN	Title1	EditionNumber	Copyright
▶	0133378713	C++ How to Program	9	2014
	0133406954	Visual Basic 2012 How to Program	6	2014
	0133379337	Visual C# 2012 How to Program	5	2014

Titles with 2014 copyright

c) Results of the "Titles ending with 'How to Program'" query

	ISBN	Title1	EditionNumber	Copyright
▶	013299044X	C How to Program	7	2013
	0133378713	C++ How to Program	9	2014
	0132151006	Internet & World Wide Web How to Program	5	2012
	0132575663	Java How to Program	9	2012
	0133406954	Visual Basic 2012 How to Program	6	2014
	0133379337	Visual C# 2012 How to Program	5	2014
	0136151574	Visual C++ 2008 How to Program	2	2008

Titles ending with "How to Program"

Fig. 12.21 | Sample execution of the **Display Query Results** app. (Part 2 of 2.)

12.6.1 Creating the Display Query Results GUI

Perform the following steps to build the **Display Query Results** app's GUI.

Step 1: Creating the Project

Perform the steps in Section 12.5.2 to create a new **Windows Forms Application** project named `DisplayQueryResult` in the same solution as the `DisplayTable` app. Rename the `Form1.vb` source file to `TitleQueries.vb`. Set the Form's **Text** property to `Display Query Results`. Be sure to set the `DisplayQueryResult` project as the startup project.

Step 2: Creating a DataGridView to Display the Titles Table

Follow *Steps 1* and *2* in Section 12.5.3 to create the data source and the `DataGridView`. For this example, select the `Title` class (rather than `Author`) as the data source, and drag the **Title** node from the **Data Sources** window onto the form. Remove the `Authors` column from the `DataGridView` as it will not be used in this example.

Step 3: Adding a ComboBox to the Form

In **Design** view, add a `ComboBox` named `queriesComboBox` below the `DataGridView` on the Form. Users will select which query to execute from this control. Set the `ComboBox`'s **Dock** property to `Bottom` and the `DataGridView`'s **Dock** property to `Fill`.

Next, you'll add the names of the queries to the `ComboBox`. Open the `ComboBox`'s **String Collection Editor** by right clicking the `ComboBox` and selecting **Edit Items…**. You can also access the **String Collection Editor** from the `ComboBox`'s *smart tag menu*. A smart tag menu provides you with quick access to common properties you might set for a control (such as the `Multiline` property of a `TextBox`), so you can set these properties directly in **Design** view, rather than in the **Properties** window. You can open a control's *smart tag menu* by clicking the small arrowhead (▣) that appears in the control's upper-right corner in **Design** view when the control is selected. In the **String Collection Editor**, add the following three items to queriesComboBox—one for each of the queries we'll create:

1. All titles

2. Titles with 2014 copyright

3. Titles ending with "How to Program"

12.6.2 Coding the **Display Query Results App**

Next you'll create the code for this app (Fig. 12.22).

Customizing the **Form's Load** Event Handler

Create the TitleQueries_Load event handler (lines 11–20) by double clicking the title bar in **Design** view. When the Form loads, it should display the complete list of books from the Titles table, sorted by title. Line 14 calls the Load extension method on the BookEntities DbContext's Titles property to load the Titles table's contents into memory. Rather than defining the same LINQ query as in lines 30–31, we can programmatically cause the queriesComboBox_SelectedIndexChanged event handler to execute simply by setting the queriesComboBox's SelectedIndex to 0 (line 19).

queriesComboBox_SelectedIndexChanged Event Handler

Next you must write code that executes the appropriate query each time the user chooses a different item from queriesComboBox. Double click queriesComboBox in **Design** view to generate a queriesComboBox_SelectedIndexChanged event handler (lines 23–49) in the TitleQueries.vb file. In the event handler, add a Select Case statement (lines 27–46). Each Case will change the TitleBindingSource's DataSource property to the results of a query that returns the correct set of data. The data bindings created by the IDE *automatically* update the TitleDataGridView *each time* we change its DataSource. The **MoveFirst** method of the BindingSource (line 48) moves to the first row of the result each time a query executes. The results of the queries in lines 31, 35–37 and 42–45 are shown in Fig. 12.21(a), (b) and (c), respectively. Because we do not modify the data in this app, each of the queries is performed on the in-memory representation of the Titles table, which is accessible through dbcontext.Titles.Local.

Ordering the Books By Title

Line 31 invokes the OrderBy extension method on dbcontext.Titles.Local to order the Title objects by their Title1 property values. As we mentioned previously, the IDE renamed the Title column of the database's Titles table as Title1 in the generated Title entity data model class to avoid a naming conflict with the class's name. Recall that Local returns an ObservableCollection(Of T) containing the row objects of the specified table—in this case, Local returns an ObservableCollection(Title). When you invoke OrderBy on an ObservableCollection(Of T), the method returns an IEnumerable(Of T). We assign that object to the TitleBindingSource's DataSource property. When the DataSource property changes, the DataGridView iterates through the contents of the IEnumerable(Of T) and displays the data.

```vb
1   ' Fig. 12.22: TitleQueries.vb
2   ' Displaying the result of a user-selected query in a DataGridView.
3   Imports System.Data.Entity
4   Imports System.Linq
5
6   Public Class TitleQueries
7      ' Entity Framework DBContext
8      Private dbcontext As New BooksExamples.BooksEntities()
9
10     ' display results of all titles query when Form loads
11     Private Sub TitleQueries_Load(sender As Object,
12        e As EventArgs) Handles MyBase.Load
13
14        dbcontext.Titles.Load() ' load Titles table into memory
15
16        ' set the ComboBox to show the default query that
17        ' selects all books from the Titles table and causes the
18        ' queriesComboBox's SelectedIndexChanged event handler to execute
19        queriesComboBox.SelectedIndex = 0
20     End Sub ' TitleQueries_Load
21
22     ' loads data into TitleBindingSource based on user-selected query
23     Private Sub queriesComboBox_SelectedIndexChanged(sender As Object,
24        e As EventArgs) Handles queriesComboBox.SelectedIndexChanged
25
26        ' set the data displayed according to what is selected
27        Select Case queriesComboBox.SelectedIndex
28           Case 0 ' all titles
29              ' use LINQ to order the books by title
30              TitleBindingSource.DataSource =
31                 dbcontext.Titles.Local.OrderBy(Function(book) book.Title1)
32           Case 1 ' titles with 2014 copyright
33              ' use LINQ to get titles with 2014 copyright and sort them
34              TitleBindingSource.DataSource =
35                 dbcontext.Titles.Local _
36                    .Where(Function(book) book.Copyright = "2014") _
37                    .OrderBy(Function(book) book.Title1)
38           Case 2 ' titles ending with "How to Program"
39              ' use LINQ to get titles ending with
40              ' "How to Program" and sort them
41              TitleBindingSource.DataSource =
42                 dbcontext.Titles.Local _
43                    .Where(Function(book) book.Title1.EndsWith(
44                       "How to Program")) _
45                    .OrderBy(Function(book) book.Title1)
46        End Select
47
48        TitleBindingSource.MoveFirst() ' move to first entry
49     End Sub ' queriesComboBox_SelectedIndexChanged
50  End Class ' TitleQueries
```

Fig. 12.22 | Displaying the result of a user-selected query in a DataGridView.

Selecting Books with 2014 Copyright

Lines 35–37 filter the titles displayed by using the **Where** extension method with the lambda

```
Function(book) book.Copyright = "2014"
```

This lambda expression takes one `Title` object (named `book`) as its parameter and uses it to check whether the given `Title`'s `Copyright` property (a `String` in the database) is equal to 2014. A lambda expression that's used with the `Where` extension method must return a `Boolean` value. Only `Title` objects for which this lambda expression returns `True` will be selected. We use `OrderBy` to order the results by the `Title1` property so the books are displayed in ascending order by title. The type of the lambda's `book` parameter is *inferred* from `dbcontext.Titles.Local`, which contains `Title` objects. As soon as the `TitleBindingSource`'s `DataSource` property changes, the `DataGridView` is updated with the query results.

Selecting Books with Titles That End in "How to Program"

Lines 42–45 filter the titles displayed by using the `Where` extension method with the lambda expression

```
Function(book) book.Title1.EndsWith("How to Program")
```

as an argument. This lambda expression takes one `Title` object (named `book`) as its parameter and uses it to check whether the given `Title`'s `Title1` property value ends with `"How to Program"`. The expression `books.Title1` returns the `String` stored in that property, then we use the string class's `EndsWith` method to perform the test. We order the results by the `Title1` property so the books are displayed in ascending order by title.

12.7 Retrieving Data from Multiple Tables with LINQ

In this section, you'll perform LINQ to Entities queries using the LINQ query syntax that was introduced in Chapter 11. In particular, you'll learn how to obtain query results that combine data from multiple tables (Fig. 12.23).

a) List of authors and the ISBNs of the books they've authored; sort the authors by last name then first name

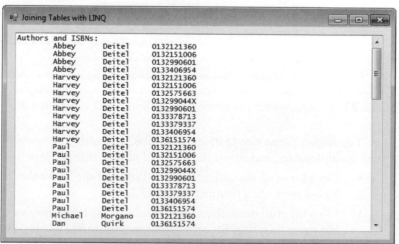

Fig. 12.23 | Outputs from the **Joining Tables with LINQ** app. (Part 1 of 2.)

b) List of authors and the titles of the book's they've authored; sort the authors by last name then first name; for a given author, sort the titles alphabetically

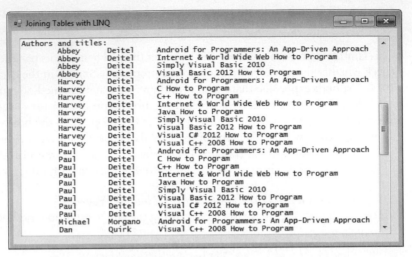

c) List of titles grouped by author; sort the authors by last name then first name; for a given author, sort the titles alphabetically

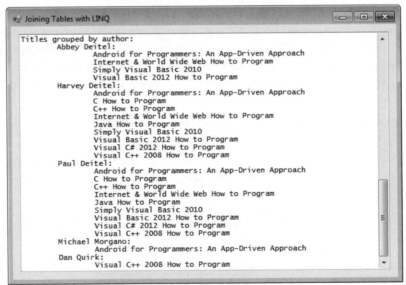

Fig. 12.23 | Outputs from the **Joining Tables with LINQ** app. (Part 2 of 2.)

The **Joining Tables with LINQ** app uses LINQ to Entities to combine and organize data from multiple tables, and shows the results of queries that perform the following tasks:

- Get a list of all the authors and the ISBNs of the books they've authored, sorted by last name then first name (Fig. 12.23(a)).

- Get a list of all the authors and the titles of the books they've authored, sorted by last name then first; for each author sort the titles alphabetically (Fig. 12.23(b)).

- Get a list of all the book titles grouped by author, sorted by last name then first; for a given author sort the titles alphabetically (Fig. 12.23(c)).

GUI *for the Joining Tables with LINQ App*

For this example (Fig. 12.24–Fig. 12.27), perform the steps in Section 12.5.2 to create a new **Windows Forms Application** project named JoinQueries in the same solution as the previous examples. Rename the Form1.vb source file to JoiningTableData.vb. Set the Form's **Text** property to Joining Tables with LINQ. Be sure to set the JoinQueries project as the startup project. We set the following properties for the outputTextBox:

- Font property: Set to Lucida Console to display the output in a fixed-width font.
- Anchor property: Set to Top, Bottom, Left, Right so that you can resize the window and the outputTextBox will resize accordingly.
- Scrollbars property: Set to Vertical, so that you can scroll through the output.

Creating the **DbContext**

The code uses the entity data model classes to combine data from the tables in the Books database and display the relationships between the authors and books in three different ways. We split the code for class JoiningTableData into several figures (Figs. 12.24–12.27) for presentation purposes. As in previous examples, the DbContext object (Fig. 12.24, line 8) allows the program to interact with the database.

```
 1   ' Fig. 12.24: JoiningTableData.vb
 2   ' Using LINQ to perform aggregate data from several tables.
 3   Public Class JoiningTableData
 4      Private Sub JoiningTableData_Load(sender As Object,
 5         e As EventArgs) Handles MyBase.Load
 6
 7         ' Entity Framework DBContext
 8         Dim database As New BooksExamples.BooksEntities()
 9
```

Fig. 12.24 | Creating the BooksDataContext for querying the Books database.

Combining Author Names with the ISBNs of the Books They've Written

The first query (Fig. 12.25, lines 12–15) *joins* data from two tables and returns a list of author names and the ISBNs representing the books they've written, sorted by LastName then FirstName. The query takes advantage of the properties in the entity data model classes that were created based on foreign-key relationships between the database's tables. These properties enable you to easily combine data from related rows in multiple tables.

```
10         ' get authors and ISBNs of each book they co-authored
11         Dim authorsAndISBNs =
12            From author In database.Authors
13            From book In author.Titles
14            Order By author.LastName, author.FirstName
15            Select author.FirstName, author.LastName, book.ISBN
16
17         outputTextBox.AppendText("Authors and ISBNs:")
18
```

Fig. 12.25 | Getting a list of authors and the ISBNs of the books they've authored. (Part 1 of 2.)

```
19        ' display authors and ISBNs in tabular format
20        For Each element In authorsAndISBNs
21           outputTextBox.AppendText(
22              String.Format("{0}{1}{2,-10} {3,-10} {4,-10}", vbCrLf, vbTab,
23                 element.FirstName, element.LastName, element.ISBN))
24        Next
25
```

Fig. 12.25 | Getting a list of authors and the ISBNs of the books they've authored. (Part 2 of 2.)

The first From clause (line 12) gets each author from the Authors table. The second From clause (line 13) uses the generated Titles property of the Author class to get the current author's books. The entity data model uses the foreign-key information stored in the database's AuthorISBN table to get the appropriate books. The combined result of the two From clauses is a collection of all the authors and the books they've authored. The two From clauses introduce *two* range variables into the scope of this query—other clauses can access both range variables to combine data from multiple tables. Line 14 orders the results by the author's LastName, then FirstName. Line 15 creates a new *anonymous type* that contains the FirstName and LastName of an author from the Authors table with the ISBN of a book in the Titles table written by that author.

Anonymous Types

Anonymous types allow you to create simple classes used to store data *without* writing a class definition. An anonymous type created as the result of a LINQ query contains the properties listed after the Select keyword—in this case, FirstName, LastName and ISBN. No class name is specified. All properties of an anonymous type are Public. Anonymous type properties are *read-only*—you cannot modify a property's value once the object is created. Each property's type is *inferred* from the values assigned to it. The class definition is generated automatically by the compiler, so you don't know the class's type name (hence the term anonymous type). Thus, you *must* use *implicitly typed local variables* to store references to objects of anonymous types (e.g., line 20). Though we are not using it here, the compiler defines a ToString method when creating the anonymous type's class definition. The method returns a String in curly braces containing a comma-separated list of *PropertyName = value* pairs. The compiler also provides an Equals method, which compares the properties of the anonymous object that calls the method and the anonymous object that it receives as an argument.

Combining Author Names with the Titles of the Books They've Written

The second query (Fig. 12.26, lines 28–31) gives similar output, but uses the foreign-key relationships to get the title of each book that an author wrote. The first From clause (line 28) gets each book from the Titles table. The second From clause (line 29) uses the generated Authors property of the Title class to get only the authors for the current book. The entity data model uses the foreign-key information stored in the database's AuthorISBN table to get the appropriate authors. The author objects give us access to the names of the current book's authors. The Select clause (line 31) uses the author and book range variables introduced earlier in the query to get the FirstName and LastName of each author from the Authors table and the title (Title1) of each book from the Titles table.

```
26          ' get authors and titles of each book they co-authored
27          Dim authorsAndTitles =
28              From book In database.Titles
29              From author In book.Authors
30              Order By author.LastName, author.FirstName, book.Title1
31              Select author.FirstName, author.LastName, book.Title1
32
33          outputTextBox.AppendText(vbCrLf & vbCrLf & "Authors and titles:")
34
35          ' display authors and titles in tabular format
36          For Each element In authorsAndTitles
37              outputTextBox.AppendText(
38                  String.Format("{0}{1}{2,-10} {3,-10} {4}", vbCrLf, vbTab,
39                      element.FirstName, element.LastName, element.Title1))
40          Next
41
```

Fig. 12.26 | Getting a list of authors and the titles of the books they've authored.

Organizing Book Titles by Author

Most queries return results with data arranged in a relational-style table of rows and columns. The last query (Fig. 12.27, lines 45–51) returns hierarchical results. Each element in the results contains the name of an Author and a list of Titles that the author wrote. The LINQ query does this by using a *nested query* in the Select clause. The outer query iterates over the authors in the database. The inner query takes a specific author and retrieves all titles that the author wrote. The Select clause (lines 47–51) creates an anonymous type with two properties:

- The property Name (line 47) combines each author's name, separating the first and last names by a space.

- The property Titles (line 48) receives the result of the nested query, which returns the title of each book written by the current author.

In this case, we're providing names for each property in the new anonymous type. When you create an anonymous type, you can specify the name for each property by using the format *name = value*.

```
42          ' get authors and titles of each book
43          ' they co-authored; group by author
44          Dim titlesByAuthor =
45              From author In database.Authors
46              Order By author.LastName, author.FirstName
47              Select Name = author.FirstName & " " & author.LastName,
48                  Titles =
49                      From book In author.Titles
50                      Order By book.Title1
51                      Select book.Title1
52
53          outputTextBox.AppendText(
54              vbCrLf & vbCrLf & "Titles grouped by author:")
```

Fig. 12.27 | Getting a list of titles grouped by authors. (Part 1 of 2.)

```
55
56             ' display titles written by each author, grouped by author
57         For Each author In titlesByAuthor
58             ' display authors
59             outputTextBox.AppendText(
60                 String.Format("{0}{1}{2}:", vbCrLf, vbTab, author.Name))
61
62             ' display titles written by that author
63             For Each title In author.Titles
64                 outputTextBox.AppendText(
65                     String.Format("{0}{1}{1}{2}", vbCrLf, vbTab, title))
66             Next title
67         Next author
68     End Sub ' JoiningTableData_Load
69 End Class ' JoiningTableData
```

Fig. 12.27 | Getting a list of titles grouped by authors. (Part 2 of 2.)

The range variable book in the nested query iterates over the current author's books using the Titles property. The Title1 property of a given book returns the Title column from that row of the Titles table in the database.

The nested foreach statements (lines 57–67) use the properties of the anonymous type created by the query to output the hierarchical results. The outer loop displays the author's name and the inner loop displays the titles of all the books written by that author.

12.8 Creating a Master/Detail View App

Figure 12.28 demonstrates a so-called master/detail view—one part of the GUI (the master) allows you to select an entry, and another part (the details) displays detailed information about that entry. When the app first loads, it displays the name of the first author in the data source and that author's books (Fig. 12.28(a)). When you use the buttons on the Binding-Navigator to change authors, the app displays the details of the books written by the corresponding author (Fig. 12.28(b)). This app only reads data from the entity data model, so we disabled the buttons in the BindingNavigator that enable the user to add and delete records.

a) **Master/Detail** app displaying books for the first author in the data source

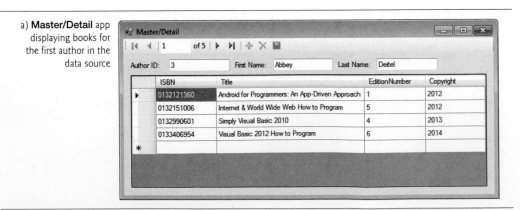

Fig. 12.28 | **Master/Detail** app. (Part 1 of 2.)

b) **Master/Detail** app displaying books for the third author in the data source

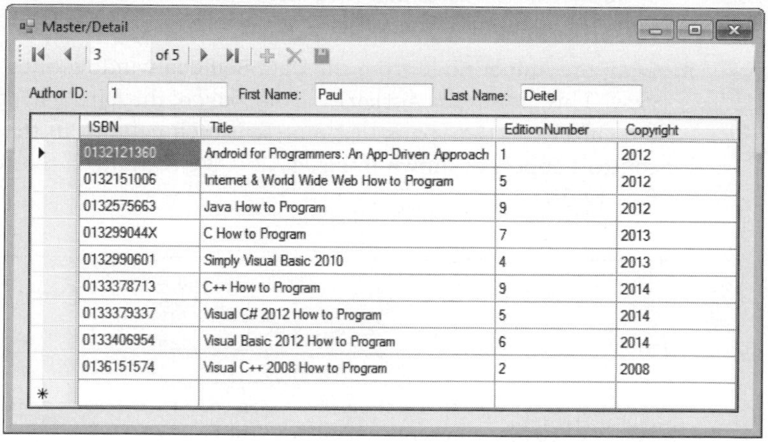

Fig. 12.28 | **Master/Detail** app. (Part 2 of 2.)

When you run the app, experiment with the BindingNavigator's controls. The DVD-player-like buttons of the BindingNavigator allow you to change the currently displayed row.

12.8.1 Creating the Master/Detail App's GUI

You've seen that the IDE can automatically generate the BindingSource, BindingNavigator and GUI elements when you drag a data source onto the Form. You'll now use two BindingSources—one for the master list of authors and one for the titles associated with a given author. Both will be generated by the IDE.

Step 1: Creating the Project
Follow the instructions in Section 12.5.2 to create and configure a new **Windows Forms Application** project called MasterDetail. Name the source file Details.vb and set the Form's Text property to **Master/Detail**.

Step 2: Adding a Data Source for the **Authors** *Table*
Follow the steps in Section 12.5.3 to add a data source for the Authors table. Although you'll be displaying records from the Titles table for each author, you do not need to add a data source for that table. The title information will be obtained from the Titles navigation property in the Author entity data model class.

Step 3: Creating GUI Elements
Next, you'll use the **Design** view to create the GUI components by dragging-and-dropping items from the **Data Sources** window onto the Form. In the earlier sections, you dragged an object from the **Data Sources** window to the Form to create a DataGridView. The IDE allows you to specify the type of control(s) that it will create when you drag and drop an object from the **Data Sources** window onto a Form. To do so:

1. Switch to **Design** view for the Form.

2. Click the **Author** node in the **Data Sources** window—it should change to a drop-down list. Open the drop-down by clicking the down arrow and select the **Details**

option—this indicates that we'd like to generate Label–TextBox pairs that represent each column of the Authors table.

3. Drag the **Author** node from the **Data Sources** window onto the Form in **Design** view. This creates the AuthorBindingSource, the AuthorBindingNavigator and the Label–TextBox pairs that represent each column in the table. Initially, the controls appear as shown in Fig. 12.29. We rearranged the controls as shown in Fig. 12.28.

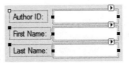

Fig. 12.29 | Details representation of an Author.

4. By default, the Titles navigation property is implemented in the entity data model classes as a HashSet(Of Title). To bind the data to GUI controls properly, you must change this to an ObservableCollection(Of Title). To do this, first ensure that the **Show All Files** (📄) button is selected in the **Solution Explorer**. Next, expand the class library project's BooksModel.edmx node in the **Solution Explorer**, then expand the BooksModel.tt node and open Author.vb in the editor. Add an Imports statement for the namespace System.Collections.ObjectModel. Then, replace the definition of the Author class's Titles property to:

```
Public Overridable Property Titles _
    As New ObservableCollection(Of Title)
```

5. Right click the class library project in the **Solution Explorer** and select **Build** to recompile the class.

6. Next, click the **Titles** node that's nested in the **Author** node in the **Data Sources** window—it should change to a drop-down list. Open the drop-down by clicking the down arrow and ensure that the DataGridView option is selected—this is the GUI control that will be used to display the data from the Titles table that corresponds to a given author.

7. Drag the **Titles** node onto the Form in **Design** view. This creates the TitlesBindingSource and the DataGridView. This control is only for *viewing* data, so set its ReadOnly property to True using the **Properties** window. Because we dragged the **Titles** node from the **Author** node in the **Data Sources** window, the DataGridView will automatically display the books for the currently selected author once we bind the author data to the AuthorBindingSource. Edit the DataGridView's columns to remove the Authors column. While still in the **Edit Columns** dialog, select the Title1 column and set its HeaderText property to Title—this text will display in the DataGridView's column head for the book title.

We used the DataGridView's Anchor property to anchor it to all four sides of the Form. We also set the Form's Size and MinimumSize properties to 550, 300 to set the Form's initial size and minimum size, respectively. The completed GUI is shown in Fig. 12.30.

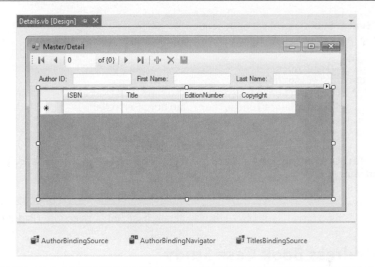

Fig. 12.30 | Finished design of the **Master/Detail** app.

12.8.2 Coding the Master/Detail App

The code to display an author and the corresponding books (Fig. 12.31) is straightforward. Line 8 creates the DbContext. The Form's Load event handler (lines 11–23) orders the Author objects by LastName (line 16) and FirstName (line 17), then loads them into memory (line 18). Next, line 21 assigns dbcontext.Authors.Local to the AuthorBindingSource's DataSource property. At this point:

- the BindingNavigator displays the number of Author objects and indicates that the first one in the results is selected,

- the TextBoxes display the currently selected Author's AuthorID, FirstName and LastName property values, and

- the currently selected Author's titles are automatically assigned to the TitlesBindingSource's DataSource, which causes the DataGridView to display those titles.

Now, when you use the BindingNavigator to change the selected Author, the corresponding titles are displayed in the DataGridView.

```
1  ' Fig. 12.31: Details.vb
2  ' Using a DataGridView to display details based on a selection.
3  Imports System.Data.Entity
4  Imports System.Linq
5
6  Public Class Details
7     ' Entity Framework DBContext
8     Private dbcontext As New BooksExamples.BooksEntities()
9
```

Fig. 12.31 | Using a DataGridView to display details based on a selection. (Part 1 of 2.)

```
10        ' initialize data sources when the Form is loaded
11       Private Sub Details_Load(sender As Object,
12          e As EventArgs) Handles MyBase.Load
13
14          ' load Authors table ordered by LastName then FirstName
15          dbcontext.Authors _
16             .OrderBy(Function(author) author.LastName) _
17             .ThenBy(Function(author) author.FirstName) _
18             .Load()
19
20          ' specify DataSource for AuthorBindingSource
21          AuthorBindingSource.DataSource = dbcontext.Authors.Local
22       End Sub ' Details_Load
23    End Class ' Details
```

Fig. 12.31 | Using a DataGridView to display details based on a selection. (Part 2 of 2.)

12.9 Address Book Case Study

Our final example (Fig. 12.32) implements a simple AddressBook app that enables users to perform the following tasks on the database AddressBook.mdf (which is included in the directory with this chapter's examples):

- Insert new contacts
- Find contacts whose last names begin with the specified letters
- Update existing contacts
- Delete contacts

We populated the database with six fictional contacts.

Rather than displaying a database table in a DataGridView, this app presents the details of one contact at a time in several TextBoxes. The BindingNavigator at the top of the window allows you to control which *row* of the table is displayed at any given time. The BindingNavigator also allows you to *add* a contact and *delete* a contact—but only

a) Use the BindingNavigator's controls to navigate through the contacts in the database

Fig. 12.32 | Manipulating an address book. (Part 1 of 2.)

b) Type a search **string** in the **Last Name:** TextBox then press **Find** to locate contacts whose last names begin with that **string**; only two names start with "Br" so the BindingNavigator indicates two matching records

c) Click **Browse All Entries** to clear the search **string** and allow browsing of all contacts in the database

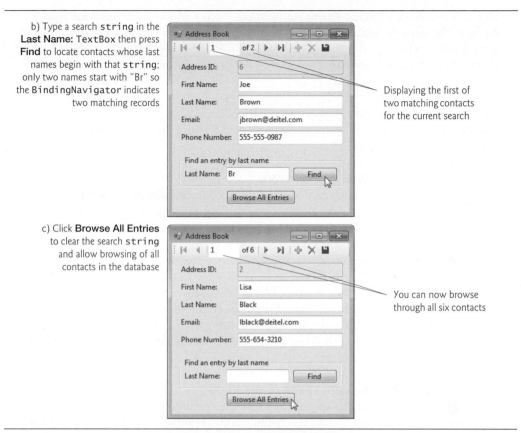

Displaying the first of two matching contacts for the current search

You can now browse through all six contacts

Fig. 12.32 | Manipulating an address book. (Part 2 of 2.)

when browsing the *complete* contact list. When you filter the contacts by last name, the app disables the **Add new** (✛) and **Delete** (✕) buttons (we'll explain why shortly). Clicking **Browse All Entries** enables these buttons again. Adding a row clears the TextBoxes and sets the TextBox to the right of **Address ID** to zero to indicate that the TextBoxes now represent a new record. When you save a new entry, the **Address ID** field is automatically changed from zero to a unique ID number by the database. No changes are made to the underlying database unless you click the **Save Data** (🖫) button.

12.9.1 Creating the Address Book App's GUI

We discuss the app's code momentarily. First you'll set up the entity data model and a Windows Forms app.

Step 1: Creating a Class Library Project for the Entity Data Model

Perform the steps in Section 12.5.1 to create a **Class Library** project named AddressExample that contains an entity data model for the AddressBook.mdf database, which contains only an Addresses table with AddressID, FirstName, LastName, Email and PhoneNumber columns. Name the entity data model AddressModel.edmx. The AddressBook.mdf database is located in the Databases folder with this chapter's examples.

Step 2: Creating a Windows Forms Application Project for the **AddressBook** App
Perform the steps in Section 12.5.2 to create a new **Windows Forms Application** project named `AddressBook` in the `AddressExample` solution. Set the `Form`'s filename to `Contacts.vb`, then set the `Form`'s **Text** property to `Address Book`. Set the `AddressBook` project as the solution's startup project.

Step 3: Adding the **Address** Object as a Data Source
Add the entity data model's `Address` object as a data source, as you did with the `Author` object in *Step 1* of Section 12.5.3.

Step 4: Displaying the Details of Each Row
In **Design** view, select the `Address` node in the **Data Sources** window. Click the `Address` node's down arrow and select the **Details** option to indicate that the IDE should create a set of `Label`–`TextBox` pairs to show the details of a single record at a time.

Step 5: Dragging the **Address** Data-Source Node to the **Form**
Drag the `Address` node from the **Data Sources** window to the `Form`. This automatically creates a `BindingNavigator` and the `Label`s and `TextBox`es corresponding to the columns of the database table. The fields are placed in alphabetical order. Reorder the components, using **Design** view, so they're in the order shown in Fig. 12.32. You'll also want to change the tab order of the controls. To do so, select **VIEW > Tab Order** then click the `TextBox`es from top to bottom in the order they appear in Fig. 12.32.

Step 6: Making the **AddressID** TextBox **ReadOnly**
The `AddressID` column of the `Addresses` table is an *autoincremented identity column*, so users should *not* be allowed to edit the values in this column. Select the `TextBox` for the `AddressID` and set its `ReadOnly` property to `True` using the **Properties** window.

Step 7: Adding Controls to Allow Users to Specify a Last Name to Locate
While the `BindingNavigator` allows you to browse the address book, it would be more convenient to be able to find a specific entry by last name. To add this functionality to the app, we must create controls to allow the user to enter a last name and provide event handlers to perform the search.

Add a `Label` named `findLabel`, a `TextBox` named `findTextBox`, and a `Button` named `findButton`. Place these controls in a `GroupBox` named `findGroupBox`, then set its **Text** property to **Find an entry by last name**. Set the **Text** property of the `Label` to `Last Name:` and set the **Text** property of the `Button` to `Find`.

Step 8: Allowing the User to Return to Browsing All Rows of the Database
To allow users to return to browsing all the contacts after searching for contacts with a specific last name, add a `Button` named `browseAllButton` below the `findGroupBox`. Set the **Text** property of `browseAllButton` to **Browse All Entries**.

12.9.2 Coding the Address Book App
The `Contacts.vb` code-behind file is split into several figures (Figs. 12.33–12.37) for presentation purposes.

Method **RefreshContacts**

As we showed in previous examples, we must connect the AddressBindingSource that controls the GUI with the DbContext that interacts with the database. In this example, we declare the AddressBookEntities DbContext object at line 9 of Fig. 12.33, but create it and initiate the data binding in the RefreshContacts method (lines 12–32), which is called from several other methods in the app. When this method is called, if dbcontext is not Nothing, we call its Dispose method, then create a new AddressBookEntities DbContext at line 19. We do this so we can re-sort the data in the entity data model. If we maintained one dbcontext.Addresses object in memory for the duration of the program and the user changed a person's last name or first name, the records would still remain in their original order in the dbcontext.Addresses object, even if that order is incorrect. Lines 23–26 order the Address objects by LastName, then FirstName and load the objects into memory. Then line 29 sets the AddressBindingSource's DataSource property to dbcontext.Addresses.Local to bind the data in memory to the GUI.

```vb
 I   ' Fig. 12.33: Contacts.vb
 2   ' Manipulating an address book.
 3   Imports System.Data.Entity
 4   Imports System.Data.Entity.Validation
 5   Imports System.Linq
 6
 7   Public Class Contacts
 8      ' LINQ to SQL data context
 9      Private dbcontext As AddressExample.AddressBookEntities = Nothing
10
11      ' fill the AddressBindingSource with all rows, ordered by name
12      Private Sub RefreshContacts()
13         ' Displose old DbContext, if any
14         If (dbcontext IsNot Nothing) Then
15            dbcontext.Dispose()
16         End If
17
18         ' create new DbContext so we can reorder records based on edits
19         dbcontext = New AddressExample.AddressBookEntities()
20
21         ' use LINQ to order the Addresses table contents
22         ' by last name, then first name
23         dbcontext.Addresses _
24            .OrderBy(Function(entry) entry.LastName) _
25            .ThenBy(Function(entry) entry.FirstName) _
26            .Load()
27
28         ' specify DataSource for AddressBindingSource
29         AddressBindingSource.DataSource = dbcontext.Addresses.Local
30         AddressBindingSource.MoveFirst() ' go to first result
31         findTextBox.Clear() ' clear the Find TextBox
32      End Sub ' RefreshContacts
33
```

Fig. 12.33 | Creating the BooksDataContext and defining method RefreshContacts for use in other methods.

Method Contacts_Load

Method Contacts_Load (Fig. 12.34) calls RefreshContacts (line 38) so that the first record is displayed when the app starts. As before, you create the Load event handler by double clicking the Form's title bar.

```
34    ' when the form loads, fill it with data from the database
35    Private Sub Contacts_Load(sender As Object,
36        e As EventArgs) Handles MyBase.Load
37
38        RefreshContacts() ' fill binding with data from database
39    End Sub ' Contacts_Load
40
```

Fig. 12.34 | Calling RefreshContacts to fill the TextBoxes when the app loads.

Method AddressBindingNavigatorSaveItem_Click

Method AddressBindingNavigatorSaveItem_Click (Fig. 12.35) saves the changes to the database when the BindingNavigator's **Save Data** Button is clicked. (Remember to enable this button.) The AddressBook database requires values for the first name, last name, phone number and e-mail. If a field is empty when you attempt to save, a DbEntityValidationException exception occurs. We call RefreshContacts (line 57) after saving to re-sort the data and move back to the first element.

```
41    ' save the changes made to the data
42    Private Sub AddressBindingNavigatorSaveItem_Click(
43        sender As Object, e As EventArgs) _
44        Handles AddressBindingNavigatorSaveItem.Click
45
46        Validate() ' validate input fields
47        AddressBindingSource.EndEdit() ' complete current edit, if any
48
49        ' try to save changes
50        Try
51            dbcontext.SaveChanges() ' write changes to database file
52        Catch ex As DbEntityValidationException
53            MessageBox.Show("Columns cannot be empty",
54                "Entity Validation Exception")
55        End Try
56
57        RefreshContacts() ' change back to initial unfiltered data on save
58    End Sub ' AddressBindingNavigatorSaveItem_Click
59
```

Fig. 12.35 | Saving changes to the database when the user clicks **Save Data**.

Method findButton_Click

Method findButton_Click (Fig. 12.36) uses LINQ query syntax (lines 67–71) to select only people whose last names start with the characters in the findTextBox. The query sorts the results by last name then first name. In LINQ to Entities, you *cannot* bind a LINQ query's results directly to a BindingSource's DataSource. So, line 74 calls the query object's

ToList method to get a List representation of the filtered data and assigns the *List* to the BindingSource's DataSource. When you convert the query result to a List, only changes to *existing* records in the DbContext are tracked by the DbContext—any records that you add or remove while viewing the filtered data would be lost. For this reason we disabled the **Add new** and **Delete** buttons when the data is filtered. When you enter a last name and click **Find**, the BindingNavigator allows the user to browse only the rows containing the matching last names. This is because the data source bound to the Form's controls (the result of the LINQ query) has changed and now contains only a limited number of rows.

```
60      ' load data for the rows with the specified
61      ' last name into the AddressBindingSource
62      Private Sub findButton_Click(sender As Object,
63         e As EventArgs) Handles findButton.Click
64
65         ' use LINQ to filter contacts with last names that
66         ' start with findTextBox contents
67         Dim lastNameQuery =
68            From address In dbcontext.Addresses
69            Where address.LastName.StartsWith(findTextBox.Text)
70            Order By address.LastName, address.FirstName
71            Select address
72
73         ' display matching contacts
74         AddressBindingSource.DataSource = lastNameQuery.ToList()
75         AddressBindingSource.MoveFirst() ' go to first result
76
77         ' don't allow add/delete when contacts are filtered
78         BindingNavigatorAddNewItem.Enabled = False
79         BindingNavigatorDeleteItem.Enabled = False
80      End Sub ' findButton_Click
81
```

Fig. 12.36 | Finding the contacts whose last names begin with a specified String.

Method *browseAllButton_Click*

Method browseAllButton_Click (Fig. 12.37) allows users to return to browsing all the rows after searching for specific rows. Double click browseAllButton to create a Click event handler. The event handler enables the **Add new** and **Delete** buttons then calls RefreshContacts to restore the data source to the full list of people (in sorted order) and clear the findTextBox.

```
82      ' reload AddressBindingSource with all rows
83      Private Sub browseAllButton_Click(sender As Object,
84         e As EventArgs) Handles browseAllButton.Click
85
86         ' allow add/delete when contacts are not filtered
87         BindingNavigatorAddNewItem.Enabled = True
88         BindingNavigatorDeleteItem.Enabled = True
```

Fig. 12.37 | Allowing the user to browse all contacts. (Part 1 of 2.)

```
89          RefreshContacts() ' change back to initial unfiltered data
90      End Sub ' browseAllButton_Click
91  End Class ' Contacts
```

Fig. 12.37 | Allowing the user to browse all contacts. (Part 2 of 2.)

12.10 Tools and Web Resources

Our LINQ Resource Center at www.deitel.com/LINQ contains many links to additional information, including blogs by Microsoft LINQ team members, sample chapters, tutorials, videos, downloads, FAQs, forums, webcasts and other resource sites.

A useful tool for learning LINQ is LINQPad (www.linqpad.net), which allows you to execute and view the results of any Visual Basic or C# expression, including LINQ queries. It also supports the ADO.NET Entity Framework and LINQ to Entities.

This chapter is meant as an introduction to databases, the ADO.NET Entity Framework and LINQ to Entities. Microsoft's Entity Framework site

> msdn.microsoft.com/en-us/data/aa937723

provides lots of additional information on working with the ADO.NET Entity Framework and LINQ to Entities, including tutorials, videos and more.

12.11 Wrap-Up

This chapter introduced the relational database model, the ADO.NET Entity Framework, LINQ to Entities and the Visual Studio 2012's visual programming tools for working with databases. You examined the contents of a simple Books database and learned about the relationships among the tables in the database. You used LINQ to Entities and the entity data model classes generated by the IDE to retrieve data from, add new data to, delete data from and update data in a SQL Server Express database.

We discussed the entity data model classes automatically generated by the IDE, such as the DbContext class that manages an app's interactions with a database. You learned how to use the IDE's tools to connect to databases and to generate entity data model classes based on an existing database's schema. You then used the IDE's drag-and-drop capabilities to automatically generate GUIs for displaying and manipulating database data.

In the next chapter, we demonstrate how to build web apps using Microsoft's ASP.NET web forms technology, which is similar similar to building Windows Forms apps, but in the context of web pages. We introduce the concept of a three-tier app, which is divided into three pieces that can reside on the same computer or be distributed among separate computers across a network such as the Internet. One of these tiers—the information tier—typically stores data in a database.

Summary

Section 12.1 Introduction
- A database is an organized collection of data.
- A database management system (DBMS) provides mechanisms for storing, organizing, retrieving and modifying data.

- SQL Server Express provides most of the features of Microsoft's full (fee-based) SQL Server product, but has some limitations, such as a maximum database size.
- A SQL Server Express database can be easily migrated to a full version of SQL Server.
- The ADO.NET Entity Framework and LINQ to Entities allow you to manipulate relational data stored in a relational database, such as a SQL Server Express database.

Section 12.2 Relational Databases
- A relational database organizes data simply in tables.
- Tables are composed of rows and columns (also called fields) in which values are stored.
- A column (or group of columns) of each row is the table's primary key—a column (or group of columns) requiring a unique value that cannot be duplicated in other rows. This guarantees that a primary key value can be used to uniquely identify a row.
- A primary key composed of two or more columns is known as a composite key.
- Each column represents a different data attribute.
- Rows are unique (by primary key) within a table, but some column values may be duplicated between rows.

Section 12.3 A Books Database
- A database's tables, their fields and the relationships between them are collectively known as a database schema.
- A foreign key is a column in one table that matches the primary-key column in another table.
- Foreign keys, which are specified when a database table is created, link the data in multiple tables.
- Every foreign-key value must appear as another table's primary-key value so the DBMS can ensure that the foreign-key value is valid.
- Foreign keys also allow related data in multiple tables to be selected from those tables—this is known as joining the data.
- There's a one-to-many relationship between a primary key and a corresponding foreign key—a foreign key can appear many times in its own table but only once (as the primary key) in another table.
- An entity-relationship (ER) diagram shows the tables in a database and their relationships.
- Every row must have a value in the primary-key column, and the value of the key must be unique in the table.

Section 12.4 LINQ to Entities and the ADO.NET Entity Framework
- With the ADO.NET Entity Framework, you interact with the database via classes that the IDE generates from the database schema when you add a new ADO.NET Entity Data Model to your project.
- The IDE creates two classes for a table. The first class represents a row of the table and contains properties for each table column. Objects of this class are called row objects and store the data from individual rows of the table. The IDE uses the singular version of a table's plural name as the row class's name. The second class represents the table itself. An object of this class stores a collection of row objects that correspond to all of the rows in the table.
- The entity data model classes have full *IntelliSense* support in the IDE.
- Navigation properties in row classes represent the relationships between tables.
- A DbContext (namespace System.Data.Entity) manages the data flow between the program and the database. When the IDE generates the entity data model's row and table classes, it also creates a derived class of DbContext that is specific to the database being manipulated. This class contains

properties that represent the database's tables. These can be used as data sources for manipulating data in LINQ queries and in GUIs.

- Changes made to the data managed by a DbContext can be saved back to the database using the DbContext's SaveChanges method.

- LINQ to Entities works through the IQueryable(Of T) interface, which inherits from the interface IEnumerable(Of T). When a LINQ to Entities query on an IQueryable(Of T) object executes against the database, the results are loaded into objects of the corresponding entity data model classes for convenient access in your code.

- The extension methods used with LINQ to Entities are defined as static methods of class Queryable (namespace System.Linq) and can be applied to any object that implements the IQueryable(Of T) interface—these include various entity data model objects and the results of LINQ to Entities queries.

Section 12.5 Querying a Database with LINQ

- The IDE provides visual programming tools and wizards that simplify accessing data in your projects. These tools establish database connections and create the objects necessary to view and manipulate the data through the GUI—a technique known as data binding.

- A DataGridView (namespace System.Windows.Forms) displays data from a data source in tabular format.

- A BindingNavigator is a collection of controls that allow you to navigate through the records displayed in a GUI. The BindingNavigator controls also allow you to add records, delete records and save your changes to the database.

Section 12.5.1 Creating the ADO.NET Entity Data Model Class Library

- An entity data model describes as Visual Basic classes the data that you'll be manipulating.

- To interact with a database, you add an ADO.NET entity data model to the project (typically a class library project for reuse). This will also configure the connection to the database.

- The ADO.NET entity data model's .edmx file contains information about the entity data model.

- When configuring the model, you create a connection to the database and choose the model's contents from the database.

- The entity connection string contains the information that the ADO.NET Entity Framework requires to connect to the database at runtime.

- SQL Server Express allows only one program at a time to connect to a database file.

- The entity data model diagram contains the selected database objects and shows the relationships between them.

Section 12.5.2 Creating a Windows Forms Project and Configuring It to Use the Entity Data Model

- To use the entity data model classes from a class library for data binding, you must first add a reference to the class library to your project. You'll also need to add references to the System.Data.Entity and EntityFramework libraries.

- The EntityFramework library is added by the IDE when you create the entity data model, but it's also required in each app that will use the entity data model. To add a reference to the EntityFramework library: Right click the solution name in the **Solution Explorer** and select **Manage NuGet Packages for Solution...** to display the **Manage NuGet Packages** dialog. In the dialog that appears, click **Manage** to display the **Select Projects** dialog, then select your project project and click **OK**. Click **Close** to close the **Manage NuGet Packages** dialog.

- Each app that will use an entity data model also requires the connection string that tells the Entity Framework how to connect to the database. The connection string is stored in the App.Config file of the project in which the entity data model is defined and must be copied into the App.Config file of the project that uses the entity data model.

Section 12.5.3 Data Bindings Between Controls and the Entity Data Model

- You must write code to enable the autogenerated GUI to interact with the entity data model.

- To use the entity data model classes for data binding, you must first add them as a data source.

- Select **VIEW > Other Windows > Data Sources** to display the **Data Sources** window at the left side of the IDE, then in that window click the **Add New Data Source...** link to display the **Data Source Configuration Wizard**. The entity data model classes are used to create objects representing the tables in the database, so use an **Object** data source. Select the object(s) you need from the model and click **Finish**. You can now drag the data source objects onto the Form in **Design** view to generate a GUI.

- The default GUI for a table is a DataGridView with column names representing all the properties of the data source object. The IDE also creates a BindingNavigator that contains Buttons for moving between entries, adding entries, deleting entries and saving changes to the database. The IDE also generates a BindingSource, which handles the transfer of data between the data source and the data-bound controls on the Form.

- Nonvisual components such as the BindingSource and the nonvisual aspects of the BindingNavigator appear in the component tray—the gray region below the Form in **Design** view.

- The IDE names the BindingNavigator and BindingSource based on the data source's name.

- To edit the columns displayed in a DataGridView, select it, then click ... button of the **Columns** property in the **Properties** window to display the **Edit Columns** dialog.

- To complete the data binding, you must create an object of the entity data model's DbContext derived class and use it to obtain data.

- The OrderBy extension method orders rows in ascending order by the property specified in its lambda expression argument.

- A lambda expression defines a simple, anonymous method. Like other Visual Basic methods, a lambda expression begins with Function if it will return a value and Sub if it will not. This is followed by a parameter list in parentheses. The parameter list is followed by the body of the function. The value produced by the expression in the lambda's body is implicitly returned by the lambda expression. You do not specify a return type for a single-line lambda expression—the return type is inferred from the return value.

- You can also create multiline lambda expressions by placing the statements on separate lines between the Function...End Function or Sub...End Sub keywords. Multiline lambdas can optionally use the As clause to specify a return type, just as in a typical method definition.

- The ThenBy extension method enables you to order results by an additional column.

- The Load extension method (defined in class DbExtensions from the namespace System.Data.Entity) loads data into memory. This data is tracked by the DbContext in local memory so that any changes made to the data can eventually be saved into the database.

- The Local property of a DbContext property is an ObservableCollection(Author) that represents the data in memory.

- When a BindingSource's DataSource property is assigned an ObservableCollection(Of T) (namespace System.Collections.ObjectModel), the GUI that's bound to the BindingSource is notified of any changes to the data so the GUI can be updated accordingly. In addition, changes made by the user to the data in the GUI will be tracked so the DbContext can eventually save those changes to the database.

- Calling EndEdit on the BindingSource forces it to save any pending changes into the DbContext model in memory.

- Calling SaveChanges on the DbContext object stores any changes into the database.

Section 12.6 Dynamically Binding Query Results

- The data bindings created by the IDE automatically update a DataGridView each time its BindingSource's DataSource changes.

- The MoveFirst method of the BindingSource moves to the first row of the data source.

- When you invoke OrderBy on an ObservableCollection(Of T), the method returns an IEnumerable(Of T).

- A lambda expression that's used with the Where extension method must return a bool value.

Section 12.7 Retrieving Data from Multiple Tables with LINQ

- To join data from multiple tables you use the properties that the entity data model contains based on foreign-key relationships between the database's tables. These properties enable you to easily access related rows in other tables.

- Most queries return results with data arranged in relational-style rows and columns. With LINQ to Entities you can create queries that return hierarchical results in which each item in the result contains a collection of other items.

- Use anonymous types to create simple classes used to store data without writing a class definition.

- An anonymous type declaration—also called an anonymous object-creation expression—begins with the keyword new followed by a member-initializer list.

- The compiler generates a new class definition based on the anonymous object-creation expression, containing the properties specified in the member-initializer list.

- All properties of an anonymous type are public.

- Properties of anonymous types are read-only.

- Each property's type is inferred from the value assigned to it.

- Objects of anonymous types are stored in implicitly typed local variables.

- The compiler defines the ToString method when creating the anonymous type's class definition. The method returns a string of comma-separated *PropertyName* = *value* pairs in curly braces.

- The Equals method, generated for any anonymous type, compares the properties of the anonymous object that calls the method and the anonymous object that it receives as an argument.

Section 12.8 Creating a **Master/Detail** View App

- In a master/detail view, one part of the GUI (the master) allows you to select an entry, and another part (the details) displays detailed information about that entry.

- The IDE allows you to specify the type of control(s) that it will create when you drag and drop an object from the **Data Sources** window onto a Form. To do so, click a data source object's node in the **Data Sources** window—it should change to a drop-down list from which you can select the controls to use on the GUI. The **Details** option indicates that the IDE should generate Label–TextBox pairs that represent each column of the data source object.

- Dragging a navigation property from a data source object in the **Data Sources** window creates a BindingSource and a GUI for the items in another table that are associated with the data source object. The items in this second BindingSource will automatically update based on the currently selected master object.

Section 12.9 Address Book Case Study

- If the data in the DbContext needs to be reordered, you'll need to call Dispose on the existing one, then create a new DbContext.

- You cannot bind a LINQ to Entities query's results directly to a BindingSource's DataSource.

- When you convert a query result to a List, only changes to existing records in the DbContext are tracked by the DbContext—any records that you add or remove while viewing the filtered data in a List would be lost.

Terminology

ADO.NET Entity Framework 435
anonymous method 452
autoincremented database column 437
BindingNavigator class 449
BindingSource class 449
column of a database table 435
composite key 435
connection to a database 443
data binding 441
Data Sources window 448
Data Source Configuration Wizard window 448
database 434
database management system (DBMS) 434
database schema 436
DataGridView class 442
DataSource property of class
    BindingSource 452
DbContext class 441
DbEntityValidationException class 453
EndEdit method of class BindingSource 453
entity data model 440
entity-relationship (ER) diagram 439
field in a database table 435
foreign key 438
identity column in a database table 437
IQueryable(Of T) interface 441
joining database tables 439

lambda expression 452
LINQ to Entities 435
Load extension method of class
    DbExtensions 452
many-to-many relationship 440
master/detail view 462
Microsoft SQL Server Express 434
MoveFirst method of class BindingSource 455
navigation property 440
Object data source 448
ObservableCollection(Of T) class 452
one-to-many relationship 439
OrderBy extension method of class
    Queryable 452
primary key 435
query 434
Queryable class 441
relational database 435
row object 440
row of a database table 435
SaveChanges method of a DbContext 441
smart tag menu 454
System.Data.Entity 441
table in a database 435
ThenBy extension method of class
    Queryable 452
Where extension method of class Queryable 457

Self-Review Exercises

12.1 Fill in the blanks in each of the following statements:

    a) A table in a relational database consists of _____ and _____ in which values are stored.

    b) The _____ uniquely identifies each row in a relational database table.

    c) A relational database can be manipulated with the ADO.NET Entity Framework via an object of a derived class of _____, which contains properties for accessing each table in the database.

    d) The _____ control (presented in this chapter) displays data in rows and columns that correspond to the rows and columns of a data source.

    e) Merging data from multiple relational database tables is called _____ the data.

     f) A(n) _____ is a column (or group of columns) in a relational database table that matches the primary-key column (or group of columns) in another table.

     g) A(n) _____ object serves as an intermediary between a data source and its corresponding data-bound GUI control.

     h) The _____ property of a control specifies where it gets the data it displays.

12.2 State whether each of the following is *true* or *false*. If *false*, explain why.

     a) Providing the same value for a foreign key in multiple rows causes the DBMS to report an error.

     b) Providing a foreign-key value that does not appear as a primary-key value in another table is an error.

     c) The result of a query can be sorted in ascending or descending order.

     d) A `BindingNavigator` object can extract data from a database.

     e) A `DbContext` automatically saves changes made back to the database.

Answers to Self-Review Exercises

12.1 a) rows, columns. b) primary key. c) `DbContext`. d) `DataGridView`. e) joining. f) foreign key. g) `BindingSource`. h) `DataSource`.

12.2 a) False. Multiple rows can have the same value for a foreign key. Providing the same value for the primary key in multiple rows causes the DBMS to report an error, because duplicate primary keys would prevent each row from being identified uniquely. b) True. c) True. d) False. A `Binding-Navigator` allows users to browse and manipulate data displayed by another GUI control. A `DbContext` can extract data from a database. e) False. You must call the `SaveChanges` method of the `DbContext` to save the changes made back to the database.

Exercises

12.3 *(Display Authors Table App Modification)* Modify the app in Section 12.5 to contain a Text-Box and a Button that allow the user to search for specific authors by last name. Include a `Label` to identify the `TextBox`. Using the techniques presented in Section 12.9, create a LINQ query and change the `DataSource` property of `AuthorBindingSource` to contain only the specified authors. Also, provide a Button that enables the user to return to browsing the complete set of authors.

12.4 *(Display Query Results App Modification)* Modify the app in Section 12.6 to contain a Text-Box and a Button that allow the user to perform a search of the book titles in the `Titles` table of the Books database. Use a `Label` to identify the `TextBox`. When the user clicks the Button, the app should execute and display the result of a query that selects all the rows in which the search term entered by the user in the `TextBox` appears anywhere in the `Title` column. For example, if the user enters the search term "Visual," the `DataGridView` should display the rows for *Simply Visual Basic 2010*, *Visual Basic 2012 How to Program*, *Visual C# 2012 How to Program* and *Visual C++ 2008 How to Program*. If the user enters "Simply," the `DataGridView` should display only the row for *Simply Visual Basic 2012*. [*Hint:* Use the `Contains` method of the `String` class.] Also, provide a Button that enables the user to return to browsing the complete set of titles.

12.5 *(Joining Tables with LINQ App Modification)* Create an app like the one in Section 12.7 that uses the Books database and displays the results of the following queries:

     a) Get a list of all the titles and the authors who wrote them. Sort the results by title.

     b) Get a list of all the titles and the authors who wrote them. Sort the results by title. For each title sort the authors alphabetically by last name, then first name.

     c) Get a list of all the authors grouped by title, sorted by title; for a given title sort the author names alphabetically by last name then first name.

12.6   *(Baseball Database App)* Build an app that executes a query against the Players table of the Baseball database included in the Databases folder with this chapter's examples. Display the table in a DataGridView, and add a TextBox and Button to allow the user to search for a specific player by last name. Use a Label to identify the TextBox. Clicking the Button should execute the appropriate query. Also, provide a Button that enables the user to return to browsing the complete set of players.

12.7   *(Baseball Database App Modification)* Modify Exercise 12.6 to allow the user to locate players with batting averages in a specific range. Add a minimumTextBox for the minimum batting average (0.000 by default) and a maximumTextBox for the maximum batting average (1.000 by default). Use a Label to identify each TextBox. Add a Button for executing a query that selects rows from the Players table in which the BattingAverage column is greater than or equal to the specified minimum value and less than or equal to the specified maximum value.

13

Web App Development with ASP.NET

If any man will draw up his case, and put his name at the foot of the first page, I will give him an immediate reply. Where he compels me to turn over the sheet, he must wait my leisure.
—Lord Sandwich

Objectives

In this chapter you'll learn:

- Web app development using ASP.NET.

- To handle the events from a Web Form's controls.

- To use validation controls to ensure that data is in the correct format before it's sent from a client to the server.

- To maintain user-specific information.

- To create a data-driven web app using ASP.NET and the ADO.NET Entity Framework.

Outline

13.1 Introduction

In this chapter, we introduce web-app development with Microsoft's ASP.NET technology. Web-based apps create web content for web-browser clients.

We present several examples that demonstrate web-app development using Web Forms, web controls (also called ASP.NET server controls) and Visual Basic programming. Web Form files have the filename extension .aspx and contain the web page's GUI. You customize Web Forms by adding web controls including labels, textboxes, images, buttons and other GUI components. The Web Form file represents the web page that's sent to the client browser. We often refer to Web Form files as ASPX files.

An ASPX file created in Visual Studio has a corresponding class written in a .NET language—we use Visual Basic in this book. This class contains event handlers, initialization code, utility methods and other supporting code. The file that contains this class is called the code-behind file and provides the ASPX file's programmatic implementation.

Software Used in This Chapter

To develop the code and GUIs in this chapter, we used Microsoft's Visual Studio Express 2012 for Web—a free IDE designed for developing ASP.NET web apps. The full version of Visual Studio 2012 includes the functionality of Visual Studio Express 2012 for Web, so the instructions we present in this chapter also apply to Visual Studio 2012. See the Before You Begin section that follows the Preface for additional information on downloading and installing the software for this chapter.

Online Chapter—Web App Development with ASP.NET: A Deeper Look

In the online Chapter 24, Web App Development with ASP.NET: A Deeper Look, we present several additional web-app development topics, including:

- master pages to maintain a uniform look-and-feel across the pages in a web app

- creating password-protected websites with registration and login capabilities

- using the **Web Site Administration Tool** to specify which parts of a website are pass-word protected

- using ASP.NET AJAX to quickly and easily improve the user experience for your web apps, giving them responsiveness comparable to that of desktop apps.

13.2 Web Basics

In this section, we discuss what occurs when a user requests a web page in a browser. In its simplest form, a *web page* is nothing more than an *HTML (HyperText Markup Language) document* (with the extension `.html` or `.htm`) that describes to a web browser the document's content and how to format it.

HTML documents normally contain *hyperlinks* that link to different pages or to other parts of the same page. When the user clicks a hyperlink, a **web server** locates the requested web page and sends it to the user's web browser. Similarly, the user can type the *address of a web page* into the browser's *address field* and press *Enter* to view the specified page.

In this chapter, we develop web apps using visual development techniques that are similar to those you've used with Windows Forms. To take full advantage of web app development, you'll also want to learn HTML5, CSS and JavaScript—topics that we cover in our textbook *Internet & World Wide Web How to Program, 5/e.* You can learn more about this book at `deitel.com/books/iw3htp5`.

URIs and URLs

URIs (Uniform Resource Identifiers) identify resources on the Internet. URIs that start with `http://` are called *URLs (Uniform Resource Locators)*. Common URLs refer to files, directories or server-side code that performs tasks such as database lookups, Internet searches and business application processing. If you know the URL of a publicly available resource anywhere on the web, you can enter that URL into a web browser's address field and the browser can access that resource.

Parts of a URL

A URL contains information that directs a browser to the resource that the user wishes to access. Web servers make such resources available to web clients. Popular web servers include Microsoft's Internet Information Services (IIS), Apache's HTTP Server and Nginx.[1]

Let's examine the components of the URL

```
http://www.deitel.com/books/downloads.html
```

The `http://` indicates that the HyperText Transfer Protocol (HTTP) should be used to obtain the resource. HTTP is the web protocol that enables clients and servers to communicate. Next in the URL is the server's fully qualified **hostname** (`www.deitel.com`)—the name of the web server computer on which the resource resides. This computer is referred to as the **host**, because it houses and maintains resources. The hostname `www.deitel.com` is translated into an **IP (Internet Protocol) address**—a numerical value that uniquely identifies the server on the Internet. A **Domain Name System (DNS) server** maintains a database of hostnames and their corresponding IP addresses, and performs the translations automatically.

---

1. w3techs.com/.

The remainder of the URL (`/books/downloads.html`) specifies the resource's location (`/books`) and name (`downloads.html`) on the web server. The location could represent an actual directory on the web server's file system. For *security* reasons, however, the location is typically a *virtual directory*. The web server translates the virtual directory into a real location on the server, thus hiding the resource's true location.

Making a Request and Receiving a Response

When given a URL, a web browser uses HTTP to retrieve the resource found at that address. Figure 13.1 shows a web browser sending a request to a web server. Figure 13.2 shows the web server responding to that request.

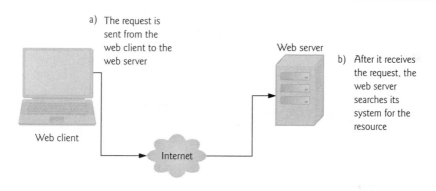

Fig. 13.1 | Client requesting a resource from a web server.

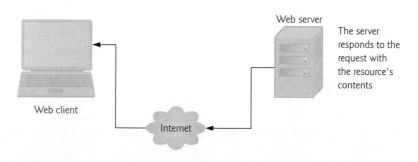

Fig. 13.2 | Client receiving a response from the web server.

13.3 Multitier App Architecture

Web-based apps are **multitier apps** (sometimes referred to as *n*-tier apps). Multitier apps divide functionality into separate **tiers** (that is, logical groupings of functionality). Although tiers can be located on the *same* computer, the tiers of web-based apps commonly reside on *separate* computers for *security* and *scalability*. Figure 13.3 presents the basic architecture of a three-tier web-based app.

Information Tier

The **bottom tier** (also called the **information tier**) maintains the app's data. This tier typically stores data in a relational database management system. For example, a retail store might have a database for storing product information, such as descriptions, prices and quantities in stock. The same database also might contain customer information, such as user names, billing addresses and credit card numbers. This tier can contain multiple databases, which together comprise the data needed for an app.

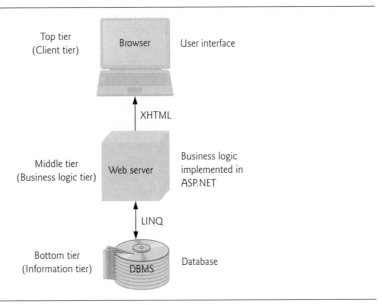

Fig. 13.3 | Three-tier architecture.

Business Logic

The **middle tier** implements **business logic**, **controller logic** and **presentation logic** to control interactions between the app's clients and its data. The middle tier acts as an intermediary between data in the information tier and the app's clients. The middle-tier controller logic processes client requests (such as requests to view a product catalog) and retrieves data from the database. The middle-tier presentation logic then processes data from the information tier and presents the content to the client. Web apps present data to clients as web pages.

Business logic in the middle tier enforces *business rules* and ensures that data is reliable before the server app updates the database or presents the data to users. Business rules dictate how clients can and cannot access app data, and how apps process data. For example, a business rule in the middle tier of a retail store's web-based app might ensure that all product quantities remain positive. A client request to set a negative quantity in the bottom tier's product information database would be rejected by the middle tier's business logic.

Client Tier

The **top tier**, or **client tier**, is the app's user interface, which gathers input and displays output. Users interact directly with the app through the user interface (typically viewed in a web browser), keyboard and mouse. In response to user actions (for example, clicking a hyperlink), the client tier interacts with the middle tier to make requests and to retrieve data from the information tier. The client tier then displays to the user the data retrieved from the middle tier. The client tier *never* directly interacts with the information tier.

13.4 Your First Web App

Our first example displays the web server's time of day in a browser window (Fig. 13.4). When this app executes—that is, a web browser requests the app's web page—the web server executes the app's code, which gets the current time and displays it in a `Label`. The web server then returns the result to the web browser that made the request, and the web browser *renders* the web page containing the time. We executed this app in both the *Internet Explorer* and *Firefox* web browsers to show you that the web page renders identically in different browsers—the page should look the same in most Web browsers.

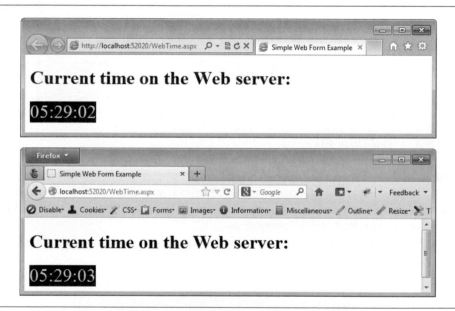

Fig. 13.4 | WebTime web app running in both Internet Explorer and Firefox.

Testing the App in Your Default Web Browser
To test this app in your default web browser, perform the following steps:

1. Open Visual Studio Express For Web.

2. Select **Open Web Site...** from the **FILE** menu.

3. In the **Open Web Site** dialog (Fig. 13.5), ensure that **File System** is selected, then navigate to this chapter's examples, select the WebTime folder and click the **Open** Button.

4. Select WebTime.aspx in the **Solution Explorer**, then type *Ctrl* + *F5* to execute the web app.

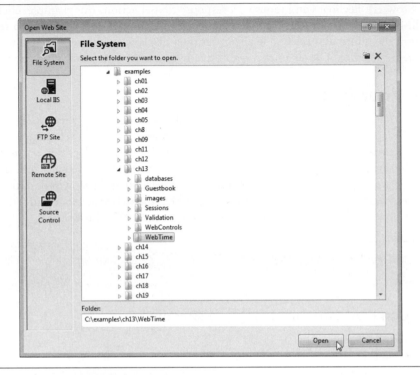

Fig. 13.5 | Open Web Site dialog.

Testing the App in a Selected Web Browser

If you wish to execute the app in another web browser, you can copy the web page's address from your default browser's address field and paste it into another browser's address field, or you can perform the following steps:

1. In the **Solution Explorer**, right click WebTime.aspx and select **Browse With...** to display the **Browse With** dialog (Fig. 13.6).

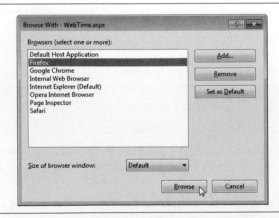

Fig. 13.6 | Selecting another web browser to execute the web app.

2. From the **Browsers** list, select the browser in which you'd like to test the web app and click the **Browse** Button.

If the browser you wish to use is not listed, you can use the **Browse With** dialog to add items to or remove items from the list of web browsers.

13.4.1 Building the WebTime App

Now that you've tested the app, let's create it in Visual Studio Express For Web.

Step 1: Creating the Web Site Project
Select **FILE > New Web Site...** to display the **New Web Site** dialog (Fig. 13.7). In the left column of this dialog, ensure that **Visual Basic** is selected, then select **ASP.NET Empty Web Site** in the middle column. At the bottom of the dialog you can specify the location and name of the web app.

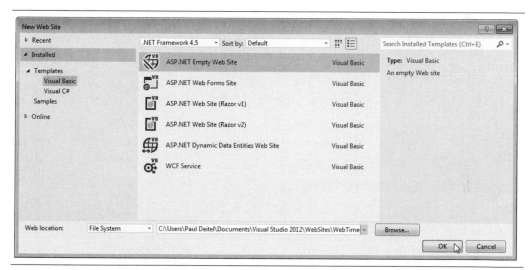

Fig. 13.7 │ Creating an **ASP.NET Web Site** in Visual Studio Express For Web.

The **Web location:** ComboBox provides the following options:

- **File System:** Creates a new website for testing on your local computer. Such websites execute on your local machine in IIS Express and can be accessed only by web browsers running on the same computer. IIS Express is a version of Microsoft's Internet Information Services (IIS) web server that allows you to test your web apps locally. You can later publish your website to a production IIS web server for access via a local network or the Internet. Each example in this chapter uses the **File System** option, so select it now.

- **HTTP:** Creates a new website on an IIS web server and uses HTTP to allow you to put your website's files on the server. IIS is Microsoft's software that's used to run production websites. If you own a website and have your own web server, you might use this to build a new website directly on that server computer. You must be an Administrator on the computer running IIS to use this option.

- **FTP:** Uses File Transfer Protocol (FTP) to allow you to put your website's files on the server. The server administrator must first create the website on the server for you. FTP is commonly used by so-called "hosting providers" to allow website owners to share a server computer that runs many websites.

Change the name of the web app from WebSite1 to WebTime, then click **OK** to create the website.

Step 2: Adding a Web Form to the Website and Examining the Solution Explorer
A Web Form represents one page in a web app—we'll often use the terms "page" and "Web Form" interchangeably. A Web Form contains a web app's GUI. To create the WebTime.aspx Web Form:

1. Right click the project name in the **Solution Explorer** and select **Add > Add New Item...** to display the **Add New Item** dialog (Fig. 13.8).

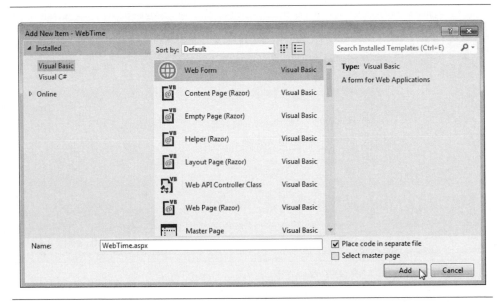

Fig. 13.8 | Adding a new **Web Form** to the website with the **Add New Item** dialog.

2. In the left column, ensure that **Visual Basic** is selected, then select **Web Form** in the middle column.

3. In the **Name:** TextBox, change the file name to WebTime.aspx, then click the **Add** Button.

After you add the Web Form, the IDE opens it in **Source** view by default (Fig. 13.9). This view displays the markup for the Web Form. As you become more familiar with ASP.NET and building web sites in general, you might use **Source** view to perform high precision adjustments to your design (in HTML and/or CSS) or to program in the JavaScript language that executes in web browsers. For the purposes of this chapter, we'll keep things simple by working exclusively in **Design** mode. To switch to **Design** mode, you can click the **Design** Button at the bottom of the code editor window.

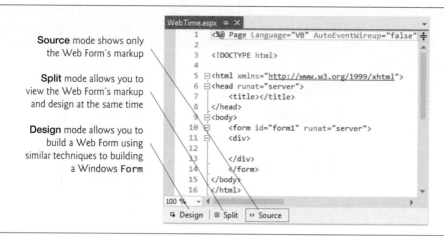

Source mode shows only the Web Form's markup

Split mode allows you to view the Web Form's markup and design at the same time

Design mode allows you to build a Web Form using similar techniques to building a Windows **Form**

Fig. 13.9 | Web Form in **Source** view.

The Solution Explorer

The **Solution Explorer** (Fig. 13.10) shows the contents of the website. We expanded the node for WebTime.aspx to show you its *code-behind file* WebTime.aspx.vb. Visual Studio Express For Web's **Solution Explorer** contains a **Nest Related Files** button that organizes each Web Form and its code-behind file.

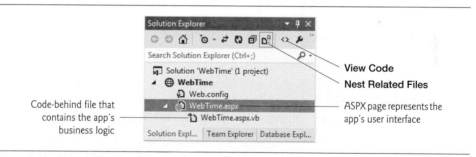

View Code
Nest Related Files

Code-behind file that contains the app's business logic

ASPX page represents the app's user interface

Fig. 13.10 | **Solution Explorer** window for an **Empty Web Site** project after adding the Web Form WebTime.aspx.

If the ASPX file is not open in the IDE, you can open it in **Design** mode by double clicking it in the **Solution Explorer** then selecting the **Design** tab, or by right clicking it in the **Solution Explorer** and selecting **View Designer**. To open the code-behind file in the code editor, you can double click it in the **Solution Explorer** or

- select the ASPX file in the **Solution Explorer**, then click the **View Code** (**<>**) Button
- right click the ASPX file in the **Solution Explorer**, then select **View Code**
- right click the code-behind file in the **Solution Explorer** and select **Open**

The Toolbox

Figure 13.11 shows the **Toolbox** displayed in the IDE when the project loads. Part (a) displays the beginning of the **Standard** list of web controls, and part (b) displays the remaining web controls and the list of other control groups. We discuss specific controls listed in Fig. 13.11 as they're used throughout the chapter. Many of the controls have similar or identical names to Windows Forms controls presented earlier in the book.

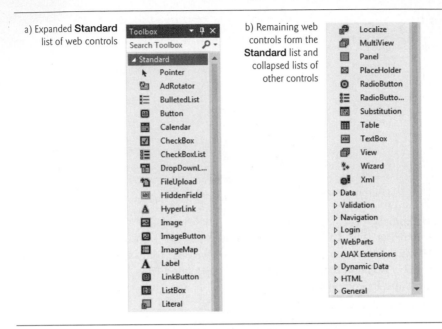

Fig. 13.11 | Toolbox in Visual Studio Express For Web.

The Web Forms Designer

Figure 13.12 shows the initial Web Form in **Design** mode. You can drag and drop controls from the **Toolbox** onto the Web Form. You can also type at the current cursor location to add so-called *static text* to the web page. In response to such actions, the IDE generates the appropriate markup in the ASPX file.

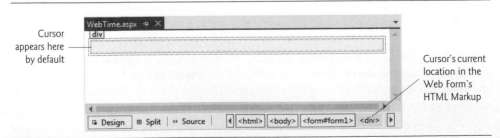

Fig. 13.12 | Design mode of the Web Forms Designer.

Step 3: Changing the Title of the Page

Before designing the Web Form's content, you'll change its title to `Simple Web Form Example`. This title is typically displayed in the web browser's title bar or on the browser tab that is displaying the page (see Fig. 13.4). It's also used by search engines like Google and

Bing when they index real websites for searching. Every page should have a title. To change the title:

1. Ensure that the ASPX file is open in **Design** view.

2. In the **Properties** window's drop-down list, view the Web Form's properties by selecting DOCUMENT, which represents the Web Form. A web page is often called a document.

3. Modify the page's Title property by setting it to Simple Web Form Example.

Designing a Page

Designing a Web Form is similar to designing a Windows Form. To add controls to the page, drag-and-drop them from the **Toolbox** onto the Web Form in **Design** view. The Web Form itself and the control's you add to the Web Form are objects that have properties, methods and events. You can set these properties visually using the **Properties** window, programmatically in the code-behind file or by editing the markup directly in the .aspx file. You can also type text directly on a Web Form at the cursor location.

Controls and other elements are placed sequentially on a Web Form one after another in the order in which you drag-and-drop them onto the Web Form. The cursor indicates the insertion point in the page. If you want to position a control between existing text or controls, you can drop the control at a specific position between existing page elements. You can also rearrange controls with drag-and-drop actions in **Design** view. The positions of controls and other elements are relative to the Web Form's upper-left corner. This type of layout is known as *relative positioning* and it allows the browser to move elements and resize them based on the size of the browser window. Relative positioning is the *default*, and we'll use it throughout this chapter.

For precise control over the location and size of elements, you can use absolute positioning in which controls are located exactly where you drop them on the Web Form. If you wish to use absolute positioning:

1. Select **TOOLS > Options....**, to display the **Options** dialog.

2. Expand the **HTML Designer** node, select the **CSS Styling** node and ensure that the checkbox labeled **Change positioning to absolute for controls added using Toolbox, paste or drag and drop** is selected.

Step 4: Adding Text and a **Label**

You'll now add some text and a Label to the Web Form. Perform the following steps to add the text:

1. Ensure that the Web Form is open in **Design** mode.

2. Type the following text at the current cursor location:

Current time on the Web server:

3. Select the text you just typed, then select **Heading 1** from the **Block Format** Combo-Box (Fig. 13.13) in the IDE's **Formatting** toolbar. This formats the text as a first-level heading that typically appears in a larger bold font. In more complex pages, headings help you specify the relative importance of parts of the content—like chapters in a book and sections in a chapter.

Block Format ComboBox on the Formatting toolbar

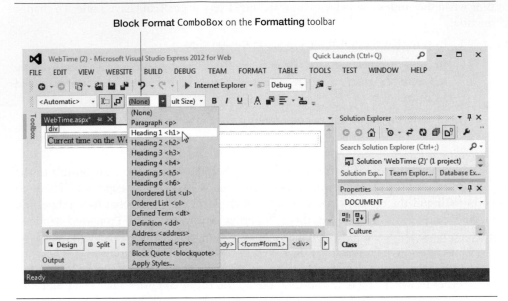

Fig. 13.13 | Changing the text to **Heading 1** heading.

4. Click to the right of the text you just typed and press the *Enter* key to start a new paragraph in the page. The Web Form should now appear as in Fig. 13.14.

The cursor is positioned here after inserting a new paragraph by pressing *Enter*

Fig. 13.14 | WebTime.aspx after inserting text and a new paragraph.

5. Next, drag a Label control from the **Toolbox** into the new paragraph or double click the Label control in the **Toolbox** to insert the Label at the current cursor position.

6. Using the **Properties** window, set the Label's (ID) property to timeLabel. This specifies the variable name that will be used to *programmatically* change the Label's Text.

7. Because, the Label's Text will be set programmatically, delete the current value of the Label's Text property. When a Label does not contain text, its name is displayed in square brackets in **Design** view (Fig. 13.15) as a placeholder for design and layout purposes. This text is not displayed at execution time.

Label control
currently selected in
Design view

Fig. 13.15 | WebTime.aspx after adding a Label.

Step 5: Formatting the Label

Formatting in a web page is performed with *CSS (Cascading Style Sheets)*. The details of CSS are beyond the scope of this book. However, it's easy to use CSS to format text and elements in a Web Form via the tools built into Visual Studio Express For Web. In this example, we'd like to change the Label's *background color* to black, its *foreground color* to yellow and make its *text size* larger. To format the Label, perform the following steps:

1. Click the Label in **Design** view to ensure that it's selected.

2. Select **VIEW > CSS Properties** to display the **CSS Properties** window at the left side of the IDE (Fig. 13.16).

Fig. 13.16 | CSS Properties window.

3. Right click below **Applied Rules** and select **New Style...** to display the **New Style** dialog (Fig. 13.17).

4. Type the new style's name in the **Selector:** ComboBox—we chose .timeStyle since this will be the style used to format the time that's displayed in the page. Styles that apply to specific elements must be named with a dot (.) preceding the name. Such a style is called a **CSS class**.

5. Each item you can set in the **New Style** dialog is known as a *CSS attribute*. To change timeLabel's *foreground color*, select the **Font** category from the **Category** list, then select the yellow color swatch for the **color** attribute.

6. Next, change the **font-size** attribute to xx-large.

7. To change timeLabel's *background color*, select the **Background** category, then select the black color swatch for the **background-color** attribute.

New style's name

Font category allows you to
style an element's font

Background category allows
you to specify an element's
background color or
background image

The new style will be
applied to the currently
selected element in the page

Preview of what the
style will look like

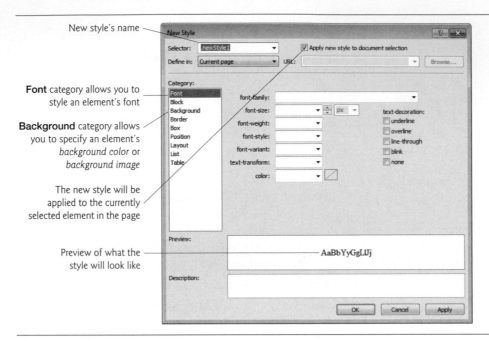

Fig. 13.17 | New Style dialog.

The **New Style** dialog should now appear as shown in Fig. 13.18. Click the **OK** Button
to apply the style to the timeLabel so that it appears as shown in Fig. 13.19. Also, notice
that the Label's *CssClass property* is now set to timeStyle in the **Properties** window.

Bold category names
indicate the categories in
which *CSS attribute* values
have been changed

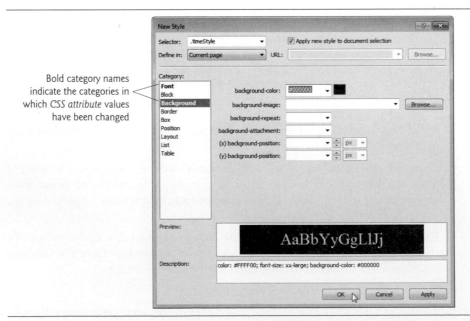

Fig. 13.18 | New Style dialog after changing the Label's style.

Fig. 13.19 | **Design** view after changing the Label's style.

Step 6: Adding Page Logic

Now that you've designed the GUI, you'll write code in the *code-behind file* to obtain the server's time and display it on the Label. Open WebTime.aspx.vb by double clicking it in the **Solution Explorer**. In this example, you'll add an event handler to the code-behind file to handle the Web Form's **Init** event, which occurs when the page is requested by a web browser. The event handler for this event—named **Page_Init**—initializes the page. The only initialization required for this example is to set the timeLabel's Text property to the time on the web server computer. To create the Page_Init event handler:

1. Select **(Page Events)** from the left ComboBox at the top of the code editor window.

2. Select **Init** from the right ComboBox at the top of the code editor window.

3. Complete the event handler by inserting the following code in the Page_Init event handler:

```
' display the server's current time in timeLabel
timeLabel.Text = DateTime.Now.ToString("hh:mm:ss")
```

Step 7: Setting the Start Page and Running the Program

To ensure that WebTime.aspx loads when you execute this app, right click it in the **Solution Explorer** and select **Set As Start Page**. You can now run the program in one of several ways. At the beginning of Fig. 13.4, you learned how to view the Web Form by typing *Ctrl + F5*. You can also right click an ASPX file in the **Solution Explorer** and select **View in Browser**. Both of these techniques execute *IIS Express*, open your *default web browser* and load the page into the browser, thus running the web app. IIS Express stops when you exit Visual Studio Express For Web.

If problems occur when running your app, you can run it in *debug mode* by selecting **DEBUG > Start Debugging**, by clicking the **Start Debugging** Button (▶) or by typing *F5* to view the web page in a web browser with *debugging enabled*. You cannot debug a web app unless debugging is *explicitly* enabled in the app's **Web.config** file—a file that's generated when you create an ASP.NET web app. This file stores the app's configuration settings. You'll rarely need to manually modify Web.config. The first time you select **DEBUG > Start Debugging** in a project, a dialog appears and asks whether you want the IDE to modify the Web.config file to enable debugging. After you click **OK**, the IDE executes the app. You can stop debugging by selecting **DEBUG > Stop Debugging**.

Regardless of how you execute the web app, the IDE will compile the project before it executes. In fact, ASP.NET compiles your web page whenever it changes between HTTP requests. For example, suppose you browse the page, then modify the ASPX file or add code to the code-behind file. When you reload the page, ASP.NET recompiles the page on the server before returning the response to the browser. This important behavior ensures that clients always see the latest version of the page. You can manually compile an entire website by selecting **Build Web Site** from the **DEBUG** menu in Visual Studio Express For Web.

13.4.2 Examining WebTime.aspx's Code-Behind File

Figure 13.20 presents the code-behind file WebTime.aspx.vb. Line 3 begins the declaration of class WebTime. A class declaration can span multiple source-code files—the separate portions of the class declaration in each file are known as **partial classes**. The **Partial** modifier indicates that the code-behind file is part of a larger class. Like Windows Forms apps, the rest of the class's code is generated for you based on your visual interactions to create the app's GUI in **Design** mode. That code is stored in other source code files as partial classes with the same name. The compiler assembles all the partial classes that have the same into a single class declaration.

```
1    ' Fig. 13.20: WebTime.aspx.vb
2    ' Code-behind file for a page that displays the current time.
3    Partial Class WebTime
4       Inherits System.Web.UI.Page
5
6       ' initializes the contents of the page
7       Protected Sub Page_Init(ByVal sender As Object, _
8          ByVal e As System.EventArgs) Handles Me.Init
9
10         ' display the server's current time in timeLabel
11         timeLabel.Text = DateTime.Now.ToString("hh:mm:ss")
12      End Sub ' Page_Init
13   End Class ' WebTime
```

Fig. 13.20 | Code-behind file for a page that displays the web server's time.

Line 4 indicates that WebTime inherits from class **Page** in namespace **System.Web.UI**. This namespace contains classes and controls for building web-based apps. Class **Page** represents the default capabilities of each page in a web app—all pages inherit directly or indirectly from this class.

Lines 7–12 define the Page_Init event handler, which initializes the page in response to the page's Init event. The only initialization required for this page is to set the time-Label's Text property to the time on the web server computer. The statement in line 11 retrieves the current time (DateTime.Now) and formats it as *hh:mm:ss*. For example, 9 AM is formatted as 09:00:00, and 2:30 PM is formatted as 02:30:00. As you'll see, variable timeLabel represents an *ASP.NET Label control*. The ASP.NET controls are defined in namespace **System.Web.UI.WebControls**.

13.5 Standard Web Controls: Designing a Form

This section introduces some of the web controls located in the **Standard** section of the **Toolbox** (Fig. 13.11). Figure 13.21 summarizes the controls used in the next example.

Web control	Description
TextBox	Gathers user input and displays text.
Button	Triggers an event when clicked.
HyperLink	Displays a hyperlink.
DropDownList	Displays a drop-down list of choices from which a user can select an item.
RadioButtonList	A group of radio buttons.
Image	Displays images (for example, PNG, GIF and JPG).

Fig. 13.21 | Commonly used web controls.

A Form Gathering User Input

Figure 13.22 depicts a form for gathering user input. This example does not perform any tasks—that is, no action occurs when the user clicks **Register**. As an exercise, we ask you to provide the functionality. Here we focus on the steps for adding these controls to a Web Form and for setting their properties. Subsequent examples demonstrate how to handle the events of many of these controls.

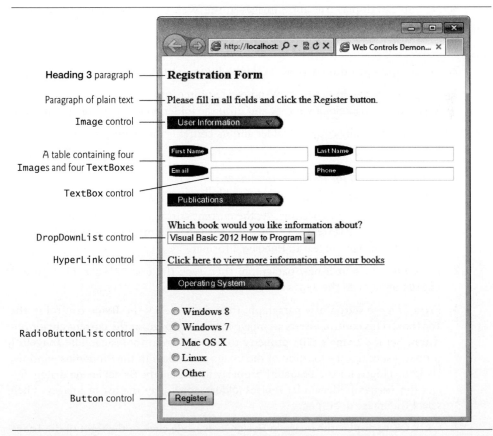

Fig. 13.22 | Web Form that demonstrates web controls.

To execute this app:

1. Select **Open Web Site...** from the **FILE** menu.

2. In the **Open Web Site** dialog, ensure that **File System** is selected, then navigate to this chapter's examples, select the WebControls folder and click the **Open** Button.

3. Select WebControls.aspx in the **Solution Explorer**, then type *Ctrl + F5* to execute the web app in your default web browser.

Step 1: Creating the Web Site

To begin, follow the steps in Section 13.4.1 to create an **Empty Web Site** named WebControls, then add a Web Form named WebControls.aspx to the project. Set the document's Title property to "Web Controls Demonstration". Right click WebControls.aspx in the **Solution Explorer** and select **Set As Start Page** to ensure that this page loads when you execute the app.

Step 2: Adding the Images to the Project

The images used in this example are located in the images folder with this chapter's examples. Before you can display this app's images in the Web Form, they must be added to your project. To add the images folder to your project:

1. Open Windows Explorer.

2. Locate and open this chapter's examples folder (ch13).

3. Drag the images folder from Windows Explorer into Visual Studio Express For Web's **Solution Explorer** window and drop the folder on the name of your project.

The IDE will automatically copy the folder and its contents into your project.

Step 3: Adding Text and an Image to the Form

Next, you'll begin creating the page. Perform the following steps:

1. First create the page's heading. At the current cursor position on the page, type the text "Registration Form", then use the **Block Format** ComboBox in the IDE's toolbar to change the text to **Heading 3** format.

2. Press *Enter* to start a new paragraph, then type the text "Please fill in all fields and click the Register button.".

3. Press *Enter* to start a new paragraph, then double click the **Image** control in the Toolbox. This control inserts an image into a web page, at the current cursor position. Set the Image's (ID) property to userInformationImage. The **ImageUrl** property specifies the location of the image to display. In the **Properties** window, click the ellipsis for the ImageUrl property to display the **Select Image** dialog. Select the images folder under **Project folders:** to display the list of images. Then select the image user.png.

4. Click **OK** to display the image in **Design** view, then click to the right of the Image and press *Enter* to start a new paragraph.

Step 4: Adding a Table to the Form
Form elements are sometimes placed in tables for layout purposes—like the elements that represent the first name, last name, e-mail and phone information in Fig. 13.22. Next, you'll create a table with two rows and two columns in **Design** mode.

1. Select **TABLE > Insert Table** to display the **Insert Table** dialog (Fig. 13.23). This dialog allows you to configure the table's options.

2. Under **Size**, ensure that the values of **Rows** and **Columns** are both 2—these are the default values.

3. Click **OK** to close the **Insert Table** dialog and create the table.

By default, the contents of a table cell are aligned *vertically* in the *middle* of the cell.

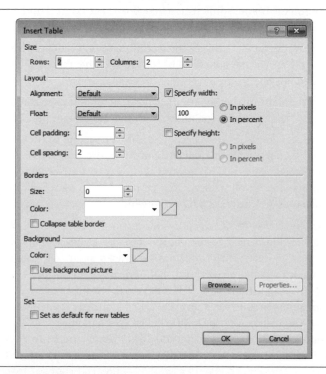

Fig. 13.23 | Insert Table dialog.

After creating the table, controls and text can be added to particular cells to create a neatly organized layout. Next, add Image and TextBox controls to each the four table cells as follows:

1. Click the table cell in the first row and first column of the table, then double click the Image control in the **Toolbox**. Set its (ID) property to firstNameImage and set its ImageUrl property to the image fname.png.

2. Next, double click the TextBox control in the **Toolbox**. Set its (ID) property to firstNameTextBox. As in Windows Forms, a **TextBox** control allows you to obtain text from the user and display text to the user.

3. Repeat this process in the first row and second column, but set the Image's (ID) property to lastNameImage and its ImageUrl property to the image lname.png, and set the TextBox's (ID) property to lastNameTextBox.

4. Repeat *Steps 1* and *2* in the second row and first column, but set the Image's (ID) property to emailImage and its ImageUrl property to the image email.png, and set the TextBox's (ID) property to emailTextBox.

5. Repeat *Steps 1* and *2* in the second row and second column, but set the Image's (ID) property to phoneImage and its ImageUrl property to the image phone.png, and set the TextBox's (ID) property to phoneTextBox.

Step 5: Creating the Publications Section of the Page

This section contains an Image, some text, a DropDownList control and a HyperLink control. Perform the following steps to create this section:

1. Click below the table, then use the techniques you've already learned in this section to add an Image named publicationsImage that displays the publications.png image.

2. Click to the right of the Image, then press *Enter* and type the text "Which book would you like information about?" in the new paragraph.

3. Hold the *Shift* key and press *Enter* to create a new line in the current paragraph, then double click the **DropDownList** control in the **Toolbox**. Set its (ID) property to booksDropDownList. This control is similar to the Windows Forms ComboBox control, but doesn't allow users to type text. When a user clicks the drop-down list, it expands and displays a list from which the user can make a selection.

4. You can add items to the DropDownList using the **ListItem Collection Editor** by clicking the ellipsis next to the DropDownList's **Items** property in the **Properties** window, or by using the **DropDownList Tasks** smart-tag menu. To open this menu, click the small arrowhead that appears in the upper-right corner of the control in **Design** mode (Fig. 13.24). Visual Studio Express 2012 for Web displays smart-tag menus for many ASP.NET controls to facilitate common tasks. Clicking **Edit Items...** in the **DropDownList Tasks** menu opens the **ListItem Collection Editor**, which allows you to add ListItem elements to the DropDownList. Add items for "Visual Basic 2012 How to Program", "Visual C# 2012 How to Program", "Java How to Program" and "C++ How to Program" by clicking the **Add Button** four times. For each item, select it, then set its Text property to one of the four book titles.

Fig. 13.24 | **DropDownList Tasks** smart-tag menu.

5. Click to the right of the DropDownList and press *Enter* to start a new paragraph, then double click the **HyperLink** control in the **Toolbox** to add a hyperlink to the web page. Set its (ID) property to booksHyperLink and its Text property to "Click here to view more information about our books". Set the **NavigateUrl** property to http://www.deitel.com. This specifies the resource or web page that will be requested when the user clicks the HyperLink. Setting the **Target** property to _blank specifies that the requested web page should open in a new tab or browser window. By default, HyperLink controls cause pages to open in the *same* browser window.

Step 6: Completing the Page

Next you'll create the **Operating System** section of the page and the **Register** Button. This section contains a **RadioButtonList** control, which provides a series of radio buttons from which the user can select only one. The **RadioButtonList Tasks** smart-tag menu provides an **Edit Items...** link to open the **ListItem Collection Editor** so that you can create the items in the list. Perform the following steps:

1. Click to the right of the HyperLink control and press *Enter* to create a new paragraph, then add an Image named osImage that displays the os.png image.

2. Click to the right of the Image and press *Enter* to create a new paragraph, then add a RadioButtonList. Set its (ID) property to osRadioButtonList. Use the **ListItem Collection Editor** to add the items shown in Fig. 13.22.

3. Finally, click to the right of the RadioButtonList and press *Enter* to create a new paragraph, then add a **Button**. A Button web control represents a button that triggers an action when clicked. Set its (ID) property to registerButton and its Text property to Register. As stated earlier, clicking the **Register** button in this example does not do anything.

You can now execute the app (*Ctrl* + *F5*) to see the Web Form in your browser.

13.6 Validation Controls

This section introduces a different type of web control, called a validation control or validator, which determines whether the *data* in another web control is in the proper *format*. For example, validators can determine whether a user has provided information in a required field or whether a zip-code field contains exactly five digits. Validators provide a mechanism for *validating user input* on the client and the server. When the page is sent to the client, the validator is converted into JavaScript that performs the validation in the client web browser. JavaScript is a scripting language that enhances the functionality of web pages and is typically executed on the client. Unfortunately, some client browsers might not support scripting or the user might disable it. For this reason, you should *always perform validation on the server*. ASP.NET validation controls can function on the *client*, on the *server* or *both*.

Validating Input in a Web Form

The Web Form in Fig. 13.25 prompts the user to enter a name, e-mail address and phone number. A website could use a form like this to collect contact information from visitors.

After the user enters any data, but before the data is sent to the web server, validators ensure that the user *entered a value in each field* and that the e-mail address and phone-number values are in an acceptable format. In this example, (555) 123-4567, 555-123-4567 and 123-4567 are all considered valid phone numbers. Once the data is submitted, the web server responds by displaying a message that repeats the submitted information. A real business app would typically store the submitted data in a database or in a file on the server. We simply send the data back to the client to demonstrate that the server received the data.

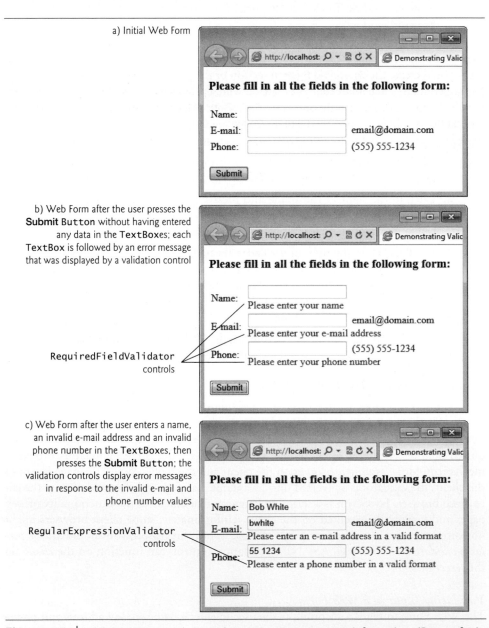

Fig. 13.25 | Validators in a Web Form that retrieves user contact information. (Part 1 of 2.)

d) The Web Form after the user enters valid values for all three `TextBox`es and presses the **Submit** Button

`outputLabel` is displayed once the user provides valid form input and submits the form

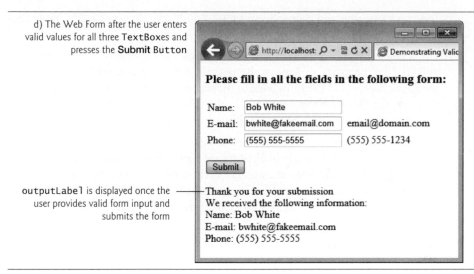

Fig. 13.25 | Validators in a Web Form that retrieves user contact information. (Part 2 of 2.)

To execute this app:

1. Select **Open Web Site...** from the **FILE** menu.

2. In the **Open Web Site** dialog, ensure that **File System** is selected, then navigate to this chapter's examples, select the `Validation` folder and click the **Open** Button.

3. Select `Validation.aspx` in the **Solution Explorer**, then type *Ctrl* + *F5* to execute the web app in your default web browser.

In the sample output:

- Fig. 13.25(a) shows the initial Web Form.

- Fig. 13.25(b) shows the result of submitting the form before typing any data in the `TextBox`es.

- Fig. 13.25(c) shows the results after entering data in each `TextBox`, but specifying an invalid e-mail address and invalid phone number.

- Fig. 13.25(d) shows the results after entering valid values for all three `TextBox`es and submitting the form.

Step 1: Creating the Web Site

To begin, follow the steps in Section 13.4.1 to create an **Empty Web Site** named `Validation`, then add a Web Form named `Validation.aspx`. Set the document's `Title` property to `"Demonstrating Validation Controls"`. To ensure that `Validation.aspx` loads when you execute this app, right click it in the **Solution Explorer** and select **Set As Start Page**.

Step 2: Creating the GUI

To create the page, perform the following steps:

1. Type `"Please fill in all the fields in the following form:"`, then use the **Block Format** ComboBox in the IDE's toolbar to change the text to **Heading 3** format and press *Enter* to create a new paragraph.

2. Insert a three-row and two-column table. You'll add elements to the table momentarily.

3. Click below the table and add a Button. Set its (ID) property to submitButton and its Text property to Submit. By default, a Button control in a Web Form sends the contents of the form back to the server for processing. Select the Button then use the **Block Format** ComboBox in the IDE's toolbar to wrap the Button in a **Paragraph** format—this places additional space above and below the Button.

4. Click to the right of the Button, then press *Enter* to create a new paragraph. Add a Label. Set its (ID) property to outputLabel and clear its Text property—you'll set it *programmatically* when the user clicks the submitButton. Set the outputLabel's Visible property to false, so the Label does *not* appear in the client's browser when the page loads for the *first* time. You'll *programmatically* display this Label after the user submits valid data.

Next you'll add text and controls to the table you created in *Step 2* above. Perform the following steps:

1. In the left column, type the text "Name:" in the first row, "E-mail:" in the second row and "Phone:" in the third row.

2. In the right column of the first row, add a TextBox and set its (ID) property to nameTextBox.

3. In the right column of the second row, add a TextBox and set its (ID) property to emailTextBox. Set its TextMode property to Email—this produces an HTML5 e-mail input field when the web page is rendered in the client web browser. Click to the right of the TextBox and type the text "email@domain.com" to show an example of what the user should enter in that TextBox.

4. In the right column of the third row, add a TextBox and set its (ID) property to phoneTextBox. Set its TextMode property to Phone—this produces an HTML5 phone input field when the web page is rendered in the client web browser. Click to the right of the TextBox and type the text "(555) 555-1234" to show an example of what the user should enter in that TextBox.

Step 3: Using *RequiredFieldValidator* Controls
We use three RequiredFieldValidator controls (found in the **Validation** section of the **Toolbox**) to ensure that the name, e-mail address and phone number TextBoxes are *not empty* when the form is submitted. A RequiredFieldValidator makes an *input control* a required field. If such a field is *empty*, validation fails. Add a RequiredFieldValidator as follows:

1. Click to the right of the nameTextBox in the table and press *Enter* to move to the next line.

2. Add a RequiredFieldValidator, set its (ID) to nameRequiredFieldValidator and set the ForeColor property to Red.

3. Set the validator's **ControlToValidate** property to nameTextBox to indicate that this validator verifies the nameTextBox's contents.

4. Set the validator's **ErrorMessage** property to "Please enter your name". This is displayed on the Web Form only if the validation fails.

5. Set the validator's `Display` property to `Dynamic`, so the validator occupies space on the Web Form only when validation fails. When this occurs, space is allocated dynamically, causing the controls below the validator to shift downward to accommodate the `ErrorMessage`, as seen in Fig. 13.25(a)–(c).

Repeat these steps to add two more `RequiredFieldValidators` in the second and third rows of the table. Set their (ID) properties to `emailRequiredFieldValidator` and `phone-RequiredFieldValidator`, respectively, and set their `ErrorMessage` properties to "`Please enter your email address`" and "`Please enter your phone number`", respectively.

Step 4: Using *RegularExpressionValidator* Controls

This example also uses two `RegularExpressionValidator` controls to ensure that the e-mail address and phone number entered by the user are in a valid format. Visual Studio Express 2012 for Web provides several *predefined* regular expressions that validate common strings like email addresses and phone numbers, which you can simply select to take advantage of this powerful validation control. Add a `RegularExpressionValidator` as follows:

1. Click to the right of the `emailRequiredFieldValidator` in the second row of the table and add a `RegularExpressionValidator`, then set its (ID) to `emailRegu-larExpressionValidator` and its `ForeColor` property to `Red`.

2. Set the `ControlToValidate` property to `emailTextBox` to indicate that this validator verifies the `emailTextBox`'s contents.

3. Set the validator's `ErrorMessage` property to "`Please enter an e-mail address in a valid format`".

4. Set the validator's `Display` property to `Dynamic`, so the validator occupies space on the Web Form only when validation fails.

Repeat the preceding steps to add another `RegularExpressionValidator` in the third row of the table. Set its (ID) property to `phoneRegularExpressionValidator` and its `ErrorMessage` property to "`Please enter a phone number in a valid format`", respectively.

A `RegularExpressionValidator`'s **`ValidationExpression`** property specifies the regular expression that validates the `ControlToValidate`'s contents. Clicking the ellipsis next to property `ValidationExpression` in the **Properties** window displays the **Regular Expression Editor** dialog, which contains a list of **Standard expressions** for phone numbers, zip codes and other formatted information. For the `emailRegularExpressionValidator`, we selected the standard expression **Internet e-mail address**. If the user enters text in the `emailTextBox` that does not have the correct format and either clicks in a different text box or attempts to submit the form, the `ErrorMessage` text is displayed in *red*.

For the `phoneRegularExpressionValidator`, we selected **U.S. phone number** to ensure that a phone number contains an optional three-digit area code either in parentheses and followed by an optional space or without parentheses and followed by a required hyphen. After an optional area code, a phone number must contain three digits, a hyphen and another four digits. For example, (555) 123-4567, 555-123-4567 and 123-4567 are all valid phone numbers.

Submitting the Web Form's Contents to the Server

If all five validators are successful (that is, each `TextBox` is filled in, and the e-mail address and phone number provided are valid), clicking the **Submit** button sends the form's data to the server. As shown in Fig. 13.25(d), the server then responds by displaying the submitted data in the outputLabel.

Examining the Code-Behind File for a Web Form That Receives User Input

Figure 13.26 shows the code-behind file for this app. Notice that this code-behind file does not contain any implementation related to the validators. We'll say more about this soon. In this example, we respond to the page's **Load** event to process the data submitted by the user. Like the Init event, the Load event occurs each time the page loads into a web browser—the difference is that you cannot access the posted data in the controls from the Init handler. The event handler for this event is **Page_Load** (lines 7–34). To create the event handler, open Validation.aspx.vb in the code editor and perform the following steps, then insert the code from lines 10–33 of Fig. 13.26:

1. Select **(Page Events)** from the left ComboBox at the top of the code editor window.

2. Select **Load** from the right ComboBox at the top of the code editor window.

```
 1  ' Fig. 13.26: Validation.aspx.vb
 2  ' Code-behind file for the form demonstrating validation controls.
 3  Partial Class Validation
 4     Inherits System.Web.UI.Page
 5
 6     ' Page_Load event handler executes when the page is loaded
 7     Protected Sub Page_Load(ByVal sender As Object,
 8        ByVal e As System.EventArgs) Handles Me.Load
 9
10        ' disable unobtrusive validation
11        UnobtrusiveValidationMode =
12           System.Web.UI.UnobtrusiveValidationMode.None
13
14        ' if this is not the first time the page is loading
15        ' (i.e., the user has already submitted form data)
16        If IsPostBack Then
17           Validate() ' validate the form
18
19           If IsValid Then
20              ' retrieve the values submitted by the user
21              Dim name As String = nameTextBox.Text
22              Dim email As String = emailTextBox.Text
23              Dim phone As String = phoneTextBox.Text
24
25              ' create a table indicating the submitted values
26              outputLabel.Text = "Thank you for your submission<br/>" &
27                 "We received the following information:<br/>"
28              outputLabel.Text &=
29                 String.Format("Name: {0}{1}E-mail:{2}{1}Phone:{3}",
30                    name, "<br/>", email, phone)
31              outputLabel.Visible = True ' display the output message
32           End If
33        End If
34     End Sub ' Page_Load
35  End Class ' Validation
```

Fig. 13.26 | Code-behind file for the form demonstrating validation controls.

ASP.NET 4.5 Unobtrusive Validation

Prior to ASP.NET 4.5, when you used the validation controls presented in this section, ASP.NET would embed substantial amounts of JavaScript code in a web page to perform the work of the validation controls in the client web browser. ASP.NET 4.5 now uses **unobtrusive validation**, which significantly reduces the amount of JavaScript that gets embedded into the web page—this, in turn, can improve the performance of your website by making pages load faster. When you create an ASP.NET Web Forms website, everything you need for unobtrusive validation is normally configured for you—*unless* you create an *ASP.NET Empty Web Site*, as we've done for the examples in this chapter so far. To enable this app to execute correctly in the web browser, lines 11–12 *disable* unobtrusive validation. In the online Chapter 24, Web App Development with ASP.NET: A Deeper Look, we'll create a website in which unobtrusive validation is properly enabled.

Differentiating Between the First Request to a Page and a Postback

Web programmers using ASP.NET often design their web pages so that the current page *reloads* when the user *submits* the form; this enables the program to receive input, process it as necessary and display the results in the same page when it's loaded the second time. These pages usually contain a form that, when submitted, sends the values of all the controls to the server and causes the current page to be requested again. This event is known as a **postback**. Line 16 uses the **IsPostBack** property of class Page to determine whether the page is being loaded due to a postback. The first time that the web page is requested, IsPostBack is false, and the page displays only the form for user input. When the postback occurs (from the user clicking **Submit**), IsPostBack is true.

Server-Side Web Form Validation

Server-side Web Form validation must be implemented *programmatically*. Line 17 calls the current Page's **Validate** method to validate the information in the request. This validates the information as specified by the validation controls in the Web Form. Line 19 uses the **IsValid** property of class Page to check whether the validation succeeded. If this property is set to True (that is, validation succeeded and the Web Form is valid), then we display the Web Form's information. Otherwise, the web page loads without any changes, except that any validator that failed now displays its ErrorMessage.

Processing the Data Entered by the User

Lines 21–23 retrieve the values of nameTextBox, emailTextBox and phoneTextBox. When data is posted to the web server, the data that the user entered is accessible to the web app through the web controls' properties. Next, lines 26–30 set outputLabel's Text to display a message that includes the name, e-mail and phone information that was submitted to the server. In lines 26, 27 and 30, notice the use of <br/> rather than \n to start new lines in the outputLabel—
 is the markup for a line break in a web page. Line 31 sets the outputLabel's Visible property to true, so the user can see the thank-you message and submitted data when the page reloads in the client web browser.

13.7 Session Tracking

Originally, critics accused the Internet and e-businesses of failing to provide the customized service typically experienced in "brick-and-mortar" stores. To address this problem, businesses established mechanisms by which they could *personalize* users' browsing experiences, tailoring content to individual users. Businesses can achieve this level of service by tracking each customer's movement through the Internet and combining the collected data with information provided by the consumer, including billing information, personal preferences, interests and hobbies.

Personalization

Personalization makes it possible for businesses to communicate effectively with their customers and also improves users' ability to locate desired products and services. Companies that provide content of particular interest to users can establish relationships with customers and build on those relationships over time. Furthermore, by targeting consumers with personal offers, recommendations, advertisements, promotions and services, businesses create customer loyalty. Websites can use sophisticated technology to allow visitors to customize home pages to suit their individual needs and preferences. Similarly, online shopping sites often store personal information for customers, tailoring notifications and special offers to their interests. Such services encourage customers to visit sites more frequently and make purchases more regularly.

Privacy

A trade-off exists between personalized business service and protection of privacy. Some consumers embrace tailored content, but others fear the possible adverse consequences if the info they provide to businesses is released or collected by tracking technologies. Consumers and privacy advocates ask: What if the business to which we give personal data sells or gives that information to other organizations without our knowledge? What if we do not want our actions on the Internet—a supposedly anonymous medium—to be tracked and recorded by unknown parties? What if unauthorized parties gain access to sensitive private data, such as credit-card numbers or medical history? These are questions that must be addressed by programmers, consumers, businesses and lawmakers alike.

Recognizing Clients

To provide personalized services to consumers, businesses must be able to recognize clients when they request information from a site. As we've discussed, the request–response system on which the web operates is facilitated by HTTP. Unfortunately, HTTP is a *stateless protocol*—it *does not* provide information that would enable web servers to maintain state information regarding particular clients. This means that web servers cannot determine whether a request comes from a particular client or whether the same or different clients generate a series of requests.

To circumvent this problem, sites can provide mechanisms by which they identify individual clients. A *session* represents a unique client on a website. If the client leaves a site and then returns later, the client will still be recognized as the same user. When the user closes the browser, the session typically ends. To help the server distinguish among clients, each client must identify itself to the server. Tracking individual clients is known as **session tracking**. One popular session-tracking technique uses cookies (discussed in Section 13.7.1); another uses ASP.NET's HttpSessionState object (used in Section 13.7.2). Additional session-tracking techniques are beyond this book's scope.

13.7.1 Cookies

Cookies provide you with a tool for personalizing web pages. A cookie is a piece of data stored by web browsers in a small text file on the user's computer. A cookie maintains information about the client during and between browser sessions. The first time a user visits the website, the user's computer might receive a cookie from the server; this cookie is then reactivated each time the user revisits that site. The collected information is intended to be an anonymous record containing data that's used to personalize the user's future visits to the site. For example, cookies in a shopping app might store unique identifiers for users. When a user adds items to an online shopping cart or performs another task resulting in a request to the web server, the server receives a cookie containing the user's unique identifier. The server then uses the unique identifier to locate the shopping cart and perform any necessary processing.

In addition to identifying users, cookies also can indicate users' shopping *preferences*. When a Web Form receives a request from a client, the Web Form can examine the cookie(s) it sent to the client during previous communications, identify the user's preferences and immediately display products of interest to the client.

Every HTTP-based interaction between a client and a server includes a header containing information either about the request (when the communication is from the client to the server) or about the response (when the communication is from the server to the client). When a Web Form receives a request, the header includes information such as the request type and any cookies that have been sent previously from the server to be stored on the client machine. When the server formulates its response, the header information contains any cookies the server wants to store on the client computer and other information, such as the type of data in the response.

The **expiration date** of a cookie determines how long the cookie remains on the client's computer. If you do not set an expiration date for a cookie, the web browser maintains the cookie for the duration of the browsing session. Otherwise, the web browser maintains the cookie until the expiration date occurs. Cookies are deleted when they **expire**.

> **Portability Tip 13.1**
> *Users may disable cookies in their web browsers to help ensure their privacy. Such users will experience difficulty using web apps that depend on cookies to maintain state information.*

13.7.2 Session Tracking with `HttpSessionState`

The next web app demonstrates session tracking using class `HttpSessionState`. When you execute this app, the `Options.aspx` page (Fig. 13.27(a)), which is the app's **Start Page**, allows the user to select a programming language from a group of radio buttons. [*Note:* You might need to right click `Options.aspx` in the **Solution Explorer** and select **Set As Start Page** before running this app.] When the user clicks **Submit**, the selection is sent to the web server for processing. The web server uses an `HttpSessionState` object to store the chosen language and the ISBN number for one of our books on that topic. Each user that visits the site has a unique `HttpSessionState` object, so the selections made by one user are maintained separately from all other users. After storing the selection, the server returns the page to the browser (Fig. 13.27(b)) and displays the user's selection and some information about the user's unique session (which we show just for demonstration purposes). The page also includes links that allow the user to choose between selecting another programming language or viewing the Recommendations.aspx page (Fig. 13.27(e)), which lists recommended books pertaining to the programming language(s) that the user selected previously. If the user clicks the link for book recommendations, the information stored in the user's unique HttpSessionState object is read and used to form the list of recommendations.

a) User selects a language from the Options.aspx page, then presses **Submit** to send the selection to the server

b) Options.aspx page is updated to hide the controls for selecting a language and to display the user's selection; the user clicks the hyperlink to return to the list of languages and make another selection

c) User selects another language from the Options.aspx page, then presses **Submit** to send the selection to the server

d) Options.aspx page is updated to hide the controls for selecting a language and to display the user's selection; the user clicks the hyperlink to get a list of book recommendations

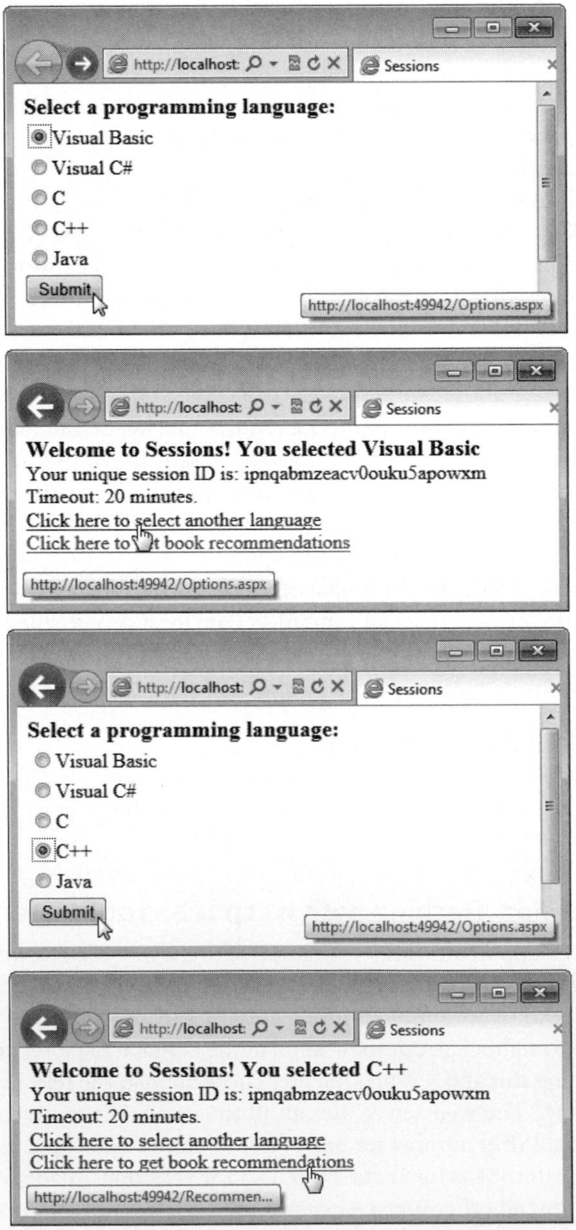

Fig. 13.27 | ASPX file that presents a list of programming languages. (Part 1 of 2.)

e) Recommendations.aspx displays the list of recommended books based on the user's selections

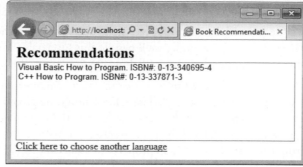

Fig. 13.27 | ASPX file that presents a list of programming languages. (Part 2 of 2.)

To test this app:

1. Select **Open Web Site...** from the **FILE** menu.

2. In the **Open Web Site** dialog, ensure that **File System** is selected, then navigate to this chapter's examples, select the Sessions folder and click the **Open** Button.

Select Options.aspx in the **Solution Explorer**, then type *Ctrl + F5* to execute the web app in your default web browser.

Creating the Web Site

To begin, follow the steps in Section 13.4.1 to create an **Empty Web Site** named Sessions, then add two Web Forms named Options.aspx and Recommendations.aspx to the project. Set the Options.aspx document's Title property to "Sessions" and the Recommendations.aspx document's Title property to "Book Recommendations". To ensure that Options.aspx is the first page to load for this app, right click it in the **Solution Explorer** and select **Set As Start Page**.

13.7.3 Options.aspx: Selecting a Programming Language

The Options.aspx page Fig. 13.27(a) contains the following controls arranged *vertically*:

1. A Label with its (ID) property set to promptLabel and its Text property set to "Select a programming language:". We used the techniques shown in *Step 5* of Section 13.4.1 to create a *CSS style* for this label named .labelStyle, and set the style's font-size attribute to large and the font-weight attribute to bold.

2. The user selects a programming language by clicking one of the radio buttons in a RadioButtonList. Each radio button has a Text property and a Value property. The Text property is displayed next to the radio button and the Value property represents a value that's sent to the server when the user selects that radio button and submits the form. In this example, we'll use the Value property to represent the ISBN for the recommended book. Create a RadioButtonList with its (ID) property set to languageList. Use the **ListItem Collection Editor** to add five radio buttons with their Text properties set to Visual Basic, Visual C#, C, C++ and Java,

and their Value properties set to 0-13-340695-4, 0-13-337933-7, 0-13-299044-X, 0-13-337871-3 and 0-13-294094-9, respectively.

3. A Button with its (ID) property set to submitButton and its Text property set to Submit. In this example, we'll handle this Button's Click event. You can create its event handler by double clicking the Button in **Design** view.

4. A Label with its (ID) property set to responseLabel and its Text property set to "Welcome to Sessions!". This Label should be placed immediately to the right of the Button so that the Label appears at the top of the page when we hide the preceding controls on the page. Reuse the CSS style you created in *Step 1* by setting this Label's CssClass property to labelStyle.

5. Two more Labels with their (ID) properties set to idLabel and timeoutLabel, respectively. Clear the text in each Label's Text property—you'll set these *programmatically* with information about the current user's session.

6. A HyperLink with its (ID) property set to languageLink and its Text property set to "Click here to choose another language". Set its NavigateUrl property by clicking the ellipsis next to the property in the **Properties** window and selecting Options.aspx from the **Select URL** dialog.

7. A HyperLink with its (ID) property set to recommendationsLink and its Text property set to "Click here to get book recommendations". Set its NavigateUrl property by clicking the ellipsis next to the property in the **Properties** window and selecting Recommendations.aspx from the **Select URL** dialog.

8. Initially, the controls in *Steps 4–7* will not be displayed, so set each control's Visible property to false.

Session Property of a Page

Every ASP.NET Web app includes a user-specific HttpSessionState object, which is accessible through property **Session** of class Page. Throughout this section, we use this property to manipulate the current user's HttpSessionState object. When the user first requests a page in a Web app, a unique HttpSessionState object is created by ASP.NET and assigned to the Page's Session property. The same object is also available to the app's other pages.

Code-Behind File for Options.aspx

Fig. 13.28 presents the code-behind file for the Options.aspx page. When this page is requested, the Page_Load event handler (lines 9–40) executes before the response is sent to the client. Since the first request to a page is *not* a *postback*, the code in lines 15–38 *does not* execute the first time the page loads.

```
1   ' Fig. 13.28: Options.aspx.vb
2   ' Process user's selection of a programming language by displaying
3   ' links and writing information in an HttpSessionState object.
```

Fig. 13.28 | Process user's selection of a programming language by displaying links and writing information in an HttpSessionState object. (Part 1 of 2.)

```
 4    Partial Class Options
 5       Inherits System.Web.UI.Page
 6
 7       ' if postback, hide form and display links to make additional
 8       ' selections or view recommendations
 9       Protected Sub Page_Load(ByVal sender As Object,
10          ByVal e As System.EventArgs) Handles Me.Load
11
12          If IsPostBack Then
13             ' user has submitted information, so display message
14             ' and appropriate hyperlinks
15             responseLabel.Visible = True
16             idLabel.Visible = True
17             timeoutLabel.Visible = True
18             languageLink.Visible = True
19             recommendationsLink.Visible = True
20
21             ' hide other controls used to make language selection
22             promptLabel.Visible = False
23             languageList.Visible = False
24             submitButton.Visible = False
25
26             ' if the user made a selection, display it in responseLabel
27             If languageList.SelectedItem IsNot Nothing Then
28                responseLabel.Text &= " You selected " &
29                   languageList.SelectedItem.Text
30             Else
31                responseLabel.Text &= "You did not select a language."
32             End If
33
34             ' display session ID
35             idLabel.Text = "Your unique session ID is: " & Session.SessionID
36
37             ' display the timeout
38             timeoutLabel.Text = "Timeout: " & Session.Timeout & " minutes."
39          End If
40       End Sub ' Page_Load
41
42       ' record the user's selection in the Session
43       Protected Sub submitButton_Click(ByVal sender As Object,
44          ByVal e As System.EventArgs) Handles submitButton.Click
45
46          ' if the user made a selection
47          If languageList.SelectedItem IsNot Nothing Then
48             ' add name/value pair to Session
49             Session.Add(languageList.SelectedItem.Text,
50                languageList.SelectedItem.Value)
51          End If
52       End Sub ' submitButton_Click
53    End Class ' Options
```

Fig. 13.28 | Process user's selection of a programming language by displaying links and writing information in an HttpSessionState object. (Part 2 of 2.)

Postback Processing

When the user presses **Submit**, a postback occurs. The form is submitted to the server and Page_Load executes. Lines 15–19 display the controls shown in Fig. 13.27(b) and lines 22–24 hide the controls shown in Fig. 13.27(a). Next, lines 27–32 ensure that the user selected a language and, if so, display a message in the responseLabel indicating the selection. Otherwise, the message "You did not select a language." is displayed.

The ASP.NET app contains information about the HttpSessionState object (property Session of the Page object) for the current client. The object's **SessionID** property (displayed in line 35) contains the **unique session ID**—a sequence of random letters and numbers. The *first* time a client connects to the web server, a unique session ID is created for that client and a temporary cookie is written to the client so the server can identify the client on subsequent requests. When the client makes additional requests, the client's session ID from that temporary cookie is compared with the session IDs stored in the web server's memory to retrieve the client's HttpSessionState object. (Since users can disable cookies in their browsers, you can also use cookieless sessions. For more information, see msdn.microsoft.com/en-us/library/aa479314.aspx.) HttpSessionState property **Timeout** (displayed in line 38) specifies the maximum amount of time that an HttpSessionState object can be inactive before it's discarded. By default, if the user does not interact with this web app for 20 minutes, the HttpSessionState object is discarded by the server and a new one will be created if the user interacts with the app again. Figure 13.29 lists some common HttpSessionState properties.

Properties	Description
Count	Specifies the number of key–value pairs in the Session object.
IsNewSession	Indicates whether this is a new session (that is, whether the session was created during loading of this page).
Keys	Returns a collection containing the Session object's keys.
SessionID	Returns the session's unique ID.
Timeout	Specifies the maximum number of minutes during which a session can be inactive (that is, no requests are made) before the session expires. By default, this property is set to 20 minutes.

Fig. 13.29 | HttpSessionState properties.

Method submitButton_Click

We store the user's selection in an HttpSessionState object when the user clicks the **Submit** Button. The submitButton_Click event handler (lines 43–52) adds a key–value pair to the HttpSessionState object for the current user, specifying the language chosen and the ISBN number for a book on that language. The HttpSessionState object is a dictionary—a data structure that stores **key–value pairs**. A program uses the key to store and retrieve the associated value in the dictionary.

The key–value pairs in an HttpSessionState object are often referred to as **session items**. They're placed in an HttpSessionState object by calling its **Add** method. If the user made a selection (line 47), lines 49–50 get the selection and its corresponding value from the languageList by accessing its SelectedItem's Text and Value properties, respectively, then call HttpSessionState method Add to add this name–value pair as a session item in the HttpSessionState object (Session).

If the app adds a session item that has the same name as an item previously stored in the HttpSessionState object, the session item is replaced—session item names *must* be unique. Another common syntax for placing a session item in the HttpSessionState object is Session(*Name*) = *Value*. For example, we could have replaced lines 49–50 with

```
Session(languageList.SelectedItem.Text) =
    languageList.SelectedItem.Value
```

Software Engineering Observation 13.1

A Web Form should not use instance variables to maintain client state information, because each new request or postback is handled by a new instance of the page. Instead, maintain client state information in HttpSessionState objects, because such objects are specific to each client.

Software Engineering Observation 13.2

A benefit of using HttpSessionState objects (rather than cookies) is that they can store any type of object (not just Strings) as attribute values. This provides you with increased flexibility in determining the type of state information to maintain for clients.

13.7.4 Recommendations.aspx: Displaying Recommendations Based on Session Values

After the postback of Options.aspx, the user may request book recommendations. The book-recommendations hyperlink forwards the user to the page Recommendations.aspx (Fig. 13.27(e)) to display the recommendations based on the user's language selections. The page contains the following controls arranged *vertically*:

1. A Label with its (ID) property set to recommendationsLabel and its Text property set to "Recommendations". We created a CSS style for this label named .labelStyle, and set the font-size attribute to x-large and the font-weight attribute to bold. (See *Step 5* in Section 13.4.1 for information on creating a CSS style.)

2. A ListBox with its (ID) property set to booksListBox. We created a CSS style for this ListBox named .listBoxStyle. In the **Position** category, we set the width attribute to 450px and the height attribute to 125px. The px indicates that the measurement is in pixels.

3. A HyperLink with its (ID) property set to languageLink and its Text property set to "Click here to choose another language". Set its NavigateUrl property by clicking the ellipsis next to the property in the **Properties** window and selecting Options.aspx from the **Select URL** dialog. When the user clicks this link, the Options.aspx page will be reloaded. Requesting the page in this manner *is not* considered a postback, so the original form in Fig. 13.27(a) will be displayed.

Code-Behind File for *Recommendations.aspx*

Figure 13.30 presents the *code-behind file* for Recommendations.aspx. Event handler Page_Init (lines 7–26) retrieves the session information. If a user has not selected a language in the Options.aspx page, the HttpSessionState object's **Count** property will be 0 (line 11). This property provides the number of session items contained in a HttpSessionState object. If the Count is 0, then we display the text **No Recommendations** (line 20), hide the ListBox (line 21) and update the Text of the HyperLink back to Options.aspx (line 24).

```vb
1   ' Fig. 13.30: Recommendations.aspx.vb
2   ' Creates book recommendations based on a Session object.
3   Partial Class Recommendations
4      Inherits System.Web.UI.Page
5
6      ' read Session items and populate ListBox with any book recommendations
7      Protected Sub Page_Init(ByVal sender As Object,
8         ByVal e As System.EventArgs) Handles Me.Init
9
10        ' determine whether Session contains any information
11        If Session.Count <> 0 Then
12           For Each keyName In Session.Keys
13              ' use keyName to display one of Session's name/value pairs
14              booksListBox.Items.Add(keyName &
15                 " How to Program. ISBN#: " & Session(keyName))
16           Next
17        Else
18           ' if there are no session items, no language was chosen, so
19           ' display appropriate message and hide booksListBox
20           recommendationsLabel.Text = "No Recommendations"
21           booksListBox.Visible = False
22
23           ' modify languageLink because no language was selected
24           languageLink.Text = "Click here to choose a language"
25        End If
26     End Sub ' Page_Init
27  End Class ' Recommendations
```

Fig. 13.30 | Session data used to provide book recommendations to the user.

If the user chose at least one language, the loop in lines 12–16 iterates through the HttpSessionState object's keys by accessing the HttpSessionState's **Keys** property, which returns a collection containing all the keys in the session. Lines 14–15 concatenate the keyName, the String " How to Program. ISBN#: " and the key's corresponding value, which is returned by Session(keyName). This String is the recommendation that's added to the ListBox.

13.8 Case Study: Database-Driven ASP.NET Guestbook

Many websites allow users to provide feedback about the website in a guestbook. Typically, users click a link on the website's home page to request the guestbook page. This page usually consists of a form that contains fields for the user's name, e-mail address, message/

feedback and so on. Data submitted on the guestbook form is then stored in a database located on the server.

In this section, we create a guestbook Web Form app. The GUI (Fig. 13.31) contains a **GridView** data control, which displays all the entries in the guestbook in tabular format. This control is located in the **Toolbox**'s **Data** section. We explain how to create and configure this data control shortly. The **GridView** displays **abc** in **Design** mode to indicate data that will be retrieved from a data source at runtime. You'll learn how to create and configure the **GridView** shortly.

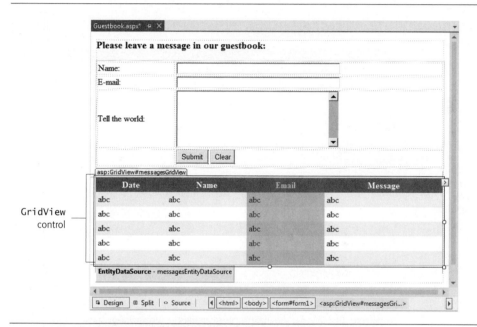

Fig. 13.31 | Guestbook app GUI in **Design** mode.

The Guestbook Database
The app stores the guestbook information in a SQL Server database called **Guestbook.mdf** located on the web server. (We provide this database in the **databases** folder with this chapter's examples.) The database contains a single table named **Messages**.

Testing the App
To test this app:

1. Select **Open Web Site...** from the **FILE** menu.

2. In the **Open Web Site** dialog, ensure that **File System** is selected, then navigate to this chapter's examples, select the **Guestbook** folder and click the **Open** Button.

3. Select **Guestbook.aspx** in the **Solution Explorer**, then type *Ctrl + F5* to execute the web app in your default web browser.

Figure 13.32(a) shows the user submitting a new entry. Figure 13.32(b) shows the new entry as the last row in the **GridView**.

a) User enters data for the name, e-mail and message, then presses **Submit** to send the data to the server

b) Server stores the data in the database, then refreshes the GridView with the updated data

Fig. 13.32 | Sample execution of the **Guestbook** app.

13.8.1 Building a Web Form that Displays Data from a Database

You'll now build this GUI and set up the data binding between the GridView control and the database. Many of these steps are similar to those performed in Chapter 12 to access and interact with a database in a Windows app. We discuss the *code-behind file* in Section 13.8.2.

Step 1: Creating the Web Site
To begin, follow the steps in Section 13.4.1 to create an **Empty Web Site** named Guestbook then add a Web Form named Guestbook.aspx to the project. Set the document's Title

property to "Guestbook". To ensure that Guestbook.aspx loads when you execute this app, right click it in the **Solution Explorer** and select **Set As Start Page**.

Step 2: Creating the Form for User Input

In **Design** mode, add the text Please leave a message in our guestbook:, then use the **Block Format** ComboBox in the IDE's toolbar to change the text to **Heading 3** format. Insert a table with four rows and two columns. Place the appropriate text (see Fig. 13.31) in the top three cells in the table's left column. Then place TextBoxes named nameTextBox, emailTextBox and messageTextBox in the top three table cells in the right column. Configure the TextBoxes as follows:

- Select **FORMAT > New Style...** to display the **New Style** dialog. In the **Selector** field, specify .textBoxWidth as the new style's name. Select the **Category** named **Position**, then set the **width:** to 300px and click **OK** to create the style and dismiss the dialog. Next set the CssClass property for both the nameTextBox and email-TextBox to textBoxWidth. This uses the style to set both TextBoxes to 300 pixels wide.

- Select **FORMAT > New Style...** to display the **New Style** dialog. In the **Selector** field, specify .textBoxHeight as the new style's name. Select the **Category** named **Position**, then set the **height:** to 100px and click **OK** to create the style and dismiss the dialog. Next set messageTextBox's CssClass property to

      textBoxWidth textBoxHeight

  This uses both the .textBoxWidth and .textBoxHeight styles to set message-TextBox's width to 300 pixels and height to 100 pixels. Also set messageTextBox's TextMode property to MultiLine so the user can type a message containing multiple lines of text.

Finally, add Buttons named submitButton and clearButton to the bottom-right table cell. Set the buttons' Text properties to Submit and Clear, respectively. We discuss the buttons' event handlers when we present the code-behind file. You can create these event handlers now by double clicking each Button in **Design** view.

Step 3: Adding a GridView Control to the Web Form

Add a GridView named messagesGridView that will display the guestbook entries. This control is located in the **Toolbox**'s **Data** section. The colors for the GridView are specified through the **Auto Format...** link in the **GridView Tasks** *smart-tag menu* that opens when you place the GridView on the page. Clicking this link displays an **AutoFormat** dialog with several choices. In this example, we chose **Professional**. We show how to set the GridView's data source (that is, where it gets the data to display in its rows and columns) shortly.

Step 4: Creating the Entity Data Model

Next, you'll add an entity data model to the project. Perform the following steps:

1. Right click the project name in the Solution Explorer and select **Add > Add New Item...** to display the **Add New Item** dialog.

2. Select **ADO.NET Entity Data Model**, change the **Name** to GuestbookModel.edmx and click **Add**. A dialog appears asking if you would like to put your new entity

data model classes in the App_Code folder; click **Yes**. The IDE will create an App_Code folder and place the entity data model classes information in that folder. For security reasons, this folder can be accessed only by the web app on the server—clients cannot access this folder over a network.

3. Next, the **Entity Data Model Wizard** dialog appears. Ensure that **Generate from database** is selected so that you can generate the model from the Guestbook.mdf database, then click **Next >**.

4. In the **Entity Data Model Wizard** dialog's **Choose Your Data Connection** step, click **New Connection...** then use the **Connection Properties** dialog to locate the Guestbook.mdf database file (included in the databases folder with this chapter's examples). Click **OK** to create the connection, then click **Next >** to complete the **Choose Your Data Connection** step.

5. A dialog appears asking if you would like to copy the database file into your project. Click **Yes**. The IDE will create an App_Data folder and place the Guestbook.mdf file in that folder. Like the App_Code folder, this folder can be accessed only by the web app on the server.

6. In the **Entity Data Model Wizard** dialog's **Choose Your Database Objects and Settings** step, select the Messages table from the database. By default, the IDE names the model GuestbookModel. Ensure that **Pluralize or singularize generated object names** is checked, keep the other default settings and click **Finish**. The IDE displays the GuestbookModel in the editor, where you can see that a Message has a MessageID, Date, Name, Email and Message1 property. Message1 was renamed from Message by the IDE so that it does not conflict with the entity data model's Message class.

7. Select **BUILD > Build Solution** to ensure that the new entity data model classes are compiled.

Step 5: Binding the GridView to the Messages Table of the Guestbook Database

You can now configure the GridView to display the database's data.

1. In the **GridView Tasks** smart-tag menu, select **<New data source...>** from the **Choose Data Source** ComboBox to display the **Data Source Configuration Wizard** dialog.

2. In this example, we use a **EntityDataSource** control that allows the app to interact with the Guestbook.mdf database. Select **Entity**, then in the **Specify an ID for the data source** field enter messagesEntityDataSource and click **OK** to begin the **Configure Data Source** wizard.

3. In the **Configure ObjectContext** step, select GuestbookEntities in the **Named Connection** ComboBox, then click **Next >**.

4. The **Configure Data Selection** screen (Fig. 13.33) allows you to specify which data the EntityDataSource should retrieve from the data context. The **EntitySetName** drop-down list contains DbContext properties that represent database's tables. For the Guestbook database, select Messages from the drop-down list. In the **Choose the properties in the query result:** pane, ensure that the **Select All** checkbox is selected to indicate that you want to retrieve all the columns in the Messages table.

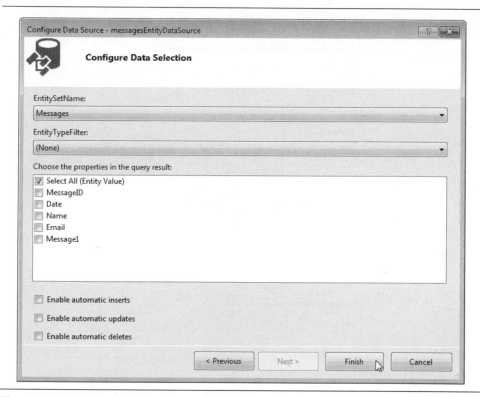

Fig. 13.33 | Configuring the `EntityDataSource`.

5. Click **Finish** to complete the wizard. A control named `messagesEntityData-Source` now appears on the Web Form directly below the `GridView`. It's represented in **Design** mode as a gray box containing its type and name. It will *not* appear on the web page—the gray box simply provides a way to manipulate the control visually through **Design** mode—similar to how the objects in the component tray are used in **Design** mode for a Windows Forms app.

6. Click the `messagesEntityDataSource`, then select **Refresh Schema** from its smart-tag menu. The `GridView` updates to display column headers that correspond to the columns in the `Messages` table (Fig. 13.34). The rows each contain either a number (which signifies an *autoincremented column*) or **abc** (which indicates string data). The actual data from the `Guestbook.mdf` database file will appear in these rows when you view the ASPX file in a web browser.

Step 6: Customizing the Columns of the Data Source Displayed in the `GridView`
It's not necessary for site visitors to see the `MessageID` column when viewing past guestbook entries—this column is merely a unique primary key required by the `Messages` table within the database. So, let's modify the `GridView` to prevent this column from displaying on the Web Form. We'll also modify the column **Message1** to read **Message**.

1. In the **GridView Tasks** *smart tag menu*, click **Edit Columns...** to display the **Fields** dialog (Fig. 13.35).

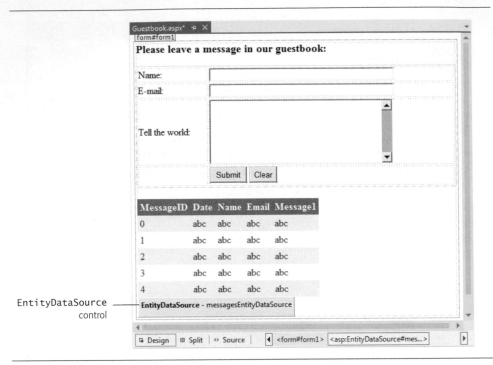

Fig. 13.34 | **Design** mode displaying EntityDataSource control for a GridView.

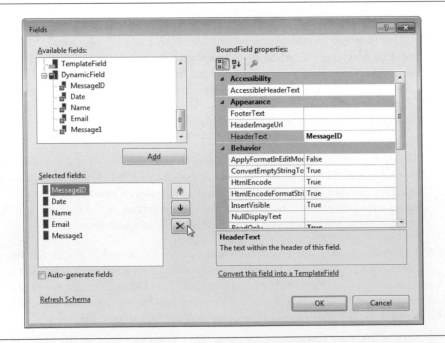

Fig. 13.35 | Removing the MessageID column from the GridView.

2. Select **MessageID** in the **Selected fields** pane, then click the ☒ Button. This removes the MessageID column from the GridView.

3. Select **Message1** in the **Selected fields** pane and change its HeaderText property to Message. The IDE renamed this field to prevent a naming conflict in the entity data model classes. Click **OK** to return to the main IDE window.

4. Next create a style to specify the width of the GridView. Select **FORMAT > New Style...** to display the **New Style** dialog. In the **Selector** field, specify .gridView-Width as the new style's name. Select the **Category** named **Position**, then set the **width:** to 650px and click **OK** to create the style and dismiss the dialog. Next set the CssClass property for the messagesGridView to gridViewWidth.

The GridView should now appear as shown in Fig. 13.31.

13.8.2 Modifying the Code-Behind File for the Guestbook App

After building the Web Form and configuring the data controls used in this example, double click the **Submit** and **Clear** buttons in **Design** view to create their corresponding Click event handlers in the code-behind file (Fig. 13.36). The IDE generates empty event handlers, so we must add the appropriate code to make these buttons work properly. The event handler for clearButton (lines 38–43) clears each TextBox by setting its Text property to an empty string. This resets the form for a new guestbook submission.

```
 1   ' Fig. 13.36: Guestbook.aspx.vb
 2   ' Code-behind file that defines event handlers for the guestbook.
 3   Partial Class Guestbook
 4      Inherits System.Web.UI.Page
 5
 6      ' Submit Button adds a new guestbook entry to the database,
 7      ' clears the form and displays the updated list of guestbook entries
 8      Protected Sub submitButton_Click(sender As Object, _
 9         e As EventArgs) Handles submitButton.Click
10
11         ' use GuestbookEntities DbContext to add a new message
12         Using dbcontext As New GuestbookEntities()
13            ' create a new Message to add to the database; Message is
14            ' the entity data model class representing a table row
15            Dim message As New Message()
16
17            ' set new Message's properties
18            message.Date = DateTime.Now.ToShortDateString()
19            message.Name = nameTextBox.Text
20            message.Email = emailTextBox.Text
21            message.Message1 = messageTextBox.Text
22
23            ' add new Message to GuestbookEntities DbContext
24            dbcontext.Messages.Add(message)
25            dbcontext.SaveChanges() ' save changes to the database
26         End Using
27
```

Fig. 13.36 | Code-behind file for the Guestbook app. (Part 1 of 2.)

```
28          ' clear the TextBoxes
29          nameTextBox.Text = String.Empty
30          emailTextBox.Text = String.Empty
31          messageTextBox.Text = String.Empty
32
33          ' update the GridView with the new database table contents
34          messagesGridView.DataBind()
35      End Sub ' submitButton_Click
36
37      ' Clear Button clears the Web Form's TextBoxes
38      Protected Sub clearButton_Click(sender As Object, _
39          e As System.EventArgs) Handles clearButton.Click
40          nameTextBox.Text = String.Empty
41          emailTextBox.Text = String.Empty
42          messageTextBox.Text = String.Empty
43      End Sub ' clearButton_Click
44  End Class ' Guestbook
```

Fig. 13.36 | Code-behind file for the Guestbook app. (Part 2 of 2.)

Lines 8–35 contain submitButton's event-handling code, which adds the user's information to the Guestbook database's Messages table. The Using statement in lines 12–26 begins by creating a GuestbookEntities object to interact with the database. Recall that the Using statement will call Dispose on this GuestbookEntities object when the Using statement terminates. This is a good practice for an ASP.NET web page request, so that we don't maintain a connection to the database beyond the request.

Line 15 creates an object of the entity data model's Message class, which represents a row in the database's Messages table. Lines 18–21 set the new Message object's properties to the values that should be stored in the database. Line 24 calls the Add method of the GuestbookEntities object's Messages property, which represents the Messages table in the database. This adds a new record to the entity data model's representation of the table. Line 25 then saves the changes into the database.

After the data is inserted into the database, lines 29–31 clear the TextBoxes, and line 34 invokes messagesGridView's **DataBind** method to refresh the data that the GridView displays. This causes messagesEntityDataSource (the GridView's data source) to obtain the Messages table's updated data from the database.

13.9 Online Case Study: ASP.NET AJAX

In the online Chapter 24, Web App Development with ASP.NET: A Deeper Look, you learn the difference between a traditional web app and an AJAX (Asynchronous JavaScript and XML) web app. You also learn how to use ASP.NET AJAX to quickly and easily improve the user experience for your web apps, giving them responsiveness comparable to that of desktop apps. To demonstrate ASP.NET AJAX capabilities, you enhance the validation example by displaying the submitted form information without reloading the entire page. The only modifications to this web app appear in Validation.aspx file. You use AJAX-enabled controls to add this feature.

13.10 Online Case Study: Password-Protected Books Database App

In the online Chapter 24, Web App Development with ASP.NET: A Deeper Look, we include a web app case study in which a user logs into a password-protected website to view a list of publications by a selected author. The app consists of several pages and provides website registration and login capabilities. You'll learn about ASP.NET master pages, which allow you to specify a common look-and-feel for all the pages in your app. We also introduce the **Web Site Administration Tool** and use it to configure the portions of the app that can be accessed only by users who are logged into the website.

13.11 Wrap-Up

In this chapter, we introduced web-app development using ASP.NET and Visual Studio Express 2012 for Web. We began by discussing the simple HTTP transactions that take place when you request and receive a web page through a web browser. You then learned about the three tiers (that is, the client or top tier, the business logic or middle tier and the information or bottom tier) that comprise most web apps.

Next, we explained the role of ASPX files (that is, Web Form files) and code-behind files, and the relationship between them. We discussed how ASP.NET compiles and executes web apps so that they can be displayed in a web browser. You also learned how to build an ASP.NET web app using Visual Studio Express For Web.

The chapter demonstrated several common ASP.NET web controls used for displaying text and images on a Web Form. We also discussed validation controls, which allow you to ensure that user input on a web page satisfies certain requirements.

We discussed the benefits of maintaining a user's state information across multiple pages of a website. We then demonstrated how you can include such functionality in a web app by using session tracking with `HttpSessionState` objects.

Finally, we built a guestbook app that allows users to submit comments about a website. You learned how to save the user input in a database and how to display past submissions on the web page.

Summary

Section 13.1 Introduction
- ASP.NET technology is Microsoft's technology for web-app development.
- Web Form files have the file-name extension `.aspx` and contain the web page's GUI. A Web Form file represents the web page that's sent to the client browser.
- The file that contains the programming logic of a Web Form is called the code-behind file.

Section 13.2 Web Basics
- URIs (Uniform Resource Identifiers) identify resources on the Internet. URIs that start with `http://` are called URLs (Uniform Resource Locators).
- A URL contains information that directs a browser to the resource that the user wishes to access. Computers that run web server software make such resources available.
- In a URL, the hostname is the name of the server on which the resource resides. This computer usually is referred to as the host, because it houses and maintains resources.

- A hostname is translated into a unique IP address that identifies the server. This translation is performed by a domain-name system (DNS) server.

- The remainder of a URL specifies the location and name of a requested resource. For security reasons, the location is normally a virtual directory. The server translates the virtual directory into a real location on the server.

- When given a URL, a web browser uses HTTP to retrieve the resource found at that address.

Section 13.3 Multitier App Architecture

- Multitier apps divide functionality into separate tiers—logical groupings of functionality—that commonly reside on separate computers for security and scalability.

- The information tier (also called the bottom tier) maintains data pertaining to the app. This tier typically stores data in a relational database management system.

- The middle tier implements business logic, controller logic and presentation logic to control interactions between the app's clients and the app's data. The middle tier acts as an intermediary between data in the information tier and the app's clients.

- Business logic in the middle tier enforces business rules and ensures that data is reliable before the server app updates the database or presents the data to users.

- The client tier, or top tier, is the app's user interface, which gathers input and displays output. Users interact directly with the app through the user interface (typically viewed in a web browser), keyboard and mouse. In response to user actions, the client tier interacts with the middle tier to make requests and to retrieve data from the information tier. The client tier then displays to the user the data retrieved from the middle tier.

Section 13.4.1 Building the WebTime App

- **File System** websites are created and tested on your local computer. Such websites execute in IIS Express and can be accessed only by web browsers running on the same computer. You can later "publish" your website to a production web server for access via a local network or the Internet.

- **HTTP** websites are created and tested on an IIS web server and use HTTP to allow you to put your website's files on the server. If you own a website and have your own web server computer, you might use this to build a new website directly on that server computer.

- **FTP** websites use File Transfer Protocol (FTP) to allow you to put your website's files on the server. The server administrator must first create the website on the server for you. FTP is commonly used by so called "hosting providers" to allow website owners to share a server computer that runs many websites.

- A Web Form represents one page in a web app and contains a web app's GUI.

- You can view the Web Form's properties by selecting DOCUMENT in the **Properties** window. The Title property specifies the title that will be displayed in the web browser's title bar when the page is loaded.

- Controls and other elements are placed sequentially on a Web Form one after another in the order in which you drag-and-drop them onto the Web Form. The cursor indicates the insertion point in the page. This type of layout is known as relative positioning. You can also use absolute positioning in which controls are located exactly where you drop them on the Web Form.

- When a Label does not contain text, its name is displayed in square brackets in **Design** view as a placeholder for design and layout purposes. This text is not displayed at execution time.

- Formatting in a web page is performed with Cascading Style Sheets (CSS).

- A Web Form's Init event occurs when the page is requested by a web browser. The event handler for this event—named Page_Init—initializes the page.

Section 13.4.2 Examining `WebTime.aspx`'s Code-Behind File

- A class declaration can span multiple source-code files—the separate portions of the class declaration in each file are known as partial classes. The `Partial` modifier indicates that the class in a particular file is part of a larger class.

- Every Web Form class inherits from class `Page` in namespace `System.Web.UI`. Class `Page` represents the default capabilities of each page in a web app.

- The ASP.NET controls are defined in namespace `System.Web.UI.WebControls`.

Section 13.5 Standard Web Controls: Designing a Form

- An `Image` control's `ImageUrl` property specifies the location of the image to display.

- A `TextBox` control allows you to obtain text from the user and display text to the user.

- A `DropDownList` control is similar to the Windows `Forms` `ComboBox` control, but doesn't allow users to type text. You can add items to the `DropDownList` using the **ListItem Collection Editor**, which you can access by clicking the ellipsis next to the `DropDownList`'s `Items` property in the **Properties** window, or by using the **DropDownList Tasks** smart-tag menu.

- A `HyperLink` control adds a hyperlink to a Web Form. The `NavigateUrl` property specifies the resource or web page that will be requested when the user clicks the `HyperLink`.

- A `RadioButtonList` control provides a series of radio buttons from which the user can select only one. The **RadioButtonList Tasks** smart-tag menu provides an **Edit Items...** link to open the **ListItem Collection Editor** so that you can create the items in the list.

- A `Button` control triggers an action when clicked.

Section 13.6 Validation Controls

- A validation control determines whether the data in another web control is in the proper format.

- When the page is sent to the client, the validator is converted into `JavaScript` that performs the validation in the client web browser.

- Some client browsers might not support scripting or the user might disable it. For this reason, you should always perform validation on the server.

- A `RequiredFieldValidator` control ensures that its `ControlToValidate` is not empty when the form is submitted. The validator's `ErrorMessage` property specifies what to display on the Web Form if the validation fails. When the validator's `Display` property is set to `Dynamic`, the validator occupies space on the Web Form only when validation fails.

- A `RegularExpressionValidator` uses a regular expression to ensure data entered by the user is in a valid format. Visual Studio Express 2012 for Web provides several predefined regular expressions that you can simply select to validate e-mail addresses, phone numbers and more. A `RegularExpressionValidator`'s `ValidationExpression` property specifies the regular expression to use for validation.

- A Web Form's `Load` event occurs each time the page loads into a web browser. The event handler for this event is `Page_Load`.

- ASP.NET pages are often designed so that the current page reloads when the user submits the form; this enables the program to receive input, process it as necessary and display the results in the same page when it's loaded the second time.

- Submitting a web form is known as a postback. Class `Page`'s `IsPostBack` property returns `true` if the page is being loaded due to a postback.

- Server-side Web Form validation must be implemented programmatically. Class `Page`'s `Validate` method validates the information in the request as specified by the Web Form's validation controls. Class `Page`'s `IsValid` property returns `true` if validation succeeded.

Section 13.7 Session Tracking

- Personalization makes it possible for e-businesses to communicate effectively with their customers and also improves users' ability to locate desired products and services.

- To provide personalized services to consumers, e-businesses must be able to recognize clients when they request information from a site.

- HTTP is a stateless protocol—it does not provide information regarding particular clients.

- Tracking individual clients is known as session tracking.

Section 13.7.1 Cookies

- A cookie is a piece of data stored in a small text file on the user's computer. A cookie maintains information about the client during and between browser sessions.

- The expiration date of a cookie determines how long the cookie remains on the client's computer. If you do not set an expiration date for a cookie, the web browser maintains the cookie for the duration of the browsing session.

Section 13.7.2 Session Tracking with **HttpSessionState**

- Session tracking is implemented with class HttpSessionState.

Section 13.7.3 **Options.aspx**: *Selecting a Programming Language*

- Each radio button in a RadioButtonList has a Text property and a Value property. The Text property is displayed next to the radio button and the Value property represents a value that's sent to the server when the user selects that radio button and submits the form.

- Every Web Form includes a user-specific HttpSessionState object, which is accessible through property Session of class Page.

- HttpSessionState property SessionID contains a client's unique session ID. The first time a client connects to the web server, a unique session ID is created for that client and a temporary cookie is written to the client so the server can identify the client on subsequent requests. When the client makes additional requests, the client's session ID from that temporary cookie is compared with the session IDs stored in the web server's memory to retrieve the client's HttpSessionState object.

- HttpSessionState property Timeout specifies the maximum amount of time that an HttpSessionState object can be inactive before it's discarded. Twenty minutes is the default.

- The HttpSessionState object is a dictionary—a data structure that stores key–value pairs. A program uses the key to store and retrieve the associated value in the dictionary.

- The key–value pairs in an HttpSessionState object are often referred to as session items. They're placed in an HttpSessionState object by calling its Add method. Another common syntax for placing a session item in the HttpSessionState object is Session(*KeyName*) = *Value*.

- If an app adds a session item that has the same name as an item previously stored in the HttpSessionState object, the session item is replaced—session items names *must* be unique.

Section 13.7.4 **Recommendations.aspx**: *Displaying Recommendations Based on Session Values*

- The Count property returns the number of session items stored in an HttpSessionState object.

- HttpSessionState's Keys property returns a collection containing all the keys in the session.

Section 13.8 Case Study: Database-Driven ASP.NET Guestbook

- A GridView data control displays data in tabular format. This control is located in the **Toolbox**'s **Data** section.

Section 13.8.1 Building a Web Form that Displays Data from a Database

- To use a SQL Server Express database file in an ASP.NET web app, you must first add the file to the project's App_Data folder. For security reasons, this folder can be accessed only by the web app on the server—clients cannot access this folder over a network. The web app interacts with the database on behalf of the client.

- An EntityDataSource control enables data bound Web Form controls to interact with a database via the ADO.NET Entity Framework.

Section 13.8.2 Modifying the Code-Behind File for the Guestbook App

- To insert data into a database from a web page, you create an object of your entity data model's class that represents a row in a table, set the object's properties, then use the Add method to add the object to the DbContext's object that represents the database table. When you call SaveChanges on the DbContext, the new row is added to the database table.

- A GridView's DataBind method refreshes the data that the GridView displays.

Terminology

Self-Review Exercises

13.1   State whether each of the following is *true* or *false*. If *false*, explain why.
  a) Web Form file names end in .aspx.
  b) App.config is a file that stores configuration settings for an ASP.NET web app.
  c) A maximum of one validation control can be placed on a Web Form.
  d) An EntityDataSource control enables data bound Web Form controls to interact with a database via the ADO.NET Entity Framework.

13.2   Fill in the blanks in each of the following statements:
  a) Web apps contain three basic tiers: _____, _____, and _____.
  b) The _____ web control is similar to the ComboBox Windows control.
  c) A control which ensures that the data in another control is in the correct format is called a(n) _____.
  d) A(n) _____ occurs when a page requests itself.
  e) Every ASP.NET page inherits from class _____.
  f) The _____ file contains the functionality for an ASP.NET page.

Answers to Self-Review Exercises

13.1   a) True. b) False. Web.config is the file that stores configuration settings for an ASP.NET web app. c) False. An unlimited number of validation controls can be placed on a Web Form. d) True.

13.2   a) bottom (information), middle (business logic), top (client). b) DropDownList. c) validator. d) postback. e) Page. f) code-behind.

Exercises

13.3   *(WebTime Modification)* Modify the WebTime app to contain drop-down lists that allow the user to modify such Label properties as BackColor, ForeColor and Font-Size. Configure these drop-down lists so that a postback occurs whenever the user makes a selection—to do this, set their AutoPostBack properties to true. When the page reloads, it should reflect the specified changes to the properties of the Label displaying the time.

13.4   *(Page Hit Counter)* Create an ASP.NET page that uses session tracking to keep track of how many times the client computer has visited the page. Set the HttpSessionState object's Timeout property to 1440 (the number of minutes in one day) to keep the session in effect for one day into the future. Display the number of page hits every time the page loads.

13.5   *(Guestbook App Modification)* Add validation to the Guestbook app in Section 13.8. Use validation controls to ensure that the user provides a name, a valid e-mail address and a message.

13.6   *(Project: WebControls Modification)* Modify the example of Section 13.5 to add functionality to the **Register** Button. When the user clicks the Button, validate all of the input fields to ensure that the user has filled out the form completely and entered a valid email address and phone number. If any of the fields are not valid, appropriate messages should be displayed by validation controls. If the fields are all valid, display a message indicating that the registration was successful followed by the registration information that was submitted from the form.

13.7   *(Project: Web-Based Address Book)* Using the techniques you learned in Section 13.8, create a web-based address book with similar functionality to the **Address Book** app that you created in Section 12.9. Display the address book's contents in a GridView. Allow the user to search for entries with a particular last name.

14

Windows Forms GUI: A Deeper Look

. . .The user should feel in control of the computer; not the other way around. This is achieved in applications that embody three qualities: responsiveness, permissiveness, and consistency.
—Apple Computer, Inc.

. . .the wisest prophets make sure of the event first.
—Horace Walpole

Objectives

In this chapter you'll learn:

- Design principles of graphical user interfaces (GUIs).

- How to process mouse and keyboard events.

- How to create and manipulate `Panel`, `ToolTip`, `MonthCalendar`, `DateTimePicker`, `LinkLabel` and `CheckedListBox` controls.

- To create menus, submenus, menu items and checked menu items.

- To create multiple document interface (MDI) programs.

- To use visual inheritance.

- To create an animation by generating events with a `Timer`.

14.1 Introduction

In this chapter, we present additional GUI components that will help you develop richer, more sophisticated GUIs. We begin with an overview of controls, components and common features of Forms. Next, we demonstrate alternate ways to create event handlers via the code editor window and the **Properties** window. Then you'll learn about common features of all controls and the IDE features for *positioning*, *aligning* and *sizing* controls.

We show how to use Panels to *group controls* and how to display visual hints called *tool tips* that are displayed when the user hovers the mouse over a control. You'll learn how to process *mouse and keyboard events*. We provide a more detailed example of menus that includes *submenus* and *checked menu items*, and discusses how to maintain a mutually exclusive set of menu items. Next, we introduce the MonthCalendar and DateTimePicker controls for manipulating dates and times in a GUI. We show how LinkLabels can be used to add *hyperlinks* to an app and demonstrate how to execute another program in response to clicking a hyperlink. We review the ListBox control and introduce the CheckedListBox control for displaying lists of items that can be *checked* or *unchecked*.

Next, we demonstrate a *multiple document interface (MDI)*—a window that can contain other windows. We introduce visual inheritance and show how to use it to maintain a consistent look-and-feel throughout an app. Finally, we demonstrate the Timer component, which is a *nonvisual component* that generates events at fixed time intervals. We use a Timer to control an *animation* that displays 20 images per second.

14.2 Controls and Components

Figure 14.1 displays the Windows Forms controls and components from the **Toolbox**. The difference between a control and a component is that a component is *not* visual at execution time. An example of a component is a Timer, which generates events at specified time intervals, but is *not* actually displayed on the screen. When you drag a component onto the Form in **Design** view, the component is placed in the *component tray* below the Form. You can select a component from the component tray to access its properties and events in the **Properties** window.

Toolbox Categories

The controls and components are organized into categories by functionality. Selecting the category **All Windows Forms** at the top of the **Toolbox** allows you to view all the controls and components from the other tabs in one list (as shown in Fig. 14.1).

Fig. 14.1 | Components and controls for Windows Forms.

The Active Window

When there are several windows on the screen, the **active window** is the *frontmost* one. A window becomes active when the user clicks inside it. The active window is said to *have the focus*. For example, in Visual Studio the active window is the **Toolbox** when you're selecting an item from it, or the **Properties** window when you're editing a control's properties.

Auto-Generated Code

As you know, a Form is a *container* for controls and components. When you drag a control or component from the **Toolbox** onto the Form, Visual Studio generates code that instantiates the object and sets its basic properties to default values. This code is updated when the control or component's properties are modified in the **Properties** window. The generated code is placed by the IDE in a separate file. Although we could write this code ourselves, it's easier to create and modify controls and components using the **Toolbox** and **Properties** windows and let Visual Studio to handle the details.

Common Properties of a Form

Figure 14.2 lists some common Form properties, methods and an event—some of which you've used in earlier chapters.

Form properties, methods and an event	Description
Common Properties	
AcceptButton	Button that's clicked when *Enter* is pressed.
AutoScroll	Boolean value that allows or disallows scrollbars when needed.
CancelButton	Button that's clicked when the *Escape* key is pressed.
FormBorderStyle	Border style for the Form (for example, none, single, three-dimensional).
Font	Font of text displayed on the Form, and the default font for controls added to the Form.
Text	Text in the Form's title bar.
Common Methods	
Close	Closes a Form and releases all resources, such as the memory used for the Form's controls and components. A closed Form cannot be reopened.
Hide	Hides a Form, but does not destroy the Form or release its resources.
Show	Displays a hidden Form.
Common Event	
Load	Occurs before a Form is displayed to the user. The handler for this event is displayed in the Visual Studio editor when you double click the Form in the Visual Studio designer.

Fig. 14.2 | Common Form properties, methods and an event.

14.3 Creating Event Handlers

In all the GUI apps you've created so far, you double clicked a control on the Form to *create an event handler* for that control. This technique creates an event handler for a control's **default event**—the event most frequently used with that control. Typically, controls can generate many different types of events, and each type can have its own event handler. For instance, you've already created Click event handlers for Buttons by double clicking a Button in design view (Click is the *default event* for a Button). However your app can also provide an event handler for a Button's MouseEnter event, which occurs when you move the mouse pointer into the Button. We now discuss how to create an event handler for an event that's not a control's default event.

Creating Event Handlers from the Code Editor Window

Visual Studio Express 2012 for Windows Desktop allows you to create event handlers from the **Code** editor. At the top of the **Code** editor window, you'll find two ComboBoxes. If you select a control in your Form from the left ComboBox (Fig. 14.3(a)), the right ComboBox is populated with all the events for that control (Fig. 14.3(b)). If you select an event from the right ComboBox, your text cursor will move to its location in the code. If the event handler does not already exist, it will be created.

a) Selecting a control in the **Code** editor window

b) Displaying the list of events for the selected control

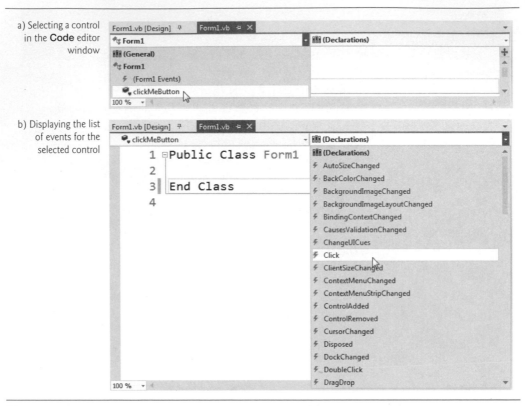

Fig. 14.3 | Viewing the events for a `Button` in the **Code** editor.

Using the Properties Window to Create Event Handlers

You can also create event handlers through the **Properties** window in **Design** view. If you select a control on the Form, then click the **Events** icon ( ) in the **Properties** window, all the events for that control are listed in the window (Fig. 14.4). You can double click an event's name to display the event handler in the editor. If the event handler does not already exist, it will be created. You can also select an event, then use the drop-down list to its right to choose an existing method that will be used as the event handler for that event. The methods that appear in this drop-down list are the class's methods that have the proper signature to be an event handler for the selected event. You can return to viewing the properties of a control by selecting the **Properties** icon.

Specifying the Same Event Handler for Multiple Controls in Design View

A single method can handle events from *many* controls. For example, to create a Click event handler that can handle the Click events of three Buttons, select all three Buttons in **Design** view, then double click the event you want to handle in the **Events** tab of the **Properties** window. If you create a new event handler this way, you should rename it appropriately, so that it does not appear to be associated with only one of the controls. You can also select each control individually and use the **Events** tab to select an existing method as the event handler. The event handler's Handles clause specifies a comma-separated list of all the events that will invoke the event handler.

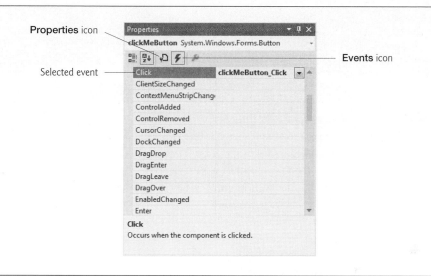

Fig. 14.4 | Viewing events for a `Button` control in the **Properties** window.

14.4 Control Properties and Layout

This section overviews properties that are common to many controls. Controls inherit from class **Control** (namespace `System.Windows.Forms`). Figure 14.5 lists some of class `Control`'s commonly used properties and methods. The properties shown here can be set for many controls. For example, the `Text` property specifies the text that appears on a control. The location of this text varies depending on the control. In a Windows Form, the text appears in the title bar, but the text of a `Button` appears on its face.

TabIndex and TabStop Properties

When you press the *Tab* key in an executing Windows app, controls receive the focus in the order specified by their **TabIndex property**. This property is set by the IDE based on the *order* in which controls are added to a `Form`, but you can modify this property to *change the tabbing order*. `TabIndex` is helpful for users who enter information in many controls, such as a set of `TextBox`es that represent a user's name, address and telephone number. The user can enter information, then quickly select the next control by pressing the *Tab* key. To prevent a control from receiving the focus in this manner, you can set its **TabStop property** to `False`.

Class **Control**'s properties and methods	Description
Common Properties	
BackColor	The control's background color.
BackgroundImage	The control's background image.

Fig. 14.5 | Class `Control`'s common properties and methods. (Part 1 of 2.)

Class **Control**'s properties and methods	Description
Enabled	Specifies whether the user can interact with the control. A disabled control typically appears "grayed out."
Focused	Indicates whether the control has the focus.
Font	The Font used to display the control's text.
ForeColor	The control's foreground color. This usually determines the color of the text in the Text property.
TabIndex	The tab order of the control. When the *Tab* key is pressed, the focus transfers between controls based on the tab order. You can set this order.
TabStop	If True, then a user can give focus to this control via the *Tab* key.
Text	The text associated with the control. The location and appearance of the text vary depending on the type of control.
Visible	Indicates whether the control is visible.
Common Methods	
Focus	Acquires the focus.
Hide	Hides the control (sets the Visible property to False).
Show	Shows the control (sets the Visible property to True).

Fig. 14.5 | Class Control's common properties and methods. (Part 2 of 2.)

Enabled *and* Visible *Properties*

The **Enabled** property indicates whether the user can interact with a control to generate an event. If a control is *disabled*, it's often because an option is unavailable to the user at that time. For example, text editor apps disable the "paste" command until the user *copies* some text. In most cases, a disabled control's text appears in *gray* (rather than in black). You can also hide a control from the user by setting the Visible property to False or by calling method Hide. In each case, the control still exists but is not visible on the Form.

Properties That Affect the Layout, Size and Position of Controls

You can use anchoring and docking to specify the layout of controls inside a container (such as a Form). **Anchoring** causes controls to remain at a fixed distance from the sides of the container even when the container is *resized*. Anchoring enhances the user experience. For example, if the user expects a control to appear in a certain corner of the app, anchoring ensures that the control will always be in that corner—even if the user resizes the Form. **Docking** attaches a control to a container such that the control stretches across an *entire side* or fills an *entire area*. For example, a button docked to the top of a container stretches across the entire top of that container regardless of the container's width.

When parent containers are resized, anchored controls move (and possibly resize) so that the distance from the sides to which they're anchored does not vary. By default, most controls are anchored to the *top-left corner* of the Form. To see the effects of anchoring a control, create a simple Windows app that contains two Buttons. Anchor one control to the right and bottom sides by setting the Anchor property as shown in Fig. 14.6. Leave the other control unanchored. Execute the app and widen the Form. The Button anchored to the bottom-right corner is always the same distance from the Form's bottom-right corner (Fig. 14.7), but the other control stays its original distance from the top-left corner of the Form.

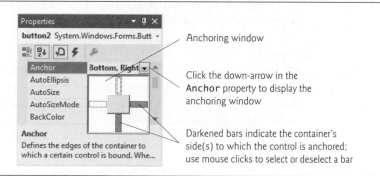

Fig. 14.6 | Manipulating the **Anchor** property of a control.

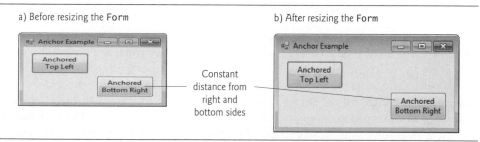

Fig. 14.7 | Anchoring demonstration.

Sometimes, it's desirable for a control to span an *entire side* of the Form, even when the Form is resized. For example, a control such as a status bar typically should remain at the bottom of the Form. Docking allows a control to span an entire side (left, right, top or bottom) of its parent container or to fill the entire container. When the parent control is resized, the docked control resizes as well. In Fig. 14.8, a Button is docked at the top of the Form. When the Form is resized, the Button is resized to the Form's new width. Forms have a **Padding** property that specifies the distance between the docked controls and the Form edges. This property specifies four values (one for each side), and each value is set to 0 by default. Some common control-layout properties are summarized in Fig. 14.9.

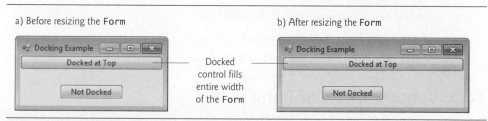

Fig. 14.8 | Docking a Button to the top of a Form.

Control layout properties	Description
Anchor	Causes a control to remain at a *fixed distance from the side(s)* of the container even when the container is resized.
Dock	Allows a control to *span one side* of its container or to *fill the remaining space* in the container.
Padding	Sets the space between a container's edges and docked controls. The default is 0, causing the control to appear flush with the container's sides.
Location	Specifies the location (as a set of coordinates) of the upper-left corner of the control, in relation to its container.
Size	Specifies the size of the control in pixels as a Size object, which has properties Width and Height.
MinimumSize, MaximumSize	Indicate the minimum and maximum sizes of a Control, respectively.

Fig. 14.9 | Control layout properties.

A Control's Anchor and Dock properties are set with respect to the Control's parent container, which could be a Form or another *parent container* (such as a Panel; discussed in Section 14.5). The minimum and maximum Form (or other Control) sizes can be set via properties MinimumSize and MaximumSize, respectively. Both are of type Size, which has properties Width and Height to specify the Form's size. Properties MinimumSize and MaximumSize allow you to design the GUI layout for a given size range. The user cannot make a Form smaller than the size specified by property MinimumSize and cannot make a Form larger than the size specified by property MaximumSize. To set a Form to a fixed size (where the Form cannot be resized by the user), set its minimum and maximum sizes to the same values or set its FormBorderStyle property to a "Fixed" value such as FixedSingle.

Using Visual Studio To Edit a GUI's Layout

Visual Studio provides tools that help you with GUI layout. In Chapter 3, you learned about the *blue snap lines* that appear to help you position a control with respect to other controls on a Form and the Form's edges. These make the control you're dragging appear to "snap into place." Visual Studio also provides the **Format** menu, which contains several options for modifying your GUI's layout. The **Format** menu appears in the IDE only in **Design** view. Some formatting features include:

• Aligning multiple controls

• Making multiple controls have the same size

• Adjusting the horizontal and vertical spacing between controls

• Centering controls on the Form horizontally or vertically

14.5 GroupBoxes and Panels

GroupBoxes (introduced in Chapter 6) and Panels arrange controls on a GUI. They're typically used to group several controls of similar functionality or several controls that are related in a GUI. All of the controls that you drag onto a GroupBox or a Panel *move together* when you move the GroupBox or Panel to a new position in the Form in **Design** view.

The primary difference between these two controls is that GroupBoxes can display a text caption and cannot have scrollbars, whereas Panels can display scrollbars but do not have a text caption. GroupBoxes have thin borders by default; Panels can be set so that they also have borders by changing their BorderStyle property. Figures 14.10 and 14.11 list some common properties of GroupBoxes and Panels, respectively.

GroupBox properties	Description
Controls	A collection of the controls that the GroupBox contains.
Text	Specifies the caption text displayed at the top of the GroupBox.

Fig. 14.10 | GroupBox properties.

Panel properties	Description
AutoScroll	Indicates whether scrollbars appear when the Panel is too small to display all of its controls. The default value is False.
BorderStyle	Sets the border of the Panel. The default value is None; other options are Fixed3D and FixedSingle.
Controls	A collection of the controls that the Panel contains.

Fig. 14.11 | Panel properties.

Look-and-Feel Observation 14.1

Panels and GroupBoxes can contain other Panels and GroupBoxes for more complex layouts.

Look-and-Feel Observation 14.2

You can organize a GUI by anchoring and docking controls inside a GroupBox or Panel. The GroupBox or Panel can then be anchored or docked inside a Form. This divides controls into functional "groups" that can be arranged easily.

When you drag new controls from the **Toolbox** into the GroupBox, they're added to the GroupBox's **Controls** property and become part of the GroupBox. The GroupBox's Text property specifies the caption.

To create a Panel, drag its icon from the **Toolbox** onto the Form. You can then add controls directly to the Panel by dragging them from the **Toolbox** onto the Panel. To enable the scrollbars, set the Panel's AutoScroll property to True. If the Panel is resized and cannot display all of its controls, scrollbars appear (Fig. 14.12). The scrollbars can be used to view all the controls in the Panel—both at design time *and* at execution time. In Fig. 14.12, we placed six Buttons vertically in a scrollable Panel. When you click one of these Buttons, the event handler (lines 5–11) changes the Text on the outputLabel to "You pressed: " followed by the Text of the clicked Button. All six Buttons' Click events are processed by this event handler. We set the Panel's BorderStyle property to FixedSingle, so you can see it on the Form. The sample output shows the results of clicking the first and last Buttons in the Panel.

```vb
1   ' Fig. 14.12: PanelDemo.vb
2   ' Displaying Buttons in a scrollable Panel.
3   Public Class PanelDemo
4      ' display which Button was pressed
5      Private Sub Button_Click(sender As Object,
6         e As EventArgs) Handles Button1.Click, Button2.Click,
7         Button3.Click, Button4.Click, Button5.Click, Button6.Click
8
9         ' display the Button's text in the outputLabel
10        outputLabel.Text = "You pressed: " & CType(sender, Button).Text
11     End Sub ' Button_Click
12  End Class ' PanelDemo
```

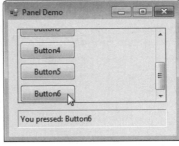

Fig. 14.12 | Using GroupBoxes and Panels to arrange Buttons.

14.6 ToolTips

In Chapter 2, we discussed tool tips—the helpful text that appears when the mouse hovers over a GUI control. The tool tips displayed in Visual Studio serve as useful reminders of each toolbar icon's functionality. Many programs use tool tips to remind users of each control's purpose. For example, Microsoft Word has tool tips that help users determine the purpose of the app's icons. This section demonstrates how to use the **ToolTip component** to add tool tips to your apps. Figure 14.13 describes common properties, a common event, and a common method of class ToolTip.

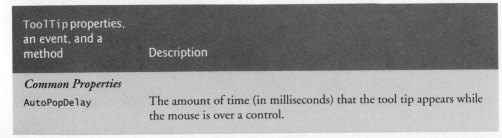

ToolTip properties, an event, and a method	Description
Common Properties	
AutoPopDelay	The amount of time (in milliseconds) that the tool tip appears while the mouse is over a control.

Fig. 14.13 | ToolTip properties, an event and a method. (Part 1 of 2.)

ToolTip properties, an event, and a method	Description
InitialDelay	The amount of time (in milliseconds) that a mouse must hover over a control before a tool tip appears.
ReshowDelay	The amount of time (in milliseconds) between which two different tool tips appear (when the mouse is moved from one control to another).
Common Event	
Draw	Raised when the tool tip is displayed. This event allows you to modify the appearance of the tool tip.
Common Method	
Show	Sets the tool tip's text and displays it.

Fig. 14.13 | ToolTip properties, an event and a method. (Part 2 of 2.)

When you add a ToolTip component from the **Toolbox**, it appears in the component tray below the Form in **Design** mode. Once a ToolTip is added to a Form, a new property appears in the **Properties** window for each of the Form's other controls. This property appears in the **Properties** window as **ToolTip on**, followed by the name of the ToolTip component. For instance, if our Form's ToolTip were named ToolTip1 (the default name), you would set a control's **ToolTip on ToolTip1** property value to specify the text that will be displayed when the user positions the mouse over that control. Figure 14.14 demonstrates the ToolTip component. For this example, we create a GUI containing a Label, a TextBox and a Button, so that we can demonstrate a different tool tip for each. The ToolTip component automatically handles the event that causes the tool tip to display for each component, so we show only the sample outputs for this program.

Fig. 14.14 | Demonstrating the ToolTip component.

In this example, we used the default name of the ToolTip component—ToolTip1. Figure 14.15 shows the ToolTip component in the component tray. We set the tool tip text for the Label to "Hovering Over the Label". Figure 14.16 demonstrates setting the tool tip text for the first Label.

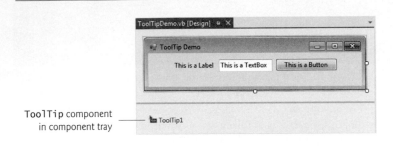

Fig. 14.15 | ToolTip component in the component tray.

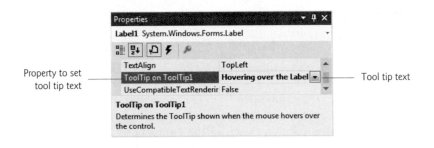

Fig. 14.16 | Setting a control's tool tip text.

14.7 Mouse-Event Handling

This section explains how to handle mouse events, such as clicks, presses and moves, which are generated when the user interacts with a control via the mouse. Mouse events can be handled for any control that derives from class System.Windows.Forms.Control. For most mouse events, information about the event is passed to the event-handling method through an object of class MouseEventArgs.

Class MouseEventArgs contains information related to the mouse event, such as the mouse pointer's *x*- and *y*-coordinates, the mouse button pressed (Right, Left or Middle) and the number of times the mouse was clicked. The *x*- and *y*-coordinates of the Mouse-EventArgs object are relative to the control that generated the event—that is, point *(0,0)* represents the *upper-left corner of the control* where the mouse event occurred. Several common mouse events and event arguments are described in Fig. 14.17.

Mouse events and event arguments
Mouse Events with Event Argument of Type EventArgs
MouseEnter   Occurs when the mouse cursor *enters* the control's boundaries.
MouseLeave   Occurs when the mouse cursor *leaves* the control's boundaries.

Fig. 14.17 | Mouse events and event arguments. (Part 1 of 2.)

Mouse events and event arguments	
Mouse Events with Event Argument of Type **MouseEventArgs**	
MouseDown	Occurs when a mouse button is pressed while the mouse cursor is within a control's boundaries.
MouseHover	Occurs when the mouse cursor hovers within the control's boundaries.
MouseMove	Occurs when the mouse cursor is moved while in the control's boundaries.
MouseUp	Occurs when a mouse button is released when the cursor is within the control's boundaries.
Class **MouseEventArgs** *Properties*	
Button	Specifies which mouse button was pressed (Left, Right, Middle or None).
Clicks	The number of times the mouse button was clicked.
X	The *x*-coordinate within the control where the event occurred.
Y	The *y*-coordinate within the control where the event occurred.

Fig. 14.17 | Mouse events and event arguments. (Part 2 of 2.)

Figure 14.18 uses mouse events to draw on a Form. Whenever the user drags the mouse (that is, moves the mouse while a mouse button is pressed), small circles appear on the Form at the position where each mouse event occurs during the drag operation. To create the event handlers in this example, select the Form in **Design** view, click the **Events** icon (⚡) in the **Properties** window then double click the event name—you'll need to do this once each for the MouseDown, MouseUp and MouseMove events.

```
 1   ' Fig. 14.18: Painter.vb
 2   ' Using the mouse to draw on a Form.
 3   Public Class Painter
 4      Private shouldPaint As Boolean = False ' determines whether to paint
 5
 6      ' should paint when mouse button is pressed down
 7      Private Sub Painter_MouseDown(sender As Object,
 8         e As MouseEventArgs) Handles MyBase.MouseDown
 9         shouldPaint = True
10      End Sub ' Painter_MouseDown
11
12      ' stop painting when mouse button is released
13      Private Sub Painter_MouseUp(sender As Object,
14         e As MouseEventArgs) Handles MyBase.MouseUp
15         shouldPaint = False
16      End Sub ' Painter_MouseUp
17
18      ' draw circle whenever mouse moves with its button held down
19      Private Sub Painter_MouseMove(sender As Object,
20         e As MouseEventArgs) Handles MyBase.MouseMove
```

Fig. 14.18 | Using the mouse to draw on a Form. (Part 1 of 2.)

```
21        ' check if mouse button is being pressed
22        If (shouldPaint) Then
23            ' draw a circle where the mouse pointer is present
24            Using g As Graphics = CreateGraphics()
25                g.FillEllipse(
26                    New SolidBrush(Color.BlueViolet), e.X, e.Y, 4, 4)
27            End Using
28        End If
29    End Sub ' Painter_MouseMove
30 End Class ' Painter
```

Fig. 14.18 | Using the mouse to draw on a Form. (Part 2 of 2.)

Line 4 declares variable shouldPaint, which determines whether to draw on the Form. We want to draw only while the mouse button is pressed (that is, held down). When the user clicks or holds down a mouse button, the system generates a MouseDown event and the event handler Painter_MouseDown (lines 7–10) sets shouldPaint to True. When the user releases the mouse button, the system generates a MouseUp event, shouldPaint is set to False in the Painter_MouseUp event handler (lines 13–16) and the program stops drawing. Unlike MouseMove events, which occur *continuously* as the user moves the mouse, the system generates a MouseDown event *only* when a mouse button is *first pressed* and generates a MouseUp event *only* when a mouse button is *released*.

Whenever the mouse moves over a control, the MouseMove event for that control occurs. Inside the Painter_MouseMove event handler (lines 19–29), the program draws only if shouldPaint is True. Line 24 calls inherited Form method **CreateGraphics** to create a **Graphics** object that allows the program to draw on the Form. Class Graphics provides methods that draw various shapes. For example, lines 25–26 use method **Fill-Ellipse** to draw a circle. The first parameter to method FillEllipse in this case is an object of class **SolidBrush**, which specifies the solid color that will fill the shape. The color is provided as an argument to class SolidBrush's constructor. Type **Color** contains many predefined color constants—we selected Color.BlueViolet. FillEllipse draws an oval in a bounding rectangle that's specified by the *x*- and *y*-coordinates of its upper-left corner, its width and its height—the final four arguments to the method. The *x*- and *y*-coordinates represent the location of the mouse event, which the event handler receives in its Mouse-EventArgs argument (e.X and e.Y). To draw a circle, we set the width and height of the bounding rectangle so that they're equal—in this example, both are 4 pixels.

Like dialog boxes, Graphics objects need to be returned to the system when they are no longer needed. For this reason, we create the Graphics object in a Using statement (lines 24–27). When the program reaches line 27, the Graphics object's Dispose method is called to return the Graphics object's resources back to the system. Classes Graphics, SolidBrush and Color are all part of the System.Drawing namespace.

14.8 Keyboard-Event Handling

Key events occur when keyboard keys are *pressed* and *released*. Such events can be handled for any control that inherits from System.Windows.Forms.Control. There are three key events—KeyPress, KeyUp and KeyDown. The **KeyPress** event occurs when the user *presses* a key that represents an ASCII character. The specific key can be determined with property **KeyChar** of the event handler's **KeyPressEventArgs** argument. ASCII is a 128-character set of alphanumeric symbols, a full listing of which can be found in Appendix D.

The KeyPress event does *not* indicate whether **modifier keys** (for example, *Shift*, *Alt* and *Ctrl*) were pressed when a key event occurred. If this information is important, the **KeyUp** or **KeyDown** events can be used. The **KeyEventArgs** argument for each of these events contains information about modifier keys. Often, modifier keys are used in conjunction with the mouse to select or highlight information. Figure 14.19 lists important key-event information. Several properties return values from the **Keys enumeration**, which provides constants that specify the various keys on a keyboard. The Keys enumeration constants can be combined to indicate multiple keys pressed at the same time.

Keyboard events and event arguments	
Key Events with Event Arguments of Type *KeyEventArgs*	
KeyDown	Generated when a key is initially pressed.
KeyUp	Generated when a key is released.
Key Event with Event Argument of Type *KeyPressEventArgs*	
KeyPress	Generated when a key is pressed.
Class *KeyPressEventArgs* properties	
KeyChar	Returns the ASCII character for the key pressed.
Handled	Indicates whether the KeyPress event was handled.
Class *KeyEventArgs* properties	
Alt	Indicates whether the *Alt* key was pressed.
Control	Indicates whether the *Ctrl* key was pressed.
Shift	Indicates whether the *Shift* key was pressed.
Handled	Indicates whether the event was handled.
KeyCode	Returns the key code for the key as a value from the Keys enumeration. This does not include modifier-key information. It's used to test for a specific key.

Fig. 14.19 | Keyboard events and event arguments. (Part 1 of 2.)

Keyboard events and event arguments	
KeyData	Returns the key code for a key combined with modifier information as a Keys value. This property contains all the information about the pressed key.
KeyValue	Returns the key code as an int, rather than as a value from the Keys enumeration. This property is used to obtain a numeric representation of the pressed key. The int value is known as a Windows virtual key code.
Modifiers	Returns a Keys value indicating any pressed modifier keys (*Alt*, *Ctrl* and *Shift*). This property is used to determine modifier-key information only.

Fig. 14.19 | Keyboard events and event arguments. (Part 2 of 2.)

Figure 14.20 demonstrates the use of the key-event handlers to display a key pressed by a user. The program is a Form with two Labels that displays the pressed key on one Label and modifier-key information on the other.

```vb
1   ' Fig. 14.20: KeyDemo
2   ' Displaying information about the key the user pressed.
3   Public Class KeyDemo
4      ' display the character pressed using KeyChar
5      Private Sub KeyDemo_KeyPress(sender As Object,
6         e As KeyPressEventArgs) Handles MyBase.KeyPress
7
8         charLabel.Text = "Key pressed: " & e.KeyChar
9      End Sub ' KeyDemo_KeyPress
10
11     ' display modifier keys, key code, key data and key value
12     Private Sub KeyDemo_KeyDown(sender As Object,
13        e As KeyEventArgs) Handles MyBase.KeyDown
14
15        If e.Alt Then ' key is Alt
16           keyInfoLabel.Text = "Alt: Yes" & vbCrLf
17        Else ' key is not Alt
18           keyInfoLabel.Text = "Alt: No" & vbCrLf
19        End If
20
21        If e.Shift Then ' key is Shift
22           keyInfoLabel.Text &= "Shift: Yes" & vbCrLf
23        Else ' key is not Shift
24           keyInfoLabel.Text &= "Shift: No" & vbCrLf
25        End If
26
27        If e.Control Then ' key is Control
28           keyInfoLabel.Text &= "Control: Yes" & vbCrLf
29        Else ' key is not Control
30           keyInfoLabel.Text &= "Control: No" & vbCrLf
31        End If
32
```

Fig. 14.20 | Demonstrating keyboard events. (Part 1 of 2.)

```
33          ' diplay key code, key data and key value
34          keyInfoLabel.Text &= "KeyCode: " & e.KeyCode.ToString() &
35          vbCrLf & "KeyData: " & e.KeyData.ToString() & vbCrLf &
36              "KeyValue: " & e.KeyValue.ToString()
37      End Sub ' KeyDemo_KeyDown
38
39      ' clear Labels when keys are released
40      Private Sub KeyDemo_KeyUp(sender As Object,
41          e As KeyEventArgs) Handles MyBase.KeyUp
42
43          charLabel.Text = String.Empty
44          keyInfoLabel.Text = String.Empty
45      End Sub ' KeyDemo_KeyUp
46  End Class ' KeyDemo
```

a) *H* pressed

b) *F1* pressed

c) *$* pressed

d) *Shift* pressed

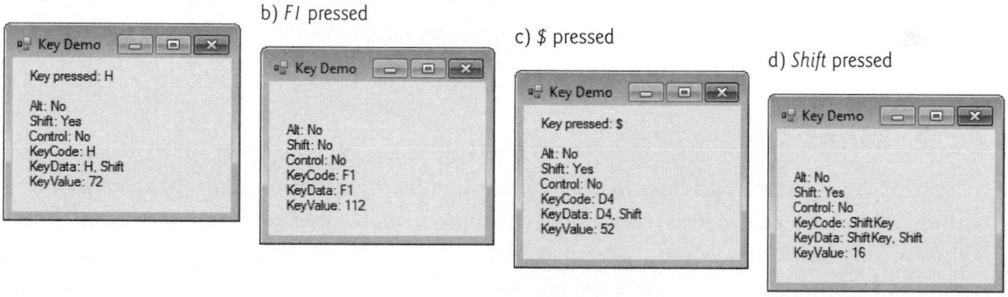

Fig. 14.20 | Demonstrating keyboard events. (Part 2 of 2.)

Initially, the two Labels (charLabel and keyInfoLabel) contain "Just press" and "a key...", respectively. When the user presses a key, charLabel displays the key's character value, and keyInfoLabel displays related information. Because the KeyDown and KeyPress events convey different information, the app handles both.

The KeyPress event handler (lines 5–9) accesses the KeyChar property of the Key-PressEventArgs object. This returns the pressed key as a Char, which we then display in charLabel (line 8). If the pressed key is not an ASCII character, then the KeyPress event will not occur, and charLabel will *not* display any text. ASCII is a common encoding format for letters, numbers, punctuation marks and other characters. It does not support keys such as the function keys (such as *F1*) or the modifier keys (*Alt, Ctrl* and *Shift*).

The KeyDown event handler (lines 12–37) displays information from its KeyEventArgs object. The event handler tests for the *Alt, Shift* and *Ctrl* keys by using the Alt, Shift and Control properties, each of which returns a Boolean value—True if the corresponding key is pressed and False if otherwise. The event handler then displays the KeyCode, KeyData and KeyValue properties.

The KeyCode property returns a Keys enumeration value (line 34). The KeyCode property returns the pressed key, but does *not* provide any information about modifier keys. Thus, both a capital "A" and a lowercase "a" are represented as the *A* key.

The KeyData property (line 35) also returns a Keys enumeration value, but this property includes data about modifier keys. Thus, if "A" is input, the KeyData shows that both the *A* key and the *Shift* key were pressed. Lastly, KeyValue (line 36) returns the key code of the pressed key as an Integer. This Integer is the **key code**, which provides an Integer value for a wide range of keys and for mouse buttons. The key code is useful when testing for non-ASCII keys (such as *F12*).

The KeyUp event handler (lines 40–45) clears both Labels when the key is released. As we can see from the output, non-ASCII keys are not displayed in charLabel, because the KeyPress event is not generated. For example, charLabel does not display any text when you press the *F1* or *Shift* keys, as shown in Fig. 14.20(b) and (d). However, the KeyDown event is still generated, and keyInfoLabel displays information about the key that's pressed. The Keys enumeration can be used to test for specific keys by comparing the key pressed to a specific KeyCode.

Software Engineering Observation 14.1

To make a control react when a particular key is pressed (such as Enter*), handle a key event for that control and test for the pressed key. To allow a* Button *to be clicked when the user presses the* Enter *key on a* Form*, set the* Form's AcceptButton *property to that* Button*.*

14.9 Menus

In Section 8.6, you learned how to create basic menus to organize groups of related commands. Although commands vary between apps, some—such as **Open** and **Save**—are common to many apps. Menus organize commands without "cluttering" the app's user interface. In this section, we take a deeper look at menus and the different types of menu items.

In Fig. 14.21, an expanded menu from Visual Studio Express 2012 for Windows Desktop lists various menu items and **submenus** (menus within a menu). Menu items are typically displayed down and indented to the right of the top-level menu, but they can be displayed to the left if there's not enough space to the right on the screen. The menu that contains a menu item is called the menu item's **parent menu**. A menu item that contains a submenu is considered to be the parent of the submenu.

Shortcut Keys

All menu items can have *Alt* key shortcuts (also called **access shortcuts** or **hotkeys**), which are accessed by pressing *Alt* and the underlined letter (for example, *Alt F* expands the **File** menu). Menus that are not top-level menus can have shortcut keys as well (combinations of *Ctrl*, *Shift*, *Alt*, *F1*, *F2*, letter keys, etc.).

To create an access shortcut (or **keyboard shortcut**), type an ampersand (&) before the character to be underlined. For example, to create the **File** menu item with the letter **F** underlined, type &File. To display an ampersand, type &&. To add other shortcut keys (like those shown in Fig. 14.21) for menu items, set the **ShortcutKeys** property of the appropriate ToolStripMenuItems. To do this, select the down arrow to the right of this property in the **Properties** window. In the window that appears (Fig. 14.22), use the CheckBoxes and drop-down list to select the shortcut keys. When you're finished, click elsewhere on the screen. You can hide the shortcut keys by setting property **Show-ShortcutKeys** to False, and you can modify how the control keys are displayed in the menu item by modifying property **ShortcutKeyDisplayString**.

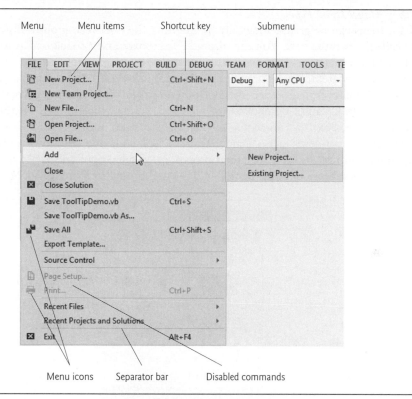

Fig. 14.21 | Menus, submenus, menu items and menu icons.

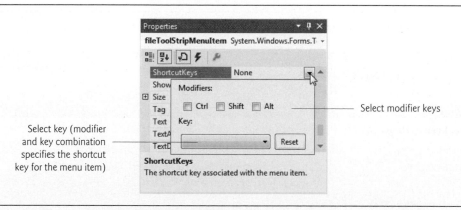

Fig. 14.22 | Setting a menu item's shortcut keys.

Look-and-Feel Observation 14.3

Buttons can have access shortcuts. Place the & symbol immediately before the desired character in the Button's text. To press the button by using its access key in the running app, press Alt and the underlined character. If the underlines are not visible at runtime, press the Alt key to display the underlines.

Other Menu Item Types

Menu items can be grouped logically by inserting lines between groups of items—these are called **separator bars**. You can also add TextBoxes and ComboBoxes as menu items. When adding an item in **Design** mode, you may have noticed that before you click to enter text for a new item, you're provided with a drop-down list. Clicking the down arrow (Fig. 14.23) allows you to select the type of item to add—**MenuItem** (of type ToolStrip-MenuItem, the default), **ComboBox** (of type ToolStripComboBox) and **TextBox** (of type ToolStripTextBox). We focus on ToolStripMenuItems. [*Note:* If you view this drop-down list for top-level menu items like the **File** menu, one additional option named **Separator** will not display.] Common properties of MenuStrip and ToolStripMenuItem and a common event of a ToolStripMenuItem are summarized in Fig. 14.24.

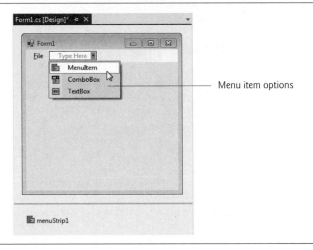

Fig. 14.23 | Menu item options.

MenuStrip and ToolStripMenuItem properties and an event	Description
MenuStrip *Properties*	
Items	Contains the top-level menu items for this MenuStrip.
RightToLeft	Causes text to display from right to left. This is useful for languages that are read from right to left.
ToolStripMenuItem *Properties*	
Checked	Indicates whether a menu item is *checked*. The default value is False, meaning that the menu item is *unchecked*.
CheckOnClick	Indicates that a menu item should appear checked or unchecked as the item is clicked.
DropDownItems	Lists the submenu items for a particular menu item.

Fig. 14.24 | MenuStrip and ToolStripMenuItem properties and an event. (Part 1 of 2.)

MenuStrip and ToolStripMenuItem properties and an event	Description
ShortcutKey- DisplayString	Specifies text that should appear beside a menu item for a short-cut key. If left blank, the key names are displayed.
ShortcutKeys	Specifies the shortcut keys for the menu item.
ShowShortcutKeys	Indicates whether shortcut keys are shown beside the menu item text. The default is True, which displays the shortcut key.
Text	Specifies the menu item's text. To create an *Alt* access shortcut, precede a character with & (for example, &File to specify a menu named **File** with the letter **F** underlined).
Common ToolStripMenuItem Event	
Click	Generated when an item is clicked or a shortcut key is used to select a menu item.

Fig. 14.24 | MenuStrip and ToolStripMenuItem properties and an event. (Part 2 of 2.)

Using Menus and Menu Items

Class MenuTest (Fig. 14.25) creates a simple menu on a Form. The Form has a top-level **File** menu with menu items **About** (which displays a MessageBox) and **Exit** (which terminates the program). The program also includes a **Format** menu, which contains menu items that change the format of the text on a Label. The **Format** menu has submenus **Color** and **Font**, which change the color and font of the text on a Label.

```vb
1    ' Fig. 14.25: MenuTest.vb
2    ' Using menus to change font colors and styles.
3    Public Class MenuTest
4
5       ' display MessageBox when About menu item is selected
6       Private Sub aboutToolStripMenuItem_Click(
7          sender As Object, e As EventArgs) _
8          Handles aboutToolStripMenuItem.Click
9
10         MessageBox.Show("This is an example" & vbNewLine &
11            "of using menus.", "About", MessageBoxButtons.OK,
12            MessageBoxIcon.Information)
13      End Sub ' aboutToolStripMenuItem_Click
14
15      ' exit program when Exit menu item is selected
16      Private Sub exitToolStripMenuItem_Click(
17         sender As Object, e As EventArgs) _
18         Handles exitToolStripMenuItem.Click
19
20         Application.Exit()
21      End Sub ' exitToolStripMenuItem_Click
22
```

Fig. 14.25 | Menus for changing text font and color. (Part 1 of 4.)

```
23        ' reset checkmarks for Color menu items
24        Private Sub ClearColor()
25           ' clear all checkmarks
26           blackToolStripMenuItem.Checked = False
27           blueToolStripMenuItem.Checked = False
28           redToolStripMenuItem.Checked = False
29           greenToolStripMenuItem.Checked = False
30        End Sub ' ClearColor
31
32        ' update Menu state and color displayLabel black
33        Private Sub blackToolStripMenuItem_Click(
34           sender As Object, e As EventArgs) _
35           Handles blackToolStripMenuItem.Click
36
37           ClearColor() ' reset checkmarks for Color menu items
38           displayLabel.ForeColor = Color.Black ' set Color to Black
39           blackToolStripMenuItem.Checked = True
40        End Sub ' blackToolStripMenuItem_Click
41
42        ' update Menu state and color displayLabel blue
43        Private Sub blueToolStripMenuItem_Click(
44           sender As Object, e As EventArgs) _
45           Handles blueToolStripMenuItem.Click
46
47           ClearColor() ' reset checkmarks for Color menu items
48           displayLabel.ForeColor = Color.Blue ' set Color to Blue
49           blueToolStripMenuItem.Checked = True
50        End Sub ' blueToolStripMenuItem_Click
51
52        ' update Menu state and color displayLabel red
53        Private Sub redToolStripMenuItem_Click(
54           sender As Object, e As EventArgs) _
55           Handles redToolStripMenuItem.Click
56
57           ClearColor() ' reset checkmarks for Color menu items
58           displayLabel.ForeColor = Color.Red ' set Color to Red
59           redToolStripMenuItem.Checked = True
60        End Sub ' redToolStripMenuItem_Click
61
62        ' update Menu state and color displayLabel green
63        Private Sub greenToolStripMenuItem_Click(
64           sender As Object, e As EventArgs) _
65           Handles greenToolStripMenuItem.Click
66
67           ClearColor() ' reset checkmarks for Color menu items
68           displayLabel.ForeColor = Color.Green ' set Color to Green
69           greenToolStripMenuItem.Checked = True
70        End Sub ' greenToolStripMenuItem_Click
71
72        ' reset checkmarks for Font menu items
73        Private Sub ClearFont()
74           timesToolStripMenuItem.Checked = False
75           courierToolStripMenuItem.Checked = False
```

Fig. 14.25 | Menus for changing text font and color. (Part 2 of 4.)

```vbnet
76          comicToolStripMenuItem.Checked = False
77      End Sub ' ClearFont
78
79      ' update Menu state and set Font to Times New Roman
80      Private Sub timesToolStripMenuItem_Click(
81          sender As Object, e As EventArgs) _
82          Handles timesToolStripMenuItem.Click
83
84          ClearFont() ' reset checkmarks for Font menu items
85          timesToolStripMenuItem.Checked = True
86
87          ' set Times New Roman font
88          displayLabel.Font =
89              New Font("Times New Roman", 14, displayLabel.Font.Style)
90      End Sub ' timesToolStripMenuItem_Click
91
92      ' update Menu state and set Font to Courier New
93      Private Sub courierToolStripMenuItem_Click(
94          sender As Object, e As EventArgs) _
95          Handles courierToolStripMenuItem.Click
96
97          ClearFont() ' reset checkmarks for Font menu items
98          courierToolStripMenuItem.Checked = True
99
100         ' set Courier font
101         displayLabel.Font =
102             New Font("Courier New", 14, displayLabel.Font.Style)
103     End Sub ' courierToolStripMenuItem_Click
104
105     ' update Menu state and set Font to Comic Sans MS
106     Private Sub comicToolStripMenuItem_Click(
107         sender As Object, e As EventArgs) _
108         Handles comicToolStripMenuItem.Click
109
110         ClearFont() ' reset checkmarks for Font menu items
111         comicToolStripMenuItem.Checked = True
112
113         ' set Comic Sans MS font
114         displayLabel.Font =
115             New Font("Comic Sans MS", 14, displayLabel.Font.Style)
116     End Sub ' comicToolStripMenuItem_Click
117
118     ' toggle checkmark and toggle bold style
119     Private Sub boldToolStripMenuItem_Click(
120         sender As Object, e As EventArgs) _
121         Handles boldToolStripMenuItem.Click
122         ' toggle menu item checkmark
123         boldToolStripMenuItem.Checked = Not boldToolStripMenuItem.Checked
124
125         ' use Xor to toggle bold, keep all other styles
126         displayLabel.Font = New Font(displayLabel.Font.FontFamily, 14,
127             displayLabel.Font.Style Xor FontStyle.Bold)
128     End Sub ' boldToolStripMenuItem_Click
```

Fig. 14.25 | Menus for changing text font and color. (Part 3 of 4.)

```
129
130      ' toggle checkmark and toggle italic style
131      Private Sub italicToolStripMenuItem_Click(
132         sender As Object, e As EventArgs) _
133         Handles italicToolStripMenuItem.Click
134         ' toggle menu item checkmark
135         italicToolStripMenuItem.Checked =
136            Not italicToolStripMenuItem.Checked
137
138         ' use Xor to toggle italic, keep all other styles
139         displayLabel.Font = New Font(displayLabel.Font.FontFamily, 14,
140            displayLabel.Font.Style Xor FontStyle.Italic)
141      End Sub ' italicToolStripMenuItem_Click
142   End Class ' MenuTest
```

a) Initial app GUI

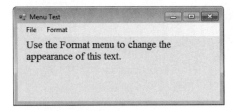

b) **Font** submenu showing **Bold** being slected

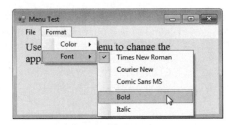

c) GUI after **Bold** was selected in part (b)

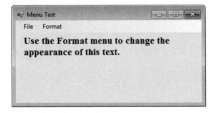

d) Selecting **Red** from **Color** submenu

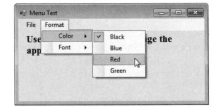

f) **About** dialog displayed by selecting **About** from the **File** menu

e) GUI after **Red** was selected in part (d)

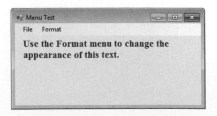

Fig. 14.25 | Menus for changing text font and color. (Part 4 of 4.)

Building the GUI

To create this GUI, drag a Label onto the Form and set its AutoSize property to False, its Font property to Times New Roman 14pt and its Text property to "Use the Format menu to change the appearance of this text." To create the menus, begin by dragging the MenuStrip from the **ToolBox** onto the Form. Then use **Design** mode to create the menu structure shown in the sample outputs. The **File** menu (fileToolStripMenuItem) has menu items **About** (aboutToolStripMenuItem) and **Exit** (exitToolStripMenuItem). The **Format** menu (formatToolStripMenuItem) has two submenus:

- **Color** (colorToolStripMenuItem) contains menu items **Black** (blackToolStrip-MenuItem), **Blue** (blueToolStripMenuItem), **Red** (redToolStripMenuItem) and **Green** (greenToolStripMenuItem). Set the **Black** menu item's Checked property to True, because at the start of the program, the text on the Form is black.

- **Font** (fontToolStripMenuItem) contains menu items **Times New Roman** (times-ToolStripMenuItem), **Courier New** (courierToolStripMenuItem), **Comic Sans MS** (comicToolStripMenuItem), a separator bar (dashToolStripMenuItem), **Bold** (boldToolStripMenuItem) and **Italic** (italicToolStripMenuItem). Set the **Times New Roman** menu item's Checked property to True, because this is the original font for the text on the Form.

Event Handlers for the About and Exit Menu Items

The **About** menu item in the **File** menu displays a MessageBox when clicked (lines 6–13). The **Exit** menu item closes the app through Shared method Exit of class **Application** (line 20). Class Application's Shared methods control program execution. Method Exit causes our app to terminate.

Event Handlers for the Color Submenu's Menu Items

We made the items in the **Color** submenu (**Black**, **Blue**, **Red** and **Green**) mutually exclusive—the user can select only one at a time. To indicate that a menu item is selected, we'll set each **Color** menu item's Checked property to True. This causes a check to appear to the left of a menu item.

Each **Color** menu item has its own Click event handler. The event handler for color **Black** is blackToolStripMenuItem_Click (lines 33–40). Similarly, the event handlers for colors **Blue**, **Red** and **Green** are blueToolStripMenuItem_Click (lines 43–50), redToolStripMenuItem_Click (lines 53–60) and greenToolStripMenuItem_Click (lines 63–70), respectively. To make the **Color** menu items mutually exclusive, each event handler calls method ClearColor (lines 24–30) before setting its corresponding Checked property to True. Method ClearColor sets the Checked property of each color MenuItem to False, effectively preventing more than one menu item from being selected at a time.

Software Engineering Observation 14.2

The mutual exclusion of menu items is not enforced by the MenuStrip. You must program this behavior.

Event Handlers for the Font Submenu's Menu Items

The **Font** menu contains three menu items for fonts (**Times New Roman**, **Courier New** and **Comic Sans MS**) and two menu items for font styles (**Bold** and **Italic**). We added a *separator bar* between the font and font-style menu items to indicate that these are separate options. A Font object can specify multiple styles at once (for example, a font can be both bold and italic). We discuss how to change the Font on the Label momentarily. We set the font menu items to display checks. As with the **Color** menu, we enforce *mutual exclusion* of these items in our event handlers.

The event handlers for menu items **Times New Roman, Courier New** and **Comic Sans MS** are `timesToolStripMenuItem_Click` (lines 80–90), `courierToolStripMenu-Item_Click` (lines 93–103) and `comicToolStripMenuItem_Click` (lines 106–116), respectively. Each event handler clears the `Checked` properties for all the font menu items by calling method `ClearFont` (lines 73–77), then sets to `True` the `Checked` property of the menu item that raised the event. This makes the font menu items mutually exclusive. The event handlers for the **Bold** and **Italic** menu items (lines 119–128 and 131–141) use the `Xor` operator to combine font styles.

*Changing the **Label**'s Font*

To change the font style on a `Label`, set its `Font` property to a new **Font** object (for example, lines 88–89). The `Font` constructor used here takes the font name, font size and font style as arguments. When we change the font in lines 88–89, 101–102 and 114–115, we change only the font name. The second and third arguments to the `Font` constructor use the `Label`'s current font size and current font style.

When we change the the font in lines 126–127 and lines 139–140, we change only the font's style. The style is specified with a member of the **FontStyle enumeration**, which contains `Regular`, `Bold`, `Italic`, `Strikeout` and `Underline`. A Font object's **Style** property is read-only, so it can be set only when the Font object is created.

Styles can be combined via **bitwise operators**—operators that perform manipulations on bits of information. All data is represented in the computer as combinations of 0s and 1s. Each 0 or 1 represents a bit. The `FontStyle` bit values are selected in a way that allows us to combine different `FontStyle` elements to create *compound styles*, using bitwise operators. These styles are *not mutually exclusive*, so we can combine different styles and remove them without affecting the combination of previous `FontStyle` elements. We can combine these various font styles using either the `Or` operator or the `Xor` operator. When the `Or` operator is applied to two bits, if at least one bit of the two has the value 1, then the result is 1. Combining styles using the `Or` operator works as follows. Assume that `Font-Style.Bold` is represented by bits 01 and that `FontStyle.Italic` is represented by bits 10. When we use the `Or` operator to combine the styles, we obtain the bits 11.

```
01  =  Bold
10  =  Italic
--
11  =  Bold and Italic
```

The `Or` operator helps create style combinations. However, what happens if we want to undo a style combination?

The `Xor` operator enables us to *combine styles* and to *undo existing style settings*. When `Xor` is applied to two bits, if both bits have the same value, then the result is 0. If both bits are different, then the result is 1.

Combining styles using `Xor` works as follows. Assume, again, that `FontStyle.Bold` is represented by bits 01 and that `FontStyle.Italic` is represented by bits 10. When we use `Xor` on both styles, we obtain the bits 11.

```
01  =  Bold
10  =  Italic
--
11  =  Bold and Italic
```

Now suppose that we would like to remove the FontStyle.Bold style from the previous combination of FontStyle.Bold and FontStyle.Italic. The easiest way to do so is to reapply the Xor operator to the compound style and FontStyle.Bold.

```
11  =  Bold and Italic
01  =  Bold
--
10  =  Italic
```

The advantages of using bitwise operators to combine FontStyle values become more evident when we consider that there are five different FontStyle values (Bold, Italic, Regular, Strikeout and Underline), resulting in 16 different FontStyle combinations. Using bitwise operators to *combine font styles* greatly reduces the amount of code required to check all possible font combinations.

In Fig. 14.25, we need to set the FontStyle so that the text appears in bold if it was not bold originally, and vice versa. Line 127 uses the Xor operator to do this. If display-Label.Font.Style is bold, then the resulting style is not bold. If the text is originally italic, the resulting style is bold and italic rather than just bold. The same applies for Font-Style.Italic in line 140.

14.10 MonthCalendar Control

Many apps manipulate dates and times. The .NET Framework provides two controls that allow an app to retrieve date and time information—MonthCalendar and DateTimePicker (Section 14.11).

The **MonthCalendar control** (Fig. 14.26) displays a monthly calendar. The user can select a date from the currently displayed month or can use the provided links to navigate to another month. When a date is selected, it's highlighted. *A range of dates can be selected* by clicking one date on the calendar, then holding the *Shift* key while clicking another date. The default event for this control is **DateChanged**, which occurs when a new date is selected. Properties are provided that allow you to modify the appearance of the calendar, how many dates can be selected at once, and the minimum and maximum dates that may be selected. MonthCalendar properties and a common event are summarized in Fig. 14.27.

Fig. 14.26 | MonthCalendar control.

MonthCalendar properties and an event	Description
MonthCalendar Properties	
FirstDayOfWeek	Sets which day of the week is the first displayed for each week.
MaxDate	The last date that can be selected.
MaxSelectionCount	The maximum number of dates that can be selected at once.
MinDate	The first date that can be selected.
MonthlyBoldedDates	An array of dates that will be displayed in bold in the calendar.
SelectionEnd	The last of the dates selected by the user.
SelectionRange	The dates selected by the user.
SelectionStart	The first of the dates selected by the user.
Common MonthCalendar Event	
DateChanged	Generated when a date is selected in the calendar.

Fig. 14.27 | MonthCalendar properties and an event.

14.11 DateTimePicker Control

The **DateTimePicker** control (see output of Fig. 14.29) is similar to the MonthCalendar control, but displays the calendar when the user clicks the control's down arrow. The Date-TimePicker can be used to retrieve date and time information from the user. The **Value** property stores a **DateTime** (namespace **System**), which always contains both date and time information. Visual Basic's **Date** primitive type is actually an alias for type DateTime. You can retrieve the date information alone by using the **Date** property of the DateTime returned by the control's Value property, and the time information alone by using the DateTime's **TimeOfDay** property. By default, this control stores the current date and time.

A DateTimePicker provides more properties than a MonthCalendar to edit the look-and-feel of the drop-down calendar. Property **Format** specifies the user's selection options using the **DateTimePickerFormat** enumeration. The values in this enumeration are Long (displays the date in long format, as in **Thursday, July 10 2008**), Short (displays the date in short format, as in **7/10/2008**), Time (displays a time value, as in **5:31:02 PM**) and Custom (indicates that a custom format will be used). If value Custom is used, the display in the DateTimePicker is specified using property **CustomFormat**. The default event for this control is **ValueChanged**, which occurs when the selected value (whether a date or a time) is changed. DateTimePicker properties and a common event are summarized in Fig. 14.28.

DateTimePicker properties and an event	Description
DateTimePicker Properties	
CalendarForeColor	Sets the text color for the calendar.

Fig. 14.28 | DateTimePicker properties and an event. (Part 1 of 2.)

DateTimePicker properties and an event	Description
CalendarMonth-Background	Sets the calendar's background color.
CustomFormat	Sets the custom format string for the date and/or time.
Format	Sets the format of the date and/or time displayed in the control.
MaxDate	The maximum date and time that can be selected.
MinDate	The minimum date and time that can be selected.
ShowCheckBox	Indicates whether a CheckBox should be displayed to the left of the selected date and time.
ShowUpDown	Used to indicate that the control should have up and down Buttons. This is helpful for instances when the DateTimePicker is used to select a time—the Buttons can be used to increase or decrease hour, minute and second values.
Value	The date and/or time selected by the user.
Common DateTimePicker Event	
ValueChanged	Generated when the Value property changes, including when the user selects a new date or time.

Fig. 14.28 | DateTimePicker properties and an event. (Part 2 of 2.)

Demonstrating a *DateTimePicker*

Figure 14.29 demonstrates using the DateTimePicker control to select an item's drop-off date. Many companies use such functionality. For instance, several online DVD-rental companies specify the day a movie is sent out, and the estimated time that the movie will arrive at your home. In this app, the user selects a drop-off day, and then an estimated arrival date is displayed. The date is always two days after drop off, three days if a Sunday is reached (mail is not delivered on Sunday).

```vb
1   ' Fig. 14.29: DateTimePickerDemo.vb
2   ' Using a DateTimePicker to select a drop off date.
3   Public Class DateTimePickerDemo
4      ' set DateTimePicker's MinDate and MaxDate properties
5      Private Sub DateTimePickerDemo_Load(sender As Object,
6         e As EventArgs) Handles MyBase.Load
7         ' user cannot select days before today
8         dropOffDateTimePicker.MinDate = DateTime.Today
9
10        ' user can select days up to one year from now
11        dropOffDateTimePicker.MaxDate = DateTime.Today.AddYears(1)
12     End Sub ' DateTimePickerDemo_Load
13
```

Fig. 14.29 | Demonstrating DateTimePicker. (Part 1 of 2.)

```
14       ' display delivery date
15     Private Sub dropOffDateTimePicker_ValueChanged(
16         sender As Object, e As EventArgs) _
17         Handles dropOffDateTimePicker.ValueChanged
18
19         Dim dropOffDate As DateTime = dropOffDateTimePicker.Value
20
21         ' add an extra day when items are dropped off Friday-Sunday
22         If dropOffDate.DayOfWeek = DayOfWeek.Friday Or
23             dropOffDate.DayOfWeek = DayOfWeek.Saturday Or
24             dropOffDate.DayOfWeek = DayOfWeek.Sunday Then
25             ' estimate three days for delivery
26             outputLabel.Text = dropOffDate.AddDays(3).ToLongDateString()
27         Else ' otherwise estimate only two days for delivery
28             outputLabel.Text = dropOffDate.AddDays(2).ToLongDateString()
29         End If
30     End Sub ' dropOffDateTimePicker_ValueChanged
31  End Class ' DateTimePickerDemo
```

a) `DateTimePicker` showing current date

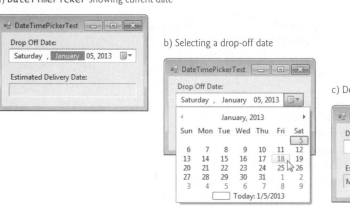

b) Selecting a drop-off date

c) Delivery date based on drop-off date

Fig. 14.29 | Demonstrating `DateTimePicker`. (Part 2 of 2.)

The `DateTimePicker` (`dropOffDateTimePicker`) has its `Format` property set to `Long`, so the user can select a date and not a time in this app. When the user selects a date, the `ValueChanged` event occurs. The event handler for this event (lines 15–30) first retrieves the selected date from the `DateTimePicker`'s `Value` property (line 19). Lines 22–24 use `DateTime`'s **DayOfWeek** property to determine the day of the week on which the selected date falls. The day values are represented using the **DayOfWeek** enumeration. Lines 26 and 28 use `DateTime`'s **AddDays** method to increase the date by three days or two days, respectively. Then a string representing the delivery date is obtained by calling method **ToLongDateString**.

In this app, we do not want the user to be able to select a drop-off day before the current day, or one that's more than a year into the future. To enforce this, we set the `DateTimePicker`'s **MinDate** and **MaxDate** properties when the `Form` is loaded (lines 8 and 11). Days from the current month that are prior to the `MinDate` are not displayed. `DateTime` property Today returns the current day, and method **AddYears** (with an argument of 1) is used to specify a date one year in the future.

Let's take a closer look at the output. This app begins by displaying the current date (Fig. 14.29(a)). In Fig. 14.29(b), we selected the 18th of January as the package drop-off date. In Fig. 14.29(c), the estimated delivery date is displayed as January 21st.

14.12 LinkLabel Control

The **LinkLabel** control displays links to other resources, such as files or web pages. A LinkLabel appears as underlined text (colored blue by default). When the mouse moves over the link, the pointer changes to a hand, just like a hyperlink in a web browser. The link can *change color* to indicate whether the link is new, previously visited or active. When clicked, the LinkLabel generates a **LinkClicked** event. Class LinkLabel is derived from class Label and therefore inherits all of class Label's functionality. Figure 14.30 lists several LinkLabel properties and a common event.

LinkLabel properties and an event	Description
Common Properties	
ActiveLinkColor	Specifies the color of the link when clicked.
LinkArea	Specifies which portion of text in the LinkLabel is part of the link.
LinkBehavior	Specifies the link's behavior, such as how the link appears when the mouse is placed over it.
LinkColor	Specifies the original color of all links before they've been visited. The default color is set by the system, but is usually blue.
LinkVisited	If True, the link appears as though it has been visited (its color is changed to that specified by property VisitedLinkColor). The default value is False.
Text	Specifies the control's text.
UseMnemonic	If True, the & character can be used in the Text property to create a shortcut (similar to the *Alt* shortcut in menus).
VisitedLinkColor	Specifies the color of visited links. The default color is set by the system, but is usually purple.
Common Event (event argument type is LinkLabelLinkClickedEventArgs)	
LinkClicked	Generated when the link is clicked.

Fig. 14.30 | LinkLabel properties and an event.

Class LinkLabelTest (Fig. 14.31) uses three LinkLabels to link to the C: drive, the Deitel website (www.deitel.com) and the Notepad app, respectively. The Text properties of the LinkLabel's cDriveLinkLabel, deitelLinkLabel and notepadLinkLabel describe each link's purpose.

```vb
1  ' Fig. 14.31: LinkLabelTest.vb
2  ' Using LinkLabels to create hyperlinks.
3  Public Class LinkLabelTest
4     ' browse C:\ drive
5     Private Sub cDriveLinkLabel_LinkClicked(sender As Object,
6        e As LinkLabelLinkClickedEventArgs) _
7        Handles cDriveLinkLabel.LinkClicked
8
9        cDriveLinkLabel.LinkVisited = True ' change LinkColor after click
10       Process.Start("C:\")
11    End Sub ' cDriveLinkLabel_LinkClicked
12
13    ' browse www.deitel.com in the default web browser
14    Private Sub deitelLinkLabel_LinkClicked(sender As Object,
15       e As LinkLabelLinkClickedEventArgs) _
16       Handles deitelLinkLabel.LinkClicked
17
18       deitelLinkLabel.LinkVisited = True ' change LinkColor after click
19       Process.Start("http://www.deitel.com")
20    End Sub ' deitelLinkLabel_LinkClicked
21
22    ' run the Notepad app
23    Private Sub notepadLinkLabel_LinkClicked(sender As Object,
24       e As LinkLabelLinkClickedEventArgs) _
25       Handles notepadLinkLabel.LinkClicked
26
27       notepadLinkLabel.LinkVisited = True ' change LinkColor after click
28       Process.Start("notepad")
29    End Sub ' notepadLinkLabel_LinkClicked
30 End Class ' LinkLabelTest
```

a) Click the first **LinkLabel** to look at contents of **C:** drive

 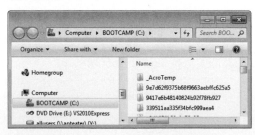

b) Click the second **LinkLabel** to display the Deitel website in your default web browser

Fig. 14.31 | LinkLabels used to link to a drive, a web page and an app. (Part 1 of 2.)

c) Click the third LinkLabel to open Notepad

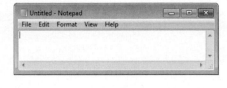

Fig. 14.31 | LinkLabels used to link to a drive, a web page and an app. (Part 2 of 2.)

The event handlers for the LinkLabels call method Start of class Process (namespace System.Diagnostics), which allows you to execute other programs from an app. Method Start can take one argument, the file to open (a String), or two arguments, the app to run and its *command-line arguments* (two Strings). Method Start's arguments can be in the same form as if they were provided for input to the Windows **Run** command (**Start > Run...**). For apps that are known to Windows (such as Notepad), full path names are *not* required, and the .exe extension often can be omitted. To open a file that has a file type that Windows recognizes, simply use the file's full path name. The Windows operating system must be able to use the app associated with the given file's extension to open the file.

The event handler for cDriveLinkLabel's LinkClicked event browses the C: drive (lines 5–11). Line 9 sets the LinkVisited property to True, which changes the link's color from blue to purple (the LinkVisited colors can be configured through the **Properties** window in Visual Studio). The event handler then passes "C:\" to method Start (line 10), which opens a **Windows Explorer** window to show the C: drive's contents.

The event handler for deitelLinkLabel's LinkClicked event (lines 14–20) opens the web page www.deitel.com in the user's default Internet browser. We achieve this by passing the web page address as a String (line 19), which opens the web page.

The event handler for notepadLinkLabel's LinkClicked event (lines 23–29) opens the Notepad app. Line 28 passes the argument "notepad" to method Start, which runs notepad.exe. In line 28, the .exe extension is not required—Windows automatically recognizes the argument given to method Start as an executable file.

14.13 ListBox and CheckedListBox Controls

The ListBox (introduced in Section 4.10) control allows the user to view and *select from multiple items in a list*. The CheckedListBox control extends a ListBox by including CheckBoxes next to each item in the list. This allows users to place checks on multiple items at once, as is possible with CheckBox controls. (Users also can select multiple items from a ListBox by setting the ListBox's **SelectionMode** property, which is discussed shortly.) In both controls, scrollbars appear if the number of items exceeds the ListBox's viewable area.

Figure 14.32 lists common ListBox properties and methods, and a common event. The SelectionMode property determines the number of items that can be selected. This property has the possible values None, One, MultiSimple and MultiExtended (from the

`SelectionMode` enumeration)—the differences among these settings are explained in Fig. 14.32. The `SelectedIndexChanged` event occurs when the user selects a new item.

ListBox properties, methods and an event	Description
Common Properties	
`Items`	The collection of items in the `ListBox`.
`MultiColumn`	Indicates whether the `ListBox` can break a list into multiple columns, which eliminates vertical scrollbars from the display.
`SelectedIndex`	Returns the index of the selected item, or -1 if no items have been selected. If the user selects multiple items, this property returns only one of the selected indices. For this reason, if multiple items are selected, you should use property `SelectedIndices`.
`SelectedIndices`	Returns a collection containing the indices of all selected items.
`SelectedItem`	Returns a reference to one of the selected items.
`SelectedItems`	Returns a collection of the selected item(s).
`SelectionMode`	Determines the number of items that can be selected and the means through which multiple items can be selected. Values `None`, `One`, `MultiSimple` (multiple selection allowed) or `MultiExtended` (multiple selection allowed using a combination of arrow keys or mouse clicks and *Shift* and *Ctrl* keys).
`Sorted`	Indicates whether items are sorted alphabetically. Setting this property's value to `True` sorts the items. The default value is `False`.
Common Methods	
`ClearSelected`	Deselects all items in the `ListBox`.
`GetSelected`	Takes an index as an argument, and returns `True` if the corresponding item is selected.
Common Event	
`SelectedIndexChanged`	Generated when the selected index changes.

Fig. 14.32 | `ListBox` properties, methods and an event.

Both the `ListBox` and `CheckedListBox` have properties `Items`, `SelectedItem` and `SelectedIndex`. Property `Items` returns all the list items as an `ObjectCollection`. Many .NET GUI components (for example, `ListBoxes`) use collections to expose lists of internal objects (for example, items contained within a `ListBox`). Property `SelectedItem` returns the `ListBox`'s currently selected item. If the user can select multiple items, use collection `SelectedItems` to obtain all the selected items as a collection. Property `SelectedIndex` returns the index of the selected item—if there could be more than one, use property `SelectedIndices`. If no items are selected, property `SelectedIndex` returns -1. Method `GetSelected` takes an index and returns `True` if the corresponding item is selected.

Adding Items Programmatically

To add items to a ListBox or to a CheckedListBox, we must add objects to its Items collection. This can be accomplished by calling method Add to add a String to the ListBox's or CheckedListBox's Items collection. For example, we could write

```
myListBox.Items.Add( myListItem )
```

to add String *myListItem* to ListBox *myListBox*. To add multiple objects, you can either call method Add multiple times or call method AddRange to add an array of objects. Classes ListBox and CheckedListBox each call the submitted object's ToString method to determine the text for the corresponding object's entry in the list. This allows you to add non-String objects to a ListBox or a CheckedListBox that later can be returned through properties SelectedItem and SelectedItems.

*Adding Items Via the **String Collection Editor***

Alternatively, you can add items to ListBoxes and CheckedListBoxes visually by examining the Items property in the **Properties** window. Clicking the ellipsis (...) button opens the **String Collection Editor**, which contains a text area for adding items; each item appears on a separate line (Fig. 14.33). The IDE then generates the code to add these Strings to the Items collection.

Fig. 14.33 | String Collection Editor.

CheckedListBox *Control*

The CheckedListBox control derives from class ListBox and includes a CheckBox next to each item. As in ListBoxes, items can be added via methods Add and AddRange or through the **String Collection Editor**. CheckedListBoxes imply that *multiple items can be selected*, and the only possible values for the SelectionMode property are None and One. One allows multiple selection, because CheckBoxes imply that there are no logical restrictions on the items—the user can select as many items as required. Thus, the only choice is whether to give the user multiple selection or no selection at all. This keeps the CheckedListBox's behavior consistent with that of CheckBoxes. Figure 14.34 lists some common properties, a common method and a common event of class CheckedListBox.

Common Programming Error 14.1

*The IDE displays an error message if you attempt to set the SelectionMode property to MultiSimple or MultiExtended in the **Properties** window of a CheckedListBox. If this value is set programmatically, a runtime error occurs.*

CheckedListBox properties, a method and an event	Description
Common Properties	*(All the ListBox properties, the method and the event are inherited by CheckedListBox.)*
CheckedItems	Contains the collection of items that are checked. This is distinct from the selected item, which is highlighted (but not necessarily checked). There can be at most one selected item at any given time.
CheckedIndices	Returns a collection of indices for all checked items.
CheckOnClick	If True, clicking an item selects it and checks/unchecks it. By default this property is False—the user must select an item, then click it again to check or uncheck it.
SelectionMode	Determines how many items can be checked. The only possible values are One (allows *multiple checks* to be placed) or None (does not allow any checks to be placed).
Common Method	
GetItemChecked	Takes an index and returns True if the corresponding item is checked.
Common Event (Event arguments ItemCheckEventArgs)	
ItemCheck	Generated when an item is checked or unchecked.
ItemCheckEventArgs Properties	
CurrentValue	Indicates whether the current item is checked or unchecked. Possible values are Checked, Unchecked and Indeterminate.
Index	Returns the zero-based index of the item that changed.
NewValue	Specifies the new state of the item.

Fig. 14.34 | CheckedListBox properties, a method and an event.

ItemCheck *Event of the* CheckedListBox *Control*

Event **ItemCheck** occurs when a user checks or unchecks a CheckedListBox item. Event argument properties CurrentValue and NewValue return CheckState values for the current and new state of the item, respectively. A comparison of these values allows you to determine whether the CheckedListBox item was *checked* or *unchecked*. The CheckedListBox control inherits the SelectedItems and SelectedIndices properties from class ListBox. It also includes properties CheckedItems and CheckedIndices, which return information about the checked items and indices.

In Fig. 14.35, class CheckedListBoxTest uses a CheckedListBox and a ListBox to display a user's book selections. The CheckedListBox allows the user to select multiple titles. In the **String Collection Editor**, we added items for some Deitel books—C, C++, Java, Internet & WWW, VB 2012, Visual C++, and Visual C# 2012 (the acronym HTP stands for "How to Program"). The ListBox (named displayListBox) displays the user's selections.

```vb
 1    ' Fig. 14.35: CheckedListBoxTest.vb
 2    ' Using the checked ListBox to add items to a display ListBox
 3    Public Class CheckedListBoxTest
 4       ' add an item to or remove an item from displayListBox
 5       Private Sub itemCheckedListBox_ItemCheck(
 6          sender As Object, e As ItemCheckEventArgs) _
 7          Handles itemCheckedListBox.ItemCheck
 8
 9          ' obtain selected item
10          Dim item As String = itemCheckedListBox.SelectedItem.ToString()
11
12          ' if the selected item is checked add it to displayListBox;
13          ' otherwise, remove it from displayListBox
14          If e.NewValue = CheckState.Checked Then
15             displayListBox.Items.Add(item)
16          Else
17             displayListBox.Items.Remove(item)
18          End If
19       End Sub ' itemCheckedListBox_ItemCheck
20    End Class ' CheckedListBoxTest
```

a) Initial GUI displayed when the app executes

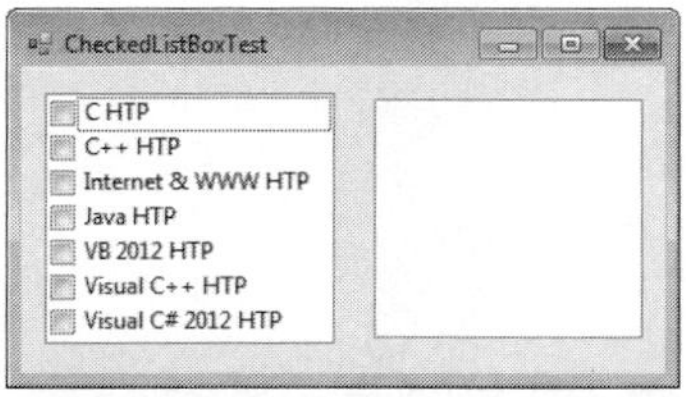

b) GUI after selecting the first three items

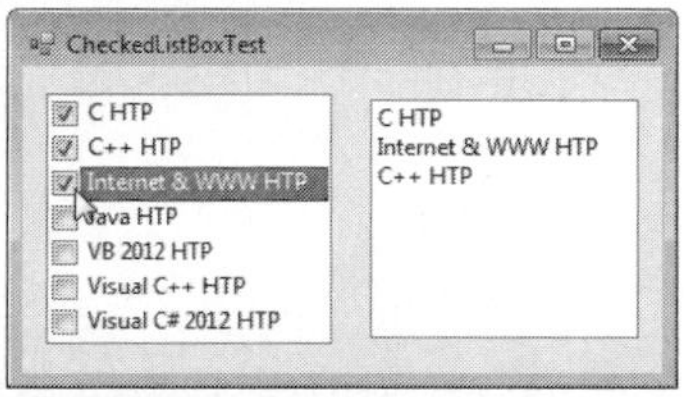

c) GUI after deselecting **C++HTP**

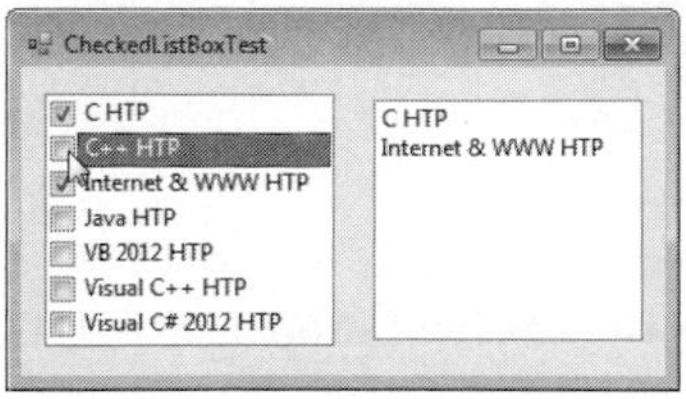

d) GUI after selecting **Visual C# 2012 HTP**

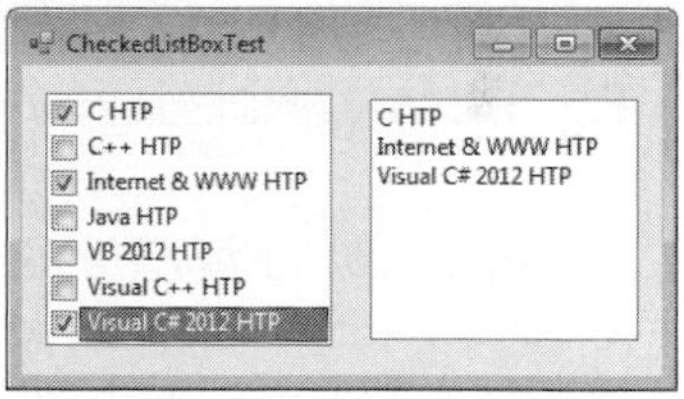

Fig. 14.35 | CheckedListBox and ListBox used in a program to display a user selection.

When the user checks or unchecks an item in itemCheckedListBox, an ItemCheck event occurs and event handler itemCheckedListBox_ItemCheck (lines 5–19) executes. An If...Else statement (lines 14–18) determines whether the user checked or unchecked an item in the CheckedListBox. Line 14 uses the ItemCheckEventArgs property NewValue to determine whether the item is being checked (CheckState.Checked). If the user checks an item, line 15 adds the checked entry to displayListBox. If the user unchecks an item, line 17 removes the corresponding item from displayListBox. This event handler was created by selecting the CheckedListBox in **Design** mode, viewing the control's events in the **Properties** window and double clicking the ItemCheck event.

14.14 Multiple Document Interface (MDI) Windows

So far, we've built only **single document interface** (SDI) apps. Such programs can support only one open window or document at a time. To work with *multiple* documents, the user must execute another instance of the SDI app. Many apps have **multiple document interfaces (MDIs)**, which allow users to work with several documents at once—for example, graphics apps like Corel PaintShop Pro and Adobe Photoshop allow you to edit *multiple* images at once.

Parent and Child Windows

The main app window of an MDI program is called the **parent window**, and each window inside the app is referred to as a **child window**. Although an MDI app can have *many* child windows, there's only one parent window. Furthermore, only *one* child window can be *active* at a time. Child windows cannot be parents themselves and cannot be moved outside their parent. In all other ways (closing, minimizing, resizing, etc.), a child window behaves like any other window. A child window's functionality can be different from the functionality of other child windows of the parent. Figure 14.36 depicts a sample MDI app.

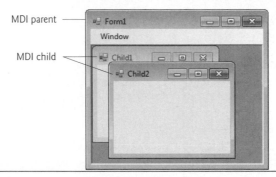

Fig. 14.36 | MDI parent window and MDI child windows.

Specifying that a **Form** is an MDI Container

To create an MDI Form, set the Form's **IsMdiContainer** property to True. The Form changes appearance, as in Fig. 14.37.

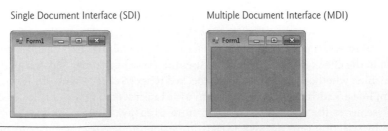

Fig. 14.37 | SDI and MDI forms.

Creating a Class for Child **Forms**

Next, create a child Form class to be added to the Form. To do this, right click the project in the **Solution Explorer**, select **Add > Windows Form…** and name the file. Edit the Form as you like. To add the child Form to the parent, we must create a new child Form object, set its `MdiParent` property to the parent Form and call the child Form's Show method. In general, to add a child Form to a parent, you would write

```
Dim childForm As New ChildFormClass()
childForm.MdiParent = parentForm
childForm.Show()
```

In most cases, the parent Form creates the child, so the *parentForm* reference is Me. The code to create a child usually resides in an event handler, which creates a new window in response to a user action. Menu selections (such as **File > New**) are commonly used to create new child windows.

MDI Container Features

Class Form property `MdiChildren` returns an array of child Form references. This is useful if the parent window wants to check the status of all its children (for example, ensuring that all are saved before the parent closes). Property `ActiveMdiChild` returns a reference to the active child window; it returns Nothing if there are no active child windows. Other features of MDI windows are described in Fig. 14.38.

MDI Form properties, a method and an event	Description
Common MDI Child Properties	
IsMdiChild	Indicates whether a Form is an MDI child. If True, the Form is an MDI child (read-only property).
MdiParent	Specifies the MDI parent Form of the child.
Common MDI Parent Properties	
ActiveMdiChild	Returns the Form that's the currently active MDI child (returns Nothing if no children are active).
IsMdiContainer	Indicates whether a Form can be an MDI parent. If True, the Form can be an MDI parent. The default value is False.
MdiChildren	Returns the MDI children as an array of Forms.
Common Method	
LayoutMdi	Arranges child forms in an MDI parent Form. The method takes as a parameter an MdiLayout enumeration constant (ArrangeIcons, Cascade, TileHorizontal or TileVertical). Figure 14.41 depicts the effects of these values.
Common Event	
MdiChildActivate	Generated when an MDI child is closed or activated.

Fig. 14.38 | MDI Form properties, a method and an event.

Manipulating Child Windows

Child windows can be minimized, maximized and closed independent of the parent window. Figure 14.39 shows two images—one containing two minimized child windows and a second containing a maximized child window. When the parent is minimized or closed, the child windows are minimized or closed as well. The title bar in Fig. 14.39(b) is **Form1 - [Child]**. When a child window is maximized, its title bar text is inserted into the parent window's title bar. When a child window is minimized or maximized, its title bar displays a *restore icon*, which can be used to return the child window to its previous size (that is, its size before it was minimized or maximized).

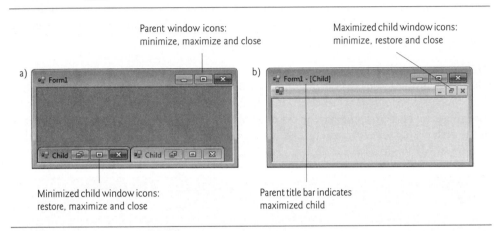

Fig. 14.39 | Minimized and maximized child windows.

Tracking Child Windows in Menus

Class `MenuStrip` provides property `MdiWindowListItem` to track which child windows are open in an MDI container. The property specifies which menu, if any, displays a list of open child windows. When a new child window is opened, an entry is added to the list (as in the first screen of Figure 14.40). If more than nine child windows are open, the list includes the option **More Windows...**, which allows the user to select a window from a list in a dialog.

> ### Good Programming Practice 14.1
>
> *When creating MDI apps, include a menu that displays a list of the open child windows. This helps the user select a child window quickly, rather than having to search for it in the parent window.*

Arranging Child Windows

MDI containers allow you to organize child windows by calling method `LayoutMdi` of the parent `Form`. Method `LayoutMdi` receives as its argument one of the `MdiLayout` enumeration constants—`ArrangeIcons`, `Cascade`, `TileHorizontal` and `TileVertical`. Tiled windows completely fill the parent and do *not* overlap; such windows can be arranged horizontally (value `TileHorizontal`) or vertically (value `TileVertical`). Cascaded windows (value `Cascade`) overlap—each is the same size and displays a *visible title bar*, if possible. Value `ArrangeIcons` arranges the icons for any minimized child windows. If minimized windows are scattered around the parent window, value `ArrangeIcons` orders them neatly at the bottom-left corner of the parent window. Figure 14.41 illustrates the values of the `MdiLayout` enumeration.

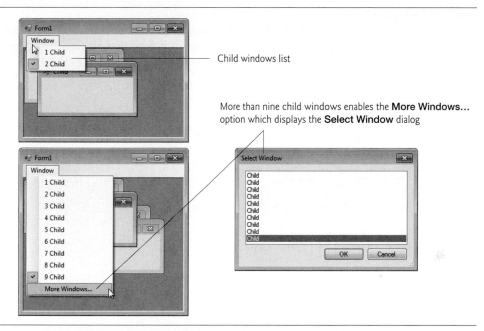

Fig. 14.40 | MenuStrip property MdiWindowListItem example.

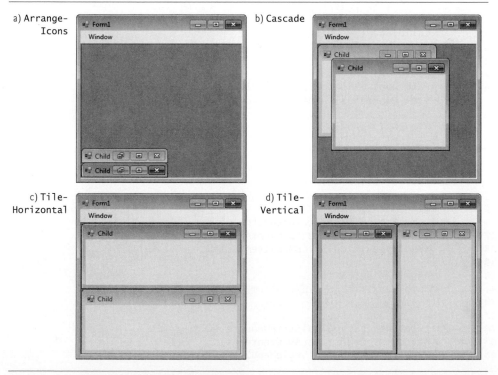

Fig. 14.41 | MdiLayout enumeration values.

Demonstrating an MDI

Class UsingMDI (Fig. 14.42) demonstrates MDI windows. It creates instances of child ChildForm (Fig. 14.43), each containing a PictureBox that displays an image. The parent MDI Form contains menus that enable users to create and arrange child Forms.

```vb
1   ' Fig. 14.42: UsingMDI.vb
2   ' MDI parent and child windows.
3   Public Class UsingMDI
4      ' create Lavender Flowers image window
5      Private Sub lavenderToolStripMenuItem_Click(sender As Object,
6         e As EventArgs) Handles lavenderToolStripMenuItem.Click
7         ' create new child
8         Dim child As New ChildForm("Lavender Flowers",
9            "lavenderflowers")
10        child.MdiParent = Me ' set parent
11        child.Show() ' display child
12     End Sub ' lavenderToolStripMenuItem_Click
13
14     ' create Purple Flowers image window
15     Private Sub purpleToolStripMenuItem_Click(
16        sender As Object, e As EventArgs) _
17        Handles purpleToolStripMenuItem.Click
18        ' create new child
19        Dim child As New ChildForm("Purple Flowers",
20           "purpleflowers")
21        child.MdiParent = Me ' set parent
22        child.Show() ' display child
23     End Sub ' purpleToolStripMenuItem_Click
24
25     ' create Yellow Flowers image window
26     Private Sub yellowToolStripMenuItem_Click(sender As Object,
27        e As EventArgs) Handles yellowToolStripMenuItem.Click
28        ' create new child
29        Dim child As New ChildForm("Yellow Flowers",
30           "yellowflowers")
31        child.MdiParent = Me ' set parent
32        child.Show() ' display child
33     End Sub ' yellowToolStripMenuItem_Click
34
35     ' exit app
36     Private Sub exitToolStripMenuItem_Click(
37        sender As Object, e As EventArgs) _
38        Handles exitToolStripMenuItem.Click
39
40        Application.Exit()
41     End Sub ' exitToolStripMenuItem_Click
42
43     ' set Cascade layout
44     Private Sub cascadeToolStripMenuItem_Click(
45        sender As Object, e As EventArgs) _
46        Handles cascadeToolStripMenuItem.Click
```

Fig. 14.42 | MDI parent-window class. (Part 1 of 2.)

```
47
48          Me.LayoutMdi(MdiLayout.Cascade)
49       End Sub ' cascadeToolStripMenuItem_Click
50
51       ' set TileHorizontal layout
52       Private Sub tileHorizontalToolStripMenuItem_Click(
53          sender As Object, e As EventArgs) _
54          Handles tileHorizontalToolStripMenuItem.Click
55
56          Me.LayoutMdi(MdiLayout.TileHorizontal)
57       End Sub ' tileHorizontalToolStripMenuItem_Click
58
59       ' set TileVertical layout
60       Private Sub tileVerticalToolStripMenuItem_Click(
61          sender As Object, e As EventArgs) _
62          Handles tileVerticalToolStripMenuItem.Click
63
64          Me.LayoutMdi(MdiLayout.TileVertical)
65       End Sub ' tileVerticalToolStripMenuItem_Click
66    End Class ' UsingMDI
```

a) Selecting a menu item that displays a child window

b) Child window displayed

c) Cascading child windows

d) Child windows cascaded

Fig. 14.42 | MDI parent-window class. (Part 2 of 2.)

UsingMDI

Class UsingMDI (Fig. 14.42) is the app's MDI parent Form. This Form is created first and contains two top-level menus. The **File** menu (fileToolStripMenuItem) contains both an **Exit** item (exitToolStripMenuItem) and a **New** submenu (newToolStripMenuItem) consisting of items for each child window. The **Window** menu (windowToolStripMenuItem), provides options for laying out the MDI children, plus a list of the active MDI children.

In the **Properties** window, we set the Form's IsMdiContainer property to True, making the Form an MDI parent. In addition, we set the MenuStrip's MdiWindowListItem property to windowToolStripMenuItem so that the **Window** menu can list the open MDI child windows.

The **Cascade** menu item's (cascadeToolStripMenuItem) event handler (lines 44–49) cascades the child windows by calling the parent Form's LayoutMdi method with the argument MdiLayout.Cascade (line 48). The **Tile Horizontal** menu item's (tileHorizontal-ToolStripMenuItem) event handler (lines 52–57) arranges the child windows horizontally by calling the parent Form's LayoutMdi method with the argument MdiLayout.TileHorizontal (line 56). Finally, the **Tile Vertical** menu item's (tileVerticalToolStripMenuItem) event handler (lines 60–65) arranges the child windows vertically by calling the parent Form's LayoutMdi method with the argument MdiLayout.TileVertical (line 64).

ChildForm

At this point, the app is still incomplete—we must define the *MDI child class*. To do this, right click the project in the **Solution Explorer** and select **Add > Windows Form…**. Name the new class in the dialog as ChildForm (Fig. 14.43). Next, add a PictureBox (displayPictureBox) to ChildForm. When you provide a constructor in a Form class, the first statement in its body *must* be a call to the base class's InitializeComponent method to ensure that the *Form* is constructed properly. In the constructor, line 7 sets the title bar text. In lines 10–14, we retrieve the appropriate image file (fileName) as a resource, convert it to an Image, and set displayPictureBox's Image property.

```vb
 1   ' Fig. 14.43: ChildForm.vb
 2   ' Child window of MDI parent.
 3   Public Class ChildForm
 4      Public Sub New(title As String, fileName As String)
 5         ' ensure that Designer generated code executes
 6         InitializeComponent()
 7         Text = title ' set title text
 8
 9         ' retrieve specific image from resources
10         Dim pictureResource = My.Resources.ResourceManager.GetObject(
11            fileName)
12
13         ' convert pictureResource to image type and load into PictureBox
14         displayPictureBox.Image = CType(pictureResource, Image)
15      End Sub ' New
16   End Class ' ChildForm
```

Fig. 14.43 | MDI child ChildForm.

The parent MDI Form (Fig. 14.42) creates new child windows using class ChildForm. The event handlers in lines 5–33 of Fig. 14.42 create a new child Form corresponding to the menu item clicked. Lines 8–9, 19–20 and 29–30 create new instances of ChildForm. Lines 10, 21 and 31 set each child's MdiParent property to the parent Form (Me). Lines 11, 22 and 32 call method Show to display each ChildForm.

14.15 Visual Inheritance

Chapter 10 discussed how to create classes by *inheriting* from other classes. In fact, you've used inheritance in every app so far, because every new Form class you create inherits from class Form. The code that indicates the inheritance relationship appears in the Form's Designer.vb file.

Inheriting from class Form is an example of visual inheritance. The derived Form class contains the functionality of its Form base class, including any base-class properties, methods, variables and controls. The derived class also inherits all visual aspects—such as size, component layout, spacing between GUI components, colors and fonts—from its base class.

Visual inheritance enables you to achieve *visual consistency* across your apps by giving them a *common look-and-feel* and makes it easier for users to move between apps. For example, you could define a base Form that contains a product's logo, a specific background color, a predefined menu bar and other elements. You then could use the base Form throughout an app for uniformity and branding.

Class *VisualInheritanceForm*

Class VisualInheritanceForm (Fig. 14.44) derives from Form. Its GUI contains two Labels with the text **Bugs, Bugs, Bugs** and **Copyright 2014 by Deitel & Associates, Inc.**, as well as one Button displaying the text **Learn More**. When a user presses the **Learn More** Button, the event handler learnMoreButton_Click (lines 5–12) displays a MessageBox that provides some informative text.

```
1    ' Fig. 14.44: VisualInheritanceForm.vb
2    ' Base Form for use with visual inheritance.
3    Public Class VisualInheritanceForm
4       ' display MessageBox when Button is clicked
5       Private Sub learnMoreButton_Click(sender As Object,
6          e As EventArgs) Handles learnMoreButton.Click
7
8          MessageBox.Show(
9             "Bugs, Bugs, Bugs is a product of Deitel & Associates, Inc.",
10            "Learn More", MessageBoxButtons.OK,
11            MessageBoxIcon.Information)
12      End Sub ' learnMoreButton_Click
13   End Class ' VisualInheritanceForm
```

Fig. 14.44 | Class VisualInheritanceForm, which inherits from class Form, contains a Button **(Learn More)**. (Part 1 of 2.)

Fig. 14.44 | Class `VisualInheritanceForm`, which inherits from class `Form`, contains a `Button` (**Learn More**). (Part 2 of 2.)

Packaging Class VisualInheritanceForm for Reuse

To allow other `Form`s to inherit from `VisualInheritanceForm`, we package it as a class library in a `.dll` file. To do so, right click the project name in the **Solution Explorer** and select **Properties**, then choose the **Application** tab. In the **Application type** drop-down list, change **Windows Forms Application** to **Class Library**. Building the project produces the `.dll`. The name of the solution that contains `VisualInheritanceForm` becomes parts of the class's *fully qualified name*—in this case, `VisualInheritance.VisualInheritance-Form`. [*Note:* A class library cannot be executed as a standalone app. The screenshots in Fig. 14.44 were taken before changing the project to be a class library.]

Visually Inheriting from Class VisualInheritanceForm

To visually inherit from `VisualInheritanceForm`, first create a new Windows Forms app named `VisualInheritanceTest` and name its `.vb` file `VisualInheritanceTest.vb`. Before you can use class `VisualInheritanceForm` in another project, you must reference its `.dll` file (also known as an assembly). This is known as adding a reference. To do so:

1. Select **Project > Add Reference…**.

2. In the **Add Reference** dialog, click **Browse…** then locate and select the `Visual-InheritanceForm.dll` file (located in the `bin\Debug` directory of the `VisualInheritance` project we created in Fig. 14.44.

3. Click **OK** to add the reference to the project.

Next, click the **Show All Files** icon (📄) in the **Solution Explorer** and expand node for `VisualInheritanceTest.vb`. Open the `VisualInheritanceTest.Designer.vb` file and modify the line

    Inherits `System.Windows.Forms.Form`

to indicate that the app's `Form` should inherit from class `VisualInheritanceForm` instead. The `Inherits` line in the `Designer.vb` file should now appear as follows:

    Inherits `VisualInheritance.VisualInheritanceForm`

You must either specify `VisualInheritanceForm`'s *fully qualified name* or use an `Imports` declaration to indicate that the new app uses classes from the namespace `VisualInheritance`. In **Design** view, the new app's `Form` now displays the inherited controls of the base class VisualInheritanceForm (as shown in Fig. 14.45). You can now add more components to the Form.

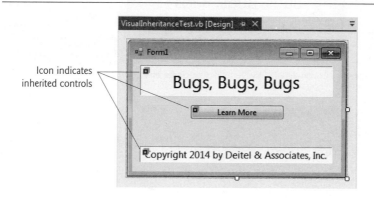

Fig. 14.45 | Form demonstrating visual inheritance.

Class *VisualInheritanceTest*

Class VisualInheritanceTest (Fig. 14.46) derives from VisualInheritanceForm (Fig. 14.44). The GUI contains the components inherited from VisualInheritanceForm and a new Button with the text **About this Program**. When the user presses this Button, the event handler aboutButton_Click (Fig. 14.46, lines 5–12) displays another MessageBox providing different informative text.

Figure 14.46 demonstrates that the components, their layouts and the functionality of base-class VisualInheritanceForm (Fig. 14.44) are inherited by VisualInheritance-Test. If a user clicks the button **Learn More**, the base class event handler learnMore-Button_Click displays a MessageBox. The derived class VisualInheritanceTest cannot modify the inherited controls—this is indicated with a lock icon on each inherited control in **Design** view.

```
1   ' Fig. 14.46: VisualInheritanceTest.vb
2   ' Derived Form using visual inheritance.
3   Public Class VisualInheritanceTest
4      ' display MessageBox when Button is clicked
5      Private Sub aboutButton_Click(sender As Object,
6         e As EventArgs) Handles aboutButton.Click
7
8         MessageBox.Show(
9            "This program was created by Deitel & Associates",
10            "About this Program", MessageBoxButtons.OK,
11            MessageBoxIcon.Information)
12      End Sub ' aboutButton_Click
13   End Class ' VisualInheritanceTest
```

Fig. 14.46 | Class VisualInheritanceTest, which inherits from class VisualInheritanceForm, contains an additional Button. (Part 1 of 2.)

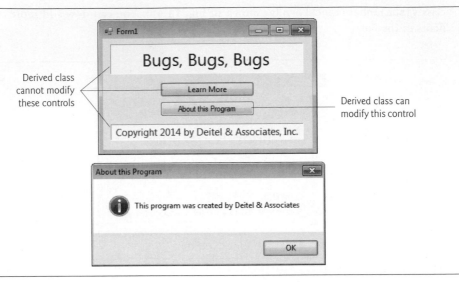

Derived class cannot modify these controls

Derived class can modify this control

Fig. 14.46 | Class `VisualInheritanceTest`, which inherits from class `VisualInheritanceForm`, contains an additional `Button`. (Part 2 of 2.)

14.16 Animation with the Timer Component

A `Timer` component generates `Tick` events at fixed time intervals. The interval is specified in the `Timer`'s `Interval` property, which defines the number of milliseconds (thousandths of a second) between events. By default, timers are disabled and do not generate events. To allow a `Timer` to generate events, set its `Enabled` property to `True`. The app in Fig. 14.47 animates a series of images by displaying a new image every 50 milliseconds. There are 30 images in the animation (included with this chapter's examples). The images were added to the project as resources that are named "`deitel`" followed by a number in the range 0–29 indicating the order in which the images are displayed.

```
 1   ' Fig. 14.47: AnimationDemo.vb
 2   ' Animating images with a Timer component.
 3   Public Class AnimationDemo
 4      Private currentImage As Integer = 0' current image number
 5      Private Const TOTAL_IMAGES = 30 ' total number of images
 6
 7      ' display next image
 8      Private Sub animationTimer_Tick(sender As Object,
 9         e As EventArgs) Handles animationTimer.Tick
10
11         ' get the resource representing the image
12         Dim pictureResource =
13            My.Resources.ResourceManager.GetObject("deitel" & currentImage)
14
15         ' convert pictureResource to type Image and load into PictureBox
16         logoPictureBox.Image = CType(pictureResource, Image)
```

Fig. 14.47 | Animating images with a `Timer` component. (Part 1 of 2.)

```
17
18          ' increment currentImage
19          currentImage = (currentImage + 1) Mod TOTAL_IMAGES
20      End Sub ' animationTimer_Tick
21  End Class ' AnimationDemo
```

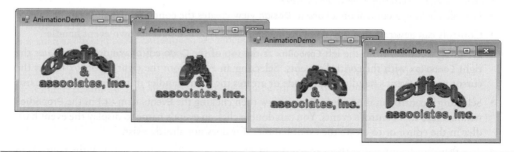

Fig. 14.47 | Animating images with a `Timer` component. (Part 2 of 2.)

Line 4 declares variable `currentImage` to represent the index of the image that will be displayed next. Line 5 declares the constant `TOTAL_IMAGES` to represent the total number of images in the animation. When the `Timer`'s `Tick` event occurs, the event handler (lines 8–20) gets the resource for the current image (lines 12–13), changes the `logoPictureBox`'s `Image` property to the new `Image` (line 16) and increments `currentImage` (line 19). When `currentImage` reaches 29, line 19 resets `currentImage` to 0 so the animation continues with the first image.

14.17 Wrap-Up

This chapter introduced additional Windows Forms GUI controls. We discussed how to create event handlers from the code editor window and the **Properties** window. You learned how to use a control's properties and Visual Studio to specify the layout of your GUI. We used `Panel`s to organize other controls. We displayed helpful text on a GUI with `ToolTip` components, and demonstrated how to handle mouse and keyboard events. We presented more detail on creating menus. You learned the `DateTimePicker` and `Month-Calendar` controls, which allow users to input date and time values quickly while minimizing input errors. We used `LinkLabel`s to open applicatons and web pages when the user clicked a hyperlink. We introduced `CheckedListBox`es for presenting lists items that can be checked or unchecked. We then introduced multiple document interfaces. The chapter concluded with demonstrations of visual inheritance and controlling an animaton with a `Timer` Control. Chapter 15 introduces graphics capabilities for drawing on an app, and multimedia capabilities for playing audio and video in apps.

Summary

Section 14.2 Controls and Components
- The difference between a control and a component is that a component is not visual at execution time. When you drag a component onto the `Form` in **Design** view, the component is placed in the component tray below the `Form`.

- `DateTimePicker` property `Format` specifies the user's selection options by using constants from the `DateTimePickerFormat` enumeration.
- The `DateTimePicker`'s `ValueChanged` event occurs when the selected value changes.

Section 14.12 LinkLabel Control
- The `LinkLabel` control displays links to other resources, such as files or web pages.
- A `LinkLabel` appears as underlined text (colored blue by default). When the mouse moves over the link, the pointer changes to a hand—similar to a hyperlink in a web page.
- The link can change color to indicate whether the link is new, previously visited or active.
- When clicked, the `LinkLabel` generates a `LinkClicked` event.

Section 14.13 ListBox and CheckedListBox Controls
- `ListBox` property `SelectionMode` determines the number of items that can be selected.
- The `SelectedIndexChanged` event of class `ListBox` occurs when the user selects a new item.
- Property `Items` returns all the list items as a collection.
- Property `SelectedItem` returns the currently selected item.
- To add items to a `ListBox`, add objects to its `Items` collection. Call method `Add` to add an object to the `ListBox`'s `Items` collection.
- You can add items to `ListBox`es and `CheckedListBox`es visually by examining the `Items` property in the **Properties** window.
- The `CheckedListBox` control extends a `ListBox` by including `CheckBox`es next to each item.
- Items can be added to a `CheckedListBox` control via methods `Add` and `AddRange` or through the **String Collection Editor**.
- `CheckedListBox`es imply that multiple items can be selected.
- An `ItemCheck` event occurs whenever a user checks or unchecks a `CheckedListBox` item.

Section 14.14 Multiple Document Interface (MDI) Windows
- Multiple document interface (MDI) programs enable users to edit multiple documents at once.
- The app window of an MDI program is called the parent window, and each window inside the app is referred to as a child window.
- Child windows cannot be parents themselves and cannot be moved outside their parent.
- To create an MDI `Form`, create a new `Form` and set its `IsMdiContainer` property to `True`.
- To add a child `Form` to the parent, create a new child `Form` object, set its `MdiParent` property to the parent `Form` and call the child `Form`'s `Show` method.
- Child windows can be minimized, maximized and closed inside the parent window.
- Property `MdiWindowListItem` of class `MenuStrip` specifies which menu, if any, displays a list of open child windows.
- The child windows in an MDI app can be arranged by calling method `LayoutMdi` of the parent `Form`.

Section 14.15 Visual Inheritance
- Visual inheritance allows you to create a new `Form` by inheriting from an existing `Form`. The derived `Form` class contains the functionality of its base class.
- Visual inheritance enables you to achieve visual consistency across apps by reusing code.

Section 14.16 Animation with the **Timer** Component

- A Timer component generates Tick events at set intervals specified by the Timer's Interval property, which defines the number of milliseconds (thousandths of a second) between events.

- A Timer's Enabled property must be set to True before the Timer will generate events.

Terminology

access shortcut 550
active window 534
ActiveMdiChild property of class Form 571
AddDays method of DateTime 562
AddYears method of DateTime 563
anchor a control 538
Application class 557
bitwise operator 558
cascaded windows 572
Checked property of class
    ToolStripMenuItem 557
CheckedListBox class 565
child window in an MDI Form 570
Color 546
Control class 537
Controls property of class GroupBox 541
CreateGraphics method of class Form 546
CustomFormat property of class
    DateTimePicker 560
Date property of type DateTime 560
DateChanged event of class MonthCalendar 559
DateTime 560
DateTimePicker control 560
DateTimePickerFormat enumeration 560
DayOfWeek enumeration 562
DayOfWeek property of DateTime 562
default event of a control 535
dock a control 538
Enabled property of class Control 538
Exit method of class Application 557
FillEllipse method of class Graphics 546
Font class 558
FontStyle enumeration 558
Format property of class DateTimePicker 560
GetSelected method of class ListBox 566
Graphics class 546
hotkey 550
Interval property of class Timer 580
IsMdiContainer property of class Form 570
ItemCheck event of class CheckedListBox 568
Items property of class ListBox 566
key code 550
key event 547

KeyChar property of class
    KeyPressEventArgs 547
KeyDown event of class Control 547
KeyEventArgs class 547
KeyPress event of class Control 547
KeyPressEventArgs class 547
Keys enumeration 547
KeyUp event of class Control 547
LayoutMdi method of class Form 572
LinkClicked event of a LinkLabel 563
LinkLabel class 563
MaxDate property of class DateTimePicker 562
MdiChildren property of class Form 571
MdiLayout enumeration 572
MdiParent property of class Form 571
MdiWindowListItem property of class
    MenuStrip 572
MinDate property of class DateTimePicker 562
modifier key 547
MonthCalendar class 559
mouse click 544
mouse event 544
mouse move 544
mouse press 544
MouseEventArgs class 544
multiple document interface (MDI) 570
ObjectCollection class 566
Padding property of class Form 539
Panel control 540
parent menu 550
parent window in an MDI Form 570
Process class 565
SelectedIndex property of class ListBox 566
SelectedIndexChanged event of class
    ListBox 566
SelectedIndices property of class ListBox 566
SelectedItem property of class ListBox 566
SelectedItems property of class ListBox 566
SelectionMode enumeration 566
SelectionMode property of class ListBox 565
separator bar in a menu 552
ShortcutKeyDisplayString property of class
    ToolStripMenuItem 550

ShortcutKeys property of class
    ToolStripMenuItem 550
ShowShortcutKeys property of class
    ToolStripMenuItem 550
single document interface (SDI) 569
SolidBrush class 546
Start method of class Process 565
Style property of class Font 558
submenu 550
System.Diagnostics namespace 565
TabIndex property of class Control 537

TabStop property of class Control 537
Tick event of class Timer 580
tiled windows 572
TimeOfDay property of type DateTime 560
Timer component 580
ToLongDateString method of DateTime 562
ToolTip component 542
Value property of class DateTimePicker 560
ValueChanged event of class
    DateTimePicker 560
visual inheritance 577

Self-Review Exercises

14.1 State whether each of the following is *true* or *false*. If *false*, explain why.
    a) The KeyData property includes data about modifier keys.
    b) A Form is a container.
    c) All mouse events use the same event arguments class.
    d) A control's tool tip text is set with the ToolTip property of class Control.
    e) Menus organize groups of related classes.
    f) Menu items can display ComboBoxes, checkmarks and access shortcuts.
    g) The ListBox control allows only a single selection (like a RadioButton).
    h) An MDI child window can have MDI children.
    i) MDI child windows can be moved outside the boundaries of their parent window.

14.2 Fill in the blanks in each of the following statements:
    a) The active control is said to have the _____.
    b) The Form acts as a(n) _____ for the controls that are added.
    c) Class _____ and class _____ help arrange controls on a GUI and provide logical groups for radio buttons.
    d) Typical mouse events include _____, _____ and _____.
    e) _____ events are generated when a key on the keyboard is pressed or released.
    f) The modifier keys we discussed in this chapter are _____, _____ and _____.
    g) Method _____ of class Process can open files and web pages.
    h) The _____ property of class MenuStrip allows a menu to display a list of child windows.
    i) The _____ window layout option makes all MDI windows the same size and layers them so that every title bar is visible (if possible).
    j) _____ are typically used to display hyperlinks to other resources, files or web pages.

Answers To Self-Review Exercises

14.1 a) True. b) True. c) False. Some mouse events use EventArgs, others use MouseEventArgs. d) False. A control's tool tip text is set using a ToolTip component that must be added to the app. e) False. Menus organize groups of related commands. f) True. g) False. The ListBox control allows single or multiple selection. h) False. Only an MDI parent window can have MDI children. An MDI parent window cannot be an MDI child. i) False. MDI child windows cannot be moved outside their parent window.

14.2 a) focus. b) container. c) GroupBox, Panel. d) mouse clicks, mouse presses, mouse moves. e) Key. f) *Shift, Ctrl, Alt.* g) Start. h) MdiWindowListItem. i) Cascade. j) LinkLabels.

Exercises

14.3 *(Enhanced Drawing App)* Extend the program of Fig. 14.18 to include options for changing the size and color of the circles drawn. Create a GUI similar to Fig. 14.48. The user should be able to draw on the app's Panel. To retrieve a Graphics object for drawing, call method *panelName*.CreateGraphics(), substituting in the name of your Panel. Remember to call the Graphics object's Dispose method when the object is no longer needed.

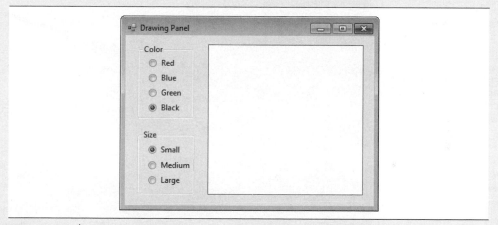

Fig. 14.48 | Drawing Panel GUI.

14.4 *(Guess the Number)* Write a program that plays "guess the number" as follows: Your program chooses the number to be guessed by selecting an Integer at random in the range 1–1000. The program then displays the following text in a label:

```
I have a number between 1 and 1000--can you guess my number?
Please enter your first guess.
```

A TextBox should be used to input the guess. As each guess is input, the background color should change to red or blue. Red indicates that the user is getting "warmer," blue that the user is getting "colder." A Label should display either "Too High" or "Too Low," to help the user zero in on the correct answer. When the user guesses the correct answer, display "Correct!" in a message box, change the Form's background color to green and disable the TextBox. Recall that a TextBox (like other controls) can be disabled by setting the control's Enabled property to False. Provide a Button that allows the user to play the game again. When the Button is clicked, generate a new random number, change the background to the default color and enable the TextBox.

14.5 *(MDI Text Editor)* Create an MDI text editor. Each child window should contain a multiline TextBox. The MDI parent should have a **Format** menu with submenus to control the size, font and color of the text in the active child window. Each submenu should have at least three options. In addition, the parent should have a **File** menu with menu items **New** (create a new child), **Close** (close the active child) and **Exit** (exit the app). The parent should have a **Window** menu to display a list of the open child windows and their layout options.

14.6 *(Enhanced Drawing App)* Modify your solution to Exercise 14.3 so that it's an MDI app with child windows in which the user can draw. Add menus to the MDI app that allow the user to modify the size and color of the paint brush. When running this app, be aware that a child window will be cleared if one of the windows overlaps another.

15

Graphics and Multimedia

One picture is worth ten thousand words.
—Chinese proverb

Nothing ever becomes real till it is experienced—even a proverb is no proverb to you till your life has illustrated it.
—John Keats

A picture shows me at a glance what it takes dozens of pages of a book to expound.
—Ivan Sergeyevich Turgenev

Objectives

In this chapter you will learn:

- To use graphics contexts and graphics objects.

- To manipulate colors and fonts.

- To understand and use GDI+ `Graphics` methods to draw lines, rectangles, `String`s and images.

- To use class `Image` to manipulate and display images.

- To draw complex shapes from simple shapes with class `GraphicsPath`.

- To use Windows Media Player to play audio and video.

- To print graphics to a printer.

15.1 Introduction

In the previous chapter, you learned more about Windows Forms GUI controls and we presented a simple animation of a spinning logo. In this chapter, we overview the traditional capabilities for incorporating graphics and multimedia into Windows Forms apps. You'll learn techniques for drawing two-dimensional shapes and for controlling colors and fonts. The drawing capabilities are part of namespace System.Drawing and the other namespaces that make up the .NET GDI+. GDI+ is an application programming interface (API) that provides classes for creating two-dimensional graphics, and manipulating fonts and images.

We start with basic drawing capabilities, then present more powerful features, such as changing the styles of the lines used to draw shapes and controlling the colors and patterns of filled shapes. Next, we explore techniques for manipulating images. Then, you'll learn how to add the Windows Media Player control to the **Toolbox** and use it to play audios and videos. The chapter concludes with an introduction to printing in which we demonstrate how to display a print preview and how to print directly to your computer's printer.

We also provide four online chapters that present Microsoft's other approaches to GUI, graphics, animation and multimedia—Windows 8 UI and Windows Presentation Foundation (WPF):

- Windows 8 UI and XAML
- Windows 8 Graphics and Multimedia
- Windows Presentation Foundation (WPF) GUI
- WPF Graphics and Multimedia

15.2 Drawing Classes and the Coordinate System

Namespaces System.Drawing and **System.Drawing.Drawing2D** contain the most commonly used GDI+ components. Class **Graphics** contains methods used for drawing Strings, lines, rectangles and other shapes. The drawing methods of class Graphics usually require a **Pen** or **Brush** object to render a specified shape. The Pen draws shape outlines; the Brush draws solid objects.

Colors and Fonts

The **Color** structure contains numerous **Shared** properties that represent the colors of various graphical components, plus methods that allow users to create new colors. A structure is like a class in that it can have attributes and behaviors, but it's a *value type* rather than a *reference type*. Class **Font** contains properties that define the characteristics of fonts. Class **FontFamily** contains methods for obtaining font information.

Coordinate System

Let's consider GDI+'s **coordinate system** (Fig. 15.1), a scheme for identifying every point on the screen. The *upper-left corner* of a GUI component (such as a **Panel** or a **Form**) has the coordinates (0, 0). A coordinate pair has both an **x-coordinate** (the **horizontal coordinate**) and a **y-coordinate** (the **vertical coordinate**). The x-coordinate is the horizontal distance *to the right* from the upper-left corner. The y-coordinate is the vertical distance *downward* from the upper-left corner. The *x-axis* defines every horizontal coordinate, and the *y-axis* defines every vertical coordinate. You position text and shapes on the screen by specifying their (x, y) coordinates. Coordinate units are measured in **pixels** ("picture elements"), which are the smallest units of resolution on a display monitor.

Portability Tip 15.1

Different display monitors have different resolutions, so the density of pixels varies among monitors. This might cause the sizes of graphics to appear different on different monitors.

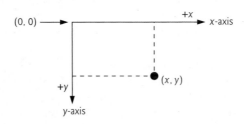

Fig. 15.1 | GDI+ coordinate system. Units are measured in pixels.

Points and Rectangles

The **System.Drawing** namespace provides several structures that represent sizes and locations in the coordinate system. The **Point** structure represents the *x–y* coordinates of a point on a two-dimensional plane. The **Rectangle** structure defines the upper-left *x–y* coordinates, width and height of a rectangular shape. The **Size** structure represents the width and height of a shape.

15.3 Graphics Contexts and Graphics Objects

A **graphics context** represents a drawing surface that enables drawing on the screen. A **Graphics** object manages a graphics context, controlling how information is drawn. **Graphics** objects contain methods for *drawing, font manipulation, color manipulation* and other graphics-related actions. Every derived class of **System.Windows.Forms.Form** inherits an **OnPaint** method in which most graphics operations are performed. The arguments to the OnPaint method include a **PaintEventArgs** object from which we can obtain a Graphics object for drawing on the Form. We must obtain the Graphics object on each call to the method, because the properties of the graphics context that the graphics object represents could change. Method OnPaint triggers the Control's **Paint** event.

Overriding *OnPaint*

When drawing on a Form, you can override method OnPaint to retrieve a Graphics object from its PaintEventArgs argument. To override the inherited OnPaint method, use the following method header:

```
Protected Overrides Sub OnPaint(PaintEventArgs e)
```

Next, call the base class's OnPaint method to execute any code in the base class's version of the method:

```
MyBase.OnPaint(e)
```

Then extract the incoming Graphics object from the argument:

```
Dim graphicsObject As Graphics = e.Graphics
```

Variable graphicsObject can now be used to draw shapes and Strings on the Form.

Handling the *Paint* Event

Rather than overriding the OnPaint method, you can add an event handler for the Paint event. Visual Studio .NET generates the Paint event handler in this format:

```
Protected Sub MyEventHandler_Paint(
    sender As Object, e As PaintEventArgs)
```

Calling *OnPaint*

You seldom call the OnPaint method directly, because drawing graphics is an event-driven process. An event—such as *covering*, *uncovering* or *resizing* a Form—calls the OnPaint method of that Form. Similarly, when any control (such as a TextBox or Label) is *displayed*, that control's OnPaint method is called.

You can force a call to OnPaint by calling a Control's **Invalidate** method, which refreshes a control and repaints all its graphical components. Class Control has several overloaded Invalidate methods that allow you to update portions of a control.

Getting a Graphics Context for a Control

Controls, such as Labels and Buttons, do not have their own graphics contexts, but you can create them. To draw on a control, first create a graphics object by invoking the control's CreateGraphics method, as in:

```
Dim graphicsObject As Graphics = controlName.CreateGraphics();
```

Now you can use the methods provided in class Graphics to draw on the control.

15.4 Colors

Colors can enhance a program's appearance and help convey meaning, just as a red traffic light indicates stop, yellow indicates caution and green indicates go. Structure Color defines methods and properties used to manipulate colors.

ARGB Values

Every color can be created from a combination of alpha, red, green and blue components (called **ARGB values**). All four ARGB components are Bytes that represent integer values in the range 0 to 255. The alpha value determines the *opacity* of the color. For example, the alpha value 0 represents a *transparent* color, and the value 255 represents an *opaque* color. Alpha values between 0 and 255 result in a weighted blending effect of the color's RGB value with that of any background color, causing a *semitransparent* effect. The first number in the RGB value defines the amount of *red* in the color, the second defines the amount of *green* and the third defines the amount of *blue*. The larger the value, the greater the amount of that color. You can choose from almost 17 million colors. If a particular computer cannot display all these colors, it will display the color closest to the one specified. Figure 15.2 summarizes some predefined Color properties (all are Public, Shared and ReadOnly), and Fig. 15.3 describes several Color methods and properties.

Constants in structure **Color**	RGB value	Constants in structure **Color**	RGB value
Orange	255, 165, 0	White	255, 255, 255
Pink	255, 192, 203	Gray	128, 128, 128
Cyan	0, 255, 255	DarkGray	169, 169, 169
Magenta	255, 0, 255	Red	255, 0, 0
Yellow	255, 255, 0	Green	0, 255, 0
Black	0, 0, 0	Blue	0, 0, 255

Fig. 15.2 | Color structure Shared ReadOnly properties and their RGB values.

Color methods and properties	Description
Common Methods	
FromArgb	A Shared method that creates a color based on red, green and blue values expressed as Integers from 0 to 255. An overloaded version allows specification of alpha, red, green and blue values.
FromName	A Shared method that creates a color from a name, passed as a String.
Common Properties	
A	A Byte between 0 and 255, representing the *alpha* component.
R	A Byte between 0 and 255, representing the *red* component.
G	A Byte between 0 and 255, representing the *green* component.
B	A Byte between 0 and 255, representing the *blue* component.

Fig. 15.3 | Color structure members.

Figure 15.3 describes two **FromArgb** method calls. One takes three Integer arguments, and one takes four Integer arguments (all argument values must be between 0 and 255, inclusive). Both take Integer arguments specifying the amount of *red*, *green* and *blue*.

a) Displa

b) Displ

Fig. 15.6

T
the use
to cha
color(

The other version also allows the user to specify the *alpha* component; the three-argument version defaults the alpha to 255 (*opaque*). Both methods return a Color object. Color properties A, R, G and B return Bytes that represent Integer values from 0 to 255, corresponding to the amounts of alpha, red, green and blue, respectively.

Pens and Brushes

You draw shapes and Strings with Pens and Brushes. A Pen is used to *draw lines*. Most drawing methods require a Pen object. The overloaded Pen constructors allow you to specify the *colors* and *widths* of the lines you wish to draw. Namespace System.Drawing also provides predefined Pens in class Pens and predefined Brushes in class Brushes. All classes derived from class Brush define objects that *color the interiors* of graphical shapes. For example, the SolidBrush constructor takes a Color object—the color to draw. In most Fill methods of class Graphics, Brushes fill a space with a *color*, *pattern* or *image*. Figure 15.4 summarizes some Brushes and their functions.

Class	Description
HatchBrush	Fills a region with a *pattern*. The pattern is defined by a member of the HatchStyle enumeration, a *foreground color* (with which the pattern is drawn) and a *background color*.
LinearGradientBrush	Fills a region with a *gradual blend* of one color to another—known as a gradient. *Linear gradients* are defined along a line. They can be specified by the two colors, the angle of the gradient (which specifies the direction) and either the width of a rectangle or two points.
SolidBrush	Fills a *region* with *one color* that's specified by a Color object.
TextureBrush	Fills a *region* by *repeating a specified* Image across the surface.

Fig. 15.4 | Classes that derive from class Brush.

Manipulating Colors

Figure 15.5 demonstrates several of the methods and properties described in Fig. 15.3. It displays two overlapping rectangles, allowing you to experiment with color values, color names and alpha values (for transparency).

When the app begins executing, its Form is displayed. This results in a call to method OnPaint to paint the Form's contents. Line 13 gets a reference to the Graphics object that's received as part of the PaintEventArgs parameter and assigns it to graphicsObject. Lines 14 and 15 create a black and a white SolidBrush for drawing solid shapes on the Form. Class SolidBrush derives from class Brush, so a SolidBrush can be passed to any method that expects a Brush parameter.

```vb
1  ' Fig. 15.5: ShowColors.vb
2  ' Color value and alpha demonstration.
3  Public Class ShowColors
4      ' color for back rectangle
5      Private backgroundColor As Color = Color.Wheat
```

Fig. 15.5 | Color value and alpha demonstration. (Part 1 of 3.)

```
17
18          ' courier new, 16 pt bold and italic
19          style = FontStyle.Bold Or FontStyle.Italic
20          Dim courierNew As New Font("Courier New", 16, style)
21
22          ' tahoma, 18 pt strikeout
23          style = FontStyle.Strikeout
24          Dim tahoma As New Font("Tahoma", 18, style)
25
26          graphicsObject.DrawString(arial.Name &
27              " 12 point bold.", arial, brush, 10, 10)
28
29          graphicsObject.DrawString(timesNewRoman.Name &
30              " 12 point plain.", timesNewRoman, brush, 10, 30)
31
32          graphicsObject.DrawString(courierNew.Name &
33              " 16 point bold and italic.", courierNew, brush, 10, 50)
34
35          graphicsObject.DrawString(tahoma.Name &
36              " 18 point strikeout.", tahoma, brush, 10, 70)
37      End Sub ' OnPaint
38  End Class ' FontDemo
```

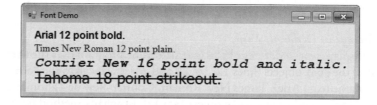

Fig. 15.8 | Fonts and FontStyles. (Part 2 of 2.)

Font Metrics

You can determine precise information about a font's **metrics** (or properties), such as **height**, **descent** (the amount that characters *dip below the baseline*), **ascent** (the amount characters *rise above the baseline*) and **leading** (the difference between the *ascent* of one line and the *descent* of the previous line). Figure 15.9 illustrates these font metrics.

Fig. 15.9 | Font metrics illustration.

Class `FontFamily` defines characteristics common to a group of related fonts. Class `FontFamily` provides several methods used to determine the *font metrics* shared by members of a particular family. These methods are summarized in Fig. 15.10.

Method	Description
GetCellAscent	Returns an Integer representing the *ascent* of a font as measured in *design units*.
GetCellDescent	Returns an Integer representing the *descent* of a font as measured in *design units*.
GetEmHeight	Returns an Integer representing the *height* of a font as measured in *design units*.
GetLineSpacing	Returns an Integer representing the *distance between two consecutive lines* (that is, the *leading*) of text as measured in *design units*.

Fig. 15.10 | `FontFamily` methods that return font-metric information.

Fig. 15.11 displays the metrics of two fonts. Line 11 creates `Font` object `arial` and sets it to 10-point Arial font. Line 12 uses `Font` property `FontFamily` to obtain object `arial`'s `FontFamily` object. Lines 15–16 output the `String` representation of the font. Lines 18–28 then use methods of class `FontFamily` to obtain the *ascent*, *descent*, *height* and *leading* of the font and draw strings containing this information. Lines 31–51 repeat the process for font `sansSerif`, which uses the Microsoft Sans Serif `FontFamily`.

```vb
1    ' Fig. 15.11: FontMetricsDemo.vb
2    ' Displaying font metric information
3    Public Class FontMetricsDemo
4       ' displays font information
5       Protected Overrides Sub OnPaint(e As PaintEventArgs)
6          MyBase.OnPaint(e) ' call base class's OnPaint
7          Dim graphicsObject As Graphics = e.Graphics
8          Dim brush As New SolidBrush(Color.DarkBlue)
9
10         ' Arial font metrics
11         Dim arial As New Font("Arial", 10)
12         Dim family As FontFamily = arial.FontFamily
13
14         ' display Arial font metrics
15         graphicsObject.DrawString("Current Font: " &
16            arial.ToString(), arial, brush, 10, 10)
17
18         graphicsObject.DrawString("Ascent: " &
19            family.GetCellAscent(FontStyle.Regular), arial, brush, 10, 30)
20
21         graphicsObject.DrawString("Descent: " &
22            family.GetCellDescent(FontStyle.Regular), arial, brush, 10, 50)
23
```

Fig. 15.11 | Displaying font metric information. (Part 1 of 2.)

```
24        graphicsObject.DrawString("Height: " &
25            family.GetEmHeight(FontStyle.Regular), arial, brush, 10, 70)
26
27        graphicsObject.DrawString("Leading: " &
28            family.GetLineSpacing(FontStyle.Regular), arial, brush, 10, 90)
29
30        ' display Sans Serif font metrics
31        Dim sanSerif As New Font("Microsoft Sans Serif",
32            12, FontStyle.Italic)
33        family = sanSerif.FontFamily
34
35        graphicsObject.DrawString("Current Font: " &
36            sanSerif.ToString(), sanSerif, brush, 10, 130)
37
38        graphicsObject.DrawString("Ascent: " &
39            family.GetCellAscent(FontStyle.Regular),
40            sanSerif, brush, 10, 150)
41
42        graphicsObject.DrawString("Descent: " &
43            family.GetCellDescent(FontStyle.Regular),
44            sanSerif, brush, 10, 170)
45
46        graphicsObject.DrawString("Height: " &
47            family.GetEmHeight(FontStyle.Regular), sanSerif, brush, 10, 190)
48
49        graphicsObject.DrawString("Leading: " &
50            family.GetLineSpacing(FontStyle.Regular),
51            sanSerif, brush, 10, 210)
52    End Sub ' OnPaint
53 End Class ' FontMetricsDemo
```

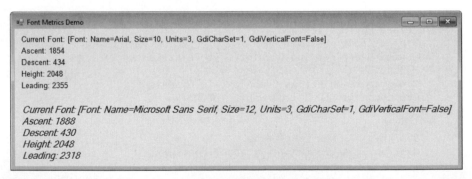

Fig. 15.11 | Displaying font metric information. (Part 2 of 2.)

15.6 Drawing Lines, Rectangles and Ovals

This section presents Graphics methods for drawing *lines*, *rectangles* and *ovals*. Each of the drawing methods has several overloaded versions. Methods that draw hollow shapes typically require as arguments

- a Pen
- four Integers

Methods that draw solid shapes typically require as arguments

- a Brush
- four Integers

The first two Integer arguments are the coordinates of the *upper-left corner* of the shape (or its enclosing area), and the last two indicate the shape's (or *enclosing area's*) *width* and *height*. Figure 15.12 summarizes several Graphics methods and their parameters.

Graphics Drawing Methods and Descriptions

`DrawLine(p As Pen, x1 As Integer, y1 As Integer,`
`  x2 As Integer, y2 As Integer)`
Draws a line from (x1, y1) to (x2, y2). The Pen determines the line's color, style and width.

`DrawRectangle(p As Pen, x As Integer, y As Integer,`
`  width As Integer, height As Integer)`
Draws a rectangle of the specified width and height. The top-left corner of the rectangle is at point (x, y). The Pen determines the rectangle's color, style and border width.

`FillRectangle(b As Brush, x As Integer, y As Integer,`
`  width As Integer, height As Integer)`
Draws a solid rectangle of the specified width and height. The top-left corner of the rectangle is at point (x, y). The Brush determines the fill pattern inside the rectangle.

`DrawEllipse(p As Pen, x As Integer, y As Integer,`
`  width As Integer, height As Integer)`
Draws an ellipse inside a bounding rectangle of the specified width and height. The top-left corner of the bounding rectangle is located at (x, y). The Pen determines the color, style and border width of the ellipse.

`FillEllipse(b As Brush, x As Integer, y As Integer,`
`  width As Integer, height As Integer)`
Draws a filled ellipse in a bounding rectangle. The top-left corner of the bounding rectangle is located at (x, y). The Brush determines the pattern inside the ellipse.

Fig. 15.12 | Graphics methods that draw lines, rectangles and ovals.

Figure 15.13 draws *lines*, *rectangles* and *ellipses*. In this app, we also demonstrate methods that draw *filled* and *unfilled shapes*.

```vb
1   ' Fig. 15.13: LinesRectanglesOvals.vb
2   ' Demonstrating lines, rectangles and ovals.
3   Public Class FrmLinesRectanglesOvals
4       ' override Form OnPaint method
5       Protected Overrides Sub OnPaint(e As PaintEventArgs)
6           MyBase.OnPaint(e) ' call base class's OnPaint
7
8           ' get graphics object
9           Dim g As Graphics = e.Graphics
```

Fig. 15.13 | Demonstration of methods that draw lines, rectangles and ellipses. (Part 1 of 2.)

```
10        Dim brush As New SolidBrush(Color.Blue)
11        Dim pen As New Pen(Color.Black)
12
13        ' create filled rectangle
14        g.FillRectangle(brush, 90, 30, 150, 90)
15
16        ' draw lines to connect rectangles
17        g.DrawLine(pen, 90, 30, 110, 40)
18        g.DrawLine(pen, 90, 120, 110, 130)
19        g.DrawLine(pen, 240, 30, 260, 40)
20        g.DrawLine(pen, 240, 120, 260, 130)
21
22        ' draw top rectangle
23        g.DrawRectangle(pen, 110, 40, 150, 90)
24
25        ' set brush to red
26        brush.Color = Color.Red
27
28        ' draw base Ellipse
29        g.FillEllipse(brush, 280, 75, 100, 50)
30
31        ' draw connecting lines
32        g.DrawLine(pen, 380, 55, 380, 100)
33        g.DrawLine(pen, 280, 55, 280, 100)
34
35        ' draw Ellipse outline
36        g.DrawEllipse(pen, 280, 30, 100, 50)
37     End Sub ' OnPaint
38  End Class ' LinesRectanglesOvals
```

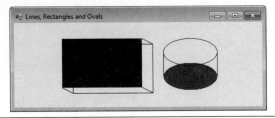

Fig. 15.13 | Demonstration of methods that draw lines, rectangles and ellipses. (Part 2 of 2.)

Methods **FillRectangle** and **DrawRectangle** (lines 14 and 23) draw rectangles on the screen. For each method, the first argument specifies the drawing object to use. The FillRectangle method uses a Brush object (in this case, an instance of SolidBrush—a class that derives from Brush), whereas the DrawRectangle method uses a Pen object. The next two arguments specify the coordinates of the *upper-left corner* of the **bounding rectangle**, which represents the area in which the rectangle will be drawn. The fourth and fifth arguments specify the rectangle's width and height. Method DrawLine (lines 17–20) takes as arguments

- a Pen
- two pairs of Integers, specifying the start and end of a line

The method then draws a line, using the Pen object.

Methods `FillEllipse` and `DrawEllipse` (lines 29 and 36) each provide overloaded versions that take five arguments

- the first argument specifies the *drawing object* to use
- the next two arguments specify the *upper-left coordinates* of the bounding rectangle representing the area in which the ellipse will be drawn
- the *last two arguments* specify the bounding rectangle's width and height

Figure 15.14 depicts an ellipse bounded by a rectangle. The ellipse touches the midpoint of each of the four sides of the bounding rectangle. The bounding rectangle is not displayed on the screen.

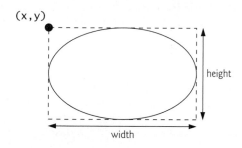

Fig. 15.14 | Ellipse bounded by a rectangle.

15.7 Drawing Arcs

Arcs are portions of ellipses and are measured in *degrees*, beginning at a **starting angle** and continuing for a specified number of degrees called the **arc angle**. An arc is said to **sweep** (*traverse*) its arc angle, *beginning* from its *starting angle*. Arcs that sweep in a clockwise direction are measured in positive degrees, whereas arcs that sweep in a counterclockwise direction are measured in negative degrees. Figure 15.15 depicts two arcs. Note that the arc at the left of the figure sweeps upward from zero degrees to approximately –110 degrees. Similarly, the arc at the right of the figure sweeps downward from zero degrees to approximately 110 degrees.

Fig. 15.15 | Positive and negative arc angles.

Note the dashed boxes around the arcs in Fig. 15.15. Each arc is drawn as part of an oval (the rest of which is not visible). When drawing an oval, we specify the oval's dimensions in the form of a *bounding rectangle* that encloses the oval. The boxes in Fig. 15.15 correspond to these bounding rectangles. The Graphics methods used to draw arcs—**DrawArc**, **DrawPie** and **FillPie**—are summarized in Fig. 15.16.

Graphics methods and descriptions

`DrawArc(p As Pen, x As Integer, y As Integer,`
    `width As Integer, height As Integer,`
    `startAngle As Integer, sweepAngle As Integer)`
Draws an *arc* beginning from angle `startAngle` (in degrees) and sweeping `sweepAngle` degrees. The *ellipse* is defined by a *bounding rectangle* of `width`, `height` and *upper-left corner* (x,y). The Pen determines the color, border width and style of the arc.

`DrawPie(p As Pen, x As Integer, y As Integer,`
    `width As Integer, height As Integer,`
    `startAngle As Integer, sweepAngle As Integer)`
Draws a pie section of an *ellipse* beginning from angle `startAngle` (in degrees) and sweeping `sweepAngle` degrees. The ellipse is defined by a *bounding rectangle* of `width`, `height` and *upper-left corner* (x,y). The Pen determines the color, border width and style of the arc.

`FillPie(b As Brush, x As Integer, y As Integer,`
    `width As Integer, height As Integer,`
    `startAngle As Integer, sweepAngle As Integer)`
Functions similarly to `DrawPie`, except draws a *solid arc* (i.e., a *sector*). The Brush determines the *fill pattern* for the *solid arc*.

Fig. 15.16 | Graphics methods for drawing arcs.

Figure 15.17 draws six images (three *arcs* and three *filled pie slices*) to demonstrate some of the arc drawing methods. To illustrate the *bounding rectangles* that determine the sizes and locations of the arcs, the arcs are displayed inside *red rectangles* that have the same *x–y* coordinates, width and height arguments as those that define the *bounding rectangles* for the *arcs*.

```
 1   ' Fig. 15.17: DrawArcs.vb
 2   ' Drawing various arcs on a Form.
 3   Public Class DrawArcs
 4      ' draw arcs
 5      Private Sub DrawArcs_Paint(sender As Object,
 6         e As PaintEventArgs) Handles Me.Paint
 7         ' get graphics object
 8         Dim graphicsObject As Graphics = e.Graphics
 9         Dim rectangle1 As New Rectangle(15, 35, 80, 80)
10         Dim brush1 As New SolidBrush(Color.Firebrick)
11         Dim pen1 As New Pen(brush1, 1)
```

Fig. 15.17 | Drawing various arcs on a Form. (Part 1 of 2.)

```
12          Dim brush2 As New SolidBrush(Color.DarkBlue)
13          Dim pen2 As New Pen(brush2, 1)
14
15          ' start at 0 and sweep 360 degrees
16          graphicsObject.DrawRectangle(pen1, rectangle1)
17          graphicsObject.DrawArc(pen2, rectangle1, 0, 360)
18
19          ' start at 0 and sweep 110 degrees
20          rectangle1.Location = New Point(100, 35)
21          graphicsObject.DrawRectangle(pen1, rectangle1)
22          graphicsObject.DrawArc(pen2, rectangle1, 0, 110)
23
24          ' start at 0 and sweep -270 degrees
25          rectangle1.Location = New Point(185, 35)
26          graphicsObject.DrawRectangle(pen1, rectangle1)
27          graphicsObject.DrawArc(pen2, rectangle1, 0, -270)
28
29          ' start at 0 and sweep 360 degrees
30          rectangle1.Location = New Point(15, 120)
31          rectangle1.Size = New Size(80, 40)
32          graphicsObject.DrawRectangle(pen1, rectangle1)
33          graphicsObject.FillPie(brush2, rectangle1, 0, 360)
34
35          ' start at 270 and sweep -90 degrees
36          rectangle1.Location = New Point(100, 120)
37          graphicsObject.DrawRectangle(pen1, rectangle1)
38          graphicsObject.FillPie(brush2, rectangle1, 270, -90)
39
40          ' start at 0 and sweep -270 degrees
41          rectangle1.Location = New Point(185, 120)
42          graphicsObject.DrawRectangle(pen1, rectangle1)
43          graphicsObject.FillPie(brush2, rectangle1, 0, -270)
44      End Sub ' DrawArcs_Paint
45  End Class ' DrawArcs
```

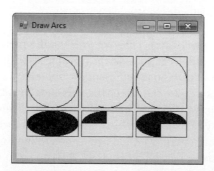

Fig. 15.17 | Drawing various arcs on a Form. (Part 2 of 2.)

Lines 8–13 create the objects that we need to draw *arcs*—a Graphics object, a Rectangle, SolidBrushes and Pens. Lines 16–17 then draw a rectangle and an arc inside the rectangle. The arc sweeps 360 degrees, forming a *circle*. Line 20 changes the location of the Rectangle by setting its Location property to a new Point. The Point constructor takes as arguments the *x*- and *y*-coordinates of the new Point. The Location property determines the *upper-left corner* of the Rectangle. After drawing the rectangle, the program draws an arc that starts at 0 degrees and sweeps 110 degrees. Because the angles increase in a *clockwise direction*, the arc sweeps *downward*. Lines 25–27 perform similar functions, except that the specified arc sweeps –270 degrees. The Size property of a Rectangle determines the arc's *height* and *width*.

Line 31 sets the Size property to a new Size object, which changes the size of the rectangle. The remainder of the program is similar to the portions described above, except that a SolidBrush is used with method FillPie. The resulting arcs, which are filled, can be seen in the bottom half of the sample output (Fig. 15.17).

15.8 Drawing Polygons and Polylines

Polygons are *multisided shapes*. There are several Graphics methods used to draw polygons—DrawLines draws a series of *connected lines*, DrawPolygon draws a *closed polygon* and FillPolygon draws a *solid polygon*. These methods are described in Fig. 15.18.

Method	Description
DrawLines	Draws a series of *connected lines*. The coordinates of each point are specified in an array of Point objects. If the last point is *different* from the first point, the figure is *not closed*.
DrawPolygon	Draws a *polygon*. The coordinates of each point are specified in an array of Point objects. If the last point is *different* from the first point, those two points are connected to *close the polygon*.
FillPolygon	Draws a *solid polygon*. The coordinates of each point are specified in an array of Point objects. If the last point is *different* from the first point, those two points are connected to *close the polygon*.

Fig. 15.18 | Graphics methods for drawing polygons.

Figure 15.19 draws *polygons* and *connected lines* via the methods listed in Fig. 15.18. In the Paint event handler, line 9 gets the Graphics object for drawing on the Form. Lines 11–16 create three arrays of Points that represent the points in a *collection of lines*, a *polygon* and a *filled polygon*. Lines 22–24 call Graphics methods DrawLines, DrawPolygon and FillPolygon. Methods DrawLines and DrawPolygon take a Pen as their first argument. Method FillPolygon takes a Brush as its first argument. All three methods take an array of Points as their second argument. Method DrawLines draws lines from one Point to the next in the array. Methods DrawPolygon and FillPolygon also draw a line from the *last point in the array* to the *first point in the array* to *close the shape*.

```
1   ' Fig. 15.19: DrawPolygons.vb
2   ' Demonstrating polygons.
3   Public Class DrawPolygons
```

Fig. 15.19 | Demonstrating polygons. (Part 1 of 2.)

```
 4      ' draw panel Paint event handler
 5      Private Sub DrawPolygons_Paint(sender As Object,
 6         e As PaintEventArgs) Handles Me.Paint
 7
 8         ' get graphics object for panel
 9         Dim graphicsObject As Graphics = e.Graphics
10
11         Dim points1() As Point = {New Point(20, 20), New Point(10, 150),
12            New Point(100, 100), New Point(50, 75)}
13         Dim points2() As Point = {New Point(120, 20), New Point(110, 150),
14            New Point(200, 100), New Point(150, 75)}
15         Dim points3() As Point = {New Point(220, 20), New Point(210, 150),
16            New Point(300, 100), New Point(250, 75)}
17
18         ' initialize default pen and brush
19         Dim pen As New Pen(Color.DarkBlue)
20         Dim brush As New SolidBrush(Color.DarkBlue)
21
22         graphicsObject.DrawLines(pen, points1)
23         graphicsObject.DrawPolygon(pen, points2)
24         graphicsObject.FillPolygon(brush, points3)
25      End Sub ' DrawPolygons_Paint
26   End Class ' DrawPolygons
```

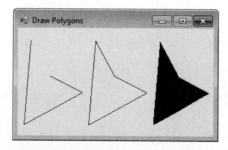

Fig. 15.19 | Demonstrating polygons. (Part 2 of 2.)

15.9 Additional Brush Types

.NET offers many other graphics capabilities. The Brush hierarchy, for example, also includes **HatchBrush**, **LinearGradientBrush**, **PathGradientBrush** and **TextureBrush**.

Gradients, Line Styles and Fill Patterns

The program in Fig. 15.20 demonstrates several graphics features, such as *dashed lines*, *thick lines* and the ability to *fill shapes with various patterns*. These represent just a few of the additional capabilities of the System.Drawing namespace.

Lines 7–73 define the DrawShapes_Paint event handler. Lines 14–15 create a LinearGradientBrush (namespace System.Drawing.Drawing2D) object named linearBrush to enable users to draw with a *color gradient*. The LinearGradientBrush used in this example takes four arguments

- a Rectangle

- two Colors
- a constant from the LinearGradientMode enumeration

Linear gradients are defined along a line that determines the *gradient endpoints*. This line can be specified either by the *start and end points* or by the *diagonal* of a rectangle. The first argument, Rectangle drawArea1, represents the *endpoints* of the linear gradient—the *upper-left corner* is the starting point, and the *bottom-right corner* is the ending point. The second and third arguments specify the *colors* the gradient will use. In this case, the color of the ellipse will gradually change from Color.Blue to Color.Yellow. The last argument, a type from the enumeration **LinearGradientMode**, specifies the linear gradient's *direction*. In our case, we use LinearGradientMode.ForwardDiagonal, which creates a gradient from the *upper-left* to the *lower-right corner*. We then use Graphics method FillEllipse in line 18 to draw an ellipse with linearBrush; the color gradually changes from blue to yellow and back to blue, as described above.

```
1   ' Fig. 15.20: DrawShapes.vb
2   ' Drawing various shapes on a Form.
3   Imports System.Drawing.Drawing2D
4
5   Public Class DrawShapes
6      ' draw various shapes on Form
7      Private Sub DrawShapes_Paint(sender As Object,
8         e As PaintEventArgs) Handles Me.Paint
9
10        Dim graphicsObject As Graphics = e.Graphics
11
12        ' ellipse rectangle and gradient brush
13        Dim drawArea1 As New Rectangle(5, 35, 30, 100)
14        Dim linearBrush As New LinearGradientBrush(drawArea1, Color.Blue,
15           Color.Yellow, LinearGradientMode.ForwardDiagonal)
16
17        ' draw ellipse filled with a blue-yellow gradient
18        graphicsObject.FillEllipse(linearBrush, 5, 30, 65, 100)
19
20        ' pen and location for red outline rectangle
21        Dim thickRedPen As New Pen(Color.Red, 10)
22        Dim drawArea2 As New Rectangle(80, 30, 65, 100)
23
24        ' draw thick rectangle outline in red
25        graphicsObject.DrawRectangle(thickRedPen, drawArea2)
26
27        ' bitmap texture
28        Dim textureBitmap As New Bitmap(10, 10)
29
30        ' get bitmap graphics
31        Dim graphicsObject2 As Graphics = Graphics.FromImage(textureBitmap)
32
33        ' brush and pen used throughout program
34        Dim solidColorBrush As New SolidBrush(Color.Red)
35        Dim coloredPen As New Pen(solidColorBrush)
```

Fig. 15.20 | Drawing various shapes on a Form. (Part 1 of 2.)

```
36
37          ' fill textureBitmap with yellow
38          solidColorBrush.Color = Color.Yellow
39          graphicsObject2.FillRectangle(solidColorBrush, 0, 0, 10, 10)
40
41          ' draw small black rectangle in textureBitmap
42          coloredPen.Color = Color.Black
43          graphicsObject2.DrawRectangle(coloredPen, 1, 1, 6, 6)
44
45          ' draw small blue rectangle in textureBitmap
46          solidColorBrush.Color = Color.Blue
47          graphicsObject2.FillRectangle(solidColorBrush, 1, 1, 3, 3)
48
49          ' draw small red square in textureBitmap
50          solidColorBrush.Color = Color.Red
51          graphicsObject2.FillRectangle(solidColorBrush, 4, 4, 3, 3)
52
53          ' create textured brush and
54          ' display textured rectangle
55          Dim texturedBrush As New TextureBrush(textureBitmap)
56          graphicsObject.FillRectangle(texturedBrush, 155, 30, 75, 100)
57
58          ' draw pie-shaped arc in white
59          coloredPen.Color = Color.White
60          coloredPen.Width = 6
61          graphicsObject.DrawPie(coloredPen, 240, 30, 75, 100, 0, 270)
62
63          ' draw lines in green and yellow
64          coloredPen.Color = Color.Green
65          coloredPen.Width = 5
66          graphicsObject.DrawLine(coloredPen, 395, 30, 320, 150)
67
68          ' draw a rounded, dashed yellow line
69          coloredPen.Color = Color.Yellow
70          coloredPen.DashCap = DashCap.Round
71          coloredPen.DashStyle = DashStyle.Dash
72          graphicsObject.DrawLine(coloredPen, 320, 30, 395, 150)
73      End Sub ' DrawShapes_Paint
74   End Class ' DrawShapes
```

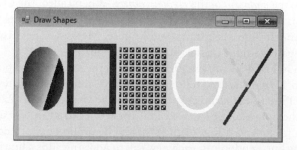

Fig. 15.20 | Drawing various shapes on a Form. (Part 2 of 2.)

In line 21, we create Pen object thickRedPen. We pass to thickRedPen's constructor Color.Red and Integer argument 10, indicating that we want thickRedPen to draw red lines that are 10 pixels wide.

Line 28 creates a new **Bitmap** image, which initially is empty. Class Bitmap can produce images in *color* and *gray scale*; this particular Bitmap is 10 pixels wide and 10 pixels tall. Method **FromImage** (line 31) is a Shared member of class Graphics and retrieves the Graphics object associated with an Image, which may be used to draw on an image. Lines 38–51 draw on the Bitmap a pattern consisting of black, blue, red and yellow rectangles. A TextureBrush is a brush that fills the interior of a shape with an image rather than a solid color. In lines 55–56, TextureBrush object textureBrush fills a rectangle with our Bitmap. The TextureBrush constructor used in line 55 takes as an argument an image that defines its *texture*.

Next, we draw a *pie-shaped* arc with a *thick white line*. Lines 59–60 set coloredPen's color to White and modify its width to be 6 pixels. We then draw the pie on the Form by specifying the Pen, the *x-coordinate*, *y-coordinate*, the *width* and *height* of the *bounding rectangle* and the *start* and *sweep angles*.

Lines 64–66 draw a green line that's five pixels wide. Finally, lines 70–71 use enumerations **DashCap** and **DashStyle** (namespace System.Drawing.Drawing2D) to specify settings for a *dashed line*. Line 70 sets the DashCap property of coloredPen (not to be confused with the DashCap enumeration) to a member of the DashCap enumeration. The DashCap enumeration specifies the styles for the ends of each dash in a dashed line. In this case, we want both ends of the *dashed line* to be *rounded*, so we use DashCap.Round. Line 71 sets the DashStyle property of coloredPen (not to be confused with the DashStyle enumeration) to DashStyle.Dash, indicating that we want our line to consist entirely of dashes.

General Paths

Our next example demonstrates a **general path**. A general path is a shape constructed from *straight lines* and *complex curves*. An object of class **GraphicsPath** (namespace System.Drawing.Drawing2D) represents a *general path*. The GraphicsPath class provides functionality that enables the creation of *complex shapes* from *vector-based primitive graphics objects*. A GraphicsPath object consists of figures defined by *simple shapes*. The *start point* of each *vector-graphics object* (such as a line or an arc) added to the path is connected by a *straight line* to the *endpoint* of the *previous object*. When called, the **CloseFigure** method attaches the final vector-graphic object endpoint to the initial starting point for the current figure by a straight line, then starts a new figure. Method **StartFigure** begins a new figure within the path without closing the previous figure.

The program in Fig. 15.21 draws *general paths* in the shape of five-pointed stars. Lines 15–16 define two Integer arrays, representing the *x*- and *y*-coordinates of the points in the star, and line 19 defines GraphicsPath object star. A loop (lines 22–25) then creates lines to connect the points of the star and adds these lines to star. We use GraphicsPath method **AddLine** to append a line to the shape. The arguments of AddLine specify the coordinates for the line's endpoints; each new call to AddLine adds a line from the previous point to the current point. Line 27 uses GraphicsPath method CloseFigure to complete the shape.

Line 30 sets the origin of the Graphics object. The arguments to method Translate-Transform indicate that the origin should be translated to the coordinates (150, 150). The loop in lines 33–40 draws the star 18 times, rotating it around the origin. Line 34 uses Graphics method **RotateTransform** to move to the next position on the Form; the argument specifies the *rotation angle* in *degrees*. Graphics method FillPath (line 39) then draws a *filled* version of the star with the Brush created in lines 36–37. The app determines the SolidBrush's color randomly, using Random method Next.

```vb
1   ' Fig. 15.21: DrawStars.vb
2   ' Using paths to draw stars on a Form.
3   Imports System.Drawing.Drawing2D
4
5   Public Class DrawStars
6      ' create path and draw stars along it
7      Private Sub DrawStars_Paint(sender As Object,
8         e As PaintEventArgs) Handles Me.Paint
9
10        Dim graphicsObject As Graphics = e.Graphics
11        Dim random As New Random()
12        Dim brush As New SolidBrush(Color.DarkMagenta)
13
14        ' x and y points of the path
15        Dim xPoints() As Integer = {55, 67, 109, 73, 83, 55, 27, 37, 1, 43}
16        Dim yPoints() As Integer = {0, 36, 36, 54, 96, 72, 96, 54, 36, 36}
17
18        ' create graphics path for star
19        Dim star As New GraphicsPath()
20
21        ' create a star from a series of points
22        For i As Integer = 0 To 8 Step 2
23           star.AddLine(xPoints(i), yPoints(i),
24              xPoints(i + 1), yPoints(i + 1))
25        Next
26
27        star.CloseFigure() ' close the shape
28
29        ' translate the origin to (150, 150)
30        graphicsObject.TranslateTransform(150, 150)
31
32        ' rotate the origin and draw the stars in random colors
33        For i As Integer = 1 To 18
34           graphicsObject.RotateTransform(20)
35
36           brush.Color = Color.FromArgb(random.Next(200, 255),
37              random.Next(255), random.Next(255), random.Next(255))
38
39           graphicsObject.FillPath(brush, star)
40        Next
41     End Sub ' DrawStars_Paint
42  End Class ' DrawStars
```

Fig. 15.21 | Paths used to draw stars on a Form. (Part 1 of 2.)

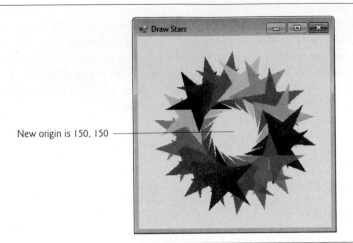

New origin is 150, 150

Fig. 15.21 | Paths used to draw stars on a Form. (Part 2 of 2.)

15.10 Loading, Displaying and Scaling Images

.NET's multimedia capabilities include *graphics*, *images*, *animations*, *audio* and *video*. This section presents image manipulation. Figure 15.22 loads an Image (System.Drawing namespace), then allows the user to *scale* the Image to a specified *width* and *height* up to 400 by 400 pixels. The "yellowflowers" image was added to the app as a resource.

```vb
1   ' Fig. 15.22: ScaleImage.vb
2   ' Displaying and resizing an image
3   Public Class ScaleImage
4      Private imageValue As Image
5      Private graphicsObject As Graphics
6
7      ' load the image and obtain the Graphics object
8      Private Sub ScaleImage_Load(sender As Object,
9         e As EventArgs) Handles Me.Load
10
11        Dim pictureResource =
12           My.Resources.ResourceManager.GetObject("yellowflowers")
13
14        imageValue = CType(pictureResource, Image)
15        graphicsObject = Me.CreateGraphics()
16     End Sub ' ScaleImage_Load
17
18     ' get NumericUpDown values and use them to size image
19     Private Sub NumericUpDown_ValueChanged(sender As Object,
20        e As EventArgs) _
21        Handles widthNumericUpDown.ValueChanged,
22           heightNumericUpDown.ValueChanged
23
```

Fig. 15.22 | Image resizing. (Part 1 of 2.)

```
24          ' clear the Form then draw the image
25          graphicsObject.Clear(Me.BackColor)
26          graphicsObject.DrawImage(imageValue, 5, 5,
27             widthNumericUpDown.Value, heightNumericUpDown.Value)
28       End Sub ' NumericUpDown_ValueChanged
29    End Class ' ScaleImage
```

a) Scaled image after setting the **Width** and **Heigth** NumericUpDowns to 100

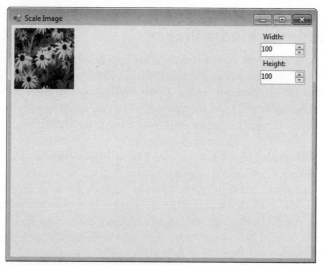

a) Scaled image after setting the **Width** NumericUpDown to 300 and the **Height** NumericUpDown to 400

Fig. 15.22 | Image resizing. (Part 2 of 2.)

Line 4 declares Image variable imageValue. Lines 11–14 in the Form's Load event handler load the Image from a resource named "yellowflowers". Line 15 uses the Form's inherited **CreateGraphics** method to create a Graphics object for drawing on the Form. When you change the value in either NumericUpDown control, lines 19–28 *scale* and *redraw* the image. Line 25 calls Graphics method **Clear** to paint the entire Form in the current background color. Lines 26–27 call Graphics method **DrawImage**, passing as arguments the *image to draw*, the *x-coordinate* of the image's *upper-left corner*, the *y-coordinate* of the image's *upper-left corner*, the *width* of the image and the *height* of the image. If the width and height do not correspond to the image's original dimensions, the image is *scaled* to fit the new width and height.

15.11 Windows Media Player

The **Windows Media Player control** enables an app to play *video* and *sound* in many multimedia formats. These include MPEG (Motion Pictures Experts Group) audio and video, AVI (audio-video interleave) video, WAV (Windows wave-file format) audio and MIDI (Musical Instrument Digital Interface) audio. You can find pre-existing audio and video on the Internet, or you can create your own files, using available sound and graphics packages.

Figure 15.23 demonstrates the Windows Media Player control. This control is not displayed in the **Toolbox** by default, so you must add it. First right click inside the **Toolbox** and select **Choose Items...** to display the **Choose Toolbox Items** dialog. Click the **COM Components** tab, then scroll down and select the option **Windows Media Player**. Click the **OK** button to dismiss the dialog. The Windows Media Player control now appears in the **Toolbox**. Drag the control onto your Form, then set the control's Dock property to Fill. Add a MenuStrip with a **File** menu that contains **Open** and **Exit** menu items. Finally, add an OpenFileDialog named openMediaFileDialog.

The Windows Media Player control provides several Buttons that allow the user to *play the current file*, *pause*, *stop*, *play the previous file*, *rewind*, *forward* and *play the next file*. The control also includes a volume control and trackbars to select a specific position in the media file.

```vb
1   ' Fig. 15.23: MediaPlayer.vb
2   ' Windows Media Player control used to play media files.
3   Public Class MediaPlayer
4      ' open new media file in Windows Media Player
5      Private Sub OpenToolStripMenuItem_Click(sender As Object,
6         e As EventArgs) Handles OpenToolStripMenuItem.Click
7
8         openMediaFileDialog.ShowDialog() ' allow user to select file
9
10        ' load and play the media clip
11        AxWindowsMediaPlayer1.URL = openMediaFileDialog.FileName
12     End Sub ' OpenToolStripMenuItem_Click
13
14        ' exit the program when the exit menu item is clicked
15     Private Sub ExitToolStripMenuItem_Click(sender As Object,
16        e As EventArgs) Handles ExitToolStripMenuItem.Click
17        Application.Exit()
18     End Sub ' ExitToolStripMenuItem_Click
19  End Class ' MediaPlayer
```

Fig. 15.23 | Windows Media Player control used to play media files. (Part 1 of 2.)

Fig. 15.23 | Windows Media Player control used to play media files. (Part 2 of 2.)

When a user chooses **Open** from the **File** menu, event handler `OpenToolStripMenu-Item_Click` (lines 5–12) displays the `openMediaFileDialog` (line 8) so the user can choose an audio or video file to play. Line 11 then sets the *URL property* of the Windows Media Player control (named `AxWindowsMediaPlayer1`) to the name of the file chosen by the user. The URL property specifies the file that Windows Media Player is currently using. We provided a sample video in the `video` folder with this chapter's examples, but you can select any video to test the program.

15.12 Printing

The next app uses the graphics techniques presented in this chapter to *print* a paycheck on your *printer.* The user inputs to a GUI (Fig. 15.24) that resembles a check: the check number, the date, the numeric amount of the check, the employee's name, the amount of the check written in words and the company's address information. Pressing the **Preview** But-

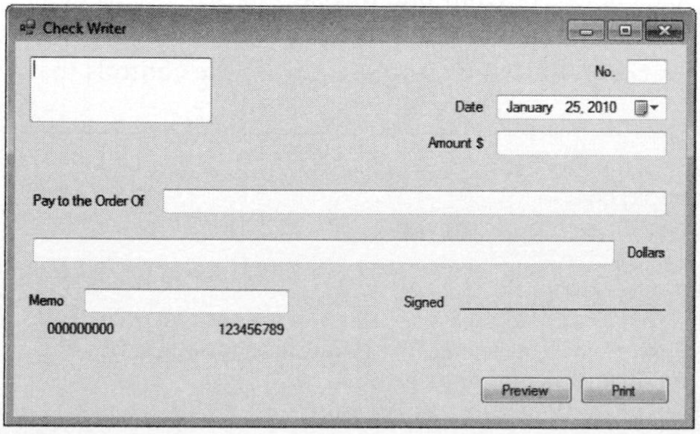

Fig. 15.24 | GUI for the **Check Writer** app.

ton displays the format of the check in a **Print preview** dialog so the user can see if the format is acceptable. Pressing the **Print** Button prints the check. To implement the printing capabilities, you'll use objects from the **Printing** section of the **Toolbox.**

GUI for the Check Writer App

The GUI consists of Labels, TextBoxes and a DateTimePicker laid out to resemble a check. The **Preview** and **Print** Buttons enable you to display a **Print preview** dialog containing the check and to print the check, respectively.

In addition to the controls shown in Fig. 15.24, we also dragged a PrintPreview-Dialog and a PrintDocument from the **Printing** section of the **Toolbox** onto the Form and named them printPreviewDialog and printDocument, respectively. A **PrintPreviewDialog** displays a dialog in which the user can view the document that will print *before* it's sent to the printer. A **PrintDocument** object allows you to specify how to print a specified document. The default event for a PrintDocument is the **PrintPage** event, which occurs when the data required to print the current page is needed—that is, when the document is printed or a print preview is generated. You can create the event handler for this event by double clicking the printDocument object in the component tray in **Design** view. In this event handler, you define what will print by using the Graphics capabilities presented in this chapter.

Coding the Check Writer App

Figure 15.25 presents the code for the **Check Writer** app. We've already presented the Graphics features used in this example, so we'll focus on the printing features. Line 3 Imports the **System.Drawing.Printing** namespace so that the app can access Windows printing services. Lines 7–81 define the PrintPage event handler for the printDocument object that specifies what will print.

Declaring the Variables Used in the PrintPage Event Handler

Line 11 declares a Font variable named fontObject that's used to specify the text font. Lines 14–15 declare Integer variables that represent the *x*- and *y*-coordinates where controls appear on the Form. Lines 18 and 21 declare Integer variables, which specify the coordinates of the left and top margins, respectively, of the page to be printed. These values are determined by using the **MarginBounds.Left** and **MarginBounds.Top** properties of the PrintPageEventArgs object (e from line 8) that's passed when the PrintPage event occurs. The MarginBounds represent the printable area of the page. Line 24 declares the String variable controlText, which stores text from the controls that will be printed.

```
1   ' Fig. 15.25: CheckWriter.vb
2   ' Printing a paycheck.
3   Imports System.Drawing.Printing
4
5   Public Class CheckWriter
6      ' PrintPage event raised for each page to be printed
7      Private Sub printDocument_PrintPage(sender As Object,
8         e As PrintPageEventArgs) _
9         Handles printDocument.PrintPage
```

Fig. 15.25 | Printing a paycheck. (Part 1 of 4.)

```
10
11          Dim fontObject As Font ' variable to store the font
12
13          ' store a control's x- and y-coordinates
14          Dim yPosition As Integer
15          Dim xPosition As Integer
16
17          ' represent the left margin of the page
18          Dim leftMargin As Integer = e.MarginBounds.Left
19
20          ' represent the top margin of the page
21          Dim topMargin As Integer = e.MarginBounds.Top
22
23          ' store a control's text
24          Dim controlText As String = Nothing
25
26          ' iterate over the controls on the Form,
27          ' printing the text displayed in each control
28          For Each controlObject In Me.Controls
29              ' do not print Buttons
30            If Not (TypeOf controlObject Is Button) Then
31                controlText = controlObject.Text
32
33              Select Case controlObject.Name
34                  Case "dateTimePicker" ' underline the date
35                      fontObject = New Font("Segoe UI", 9.0F,
36                         FontStyle.Underline)
37                  Case "amountTextBox" ' draw a box around the amount
38                      e.Graphics.DrawRectangle(Pens.Black,
39                         amountTextBox.Location.X + leftMargin,
40                         amountTextBox.Location.Y + topMargin - 2,
41                         amountTextBox.Width, amountTextBox.Height)
42                      fontObject = controlObject.Font ' default font
43                  Case Else
44                      fontObject = controlObject.Font ' default font
45              End Select
46
47              ' set the string positions relative to the page margins
48              xPosition = leftMargin + controlObject.Location.X
49              yPosition = topMargin + controlObject.Location.Y
50
51              ' draw the text in a graphics object
52              e.Graphics.DrawString(controlText, fontObject,
53                 Brushes.Black, xPosition, yPosition)
54            End If
55          Next controlObject
56
57          ' draw a line for the payee's name
58          e.Graphics.DrawLine(Pens.Black,
59             payeeTextBox.Location.X + leftMargin,
60             payeeTextBox.Location.Y + topMargin + 15,
61             payeeTextBox.Location.X + payeeTextBox.Width + leftMargin,
62             payeeTextBox.Location.Y + topMargin + 15)
```

Fig. 15.25 | Printing a paycheck. (Part 2 of 4.)

```vb
63
64          ' draw a line for the amount
65          e.Graphics.DrawLine(Pens.Black,
66             dollarsTextBox.Location.X + leftMargin,
67             dollarsTextBox.Location.Y + topMargin + 15,
68             dollarsTextBox.Location.X + dollarsTextBox.Width + leftMargin,
69             dollarsTextBox.Location.Y + topMargin + 15)
70
71          ' draw the memo line
72          e.Graphics.DrawLine(Pens.Black,
73             memoTextBox.Location.X + leftMargin,
74             memoTextBox.Location.Y + topMargin + 15,
75             memoTextBox.Location.X + memoTextBox.Width + leftMargin,
76             memoTextBox.Location.Y + topMargin + 15)
77
78          ' draw a box around the check
79          e.Graphics.DrawRectangle(Pens.Black, leftMargin,
80             topMargin, Me.Width, Me.Height - 60)
81       End Sub ' document_PrintPage
82
83       ' print the document
84       Private Sub printButton_Click(sender As Object,
85          e As EventArgs) Handles printButton.Click
86
87          ' if no printers are installed, display an error message
88          If PrinterSettings.InstalledPrinters.Count = 0 Then
89             ErrorMessage()
90          Else
91             printDocument.Print() ' print the document
92          End If
93       End Sub ' printButton_Click
94
95       ' display the document in a print preview dialog
96       Private Sub previewButton_Click(sender As Object,
97          e As EventArgs) Handles previewButton.Click
98
99          ' if no printers are installed, display an error message
100         If PrinterSettings.InstalledPrinters.Count = 0 Then
101            ErrorMessage()
102         Else
103            printPreviewDialog.Document = printDocument ' specify document
104            printPreviewDialog.ShowDialog() ' show print preview dialog
105         End If
106      End Sub ' previewButton_Click
107
108      ' display an error message to the user
109      Sub ErrorMessage()
110         MessageBox.Show("No printers installed. You must " &
111            "have a printer installed to preview or print the document.",
112            "Print Error", MessageBoxButtons.OK, MessageBoxIcon.Error)
113      End Sub ' ErrorMessage
114   End Class ' CheckWriter
```

Fig. 15.25 | Printing a paycheck. (Part 3 of 4.)

a) GUI after the user fills in the fields with the information for the check

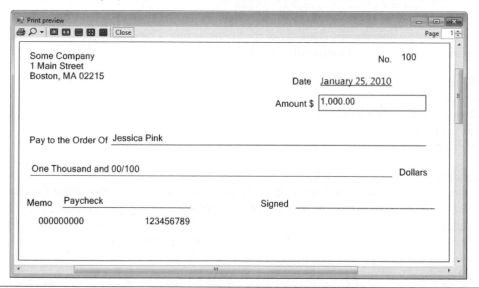

b) **Print preview** dialog that displays when the user clicks the **Preview** Button. We used the zoom button (🔍▾) to set the zoom level to 150% so the check appears as shown here. The user can click the printer icon in the upper-left corner of the dialog to print the check, or can click the **Close** Button, then click **Print** in the main GUI.

Fig. 15.25 | Printing a paycheck. (Part 4 of 4.)

Iterating Through the Controls on the Form

Lines 28–55 iterate through the controls on the Form to print the check. References to all of the Form's controls are stored in the Form's **Controls** property. The If...Then statement (lines 30–54) determines whether the current control is a Button. The **TypeOf...Is** operator returns True if the variable between TypeOf and Is refers to an object of the type specified to the right of Is. If the current control is not a Button, the body of the If...Then statement executes; otherwise, the loop continues to the next control on the Form. Line 31 stores the value of the current control's Text property—the text displayed to the user or entered by the user.

The Select Case statement (lines 33–45) specifies how each control prints. The first Case (lines 34–36) handles the dateTimePicker control. It sets fontObject to the date's font style, which underlines the text.

The second Case (lines 37–42) executes if the control is amountTextBox. This Case draws the box around the check amount. The *x*- and *y*-coordinates of the rectangle are specified by adding the TextBox's *x–y* location on the Form to variables leftMargin and topMargin, respectively. Recall that you begin printing the check at the corner of the top and left margins of the page. Adding the margin values to the Location properties ensures that amountTextBox prints in the same position as it appears on the Form. (Line 40 subtracts two points of space to center the box on the text.) Line 42 sets the font of the text to draw to the same value as the font used to display text in the control.

The third Case (lines 43–44) executes for all the other controls. This Case sets the fontObject to the same value as the font used to display text in the control.

Line 48 sets the xPosition variable to leftMargin + controlObject.Location.X. By adding the *x*-coordinate of the current control to the left margin of the printed page, you ensure that the check will not be drawn outside the left margin of the printed page. Line 49 perform a similar operation, setting yPosition to the sum of the top margin and *y*-coordinate of the control's location. Lines 52–53 call the DrawString method on the e.Graphics property to display the current control's text. The fourth and fifth arguments are the *x*- and *y*-coordinates where the first character of the String prints. The xPosition and yPosition variables cause the text of each control to print at the correct location on the page.

Drawing Lines for the Payee, Payee Amount and Memo Information
Checks contain lines for payee, payment amount and memo information. Lines 58–76 draw these lines. We added 15 pixels to the *y*-coordinates for each line because each control's *y*-coordinate represents the *top* of the control and we want to draw the line at the bottom of the control.

Drawing a Border for the Check
The Form's border is not contained in a control, so we draw a rectangle around the check to be printed (lines 79–80). Method DrawRectangle's second argument specifies the *x*-coordinate of the upper-left corner of the rectangle. We use the value leftMargin to align the rectangle with the left margin of the printed page. The third argument specifies the *y*-coordinate of the upper-left corner of the rectangle. We use the value topMargin to align the rectangle with the top margin of the printed page.

The fourth and fifth arguments specify the rectangle's width and height. The width is set to Me.Width, which returns the Form's width. The height is set to Me.Height - 60—the height of the Form minus 60 pixels. We subtract 60 because we do not want to print the space for the Buttons at the bottom of the Form. These Buttons were created to allow users to print and preview the checks—they were *not* intended to be printed on the checks.

Event Handlers for the Preview and Print Buttons
The event handlers for the **Preview** and **Print** Buttons cause the PrintPage event for the printDocument object. When the user clicks **Preview**, method previewButton_Click (lines 96–106) first checks whether your computer has any printers installed (line 100). If not, line 101 calls method ErrorMessage (lines 109–113) to display an error message. The **Print preview** dialog cannot display a preview unless there's at least one printer installed. If

there is, line 103 assigns the `printDocument` object to the `printPreviewDialog`'s **`Document`** property to specify which document will be previewed. Then line 104 calls the `printPreviewDialog`'s `ShowDialog` method to display the dialog. This causes a `PrintPage` event on the `printDocument` object, which executes the `printDocument_PrintPage` event handler in lines 7–81 to create the graphics for the preview.

Method `printButton_Click` (lines 84–93) works similarly to method `previewButton_Click`. The key difference is line 91, which calls the `printDocument`'s `Print` method to send the document to the printer. This causes a `PrintPage` event on the `printDocument` object, which executes the event handler in lines 7–81 to create the graphics that will be printed.

15.13 Wrap-Up

This chapter began with an introduction to the .NET framework's drawing capabilities. We then presented more powerful drawing capabilities, such as changing the styles of the lines used to draw shapes and controlling the colors and patterns of filled shapes.

You learned techniques for manipulating images. We discussed class `Image`, which can store and manipulate images of various formats. You also learned how to incorporate the Windows Media Player control in an app to play audio or video. Finally, we introduced printing features, showing how to display a print preview and how to print to your computer's printer

This completes the print portion of *Visual Basic 2012 How to Program*. For those who wish to continue their Visual Basic studies, we've provided bonus online chapters in PDF format at the book's Companion Website:

```
www.pearsonhighered.com/deitel/
```

These chapters extend some of the chapters in the print book and also cover intermediate and advanced Visual Basic material.

Online chapters	
16 Exception Handling: A Deeper Look	25 Web Services
17 Strings and Characters: A Deeper Look	26 Windows Azure™ Cloud Computing Case Study
18 Files and Streams: A Deeper Look	27 Windows Presentation Foundation (WPF) GUI
19 XML and LINQ to XML	28 WPF Graphics and Multimedia
20 Windows 8 UI	29 Data Structures and Generic Collections
21 Windows 8 Graphics and Multimedia	30 ATM Case Study, Part 1: Object-Oriented Design with the UML
22 Windows Phone 8 Case Study	31 ATM Case Study, Part 2: Implementing an Object-Oriented Design
23 Introduction to Concurrency: `Async` and `Await`	
24 Web App Development with ASP.NET: A Deeper Look	

Fig. 15.26 | Online chapters.

Summary

Section 15.1 Introduction

- .NET contains many sophisticated drawing capabilities as part of namespace System.Drawing and the other namespaces that make up the .NET GDI+.

- GDI+ is an API that provides classes for creating two-dimensional vector graphics, and manipulating fonts and images.

Section 15.2 Drawing Classes and the Coordinate System

- Namespaces System.Drawing and System.Drawing.Drawing2D contain the most commonly used GDI+ components.

- Class Graphics contains methods used for drawing Strings, lines, rectangles and other shapes on a Control. These methods usually require a Pen or Brush object to render a shape. A Pen draws shape outlines; a Brush draws solid objects.

- The Color structure contains numerous Shared properties that represent colors of graphical components, plus methods that allow users to create new colors.

- Class Font contains properties that define characteristics of fonts.

- Class FontFamily contains methods for obtaining font information.

- The upper-left corner of a control has the coordinates (0, 0). The *x*-coordinate is the horizontal distance to the right from the upper-left corner. The *y*-coordinate is the vertical distance downward from the upper-left corner.

- You position text and shapes on the screen by specifying their coordinates in pixels.

- The Point structure represents the *x*–*y* coordinates of a point on a two-dimensional plane.

- The Rectangle structure defines the location, width and height of a rectangular shape.

- The Size structure represents the width and height of a shape.

Section 15.3 Graphics Contexts and Graphics Objects

- A graphics context represents a drawing surface that enables drawing on the screen. A Graphics object manages a graphics context by controlling how information is drawn.

- Every derived class of Form inherits an OnPaint method in which most graphics operations are performed. The OnPaint method triggers the Control's Paint event. Instead of overriding the OnPaint method, you can add an event handler for the Paint event.

- You can force a call to OnPaint by calling a Control's Invalidate method.

- To draw on a control, first create a graphics object by invoking the control's CreateGraphics method, then use the Graphics object's methods to draw on the control.

Section 15.4 Colors

- Structure Color defines methods and constants used to manipulate colors.

- Every color can be created from a combination of alpha, red, green and blue components (called ARGB values). All four ARGB values are integer values in the range 0–255.

- The alpha value determines the opacity of the color—0 represents a transparent color and 255 represents an opaque color. Alpha values between 0 and 255 result in a weighted blending effect of the color's RGB value with that of any background color, causing a semitransparent effect.

- Method FromArgb returns a Color object based on its ARGB or RGB arguments.

- The overloaded Pen constructors allow you to specify the colors and widths of lines.

- The System.Drawing namespace provides a Pens class containing predefined Pens.

- Derived classes of Brush define objects that color the interiors of graphical shapes.
- The SolidBrush constructor takes a Color object representing the color to draw.
- Fill methods use Brushes to fill a space with a color, pattern or image.
- Graphics method FillRectangle draws a filled-in rectangle. FillRectangle takes as parameters a Brush, the *x*- and *y*-coordinates of the rectangle's upper-left corner and its width and height.
- There are several overloaded DrawString methods; one takes as arguments the String to display, the display Font, the Brush to use for drawing and the coordinates of the String's first character.
- Class Color's Shared method FromName creates a new Color object from a String.
- A ColorDialog allows users to select from a palette of available colors or to create custom colors. An app retrieves the user's selection via the ColorDialog's Color property.
- Setting ColorDialog's FullOpen property to True indicates that the dialog should display all available colors. When FullOpen is False, the dialog shows only color swatches.

Section 15.5 Fonts
- A Font's Size property returns the font size as measured in design units, whereas property SizeInPoints returns the font size as measured in points. Design units allow the font size to be specified in one of several units of measurement, such as inches or millimeters.
- Some Font constructors accept a GraphicsUnit enumeration argument that allows you to specify the unit of measurement for the font size. Members of the GraphicsUnit enumeration include Point (1/72 inch), Display (1/75 inch on the screen or 1/100 inch on a printer), Document (1/300 inch), Millimeter, Inch and Pixel.
- Most Font constructors require a font name, the font size and the font style. The font style is specified with a constant from the FontStyle enumeration (Bold, Italic, Regular, Strikeout and Underline, or a combination of these). You can combine font styles with the Or operator.
- You can determine a font's metrics, such as height, descent, ascent and leading.
- Class FontFamily defines characteristics common to a group of related fonts. Class FontFamily provides methods to determine the font metrics shared by members of a particular family.

Section 15.6 Drawing Lines, Rectangles and Ovals
- Methods that draw hollow shapes typically require as arguments a Pen and four Integers. Methods that draw solid shapes typically require as arguments a Brush and four Integers. The Integers represent the bounding box of the shape.
- Methods FillRectangle and DrawRectangle draw rectangles. For each method, the first argument specifies the drawing object to use—for FillRectangle a Brush object and for DrawRectangle method a Pen object. The last four arguments represent the rectangle's bounding box.
- Method DrawLine takes a Pen and two pairs of Integers that specify the start and end of a line. The method then draws a line, using the Pen object.
- Methods FillEllipse and DrawEllipse draw ellipses. For each method, the first argument specifies the drawing object to use. The last four arguments represent the ellipse's bounding box. The ellipse touches the midpoint of each of the four sides of the bounding rectangle.

Section 15.7 Drawing Arcs
- Arcs are portions of ellipses and are measured in degrees, beginning at a starting angle and continuing for a specified number of degrees called the arc angle. Arcs that sweep in a clockwise direction are measured in positive degrees.
- The Point constructor takes as arguments the *x*- and *y*-coordinates of the new point.

- The Location property determines the upper-left corner of the Rectangle.
- The Size property of a Rectangle determines the arc's height and width.

Section 15.8 Drawing Polygons and Polylines
- There are several Graphics methods used to draw polygons—DrawLines draws a series of connected points, DrawPolygon draws a closed polygon and FillPolygon draws a solid polygon.

Section 15.9 Additional Brush Types
- Class LinearGradientBrush (System.Drawing.Drawing2D) enables drawing with a color gradient. One of its constructors takes four arguments—a Rectangle, two Colors and a member of enumeration LinearGradientMode. All linear gradients are defined along a line that determines the gradient endpoints. This line can be specified by either the start and endpoints or the diagonal of a rectangle. The Rectangle argument represents the endpoints of the linear gradient—the upper-left corner is the starting point and the bottom-right corner is the ending point. The second and third arguments specify the colors the gradient will use. The last argument, a type from the enumeration LinearGradientMode, specifies the gradient's direction. LinearGradientMode.ForwardDiagonal creates a gradient from the upper-left to the lower-right corner.
- Class Bitmap can produce images in color and gray scale. Graphics method FromImage retrieves the Graphics object associated with an Image, which may be used to draw on the image.
- A TextureBrush is a brush that fills the interior of a shape with an image rather than a solid color. The TextureBrush constructor takes as an argument an image that defines its texture.
- A GraphicsPath (System.Drawing.Drawing2D namespace) represents a general path. The class provides functionality for creating complex shapes from vector-based primitive graphics objects.
- GraphicsPath method CloseFigure attaches the final vector-graphic object endpoint to the initial starting point for the current figure by a straight line, then starts a new figure. Method StartFigure begins a new figure within the path without closing the previous figure.
- GraphicsPath method AddLine appends a line to the shape.
- Method TranslateTransform sets the origin of a Graphics object.
- Graphics method RotateTransform enables you to rotate drawing positions around the origin.
- Graphics method FillPath draws a filled version of a GraphicsPath.

Section 15.10 Loading, Displaying and Scaling Images
- Graphics method Clear paints the entire Form in the current background color.
- Graphics method DrawImage receives as arguments the image to draw, the *x*- and *y*-coordinates of the image's upper-left corner, the width of the image and the height of the image. The image is scaled to fit the specified width and height.

Section 15.11 Windows Media Player
- The Windows Media Player control enables an app to play video and sound in many multimedia formats, including MPEG, AVI, WAV and MIDI.
- To use the Windows Media Player control, you must add the control to the **Toolbox**.
- The Windows Media Player control provides several buttons that allow the user to play the current file, pause, stop, play the previous file, rewind, forward and play the next file. The control also includes a volume control and trackbars to select a specific position in the media file.
- The URL property of a Windows Media Player control object specifies the file that Windows Media Player is currently using.

Section 15.12 Printing

- A `PrintPreviewDialog` displays a dialog in which the user can view the document that will print before it's sent to the printer.
- A `PrintDocument` object allows you to specify how to print a specified document.
- The default event for a `PrintDocument` is the `PrintPage` event, which occurs when the data required to print the current page is needed—that is, when the document is printed or a print preview is generated. In this event handler, you define what will print by using the `Graphics` capabilities presented in this chapter.
- The `MarginBounds` represent the printable area of a page.
- References to all of a `Form`'s controls are stored in its `Controls` property.
- The `TypeOf...Is` operator returns `True` if the variable between `TypeOf` and `Is` refers to an object of the type specified to the right of `Is`.
- A `PrintPreviewDialog`'s `Document` property specifies which `PrintDocument` will be previewed.
- `PrintPreviewDialog` method `ShowDialog` displays the dialog and causes a `PrintPage` event on the `PrintDocument` object specified in the `Document` property.
- `PrintDocument` method `Print` method sends a `PrintDocument` to the printer and causes a `PrintPage` event on the `PrintDocument` object.

Terminology

Self-Review Exercises

15.1 State whether each of the following is *true* or *false*. If *false*, explain why.
    a) A Font object's size can be changed by setting its Size property.
    b) In the GDI+ coordinate system, *x*-values increase from left to right.
    c) Method FillPolygon draws a solid polygon with a specified Brush.
    d) Method DrawArc allows negative angles.
    e) Font property Size returns the size of the current font in centimeters.
    f) Pixel coordinate (0, 0) is located at the exact center of the monitor.
    g) A HatchBrush is used to draw lines.
    h) A Color is defined by its alpha, red, green and violet content.
    i) Method OnPaint is inherited by every Form.

15.2 Fill in the blanks in each of the following statements:
    a) Class _____ is used to draw lines of various colors and thicknesses.
    b) Class _____ defines the fill for a shape in such a way that the fill gradually changes from one color to another.
    c) Method _____ of class Graphics draws a line between two points.
    d) ARGB is short for _____, _____, _____ and _____.
    e) Font sizes usually are measured in units called _____.
    f) Class _____ fills a shape using a pattern drawn in a Bitmap.
    g) _____ _____ _____ allows an app to play multimedia files.
    h) Class _____ defines a path consisting of lines and curves.
    i) The FCL's drawing capabilities are part of the namespaces _____ and _____.

Answers to Self-Review Exercises

15.1 a) False. Size is a read-only property. b) True. c) True. d) True. e) False. It returns the size of the current Font in design units. f) False. The coordinate (0,0) corresponds to the upper-left corner of a GUI component on which drawing occurs. g) False. A Pen is used to draw lines, a Hatch-

Brush fills a shape with a pattern defined by a member of the HatchStyle enumeration. h) False. A color is defined by its alpha, red, green and blue content. i) True.

15.2   a) Pen. b) LinearGradientBrush. c) DrawLine. d) alpha, red, green, blue. e) points. f) TextureBrush. g) Windows Media Player h) GraphicsPath i) System.Drawing, System.Drawing.Drawing2D.

Exercises

15.3   Write a program that displays the text "Graphics and Multimedia" in Arial, Times New Roman, Courier New and Tahoma fonts, with font size 12.

15.4   Write a program to determine the metrics of the Arial font such as height, descent (the amount that characters dip below the baseline), ascent (the amount characters rise above the baseline) and leading (the difference between the ascent of one line and the descent of the previous line).

15.5   *(Rectangle and Ellipse)* Write a program that draws a filled rectangle and ellipse using pen and brush.

15.6   Write a program that draws any three arcs and any three filled pie slices.

15.7   *(Polygon)* Write a program to draw the lines of a polygon, an unfilled polygon and a filled polygon.

15.8   *(Images)* Write a program to scale an image to a specified width and height upto 400 X 400 pixels.

15.9   *(Screen Saver App)* Develop an app that simulates a screen saver. This app should add random-colored, random-sized, solid and hollow shapes at random positions on the Form. The Form should have a black background and a Timer control. Each Timer event should display another random shape. Clear the Form after every 20 shapes.

Making a Difference Exercises

15.10   *(Large-Type Displays for People with Low Vision)* The accessibility of computers and the Internet to all people, regardless of disabilities, is becoming more important as these tools play increasing roles in our personal and business lives. According to a recent estimate by the World Health Organization (www.who.int/mediacentre/factsheets/fs282/en/), 246 million people worldwide have low vision. To learn more about low vision, check out the GUI-based low vision simulation at www.webaim.org/simulations/lowvision.php. People with low vision might prefer to choose a different font and/or a larger font size when reading electronic documents and web pages. Write an app that provides a TextBox in which the user can type text. Allow the user to select Times New Roman, Arial or Courier New from a ComboBox. Provide a **Bold** CheckBox, which, if checked, makes the text bold. Include **Increase Font Size** and **Decrease Font Size** Buttons that allow the user to scale the size of the font up or down, respectively, by one point at a time. Start with a font size of 18 points. For the purposes of this exercise, set the font size on the ComboBox, Buttons and CheckBox to 20 points so that a person with low vision will be able to read the text on them.

15.11   *(Ecofont)* Ecofont—developed by SPRANQ (a Netherlands-based company)—is a font designed to reduce by as much as 20% the amount of ink used for printing, thus reducing also the number of ink cartridges used and the environmental impact of the manufacturing and shipping processes (using less energy, less fuel for shipping, and so on). The font, based on sans-serif Verdana, has small circular "holes" in the letters that are not visible in smaller sizes—such as the 9- or 10-point type frequently used. Download the free version of Ecofont (www.ecofont.com/en/products/green/font/download-the-ink-saving-font.html), then install the font file ecofont_vera_sans_regular.ttf using the instructions from the Ecofont website. Next, develop a GUI-based program that allows you to type text in a TextBox to be displayed in the Ecofont. Create **Increase Font Size** and **Decrease Font Size** buttons that allow you to scale up or down by one point at a time. Set the TextBox's Font property to 9 point Ecofont. Set the TextBox's MultiLine property to true so the user can enter multiple lines of text. As you scale up the font, you'll be able to see the holes in the letters more clearly. As you scale down, the holes will be less apparent. To change the TextBox's font programmatically, use a statement of the form:

```
inputTextBox.Font = New Font( inputTextBox.Font.FontFamily,
    inputTextBox.Font.SizeInPoints + 1 )
```

This changes the TextBox's Font property to a new Font object that uses the TextBox's current font, but adds 1 to its SizeInPoints property to increase the font size. A similar statement can be used to decrease the font size. What is the smallest font size at which you begin to notice the holes?

Online Chapters

This book's Companion Website

www.pearsoninternationaleditions.com/deitel

contains PDFs of the following:

- Chapter 16, Exception Handling: A Deeper Look
- Chapter 17, Strings and Characters: A Deeper Look
- Chapter 18, Files and Streams: A Deeper Look
- Chapter 19, XML and LINQ to XML
- Chapter 20, Windows 8 UI
- Chapter 21, Windows 8 Graphics and Multimedia
- Chapter 22, Windows Phone 8 Case Study
- Chapter 23, Introduction to Concurrency: `Async` and `Await`
- Chapter 24, Web App Development with ASP.NET: A Deeper Look
- Chapter 25, Web Services
- Chapter 26, Windows Azure™ Cloud Computing Case Study
- Chapter 27, Windows Presentation Foundation (WPF) GUI
- Chapter 28, WPF Graphics and Multimedia
- Chapter 29, Data Structures and Generic Collections
- Chapter 30, ATM Case Study, Part 1: Object-Oriented Design with the UML
- Chapter 31, ATM Case Study, Part 2: Implementing an Object-Oriented Design
- Index of Print and Online Chapters

These files can be viewed in Adobe® Reader® (`get.adobe.com/reader`). Several of the online chapters extend those in the print book. All of the online chapters cover intermediate and advanced Visual Basic material. The online index contains entries for the entire book—the index in the printed book contains entries for only the content in Chapters 1–15 and the appendices.

New copies of this book come with a Companion Website access code that is located on the the book's inside front cover. If the access code is visible or there is no access code, you purchased a used book or an edition that does not come with an access code. In this case, you can purchase access directly from the Companion Website.

A

Operator Precedence Chart

Operators are shown in decreasing order of precedence from top to bottom, with each level of precedence separated by a horizontal line. Visual Basic operators associate from left to right.

Operator	Type
TypeOf	type comparison
^	exponentiation
+	unary plus
–	unary minus
*	multiplication
/	division
\	integer division
Mod	modulus
+	addition
–	subtraction
&	concatenation
<<	bitwise left shift
>>	bitwise right shift
=	relational is equal to
<>	relational is not equal to
<	relational less than
<=	relational less than or equal to
>	relational greater than
>=	relational greater than or equal to
Like	pattern matching
Is	reference comparison
IsNot	reference comparison
Not	logical negation
And	logical AND without short-circuit evaluation
AndAlso	logical AND with short-circuit evaluation

Fig. A.1 | Operator precedence chart. (Part 1 of 2.)

Operator	Type
Or	logical inclusive OR without short-circuit evaluation
OrElse	logical inclusive OR with short-circuit evaluation
Xor	logical exclusive OR

Fig. A.1 | Operator precedence chart. (Part 2 of 2.)

Primitive Types

Type	Size in bytes	Value range
SByte	1	−128 to 127, inclusive
Byte	1	0 to 255, inclusive
Boolean	2	True or False
Char	2	0 to 65,535, inclusive (representing the Unicode character set)
Short	2	−32,768 to 32,767, inclusive
UShort	2	0 to 65,535, inclusive
Integer	4	−2,147,483,648 to 2,147,483,647, inclusive
UInteger	4	0 to 4,294,967,295, inclusive
Single	4	negative range: −3.4028235E+38 to −1.401298E-45 positive range: 1.401298E−45 to 3.4028235E+38
Long	8	−9,223,372,036,854,775,808 to 9,223,372,036,854,775,807, inclusive
ULong	8	0 to 18,446,744,073,709,551,615, inclusive
Double	8	negative range: −1.79769313486231570E+308 to −4.94065645841246544E−324 positive range: 4.94065645841246544E−324 to 1.79769313486231570E+308
Date	8	0:00:00 on 1 January 0001 to 23:59:59 on 31 December 9999
Decimal	16	Range with no decimal point: ±79,228,162,514,264,337,593,543,950,335 Range with 28 places to the right of the decimal point: ±7.9228162514264337593543950335 The smallest nonzero number is ±0.0000000000000000000000000001 (±1E−28)
String		Up to approximately 2 billion Unicode characters

Fig. B.1 | Primitive types.

To promote portability, Microsoft uses internationally recognized standards for character formats (Unicode, www.unicode.org) and floating-point numbers (IEEE 754, grouper.ieee.org/groups/754/). We discuss Unicode in Appendix E, Unicode®.

Number Systems

C

Objectives

In this appendix you'll learn:

- Basic number-systems concepts, such as base, positional value and symbol value.
- How to work with numbers represented in the binary, octal and hexadecimal number systems.
- To abbreviate binary numbers as octal or hexadecimal numbers.
- To convert octal and hexadecimal numbers to binary.
- To convert between decimal values and their binary, octal and hexadecimal equivalents.
- To understand binary arithmetic and how negative binary numbers are represented using two's-complement notation.

C.1 Introduction

In this appendix, we introduce the key number systems that programmers use, especially when they're working on software projects that require close interaction with machine-level hardware. Projects like this include operating systems, computer networking software, compilers, database systems and applications requiring high performance.

When we write an integer such as 227 or –63 in a program, the number is assumed to be in the decimal (base-10) number system. The digits in the decimal number system are 0, 1, 2, 3, 4, 5, 6, 7, 8 and 9. The lowest digit is 0 and the highest is 9—one less than the base of 10. Internally, computers use the binary (base-2) number system. The binary number system has only two digits, namely 0 and 1. Its lowest digit is 0 and its highest is 1—one less than the base of 2.

As you'll see, binary numbers tend to be much longer than their decimal equivalents. Programmers who work in assembly languages and in high-level languages that enable programmers to reach down to the machine level find it cumbersome to work with binary numbers. So, two other number systems—the octal number system (base 8) and the hexadecimal number system (base 16)—are popular primarily because they make it convenient to abbreviate binary numbers.

In the octal number system, the digits range from 0 to 7. Because both the binary and the octal number systems have fewer digits than the decimal number system, their digits are the same as the corresponding digits in decimal.

The hexadecimal number system poses a problem because it requires 16 digits—a lowest digit of 0 and a highest digit with a value equivalent to decimal 15 (one less than the base of 16). By convention, the letters A through F represent the hexadecimal digits corresponding to decimal values 10 through 15. Thus, in hexadecimal, you can have numbers like 876 consisting solely of decimal-like digits, numbers like 8A55F consisting of digits and letters and numbers like FFE consisting solely of letters. Occasionally, a hexadecimal number spells a common word such as FACE or FEED—this can appear strange to programmers accustomed to working with numbers. The digits of the binary, octal, decimal and hexadecimal number systems are summarized in Figs. C.1 and C.2.

Each of these number systems uses positional notation—each position in which a digit is written has a different positional value. For example, in the decimal number 937 (the 9, the 3 and the 7 are referred to as symbol values), we say that the 7 is written in the ones position, the 3 is written in the tens position and the 9 is written in the hundreds position. Each of these positions is a power of the base (base 10) and that these powers begin at 0 and increase by 1 as we move left in the number (Fig. C.3).

Binary digit	Octal digit	Decimal digit	Hexadecimal digit
0	0	0	0
1	1	1	1
	2	2	2
	3	3	3
	4	4	4
	5	5	5
	6	6	6
	7	7	7
		8	8
		9	9
			A (decimal value of 10)
			B (decimal value of 11)
			C (decimal value of 12)
			D (decimal value of 13)
			E (decimal value of 14)
			F (decimal value of 15)

Fig. C.1 | Digits of the binary, octal, decimal and hexadecimal number systems.

Attribute	Binary	Octal	Decimal	Hexadecimal
Base	2	8	10	16
Lowest digit	0	0	0	0
Highest digit	1	7	9	F

Fig. C.2 | Comparing the binary, octal, decimal and hexadecimal number systems.

Positional values in the decimal number system			
Decimal digit	9	3	7
Position name	Hundreds	Tens	Ones
Positional value	100	10	1
Positional value as a power of the base (10)	10^2	10^1	10^0

Fig. C.3 | Positional values in the decimal number system.

For longer decimal numbers, the next positions to the left would be the thousands position (10 to the 3rd power), the ten-thousands position (10 to the 4th power), the hundred-thousands position (10 to the 5th power), the millions position (10 to the 6th power), the ten-millions position (10 to the 7th power) and so on.

In the binary number 101, the rightmost 1 is written in the ones position, the 0 is written in the twos position and the leftmost 1 is written in the fours position. Each position is a power of the base (base 2), and these powers begin at 0 and increase by 1 as we move left in the number (Fig. C.4). So, $101 = 1 * 2^2 + 0 * 2^1 + 1 * 2^0 = 4 + 0 + 1 = 5$.

For longer binary numbers, the next positions to the left would be the eights position (2 to the 3rd power), the sixteens position (2 to the 4th power), the thirty-twos position (2 to the 5th power), the sixty-fours position (2 to the 6th power) and so on.

In the octal number 425, we say that the 5 is written in the ones position, the 2 is written in the eights position and the 4 is written in the sixty-fours position. Each of these positions is a power of the base (base 8) and that these powers begin at 0 and increase by 1 as we move left in the number (Fig. C.5).

For longer octal numbers, the next positions to the left would be the five-hundred-and-twelves position (8 to the 3rd power), the four-thousand-and-ninety-sixes position (8 to the 4th power), the thirty-two-thousand-seven-hundred-and-sixty-eights position (8 to the 5th power) and so on.

In the hexadecimal number 3DA, we say that the A is written in the ones position, the D is written in the sixteens position and the 3 is written in the two-hundred-and-fifty-sixes position. Each of these positions is a power of the base (base 16) and that these powers begin at 0 and increase by 1 as we move left in the number (Fig. C.6).

For longer hexadecimal numbers, the next positions to the left would be the four-thousand-and-ninety-sixes position (16 to the 3rd power), the sixty-five-thousand-five-hundred-and-thirty-sixes position (16 to the 4th power) and so on.

Positional values in the binary number system			
Binary digit	1	0	1
Position name	Fours	Twos	Ones
Positional value	4	2	1
Positional value as a power of the base (2)	2^2	2^1	2^0

Fig. C.4 | Positional values in the binary number system.

Positional values in the octal number system			
Decimal digit	4	2	5
Position name	Sixty-fours	Eights	Ones
Positional value	64	8	1
Positional value as a power of the base (8)	8^2	8^1	8^0

Fig. C.5 | Positional values in the octal number system.

Positional values in the hexadecimal number system			
Decimal digit	3	D	A
Position name	Two-hundred-and-fifty-sixes	Sixteens	Ones
Positional value	256	16	1
Positional value as a power of the base (16)	16^2	16^1	16^0

Fig. C.6 | Positional values in the hexadecimal number system.

C.2 Abbreviating Binary Numbers as Octal and Hexadecimal Numbers

The main use for octal and hexadecimal numbers in computing is for abbreviating lengthy binary representations. Figure C.7 highlights the fact that lengthy binary numbers can be expressed concisely in number systems with higher bases than the binary number system.

Decimal number	Binary representation	Octal representation	Hexadecimal representation
0	0	0	0
1	1	1	1
2	10	2	2
3	11	3	3
4	100	4	4
5	101	5	5
6	110	6	6
7	111	7	7
8	1000	10	8
9	1001	11	9
10	1010	12	A
11	1011	13	B
12	1100	14	C
13	1101	15	D
14	1110	16	E
15	1111	17	F
16	10000	20	10

Fig. C.7 | Decimal, binary, octal and hexadecimal equivalents.

A particularly important relationship that both the octal and the hexadecimal number system have to the binary system is that the bases of octal and hexadecimal (8 and 16, respectively) are powers of the base of the binary number system (base 2). Consider the following 12-digit binary number and its octal and hexadecimal equivalents. See if you can determine how this relationship makes it convenient to abbreviate binary numbers in octal or hexadecimal. The answer follows the numbers.

Binary number	Octal equivalent	Hexadecimal equivalent
100011010001	4321	8D1

To see how the binary number converts easily to octal, simply break the 12-digit binary number into groups of three consecutive bits each and write those groups over the corresponding digits of the octal number as follows:

100	011	010	001
4	3	2	1

The octal digit you have written under each group of three bits corresponds precisely to the octal equivalent of that 3-digit binary number, as shown in Fig. C.7.

The same kind of relationship can be observed in converting from binary to hexadecimal. Break the 12-digit binary number into groups of four consecutive bits each and write those groups over the corresponding digits of the hexadecimal number, as follows:

1000	1101	0001
8	D	1

Notice that the hexadecimal digit you wrote under each group of four bits corresponds precisely to the hexadecimal equivalent of that 4-digit binary number as shown in Fig. C.7.

C.3 Converting Octal and Hexadecimal Numbers to Binary Numbers

In the previous section, you learned how to convert binary numbers to their octal and hexadecimal equivalents by forming groups of binary digits and simply rewriting them as their equivalent octal digit values or hexadecimal digit values. This process may be used in reverse to produce the binary equivalent of a given octal or hexadecimal number.

For example, the octal number 653 is converted to binary simply by writing the 6 as its 3-digit binary equivalent 110, the 5 as its 3-digit binary equivalent 101 and the 3 as its 3-digit binary equivalent 011 to form the 9-digit binary number 110101011.

The hexadecimal number FAD5 is converted to binary simply by writing the F as its 4-digit binary equivalent 1111, the A as its 4-digit binary equivalent 1010, the D as its 4-digit binary equivalent 1101 and the 5 as its 4-digit binary equivalent 0101 to form the 16-digit binary number 1111101011010101.

C.4 Converting from Binary, Octal or Hexadecimal to Decimal

We're accustomed to working in decimal, and therefore it is often convenient to convert a binary, octal, or hexadecimal number to decimal to get a sense of what the number is "really" worth. Our diagrams in Section C.1 express the positional values in decimal. To convert a number to decimal from another base, multiply the decimal equivalent of each digit by its positional value and sum these products. For example, the binary number 110101 is converted to decimal 53, as shown in Fig. C.8.

To convert octal 7614 to decimal 3980, we use the same technique, this time using appropriate octal positional values, as shown in Fig. C.9.

To convert hexadecimal AD3B to decimal 44347, we use the same technique, this time using appropriate hexadecimal positional values, as shown in Fig. C.10.

Converting a binary number to decimal					
Positional values:	32	16	8	4	2	1
Symbol values:	1	1	0	1	0	1
Products:	1*32=32	1*16=16	0*8=0	1*4=4	0*2=0	1*1=1
Sum:	= 32 + 16 + 0 + 4 + 0s + 1 = 53					

Fig. C.8 | Converting a binary number to decimal.

Converting an octal number to decimal			
Positional values:	512	64	8	1
Symbol values:	7	6	1	4
Products	7*512=3584	6*64=384	1*8=8	4*1=4
Sum:	= 3584 + 384 + 8 + 4 = 3980			

Fig. C.9 | Converting an octal number to decimal.

Converting a hexadecimal number to decimal			
Positional values:	4096	256	16	1
Symbol values:	A	D	3	B
Products	A*4096=40960	D*256=3328	3*16=48	B*1=11
Sum:	= 40960 + 3328 + 48 + 11 = 44347			

Fig. C.10 | Converting a hexadecimal number to decimal.

C.5 Converting from Decimal to Binary, Octal or Hexadecimal

The conversions in Section C.4 follow naturally from the positional notation conventions. Converting from decimal to binary, octal, or hexadecimal also follows these conventions.

Suppose we wish to convert decimal 57 to binary. We write the positional values of the columns right to left until we reach a column whose positional value is greater than the decimal number. We don't need that column, so we discard it. Thus, we first write:

Positional values:	64	32	16	8	4	2	1

Then we discard the column with positional value 64, leaving:

Positional values:	32	16	8	4	2	1

Next we work from the leftmost column to the right. We divide 32 into 57 and observe that there is one 32 in 57 with a remainder of 25, so we write 1 in the 32 column. We divide 16 into 25 and observe that there is one 16 in 25 with a remainder of 9 and write 1 in the 16 column. We divide 8 into 9 and observe that there is one 8 in 9 with a remainder of 1. The next two columns each produce quotients of 0 when their positional values are divided into 1, so we write 0s in the 4 and 2 columns. Finally, 1 into 1 is 1, so we write 1 in the 1 column. This yields:

Positional values:	32	16	8	4	2	1
Symbol values:	1	1	1	0	0	1

and thus decimal 57 is equivalent to binary 111001.

To convert decimal 103 to octal, we write the positional values of the columns until we reach a column whose positional value is greater than the decimal number. We do not need that column, so we discard it. Thus, we first write:

Positional values:	512	64	8	1

Then we discard the column with positional value 512, yielding:

Positional values:	64	8	1

Next we work from the leftmost column to the right. We divide 64 into 103 and observe that there is one 64 in 103 with a remainder of 39, so we write 1 in the 64 column. We divide 8 into 39 and observe that there are four 8s in 39 with a remainder of 7, so we write 4 in the 8 column. Finally, we divide 1 into 7 and observe that there are seven 1s in 7 with no remainder, so we write 7 in the 1 column. This yields:

Positional values:	64	8	1
Symbol values:	1	4	7

and thus decimal 103 is equivalent to octal 147.

To convert decimal 375 to hexadecimal, we write the positional values of the columns until we reach a column whose positional value is greater than the decimal number. We do not need that column, so we discard it. Thus, we first write:

Positional values:	4096	256	16	1

Then we discard the column with positional value 4096, yielding:

Positional values:	256	16	1

Next we work from the leftmost column to the right. We divide 256 into 375 and observe that there is one 256 in 375 with a remainder of 119, so we write 1 in the 256 column. We divide 16 into 119 and observe that there are seven 16s in 119 with a remainder of 7, so we write 7 in the 16 column. Finally, we divide 1 into 7 and observe that there are seven 1s in 7 with no remainder, so we write 7 in the 1 column. This yields:

Positional values:	256	16	1
Symbol values:	1	7	7

and thus decimal 375 is equivalent to hexadecimal 177.

C.6 Negative Binary Numbers: Two's-Complement Notation

The discussion so far in this appendix has focused on positive numbers. In this section, we explain how computers represent negative numbers using *two's-complement notation*. First we explain how the two's complement of a binary number is formed, then we show why it represents the negative value of the given binary number.

Consider a machine with 32-bit integers. Suppose

```
Dim value As Integer = 13
```

The 32-bit representation of value is

```
00000000 00000000 00000000 00001101
```

To form the negative of value we first form its *one's complement* by combining value with &H7FFFFFFF using Visual Basic's Xor operator, as in:

```
onesComplement = value Xor &H7FFFFFFF
```

Internally, onesComplement is now value with each of its bits reversed—ones become zeros and zeros become ones, as follows:

```
value:
00000000 00000000 00000000 00001101
onesComplement
11111111 11111111 11111111 11110010
```

To form the two's complement of value, we simply add 1 to value's one's complement, which produces

```
Two's complement of value:
11111111 11111111 11111111 11110011
```

Now if this is in fact equal to −13, we should be able to add it to binary 13 and obtain a result of 0. Let us try this:

```
  00000000 00000000 00000000 00001101
+ 11111111 11111111 11111111 11110011
-------------------------------------
  00000000 00000000 00000000 00000000
```

The carry bit coming out of the leftmost column is discarded and we indeed get 0 as a result. If we add the one's complement of a number to the number, the result will be all 1s. The key to getting a result of all zeros is that the two's complement is one more than the one's complement. The addition of 1 causes each column to add to 0 with a carry of 1. The carry keeps moving leftward until it is discarded from the leftmost bit, and thus the resulting number is all zeros.

Computers actually perform a subtraction, such as

```
x = a - value;
```

by adding the two's complement of value to a, as follows:

```
x = a + (onesComplement + 1);
```

Suppose a is 27 and `value` is 13, as before. If the two's complement of `value` is actually the negative of `value`, then adding the two's complement of value to a should produce the result 14. Let us try this:

```
  a (that is, 27)           00000000 00000000 00000000 00011011
 +(onesComplement + 1)     +11111111 11111111 11111111 11110011
                           -------------------------------------
                            00000000 00000000 00000000 00001110
```

which is indeed equal to 14.

Self-Review Exercises

C.1 Fill in the blanks in each of the following statements:
   a) The bases of the decimal, binary, octal and hexadecimal number systems are _____, _____, _____ and _____, respectively.
   b) The positional value of the rightmost digit of any number in either binary, octal, decimal or hexadecimal is always _____.
   c) The positional value of the digit to the left of the rightmost digit of any number in binary, octal, decimal or hexadecimal is always equal to _____.

C.2 State whether each of the following is *true* or *false*. If *false*, explain why.
   a) A popular reason for using the decimal number system is that it forms a convenient notation for abbreviating binary numbers simply by substituting one decimal digit per group of four binary bits.
   b) The highest digit in any base is one more than the base.
   c) The lowest digit in any base is one less than the base.

C.3 In general, the decimal, octal and hexadecimal representations of a given binary number contain (more/fewer) digits than the binary number contains.

C.4 The (octal / hexadecimal / decimal) representation of a large binary value is the most concise (of the given alternatives).

C.5 Fill in the missing values in this chart of positional values for the rightmost four positions in each of the indicated number systems:

decimal	1000	100	10	1
hexadecimal	...	256	...	...
binary	...	...	...	...
octal	512	...	8	...

C.6 Convert binary 110101011000 to octal and to hexadecimal.

C.7 Convert hexadecimal FACE to binary.

C.8 Convert octal 7316 to binary.

C.9 Convert hexadecimal 4FEC to octal. [*Hint:* First convert 4FEC to binary, then convert that binary number to octal.]

C.10 Convert binary 1101110 to decimal.

C.11 Convert octal 317 to decimal.

C.12 Convert hexadecimal EFD4 to decimal.

C.13 Convert decimal 177 to binary, to octal and to hexadecimal.

C.14 Show the binary representation of decimal 417. Then show the one's complement of 417 and the two's complement of 417.

C.15 What is the result when a number and its two's complement are added to each other?

Answers to Self-Review Exercises

C.1 a) 10, 2, 8, 16. b) 1 (the base raised to the zeroth power). c) The base of the number system.

C.2 a) False. Hexadecimal does this. b) False. The highest digit in any base is one less than the base. c) False. The lowest digit in any base is zero.

C.3 Fewer.

C.4 Hexadecimal.

C.5 Fill in the missing values in this chart of positional values for the rightmost four positions in each of the indicated number systems:

decimal	1000	100	10	1
hexadecimal	4096	256	16	1
binary	8	4	2	1
octal	512	64	8	1

C.6 Octal 6530; Hexadecimal D58.

C.7 Binary 1111 1010 1100 1110.

C.8 Binary 111 011 001 110.

C.9 Binary 0 100 111 111 101 100; Octal 47754.

C.10 Decimal 2 + 4 + 8 + 32 + 64 = 110.

C.11 Decimal 7 + 1 * 8 + 3 * 64 = 7 + 8 + 192 = 207.

C.12 Decimal 4 + 13 * 16 + 15 * 256 + 14 * 4096 = 61396.

C.13 Decimal 177
to binary:

```
256 128 64 32 16 8 4 2 1
128 64 32 16 8 4 2 1
(1*128)+(0*64)+(1*32)+(1*16)+(0*8)+(0*4)+(0*2)+(1*1)
10110001
```

to octal:

```
512 64 8 1
64 8 1
(2*64)+(6*8)+(1*1)
261
```

to hexadecimal:

```
256 16 1
16 1
(11*16)+(1*1)
(B*16)+(1*1)
B1
```

C.14 Binary:

```
512 256 128 64 32 16 8 4 2 1
256 128 64 32 16 8 4 2 1
(1*256)+(1*128)+(0*64)+(1*32)+(0*16)+(0*8)+(0*4)+(0*2)+(1*1)
110100001
```

```
One's complement: 001011110
Two's complement: 001011111
Check: Original binary number + its two's complement
```

```
110100001
001011111
---------
000000000
```

C.15 Zero.

Exercises

C.16 Some people argue that many of our calculations would be easier in the base-12 number system because 12 is divisible by so many more numbers than 10 (for base 10). What is the lowest digit in base 12? What would be the highest symbol for the digit in base 12? What are the positional values of the rightmost four positions of any number in the base-12 number system?

C.17 Complete the following chart of positional values for the rightmost four positions in each of the indicated number systems:

decimal	1000	100	10	1
base 6	...	...	6	...
base 13	...	169	...	...
base 3	27	...	...	...

C.18 Convert binary 100101111010 to octal and to hexadecimal.

C.19 Convert hexadecimal 3A7D to binary.

C.20 Convert hexadecimal 765F to octal. (*Hint:* First convert 765F to binary, then convert that binary number to octal.)

C.21 Convert binary 1011110 to decimal.

C.22 Convert octal 426 to decimal.

C.23 Convert hexadecimal FFFF to decimal.

C.24 Convert decimal 299 to binary, to octal and to hexadecimal.

C.25 Show the binary representation of decimal 779. Then show the one's complement of 779 and the two's complement of 779.

C.26 Show the two's complement of integer value –1 on a machine with 32-bit integers.

ASCII Character Set

ASCII character set										
	0	1	2	3	4	5	6	7	8	9
0	nul	soh	stx	etx	eot	enq	ack	bel	bs	ht
1	lf	vt	ff	cr	so	si	dle	dc1	dc2	dc3
2	dc4	nak	syn	etb	can	em	sub	esc	fs	gs
3	rs	us	sp	!	"	#	$	%	&	'
4	(	)	*	+	,	-	.	/	0	1
5	2	3	4	5	6	7	8	9	:	;
6	<	=	>	?	@	A	B	C	D	E
7	F	G	H	I	J	K	L	M	N	O
8	P	Q	R	S	T	U	V	W	X	Y
9	Z	[	\	]	^	_	`	a	b	c
10	d	e	f	g	h	i	j	k	l	m
11	n	o	p	q	r	s	t	u	v	w
12	x	y	z	{	|	}	~	del		

Fig. D.1 | ASCII character set.

The digits at the left of the table are the left digits of the decimal equivalent (0–127) of the character code, and the digits at the top of the table are the right digits of the character code. For example, the character "F" is in row 7 and column 0, so its character code is 70. Similarly, the character "&" is in row 3 and column 8, so its character code is 38.

Most users of this book are interested in the ASCII character set used to represent English characters on many computers. The ASCII character set is a subset of the Unicode character set used by Visual Basic to represent characters from most of the world's languages. For more information on the Unicode character set, see Appendix E.

E

Unicode®

E.1 Introduction

The use of inconsistent character **encodings** (that is, numeric values associated with characters) in the developing of global software products causes serious problems, because computers process information as numbers. For instance, the character "a" is converted to a numeric value so that a computer can manipulate that piece of data. Many countries and corporations have developed their own encoding systems that are incompatible with the encoding systems of other countries and corporations. For example, the Microsoft Windows operating system assigns the value 0xC0 to the character "A with a grave accent"; the Apple Macintosh operating system assigns that same value to an upside-down question mark. This results in the misrepresentation and possible corruption of data when it is not processed as intended.

In the absence of a widely implemented universal character-encoding standard, global software developers had to **localize** their products extensively before distribution. Localization includes the language translation and cultural adaptation of content. The process of localization usually includes significant modifications to the source code (such as the conversion of numeric values and the underlying assumptions made by programmers), which results in increased costs and delays releasing the software. For example, some English-speaking programmers might design global software products assuming that a single character can be represented by one byte. However, when those products are localized for Asian markets, the programmer's assumptions are no longer valid; thus, the majority, if not the entirety, of the code needs to be rewritten. Localization is necessary with each release of a version. By the time a software product is localized for a particular market, a newer version, which needs to be localized as well, may be ready for distribution. As a result, it is cumbersome and costly to produce and distribute global software products in a market where there is no universal character-encoding standard.

In response to this situation, the **Unicode Standard**, an encoding standard that facilitates the production and distribution of software, was created. The Unicode Standard outlines a specification to produce consistent encoding of the world's characters and symbols. Software products that handle text encoded in the Unicode Standard need to be localized, but the localization process is simpler and more efficient, because the numeric values need not be converted and the assumptions made by programmers about the character encoding are universal. The Unicode Standard is maintained by a nonprofit organization called the **Unicode Consortium**, whose members include Apple, IBM, Microsoft, Oracle, Sun Microsystems, Sybase and many others.

When the Consortium envisioned and developed the Unicode Standard, they wanted an encoding system that was **universal, efficient, uniform** and **unambiguous**. A universal encoding system encompasses all commonly used characters. An efficient encoding system allows text files to be parsed easily. A uniform encoding system assigns fixed values to all characters. An unambiguous encoding system represents a given character in a consistent manner. These four terms are referred to as the Unicode Standard **design basis**.

E.2 Unicode Transformation Formats

Although Unicode incorporates the limited ASCII character set (that is, a collection of characters), it encompasses a more comprehensive character set. In ASCII each character is represented by a byte containing 0s and 1s. One byte is capable of storing the binary numbers from 0 to 255. Each character is assigned a number between 0 and 255; thus, ASCII-based systems can support only 256 characters, a tiny fraction of world's characters. Unicode extends the ASCII character set by encoding the vast majority of the world's characters. The Unicode Standard encodes all of those characters in a uniform numerical space from 0 to 10FFFF hexadecimal. An implementation will express these numbers in one of several transformation formats, choosing the one that best fits the particular application at hand.

Three such formats are in use, called **UTF-8**, **UTF-16** and **UTF-32**, depending on the size of the units—in bits—being used. UTF-8, a variable-width encoding form, requires one to four bytes to express each Unicode character. UTF-8 data consists of 8-bit bytes (sequences of one, two, three or four bytes depending on the character being encoded) and is well suited for ASCII-based systems, where there is a predominance of one-byte characters (ASCII represents characters as one byte). Currently, UTF-8 is widely implemented in UNIX systems and in databases.

The variable-width UTF-16 encoding form expresses Unicode characters in units of 16 bits (that is, as two adjacent bytes, or a short integer in many machines). Most characters of Unicode are expressed in a single 16-bit unit. However, characters with values above FFFF hexadecimal are expressed with an ordered pair of 16-bit units called **surrogates**. Surrogates are 16-bit integers in the range D800 through DFFF, which are used solely for the purpose of "escaping" into higher-numbered characters. Approximately one million characters can be expressed in this manner. Although a surrogate pair requires 32 bits to represent characters, it is space efficient to use these 16-bit units. Surrogates are rare characters in current implementations. Many string-handling implementations are written in terms of UTF-16. [*Note:* Details and sample code for UTF-16 handling are available on the Unicode Consortium website at www.unicode.org.]

Implementations that require significant use of rare characters or entire scripts encoded above FFFF hexadecimal should use UTF-32, a 32-bit, fixed-width encoding form that usually requires twice as much memory as UTF-16 encoded characters. The major advantage of the fixed-width UTF-32 encoding form is that it expresses all characters uniformly, so it is easy to handle in arrays.

There are few guidelines that state when to use a particular encoding form. The best encoding form to use depends on computer systems and business protocols, not on the data itself. Typically, the UTF-8 encoding form should be used where computer systems and business protocols require data to be handled in 8-bit units, particularly in legacy systems being upgraded, because it often simplifies changes to existing programs. For this reason, UTF-8 has become the encoding form of choice on the Internet. Likewise, UTF-

16 is the encoding form of choice on Microsoft Windows applications. UTF-32 is likely to become more widely used in the future, as more characters are encoded with values above FFFF hexadecimal. Also, UTF-32 requires less sophisticated handling than UTF-16 in the presence of surrogate pairs. Figure E.1 shows the different ways in which the three encoding forms handle character encoding.

Character	UTF-8	UTF-16	UTF-32
Latin Capital Letter A	0x41	0x0041	0x00000041
Greek Capital Letter Alpha	0xCD 0x91	0x0391	0x00000391
CJK Unified Ideograph-4e95	0xE4 0xBA 0x95	0x4E95	0x00004E95
Old Italic Letter A	0xF0 0x80 0x83 0x80	0xDC00 0xDF00	0x00010300

Fig. E.1 | Correlation between the three encoding forms.

E.3 Characters and Glyphs

The Unicode Standard consists of characters, written components (that is, alphabetic letters, numerals, punctuation marks, accent marks, and so on) that can be represented by numeric values. Examples of characters include: U+0041 LATIN CAPITAL LETTER A. In the first character representation, U+*yyyy* is a **code value**, in which U+ refers to Unicode code values, as opposed to other hexadecimal values. The *yyyy* represents a four-digit hexadecimal number of an encoded character. Code values are bit combinations that represent encoded characters. Characters are represented with **glyphs**, various shapes, fonts and sizes for displaying characters. There are no code values for glyphs in the Unicode Standard. Examples of glyphs are shown in Fig. E.2.

Fig. E.2 | Various glyphs of the character A.

The Unicode Standard encompasses the alphabets, ideographs, syllabaries, punctuation marks, **diacritics**, mathematical operators and so on that comprise the written languages and scripts of the world. A diacritic is a special mark added to a character to distinguish it from another letter or to indicate an accent (for example, in Spanish, the tilde "~" above the character "n"). Currently, Unicode provides code values for 94,140 character representations, with more than 880,000 code values reserved for future expansion.

E.4 Advantages/Disadvantages of Unicode

The Unicode Standard has several significant advantages that promote its use. One is its impact on the performance of the international economy. Unicode standardizes the characters for the world's writing systems to a uniform model that promotes transferring and sharing data. Programs developed using such a schema maintain their accuracy, because each character has a single definition (that is, *a* is always U+0061, % is always U+0025). This enables corporations to manage the high demands of international markets by processing different writing systems at the same time. Also, all characters can be managed in an identical manner, thus avoiding any confusion caused by different character-code architectures. Moreover, managing data in a consistent manner eliminates data corruption, because data can be sorted, searched and manipulated via a consistent process.

Another advantage of the Unicode Standard is portability (that is, the ability to execute software on disparate computers or with disparate operating systems). Most operating systems, databases, programming languages and web browsers currently support, or are planning to support, Unicode. Additionally, Unicode includes more characters than any other character set in common use (although it does not yet include all of the world's characters).

A disadvantage of the Unicode Standard is the amount of memory required by UTF-16 and UTF-32. ASCII character sets are 8 bits in length, so they require less storage than the default 16-bit Unicode character set. However, the **double-byte character set** (DBCS) and the **multibyte character set** (MBCS) that encode Asian characters (ideographs) require two to four bytes, respectively. In such instances, the UTF-16 or the UTF-32 encoding forms may be used with little hindrance to memory and performance.

E.5 Using Unicode

Visual Studio uses Unicode UTF-16 encoding to represent all characters. Figure E.3 uses Visual Basic to display the text "Welcome to Unicode!" in eight different languages: English, French, German, Japanese, Portuguese, Russian, Spanish and Traditional Chinese.

```
 1   ' Fig. E.3: UnicodeDemo.vb
 2   ' Using Unicode encoding.
 3   Public Class UnicodeDemo
 4      Private Sub UnicodeDemo_Load(ByVal sender As System.Object, _
 5         ByVal e As System.EventArgs) Handles MyBase.Load
 6         'English
 7         englishLabel.Text = ChrW(&H57) & ChrW(&H65) & ChrW(&H6C) & _
 8            ChrW(&H63) & ChrW(&H6F) & ChrW(&H6D) & ChrW(&H65) & _
 9            ChrW(&H20) & ChrW(&H74) & ChrW(&H6F) & ChrW(&H20) & _
10            "Unicode" & ChrW(&H21)
11
12         ' French
13         frenchLabel.Text = ChrW(&H42) & ChrW(&H69) & ChrW(&H65) & _
14            ChrW(&H6E) & ChrW(&H76) & ChrW(&H65) & ChrW(&H6E) & _
15            ChrW(&H75) & ChrW(&H65) & ChrW(&H20) & ChrW(&H61) & _
16            ChrW(&H75) & ChrW(&H20) & "Unicode" & ChrW(&H21)
```

Fig. E.3 | Windows application demonstrating Unicode encoding. (Part 1 of 2.)

```
17
18          ' German
19          germanLabel.Text = ChrW(&H57) & ChrW(&H69) & ChrW(&H6C) & _
20              ChrW(&H6B) & ChrW(&H6F) & ChrW(&H6D) & ChrW(&H6D) & _
21              ChrW(&H65) & ChrW(&H6E) & ChrW(&H20) & ChrW(&H7A) & _
22              ChrW(&H75) & ChrW(&H20) & "Unicode" & ChrW(&H21)
23
24          ' Japanese
25          japaneseLabel.Text = "Unicode " & ChrW(&H3078) & _
26              ChrW(&H3087) & ChrW(&H3045) & ChrW(&H3053) & _
27              ChrW(&H305D) & ChrW(&H21)
28
29          ' Portuguese
30          portugueseLabel.Text = ChrW(&H53) & ChrW(&HE9) & ChrW(&H6A) & _
31              ChrW(&H61) & ChrW(&H20) & ChrW(&H42) & _
32              ChrW(&H65) & ChrW(&H6D) & ChrW(&H76) & _
33              ChrW(&H69) & ChrW(&H6E) & ChrW(&H64) & _
34              ChrW(&H6F) & ChrW(&H20) & "Unicode" & ChrW(&H21)
35
36          ' Russian
37          russianLabel.Text = ChrW(&H414) & ChrW(&H43E) & ChrW(&H431) & _
38              ChrW(&H440) & ChrW(&H43E) & ChrW(&H20) & _
39              ChrW(&H43F) & ChrW(&H43E) & ChrW(&H436) & _
40              ChrW(&H430) & ChrW(&H43B) & ChrW(&H43E) & _
41              ChrW(&H432) & ChrW(&H430) & ChrW(&H442) & _
42              ChrW(&H44A) & ChrW(&H20) & ChrW(&H432) & _
43              ChrW(&H20) & "Unicode" & ChrW(&H21)
44
45          ' Spanish
46          spanishLabel.Text = ChrW(&H42) & ChrW(&H69) & ChrW(&H65) & _
47              ChrW(&H6E) & ChrW(&H76) & ChrW(&H65) & _
48              ChrW(&H6E) & ChrW(&H69) & ChrW(&H64) & _
49              ChrW(&H61) & ChrW(&H20) & ChrW(&H61) & _
50              ChrW(&H20) & "Unicode" & ChrW(&H21)
51
52          ' Traditional Chinese
53          chineseLabel.Text = ChrW(&H6B22) & ChrW(&H8FCE) & _
54              ChrW(&H4F7F) & ChrW(&H7528) & ChrW(&H20) & _
55              "Unicode" & ChrW(&H21)
56      End Sub ' UnicodeDemo_Load
57  End Class ' UnicodeDemo
```

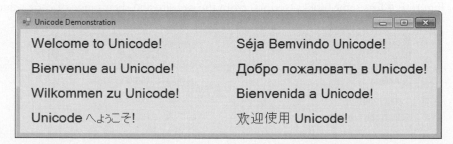

Fig. E.3 | Windows application demonstrating Unicode encoding. (Part 2 of 2.)

The first welcome message (lines 7–10) contains the hexadecimal codes for the English text. The **Code Charts** page on the Unicode Consortium website contains a document that lists the code values for the **Basic Latin** block (or category), which includes the English alphabet. The hexadecimal codes in lines 7–8 equate to "Welcome." When using Unicode characters in Visual Basic, the format &H*yyyy* is used, where *yyyy* represents the hexadecimal Unicode encoding. For example, the letter "W" (in "Welcome") is denoted by &H57. [*Note:* The actual code for the letter "W" is &H0057, but Visual Studio removes the two zeros.] Line 9 contains the hexadecimal for the *space* character (&H20). The hexadecimal value for the word "to" is on lines 9, and the word "Unicode" is on line 10. "Unicode" is not encoded because it is a registered trademark and has no equivalent translation in most languages. Line 10 also contains the &H21 notation for the exclamation mark (!).

The remaining welcome messages (lines 13–55) contain the hexadecimal codes for the other seven languages. The code values used for the French, German, Portuguese and Spanish text are located in the **Basic Latin** block, the code values used for the Traditional Chinese text are located in the **CJK Unified Ideographs** block, the code values used for the Russian text are located in the **Cyrillic** block and the code values used for the Japanese text are located in the **Hiragana** block.

[*Note:* To render the Asian characters in a Windows app, you would need to install the proper language files on your computer. To do this, open the **Regional Options** dialog from the **Control Panel** (**Start > Control Panel > Clock, Language, and Region**). Under the **Keyboard and Languages** tab, click the **Change Keyboards...** button. At the bottom of the **General** tab is a list of languages. Click **Add...** then search the tree view for the **Japanese** and the **Traditional Chinese** checkboxes and press **OK**. Follow the directions of the install wizard to install the languages. For additional assistance, visit `www.unicode.org/help/display_problems.html`.]

E.6 Character Ranges

The Unicode Standard assigns code values, which range from 0000 (**Basic Latin**) to E007F (**Tags**), to the written characters of the world. Currently, there are code values for 94,140 characters. To simplify the search for a character and its associated code value, the Unicode Standard generally groups code values by script and function (that is, Latin characters are grouped in a block, mathematical operators are grouped in another block, and so on). As a rule, a script is a single writing system that is used for multiple languages (for example, the Latin script is used for English, French, Spanish, and so on). The **Code Charts** page on the Unicode Consortium website lists all the defined blocks and their respective code values. Figure E.4 lists some blocks (scripts) from the website and their range of code values.

Script	Range of code values
Arabic	U+0600–U+06FF
Basic Latin	U+0000–U+007F
Bengali (India)	U+0980–U+09FF
Cherokee (Native America)	U+13A0–U+13FF

Fig. E.4 | Some character ranges. (Part 1 of 2.)

Script	Range of code values
CJK Unified Ideographs (East Asia)	U+4E00–U+9FAF
Cyrillic (Russia and Eastern Europe)	U+0400–U+04FF
Ethiopic	U+1200–U+137F
Greek	U+0370–U+03FF
Hangul Jamo (Korea)	U+1100–U+11FF
Hebrew	U+0590–U+05FF
Hiragana (Japan)	U+3040–U+309F
Khmer (Cambodia)	U+1780–U+17FF
Lao (Laos)	U+0E80–U+0EFF
Mongolian	U+1800–U+18AF
Myanmar	U+1000–U+109F
Ogham (Ireland)	U+1680–U+169F
Runic (Germany and Scandinavia)	U+16A0–U+16FF
Sinhala (Sri Lanka)	U+0D80–U+0DFF
Telugu (India)	U+0C00–U+0C7F
Thai	U+0E00–U+0E7F

Fig. E.4 | Some character ranges. (Part 2 of 2.)

Summary

- Before Unicode, software developers were plagued by the use of inconsistent character encoding (that is, numeric values for characters). Most countries and organizations had their own encoding systems, which were incompatible. A good example is the individual encoding systems on the Windows and Macintosh platforms.

- Computers process data by converting characters to numeric values. For instance, the character "a" is converted to a numeric value so that a computer can manipulate that piece of data.

- Without Unicode, localization of global software requires significant modifications to the source code, which results in increased cost and delays in releasing the product.

- Localization is necessary with each release of a version. By the time a software product is localized for a particular market, a newer version, which needs to be localized as well, is ready for distribution. As a result, it is cumbersome and costly to produce and distribute global software products in a market where there is no universal character-encoding standard.

- The Unicode Consortium developed the Unicode Standard in response to the serious problems created by multiple character encodings and the use of those encodings.

- The Unicode Standard facilitates the production and distribution of localized software. It outlines a specification for the consistent encoding of the world's characters and symbols.

- Software products that handle text encoded in the Unicode Standard need to be localized, but the localization process is simpler and more efficient because the numeric values need not be converted.

- The Unicode Standard is designed to be universal, efficient, uniform and unambiguous.

- A universal encoding system encompasses all commonly used characters; an efficient encoding system parses text files easily; a uniform encoding system assigns fixed values to all characters; and an unambiguous encoding system represents the same character for any given value.

- Unicode extends the limited ASCII character set to include all the major characters of the world.

- Unicode makes use of three Unicode Transformation Formats (UTF): UTF-8, UTF-16 and UTF-32, each of which may be appropriate for use in different contexts.

- UTF-8 data consists of 8-bit bytes (sequences of one, two, three or four bytes depending on the character being encoded) and is well suited for ASCII-based systems, where there is a predominance of one-byte characters (ASCII represents characters as one byte).

- UTF-8 is a variable-width encoding form that is more compact for text involving mostly Latin characters and ASCII punctuation.

- UTF-16 is the default encoding form of the Unicode Standard. It is a variable-width encoding form that uses 16-bit code units instead of bytes. Most characters are represented by a single unit, but some characters require surrogate pairs.

- Surrogates are 16-bit integers in the range D800 through DFFF, which are used solely for the purpose of "escaping" into higher-numbered characters.

- Without surrogate pairs, the UTF-16 encoding form can encompass only 65,000 characters, but with the surrogate pairs, this is expanded to include over a million characters.

- UTF-32 is a 32-bit encoding form. The major advantage of the fixed-width encoding form is that it uniformly expresses all characters, so that they're easy to handle in arrays and so forth.

- The Unicode Standard consists of characters. A character is any written component that can be represented by a numeric value.

- Characters are represented with glyphs (various shapes, fonts and sizes for displaying characters).

- Code values are bit combinations that represent encoded characters. The Unicode notation for a code value is U+$yyyy$, in which U+ refers to the Unicode code values, as opposed to other hexadecimal values. The $yyyy$ represents a four-digit hexadecimal number.

- An advantage of the Unicode Standard is its impact on the overall performance of the international economy. Applications that conform to an encoding standard can be processed easily by computers anywhere.

- Another advantage of the Unicode Standard is its portability. Applications written in Unicode can be easily transferred to different operating systems, databases, web browsers and so on. Most companies currently support, or are planning to support, Unicode.

- To obtain more information about the Unicode Standard and the Unicode Consortium, visit www.unicode.org. It contains a link to the code charts, which contain the 16-bit code values for the currently encoded characters.

- The Unicode Standard has become the default encoding system for XML and any language derived from XML.

- The Visual Basic IDE uses Unicode UTF-16 encoding to represent all characters.

- In the marking up of Visual Basic documents, the entity reference &H$yyyy$ is used, where $yyyy$ represents the hexadecimal code value.

Terminology

&H$yyyy$ notation	character
ASCII	character set
block	code value

diacritic
double-byte character set (DBCS)
efficient (Unicode design basis)
encode
entity reference
glyph
hexadecimal notation
localization
multibyte character set (MBCS)
portability
script
surrogate

symbol
unambiguous (Unicode design basis)
Unicode Consortium
Unicode design basis
Unicode Standard
Unicode Transformation Format (UTF)
uniform (Unicode design basis)
universal (Unicode design basis)
UTF-8
UTF-16
UTF-32

Self-Review Exercises

E.1 Fill in the blanks in each of the following.
   a) Global software developers had to _____ their products to a specific market before distribution.
   b) The Unicode Standard is a(n) _____ standard that facilitates the uniform production and distribution of software products.
   c) The four design bases that constitute the Unicode Standard are: _____, _____, _____ and _____.
   d) A(n) _____ is the smallest written component that can be represented with a numeric value.
   e) Software that can execute on different operating systems is said to be _____.

E.2 State whether each of the following is *true* or *false*. If *false*, explain why.
   a) The Unicode Standard encompasses all the world's characters.
   b) A Unicode code value is represented as U+*yyyy*, where *yyyy* represents a number in binary notation.
   c) A diacritic is a character with a special mark that emphasizes an accent.
   d) Unicode is portable.
   e) When designing Visual Basic programs, the entity reference is denoted by #U+*yyyy*.

Answers to Self-Review exercises

E.1 a) localize. b) encoding. c) universal, efficient, uniform, unambiguous. d) character. e) portable.

E.2 a) False. It encompasses the majority of the world's characters. b) False. The *yyyy* represents a hexadecimal number. c) False. A diacritic is a special mark added to a character to distinguish it from another letter or to indicate an accent. d) True. e) False. The entity reference is denoted by &H*yyyy*.

Exercises

E.3 Navigate to the Unicode Consortium website (www.unicode.org) and write the hexadecimal code values for the following characters. In which block are they located?
   a) Latin letter 'Z.'
   b) Latin letter 'n' with the 'tilde (~).'
   c) Greek letter 'delta.'
   d) Mathematical operator 'less than or equal to.'
   e) Punctuation symbol 'open quote (").'

E.4 Describe the Unicode Standard design basis.

E.5 Define the following terms:
a) code value.
b) surrogates.
c) Unicode Standard.
d) UTF-8.
e) UTF-16.
f) UTF-32.

E.6 Describe a scenario where it is optimal to store your data in UTF-16 format.

E.7 Using the Unicode Standard code values, create a program that prints your first and last name. If you know other writing systems, print your first and last name in those as well. Use a Label to display your name.

E.8 Write an ASP.NET program that prints "Welcome to Unicode!" in English, French, German, Japanese, Portuguese, Russian, Spanish and Traditional Chinese. Use the code values provided in Fig. E.3. In ASP.NET, a code value is represented the same way as in a Windows app (&H*yyyy*, where *yyyy* is a four-digit hexadecimal number).

Creating Console Applications

F.1 Introduction

Several of our online chapters use console applications that display text in and receive user input from a **Command Prompt** window. In this appendix, we present a simple console application that displays a line of text, then show the steps for building a console application.

F.2 A Simple Console Application

We begin by considering a simple program (Fig. F.1) that displays a line of text. When this program runs, its output appears in a **Command Prompt** window (also known as the **Console** window). We show such output in a box following the program listing. You'll see exactly what a **Command Prompt** window looks like later in this section, when we guide you step-by-step through the process of creating a console application.

```
1    ' Fig. F.1: Welcome1.vb
2    ' Simple Visual Basic program.
3    Module Welcome1
4        Sub Main()
5            Console.WriteLine("Welcome to Visual Basic!")
6        End Sub ' Main
7    End Module ' Welcome1
```

```
Welcome to Visual Basic!
```

Fig. F.1 | Simple Visual Basic program.

Analyzing the Program

Each console application contains at least a **Module** (lines 3–7), a logical grouping of methods that simplifies program organization. All methods in a Module are implicitly Shared. Like classes, each Module has a name, which can be any valid identifier. Lines 4–6 define the Main method. Every console application begins executing at **Main**, which is known as the **entry point of the program**. Main must be declared as shown in line 4.

Using Console.WriteLine to Display Text

Line 5 displays the string Welcome to Visual Basic! on the screen. The **Console** class contains Shared methods, such as **WriteLine**, that communicate with users via the **Console** window. When method `WriteLine` completes its task, it positions the **output cursor** (the location where the next output character will be displayed) at the beginning of the next line in the **Console** window. This behavior is similar to what happens when you press the *Enter* key when typing in a text editor window—the cursor is repositioned at the beginning of the next line. Program execution terminates when the program encounters the keywords `End Sub` in line 6.

F.3 Creating a Console Application

Perform the following steps to create and run a console application using Visual Studio Express 2012 for Windows Desktop.

Creating the Console Application
Select **FILE > New Project…** to display the **New Project** dialog (Fig. F.2). Select the **Console Application** template. In the dialog's **Name** field, type `Welcome1`. Click **OK** to create the project. The IDE now contains the open console application, as shown in Fig. F.3.

Changing the Name of the Program File
We change the name of the program file (i.e., `Module1.vb`) to a more descriptive name for each application we develop. To rename the file, click `Module1.vb` in the **Solution Explorer** window. This displays the program file's properties in the **Properties** window. Change the **File Name** property to `Welcome1.vb`. Notice that the name of the module in the source code changes to `Welcome1` to match the file name.

Entering the `Console.WriteLine` Statement
Insert the cursor in the `Main` method and type the statement in line 5 of Fig. F.1.

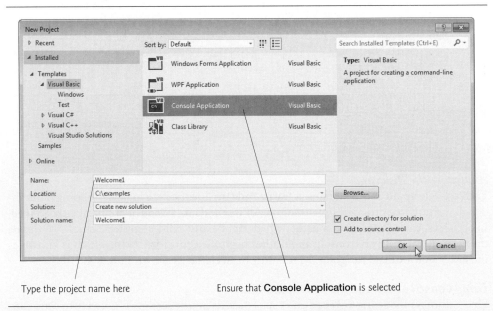

Type the project name here   Ensure that **Console Application** is selected

Fig. F.2 | Creating a **Console Application** with the **New Project** dialog.

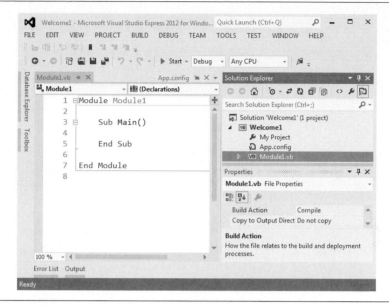

Fig. F.3 | IDE with an open console application.

Saving the Program
Select **FILE > Save All** to save the app.

Compiling and Running the Program
To execute this console application, select **Debug > Start Debugging** (or press *F5*), which invokes the Main method. The Console.WriteLine statement in Main displays Welcome to Visual Basic! however, the **Command Prompt** window appears, then disappears immediately. To enable the window to remain on the screen so you can view the results, you can execute the application by typing *Ctrl + F5*. The window showing the results (Fig. F.4) will remain on the screen until you press a key or click the window's close box. [*Note:* **Command Prompt** windows normally have black backgrounds and white text. We adjusted these settings in our environment to make our screen captures more readable.]

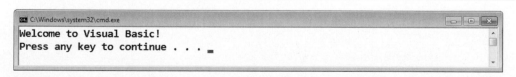

Fig. F.4 | Welcome1 application executed by typing *Ctrl + F5* in the IDE.

Index